LAW, ORDER AND FREEDOM

Law and Philosophy Library

VOLUME 94

For further volumes:
http://www.springer.com/series/6210

LAW, ORDER AND FREEDOM

A Historical Introduction to Legal Philosophy

Editors

Cees Maris

Faculty of Law, University of Amsterdam, Netherlands

Frans Jacobs

Faculty of the Humanities, University of Amsterdam, Netherlands

Translated by

Jacques de Ville

Faculty of Law, University of the Western Cape, South Africa

Springer

Editors
Cees Maris
University of Amsterdam
Faculty of Law
Oudemanhuispoort 4-6
1012 CN Amsterdam
Netherlands
c.w.maris@uva.nl

Frans Jacobs
University of Amsterdam
Faculty of the Humanities
Department of Philosophy
Nieuwe Doelenstraat 15
1012 CP Amsterdam
Netherlands
f.c.l.m.jacobs@uva.nl

Translator
Jacques de Ville
University of the Western Cape
Faculty of Law
Private Bag X17
7535 Bellville, Cape Town
South Africa
jdeville@uwc.ac.za

Translated by J.R. de Ville from the original version in Dutch

Recht, Orde en Vrijheid
Prof.mr. C.W. Maris and Prof.dr. F.C.L.M. Jacobs
01 August 1997
Kluwer B.V

ISSN 1572-4395
ISBN 978-94-007-1456-4 e-ISBN 978-94-007-1457-1
DOI 10.1007/978-94-007-1457-1
Springer Dordrecht Heidelberg London New York

Library of Congress Control Number: 2011928954

Printed on acid-free paper

Springer is part of Springer Science+Business Media (www.springer.com)

Preface

Law, Order and Freedom gives an account of the history of Western legal and political philosophy. It focuses on *law* as a system of norms which aspires to provide a fair balance between *order* and *freedom*. This liberal ideal of law and justice is a distinctive feature of many present-day constitutions, specifically in Western culture. Western legal orders are permeated with the principles of Enlightenment philosophy, that is, liberty, equality, and (to a lesser degree) fraternity, which have been translated into the institutions of the democratic constitutional state with its characteristic rule of law, separation of powers and human rights. Judicial interpretation too takes place within this spirit.

The core value of Enlightenment ethics is individual autonomy. In constitutional terms autonomy is guaranteed by the classical freedom rights, while social rights must ensure that every individual can adequately make use of his liberties. In public deliberation everyone has an equal voice. As a consequence of the emphasis on individual autonomy, the state is accorded a much narrower moral role than during the time when Enlightenment values were not yet incorporated into law. In earlier periods it appeared self-evident that the government should mould citizens into virtuous members of society. In the liberal view, in contrast, it is the individual's responsibility to give shape to his life in conformity with his own ideals. The state should be neutral in ideological respect, refraining from interference on moral grounds. Moreover, in present-day plural societies consensus about ideals of life is lacking, calling for restraint rather than legal moralism, as the latter can easily degenerate into forms of oppression that endanger social peace. Individual liberty should find its limits only in the equal liberty of others. Liberal legal systems, then, aim at safeguarding the equal freedom of all citizens in an orderly way. In the second half of the 20th century, the Enlightenment values have been declared universally valid by the Universal Declaration of Human Rights of the United Nations, and have subsequently been laid down in several international treaties on human rights. Nowadays they have acquired the status of apparent self-evidence, at least in the Western world.

Viewed historically, however, liberal freedom is a recent phenomenon that emerged only with the scientific revolution and Enlightenment philosophy in the early modern period from the 16th century onwards. In antiquity and medieval times, man was viewed as part of a comprehensive cosmic hierarchy that should be reflected in the legal order. Individual freedom to think and act as one wishes is then out of the question, as is equality. In modern times, too, equal freedom on closer inspection is not at all that self-evident. Liberal individualism has been met with strong criticism. According to moralists, liberalism wrongfully claims that its narrow state ideal is neutral. Adherents of conflict theory assert that law merely reflects political power struggles. Advocates of order theory warn that it is better for law to concentrate on the maintenance of order, because freedom undermines social peace. Anarchists see the state as an illegitimate violation of freedom. Communitarians stress the value of communal life and solidarity. Cultural relativists accuse liberals of an ethnocentric bias and deny that so-called human rights are really universal. Asian critics advocate 'Asian values' as a perfect alternative. Orthodox believers of various creeds reject liberal freedom as immoral heresy. Sceptics doubt the rationality of any theory of justice. All things considered, therefore, the prevailing legal values call for a critical historical analysis.

Law, Order and Freedom chronicles liberal legal morality and its critics. Focusing on the developments in Western thinking from ancient Greek philosophy to the present day, this historiography has admittedly been written from an ethnocentric perspective. *Law, Order and Freedom* may also entail some moral bias. It can be read as a defence of political liberalism, viewed as the outcome of a historical learning process that enables us to deal fairly with deep conflicts of interests and ideals.

Chapter 1 opens with a sketch of the present state of the art in the philosophy of law. It lists the central problems of legal philosophy (What is law, and why should one follow its rules? What is the connection between law and morals, particularly justice, on the one hand, and between law and power, on the other? What does justice entail?), as well as the various philosophical accounts of them (natural law, legal positivism, and their critics). In the successive historical Chapters 2, 3, 4, 5, 6, 7, 8, and 9, the central topics of legal and political philosophy are embedded in discussions of the relevant philosophical systems as a whole. Plato's theory of justice, for example, can be understood only from within the larger framework of his metaphysics and epistemology (Chapter 2). Derrida's 'hyper-ethics' results from his effort to go beyond metaphysics (Chapter 9). Likewise, Rawls's liberal theory of justice stems from his epistemological insight that in modern plural and open societies people may reasonably disagree about worldviews and ideals of the good life (but still have to cooperate in a peaceful way) (Chapter 10).

Each historical chapter starts with an introductory section that sketches the period concerned, continuing with an overview of the philosophical theories which are discussed more extensively in the sections that follow (so that the impatient reader may jump over the latter to continue with the next chapter). Sequentially, the chapters present the philosophies of Antiquity and the Middle Ages: the Pre-Socratics, the Sophists, Plato, Aristotle, the Stoa, Thomas Aquinas, William of Ockham, Marsilius of Padua (Chapter 2); the early Modern Age: Calvinism, Machiavelli, Descartes, Grotius (Chapter 3); Hobbes, Locke and Spinoza (Chapter 4); the 18th-century French Enlightenment: Montesquieu, Rousseau, Beccaria (Chapter 5); Kant (Chapter 6); the 19th century: utilitarianism, Hegel, Marx, Nietzsche (Chapter 7); the 20th century, 1900–1945: Freud's psycho-analysis, logical positivism, Popper's critical rationalism, hermeneutics (Chapter 8); the 20th century, 1945–2000: communitarianism, linguistic philosophy, postmodernism, Critical Theory, Nussbaum's neo-Aristotelianism, and Derrida's deconstruction (Chapter 9). The concluding Chapter 10 summarises the historical developments of the preceding chapters in light of the central problems of legal philosophy as elaborated on in Chapter 1. It proceeds to discuss whether political liberalism, which has found its most impressive articulation in the theory of justice of John Rawls, gives an adequate answer to these problems. It concludes that, although there certainly is no such thing as a liberal End of History, for the time being political liberalism emerges from historical experience as providing law with the most reasonable balance between order and freedom available.

Law, Order and Freedom is partly the translation of a book that was originally published in the Netherlands in 1991 (second edition 1997), which has since been used at several Dutch universities. Most of it was written by a group of legal philosophers who at the time collaborated at the University of Amsterdam. The present English text was substantially revised and updated in 2010. It was edited by Cees Maris (professor of legal philosophy, University of Amsterdam) and Frans Jacobs (professor of practical philosophy, University of Amsterdam). Both also contributed as authors. Other authors who contributed include Herman van Erp (associate professor of social philosophy, University of Tilburg), Govert den Hartogh (professor of practical philosophy, University of Amsterdam), Hendrik Kaptein (associate professor of legal philosophy, University of Leiden), Jacques de Ville (professor of law, University of the Western Cape), and Joep van der Vliet (associate professor of legal philosophy, University of Amsterdam). The English translation was undertaken by Jacques de Ville.[1]

References to events that have a particular Dutch connotation have been preserved in the English translation in as far as they are illustrative of more general themes. The book begins, for instance, with a discussion of the legitimacy of the former Dutch colonial legal system in Indonesia, as an illustration of the problematic relationship between law and morals. Yet, although *Law, Order and Freedom* is admittedly ethnocentric, it is not chauvinistic. The Dutch Republic during its Golden Age was, in the tradition of Erasmus, certainly a unique social laboratory of experiments with tolerance. Foreign philosophers such as Descartes and Locke, who were about to turn the world upside-down, could take refuge there; other philosophers of the Enlightenment could have their books printed there while they were censured back home. On the other hand, the pragmatic Dutch did not particularly excel in philosophy.[2] Well-known Dutch philosophers, notably Grotius and Spinoza, are

---

[1] We are thankful to Solly Leeman for his proofreading of the present text.

[2] See, however, Jonathan Israel's *Radical Enlightenment Philosophy and the Making of Modernity 1650–1750* (2001), which places the spotlight on Spinoza and his Dutch followers who, as the philosophical vanguard, brought the Enlightenment project to its radical conclusion.

accorded space in proportion to their international reputation. In this sense, *Law, Order and Freedom* has a cosmopolitan spirit.

The various chapters were (co-)written by the various authors as follows:

Chapter 1, *Legal Philosophy: The Most Important Controversies*: Maris.
Chapter 2, *Antiquity and the Middle Ages*: Van der Vliet (Sections 2.1–2.4, with contributions by Maris), Jacobs (Sections 2.5–2.8, with contributions by Van der Vliet).
Chapter 3, *The Commencement of the Modern Age*: Den Hartogh, with an introduction by Maris.
Chapter 4, *Hobbes, Locke and Spinoza*: Den Hartogh (Sections 4.1, 4.2, 4.4), Jacobs (Section 4.3).
Chapter 5, *Eighteenth-Century French Enlightenment*: Kaptein (Sections 5.1–5.7; Section 5.6 partly by Maris).
Chapter 6, *The Synthesis of Kant*: Maris (Sections 6.1, 6.2, 6.5), Jacobs (Sections 6.3, 6.4.3, 6.6), Van der Vliet (Sections 6.4.1, 6.4.2).
Chapter 7, *Nineteenth Century*: Maris (Sections 7.1, 7.4.1–7.4.5, 7.4.7, 7.5), Jacobs (Sections 7.2, 7.4.6), Van Erp (Section 7.3).
Chapter 8, *Twentieth Century: 1900–1945*: Maris (Sections 8.1, 8.3–8.5), De Ville (Section 8.2).
Chapter 9, *Twentieth Century: 1945–2000*: Maris (Sections 9.1–9.4), De Ville (Section 9.5).
Chapter 10, *Conclusion: Law, Order and Freedom*: Jacobs (Sections 10.1–10.5, 10.9–10.10, with contributions by Maris), Maris (Sections 10.6–10.8).

Amsterdam, The Netherlands
May 2011

Cees Maris
Frans Jacobs

Contents

Chapter 1
Legal Philosophy: The Most Important Controversies

1.1 Introduction

> According to the idea generally held over almost all Asia the subject, with all he possesses, belongs to the Prince. ... Accordingly, nothing is more normal than that hundreds of families should be summoned from a great distance to work, *without payment*, on fields that belong to the Regent. Nothing is more normal than the supply, unpaid for, of food for the Regent's court. And should the horse, the buffalo, the daughter, the wife of the common man find favour in the Regent's sight, it would be unheard-of for the possessor to refuse to give up the desired object unconditionally.... This is known to the [Dutch colonial] Government; and when you read the official gazette containing the laws and instructions and advice for the functionaries, you applaud the humanity that appears to have presided at their framing. Everywhere the European who is clothed with authority in the interior is enjoined, as one of his most sacred duties, to protect the population against their own docility and the rapacity of their chiefs (Multatuli 1987, pp. 74–76).

This passage in the novel *Max Havelaar* was written in 1856 by the Dutch author Douwes Dekker under the pen name Multatuli. Max Havelaar, the novel's main character, attempts to protect the Asian population in the former Dutch India (now Indonesia) against the abuse of power by the indigenous elite by appealing to the 'humane' European laws mentioned above, but in vain. *Max Havelaar* is in part autobiographical. Douwes Dekker was himself an official in Sunda (in the western part of the Indonesian island Java). He did not reject colonialism as such, because in his view it could be to the benefit of the local population: an enlightened colonial regime could break down the indigenous suppressive hierarchies based on superstition, and bring about a society based on justice instead. As assistant-commissioner he took seriously his official oath 'to protect the population against exploitation and extortion', and accused the indigenous ruler of abuses of power vis-à-vis his own subjects. The colonial superiors of Douwes Dekker were not pleased with this, for the interests of the Netherlands were not always furthered through compliance with fair laws. The colonial government regarded it as more efficient for pre-colonial indigenous feudal relations to remain in place, and then to enforce its will on the population via the old dynasties. The actions of Douwes Dekker, therefore, ended in

C.W. Maris, F.C.L.M. Jacobs (eds.), *Law, Order and Freedom*, Law and Philosophy Library 94, DOI 10.1007/978-94-007-1457-1_1, © Springer Science+Business Media B.V. 2011

his dismissal and not in measures against the Sundanese ruler. The *J'accuse* of *Max Havelaar* constitutes Multatuli's literary revenge.[1]

Nowadays the actions of Douwes Dekker are challenged for other reasons too:[2] he would have made himself guilty of spiritual colonialism by forcing Western values upon another culture, and thus have undermined the inherent value and identity of the Sundanese culture on the basis of a misplaced feeling of superiority. According to the local customary law the ruling authority was regarded as sacred, so that the absolute rights of the ruler were not deemed unjust.

The conflict between two legal orders based upon incompatible principles, both of which claim obedience, raises a number of philosophical questions: Which of the two legal systems deserves to be followed? Why should one comply with the law at all when it can apparently be given content in such incompatible ways? Is the law primarily an instrument of power aimed at maintaining *order* (the view of the Dutch colonial administration)? However, if I were an Indonesian without any interest in colonial order, why should I then have to obey it? Or should the law satisfy a number of substantial moral requirements? In other words, is a legal order only legitimate if it guarantees a *just* order? And if so, which justice precisely? The European ideal of justice that Douwes Dekker advocated? In that case, must one ignore local customary law if it conflicts with this view of justice – for the benefit of the local population, even though they do not themselves realise this? Or does the traditional Asian, hierarchical view of justice have as much, or even more, value than the European rule of law? And in this case, does Douwes Dekker's reliance on Dutch colonial law not simply amount to an expression of power without any legitimacy?

Presently in Western culture the moral values of freedom and equality, as well as the complementary constitutional ideal of democracy and the rule of law are self-evident to a great degree. These principles were formulated during the 18th-century Enlightenment, a movement which propagated a modern, 'enlightened' conception of man and society. As its central value it emphasizes the autonomy of the individual to define his own life. This leads to the constitutional ideal of *democracy*: everyone should have an equal vote in the design of society. Furthermore, the individual is protected against the power of the government through the *rule of law* which, defined broadly, consists of three complementary elements: (1) the government is itself bound by its own laws; (2) this is controlled by an independent judiciary, in accordance with the principle of separation of powers which likewise aims at limiting state power; and (3) in addition, the law must guarantee the equal individual freedom of all citizens, as determined in the classical fundamental rights. Government and law may only interfere with this freedom in order to safeguard that very freedom right for everyone – by means of the protection of the classical fundamental rights and the realization of social fundamental rights. The Enlightenment values,

[1] Douwes Dekker himself, incidentally, advocated an authoritarian anti-parliamentarianism.

[2] For example by Nieuwenhuys (1987).

therefore, imply a liberal view of law, not a moralistic one: the government does not have the function of ensuring that legal subjects lead a morally perfect way of life.

As a result of this liberal tendency, the modern Western ideal of law deviates significantly from the concepts of law in most non-Western and pre-modern European societies. These views of law assign a much broader moral task to the state. In Europe, during the Middle Ages, for example, the law was expected to impose Christian virtues. The freedom to live in accordance with non-Christian ideals was regarded as immoral and, therefore, had to be combated by the law with all its might.

Freedom and equality thus were not always the same self-evident values as they now appear to be in Western culture. The philosophers of the Enlightenment formulated these ideas in the 18th century as criticism of the law of that time, which was still based on the feudal traditions of the Middle Ages and on the monarchical absolutism of the 17th century (with its characteristic features of inequality and lack of individual freedom). These new liberal ideas coincided with an emerging belief in human progress. People expected that the growth of scientific knowledge would promote social and moral progress: to emancipation from the superstitious fears and suppressive traditions of the 'dark' Middle Ages. This would lead to an autonomous, consciously chosen way of life for both the individual and society. Later, the Enlightenment ideals were incorporated in most national legal systems of the West and in a great number of international treaties. As a result they now increasingly serve as the standard against which the legislation and judicial decisions of Western countries are measured. Moreover, since the Enlightenment the principles of freedom and equality have been accorded a supra-cultural, universal significance: they should form the basis of every modern society. In this view, societies which are based on illiberal values are regarded as 'primitive' and must, for their own sake, be modernised and 'enlightened'.

It is, however, controversial whether the liberal principles of the Enlightenment can indeed serve as the universal basis for society and law. Critics argue that they are just an accidental and fleeting product of Western culture and can, therefore, make no claim to universal validity. If this criticism is applied to the Max Havelaar dispute mentioned above, the indigenous customary law would deserve to be preferred to the colonial legal order (supposing that the latter was an expression of the liberal idea of justice, as Douwes Dekker, not very convincingly, argued). Another criticism is that the liberal emphasis on individual freedom leads to social disintegration, because individualism would undermine the solidarity that is required for social life. Liberal values would, therefore, fail to provide a sufficient basis for society and law.

This discussion about freedom and equality constitutes a central theme of this book. In *Law, Order and Freedom* the fundamental question of legal philosophy, what is the relation between law and morals?, focuses on the liberal values of the Western Enlightenment. To what extent can the principle of equal freedom serve as the universal standard for law: should *law* guarantee a social *order* that serves as a framework for the equal exercise by all citizens of their *freedom*? This problem is placed within the context of the history of Western legal and political philosophy, or the development from the moralistic view of law in classical Greek philosophy to the liberal view of modern times.

Thus, this book approaches history from a modern viewpoint with its associated conceptual tools, as sketched in the introductory methodological Section 1.4. This may involve anachronistic comparisons, such as: for which reasons does the ideal state of Plato differ so radically from the modern democratic constitution with its liberal fundamental rights? – obviously Plato himself was not acquainted with modern liberalism. The central question examined in this book also implies specific criteria for the selection of material: it focuses on those parts of the history of Western legal philosophy which either have led to present-day liberalism, or serve as its counter-model. This in the hope that we can learn from history, and that in this way historiography may clarify fundamental problems of actual legal orders.

1.2 Legal Philosophy

1.2.1 What is Law?

1.2.1.1 Introduction

Legal philosophy concerns the previously mentioned fundamental questions of law: What is law? To what extent does law relate to morality, more specifically to justice? To what extent is law simply an instrument of power? How can the enforcement of law be justified, for example, by means of punishment? When should one obey law? What is the extent to which the state may interfere in the lives of citizens? In asking these questions, legal philosophy offers a critical view of everyday legal practice.

The most central question of traditional legal philosophy pertains to the nature of law. The answer to this question may also determine how one answers the other questions, such as the extent to which positive law deserves to be obeyed, and when legal force is legitimate.

In colloquial speech the meaning of the concept 'law' is ambiguous. On the one hand, it is used to point to the existing positive legal order, while, on the other hand, it refers to the moral concept of justice. These two meanings may overlap in so far as positive law has a just content. This is not, however, necessarily the case. The ambiguity of the concept 'law' comes to light most clearly in the event of unjust positive law. This can lead to paradoxical statements, such as: 'The law of Nazi Germany was not real *law*.' The question 'what is law?' can thus focus on whether the concept 'law' refers to every legal order which is in fact effective within a specific territory, irrespective of its content (and which is thus in important respects determined by power), *or* whether a necessary relation exists between law and morality. Nowadays it is, however, contended that such problems of definition are of secondary importance. However one defines the concept 'law', the central question is a moral one: under what conditions is the claim of law to obedience legitimate?

1.2.1.2 Law, Order and Morality

Viewed historically, undoubtedly a close factual relation obtains between law and morality. At the origin of human history man lived in simple small groups, mostly an extended family under the leadership of the older men (in the 21st century this mode of life is still maintained in certain parts of the world, such as Australia and Canada). These groups survive by means of gathering and hunting. In such a society law forms an undifferentiated whole with traditional morality and religion. One can actually ask whether such societies know of 'law' in our sense, as specific legal institutions, such as a legislature, judicial power and police are lacking. General norms do exist, but taboos and traditions are sufficient to ensure compliance. The groups are so small that everyone knows each other. The breach of the norms thus has immediate negative social consequences, so that social control suffices (in addition to the belief in supernatural sanctions).

Only when larger and more complicated societal structures come into being, because of conquest or extending family relations, does social control through kinship ties become insufficient. People no longer know each other personally; in subgroups different traditions come into being, and as a result of accelerated social changes, traditional norms do not keep up with social needs. To ensure a peaceful and orderly society in such circumstances, institutions of a specific legal character evolve. Thus, it was impossible for the agricultural societies that came into being from 6500 BC to function without purposive legal regulation. Sowing, irrigation, and harvesting require rules for an extensive co-ordination of activities. Commerce requires safe trade routes, reliable contracts, and money as a means of exchange. A central authority then comes into being which co-ordinates social life, for instance, by enacting general rules. As a result of the new agricultural techniques, surpluses arise which provide the opportunity to exempt from the daily work a class of priests who specialise in legal knowledge and legislation (and who are the only ones able to write). The central enactment of a number of fundamental norms for social exchange now compensates for the lack of generally shared traditions, and enables quick adaptations to new social conditions. A specific judicial institution concerns itself with the final settlement of legal disputes. Because compliance with such non-traditional norms is not customary, a specialised group is formed which concerns itself with the maintenance of legal rules, through violence, if necessary. In short, as time goes by, specific legal institutions develop, which specialise in legislation, judicial decisions, and policing functions. These institutions ensure social order by establishing central rules that are clear to everyone, and maintain them through a monopoly on violence.

Critics of Enlightenment philosophy point out that this kind of development should not be taken as social progress from an inferior 'primitive' form of society to a superior modern civilization. According to them, all that happens is an evolution from simpler to more complex forms of society, in which, as a result of the process of division of labour, still more specialised social institutions develop. This does not per se mean progress in a moral or rational sense. It is, for example, equally possible to perceive in less complex societies a purity that has been lost in modern society. Furthermore, what is rational for a society of hunters is not per se rational in an industrialised society.

This development, moreover, does not take place in a straight line and differs in each cultural sphere. In Western Europe, the invasions of the Germanic tribes in the 4th century AD led to the demise of the Western Roman Empire. Because of this, the Roman legal order, and with that also the unity of Roman law, was lost (although it did continue to develop in the Eastern Roman Empire where it was codified by the emperor Justinian in approximately 530 AD). The professional practice of law then provisionally came to an end. In its place came the unwritten customary law of the different Germanic tribes which was maintained by the group itself. Only in the 13th century, in Italian universities, was the scientific study of Roman legal texts revived. At the end of the Middle Ages, lawyers, having completed their studies, started playing an increasingly important role in state administration, which from the 15th century slowly developed in the direction of centrally organised monarchical states (with the federal Netherlands as the exception). Central legislation and jurisprudence came into being to direct the booming trade and colonial expansion, and to increase the power of the king. The success of natural science, moreover, led to the idea that man can control his own environment and life, adapting them to his will. Consistent with the belief in progress of 18th-century Enlightenment philosophy, man, by means of legislation, could fashion society in accordance with his ideals. The Enlightenment ideals of freedom, equality and democratic deliberation, therefore, had to be anchored in a constitution, and be elaborated in more detail in codes that were comprehensible to all citizens. After the French revolution in 1789, French law was indeed codified in the *Code Civil* and other codes, which served as examples for similar codifications in the rest of Europe. Later 19th-century legislation stressed the principle of freedom, so that the modest task remained for law to regulate the freedom rights of everyone in an orderly fashion. Gradually, however, it became apparent that this leads to an extremely unfair distribution of the opportunities to use one's liberties. In this revised liberal view, state and law were allocated a much broader task, particularly in the field of social legislation, which in the second half of the 20th century led to the welfare state. This process went hand in hand with the development of an expansive bureaucracy, the 'fourth branch', in addition to the legislature, executive and judiciary. The law now extended significantly into important parts of social life. Nonetheless, it remains central to the liberal view that law does not have the function of enforcing a morally good way of life, since every individual should be free to establish how he arranges his own life.

With the increasing complexity of society, law and morality thus gradually grow apart. The law breaks away from the old moral traditions, as it is centrally established, and changes in accordance with practical circumstances and political priorities. Morality, for its part, can develop into a critical ethics, which distances itself from inherited moral values and can even call for radical social change. Moreover, law and morality grow apart in substance as law primarily focuses on the *orderly* course of social life.

Since law is distinguished from morality by its ordering function, one can now specify the following ideal-typical differences between them. Law is tied to impersonal social institutions that centrally regulate its establishment and maintenance.

Legal norms can be identified with reference to clear formal characteristics (procedures for creation, proclamation, etc), and consequently can become known by everyone, as is required by legal certainty. Legal norms apply to all participants in the legal order, and in the case of deviating behaviour may be maintained by force. Moral rules, on the other hand, are less clearly determined, as they are not decreed by a central institution. They can, therefore, differ per group, or even per person. They are dependent for their compliance upon individual goodwill, instead of external force. To be sure, the moral views of most people are determined by generally shared cultural traditions, and transgressions of traditional morality are punished with social sanctions. It is, nonetheless, possible that an individual with a critical attitude propagates deviating moral views that conflict with dominant values. Jesus and Muhammad are good examples: they gave a radical reinterpretation of the traditions of their times (whilst claiming that they were bringing to the fore what was most fundamental to those traditions). The law, furthermore, primarily requires conduct which externally conforms to norms, whereas morality addresses someone's motives, too. (From a moral perspective, it is insufficient that one refrains from stealing out of egoistic motives, such as fear of punishment.) Moreover, in contrast to law, morality often requires more than is necessary for orderly social relations. Hence, dishonesty is regarded as morally prohibited as such, but its legal sanction is limited to the non-fulfilment of contracts, committing forgery, etc. On the other hand, law sometimes requires more than morality: it aims at conduct which is indifferent from a moral point of view, but that is required by the social order, such as the right of way in traffic rules.

The consequence of this segregation of law and morality into different normative areas is that legal authorities can give law a content which, from a critical-ethical perspective, is utterly immoral. Since those in power dispose over specialised legal institutions to transform their interests and values into legal rules, law is indeed an efficient instrument to impose injustice. Certain legal philosophers argue that one should still obey unjust laws because the maintenance of social order is the primary requirement for human survival. They reject the counter-argument that a duty of obedience exists only when law is substantially just: if everyone could disobey the law whenever he considers it unjust, there would be social chaos. The function of ensuring order relies precisely on the *central*, generally binding establishment and maintenance of law. In other words, a bad order is better than no order at all. These legal philosophers thus primarily accord to law the function of ensuring order, which is not tied to additional moral requirements. However, this equation of law and order gives a somewhat extreme view of the differences between law and morality. Despite the differentiation of the legal and moral spheres, a number of similarities remain. In substance, law and morality will almost always share certain central norms. The general norm 'You may not kill', for example, is not only central to most moral systems, but also to every legal order (with the reservation: unless the prohibition to kill is overruled by another norm, for example, that killing is allowed in the case of self-defence). Here the requirements of morality and order coincide because society would not be possible if everyone was about to kill each other. Moreover, like morality, law sometimes takes account of motives, as in the case of the criminal fault or intention requirement. Certain legal fields, such as customary law and international law, are institutionalised to a lesser extent than others. The differences with traditional morality are, therefore, smaller here. In addition, written law frequently mirrors existing moral views. Consequently, law is constantly subject to the ongoing social debate concerning the moral question of how society and law should be structured. Furthermore, often the meaning of written law is much less clear than was suggested above, so that its application requires detailed interpretation. In many instances judges let their reading be guided by their sense of justice.

In brief, in many societies a great number of legal subjects, specifically the political elite, at least have the subjective sense that they *should* obey the law, irrespective of any threat of sanction. Furthermore, the authorities will never publicly present their norms as purely based on power. For strategic reasons they will at least attempt to create the façade of justice. They do not only say 'do this or else...', but also attempt to give (moral or other) reasons why it is good to act in the required manner. In doing this, they open themselves to moral criticism, which tests their legislation against its own pretences of legitimacy. Due to this, legal and moral discussions overlap. Nonetheless, as a consequence of the differences between law and morality, positive law may primarily serve the interests of the powerful, and fundamentally conflict with the requirements of a critical ethics.

1.2.1.3 Natural Law and Legal Positivism

Because of this demarcation between law and morality, the question 'What is law?' is answered in diverse ways. Certain legal philosophers regard the ordering function of law as characteristic, seeing that a number of unjust positive legal orders exist as well. Others retain the view that the law by its nature is aimed at the realisation of a just order. This controversy about the nature of law is central to the debate between the two most important movements in legal philosophy: the natural-law doctrine and legal positivism.

According to the *natural-law doctrine*, 'law' conceptually implies a necessary relation with morality, specifically justice. This relation exists 'by nature', thus independently of, and preceding, human legislation. For this reason the concept of law provides a critical standard by which to test positive law. According to the classical natural-law doctrine, manifestly immoral positive law can make no claim to the status of 'law' in the full sense of the term, and can, therefore, also not require obedience.

Legal positivism on the other hand denies any relation between law and morality which is more than accidental. Law is simply what is posited and maintained as such by competent state organs, even if it is substantially unjust. According to this view, law reflects power rather than morality. According to many legal positivists this does not, however, mean that one ought to obey positive law unconditionally. *Normative* legal positivism does indeed associate a duty of obedience with law's function of ensuring order. In accordance with this view, legal certainty is so important that one should obey unjust law, too. These positivists thus actually do connect legal positivism with a moral argument: a chaotic society is worse than an unjust society, *ergo* an absolute duty of obedience to positive law.

Descriptive legal positivism, on the other hand, advocates a complete separation of law and morals. It only intends to give a neutral description of law as a factual societal phenomenon, for example: law is what the legal authorities command and maintain effectively in a certain territory, irrespective of the content of their prescriptions. This neutral analysis of what a positive legal order entails does not imply any moral duty to obey it. The latter question is viewed as a separate moral problem. In this variant of legal positivism, positive law can indeed be criticised and disobeyed on moral grounds. In this regard descriptive legal positivists agree with the adherents of natural law. Their basic disagreement with the natural-law doctrine is that this critique is not a *legal*, but an extra-legal *moral* issue.

1.2.2 The Natural-Law Doctrine

1.2.2.1 Classical Natural Law

The classical doctrine of *natural law* is grounded in a presupposed fundamental 'nature' or essence of man: man displays a number of essential characteristics from which societal rules follow, which always and everywhere should constitute the nucleus of positive law. The content of these natural-law norms can be determined prior to the study of any positive legal order, because natural law can be derived directly from insights into human nature. This means that one can, independently of positive law, determine what the concept of law entails at its core. From this, natural-law theory concludes that a positive legal order only has the status of genuine 'law' when it does not substantially deviate from natural law.

A modern version of classical natural law reflecting the values of the Enlightenment was proclaimed in the American Declaration of Independence of 1776:

> We hold these truths to be self-evident, that all men are created equal, that they are endowed by their Creator with certain unalienable Rights, that among these are Life, Liberty and the pursuit of Happiness. — That to secure these rights, Governments are instituted among Men, deriving their just powers from the consent of the governed, — That whenever any Form of Government becomes destructive of these ends, it is the Right of the People to alter or to abolish it.

The truth claims of natural-law theories are, however, subject to a number of objections. The most important problem is how to establish what the essential nature of man entails. The American Declaration of Independence posits a number of 'evident truths', such as the truth that all people are (created) equal, and that as such they have a right to freedom. However, when one examines the world as it is, one sees that in fact people are indeed the same (equal) in many respects; but then again, they are very different (unequal) in other respects. For example, on average human beings are much more intelligent than animals, but among themselves they show great varieties in intelligence. On what basis can one claim that the similarities are more decisive, or more 'essential', than the differences?

Moreover, how can one actually speak of inalienable 'rights' which people would possess 'by nature', thus preceding legislation? Do such rights exist in an objective way? If so, where and how? How can this be proved to someone who doubts it?

Generally, advocates of classical natural law state that such rights belong to that which makes human life 'dignified'. But what can be the basis of such a normative claim? Do animals then have no 'right' to freedom and happiness? Often the natural-law doctrine's response to this is that man *as* man is to be distinguished from animals owing to a number of characteristics: specifically, because of his intellectual abilities that enable him to distance himself from his immediate environment, in order to establish the course of his life himself. Man, in brief, differs from animals because of his reason and freedom. To this is added that human beings develop these characteristics in cooperation with others; thus, in a society. According to this view, state and law are social institutions which should guarantee the development of these essential human traits. Therefore, in the liberal version of natural law, the state should exercise coercion when people infringe each other's freedom rights.

The question, however, is whether this concept of man is not based on an arbitrary selection from the set of characteristics which human beings actually possess. After all, in some respects they are equal; but in other respects they are unequal. They may appear to be free at first sight, but on reflection their actions may turn out to be closer to the instinctively determined animal way of life. Moreover, is the idea of a 'natural' supra-positive law not a projection of human thinking onto nature? Nature after all primarily seems to be the arena where the 'right' of the strongest prevails.

Opponents of classical natural-law thinking, therefore, frequently state that nature as such is without norms and thus amoral. It consists of all the phenomena that manifest themselves in nature – thus, of life and death, cooperation and aggression, equality and inequality, and freedom and lack of freedom. It entails no rights, but only the amoral 'law of the jungle', that is to say, the struggle for survival. This of course does not mean that all individuals are by nature involved in some mutual physical struggle. Survival of the species can be equally promoted by means of close cooperation. Yet in mammals that live together in groups, and in most human societies as well, cooperation takes place in a strict hierarchy; thus, in relations of fundamental inequality and lack of freedom. Moreover, in most human societies, not only cooperation, but also competition and aggression, stimulate progress. According to this criticism, an advocate of classical natural law who selects specific natural phenomena from the whole of nature as 'essential', simply projects his own normative preferences onto amoral nature

The American Declaration of Independence, quoted above, claims to provide a response to this criticism. It appeals to the order which God conceived in his creation of nature. Indeed, in the Christian view a normative order can be discovered in nature (see Section 2.7). This divine creation plan cannot be observed directly in the natural phenomena as such, because through the acts of Evil, immoral phenomena are part of reality as well. Therefore, the actual actions of mankind may diverge from God's plan. However, by taking note of God's revelation, specifically via the Bible, we can still know which of our characteristics should be promoted and which we should fight against. According to the traditional Christian worldview, God's creation implies a normative hierarchy: lifeless nature and animals take the lower positions, God himself is placed at the top, while mankind occupies a position in-between. Man, then, partly has an animal nature that links him to the material world; but because of his immortal, immaterial soul, he at the same time resembles God. This latter aspect constitutes the origin of human reason and freedom. This hierarchical order makes it easy to decide what we should do: suppress our bestial (instinctive, materialistic) side and live in accordance with our reasonable free will, aimed at God's Commandments.

Critics object to this argument because it is based on indemonstrable metaphysical speculation, and ultimately on faith. Christian metaphysics claims a hierarchy which is hidden behind, and in, natural phenomena, but which is not directly observable. How could a Christian prove to an unbeliever that God exists, and that, if he exists, the Bible is his word? This objection may be strengthened by pointing at competing metaphysical theories that are incompatible with Christian natural law. The Greek philosopher Plato (428–347 BC), for example, likewise contends that nature consists of more than the world of observable phenomena (see Section 2.4). Plato states that man can, via his intelligence, take part in a rational world of eternal truths. This 'world of Ideas' functions as an ideal model for our imperfect everyday world. On the other hand, man, owing to his body, equally belongs to the material world of things and animals. Like Christianity, Plato derives from this hierarchical division of nature as a whole, and of human nature specifically, the following norms: live reasonably, and allow intelligence to control physical inclinations. Plato, however, then arrives at a version of natural law with values that are the complete inverse of those of the American Declaration of Independence. According to him, only an intellectual elite is capable of the rational insight that is required for emancipation from our animal instincts. The masses, on the other hand, are by nature irrational. The best form of government is, therefore, a benevolent, but absolutist and paternalistic one of a wise elite ruling over the dumb majority, in their own best interests. On the basis of his hierarchical metaphysics Plato thus denies that all human beings are by nature equal and possess inalienable freedom rights. According to his theory, a democratic constitution, such as that of the United States, would fundamentally conflict with human nature. Because of its immorality and irrationality, it could make no claim to obedience at all.

The central problem of the classical natural-law doctrine, then, is that, on the one hand, empirical nature as such, as a consequence of its value-free character, does not appear to involve any (legal) norms; but that, on the other hand, each appeal to an underlying 'essence' that is not directly observable relies on indemonstrable metaphysics.

1.2.2.2 Naturalistic Natural Law: The Biological Model

Nonetheless, some natural-law theories are more acceptable to contemporary readers because they have a less metaphysical character. They advocate a conception of nature that is inspired by a biological model that takes a middle position between conceptions that are completely value-free, on the one hand, and conceptions of a comprehensive normative-metaphysical character, on the other hand. According to this view – which is, for instance, to be found in the philosophy of Plato's pupil Aristotle (Section 2.5) – the diverse forms of life in (living) nature each show their own developmental design. A wholly mature human being has a different way of life than a mature ant. It is, therefore, possible to determine for each natural species which mode of life best serves its development. It is, however, questionable whether this view of nature can succeed in providing uncontroversial critical standards for the law.

Minimal forms of this model of natural law base their arguments on a simple biological fact: the human instinct for survival (Hobbes, Section 4.1; Hart, Section 1.2.3.2): in order to survive, man requires social organisation; because people, in addition to their social dispositions, equally display egotistical and aggressive characteristics, social life requires enforceable rules that prohibit violence, theft and the breach of contracts. This minimal natural law must, in other words, guarantee everyone's physical integrity, the right to property and contractual rights, if necessary through sanctions. However, this version of natural law is very minimal indeed. It is too meagre to provide a basis for the Enlightenment values of freedom and equality. Human beings can after all also survive in inequality and without liberties. In fact, in most cultures people live like this.

A less minimal version of natural law which does implicate the Enlightenment values must, therefore, contend that man prospers best in a society which is based on freedom and equality.[3] In this line of reasoning, the tendency to survive in groups is characteristic of many kinds of animals, and thus not specifically of man. People and ants both require social organisation. As a consequence of his greater intelligence, the *human* species is distinguished by a unique mode of organisation. Ants live in accordance with firmly established instinctive patterns, in a rigid, hierarchical organisation, organised in fixed classes (workers, soldiers and queen). In comparison, people are lacking in instinct, but compensate for this by means of their intelligence: they can learn from their mistakes; owing to their use of language they have access to information based on the experience of previous generations, and which helps them to determine which mode of action would best serve their goals in the long run. The social organisation of human beings, therefore, functions best when it is flexible and provides sufficient space for intelligent adaptation to new information. A problem for man is, however, that he can likewise use this free space in irrational ways, as his immediate instinctive reactions and spontaneous emotions are often not in harmony with his intellectual insights. (According to the theory of evolution, the layers of the brain where intelligence is situated have only recently been added to the older, 'animal' layers which constitute the source of emotions and instincts. Because of this, the intellect is in many instances too weak to control

[3]See, for example, Locke, Chapter 4, although one also finds that some of his arguments tend to remind one of classical natural law, specifically his appeal to God's will.

the emotions.) Acting instinctively one may become a chain smoker, even though anyone who takes his rational self-interest into account knows that in the long run he had better stop smoking. Nonetheless, many smokers are not able to follow their intellectual insight. Likewise, many people act in an asocial manner, although in the long run they cannot do without society. Therefore, it is necessary that people be compelled to discipline themselves by social rules and by sanctions, so that they fulfil the social roles that a well-ordered society requires. This serves their own well-being in the long run as well. Human societies must, therefore, on the one hand, limit individual freedom, but, on the other hand, grant enough space for free acquisition of information and for social dynamics.

Extending this reasoning, liberals contend that it is essential for the welfare of both individual and society that each person has equal freedom to think as he wishes, to express his thoughts, and to act accordingly. These liberties should be limited only if they infringe the like rights of others. Individuals can then develop their personality in accordance with their own insights, while society benefits as freedom furthers the growth of knowledge and new social initiatives.

However, conservatives argue against this that the Enlightenment philosophy allows for too much free space because it greatly overestimates human rationality and autonomy. In the conservative view, in reality man's intellectual abilities are extremely limited, so that he can hardly overcome his irrational emotions. Consequently, 'rational' attempts to transform society have ill effects. To orientate himself in the world man should rely on the traditional modes of life which are shaped by the experience of previous generations. Freedom to deviate from the traditions endangers the survival of the human species, the conservative critics conclude.

Even when this overestimation of human intelligence does not apply to everyone, critics of liberalism maintain that freedom is typically an ideal for intellectuals. The majority, by contrast, apparently feels more at ease in conforming with the prevailing traditions. Free criticism of traditions could under certain circumstances even lead to the loss of a communal sense of values and of solidarity, and hence to social disintegration. This at least would count against *equal* freedom for all: freedom is suitable only for an intellectual elite, not for the whole of the human species.

The advocate of freedom can still attempt to save his position with the contention that the intellectual mode of life constitutes the most complete stage of human development. However, the counter-argument may run as follows: are intellectuals not the very same persons who, while proclaiming unworldly ideas, make chairs fall over, get the food burnt and mess coffee on their clothes? Moreover, nothing guarantees that intellectuals will indeed use their freedom for increasing knowledge and developing new initiatives, and not for asocial conduct. Freedom, then, should be granted only to wise people who will definitely realise their liberties in a positive way (and who are thus in this sense not free). Thus runs the reasoning of Plato, whose elitist state ideal moreover includes inequality and a lack of freedom. The ideal of equal individual freedom is, in other words, deeply controversial.

1.2.2.3 Natural Law According to the Communication Model

Another contemporary version of natural law bases the universal validity of Enlightenment values on the non-metaphysical fact that man typically orients himself in the world through communication via language (among others, Habermas, Section 9.3). People determine their lives, consciously or subconsciously, on the basis of information based on the still growing life experience of successive generations, and which is passed on by means of language. Language enables people to convey new information, to argue about it, and, consequently, to strive toward a better way of life. This means that man, as a result of communication with others, can in the long run free himself from domination by nature and from oppressing social traditions. From this it follows that for his development man is reliant on social intercourse with others in a 'communication society'. Communication in its full sense can succeed only if certain conditions are complied with. The communication partners must rightfully expect of each other that they are sincere and that they are speaking the truth. (To lie now and then is acceptable, but this works only by virtue of the fact that people in general can expect honesty from each other.) Moreover, in ideal communication, one must appeal only to arguments which are acceptable to all participants. Inequalities in status and power may not play any role. In most actual societies these conditions are not complied with, which hinders full human development. From communicative human nature follows the normative ideal that actual societies must be reorganised in a way that enables an unlimited and truthful exchange of information and arguments, not influenced by inequalities in power or by indoctrination. This version of natural law implies that society and law are built upon a democratic deliberation procedure, based on the principles of freedom and equality. Societies which do not comply with this must be emancipated toward such an ideal, power free, communication community.

According to this view, the criterion of impartial argumentation and decision-making would, moreover, be immanent in legal reality as such: in the institution of an independent judiciary, the hearing of all parties, the distribution of the onus of proof, and the requirement that judicial sentences be adequately motivated. Admittedly, actual judicial decisions may frequently be influenced by social prejudices and partial interests. Nonetheless, as soon as these biases come to light, this will evoke criticism. Law's characteristic claim to impartiality implies a critical standard for testing positive legislation and jurisprudence: is this law or sentence justifiable from a neutral point of view, that is, can it be the outcome of a reasonable discussion between free and equal parties?

Critics of this variant of natural law argue that it, too, is based on an arbitrary selection from the totality of human characteristics. Open argumentation on an equal footing is viewed as the essence of human communication, which in turn constitutes the essence of human nature. But, in fact, people use language equally to manipulate, to defraud, to command, in short, as an instrument of power.

In general, the reproach is that natural law makes itself guilty of 'top hat' reasoning: the natural law advocate first inserts his moral preferences into his definition of nature, and subsequently in triumph derives his morality from nature thus defined, just like a magician who conjures a rabbit out of his top hat after himself first concealing it there.

1.2.3 Descriptive Legal Positivism and Its Critics

In reaction to the indemonstrable metaphysical character which is often ascribed to traditional natural-law theories, *legal positivism* wishes to determine the concept of law exclusively on the basis of the concrete legal phenomena of everyday social reality. This movement identifies 'law' with positive legal orders, rejecting any reference to preceding legal values. Because actual positive legal orders can be very unjust, measured against the traditional natural-law theories, this approach has the consequence that immoral law is regarded as 'law', too.

The most important task of legal positivism then becomes to develop a theory of law which records all phenomena of positive law, and distinguishes these from non-legal social phenomena, such as etiquette, morality and politics. That this is a difficult task appears from the disagreements between the successive positivistic theories of law and between the positivists and their critics, which will be discussed in this section. The theory of John Austin gives a simple, and at first sight plausible, description of law: law consists of commands of the sovereign who enforces them through sanctions. On closer inspection, however, Austin's theory requires refining, which is provided by the theory of Herbert Hart: law is not merely based on power, for the competence of the highest legal authorities, such as the legislature, itself again is based on rules that invest them with authority.

To this Ronald Dworkin has reacted with a third legal theory which entails so many corrections to Hart's positivism that it no longer wishes to be called 'legal-positivist'. This latter theory reintroduces a necessary relation between law and morality, without, however, reverting to traditional natural-law metaphysics. It concludes that it is impossible to make an absolute distinction between law and morality, because, in the practice of positive law, moral principles inevitably play a role, particularly in the interpretation of legal rules. According to Dworkin, judicial interpretation should be regulated by the liberal principle of equal concern and respect.

Subsequently this ethical turn of legal philosophy has been criticised by the Critical Legal Studies (CLS) movement because of Dworkin's denial of social and legal reality. In fact, these critics contend, law is nothing other than a continuation of the political struggle, but with other weapons. All reference to justice only masks partial interests. If the distinction between law and politics were indeed to be that fluid, it would subvert the association of law with the morals of natural law, as well as the claim of legal positivism that law is a self-standing system which can be identified by formal criteria. Incidentally, leading critics of CLS favour a politics of emancipation that has been called 'super-liberalism'.

1.2.3.1 Austin: Law as Commands of the Government

The legal positivist John Austin (1790–1859) gives a simple, and at first sight acceptable, description of law as a social phenomenon. First, law consists of commands to act in a specific way. However, this description equally applies to other social phenomena, such as morality and etiquette. Legal norms distinguish themselves from these by their institutional character: they derive from a central institution. Austin calls this institution the 'sovereign', being the supreme authority in society. (In many legal orders local authorities, for example, derive their legislative powers from a central legislature, which is the highest legal authority.) Austin defines the 'sovereign' as the person or group whose commands the members of a society are in the habit of obeying, without itself owing obedience to any higher authority.

Moreover, unlike morality and etiquette, law has the function of ensuring that social interaction takes an orderly course. Law must, therefore, be effective. As appears from Austin's definition of the sovereign, law's effectiveness is partly guaranteed by the fact that citizens are accustomed to obey the commands of the highest authority. Yet, legal certainty requires more: people who nonetheless deviate from the norms, must be called to order by means of coercion. Thus, Austin defines law as the commands of the sovereign, maintained through the force of sanctions.

This positivistic definition implies that law may consist of very unjust commands. As long as the sovereign manages to enforce his decrees, then in Austin's view one can speak of law. This does not, however, mean that the moral evaluation of law is impossible. Austin simply states that this is not a legal matter. His positivistic concept of law wishes to be completely value-free. In other words, the determination of what law is, in this positivistic legal theory, is of a completely different order than the evaluation or moral merit of positive law. The question of when one ought to obey the law likewise belongs to the non-legal, moral perspective. The positivistic statement that, for example, the law of Nazi Germany is 'law' in its full sense, does not imply that it should be obeyed. It simply reflects a neutral observation of social facts.

In short, Austin emphasizes the social function of law of ensuring order: a central institution establishes its content, so that everyone knows what he has to comply with – in contrast to the much more diffuse and heterogeneous normative systems of morality and etiquette, which are not centrally organised. Furthermore, those who deviate from legal norms are kept under control by means of organised state force, which is absent in the case of morality and etiquette.

1.2.3.2 Hart: Primary and Secondary Rules

According to the legal positivist H.L.A. Hart (1907–1992), Austin's legal theory can give no account of a number of characteristics of positive law. Hart attempts to capture these shortcomings in a more nuanced theory. In *The Concept of Law* (1961) he contends that law is more than simply obedience to a sovereign government, caused by the threat of sanction and conformity to custom. A first objection against

Austin's legal theory states that custom and enforcement are insufficient to explain obedience to the law. A stable legal order requires that at least a number of legal subjects – specifically the authorities themselves – consciously accept the legal order as authoritative. On the basis of this objection, Hart substitutes the concept 'rule' for Austin's 'commands' and 'custom'.

The concept 'custom' refers only to an externally observable regularity in conduct. A 'rule', in addition, includes the awareness that the conduct ought to take place in that way. This normative consciousness constitutes what Hart refers to as the 'inner aspect' of the law. A rule, then, exists when the members of a group manifest a specific external conduct with regularity, and also accept a standard implied therein as correct. The latter appears when they criticise others (as well as themselves) for deviating conduct. By contrast, deviation from a custom is generally not a ground for criticism. When somebody occasionally deviates from his custom of sleeping on his right side, he will not be called to account by himself or by others. 'Not stealing' is, on the other hand, associated with the consciousness that one ought to respect what belongs to someone else. Therefore, theft implies the transgression of a rule, resulting in the attribution of blame. For that matter, in Hart's view the acceptance of a legal rule is not necessarily based on moral convictions. Conformism or self-interest can serve as motivation, too. Moreover, Hart does not require that, for a legal order to exist, *all* members of society need to accept it as authoritative. As social reality frequently shows, a legal order can function efficiently, even though a large part of the population experiences it as oppressive. For the actual existence of law it is sufficient that the majority in a society conform to the rules only in their external conduct (for example, because of fear of sanctions), as long as at least a number of its members, particularly the legal authorities, accept these rules as the standard for conduct.

A second objection to Austin's legal conception declares that the state, in turn, derives its powers to sanction from legal rules that regulate its competence. In this respect Austin's legal definition is circular: he defines law as the commands of the sovereign, but then it appears that the sovereign itself is defined by means of law. Moreover, legal rules that assign authority can hardly be described as commands backed by the threat of sanctions.

In conformity with this second objection, a further criticism of Austin states that he does not do justice to the specific structure of law in describing it as the 'commands of the sovereign'. As already mentioned, the institution of the sovereign is itself a legal figure, the power of which is determined by rules that assign authority. Apart from rules relating to legal subjects, law thus equally consists of rules which concern the legal institution itself. In other words, the legal norms that regulate the conduct of the legal subjects derive their own legal validity from higher norms that regulate the competence of the legal authorities. Law thus exhibits a layered, hierarchical structure of rules. The rules concerning the competences of the legal institutions likewise have a layered, hierarchical structure. In many legal systems, norms that confer authority themselves obtain their validity in turn from an aggregate of co-ordinating highest norms: the constitution.

For these reasons, Hart describes the law as a system of two kinds of rules. First, there are 'primary rules', which contain prescriptions for the members of society. In the latter respect they are akin to Austin's commands. Additionally, Hart distinguishes 'secondary rules'. These are rules which regulate the validity of the first kind of rules. They include the rules which identify the legal authorities, such as the legislature, the judiciary and the police. These secondary rules regulate the coming into effect and application of the law (and thus replace Austin's 'sovereign').

Differing from Austin, Hart consequently pays ample attention to the normative, internal aspect of law: to the fact that, at least for a number of participants, the legal order is more than mere force, as they are convinced that the law should be obeyed. Ultimately however, he still derives the legal order from a social fact. This happens when he asks whence the highest authority-assigning legal rules (the constitution) derive their authority. Hart then does not refer to a still higher natural-law norm, but to the actual acceptance of these rules by the authorities, and thus to a social fact.

Unlike classical natural-law doctrine, Hart thus rejects the view that normative legal consciousness – the subjective awareness of the participants in a legal order that the law should be obeyed even when there is no coercion – refers to an objective supra-positive, natural-law norm. At issue is a subjective conviction, which applies only to the 'internal point of view' of the participants in a legal order who accept its norms as correct. From the 'external perspective' of a scientist, who investigates the specific legal order like a sociologist or cultural anthropologist, such norms are not legitimate or illegitimate. An anthropologist can, for example, give a value-free description and explanation of the social fact *that* in some Inuit communities it is regarded as appropriate to send older members of the group to freeze to death, without subscribing to that norm himself. In this respect legal rules are comparable to the rules of a game. The participants in a boxing match will accept the rules of the game and complain when one hits the other below the belt. Just like a judge, a referee cannot function when he does not accept the validity of the rules. However, a neutral spectator will simply ascertain that some people clearly find pleasure in beating each other up in accordance with specific rules, without himself accepting these rules as fair.

Furthermore, from the perspective of a critical ethics, the norms which the participants in a legal order accept as right may be rejected as utterly immoral. Hence, most members of the classical Greek legal order advocated slavery, whereas according to most modern ethicists this is unquestionably unjust. According to Hart's legal positivism, a legal order which is viewed as unjust in this way, nonetheless qualifies as 'law' as long as (a sufficient number of) participants accept its authority. Hart endorses the thesis of Austin's legal positivism that the existence of law is to be distinguished from its moral merit.

Hart nonetheless speaks of a 'minimal natural law'. He contends that all existing legal orders must at least contain a number of fundamental norms, such as a prohibition against violence, because this is necessary for every human society. This minimalistic version of natural law is not derived from a metaphysical, essentialist conception of man, but from human nature as it is observable by anyone. Hart points to empirical characteristics of man, such as his instinct for survival, his dependence on cooperation with others, and his egoism, which conflict with this; as well as to the condition of the world within which man must live, particularly the existence of scarcity. Hart's minimal natural law consists of rules which make communal life possible by reining in egoism, and preventing conflict about the distribution of scarce goods: rules which prescribe respect for everyone's physical integrity and property, rules for compliance with contracts, and the enforcement of rule-conforming conduct. Hart's minimal natural law does not consist of eternal, unchanging metaphysical laws. It is possible for empirical circumstances to change, and with that the rules which are necessary for the survival of man. If there were no scarcity, the need for property would be less urgent. Should people become more altruistic, sanctions might be superfluous. But as long as human life remains as it is, every human society will be based on this minimum natural law.

However, on the basis of these empirical characteristics of human life, at most a very minimal morality or natural law can be posited (of the kind that was referred to above as 'naturalistic natural law'). At stake is staying alive, not *good* living. The advantage is that the simple biological fact of the instinct for survival is for most people a plausible and uncontroversial starting point, whereas the conceptions as to what a good life entails diverge diametrically. (Although in proceeding thus, one has already excluded from discussion a fundamental problem, which Camus in his *Le Mythe de Sisyphe* (The Myth of Sisyphus, 1942) referred to as the most fundamental: 'There is but one truly serious philosophical problem, and that is suicide' (Camus 1991, p. 3).[4] Hart countered this objection by remarking that law is not meant for a suicide club.) The disadvantage is, however, that this minimal assumption provides an insufficient basis for a morality in the full sense, which can serve as critical standard for positive law, as traditional natural-law theory would want. Hart acknowledges that a legal order which complies with his requirements can nonetheless be very unjust. Survival in a group, for example, indeed requires the existence of the institution of property, but not that property be justly distributed. Even a society that is based on slavery, thus on inequality and a lack of freedom, is compatible with his minimal natural law. According to Hart, survival in a legal order after all does not require that *all* members of the society accept the existing rules as fair. It is even sufficient when a powerful minority does so, while the majority conforms to the rules only under the pressure of coercion. Such a system of norms Hart calls 'law', even if it is unjust and oppressive.

For these reasons Hart is an adherent of legal positivism: 'law' exists when in a specific area an aggregate of primary and secondary rules is accepted, at least by the authorities, and in general is efficiently enforced on the rest of the population. Law bears no necessary relation to morality, except in so far as each legal system will contain the rules of Hart's minimal natural law, as they are a necessary condition for

[4]See further in this respect, Sections 8.2.4 (psychoanalysis) and 9.5.1 (deconstruction) on the death drive.

social and legal order. However, these minimal rules of natural law cannot serve as a critical moral standard for the law, as they guarantee only order, and not a just order. Moreover, they do not constitute a meaningful critical standard, because, as a sociological fact, they will already be present in every stable legal order. In all societies there are such things as property, contracts and punishment. (One may add to this that the co-ordination of social action in more complex societies requires that the legal rules are published, that they are clear, that they are not changed at random, and that they are interpreted consistently. In *The Morality of Law* (1964, 1969), Lon Fuller summarized such principles as 'the inner morality of law'. However, Hart points out that they only guarantee legality and efficacy, not justice. Fuller's argument that the requirement of publication would prevent the enactment of unjust laws fails. In societies where slavery is generally accepted, nothing impedes the publishing of slave-enactments.) Under the concept 'law', Hart thus includes all actual legal systems. Legal science must analyse their content in a value-free manner. Hart points to the pragmatic importance of taking stock of the positive legal order as a whole, even when it appears partially unjust. It would, for example, be impractical if someone who seeks legal advice obtains information only concerning the just part of positive law, or if a law student would study only the morally just part of a specific legal order because only this part is real 'law' (as natural law would have it). As in the case of Austin, the moral valuation of law falls outside of Hart's legal positivistic programme: it is a non-legal issue, which is not, however, less meaningful.

Hart's legal positivism, in short, corresponds with Austin's in its separation of law and morals: law is what the legal authorities posit as such; it can accidentally be just, but equally, unjust. Hart improves on Austin, as his theory, by means of the introduction of the concept 'rule', takes account of the important social role of normative (legal) consciousness – even if this does not refer to something objective. He furthermore gives an account of the layered structure of law – the validity of rules lower in the hierarchy depends on those that are higher – due to the distinction between primary and secondary rules.

1.2.3.3 Dworkin's Criticism: Rules and Principles

Subsequently Ronald Dworkin pointed out in *Taking Rights Seriously* (1977) that Hart's depiction of law as a social phenomenon is also too simplistic. Dworkin rejects positivism, and specifically accuses it of unjustly taking for granted that law and morals are separate. He bases his criticism on an analysis of how judges proceed in solving hard cases which are not unambiguously covered by laws and precedent. Dworkin bases his analysis mainly on American law, where the Supreme Court plays an important role because of its power to test the constitutional validity of laws. The American Supreme Court therefore participates to a much greater extent in public moral debate than is the case in countries without constitutional review.

Thus, a number of legal phenomena that are considered as contingent by Hart, are promoted to essential characteristics in Dworkin's concept of law. Hart recognises that the interpretation by judges is often –

> guided by an assumption that the purpose of the rules which they are interpreting is a reasonable one, so that the rules are not intended to work injustice or offend settled moral principles. Judicial decision, especially on matters of high constitutional import, often involves a choice between moral values.... No doubt because a plurality of such principles is always possible it cannot be *demonstrated* that a decision is uniquely correct: but it may be acceptable as the reasoned product of informed impartial choice. In all this we have the 'weighing' and 'balancing' characteristic of the effort to do justice between competing interests (Hart 1961, p. 200).

However, Hart (1961, p. 201) maintains, this does not prove a *necessary* connection between law and morals because 'the same principles have been honoured nearly as much in the breach as in the observance'. In Dworkin's view, it is characteristic of judicial practice as such that judges are looking for right answers in hard cases by balancing the moral principles that provide the legal rules with a reasonable purpose. Dworkin, moreover, claims that adequate interpretation can indeed yield the right answer for any hard case. Hart, by contrast, maintains that in many cases law is far too indeterminate for that.

> In these cases it is clear that the rule-making authority must exercise a discretion, and there is no possibility of treating the question raised by the various cases as if there were one uniquely correct answer to be found (Hart 1961, p. 128).

Likewise, Hart (1961, p. 196) recognises that all modern states at least pay lip service to the moral principle that 'all human beings are entitled to be treated alike'. However, this connection between law and morals is contingent, because many legal systems have excluded large classes of people from their protection. To be sure, the legal order of any society will be influenced by the prevailing moral traditions. But again, the accepted morality may very well rest on superstition and withhold its benefits from slaves or subjected classes. It is not necessary at all that it coincides with 'standards which are enlightened in the sense that they rest on rational beliefs as to matters of fact, and accept all human beings as entitled to equal consideration and respect' (Hart 1961, p. 201). Dworkin, by contrast, contends that judges should find their right answers by interpreting legal rules from the perspective of the highest principles of (American) law: equal concern and respect – or the liberal triad equality, brotherhood and liberty.

Like Dworkin, legal positivists nowadays agree that law consists of more than legislation: the judge must interpret legislation and supplement it in cases that were not foreseen by the legislature. Dworkin, however, disagrees with legal positivists as to the nature of judicial decision-making. According to Hart's positivistic theory, the judge creates new law when he decides hard cases, on the basis of his discretionary power. Legal positivism, after all, states that 'law' is what is acknowledged to be such by legal authorities, specifically the legislator and the judiciary. Law does not exist prior to its determination, so that the law comes into being only *by means of* the decision of the judge that solves a hard case which is not yet covered by law and precedent. In other words, in a hard case a judge does not find the law, but creates it. Dworkin objects to this view with the response that judges themselves see this differently. The judge does not view his decision in a hard case as a creation out of nothing that rests on his subjective choice. He tries to anchor it in existing law, for example, by way of systematic interpretation, or by reasoning analogically or *a contrario* (pointing at a relevant difference). To be sure, he has the free space to choose whether to regard the law as applicable to the hard case by analogy, or *a contrario* to regard it as non-applicable, and thus to formulate judgments with opposing outcomes. His choice in favour of analogical or *a contrario* reasoning is, however, not arbitrary, but remains bound to the legal system. Judges wish to judge as justly as possible, not on the basis of their personal view of justice, but in accordance with the 'spirit' of the positive law. (The personal preferences of a judge of course in fact sometimes also influence his decision. But in his role as judge, he cannot use them explicitly to justify his decision. Judgments which are too subjective would be open to criticism.)

Dworkin, therefore, views the law as a unity consisting of more than written laws and judge-made law. The spirit of the law is hidden in the moral-legal principles which constitute the background motive of legislation and judicial decisions. Legislation is after all an attempt to give shape to a political community in accordance with certain moral ideals – at least in the Western world.

Dworkin concludes that Hart's 'rule' model of the law is too simplistic. Positive law consists not only of rules, but also of *principles*. While rules provide direct and clear-cut indications (which, for example, prohibit murder or regulate the powers of the public prosecutor), principles rather provide a background orientation for the interpretation of rules. For instance, in the United States the principle of equality constitutes the basis of legislation, and ranks as a guiding principle for all judicial decisions.

Such moral-legal background principles often do not explicitly form part of positive law. They, for example, do not have to be formulated in the constitution. Legislators are sometimes not even aware of such principles, often precisely because they appear self-evident to the legal community in question. Dworkin nonetheless does not allude to objectively existing natural-law values which precede positive law. His principles are tied to the existence of a positive legal order in a specific legal culture: they constitute its silent background ideology, and according to Dworkin form part of positive law itself. They, therefore, differ per culture and per legal system.

The lawyer can trace such basic principles by means of a systematic interpretation of the legal order as a whole: he must reconstruct it as a hierarchical normative structure, by formulating foundational principles that can summarize and justify as many legal rules as possible under their heading. He must, therefore, construct a moral theory which makes explicit the implicit coherence and purpose of laws and judicial decisions. Dworkin refers to this as the dimension of *fit*: the reconstruction must befit most of the laws and legal decisions that occurred in the past. But interpretation is forward looking as well. The legal system does not constitute a closed dogmatic whole, but an open system which develops into the future: within the possibilities of the existing law, the judge aligns himself in a hard case with the solution which is most justifiable in light of the general moral principles of his legal culture. Dworkin, therefore, gives the element of *justification* an additional role in the ideal judicial reconstruction: in cases that allow for several reconstructions that, in accordance with the *fit* criterion, suit the existing law equally well, the judge must choose that reconstruction which can best be justified from the perspective of the ideals of justice of the specific society. After the lawyer has reconstructed the legal order in this vein, he should use the foundational principles thus discovered as guidelines for the further interpretation of the law in concrete hard cases.

As already mentioned, Dworkin bases this conception of the law on the way in which judges actually justify their decisions in hard cases: by connecting with the spirit of the law, as this appears from overt laws and precedent. Drawing upon the radical consequences of this discovery, Dworkin then proposes that judges should take this approach even more seriously in the future: judges should always decide the law through an analysis of the central principles of their legal order as a whole. These principles should not only give direction to each judicial interpretation; according to Dworkin they also ensure that the law already implies a right answer to hard cases before the decision has been made (even though this is not made explicit until the judgment). Citizens can, therefore, likewise have subjective legal rights without these being expressly proclaimed: they nonetheless follow from the legal system viewed as a coherent whole. Differing from legal positivism, such rights are not created *by means of* the judicial decision. Dworkin, therefore, contends that an actual judicial decision which is in conflict with fundamental legal principles, does not constitute 'law', or, at any rate, is legally wrong.

Dworkin recognises that in reality lawyers often disagree about the best interpretation of the law. Different interpreters can point to divergent principles as foundation of the legal order. Hence, one lawyer may regard the equality principle as the most fundamental in a specific legal system, and another the principle of freedom. However, as Dworkin points out, such disagreements do not imply that there is not one right interpretation. On the contrary, the very fact that lawyers discuss alternative interpretations with each other proves that they all assume their own answer to be the right one. Otherwise argumentation would make no sense. Even if final agreement will never be reached, the striving toward the best, most coherent interpretation is included in the actual practice of lawyers. In this spirit they should go on developing the law.

In contrast to legal positivism, Dworkin states that the interpretative role of the judge implies a necessary relation between positive law and morality. After all, the judge searches for the background principles that legitimise the legal order as just. He cannot, therefore, engage in a legal discussion without becoming involved in a moral discussion as well. The moral-legal principles consequently determine his interpretation of the law in concrete cases. According to Dworkin a systematic analysis of American law would point to the principle of equality as its fundamental principle. This does not entail the uniform treatment of all citizens, but a right to be treated as equals, or to equal concern and respect – Dworkin's rephrasing of the liberal principles of equality, fraternity and liberty (*respect* for a person's autonomy).

Does this not imply that jurisprudence assumes a political character that infects its claim to impartiality? Dworkin concedes that his approach will often lead to judicial decisions that are politically controversial, for instance, in cases concerning abortion or euthanasia. In this sense, good judges are indeed involved in politics. However, they do not judge on the basis of party politics, nor are they influenced by their own political preferences. Their interpretation is still impartial, as it is guided by the immanent moral principles of the legal system. Thus in Dworkin's view, it belongs to the core tasks of the judicial power to protect the constitutional rights of individuals. Even if in constitutional review majority decisions of the legislature are overruled, this does not turn the judges into political activists.

Dworkin does not appeal to eternal and universal natural-law values, but to values which are implied in the existing legal system and the encompassing legal culture. He thus rejects the positivistic separation of law and morality. Nevertheless, he distinguishes these normative spheres from each other: in contrast to morality, law is institutionalised. Because of its function of ensuring social order, its content is to an important extent determined by central legal institutions, such as the legislature and judiciary. The content of the central legal principles must, therefore, primarily be derived from positive law as determined by the legal authorities – the dimension of *fit* in judicial interpretation.

This, however, means that the relation between law and (liberal) morality in Dworkin's theory is quite fragile. Dworkin himself realises this insufficiently because of his focus on American law. An analysis of the American Bill of Rights and other legal domains will certainly reveal that equal individual freedom is its founding principle. However, following the Dworkinian method of interpretation, the anti-Semitic legal system of Nazi Germany, as well as of the apartheid system in South Africa until 1994, would be traced back to a principle of fundamental *in*equality.

From this follows that Dworkin's legal theory only allows for immanent moral criticism of the positive law in a specific legal culture: legal rules lower down in the hierarchy can be rejected should they conflict with the fundamental principles of the same legal system. Criticism of the moral quality of the foundational principles themselves is, however, excluded. Such criticism would, in Dworkin's legal theory at any rate, not be of a legal, but of a purely moral nature. In contrast with the natural-law tradition, Dworkin's legal theory is, therefore, unsuitable to serve as a critical standard for a legal system, such as that of Nazi Germany, which is viewed as immoral in its entirety. In this regard Dworkin himself states only that, from the moral perspective of American legal culture, the normative system of the Nazis is simply something incomprehensible, and can be understood only as a perversion of law. However, from the perspective of the Nazi legal culture, the liberal principles of American law will equally appear as a perversion of law. By taking this relativistic view, Dworkin abandons any open discussion with cultures that have ideals which conflict with the American liberal values.

Since the Dworkinian principles are closely connected to positivised laws and case law, it has been contended that Dworkin's objections against Hart can be overcome quite well in a more nuanced version of the legal positivist programme that includes legal principles. The point of departure is positive law, identifiable by its establishment in accordance with the secondary rules which regulate legislation and judicial decisions. Rational reconstruction then yields the unwritten central moral principles which are inherent in the positive legal system, and which can thus be indirectly identified in a positivist way. Next, these principles determine how a judge should interpret hard cases. Thus, what law entails is not determined by moral standards but, in an indirect way, by means of formal criteria. So far, legal positivism may be able to accommodate Dworkin's critique, without having to admit that the law implies right answers for all hard cases. Positivists may still maintain that judges often have to complement the incoherency of the legal system by the use of their discretionary power.

However, this extended version of positivism would only include the principles that belong to Dworkin's dimension of *fit*. In Dworkin's view, positive law does not constitute a closed system that can be identified by means of formal criteria. Indeed, as a *relatively* autonomous system, law is open to its social environment and to future social developments. Therefore, a judge cannot avoid taking notice of the dimension of *justification*: positive law can be understood only in the light of a broader moral discussion concerning what the law ought to be. The moral principles of the social environment that play a role here cannot be identified with the formal criteria of legal positivism. On the other hand, legal systems being relatively *autonomous*, ideal-typically 'law' can still be defined in a positivist way, for the bulk of its rules and principles can be identified formally. The remaining topic under discussion is whether social principles that do not fit, but yet influence, jurisprudence are to be conceived as legal standards, or whether they rather have an extra-legal, moral status.

1.2.3.4 Critical Legal Studies

Dworkin's legal theory, and particularly his association of law with morals, has been criticized by the Critical Legal Studies (CLS) movement, consisting of legal scholars, such as Duncan Kennedy, Roberto Unger and Peter Goodrich, who adopt a critical stance towards law under the influence of Critical Theory (see Section 9.1.5), postmodernism (Section 9.1.4) and deconstruction (Section 9.5).[5] The Crits purport to unmask the claims to objectivity and justice of the law, unveiling the suppression of the socially weak that lies behind it. This 'ideology critique' is intended to open the way to emancipation for oppressed groups.

Against Dworkin, the Crits argue that law does not at all constitute a coherent whole that generates right answers for hard cases. This should not come as a surprise when one takes a realistic look at the process of legislation. Indeed, even democratic laws are products of power politics: political compromises in which diverse political parties invest their conflicting interests. Parties with a libertarian program will

[5] We have as a rule refrained from capitalising philosophical and legal movements, except in instances where capitalisation is required to point out that a specific movement is at stake; in other words, in order to avoid confusion.

stress freedom, egalitarian parties will place emphasis on equality, communitarians will favour solidarity. As a consequence, legal codes comprise a patchwork of conflicting ideological aims. In their interpretation of the law, judges must inevitably make ideological choices in favour of one of these political agendas. Therefore, the Crits conclude, jurisprudence will reflect the political controversies of the legislature. Their critical view on the genesis of the law is thus linked to a claim in the field of justification: the fact that law forms a patchwork of contradictory values renders it impossible to rationally reconstruct it in a coherent way on the basis of immanent moral principles. And even if that would be possible, the Crits argue, actual judges would fall so far short of Dworkin's ideal of the perfect judge that their interpretations would still be partisan. In the radical version of this critical view, legal reasoning turns out to be mere rhetoric. Jurisprudence is not just political-yet-ethical in the sense of Dworkin, but brutally political, being the amoral product of power relationships. From behind its cloak of impartiality, the law is exposed as nothing but a continuation of social suppression by legal means.

Kennedy's summary of his critical studies, *A Critique of Adjudication*, contains an extensive critique of Dworkin, precisely because he is 'the emblematic modern American legal theorist' (Kennedy 1997, p. 75).[6] Kennedy appreciates Dworkin's theory as the most 'realistic' within liberalism, because Dworkin concedes that adjudication does not confine itself to the neutral interpretation of the legal material. His ideal judge not only justifies his decision by *fit* with the legal system, but also by coherence with the general views about justice that are prevalent in society. So far so good. But Dworkin's theory contains the further unrealistic assumption that these dimensions of 'fit' and 'justification' can be combined in a coherent and legitimate reconstruction of positive law. At this point Kennedy launches his critique.

First, *fit* is impossible because laws and precedents are themselves the incoherent outcomes of ideological struggle. Although the legal material does constrain the judge to a certain degree, it leaves him plenty of room to interpret it according to his own political preferences. The dimension of *justification* is not of much help either, for in modern societies general political and ethical views on justice tend to be controversial as well.

The most striking ideological struggle Kennedy exposes in American law is that between conservatism and liberalism. Unlike other ideologies, such as anarchism, communism and fascism, both opponents here are in agreement on the fundamental values of Western legal order. They endorse democracy based on majority rule, the rule of law, individual rights, a regulated market economy complete with safety nets, and a Judeo-Christian moral system. At a more concrete level, however, there are profound differences in the way that conservatives and liberals interpret these institutions. Liberals favour the equal treatment of underprivileged groups, such as workers, women and blacks, and are concerned with combating discrimination. Conservatives, on the contrary, try to preserve the traditional distinctions of status because, in their view, they reflect the natural order. Liberals are tolerant of pluralism

[6] This passage is derived from Maris (2002).

and strive for a more participatory democracy; conservatives want to maintain law and order in an authoritarian fashion. Conservatives choose the side of Capital and the free market; liberals defend the rights of Labour and of consumers, and support legislation to protect the environment against the economic power of the capitalists.

Each of these two ideological parties, moreover, is internally incoherent in the ways that they try to realise their ideological preferences. Egalitarian liberals, for instance, reject a paternalistic attitude towards deviant lifestyles, while in the economic field they advocate paternalistic protection. They invoke the needs of the majority against rights that protect traditional privileges, but appeal to individual liberty rights where these conflict with majority interests; conservatives do the opposite. Moreover, there are numerous situations where fundamental liberal principles, such as liberty and equality, are actually in contradiction with each other. Under the influence of his commitment to racial justice, for instance, a liberal will tend to prohibit hate speech, but at the same time he will be inclined to tolerate it in the name of civil liberties. A liberal judge will not even be able to find a right answer within his own ideology. Judges then, regardless of whether they are liberal or conservative, may arrive at completely conflicting answers.

Kennedy devotes special critical attention to private law. In his pioneering work, *Form and Substance in Private Law Adjudication* (1976), he maintains that in the legal relations between private citizens, two incompatible ideologies, that is, individualism and altruism, each of which sports its own legal uniform, are in a state of permanent war. Legislatures with an individualistic bias tend to make laws in the form of rigid formal 'rules', furthering predictability as a necessary condition for each individual for purposes of rational planning and the optimizing of his or her well-being. Altruistic lawmakers, on the other hand, prefer the form of open 'standards' of a more substantial tenor, such as 'good faith' or 'fairness'. Between contract partners, for instance, such standards implicate mutual obligations that go much further than the parties have explicitly agreed upon. The contractual relation requires, therefore, more solidarity than is implied in the free will and self-interest of the parties concerned.

According to Kennedy, all legal talk about rights and the rule of law, as if they were objective goods, conceals partial group interests. Kennedy speaks of an ideological struggle in which each party invokes a doctrine that legitimizes its own interests as universal values. Dworkin's liberal reconstruction of law is also an example of 'fancy theory', as is 'the project of the milieu of elite academic intellectuals self-consciously concerned with universalising the interests of various oppressed or disadvantaged groups' (Kennedy 1997, p. 300). Apart from representing partial group interests, legal intelligentsias, moreover, have autonomous interests of their own. The legal system gives them privileged access to the courts, which empowers them 'to settle ideologized group conflicts, through a mystified adjudication process' (Kennedy 1997, p. 224). They further their status by keeping up the appearance of being engaged in a neutral adjudication process; in this way they preserve the legal status quo, in the heat of the ideological combat in which they are an active party.

Unsurprisingly, Kennedy disagrees with Dworkin's contention that we should take judges seriously in their self-interpretation, as being impartial arbiters reaching for right answers. This pretension is mere window dressing. Kennedy reverses Dworkin's argument that the burden of proof to the contrary lies with the sceptics. Indeed, the deep ideological controversies about interpretation make the possibility of coherence very implausible. Up till now nobody has found a right answer, nor is it likely that someone will do so in the future. According to Kennedy, the self-concept of the judiciary is a form of self-deception caused by wishful thinking. Although judges are dimly aware that their judgments are not impartial, they conceal this from themselves and from the outside world. The general public displays the same attitude, because ordinary citizens also have an interest in keeping up the appearance of neutral arbitration: 'People want coherence for its own sake. . .because it is a pleasure, it is release from a kind of terror' (Kennedy 1997, p. 207).

Yet this inclination has undesirable consequences, Kennedy maintains. Due to the law's pretensions to objectivity, its rule is generally accepted as being natural and just, and it does not, therefore, provoke revolt. The sad by-product of this assumption has been lasting social inequality, and discrimination against weaker groups, such as the second (and third) sex, immigrants from the third world, and members of the fourth estate, or women, homosexuals, blacks and workers.

Kennedy (1997, p. 17) presents his subversive critique of adjudication as a 'project for changing the world'. He and other critics of CLS intend 'to delegitimate the outcomes achieved through the legal system by exposing them as political when they masquerade as neutral' (Kennedy 1997, p. 280). His critical characterizations of the legal system are intended to undermine the dominant belief in law as a natural and just order which impedes 'our efforts to realize justice and liveliness by falsely making it appear that they can't be realized' (Kennedy 1997, p. 17). In a positive sense, he wants to bring about a better world by empowering suppressed groups, so that they can participate in society on equal terms.

So far, Kennedy's approach is compatible with the Marxist critique of ideology (see Section 7.4). But his postmodern perspective also places him at a critical distance from the orthodox and neo-Marxist left. His critique is an internal one and has the aim of showing that current legal doctrines are incapable of living up to their own pretensions. He does not develop a Grand Theory, in the style of the Marxist explanation of law as a reflection of economic interests; nor does he offer any Utopian alternative. Kennedy's postmodern writings hint at a more aesthetic kind of liberation, to be attained by a permanent spiritual revolution. His critical studies intend to break up the rationalistic clusters of bourgeois culture, thus liberating suppressed vital irrational energies. They deploy –

> internal critique to loosen the sense of closure or necessity that legal and rights analyses try to generate. But rather than putting a new theory in place, it looks to induce, through the artificial construction of the critique, the modernist emotions associated with the death of reason - ecstasy, irony, depression, and so forth (Kennedy 1997, p. 342).

Kennedy recognises that this critique bites its own tail. If you deny that rational argument is possible, that very denial must be irrational too. And if all moral statements lack objectivity, your moral alternative likewise just expresses one more emotional preference. From this radical conclusion Kennedy recoils. In the end he confesses to be closer to American pragmatism than to European postmodernist scepticism. Instead of doing away with legal reasoning completely, he rather embraces the pragmatist assumption that competing legal conceptions can be compared for their practical success. For instance, appeals to 'rights' have proved useful to oppressed groups. Therefore, the oppressed may go on using 'their rights rhetoric, when it operates effectively' (Kennedy 1997, p. 335).

More generally, Kennedy declares his belief in the rule of law, albeit with certain provisos. He agrees with liberals like Dworkin that there should be legal restraints in the relations between private persons and between public authorities and private persons. These rules should be enforced by independent judges who feel bound by the legal material. Surprisingly, Kennedy (1997, p. 13) concludes not only that citizens have rights, but also that such rights ' "exist", even if there is no Bill of Rights . . . and no legal recognition of the particular rights that particular countries consider "fundamental" '. His main proviso is that the liberal democratic rule of law cannot claim universal validity, since it has proven its relevance mainly in the context of Western culture. In short, Kennedy still believes in the rule of law, human rights, democracy and separation of powers as a desirable alternative to fascism and communism, provided that those concepts are not reified. So it seems that Kennedy's critical studies do not so much present a sceptical program, but rather a radicalization of the liberal project aimed at empowering excluded groups. (Likewise, in his later work Unger (1986, p. 41) labels his own critical program as 'super-liberalism'.)

On the other hand, Kennedy remains sceptical of Dworkin's claim that law can be rationally reconstructed into a coherent whole which renders a right answer for each legal dispute. Dworkin has responded to this critique, noting that the obvious fact that the law contains conflicting principles does not disprove his right-answer thesis. In private law, for instance, the judge should find the right solution by establishing a fair balance between individualistic and altruistic principles. This would indeed be impossible if such principles were incompatible, Dworkin maintains, but *that* CLS has failed to prove. Yet, Kennedy may very well be right in his critique that, in a dynamic plural world, judicial decisions are underdetermined by the legal rules and principles. But even if in major hard cases different decisions could be reasonably defended, this would not subvert the liberal rule of law. One way or another, such indeterminate cases are to be decided according to the formal procedures of adjudication. As long as the judge has adequately anchored his decision in the legal system, citizens should accept his arbitration as binding, even if they do not agree with its substance.

In summary, legal positivism may, at least partly, be saved from Dworkin's critique by incorporating moral principles that fit the legal system. Even if Dworkin is right in saying that legal systems are relatively open to their social context and its prevailing values, this would only allow for immanent moral criticism. The Dworkinian method of interpretation cannot overcome the boundaries of local legal cultures. Hart, then, is right in his thesis that law does not have a necessary connection with an objective morality as the advocates of natural law maintain, nor with any critical morality that can claim universal validity. On the other hand, the identification of law and power politics of CLS would hit the mark only if their scepsis of rational ethical discussion holds. If, by contrast, it is assumed that we can learn from history, criteria for rational and moral progress in the sense of the Enlightenment may emerge from the political struggles, even if these cannot claim to represent eternal truths. This seems to be the pragmatic conclusion of Kennedy, too. In that case, the immanent claim of law to impartiality and justice can be met with a liberal standard that comes close to Dworkin's principle of equal respect. Anyhow, legal philosophers of all kinds, positivists included, will acknowledge that in modern Western societies law happens to coincide with liberal morality, albeit in a far from perfect way.

1.3 Law Between Power and Morality

In the 19th and 20th centuries legal positivism increasingly pushed aside natural-law theory. The reason for this lies partly in the ideal of a value-free science and partly in waning confidence in the possibility of formulating generally valid standards for law. Within legal positivism, as already mentioned, two variants are to be found: the one, normative, and the other, descriptive.

The descriptive version of legal positivism of Austin and Hart views the study of a legal system as a value-free scientific activity, comparable to the procedure adopted by a natural scientist who formulates a theory of atoms. It thus wants to make the study of law independent of the moral discussion concerning what law should be and when it should be obeyed. In addition, according to the descriptive positivists, law may be critically evaluated in terms of independent moral criteria. Just as the atom physicist, after the formulation of his theory, can concern himself, from a moral point of view, with the social consequences of his enquiry (for example, about the production of atom bombs), the lawyer can, from a non-legal, moral point of view, furnish commentary on the claim to obedience of the positive legal system.

Normative legal positivism bases the distinction between law and morality primarily in the certainty that the positive legal order offers, in contrast with the uncertainty regarding generally valid standards in a moral discussion. For this reason, unlike descriptive legal positivism, it attaches a normative conclusion to the establishment of what the positive law is. Because of the importance of social certainty and order, it argues in favour of an absolute duty of obedience to the rules issued by the central government, whatever their content.

The German philosopher Radbruch (1878–1949), for example, argued in the first half of the 20th century that law is directed at three aims: justice, legal certainty and effectiveness. This relation between law and justice suggests a natural-law conception. However, because of the fundamental disagreements about the substance of 'justice', according to Radbruch in social practice the principle of justice cannot serve as a critical moral standard for the law. Instead, he regards legal certainty as the ultimate legal principle. Broad agreement, after all, does exist concerning the function of law of ensuring order: it must at least guarantee the orderly functioning of society. For that reason legal subjects must know which norms they need to comply with, in accordance with the principle of legal certainty. The indeterminacy of the concept of justice stands in tension with this. If everyone were to interpret the law according to his own moral convictions, chaos and conflict would quickly make an end to all order. The fundamental social importance of clear legal norms made Radbruch adopt a legal positivistic position, even though personally he was of a liberal social-democratic conviction: law is what the legislator lays down to be such, irrespective of its content. He added to this the normative prescription that the judge should always apply the law, even if he considers it unjust.

Radbruch, however, later made an about-turn in this respect. Towards the middle of the 20th century he was confronted with the German Nazi regime, which enacted law that in the view of liberals like himself was extremely unjust. To Radbruch's dismay, former law students who had been educated in normative positivism, as judges uncritically accepted the dictatorial, anti-Semitic Nazi laws. Absolute obedience to such a completely immoral order Radbruch now found to be unacceptable. For this reason he wanted to make the duty of obedience dependent upon moral criteria. He did not do this in the way of the descriptive positivists by arguing for an independent moral discussion concerning the merits of the law, in addition to a value-free legal analysis. After the Second World War Radbruch rejected not only the absolute duty of obedience, which German legal philosophy had associated with positivism, but also legal positivism as such. He searched for the solution in a revised natural-law doctrine, which emphasises the link between law and justice, now equating justice with human rights.

The atrocities of the Second World War led to a general revival of natural-law philosophy. In the Netherlands, for example, natural law made a comeback in reaction to the uncritical attitude of the Dutch Supreme Court between 1940 and 1945 regarding countless unjust measures of the German occupiers. In 1942 the Supreme Court had agreed with the repeal of section 1 of the Criminal Code which entailed the principle of legality (permitting punishment only on the basis of a previously existing criminal provision), making punishable all conduct that is regarded as dangerous for the social order and in conflict with the 'sound opinions' of the people. This opened the gates for great arbitrariness on the part of the occupiers. For this reason there was a need after the war for critical standards against which to measure the law. The renewed call for a moral infrastructure for the law likewise appeared during the processes at Nuremberg. In the course of these processes, Nazi war criminals were punished because of 'crimes against humanity', which, when they were committed, were not as yet positivised as crimes. This meant a violation of the principle 'no punishment without a previously existing penal law'. The trial was nonetheless justified with the natural-law argument that the Nazis could have known even before the positivisation that their inhuman conduct was criminal.[7]

[7] Against the processes at Nuremberg, it is contended that they amount to one-sided victor's law. Hence, no prosecution was instituted against war crimes of which the allied forces also made themselves guilty, such as the bombardment of civilians.

Currently the view of normative positivism that positive law has to be obeyed unconditionally is practically never proclaimed. Because of this the traditional discussion between natural-law doctrine and (descriptive) legal positivism has lost much of its practical significance. Both movements after all connect the duty to obey the law with an evaluation against moral criteria. Moreover, most of the followers of the two movements acknowledge the importance of the function of law in maintaining order, and of legal certainty. For this reason, even the adherents of natural law argue that one may be disobedient only if the legal order as a whole is fundamentally immoral. A mildly unjust order one must, on the other hand, attempt to change by legal means, because it is still better than disorder and conflict.

The remaining disagreement between legal positivists and the adherents of natural law relate primarily to the question whether moral criticism should be included within the concept of law. In so far as the relation between law and morality is concerned, the modern legal positivism of Hart has indeed come somewhat closer to natural law, although it retains the thesis that law does not have a necessary relation with morality. Differing from Austin, Hart points out that the efficient functioning of the legal order requires that a section of the participants, particularly the legal authorities, must regard the prevailing law as binding. In a subjective way, something like a normative consciousness thus plays a role in positive law, too. Furthermore, legal authorities, simply for considerations of efficiency, will always present their normative system externally as just and never simply as pure power. Both the German Nazis and the National Party in South Africa attempted to give an ideological justification for their laws. The holders of power, in doing this, open themselves to criticism based on these pretences. In short, even the legislature and the judge in an immoral legal order will never be able to withdraw themselves completely from a moral discussion. Moreover, contemporary legal positivism has integrated the criticism of Dworkin: that the law should be understood from its immanent moral background principles, and that this affects judicial decision-making. In general, the current view in most jurisdictions as to the function of a judge entails that in his interpretation he should search for a solution which is as just as possible within the system of law. This task is even more important in those legal systems where judges, because of judicial review on the basis of an enforceable Bill of Rights, have to solve political-moral problems that previously belonged to the domain of the legislature, such as the death penalty, abortion, and euthanasia.

The gulf between legal positivism and natural-law doctrine in Western culture has, moreover, been narrowed by the fact that contemporary Western legal systems have adopted the form of the democratic constitutional state, and have positivised a number of moral values which were previously developed by moral philosophers, particularly the Enlightenment values of freedom and equality. The American Declaration of Independence is an example of this. The moral principle of equality has, moreover, been positivised in the legal orders of most countries with Bills of Rights. Because of this, moral discussion has become part of positive law, even according to the criteria of legal positivism. Hence, the formulation of the right to equality in constitutions often leaves open *which* instances are to be regarded as similar for purposes of determining equal treatment. The judge or lawyer must, therefore, give a more detailed interpretation of the principle of equality, and then necessarily has to engage in an act of moral balancing. Most people agree that the formula ‘Equal cases should be treated equally’ does not mean that all people deserve absolutely identical treatment. A person who is sick, for example, requires different treatment from one who is healthy. Criteria of relevance thus need to be found to distinguish justified differences in treatment from those that are unjustified. And with the question of which differences are justified in which contexts, a judge finds himself at the centre of ethical debates. The right to equality as protected in a constitution can furthermore conflict with other moral principles that have been enacted, such as the rights to education and freedom of religion. This could lead to problems of priority between the principles of freedom and equality: may, for example, a school founded on religious grounds make a distinction based on sexual orientation when selecting applicants for the teaching profession? Because constitutions often do not establish a hierarchy between these principles, one here has to revert to the ethical question whether freedom or equality deserves priority. The theory of justice of Rawls (Sections 10.5 and 10.6) attempts to give an answer to questions such as these.

Specific subdivisions of positive law likewise contain more broad, morally laden terms, such as ‘good faith’, ‘reasonableness and fairness’, and ‘unlawfulness’, which require more detailed interpretation.

In consequence of all of this, the central question of legal philosophy concerning the relation between law and morality remains an actual one, both for the legal positivist and for the adherent of natural law. No one can withdraw himself from the question of when law is legitimate, and whether it is possible to criticise the law from a rational, moral perspective. The next question then is: what precisely does ‘justice’ entail, and how can one determine its content? The problems of legal philosophy are, therefore, to be answered within the framework of ethics in general.

However, in ethics the same problem returns that came to the fore in the discussion of natural-law theory: how to justify a generally valid ethics when metaphysical worldviews, such as that of Christianity or of Plato, have lost their plausibility? The rise of scientific thinking has strongly affected the persuasiveness of such metaphysical views. Moreover, contrary to the position during the classical period and the Middle Ages, currently no self-evident consensus exists regarding human nature and the morally good life. Individuals and groups living within the same society have very diverse moral convictions. In many European countries, for example, a large majority subscribes to the values of freedom and equality, but at the same time these countries host cultural minorities who regard such values as immoral. Besides, the Enlightenment ideals can be weighed up against each other in different ways: more equality often implies less freedom. The central question therefore is whether the modern worldview can nevertheless furnish a sufficient basis for a generally accepted ethics and concept of law, which enable people to live together in a peaceful and fair way, in spite of their conflicting ideals.

This is, moreover, a global problem, because as a result of more efficient means of communication, cultures with completely opposing worldviews increasingly come into contact with each other. The adherents of the Enlightenment contend that it is precisely the ideal of equal individual freedom that provides an answer to the problem. Their emphasis on freedom and autonomy after all allows everyone optimal space to live according to his own convictions, as long as the equal freedom of others is not affected. The law, in their view, has as function to guarantee this equal freedom. The law may, on the other hand, not enforce one particular view of the good moral life. Opponents argue against this that the liberal emphasis on individual autonomy itself likewise involves a moral preference which is not superior to other conceptions of law and morality. They even regard the ideal of freedom as inferior, because it allows freedom for an immoral mode of life as well. It would, moreover, encourage individual egoism and undermine all communal spirit. In their view, the core function of the law is to suppress immoral conduct and egoism.

The central question *Law, Order and Freedom* raises is the extent to which the liberal Enlightenment values can serve as universal foundation for law. On the one hand, most people have a basic intuition that specific moral views are better than others, and that one can even speak of moral progress in law. Consequently, most people in the West, but also elsewhere, will reject as 'primitive' or as 'inhumane' legal systems which punish theft with the cutting off of a hand, or which allow for racial segregation, or significant inequalities between men and women. This means that they actually regard a legal system which recognises the ideals of freedom, equality and fraternity, democracy and human rights, as superior to a legal system where opposing moral values find expression. On the other hand, many people nowadays incline towards a relativistic view regarding morality. They acknowledge that they can give no objective, generally valid arguments for their moral intuitions.

The question as to whether moral convictions, and particularly those of the Enlightenment ethics, can be objectively justified, can be answered only against the background of general philosophical conceptions of man and reality (the nature of being, or *ontology*, *metaphysics*) and of the possibility of knowledge of reality (theory of knowledge, or *epistemology*). In the rest of this book such general philosophical questions will be discussed within the framework of a history of Western legal philosophy.

1.4 Conceptual Framework and Brief Overview of the Subsequent Chapters

In the chapters that follow, three periods will be discussed, each with its own worldview that is characterised by a specific relation between ontology, epistemology, ethics and legal philosophy: the Greek-Roman period (having experienced its Golden Age of philosophy in the 4th and 3rd centuries BC), the Christian Middle Ages (500–1500 AD), and the Modern Age (16th century until today). In broad terms, the following historical line will be sketched: a development has taken place from the worldviews of the classical period and the Middle Ages, which presupposed a coherent unity and purpose in the universe, to the worldview of the Modern Age, which is characterised by increasing fragmentation, individualisation and relativisation. In the domain of ethics this entails the transition from a *broad* notion of ethics which concerns the whole of human life and a natural-law doctrine derived therefrom, to a more restrained, *narrower* notion of ethics, which restricts itself to rules which are necessary for living together peacefully and fairly. This can, in law, take the form of either a liberal natural-law doctrine or a descriptive legal positivist view, the latter possibly combined with a liberal ethics.

In the Greek-Roman period and in the Middle Ages people took for granted that behind the phenomenal world within which man leads his everyday life, a higher spiritual order is concealed. This spiritual world gives unity and meaning to empirical reality. Since the empirical world is viewed as an imperfect materialisation of the spiritual world, the latter serves as the standard by which to perfect the former. According to the idealistic worldview, the good is thus objectively present in (the higher sphere of) nature. Hence, in Christianity man is conceived as a being who is, on the one hand, created in the likeness of God, but who, on the other hand, does not share in God's perfection. Therefore, in this conception man must strive to develop those aspects that he shares with God. This implies a *broad, perfectionist* concept of ethics, which commands man to align himself fully with an ideal of perfection. (Natural) law, in this view, serves to enforce compliance with this perfectionist morality, and thus to ensure that man lives in accordance with his essential nature. Plato consequently developed a theory of the ideal state with detailed prescriptions for the mode of life of all subjects, depending on their social position. The aim of Plato's state was the perfection of the populace. Such a perfectionist ethics does not make provision for any individual freedom to arrange one's life according to one's own convictions. How one must live *as* man is after all objectively determined in nature, and is not left to individual choice. In this conception there is, therefore, no place for liberal freedom rights. Plato, moreover, rejects democracy, because in this regime every person's views count equally, irrespective of whether these are in accordance with the objective standards of a just and perfect life.

Characteristic of the Modern Age is the rise of *natural science*. Modern natural science restricts itself to an explanation of empirical phenomena. The idealistic assumption that, behind the phenomenal world, another non-observable spiritual world would be concealed, is rejected as indemonstrable metaphysics. In ethics and legal philosophy this worldview has led to two contradictory tendencies: one *emancipatory*, and the other, *nihilistic*. On the one hand, people think that emancipation can take place on the basis of scientific knowledge of nature and of man: by means of objective knowledge man will be able to free himself from religious prejudices and the feudal power asymmetries of the dark Middle Ages. On the basis of a realistic view of the world, he will be able to arrive at an independently chosen mode of life. In an ethical respect, emancipation implies that each individual has an equal value as a free and autonomous person. This leads to the ideal of a society of self-conscious individuals, who in free and equal deliberation with others can establish the course of their own lives. These emancipatory ideals are most strikingly formulated in the values of freedom and equality of the 18th-century Enlightenment, and the related constitutional ideals of democracy, the rule of law and human rights (Chapter 5). This ethics is directly opposed to the ethics of Plato and Thomas Aquinas, who regard an individual definition of life as utterly immoral. The Enlightenment philosophers, on their part, in general wish to challenge the authoritarian tendencies in the ethics of Plato and Thomas Aquinas.

This emphasis on individual autonomy implies a *narrow*, *liberal* notion of morality. The individual is responsible for arranging his own life. For this reason morality does not prescribe a specific mode of life on the basis of an ideal of the perfect man, as in the classical and Christian broad, perfectionist concept of ethics, but leaves man free in his choices. In this modern conception, man's autonomy, his ability of self-legislation, constitutes the core of human dignity. Because of its limited claims, this modern morality is referred to as a 'narrow morality'. Government and law, in this view, likewise have a limited function. They must not impose a virtuous life in a perfectionist sense on all citizens, but limit themselves to creating the conditions for the equal freedom of all. Differing from anarchism, which regards *every* governmental limitation of individual freedom as evil, liberalism does assign certain organising functions to law that restrict liberties. It is sceptical about the anarchic presupposition that free persons will spontaneously respect each other, and takes account of the possibility that people may instead infringe each other's freedom rights and harm each other's interests. However, the liberal legal order may limit the freedom of citizens only to regulate their conflicting interests and to protect their freedom rights. It may, apart from this, not enforce a specific mode of life simply because the authorities regard it as morally good (*moralism* or *perfectionism*). The state may also not force an individual to act in a certain way because that would serve his own interests (*paternalism*). Law and morality in the liberal view thus have an internal connection, but of a specific, limited nature. Individual freedom finds its limit in the legal order which protects the equal freedom of all others, and the legal order finds its limit, in turn, in the freedom rights of the individual citizen. Individual autonomy is protected by the classical human rights, which guarantee freedom from state interference. The government may promote only the virtues which are presupposed by a liberal legal order, such as respect for the person and property of others (and possibly even virtues which are presupposed in an autonomous mode of life, such as independent thinking and openness to information). Such a narrow legal philosophy, based on the autonomy ideal, is to be found with Locke and Kant (Section 4.2 and Chapter 6). This is not to say that liberals do not support a more far-reaching ideal of human perfection than simply that everyone should be autonomous. Liberal negative freedom is not an aim in itself: it must still be realised in greater detail. Every individual should do this according to his own representation of human perfection. Almost nobody simply follows his wishes uncritically as these present themselves to him: most people organise their preferences from the perspective of life ideals which extend over a longer period. For example, even someone who is addicted to the smoking of nicotine will, on being asked, acknowledge that he would actually prefer to kick the habit because of the health risks. On a personal level everyone is thus a perfectionist in his own way. Liberals can, moreover, support more far-reaching perfectionist ideals for all persons, for example, 'you should never lie' or 'cultural development is desirable'. However, on the level of political and legal philosophy they do not see here any task for the state, since it concerns a question of individual responsibility. One may of course still attempt to convince others of one's ideal by means of argument. Liberalism is, in other words, primarily concerned with the social conditions enabling an independent life.

The worldview of natural science, however, implies an opposing nihilistic tendency as well: values, such as those of the Enlightenment, are difficult to ground in nature as it is understood by modern science. Natural science after all limits its knowledge to nature as it is observed by the senses. The modern ideal of science implies that theoretical hypotheses must be capable of being tested by means of empirical experiments. Platonic and Christian metaphysics, which assume the existence of a higher world behind the empirical world, are, therefore, regarded as indemonstrable speculation. And it is seriously doubted whether an ethics can have its *only* foundation in the observable world. The empirical world after all equally exhibits phenomena which rate as immoral and phenomena which are regarded as morally good. The very function of ethics is making a distinction between these phenomena. Objective values are not observable *in* the empirical world. For this reason one can, according to the model of natural science, speak objectively only about observable facts, not about norms. This means that one can, equally, choose lack of freedom and inequality or favour the Enlightenment ideals. Viewed thus, the scientific worldview tends towards moral *non-cognitivism*.[8] In its most radical form, this tendency can result in moral *nihilism*: there is no objective morality; one lives only once, thus why would one place restrictions on oneself? Why would one actually take account of others? Why not live egoistically and aggressively if this is how things are? The optimistic belief in progress of Enlightenment thinking thus stands in contrast to the fundamental meta-ethical problem of the Modern Age: how can these Enlightenment ideals underpin their claim to universal validity? Does the Enlightenment really amount to objective moral progress in comparison with Greek ethics?

Non-cognitivism nonetheless does not necessarily have to lead to nihilism: it can in its turn serve as the basis for a *narrow morality*, which to a certain extent corresponds with the Enlightenment values. This may be argued for as follows. Although there are no objective moral values, people need shared rules as they have to live with each other. Therefore, one has to search for a less far-reaching system of norms that is acceptable to all members of society. One then arrives at a narrow morality that limits itself to the rules that are necessary for peaceful social life. For the rest, everyone must live in accordance with his own convictions, as a 'broader' morality cannot be objectively founded. Here a liberal view of ethics and law is thus presented as a moral solution of the 'second order' for the problem that people must live together, although they have conflicting views of the 'first order' regarding the good life (see the liberal theory of justice of John Rawls, Section 10.5 and 10.6).

---

[8]The thesis that moral knowledge is impossible.

One problem, however, is that this second order ethics works only when all are prepared to compromise – social stability may even require that all endorse a meta-ethics of tolerance. It does not provide an argument against a powerful group that has the will and the ability to impose its views on the rest of the members of society.

One point of criticism of adherents of a broader morality against the narrow, liberal morality is, moreover, that it provides an insufficient basis for social cohesion. In contemporary thinking this criticism of liberalism is expressed by communitarians, such as MacIntyre (Section 9.1.2), and partly by neo-Marxists (Section 9.3.1). From the time of the Enlightenment they were preceded by philosophers, such as Rousseau (Section 5.5), Hegel (Section 7.3) and Marx (Section 7.4). These opponents of liberalism object to the individualism of Enlightenment thinking. According to them it encroaches upon the solidarity which is required for social life. Moreover, according to this criticism, liberalism is based on an overvaluation of the value of autonomy: in fact, individuals are not at all capable of determining their lives autonomously, independently of the communal traditions in which they grow up. Communal life, therefore, has a higher value than individual freedom. Only in a community with others can one arrive at full maturity. These anti-liberals in many instances revert to classical perfectionist views, contending that the legal order should greatly restrict individual freedom on moral grounds. When individuals have the freedom to do what they want, according to the perfectionists, they often make short-sighted choices that hinder them in their further development. Addicts of nicotine, gambling, drugs or television, for example, make themselves the slaves of their own desires, which means that they are not *really* free. Perfectionists, therefore, distance themselves from the liberal view of freedom, which entails freedom *from* external hindrances (such as state force), and which leaves it open to the individual to decide how to fill in this free space (*negative freedom*). In opposition to this they propose a completely different, metaphysical concept of freedom: one is free when one can unimpededly develop one's true nature (*essential freedom*). According to them, the state must, if necessary by means of coercion, ensure that man is free in a complete sense: free to develop an attitude to life in which he finds the full development of his true humanity, unrestricted by his own internal irrational tendencies. The law then serves to perfect man in this direction.

The following conceptual schema explains the diverse views on freedom:

X is free from Y toward Z

X stands for the *bearer* of freedom, for example, a person or an organisation. Y stands for *restrictions* on freedom. Z stands for the *goal* which freedom is meant to serve. Freedom is, in other words, a relational concept. One must always ask oneself: who is free from what for the attainment of which goal? This book focuses on the role that the law must play in this regard. On the one hand, law creates order, by means of which it restricts everyone's negative freedom. On the other hand, everyone, with the exception of radical anarchists, is convinced that freedom without law is not possible either. In the liberal conception, law specifically serves to guarantee everyone's equal, negative freedom against unjustified infringement by others.

In accordance with the classical version of liberalism, the human individual is the subject of this freedom (X). The individual is himself responsible for the determination of his ideals and other goals (Z). Classical liberalism deduces this from a specific concept of man: characteristic of man is his autonomy. This implies a liberal standard of human perfection: one's life is imperfect when one cannot plan it oneself.

From this, moreover, follows how liberals define restrictions of individual freedom (Y): external restrictions which stand between oneself and one's goals. Freedom is then freedom *from* such restrictions. Classical liberals refer in this respect primarily to restrictions such as physical force by the state or fellow human beings. Later liberals, however, arrived at the insight that one can equally be impeded by the *lack* of goods, such as sufficient food, health, knowledge or income. Hence the distinction between *negative* freedom from *positive* restrictions, or freedom from the disagreeable presence of something; and *positive* freedom from *negative restrictions*, or freedom from the disagreeable absence of something.[9] Negative freedom is protected by means of the classical freedom or preventive rights. When the state restricts its actions to this, one has the 19th-century minimal state. Positive freedom is guaranteed by social human rights, as advocated by social-democratic liberals: otherwise there cannot be any *equal* freedom. In the 20th century, the social-democratic version of liberalism led to a comprehensive welfare state. State and law now concern themselves more intensely with social and individual life than in the preceding century.

Should one wish to indicate the goals (Z) for which someone can use his freedom, one can draw a further distinction between 'wish-directed preferences' and 'ideal-directed preferences'. Someone who subscribes to *ideal-directed* preferences, subjects his factual wishes to a qualitative judgment, for example: 'With the type of person I want to be it is not compatible that I spend my time with pornography or drugs.' Addiction to drugs then amounts to an internal impediment to what he actually wants, or even to the development of his professed essential nature. Someone who does not make such distinctions between wishes and ideals only has *wish-directed* preferences. He acts according to all his wishes, as these thrust themselves upon him.

Almost everyone in his *own* life makes qualitative distinctions between his wishes, which result in ideal-directed preferences. Almost all people are, in other

[9] Isaiah Berlin, in his famous essay *Two Concepts of Liberty* (1958), gives a different definition of 'negative' and 'positive freedom'. Regarding negative freedom he thinks only of freedom *from* external hindrances, irrespective of the purpose. His negative concept of freedom can, therefore, also include what was described above as 'positive freedom'. On the disagreeable absence of things, he did not express himself, so that he had no need for this conceptual differentiation. Berlin's 'positive freedom' is concerned with freedom *towards* something else, and thus with the realisation of the content of the concept of freedom. Berlin, as a liberal, contests especially the version of freedom which was referred to above as *essential freedom*.

words, in their own lives perfectionists: they posit certain ideals for themselves in accordance with which they attempt to live. It only becomes problematic when *the state* is granted the task of evaluating the wishes of its citizens. Only in this political sphere does the real controversy arise between perfectionists and liberals.

According to perfectionists, it is a central task of the state to 'perfect' the preferences of citizens in the direction of some ideal of human perfection. The state then determines coercively what is good for an individual, or the 'Z' in the schema. True freedom is here again *essential freedom*: the freedom to thrive fully according to one's essential nature without impediment. Ideals of the good life are in this view objectively given with human nature and are, therefore, not dependent on the choice of the individual. According to Aristotle, this entails the nurturing of the reasonable and social nature of man that distinguishes him from the animal. Thomas Aquinas thinks of the development of the characteristics which man shares with his Creator. At issue in both instances is the elevation of the spirit over the body. Vile, animal instincts can, after all, impede higher, truly human aspirations. The internal disturbances of the vile, animal instincts can be so strong that the individual can no longer cope on his own. Liberal negative freedom of choice then precisely means an immoral restriction of one's essential freedom: it permits one to be dragged along by irrational impulses. In such an instance the state must by enforcement of the law provide for the orderly management of the internal organisation of the individual life, not only for the peaceful external relations between legal subjects. Thomas Aquinas for this reason argues for strict laws against all sexual preferences which are not aimed at procreation within marriage. Moreover, from the perspective of their Z ideal, non-liberal perfectionists define the subject of freedom (X) not as an autonomous individual, but as a member of a community. According to Aristotle, one attains one's true freedom via active participation in political life. In this collectivist view regarding X and Z, individual freedom of choice and negative preventive rights against others can thus be understood as immoral impediments to one's essential freedom.

State perfectionism finds expression in both elitist and egalitarian forms. According to classical perfectionists, such as Plato and Aristotle, only a small group is par excellence the bearer (X) of the essential characteristics of man, such as reasonableness, and thus of *essential freedom* (Z): for Plato, the philosophers; for Aristotle, the free male citizens. Other human beings are inferior, and, therefore, not X. Workers (and, with Aristotle, women) exist only to serve the elite slavishly, and thus know neither negative freedom nor essential freedom, and consequently not any impediments to freedom either. The elite must rule over the rest in a *paternalistic* and *moralistic* way. Modern philosophers, such as Rousseau (Section 5.5) and Marx (Section 7.4), on the other hand, often combine their perfectionism with an ideal of equality: one must live with all others in a fraternal community. Rousseau's *fraternal* human ideal indeed includes equality, but no individual negative freedom vis-à-vis the community. Marx's fraternalism likewise entails no negative freedom rights, but does combine fraternity with positive freedom: state care guarantees that the means to satisfy the most important necessities of life are not lacking.

Someone who on principle rejects state perfectionism is a liberal. From his perspective all these variants of legal enforcement of *essential freedom* entail positive impediments to individual autonomy, thus lack of negative freedom: suppression from which one should emancipate oneself as quickly as possible. The state must respect the wishes of citizens, whatever content they may have. Even when a liberal thinks he knows what is best for others, he deprives himself of the right to enforce his moral views upon them. Every citizen is in this domain, in the determination of Z, his own legislature. Nonetheless, the liberal state does have a task here: it must sift and bring into harmony conflicting wishes. In doing this, it, however, makes use of a narrow criterion: it prohibits only the realisation of wishes that cause impermissible harm to others. Moreover, it may actively create the conditions for the realisation of the goals of each person by eliminating negative impediments.

In summary, the views concerning X, Y and Z, and thus concerning Law, Order and Freedom, currently still are sharply divided. Hence, the question is: to which extent can the liberal principles of the Enlightenment serve as the foundation for law and society? According to (normative) legal positivism, *law* at least brings about *order*. Is it possible to argue that the order of law must, moreover, regulate the equal (negative) *freedom* of everyone, and find its limit there, too? Or do state and law have an additional moral task? Or do they perhaps have a task which goes beyond morality? History will teach this – one would hope. But perhaps my history is not yours. And your legal order not mine.

Chapter 2
Antiquity and the Middle Ages

2.1 Introduction to Greek Philosophy

Greek antiquity and Christianity are regarded as the two major sources of Western civilization. Since the Renaissance, Greek culture between the sixth and the third centuries before Christ has been referred to as 'classical antiquity', and Greek philosophy since Socrates as 'classical philosophy'. The term 'classical' attributes to Greek civilization a certain exemplary significance. It specifically had an important influence on the poetry, painting, architecture and philosophy of the fourteenth and fifteenth centuries.

The exemplary character of Greek civilization is, however, easily exaggerated. In the standard view, aesthetics, harmony and rationality held a prominent place. Greek civilization was, however, at the same time characterised by war, slavery, decadence, animism and the consultation of oracles. The notions of 'Greek antiquity' and 'Christianity', furthermore, have a less univocal meaning than is often assumed. Greek philosophy in fact consists of a variety of many different, sometimes completely contradictory, philosophical viewpoints. We furthermore have to rely on very incomplete information. Regarding some periods of Greek civilization not much is known. Of certain Greek philosophers, no works at all have survived; of others, only fragments. In such cases we have to rely on what others wrote about them. Philosophers are, however, rarely a reliable source when they write about other philosophers. There is, therefore, a dearth of information, and what is known does not point to a harmony in thinking which would justify speaking of 'the' Greek philosophy.

In writing the history of Greek philosophy we thus have to remember that we are inadequately informed. We furthermore tend to be selective regarding the materials that have been handed down to us. We after all write history from our point of view, with the help of our language, our concepts and the meaning that we attach to them. In writing the history of Greek philosophy the emphasis is usually placed on its *rationalism*. This characteristic, however, requires considerable qualification. When Plato or Aristotle presents us with a system of Ideas or forms between which, for us, understandable relations exist – for example, mathematical or logical relations – we regard their philosophy as 'rational' – in terms of our standards. When Pythagoras

C.W. Maris, F.C.L.M. Jacobs (eds.), *Law, Order and Freedom*, Law and Philosophy Library 94, DOI 10.1007/978-94-007-1457-1_2, © Springer Science+Business Media B.V. 2011

says that the order of the universe can be expressed in numerical, mathematical relations, this appears rational also from our point of view. This changes when the same Pythagoras by way of a (dietary) regimen for the community established by him, orders its members to abstain from harming a white cock, from eating from a whole loaf of bread and from eating beans, or when Aristotle states that it is best to conceive children in winter and when the north wind blows. Such statements do not at all fit into the Western worldview, and also not into our views of what rationality entails. One instead tends to disregard these as irrational superstitions. For the above-mentioned philosophers and their contemporaries these statements were, however, not at all irrational. These examples may appear trivial, but there are important matters to which the same applies. The Greek philosophers, for example, understood under 'democracy' a form of government where officials and judges are appointed by way of a lottery from among the ranks of the people. Competence played no role in this regard. Slaves and women were, moreover, excluded from having any say in society. The Greek concept of democracy is, therefore, difficult to compare with the modern concept. In brief, the world of the Greeks was in many ways different from our present world. We, therefore, have to realise that we cannot transpose ourselves completely into their way of thinking and life. Historiography amounts to the selective reproduction of what has been handed down in so far as, and to the extent that, it can be conceptualised by us.

It is difficult to take account of all such problems and still write a history of philosophy. We cannot escape from simplifying, selecting, and disregarding the conditions under which philosophical ideas came about, and as a result do them an injustice. It is nonetheless important for us to have some insight into Greek philosophy, as the source of Western philosophy is to be found there. It has been suggested that the history of European philosophy is actually a long commentary on the work of Plato. Kant stated in this regard that in the domain of logic there has been no progress since Aristotle. Specifically Plato and Aristotle had a major influence on the Western philosophical tradition.

With the qualification that this amounts to a somewhat selective characterisation, one could call the Greek worldview *rationalistic*: in the universe a rational order exists in which everything and everyone has its proper place and function.[1] This orderly coherence shows some correspondence with an organism: the parts are dependent on the whole and subject to it. The individual person, for example, has a set function within the political community, whilst humanity as a whole has its

[1] Greek life also knows an explicit irrational counter-movement. Many Greeks were followers of an animistic religion which was associated with sacrifice. In particular, their worship of Dionysus or Bacchus stands in opposition to rationalism. This Bacchian religion was all but serene, virtuous and rational. It was thought that through excessive drinking and ecstatic rites it was possible to become one with the god. Perhaps the emphasis in Greek philosophy on reasonableness and a harmonious order was so great in order to serve as a counterweight to these passionate, irrational features of Greek culture: in ethics it is specifically emphasized that the passions need to be controlled through reason. Nietzsche (Section 7.5) emphasized strongly this counter-side of Greek culture.

proper place in the universe. This rational order is to a certain extent knowable to human reason. Living a 'good' or 'virtuous' life means living in accordance with one's proper place and function in this order. Everyone must do what is 'proper'. Greek philosophy thus entails a rationalistic ontology, ethics and epistemology: being, the good, and reflection on it, constitute one rational, connected whole.

In general this means a hierarchical division of reality: the reasonable and spiritual sphere represents what is higher; the discordant sphere of the material and physical, what is lower. In man both spheres combine. The good for man means that he unites with the rational world order by developing his reasonable side. Reasonable thinking counts in this rational view as the highest form of human activity, and, therefore, other aspects of human existence, such as bodily instincts, feelings and needs, have to be made subject to reason. Only in this way can harmony with the rational order of the universe be attained. Ethics in this worldview is thus based on an order which really exists, even though it is not directly perceivable by the senses.

This view of human existence as belonging to one universal order, and of the individual as part of the whole, leads to a broad conception of ethics. Such ethics in principle leaves no single aspect of life untouched, neither that of the individual, nor that of the community as a whole. Greek ethics is, moreover, *perfectionist*: everyone should strive for an ideal of human perfection. In conformity with this the Greeks also developed a doctrine of *natural law*: nature determines the higher purpose of man, that is, the development of his reasonable abilities in community with others; law must state the rules that are necessary to perfect the members of society in attaining rational virtue.

This view of man and world deviates greatly from the modern Western liberal worldview. The modern idea of individual, personal 'negative' freedom, in the sense that one can do what one wants, does not appear in the thinking of Greek philosophers. For the latter, this idea would certainly lead to irrational and short-sighted egoism. Freedom for the Greek philosophers meant *essential freedom*: to free oneself from irrational desires so that one can live in accordance with one's reasonable human nature. The state was, moreover, contrary to the contemporary liberal view, not regarded as a necessary arrangement for the protection of individual rights. A positive meaning was attached to life in the community. The individual can, in this view, only be a complete human being in a political community. Virtues, therefore, above all had a social meaning; the duties of citizens were emphasized, not freedom rights.

The Golden Age of Greek philosophy is often divided into two periods, with Socrates (469–399 BC) bridging the divide between them. In brief, Greek philosophy provides us with the following scenario. In the period before Socrates, a development takes place from *mythos* (magical-mythical thinking) to *logos* (rational-logical thinking). Under the influence of great culture shocks the Greeks lost the self-evidence of their traditional mythological worldview. From the sixth century BC the pre-Socratic philosophers, by independent critical thinking, attempted to determine how the world fits together. The first, still primitive theories derived all phenomena from one natural phenomenon which would be the source of all others: according to one, air; according to another, fire; according to a third, water. The various philosophers thus contradicted each other.

This is why a next generation of philosophers, the *Sophists*, by way of critical reflection, arrived at the relativistic or sceptical view that truth is dependent on the viewpoint of the speaker, or even not knowable at all. They furthermore provide more specific arguments in this regard. A person who is sensitive to the cold would, for example, experience something as cold which another would call warm. Protagoras, therefore, concludes that man is the measure of all things. A universally valid natural law is, in terms of this view, impossible. According to the Sophists the law is simply something made by human beings. From a political perspective this relativising of truth can have two different results. It can either lead to *democracy*: as there is no absolute truth, all opinions are of equal value; therefore, all opinions should count equally in political decision-making. Or it can lead to *tyranny*: as all opinions are arbitrary, the view of the most powerful should determine the outcome.

With Socrates as intermediate figure, his pupil Plato (428–347 BC) entered into a polemic with Sophist relativism with the assertion that absolute knowledge of reality and a rational state order are indeed possible. Plato had personal experience of the dreadful consequences of the two state forms to which sophism leads: a tyranny which is ruled only by self-interest, and a democracy in which an irrational majority unjustly sentenced Socrates to death. In the *Politeia* (the Republic) he formulated an alternative to overcome the shortcomings of these state forms. A state institution, according to Plato, is *just*, when everyone occupies his proper place in the social hierarchy. Plato sees this hierarchical order as a reflection of a cosmic hierarchical order. According to his metaphysical ontology the world consists of more than merely the empirically observable, material reality of everyday life. Behind this hides a higher, rationally ordered world of *Ideas*, which provides the standard for the imperfect empirical world. One finds this dualism in man too: he consists of a lower part, the perishable body; and a higher part, the imperishable reasonable soul, which can obtain insight into the world of Ideas. Spiritual abilities are unequally distributed: only a small wise elite of philosophers are, according to Plato, able to obtain knowledge of the rational basic structure of reality. He regards the masses as without reason: they are led by irrational bodily inclinations. This distinction in relation to the faculty of cognition is also found in Plato's ethics as well as in his state doctrine. Human virtues differ depending on the group a person belongs to: whereas the elite eclipse everyone because of their wisdom, the masses should by means of self-control, simply rein in their own irrational instincts. The just state order is, therefore, at the same time a hierarchical order: governing power belongs exclusively to the reasonable elite. The philosopher-kings are supported by a class of guardians who excel in courage and strength of will. The everyday physical work is performed by the unwise masses. This class-state thus appears similar to the later Middle Ages with its tripartite division of clergy, nobility and peasantry. Apart from his rejection of equality, Plato also rejects freedom. With most people freedom would all too quickly degenerate into immoral licentiousness. Democracy is similarly to be rejected: there the stupidity of the majority rules, in accordance with the fashion of the times. The wise elite should, therefore, by means of state power and indoctrination force a rational way of life onto the masses. The best form of government is, in brief, *aristocracy* in the literal meaning of the word: government by the best. Therefore, quality is important, rather than democratic quantity. In contrast with tyranny, an aristocratic government places itself, without self-interest, in the service of a just order. As philosophers, those who govern are after all motivated by their impartial love for the truth.

Plato's student Aristotle (384–322 BC) gave a more detailed definition of distributive *justice*: those who are equal must be treated equally, and those who are unequal, unequally in proportion to their (in)equality. Aristotle too, consequently concludes that a just society entails fundamental inequality, as different categories of people deserve unequal treatment. He likewise bases this ideal of inequality on a metaphysical worldview where rationality reigns supreme. Aristotle's ontology differs from that of Plato in that he concentrates on the changing earthly world. However, according to him, behind all the changes actually hides a fixed rational order. The worldview of Aristotle is *teleological*: all phenomena, according to him, have their own aim, goal or purpose. Consequently an acorn has the inherent purpose of growing into an oak tree. In the world a hierarchical order, moreover, exists between the aims of the diverse phenomena, depending on their position on a scale between matter and reasonableness. Man constitutes the highest category: he distinguishes himself from the animal owing to his reason, with which he can arrange his life rationally. Aristotle's ontology at the same time implies an ethics: *good* for every phenomenon is what assists in attaining its natural goal; in other words, what serves its full development. For man the good is then that he must perfect his reasonable essential nature; in other words, rise above his instinctive inclinations.

According to Aristotle this leads to inequalities in kind between people, a social division of labour which corresponds to the unequal distribution of their rational abilities. Free Greek men like himself are capable of complete intellectual virtue. The barbarian strangers, due to their low intelligence, have a natural capacity for slave labour. Women must restrict themselves to domestic work under the leadership of men. On the grounds of such differences within humanity, Aristotle distinguishes four kinds of legal relations. The economic relations between (Greek) men are equal; principally unequal are the relations between parents and children, husband and wife, and master and (barbarian) slave. This inequality in the domestic context is continued in political life, because in the ideal constitutional state naturally only reasonable, free men have a vote. To be sure, the Athens of that time knew the democratic state form, but in accordance with Aristotle's state doctrine only free Greek men counted.

Of the thinkers who came after Aristotle, we furthermore discuss the Stoics here. The Stoa came to the fore after the conquests of Alexander the Great (356–323 BC), who in his short life managed to conquer a large part of the then-known world. He wanted to unite the whole world in a common 'Hellenic' culture (hence the name 'Hellenistic' for the period of Greek civilization after Alexander the Great). The

Stoics wanted to free people from their irrational fears (for example, the fear of death and of the uncertainty regarding their destiny) by showing that the cosmos fitted together rationally. Man could obtain freedom by forsaking irrational desires (such as living eternally and obtaining power) which bring him into conflict with the rationality of the cosmos. From a legal-philosophical perspective the Stoics are especially interesting because they, starting from the presupposition of the moral equality of all people, broke with the traditional Greek ethnocentrism and advocated cosmopolitanism. The 'Hellenic' character of this cosmopolitanism, however to some extent devalued this idea.

The Middle Ages in this book is represented by the figure of Thomas Aquinas (1225–1274), who according to many was the greatest of the theologians and philosophers of the Middle Ages. He wanted to bring about a synthesis between Aristotelian thinking and Christian thinking. Like Aristotle, Aquinas employs a teleological worldview: everything is, because of its inner essential nature, aimed at its own perfection. For Thomas, man ultimately aims at beholding God. Thomas fits his views regarding law into his creation theology: human laws are via natural laws derived from divine law, which governs everything. From a legal-philosophical perspective, the thinking of Thomas Aquinas is especially interesting as an example of naturalistic natural law with a perfectionist tendency.

Towards the end of the Middle Ages Thomist thinking, which united faith and reason, was ripped apart. In concluding this chapter we deal briefly with Duns Scotus (ca. 1266–1308), and in somewhat more detail, with William of Ockham (ca. 1300 – ca. 1350) and Marsilius of Padua (ca. 1290 – ca. 1343). Duns Scotus separated faith from reason. We cannot reach God by way of the heathen rationalism of Aristotle, but only through humble faith. William of Ockham was of the view that humility requires that we, as believers, must at the same time give up on every attempt to understand something of God: we must submissively bow our heads to his inscrutable decrees. Marsilius of Padua derived radical political and legal-philosophical consequences from these ideas: pope and church should restrict themselves to the supernatural; the natural belongs integrally to the jurisdiction of the state. Marsilius of Padua is interesting because in his thinking we find ideas that would later, in the modern period which follows upon the Middle Ages, be worked out in the doctrines of the social contract as well as state absolutism.

2.2 Pre-Socratics

Greek philosophy – and thus the pre-Socratic period – begins in approximately 585 BC with the appearance of the philosopher Thales: not in contemporary Greece, but in Miletus, a city in Asia Minor (now Turkey). At that time, in the area of contemporary Greece, a number of autonomous city states existed with very different social and political systems. The mountainous landscape made mutual influence difficult. This led to the city states on the coast choosing seafaring rather than trading across land which was only passable with difficulty. Seafaring brought the Greeks to Southern Italy and Asia Minor, where colonies were established.

In Asia Minor the Greeks were confronted with the highly developed civilizations of Mesopotamia and Egypt which came into existence many centuries earlier in the fertile areas around the estuaries of the Nile, Euphrates and Tigris. Because of this confrontation with cultures with completely different worldviews, the Greek emigrants lost faith in their own mythological traditions. This meant the start of philosophical thinking, or the development from *mythos* to *logos*: man started reflecting independently and critically about the true nature of reality. Many of the early theories now appear primitive, but they provided the basis for the classical philosophical systems of Plato and Aristotle. A first generation of *natural philosophers* attempted to explain reality with reference to a single natural principle. Thus, Thales contended that water is the basic principle of all phenomena in the universe. Other natural philosophers pointed to the earth or air as the primordial element. Later generations formulated theories of an even more abstract nature, although mythological thinking continued having a clear influence. So, for example, Pythagoras stated that the universe is composed of mathematical relations. Behind observable reality, thus, hides a harmonious rational order, which is reflected in the mathematical thinking of man.

From the above discussion the rationalistic tendency of Greek philosophy is apparent: the reasonable stands above what is perceived by the senses, the spirit stands above the body, and knowledge comes into existence through thinking, not sensory perception. In the fifth century BC, Heraclitus and Parmenides worked out this rationalism in opposing ways. According to the conflict theory of Heraclitus, the rational order of the cosmos consists of a dynamic equilibrium of opposing forces ('War is the father of all'). This equilibrium is, therefore, subject to continuous change ('All is flux, nothing stays still'). It concerns the battle between principles, such as coming into existence and perishing, life and death, hate and love, man and woman, day and night. Such opposing principles cannot do without each other: the good only exists in contrast with the bad. Heraclitus saw law as a consequence of this rational cosmic combat. In human society this battle leads to a (temporary) hierarchical order in which individuals and groups find their proper place. This is reflected in law. Law is part of the same cosmic justice which at the same time determines the proper relation between the heavenly bodies:

> The sun will not overstep his measures; otherwise the Erinyes, ministers of Justice, will find him out (McKirahan 1994, p. 125).

By contrast, according to the static model of Parmenides, all change in the observable world is an illusion. Behind this hides a rational reality which always remains at one with itself. This was the solution of Parmenides to the fundamental philosophical problem of the relation between thinking (knowledge) and reality. Thinking requires fixed concepts which remain at one with themselves. It must be certain what a person means with the concept 'table'. If 'table' could at the same time mean 'ostrich' or 'wine', no one would know what one is talking about. However, observable reality changes constantly, as Heraclitus indicated with his opposing conceptual pairs: day becomes night, young becomes old, love turns into hate. It is, therefore, difficult to determine whether thinking can indeed acquire a sufficient grasp of reality. Parmenides drew a radical conclusion from this: the world is only conceivable and rational if it remains completely at one with itself. And because the real world, according to the rationalist viewpoint, must correspond with what is conceivable, the changing world which we observe daily must rest on an illusion. True reality must consist of a rational unchangeable world. This equation between thought and being is characteristic of the rationalistic worldview.

2.3 The Sophists

2.3.1 Scepticism and Relativism

The first Greek philosophers thus developed a variety of mutually conflicting theories concerning the nature of reality. These could impossibly all be true at the same time. In the fifth century BC, this led to the sceptical, anti-rationalistic philosophical movement of the *Sophists*.

In the rationally oriented philosophy which preceded the Sophists, doubt was generally expressed regarding sensory perception as a source of knowledge. The Sophists now likewise expressed doubt concerning the reliability of reason, and as a result arrived at a sceptical theory of knowledge. In their opinion objective truth was unattainable. The Sophists nonetheless had different views regarding the degree of doubt. Some drew a radically sceptical conclusion. Cratylus, for example, contended that reality was so changeable and chaotic that it could not provide any support for thinking. His ontology is, therefore, related to that of Heraclitus, but it denies the assumption of an underlying rational order. For this reason, knowledge of facts and norms is, according to Cratylus, impossible. As a consequence, he refused all further discussion.

Other Sophists drew a less radical conclusion and arrived at a relativistic view of knowledge. They denied, like Cratylus, the existence of any rational order behind observable phenomena. If this universe existed, it would be unknowable. Of the world as it appears to our senses, only relative knowledge is possible. Relative standards do not straightforwardly apply to everyone and for all times. Partly because of this, *rhetoric*, as the art of persuasion, will play an important role in Sophist philosophy. The achievement of victory in a debate is the criterion by means of which different relative 'truths' are measured. The Sophists, therefore, acted as travelling teachers, who gave instruction in the art of persuasion.

We know the philosophy of the Sophists primarily from the works of Plato. These are mostly written in the form of dialogues in which the Sophists often act as opponents of Plato's teacher, Socrates. Plato is frequently unfair towards the Sophists. He cuts them down to size so that Socrates – who defends Plato's views – has no difficulty in defeating their arguments. Plato in many instances does not mention arguments which could have been used in favour of their position. The Sophists, at face value, actually have too much against them to deserve just treatment. They let go of objective criteria so that true and false, good and bad, are no longer ascertainable. Hence the natural rational order in the world and in society, which was presupposed by the Greek rationalist worldview, became unsettled. Because of their relativising of the truth they also had no interest in the true and the good, but simply in success and power. Moreover, they required payment for the instruction they offered. Paid labour was regarded as unworthy in Athens where the greatest part of the population consisted of slaves who did all the work. Their critical philosophy nonetheless deserves more attention than Plato gave it.

The most important representative of the Sophists is Protagoras (480–410 BC). He appeared in the Golden Era of Greek civilization, which lasted from 490 to 431 BC. This period, at the end of which the legendary Pericles ruled Athens, ended with the Peloponnesian war (431–404 BC) which Athens dramatically lost. Under Pericles the state institution of Athens was aristocratic. In the course of this war, due to the fact that decadence among the rich increased and, furthermore, the plague broke out, the already existing democratic resistance against the aristocracy increased. After democracy was established, both political and judicial decision-making were left in the hands of large groups of citizens. Hence the art of persuading others became of the greatest importance. The Sophists were instructors in rhetoric. They defended the view that 'truth' and the 'good' are illusions. According to the Sophists, even if one did not have right on one's side, one could still win the argument. They, therefore, developed the art of public debate. Plato consequently accused the Sophists of a scandalous play with words. Regarding Protagoras, the story is told that he came to an agreement with a pupil that the latter would only have to pay him for his instruction after he won his first case. Protagoras, thereupon, asserted a claim in court to obtain payment for his instruction.

From Protagoras comes the famous statement that man is the measure of all things. With this statement he denies all objective truth. Some opinions can be better than others, but not 'more true'. The statement that man is the measure of all things, can relate to the single individual or to man in general. In the first case, everyone would have 'his own truth', and everyone would establish completely subjectively what is good and what is bad. This interpretation is, however, not defensible in light of two other statements of Protagoras. The first is to the effect that in relation to each topic contrary arguments can be defended equally well. The second is that there is no objective criterion independent of man with which to decide between opposing positions, but that consensus is indeed possible following upon rational discussion. This means that there is no absolutely objective truth in the sense of correspondence with reality, but that truth is possible in the sense of intersubjective agreement between participants in a discussion. A truth like that is bound to time and place, because it must be determined on the basis of the subjective views which people hold at that moment. For this reason rhetorical argument becomes extremely important.

Protagoras illustrates these Sophistic statements with reference to the opposing theories of the earlier natural philosophers: the one derives the whole world from the primordial element of water, another from air, and a third from fire. Similar to the two statements mentioned above, none of these contentions can ever be confirmed by way of human experience. Even if there should be one primordial principle, it is not knowable to human beings. This applies to conflicting ethical theories too, each of which prescribes a different way in which to become one with the rationally true Being. For this reason, ontology and ethics are in practice of little relevance to everyday life. Absolute, unchanging truths are beyond our reach. The only way to test conflicting views is comparing them critically with each other and discussing them. According to Protagoras, man has, for this purpose, a certain rational ability and a sense of justice that can be developed through ongoing discussion. As a result people can within a society in each instance reach a temporary consensus concerning issues of ethics and law. The content of their consensus is based on what has proven successful in the society in question: the knowledge and norms which best enable human beings to adapt to their environment and achieve their purposes. It will, however, recurrently appear that the consensus that was reached is deficient in certain respects. Dissenting, opposing opinions are then voiced anew. By way of discussion the new position can prevail and, in turn, acquire general consensus. The new position will appear to be better than the previous one when it solves more problems or solves them more successfully.

The importance of Protagoras lies in the fact that he was the first defender of a view that is again taking root today, and which many find greatly unattractive: a relativistic position.

2.3.2 Law as Convention

The scepticism and relativism of the Sophists extend also to law. Earlier philosophers regarded law as a subdivision of a divine cosmic order which is knowable to human beings to a certain extent, and which serves as norm for man. The Sophists deny the existence of such an order, or at least the possibility of knowledge thereof. As a result, the interest shifts from the impersonal, rational world order to the subjective world of man. Human society is no longer viewed as the result of a natural order which controls everything, but as a human product. Man is not only able, but required, to himself make rules for an orderly society. The Sophists were thus the first to make a distinction between *nature* and *convention,* or nature and culture. Law is no longer 'found' by man in the rational order, but made by man himself.

Different Sophists developed diverse interpretations of law as a conventional system of rules. In the absence of an objective moral standard, some sought the solution in *democratic* decision-making with which as many as possible legal subjects could agree. Others saw law simply as the result of the interests of the *most powerful* in society.

Protagoras defended a moderate relativism, in accordance with his statement that 'man is the measure of all things'. Applied to law, this rule means the following: what people in a specific state regard as fair and good *is* such within that state. Law, therefore, differs depending on time and place. In line with Protagoras's consensus model the majority of citizens must decide about the content of law in an assembly of the people. For this reason the manipulation of decision-making in the people's assembly, and in legal decision-making, is of the greatest importance. Protagoras saw in this a task set aside for instructors and public orators, and compares their task with that of a doctor. He saw as the aim of his teaching specifically the development of statecraft.

Other Sophists defended a much more extreme relativism. They denied the existence of any objective moral standard against which positive law could be tested. They did not seek the solution in discussion and in the reaching of consensus where all legal subjects participate equally. According to them law is simply the exercise of power. Thus, for example, Callicles defended a natural right of the strongest in a manner that is later again found in Nietzsche (Section 7.5). In reality conventional laws often conflict with the laws of nature. They are the product of a conspiracy of the weak masses to disempower the strong: inferior people have a base interest in referring to the natural striving for superiority of those who excel as 'injustice':

> We mold the best and the most powerful among us, taking them while they are still young, like lion cubs, and with charms and incantations we subdue them into slavery, telling them that one is supposed to get no more than his fair share, and that that's what's admirable and just. But surely, if a man whose nature is equal to it arises, he will shake off, tear apart, and escape all this, he will trample underfoot our documents, our tricks and charms, and all our laws that violate nature. He, the slave, will rise up and be revealed as our master, and here the justice of nature will shine forth (Plato 1997, *Gorgias* 484a–b).

A state institution in which the natural inequalities between people are not given effect to, a democracy in which everyone is treated as an equal, is therefore wrong. A strong man has to rise up to reclaim his natural right as master of the people.

Thrasymachus claimed that law simply gives expression to the interests of those who rule: in one country this is a single tyrant, elsewhere a small elite, farther away a democratic majority. Whoever thus has the legislative power in hand enacts laws which are called just in so far as they serve his interests: 'Justice is nothing but what is to the benefit of the strongest.' We later come across a similar statement by Marx (Section 7.4).

The Sophists were extremely important for the development of thinking about law. They untied the law from a presupposed cosmic order and regarded it as a changing human product determined by time and place. This was the start of the philosophical discussion between legal positivism and natural-law doctrine concerning the question whether positive law is simply a consequence of human convention, or whether it can be tested against a preceding, naturally valid ideal law. In so far as the first possibility is concerned, the Sophists additionally distinguished between two further possibilities: such conventions could either still be tested against the standard of intersubjective agreement, or they would simply be based on power (of a single person or of a majority).

Plato and Aristotle subsequently opposed the relativism of the Sophists and gave a new impulse to natural-law doctrine. According to them it is indeed possible to determine objectively what is just and good, independently of human consensus or striving for power.

2.4 Plato

2.4.1 Introduction

Plato was born in 428 BC in Athens. He studied under Socrates, who acted as a philosophical teacher at the same time period as the Sophists. According to tradition, Socrates each day started discussions in the street with any person he met regarding any topic that could provide insight into the nature of human existence. He concerned himself especially with questions of justice, truth and virtue. Socrates attempted to take a stance midway between dogmatism (which adopts one unproven statement as the basis of all truth) and the complete relativism of the Sophists.

Thus he, for example, attacked the Sophists for their relativistic view concerning the virtues. Under virtues more was then understood than would be regarded as such in the Western world today due to the influence of Christianity. Virtue, for example, included craftsmanship. It included all the characteristics which make people fit for their tasks. Socrates attempted to cause problems for the Sophists in the following way. He would ask them what they understand under 'virtue'. The Sophist would answer with concrete examples: the virtue of the carpenter, for example, consists in his ability to be good at carpentry; that of a doctor, in the healing of people, etc. Socrates would argue against this that there must be something which is common to all the examples, by means of which the Sophist can recognise them as examples of the same, *as* virtue. Stated more abstractly, the particular (relative) supposes the general (absolute). Socrates would, moreover, point out that the virtues that have been mentioned are not ends in themselves, but that they serve further ends. Hence, good carpentry or healing people is good in the full sense only if people can, because of this, live a more virtuous life. And a good human life, for its part, only has meaning when it constitutes a harmonious component of a natural order. It is, therefore, meaningful to speak about virtues only when we assume that these ultimately have a place in a cosmic order.

Socrates, differing from Plato after him, however developed no doctrine of virtue. Tradition records the following statement by Socrates: 'I know only that I know nothing.' With this he wanted to stimulate a critical attitude, so that people would in future be able to take their own well considered decisions. Socrates never put anything down in writing. His views became known especially through the writings of his pupil, Plato.

Plato continued Socrates's battle against the Sophists. He chose the pursuit of philosophy, although he could have had a political career as he belonged to one of the most prominent families of Athens. He was actually invited to do this, but due to the serious corruption in public affairs he declined the offer. After travelling for approximately 10 years, he established in Athens, at the age of 40, the platonic Academy, where he, like Socrates, gave free instruction. Teaching was for Plato the most important. Despite his many writings which are known to us, he stated that the core of his philosophy was never consigned to paper. With this he sought to give expression to the view that the words of language are inadequate to impart real insight. The extent to which Socrates's voice really finds expression in Plato's work cannot be established. It seems certain that Plato wanted to elaborate on what he had learned from Socrates, but added a lot to this, as he had more faith in the possibility of objective knowledge.

2.4.2 State Doctrine

The state is, according to Plato, established due to the fact that every individual person by himself is deficient, needy and inadequate. For this reason people have to live together in a *polis* (city state). The diverse abilities of different people complement each other, and for this reason a natural division of labour is established in accordance with communal needs. The *polis* must in each instance provide for the need for food, clothing and housing. In addition, the need arises for leadership and the defence of the state. Plato, therefore, distinguishes three main functions of the state: government, maintaining order, and productive labour. These must be carried out by those who are most suitable for these tasks. According to Plato the required virtues, such as wisdom and courage, are unequally shared amongst people. For this reason all members of a state community must, depending on their characteristics, be divided into three classes. Governing must be performed by a class of people who excel in the virtue of wisdom. Those who have courage as main attribute constitute the class which carries out the tasks of defence and policing. Finally, the class of workers is constituted by the majority who are neither particularly intelligent nor particularly courageous. The most important virtue of these workers is that they use their bodily energy by way of self-discipline in a productive manner. These classes stand in a hierarchical order in relation to each other. In the same way in which every individual person must allow his bodily instincts to be led by reason, in the state the class of the wise must, via the guardians of order, rule over the class of workers. Only with such a hierarchical order of classes can there, according to Plato, be a just state.

In the state doctrine which Plato develops in the *Republic*, he consequently defends an aristocratic state ideal, in the literal sense of government by the best.[2] He joins issue, also in this domain, with the Sophists, both as regards their doctrine of democracy and their view of law as the means of the power of the strongest. It is likely that Plato's political philosophy was influenced by a number of events which led to drastic changes in the Athenian world. After Athens lost the Peloponnesian war with Sparta, the victorious city state appointed an *oligarchy* (government by the

[2]Greek: *aristoi* = the best.

few) which consisted of the Athenian elite. The dictatorial and corrupt rule of the 'Thirty Tyrants' turned them into an object of hate. Their regime was overthrown within a year and replaced by a democracy. Deep resentment prevailed against the aristocrats who constituted the oligarchic government. During this democratic period, also, an action was begun against Socrates for his ruining of the Athenian youth, and for his dishonourable conduct towards the gods. In his role as philosophical teacher, Socrates had members of the aristocratic party as his pupils, which included a number of later tyrants. The grudge against these tyrants was probably turned against Socrates as well. The democratic people's court sentenced Socrates to death after a demagogic process. In 399 BC he was executed by being forced to drink a cup of poison. This course of events probably made Plato aware of a number of disadvantages of the democratic form of government. On the other hand, he also despised the corrupt and decadent regime of the Thirty Tyrants, although a number of his relatives were part of this regime.

Plato thus rejects both tyranny and democracy. He rejects democratic decision-making because in this model everybody participates, and ultimately the majority decides. He strongly resists such a simple criterion of number. He regards it as fundamentally unjustified that all views count irrespective of their content, and argues for a qualitative test. A ship is after all not sailed by the passengers, but by an expert: the captain. Only people with a *rational* ability to judge should govern the state. The majority are, according to Plato, not capable of this. They live according to the fashion of the day and allow themselves to be drawn along by fluctuating irrational desires, as occurred during the case against Socrates. The government must, therefore, be formed by the elite. Contrary to what some Sophists contended, this elite should not consist of the powerful. The latter are after all as irrational and selfish as the masses, so that a tyranny would quickly be established, as was shown by the regime of the Thirty Tyrants. In Plato's ideal society an elite of wise and unselfish men and women would rule, so that the disadvantages of both democracy and tyranny would be avoided.

Plato's authoritarian state ideal is based on a sharp distinction between the wise elite and the irrational masses. His emphasis on the need for a paternalistic government of wise experts can be understood only in light of his theory of knowledge. According to Plato most people live in a world of appearances, because of which they are not capable of rational knowledge. It would, therefore, not make sense to entrust them with the leadership of the state. True knowledge is to be acquired only by means of strict philosophical schooling. For this reason only philosophers are capable of governing.

2.4.3 Rationalistic Theory of Knowledge and Ontology

In the domain of epistemology, Plato contests, in line with the teachings of Socrates, the relativism of the Sophists. However, differing from Socrates, Plato places unquestionable knowledge in opposition to relativism. Man would, owing to his reason, be able to obtain insight into absolute truths.

Absolutely certain knowledge is, according to him, not to be found in the perceptible world of the senses. This is impossible, in the first place, because all observation is dependent upon the position and constitution of the observer. In the second place, this is impossible because what is observed is itself changeable and perishable, and thus provides insufficient certainty. Hence an object which first appears as red can in a different light appear as grey. On the basis of sensory experience, the best that can, therefore, be obtained, is uncertain, changeable *opinion*.

We arrange the changeable observable phenomena into general concepts, which do remain equal to themselves. A human being, for example, grows from a baby into an adult, and then shrinks again in old age, but despite all these changes remains included within the same concept of the 'human'. However, all cells from which he was originally constituted are in the meantime renewed completely a number of times, and he, therefore, cannot actually be said to have a fixed bodily identity over the course of time. We, moreover, still know what 'red' is even though the actual colours which we observe around us constantly change. Only because we have such fixed concepts can we bring order to changing empirical reality. According to Plato, such fixed concepts can, therefore, never derive from observable reality itself. We must already in advance have an idea of what a 'human being' or 'redness' entails, to be able to identify all the diverse particular instances which fall under such general concepts as 'human being' or 'red'. Stated differently, every comparison presumes a third, a standard by means of which comparisons can be drawn. How else would we be able to identify stick insects, human beings, bats and sloths all as 'animals'? This applies even more so to general moral and aesthetic concepts such as 'justice' and 'beauty', which are not to be found as such in observable reality. The beauty of a painting and the beauty of a piece of music are, for example, each based on very different empirical characteristics (forms and colours, on the one hand, and sounds, on the other). All material beauty, moreover, perishes with time. In addition, all things in the empirical world are not only changeable and perishable, but also imperfect and relative. In sensory observable reality, nothing is, for example, in all respects perfectly beautiful or good. To repeat, we must, therefore, know such ethical and aesthetic concepts before we can apply them to observable phenomena. (Socrates already anticipated this in his criticism of the relativistic doctrine of virtue of the Sophists.) Plato furthermore points to the universal validity and certainty of mathematical knowledge, which is independent of empirical observation. $224 + 631 = 855$ is always true, independently of the counting of observable beads on an abacus. It was, moreover, already true before anybody had factually calculated this. And it always remains true, even if all the material things on which we base such abstract calculations are lost. Our mathematical ideas can, therefore, not be derivable from the empirical world.

From this Plato concludes that such general concepts must actually exist in a separate spiritual world, preceding material reality and human thinking. He contends that the empirically observable and changeable reality is simply a world of appearance. Behind this hides a world of *Ideas* which is unchangeable and forever equal to itself, which already existed before we obtained knowledge of it. The fundamental problem which Plato's rationalistic metaphysics attempts to solve is the same as that of Parmenides (see Section 2.2): our thinking requires fixed concepts remaining equal to themselves. Observable reality is, however, changeable, and thus not graspable by means of thinking. This raises the question of the extent to which we can succeed in obtaining a grasp of reality with our thinking. Plato solves this question in the same way as Parmenides by presupposing that true reality must coincide with what is thinkable: it must be as unchangeable as the thinking about it. The observable world is unthinkable, and, therefore, unreal.

Knowledge of such Ideas can, according to Plato, only be attained by way of a proper use of reason. The senses, which form part of the inferior material world, can provide only subjective *opinions*. The everyday views concerning matters of good and bad, true and false, beautiful and ugly, are, therefore, determined by differences in taste, personal interests, societal prejudices and so forth.

Plato, thus, defends a dualistic worldview: the materially observable world is not all there is, but constitutes a mirror image of a separate, immaterial world. These two worlds stand in a hierarchical relation to each other: the perfect, rational world of Ideas serves as ideal model for the everyday, imperfect, empirical world. The Ideas have two aspects: they constitute the meaning of general ideas, but are at the same time the ideal of perfection. The word 'cat' has a general meaning which is illustrated by all different, existing cats. However, according to Plato, 'cat' is also the ideal cat, the Idea of perfection which all different, visible cats never completely comply with. The *true* (ideal) reality thus coincides with the *good*.

According to Plato, a hierarchical order prevails in the World of Ideas itself as well. At the bottom of the hierarchy are the most particular Ideas, at the top, the most general, co-ordinating, abstract concepts. This conceptual order, for example, ascends from sub-species to species, and so on; for example: elephant → mammal → animal. Regarding the precise design of this hierarchical order, specifically the issue of how the Ideas relate to each other, Plato gave no clear explanation. He did, however, state that at the top of the hierarchy of Ideas is the Idea of the True, the Beautiful and the Good. By means of this metaphysical assumption of a normative ideal reality, Plato could escape from the relativism of the Sophists. Knowledge of the general Ideas provides an objective standard in accordance with which to organise and evaluate the changing world.

With this dualism, Plato made a distinction which is characteristic of Greek rationalistic ontology, and which afterwards deeply influenced Western philosophy: between, on the one hand, a true, reasonable world which corresponds with thinking and of which knowledge is possible via human reason, and, on the other hand, the changeable empirically observable world where only appearance prevails. Reason is thus regarded as the source of knowledge by means of which truth can be obtained. 'Knowledge' which is obtained by way of sensory observation (or what Plato calls 'opinion') is, by contrast, simply a source of error. With our senses we after all observe change and development, which cannot be grasped in fixed, reasonable categories. To be sure, the observable world exists, but not in the full sense: it is based on the fraudulent functioning of our senses, which themselves form a component of our imperfect bodies. Most people are aware only of this imperfect material existence, and lack any understanding of the higher, rational reality.

Plato depicted this theory of knowledge in his famous metaphor of the cave. He compares people who only live in the world of sensory observable phenomena with persons who for all their lives have been sitting chained in a cave, with their backs to the opening. When shadows appear on the back wall of the cave as a result of human beings and objects that move at the opening behind the backs of those who are chained, the cave dwellers would regard the shadows as real, instead of the things which cause the shadows. Only when people by means of reason free themselves from the physically bound perspective of the senses, can they see the true reality in the full sunlight outside the cave: then the reality of the Ideas shows itself to them in the light of the highest Idea of the True, the Beautiful and the Good. Only then does one realise that what one all the time regarded as reality is simply a silhouette of the higher reality.

Access to this ideal truth is only to be obtained by way of rigorous intellectual as well as physical and ethical training: human beings should free themselves from their physically restricted viewpoint which is distorted by selfish desires. Only if people are capable of an impartial and unselfish (and thus moral) point of view, can they obtain an understanding of the rational Ideas with their own generally valid (thus supra-personal) nature. After all, because these Ideas are universal, and not affected by an egocentric and perverted perspective, they themselves, in addition to being true, also have a moral side. Because truth is, according to Plato's epistemology, only obtainable by a few after a rigorous intellectual and moral education, his political philosophy assumes a radically elitist and authoritarian format.

2.4.4 Moral Perfectionism

2.4.4.1 Perfectionist Individual Ethics

The sharp dichotomy between the inferior empirical world and the superior spiritual world of the Ideas which characterises Plato's ontology is reflected both in his individual ethics and in his hierarchical state ideal. Man forms part of both worlds: he consists of body and soul. Plato's perfectionist *virtue ethics* for one's personal life are based on this twofold position, which is analogous to his perfectionist political doctrine for communal life in the state.

Plato takes the following view on man. With our souls we are capable of rational knowledge. On the other hand, with our perishable bodies and the needs and urges which belong to them we also belong to the inferior material world. Plato calls the body the grave of the soul. He distinguishes, as the mediator between reason and passionate physical inclinations, will-power as a third dimension of man, which has as its function bringing the bodily tendencies under the control of reason. Man is, thus, characterised by three levels. The lowest level, which we share with animals, is that of sensual animal urges. The need for food and the sexual urge belong here. The second level is that of will-power. To the latter belong ambition, courage and hope. The highest level is reason, by means of which man has access to the perfect realm of the Ideas.

Virtues serve to perfect the higher dimensions of man. Plato distinguishes between four virtues, which correspond to his tripartite portrayal of mankind. With the lower bodily instincts corresponds the virtue of *self-control*. With the higher abilities of reason corresponds the virtue of *wisdom*. Between them resides the virtue of *courage*, which via the will has to ensure that self-control is subjected to wisdom. As overarching fourth virtue Plato mentions *justice*, which he defines as 'to each what is due to him': a situation is just if everything has its proper place in accordance with Plato's hierarchical doctrine of Ideas. In casu this means that the virtues have to relate to each other in accordance with the proper hierarchical order: wisdom must guide the other virtues. Wisdom is the highest virtue because it provides an understanding of the Idea of the Beautiful and the Good, the highest Idea in Plato's realm of Ideas and the final aim of the universe. Only by way of this insight is it possible for man to perfect himself.

According to Plato, the Good, thus, does not consist in bodily pleasure, but in the complete realisation of man's rationality, that is, an understanding of the true aim of life, knowledge of the Good. For this reason the spirit has to untie itself from the material world of appearance and direct itself towards the realm of the perfect ideal reality. The knowledge thus obtained henceforth determines all desires and actions. Plato never gave a more specific definition of the Good. He was of the view that an understanding of the Good can be acquired only after long intellectual exercise and self-discipline. In addition, physical existence must be subjected to reason by means of the moderation of needs, urges and inclinations. Man only needs to strive towards satisfaction of needs in so far as this is necessary to remain alive. By subjecting need to rational control, by exercising the will, one can escape from the imprisonment of one's bodily existence: those who are chained escape from the cave. This enables one to strive for wisdom, and ultimately for justice, by way of insight into the proper relation between the virtues and the levels of the soul which correspond with them.

However, according to Plato, most people are not able to do this. They only strive for physical pleasure and wealth. They harbour no love for wisdom and, therefore, do not attempt to escape from their 'cave'. As Heraclitus said, asses prefer hay over gold. Only philosophers live in the World of Ideas, the truly perfect reality. Therefore, only they are capable of perfecting the community as a whole in accordance with normative Ideas. Philosophers are separated by a great divide from all others. The majority will never of their own accord believe the philosophers, and, even less, understand them. Socrates, therefore, also states that in a world of fools, philosophers will undoubtedly appear to be mad.

2.4.4.2 Perfectionist Political Theory

From the above follows Plato's perfectionist aristocratic *political philosophy*. As in the case of his virtue ethics, 'justice' is here the overarching virtue: 'everything in its proper place'. Because people, according to Plato, differ greatly from each other in so far as individual virtue is concerned, they likewise deserve an unequal position in political life. Someone's proper place in society is determined by the extent to which he excels in one of the three other platonic virtues: wisdom, courage or self-control. In his ideal class state the government is formed by a wise spiritual elite, the maintenance of order lies in the hands of the courageous, whereas the non-wise, non-courageous masses, who are barely able to control their base instincts, must work to provide for the material needs of the elite.

As only well-educated philosophers have knowledge of what is good for man and society, only they can govern the state and make citizens attain perfect virtue. Therefore, the ideal rulers are 'philosopher-kings'. A philosopher is someone who has a love for wisdom and who makes this into a way of life. He lives in the reality of thinking, of the Ideas, not in the façade of the observable world. Plato's philosopher-kings endured until their 60th birthday a long and difficult training, which had to guarantee their development on the way to perfect rationality. In addition, they had to permanently relinquish earthly physical pleasure as an independent value. They relinquished all wealth, all personal possessions, all personal relations; they did not know who their children were; all of this to prevent them from being impeded in their aspiration for wisdom because of selfish inclinations. The workers and guardians, on the other hand, would have private property and personal relations with women and children. They are then, because of their partiality, excluded from all political power. Those who endure all difficult training must undoubtedly possess a great love of wisdom and really have made virtue their own. The life of the highest class is, from the perspective of those who are 'chained' to their physical pleasures, after all very unattractive. Opportunists or those hungry for power would not survive the selection process. Therefore, according to Plato, there is no chance that the government of philosophers could degenerate into tyranny.

The selection of leaders is based only on quality. Everyone with adequate talents has an equal chance of becoming a ruler. All children receive until their twentieth year the same schooling, irrespective of their birth. This education begins with music and physical exercise. Plato attempts with these methods to form a balanced and moderate character. The next stage consists of education in mathematics and dialectics in the formation of the intellect, in the hardening of the body, in deprivations for the purpose of exercising will-power and the ability to sacrifice. Those who pass selection, continue their education in the same manner. The rest fall into the class of workers. After 10 years another selection takes place, followed by another 5 years of philosophical education. Thereafter the educated undergo an apprenticeship of 20 years. They must acquire experience in all aspects of a full life, including military battle. They must learn about social life to which they would later give leadership, and gain experience in leadership functions. Those who successfully survive this apprenticeship as well, gain access to the highest class.

The philosopher-kings govern solely by virtue of a sense of duty. Not power and governing as such, but wisdom, is what they love. The state led by them specifically has the education of citizens as its task. This education is aimed at the raising of self-awareness, reflection, and the forming of citizens according to the rationalistic model. The wise rulers govern with absolute power over the other classes, who have to unconditionally conform to the unequal political and class relationships. The rulers are subject to no other limitation than that of their wisdom. They must, among other things, strictly censure pieces of writing presenting irrational views which incite urges, needs and inclinations. Theatre and poetry are forbidden as they affect the emotions rather than the intellect. When necessary the rulers may even spread lies to ensure that citizens live in accordance with the good life. They can, for example, justify their own authority by propagating the myth that they are of divine origin. Truth and reasonable arguments derived from the doctrine of Ideas are after all incomprehensible to the masses. As Heraclitus said, the herd has to be driven to pasture by flogging.

Against Plato's state model it is often contended that the individual disappears completely for the sake of the whole. Plato, after all, mentions that the state cannot be in the service of individual interests. Moreover, in his state no individual freedom exists. Yet, the state must serve the interests which are shared by citizens. The aim is ultimately to lead citizens by means of a virtuous life to their 'natural' destiny. In Plato's theory no essential contradiction exists between individual and society, because he presupposes the existence of a universal harmonious order. The instinctive inclinations of one individual can indeed conflict with communal interests, but, in accordance with his higher essential nature, the individual person fits perfectly into the organic whole of society. The inequality between different groups of people, which is the consequence of Plato's hierarchical class state and of his elitist view of government, can similarly be justified by invoking the harmonious natural order which controls the world in line with Plato's ontology. Plato regards the hierarchical structure of his state ideal not as tyrannical, but as providing for a just division of labour. The workers are for their defence dependent on the guardians, and for their administration, on the rulers. But guardians and rulers are for their livelihood dependent on the workers. According to Plato, a kind of balance exists in reality between the three classes, which is dictated by justice. A just relationship, in other words, exists between different groups of people, based on their different natural talents. Freedom and equality, democracy and a constitutional state, are, on the other hand, pre-eminently unjust.

The ideal state, as Plato envisages it, provides the standard with which actual states have to comply, if they do not wish to degenerate. Hence, if the rulers receive inadequate philosophical education, the (ideally) just aristocracy will degenerate into a military dictatorship. From the enrichment and weakening of the rulers, an 'oligarchy' would result, as well as increasing conflict between rich and poor. Eventually the people will revolt, kill the rich, and establish 'democracy'. Now every subjective opinion is regarded as equally valid and worthy of respect. In such circumstances demagogues emerge who can turn democracy into its converse, 'tyranny'. The tyrant can at first satisfy the needs of the people. When this no longer works, he must, in order to avert attention, wage war. The cycle is completed when in this hopeless situation a wise man arises, and, with the help of the good-natured, founds the state anew.

2.4.5 Commentary

Following upon this analysis, Plato in the *Republic* arrives at a 'broad' perfectionist ethics for individual and political life. The whole of state life is aimed at the moral education of all citizens into virtuous human beings. For this purpose Plato designs an authoritarian form of government which stands at odds with the modern ideal of the democratic constitutional state and the principles of (negative) freedom and equality – which Plato, of course, did not know himself. From the anachronistic perspective of contemporary liberalism, the absolute power of the philosopher-kings brings about a significant degree of inequality between the three classes and, moreover, leaves no room for individual autonomy. Democracy, the constitutional state, separation of powers, freedom of speech, and other rights of the individual citizen are out of the question. Instead of liberal negative freedom, Plato advocates *essential freedom*: thanks to the wise paternalistic leadership of the philosophers, humanity achieves freedom *from* their own irrational inclinations *for* the purpose of a rational way of life.

Plato's arguments in favour of this model can, in modern terms, be summarised as follows:

1. Knowledge of the perfect human way of life is possible via an understanding of a higher rational reality.
2. This knowledge is, however, only accessible to an intellectual elite. The majority, on the other hand, allow themselves to be led by irrational desires which are in conflict with a true, humane, reasonable way of life.
3. The elite which attain this knowledge will use it in an unbiased, unselfish way, uncorrupted by power.
4. For this reason the elite must lead the masses and educate them in virtues which perfect human talent as far as possible. For this purpose a strict hierarchical state structure is required.
5. Because of (3), the institution of the constitutional state, which aims at restricting governmental power, is superfluous and undesirable.
6. Because of (2) and (4), the democratic form of state is irrational and immoral.
7. Because of (2), the freedom principle is likewise irrational and immoral: most people lack the required maturity.
8. Because of (2), (4), (6) and (7), the principle of equality is similarly unfounded.
9. Because of (1)–(8), a just state institution requires a lack of freedom, and inequality, in principle, for the benefit of all.

In Plato's view of the ideal rulers hides an important insight: people who are ensconced in a certain societal position, with all the attached prejudices, conventions, need and value patterns, cannot be unbiased. Their views of ethical and political matters are prejudiced. For this reason a democratic decision-making procedure does not guarantee equitable outcomes. Plato realises that it is necessary to subject oneself to a very thorough self-enquiry and very strict discipline in order to approach impartiality.

The defence of Plato's absolutist state doctrine, however, stands or falls with the tenability of his rationalistic ontology (1). The objection against this is that it is too speculative. Man lives in an imperfect world, and his ability to attain knowledge is imperfect as well. That he could nonetheless attain knowledge of a perfect supernatural world is an understandable desire; but perchance wish is the father of this thought. Perhaps abstract mathematical truths and 'absolute' Ideas, such as those of the Good and the Beautiful, are simply human constructions: idealised generalisations of what we know from our experiences and from the imperfect empirical world. That we have such ideas, therefore, does not prove that they exist independently of human thinking in an eternal world of Ideas.

If one regards the existence of a higher world of Ideas as indemonstrable, only empirical reality remains, in relation to which only uncertain 'opinions' are possible. With this the justification of a government of the wise, who have an exclusive understanding of a higher truth concerning world and values (2), would likewise disappear. When one assumes that all human knowledge is fallible – and thus relativises Plato's absolute opposition between 'knowledge' and 'opinions' – one rather arrives at a democratic view of the state in line with the ideals of freedom and equality: everyone's knowledge is in principle equally uncertain and provisional. There is no privileged elite who possesses all wisdom, so that everyone should be able to participate in a critical discussion (4). If certain knowledge concerning the absolute good is not settled, and if there is no fixed harmony between individual and community, reason seems to require that individuals be given as much as possible autonomous scope to determine their own way of life, as long as they do not disregard the equal autonomy of others. This requires a democratic state form (6) with equal freedom rights (7, 8). One is then back again with the Sophists. Experience, moreover, shows that power often corrupts (3). For this reason one can succeed better in restricting state power by means of the institutions of the democratic constitutional state with its separation of powers (5). In the twentieth century this position was defended by Popper (Section 8.4). In other words, from Plato's rationalist metaphysics a 'broad morality' can be derived. But if one is doubtful about this metaphysics, it appears possible only to arrive at a 'narrow morality'. We will, however, see that there are also philosophers who specifically do not base a narrow morality on scepticism or relativism, but on the insight that the truth can be realised only if it is not imposed through force (see specifically Locke, Section 4.2).

Plato realised that the perfect rational state is an ideal which is in reality very difficult to achieve. In a later period he started to think that the political model in the *Republic* was perhaps conceived at too high a level. The selection of rulers, for instance, will pose insurmountable difficulties. He came to the conviction that no person can be protected completely from becoming unjust. However, if there are no absolutely just kings, there is no greater horror than an absolute ruler who is not subject to the law, but subjects the law completely to his authority. Therefore, in a later work, *Nomoi* (the Laws), Plato abandons the ideal of a community with a hierarchical class structure. He then apparently adopts the position that, depending on the circumstances, different forms of government can be effective. In the *Laws* he advocates, among other things, a legal order enacted by a democratic people's assembly. The government itself should be subject to the rule of law.

2.5 Aristotle

Aristotle (384–322 BC) was for many years a student of Plato's Academy, and knew Plato personally. He was later asked by the king of Macedonia to take responsibility for the education of his son Alexander (the Great). Aristotle thereafter returned to Athens and established his own school there.

Aristotle's philosophy starts from amazement: how does it come about that things are the way they are? This is not a question with any practical utility. Aristotle furthermore emphasises that philosophical questions concerning the nature and origin of reality can only arise when the necessities of life have been provided for. Aristotle marvelled, among other things, at our ability to obtain knowledge: how is it possible that we can come to certain knowledge of the world, whereas the latter is continually subject to change? How can we regard things as the same, whereas in reality there is nothing that is completely equal to anything else? This question was also posed by Parmenides and Plato, but Aristotle provides a different answer which ties in more closely with empirical reality. He rejects the idea of a separate world of Ideas. Aristotle's answer is that experience teaches us that in all things an essential core is present, which reveals itself in each instance in a concrete manner, and which is often subject to historical development. Take an acorn. When it finds itself in favourable circumstances, it will develop into an oak tree. This is the natural destiny of an acorn. One will never see that an apple tree grows from an acorn, and if such monsters would appear, we would reject them as unnatural. Apparently the essence of the oak tree is from the beginning of the process present in the acorn, so that the distinction between species is a natural necessity. Aristotle's 'biomorph' worldview implies that he regards the whole of reality as analogous to an acorn: things are aimed at the development of their natural capacity. In the mutual relationship between things likewise natural patterns can be discerned. Hence, plants serve to be eaten by animals, whilst animals are at the service of man. (Some people similarly appear by nature to be suitable for subjection, whereas others by nature rule over them: Aristotle thus both explains *and* justifies slavery.) Aristotle's biomorph worldview makes him an adherent of a specific form of natural law, of what we in the first chapter referred to as the biological model. Law is allocated the function of advancing the purposes active in human nature.

Contrary to Plato, Aristotle subscribes to empirical, scientific enquiry. This difference is closely connected to Aristotle's philosophy, which criticises the doctrine of Ideas of his teacher. Aristotle stands closer to what we today refer to as empirical science; he can also be said to stand closer to *common sense* than Plato. He deals with arguments against Plato's doctrine of Ideas which are partly presented by Plato himself in his dialogue *Parmenides*. The strongest of these is the argument of the 'third man'. Simply stated, it boils down to the following. Plato originally uses as argument for the existence of his Ideas that without the Ideas we would not be able to know a cat as an example of 'cat' or a man as an example of 'man'. We do not, according to Plato, in the first instance arrive at the Idea 'cat' or 'man' by comparing cats and men. The objection against this argument is that the problem repeats itself. If we need the Idea 'man' to recognise two men as specimens of the same kind, then we need a third, more ideal 'man', to similarly be able to compare the man and the Idea 'man'.

2.5.1 Ontology

One of the most important points of Aristotle's criticism against Plato relates to the place the latter accords to the Ideas: situated in a separate unchanging realm. This has the consequence that observable reality is reduced to appearance. Plato assumes that truth must be unchanging and perfect, whereas all material forms of existence are changing and imperfect.

Aristotle raises the objection that these Ideas or general concepts can exist only *in*, and because of, concrete, bodily forms of existence. What we trace in our general concepts are general Ideas or 'forms' which are active in the particular specimen. Expressed technically, in Plato the Ideas are 'transcendent'; in Aristotle they are 'immanent'.

Plato states that in order to be able to recognise two differently shaped objects as chairs we must already have at our disposal the Idea 'chair'. His method of reasoning is *deductive*: he derives the specific (the concrete examples) from the general (the shared Idea). Aristotle argues that we take the reverse (*inductive*) course and derive the general concept from the separate specimen. On the basis of the particular specimens which we observe, we form a general concept. In the latter the common characteristics of all specimens of one kind are contained, which distinguishes this kind from others. Aristotle realises that in this manner absolute certainty cannot be attained. But like Plato in his later years, Aristotle accepts that such complete certainty is illusory.

Aristotle thus, like Plato, takes for granted a dualism of general form, essence or Idea, on the one hand, and, on the other, substance or matter. However, because Aristotle locates form in material things, he is to a lesser extent subject to the critique raised against Plato that there is an inexplicable gap between the ideal and the material world.

Aristotle can, moreover, in this manner explain changes in the observable world, which Plato with his static world of Ideas rejects as mere appearance. Every specific thing, according to Aristotle, consists of a combination of form (or Idea) and substance. Substance in itself he regards as unformed, passive matter. Matter only takes on the form of a tree, a dog or a man, because the general form or Idea is at work within it, and because of which potentiality turns into actuality. This is why a human embryo grows into an adult man. Aristotle takes this biological process as model for all development and change in nature.

Aristotle also refers to ‘form’, because of its creative role, as the *final* or *purposive cause*. The final purpose of development is, in other words, in potentiality already present in the form, preceding its realisation. The immanent final purpose is the cause of the development towards a fully grown specimen of the kind. The inherent Idea ‘man’, for example, functions as purposive cause, so that the baby takes on more and more the features which are characteristic of its being human, that is, those characteristics by means of which man distinguishes himself from other living beings, and which, therefore, constitute his essence. The distinguishing characteristic of man is, according to Aristotle, the possession of reason. A human embryo has not as yet developed this, but already possesses it as potentiality. It must clearly possess this potentiality, because why would it always grow into a human being and not now and then into a Danish dog or a canary?

Such a purposive cause or essence has a *normative* import as well: it is at the same time a norm for the most proper development. If the potentiality or form in a particular specimen does not come to perfect realisation, this is, according to Aristotle, caused by the resistance which matter presents. Everywhere in nature and in human existence where movement or development is observed, this is a sign that the form is not as yet completely realised, and, thus, of imperfection. Aristotle’s ontology thus implies, like Plato’s, an ethics.

The hypothesis that all existence has a form in itself which is the potentiality for, and the source of, all its development, is, according to Aristotle, confirmed by an observable teleology in the whole of nature. Polar bears are, for example, because of their white fur adapted to snow, and giraffes can because of their long necks reach up high in trees. He does not only see teleology in every form of existence in itself, but in nature as a whole: the latter, according to him, constitutes a purposively ordered hierarchical unity. Lower kinds are in the service of the higher. Grass has the natural function of serving as food for cattle, whereas cattle exist to be eaten by man. Such a worldview is referred to as *teleological*.[3] The different kinds, according to Aristotle, find themselves higher up in the hierarchical order depending on the extent to which they are less material and more spiritual: for this reason the lifeless things are at the bottom, thereafter come the plants, next the animals, and finally man. Every higher kind has all the characteristics of the lower kinds in itself. They distinguish themselves from the lower species by an individual, characteristic quality which stands in a looser relationship with lifeless matter depending on the extent to which the kind in issue is a higher one: animals, for example, consume food, similarly to plants, but they can in addition move freely; man has all the animal characteristics, but distinguishes himself from them through his rational abilities, enabling him to free himself from his instincts. Thinking is the highest form of activity; contemplation is the uppermost that has been given to the human soul. As highest source and purpose of all these developments, Aristotle presupposes an ‘Unmoved Mover’ or ‘thought thinking itself’: a pure rational form, which thinks all substance ‘towards itself’. The harmonious hierarchy of Plato’s World of Ideas, in Aristotle’s theory

[3] Greek: *telos* = purpose.

thus returns *in* the world. With Aristotle we find nothing of the mystical-religious and utopian elements of Plato's philosophy.

2.5.2 Ethics

Because the 'forms', 'essences' or 'purposive causes' of every form of existence lead to the development of its essential nature and because all kinds in the universe are aimed at one common highest purpose, Aristotle's ontology at the same time provides a basis for his *ethics*: the good for each being is the perfection of its immanent potentiality, thus of what characterises the kind. As a result it can fulfil its natural function in the universe. Because man distinguishes himself from the rest of nature through his reason, the good for him is to attain harmony and happiness by means of a mode of life which is as reasonable as possible.

Happiness (*eudaimonia*) is the name which Aristotle gives to the highest good that is achievable by man. This word is tainted by a number of associations, and Aristotle knows this quite well: he, therefore, specifically points out that one should not let oneself be misled by this notion. Its meaning is not the same as the usual meaning (happiness as a situation of individual satisfaction), but ties in with Aristotle's own theory concerning the typical human aspiration for the highest achievable good – a reasonable way of life – to which he gives the conventional name 'happiness'. Aristotle describes happiness as follows:

> [T]he good for man is an activity of the soul in accordance with virtue, or if there are more kinds of virtue than one, in accordance with the best and most perfect kind (Aristotle 2004, p. 1098a (15)).

Regarding the elements of this description we provide a few comments.

Like every being, man has a task unique to him, and this entails completing the task well. Whoever completes this task in a good, or rather, in the best possible way, deserves to be referred to as happy (Aristotle is no 'hedonist',[4] but like Plato, a 'perfectionist'). Where is the highest good to be found? In the first book of his main work on ethics, *Nicomachean Ethics*, Aristotle responds: in politics. In the last book: in philosophical contemplation. Commentators accuse Aristotle of incoherence. His thinking is not, however, incoherent. He wants to show that an exclusive emphasis either on practical action, or a life of enjoyment, or else a life according to the intellect, is undesirable. Happiness consists in a *combination* of these: and the nature of this he wants to illustrate. Aristotle investigates how the same person has a function to fulfil, both in the domain of moral-political action and in the domain of contemplation, and how fulfilling this function well, brings along with it a specific feeling of well-being. These three elements (tasks in relation to moral-political

[4]Greek: *hèdonè* = enjoyment; a hedonist is someone who regards enjoyment as the highest goal. This Aristotle does not do: enjoyment is a natural consequence of the achievement of virtuous perfection.

action, contemplation, and the feeling of well-being that goes with it) are described in more detail in what follows.

The problem with *moral-political action* is the following: how can a reasonable soul that is bound to a desiring body, which in turn is unreasonable, properly fulfil its peculiar task (being rational)? The reasonable soul must in one way or another give direction to the irrational desires, so that the soul influences the body. But there is also an interchanging movement: the body provides the reasonable soul with the impulse to want to fulfil its peculiar task. According to Aristotle, reason itself is simply passively contemplative, and does not provide active motives for conduct. Such motives still find their source in our desires and yearnings. Hence a form of cooperation is established between the reasonable and the instinctive parts of man, which finds expression in every concrete virtue. This cooperation finds its high point in 'moral wisdom' (*phronèsis*, the virtue of the practical intellect), which dictates to us how we should act in a concrete instance.

This moral wisdom is called an 'intellectual' virtue because it relates to the practical *intellect*. It is called 'virtue' because it contributes to the ability of man to complete his task well (the exercise of his rationality). It has an adjudicating task: it must provide man with knowledge of the rules of conduct. The judgment of moral wisdom attains the form of a command, and more specifically a command directed at desire. Through compliance with the commands of moral wisdom, desires are changed into *moral virtues*. By means of the performance of conduct that is good, in the long run an inner, self-evident *habit* in favour of the performance of good conduct is established in man; in the long run man performs virtuous actions because of their immanent beauty: then these actions are performed simply because he realises that it is good to perform them. And this beauty is desired: the rationalisation of the instincts due to moral understanding derives at the same time from the instincts the desire to achieve the purpose of *phronèsis*.

According to Aristotle, moral virtues consist of the golden mean between two extremes or vices. Hence, bravery is the middle path between cowardice and recklessness, pride the middle path between vanity and modesty. Of importance are the proper relations. The best man, according to Aristotle, is someone who has an appropriate measure of pride, who does not underestimate himself, who despises whoever deserves to be despised, who has a sense of honour, who is great in every virtue, and who has a noble and good character. The best man does not avoid danger, he performs good deeds and grants favours, but prefers not to receive these (he is a superior person vis-à-vis those who are inferior), he gives assistance, but asks for nothing, he does not admire anything or anyone and has more of an interest in beautiful things than in useful things which eventually bring in money.

Whereas *phronèsis*, the virtue of practical knowledge, gives direction to the 'lower instincts', philosophy, the virtue of theoretical knowledge (which like *phronèsis* has the task of making the soul fulfil its own rational activity), is in the service of the higher, that is, of *contemplation*. Theory is knowledge for the sake of knowledge itself, without the will to influence what is known. This consideration of the higher is separated from the body, so that no desire needs to be rationalised. Philosophy is thus a habit which comes to completion only in the activity of contemplation. Here man achieves his highest point of perfection, which is rarely attained, and then only by a few. From this it follows that not all people should strive for an introverted, celibate and contemplative life. A life of continual contemplation is not reserved for ordinary mortals. Some can accomplish this during a part of their life, most not at all. The contemplative life in accordance with the intellect ideally has priority over the active life in accordance with the moral virtues: a kind of ontological hierarchy, in which the latter is simply an indirect means for achieving the first mentioned (compare, for example, Aristotle's praise of contemplative life as 'the best and the most perfect of the virtues').

As to *satisfaction*, which typically accompanies action and contemplation, Aristotle rejects the idea that pleasure is uniform: different forms of pleasure are specifically to be distinguished from each other. Contemplation and action bring about true pleasure: man finds pleasure in fulfilling his task as rational being by means of his practical conduct and contemplation. Although he regards contemplation as the highest activity, the ethics of Aristotle can hardly be regarded as ascetic. Happiness is not to be equated with pleasure or enjoyment, but happiness without pleasure is impossible. A person who is tortured cannot be happy.

According to Aristotle, ethics as science has a very limited precision. It is not in all instances clear exactly which conduct it prescribes; it is thus not always certain what is required by the virtues. One of the reasons for this is the general character of ethical judgments. They can apply only 'in most instances', subject to exceptions or changed circumstances. Circumstances can vary infinitely. Every general moral rule will, therefore, be confronted with situations to which it is not applicable. The same applies to legal rules. Certainly, laws are generally formulated, but they must not be strictly applied in all instances. This should specifically not happen where application of the law would come into conflict with justice. Application of laws always requires equity for the concrete case.

Ethics according to Aristotle, therefore, does not consist solely of a limited number of fixed universal rules or principles. Each of these contains exceptions, so that every universal ethical judgment is imperfect. Ethics is capable only of provisional, more or less adequate generalisations, which must in concrete instances be corrected by considerations of equity. Where they fall short, we can let go of them to look for new, better ones, or realise our own inability to make a moral judgment in this particular instance. Our ethical knowledge is in any event, according to Aristotle's philosophy, limited, as the normative Idea – the purposive cause – is immanent. There is, thus, no possibility of rational insight into independent Ideas, as with Plato. With Aristotle we have to depend on the observation of still imperfect developments. Preceding the complete realisation of the *telos*, there can be no complete knowledge of the norm. On the other hand, we can on the basis of factual developments certainly have some knowledge of the immanent purposes of nature so that for Aristotle, ethics likewise does not depend completely on human arbitrariness and convention as it does for the Sophists.

2.5.3 Political Philosophy and Legal Philosophy

In the preceding discussion we considered the main features of Aristotle's individual ethics, distinct from the rest of his practical philosophy, which entails a political-social ethics, including a legal philosophy.

In so far as his legal philosophy is concerned, the most important virtue of law is justice. In general, justice entails that one gives to each his own: equals must be treated equally, and those who are unequal, unequally, according to the measure of their inequality. According to the fifth book of *Nicomachean Ethics* this can take two forms: distributive and corrective justice; a distinction which has been adopted by a number of later thinkers.

In the first place, there is *distributive justice*. Aristotle accepts that people differ in a number of respects from each other. The one is rich, the other poor, the one is of noble origin, the other does not amount to much. The differences are not a private matter, but result in different forms of treatment. In a democratic society, those who are born free deserve to participate in the administration of the city or state administration; in an aristocracy, virtue forms the basis of respect. That the free-born or the virtuous is treated with the appropriate respect, is a matter of distributive justice. This form of justice includes the principle of proportionality: man receives in accordance with what he merits, and merit is distributed unequally among people.

Secondly, there is *corrective* or *rectificatory justice*. The point of departure here is the fact that people conclude a variety of transactions with each other. Some of these are voluntary, such as buying and selling, and the taking of loans. Things which people buy and sell must in some way or another be capable of comparison with each other. For this purpose their value must be established, which finds concrete expression in a price. When people buy and sell in an honest manner, it is a question of reciprocity: what they give and receive are of equal value. Sometimes, however, someone sells a pig in a poke. If the buyer realises this, he can complain before a judge, after which he receives what he had a right to, that is, corrective justice takes place. When someone buys a pig in a poke, the transaction for his part contains an involuntary element; the perpetrator after all attempts to prevent that the one who is prejudiced is aware of what happens to him. There are many more involuntary transactions which take place on the sly: theft, adultery, false testimony. Involuntary transactions can, however, take place openly too. Aristotle gives as examples, violence, murder, and defamatory language. In these instances too, corrective action has to take place. The judge who intervenes correctively does not act proportionally, but relies on an absolute principle of equality: the injustice is compensated for without taking account of the persons concerned.[5]

[5] Such an outcome is, viewed from a greater moral distance, only just when the preceding distribution was just: in the case of a very unjust distribution of wealth, theft can, on the other hand, be legitimate.

Aristotle's legal philosophy is a branch of his political-social philosophy. One can see this in the way in which he deals with distributive justice. Those treatments are 'just' which respect the existing socio-political divisions. Aristotle's ethics is similarly a branch of his social-political philosophy: political ethics have priority over individual ethics. A radically individual human being is a non-existing abstraction: man has an essentially social character. This does not only mean that people are for a reasonable and virtuous life dependent upon the community. One would still be able to describe this in individualistic terms: individuals need other individuals to develop their individuality; viewed thus the community would simply be an 'extrinsic'[6] good, a means for individual development. That people are social beings means specifically that being part of a community is an 'intrinsic' good, something which is in itself good and to be aspired to. Because the essential human characteristics can, according to Aristotle, only realise themselves in a community, he states that the *polis* (the whole) in logical and normative respects precedes the constitutive parts (the individuals). Consequently the whole acquires as main task the education of individuals to become good socio-political beings: moral education is essentially political education. Aristotle does not at all share the modern liberal belief that morality cannot be legally imposed, but proclaims a perfectionist view of ethics and law. When the good human being needs to coincide with the good citizen, as Aristotle contends, the authority which has the final say in the political domain has an important say in the moral domain, too. It then makes sense to prescribe moral virtues, specifically to those who do not understand the meaning of such virtues or who do not want to follow them. After all, the virtues are internalised by acting in accordance with them. By acting in a just way – for whatever reason – one becomes just.

Law is required in every form of society. The purpose of law, according to Aristotle, is the promotion of the good of man, happiness in accordance with his essential nature. Aristotle, thus, presupposes a natural law which is based on the essential nature of man, and which applies everywhere irrespective of whether it has been positivised. Positive law created by people can be tested against this natural law. Aristotle, then, maintains a strict opposition between natural law and positive law.

In general one should, according to Aristotle, obey positive law. Man is after all, in accordance with his essential nature, a communal being. From this follows the duty to live in a community. And from this follows, in turn, the duty to be obedient to the communal order. Aristotle, moreover, contends that without a duty of obedience no community would be able to exist. The duty of obedience is, however, not unconditional. The only legitimate purpose of a community is to create the conditions for the realisation of the essential human nature of its members. The duty of obedience, thus, comes to an end when the law conflicts with communal well-being.

---

[6] *Extrinsic good* = good, but exclusively as a means to achieve another good; as opposed to an *intrinsic* good that is good as such.

Aristotle's political ethics and natural-law doctrine are, furthermore, not static: Aristotle is fully aware that the laws of a successful political dispensation cannot be determined once and for all. The philosopher can only furnish the broad outlines within which politics should operate; for the rest one is dependent upon what one could refer to as local experimentation. Aristotle's school consequently engaged in an extensive comparative enquiry into the various state forms. The results of this enquiry are not known to us, although tradition has it that more than two hundred forms of government were described and studied. This enquiry provides an example of how Aristotle wanted to establish insight into the real essence by way of empirical enquiry. Aristotle ultimately distinguishes between three forms of government: monarchy, aristocracy, and the democratic state. Under certain circumstances each form can degenerate into a bad variant, respectively, tyranny, oligarchy, and democracy in imperfect form.

A government is good if it looks after the well-being of the community, and the quality of a government is determined by the ethical qualities of those who govern. The best rulers are those with a highly cultivated spirit, a well-formed character, and moderate wealth. An aristocracy – government by the best – would, viewed thus, deserve preference. However, the pursuit of an aristocracy easily results in oligarchy: government by the wealthiest. And the wealthiest disregard the interests of the poorest. Aristotle notes that in certain city states the ruling oligarchs even swore an oath that they would be the enemy of the people.

Because people are not perfect – often not even good – democracy is, comparatively, the best form of government. Aristotle's view of democracy, however, excludes the majority of the population from political participation. Only the free men count. Aristotle assumes that people are unequal by nature. Rationality constitutes the essence of human beings, but according to him different kinds of people have an unequal share of this. Specifically in the case of women and (non-Greek) barbarians, the instinctive bodily side rules over the reasonable side. For this reason they should, in their own best interests, be ruled by free men in the same way in which the passions must be ruled by reason: absolutely. This can likewise be justified as a consequence of distributive justice in the political domain: political power is shared in proportion to the fundamentally unequal abilities of people.

2.5.4 Commentary

A common criticism that is voiced against Aristotle is that his worldview suffers from an indemonstrable *essentialism*. He is erroneously of the view that objective essences are to be found in nature: a number of the characteristics of a phenomenon would constitute its essence; the other characteristics would simply be accidental. Hence his rational and social dispositions would constitute the essence of man. Nature as a whole would, moreover, consist of a hierarchical order of such essences. Critics argue against Aristotle that such a selection and hierarchical ordering of essences from the totality of natural characteristics cannot be proved. It is just as feasible to make a different choice. Why would one, for example, not be able to say, with Nietzsche (Section 7.5), that the irrational and instinctive side of man is more important than the intellectual side, and, in addition, that the individual development of a genial individual deserves preference independently of the equalising community of the 'all too many'? Moreover, nature in reality does not allow for any harmony of purposes to be seen. The purpose of the mouse is, for example, in conflict with that of the cat. Aristotle would in fact simply have projected his own subjective normative preferences onto nature, in order to subsequently again derive them from nature as 'objective', because they are 'natural'.

Opponents contend against Aristotle's essentialism that many forms of categorisation of the world are possible, depending on one's point of view. There is not *one* essential, exclusively just way of categorising. A sociologist, a psychologist and a jurist would, for example, conceptualise the same act of theft in completely different ways. Such categorisations are human constructions which are based on a selection from a specific point of view. These critics regard a non-observable, but nevertheless objective order of 'essences' behind the empirical appearances as indemonstrable. It is then self-evidently also impossible to derive an ethics and a legal philosophy from such an indemonstrable metaphysical order. It is no longer possible to equate, as Aristotle did, the 'natural' with the 'good', because empirical nature also contains irrational and asocial phenomena.

2.6 The Stoics

The origins of Stoicism lie in the fourth century BC in Athens, when Zeno of Citium (Cyprus) started spreading his doctrine and established a school. No books have been handed down to us of any of the Greek Stoic thinkers. We know about them only from the summaries and quotations of others, written often long after they had lived. We know much more of the Roman Stoics, who came to bloom much later. Important Roman representatives were Seneca, emperor Marcus Aurelius, and the slave Epictetus. Stoicism arose in the period after Alexander the Great had replaced Greek democracy with an authoritarian regime. Because participation in political deliberation was no longer possible, philosophy turned inward: henceforth philosophy aimed specifically at attaining inner spiritual balance.

The Stoics elaborated on Aristotle's natural-law doctrine. They likewise based their natural-law doctrine on a rational ontology. The movement presupposed the existence of a rational *logos* in the role of a providence which predetermines all events. *Logos* is the general, reasonable law which permeates the whole of the cosmos: nature, as well as man and his ethics and law. For this reason, *logos* is the norm by which man must let himself be guided. Man himself is capable of this, because by means of his reason he shares in the rational world principle. Everyone can, therefore, in his own reason find the ethical prescriptions of natural law. The central command is 'to live according to nature'. Every person must, therefore, live in accordance with his reasonable essential nature.

This sounds very abstract. Let us concretise it somewhat. When one asks someone what makes life worth living, he would typically point to a satisfying relationship, good health, a long life, sufficient means of subsistence, and having a say regarding his own existence. Bad would be a boring life, sickness, a premature death, poverty, and powerlessness. The good things, people however mostly do not have in their power; because of a happy coincidence we may obtain a share in this; an unhappy coincidence can take it away. When, in efforts to attain happiness, one attaches oneself to things over which one has no control, disaster will follow. When this happens, one should not curse one's destiny but oneself: blinded by one's own immoderate desires, one caused one's own unhappiness. Seneca conveys in this regard, in his *Letters to Lucilius*, the answer Panaetius gave to a young man who asked whether a wise person could be in love:

> As to the wise man, we shall see later; but you and I, who are as yet far removed from wisdom, should not trust ourselves to fall into a state that is disordered, uncontrolled, enslaved to another, contemptible to itself. If our love be not spurned, we are excited by its kindness; if it be scorned, we are kindled by our pride. An easily won love hurts us as much as one which is difficult to win; we are captured by that which is compliant, and we struggle with that which is hard. Therefore, knowing our weakness, let us remain quiet. Let us not expose this unstable spirit to the temptations of drink, or beauty, or flattery, or anything that coaxes and allures (Seneca *Epistles* Volume 3 CXVI).

Matters which we cannot control can, therefore, according to the Stoic doctrine, not be called good or bad; because their goodness or badness depends on our own desires. For this reason a satisfying relationship, good health, a long life, sufficient means of subsistence, and having a say in one's own existence, are in themselves as indifferent as a boring life, sickness, a premature death, poverty, and powerlessness. These become bad only when we allow our peace of mind to become dependent upon them. Good, on the other hand, are virtues, such as courage and moderation, by means of which we can control our desires. Wisdom is true health, and philosophy is the art of controlling what happens to one. According to Marcus Aurelius in his *Meditations*:

> [I]n external happenings either chance or providence is at work, and one should not blame chance or indict providence (2006, p. 120).

We can from this extract the ideal of freedom of the Stoics. One is free when one is unhampered by one's desire for 'indifferent things', which are external to one, and over which one does not have power; and likewise if one desires and comes into possession of the 'good things', which one has in one's power because they belong intimately to one. One is, on the other hand, unfree when one is in the grip of one's desire for indifferent things, and because of this cannot obtain enjoyment of the good things.

This ideal of freedom thus emphasises especially 'internal hindrances' and relativises 'external hindrances' about which people mostly complain when they feel unfree. One is, according to the Stoics, not simply free when one can do what one wants to do (for example, one wants to become rich, and finds a treasure in one's garden), but when one has control over one's desires. Whoever laments that he is poor or that he is politically suppressed, must not strive for any economic or political change, but must withdraw himself to that domain which he can control: the management of his own passions.[7]

Epictetus expresses this idea as follows:

> Of things some are in our power, and others are not. In our power are opinion, movement toward a thing, desire, aversion (turning from a thing); and in a word, whatever are our own acts: not in our power are the body, property, reputation, offices (magisterial power), and in a word, whatever are not our own acts. And the things in our power are by nature free (Epictetus 1955, p. 11).

You are really free (in the sense of the *essential freedom* of Section 1.4) when you do not allow yourself to be dragged along by stupid, impossible, immoral, short-lived and addictive desires, but know how to eliminate them. This results in *apathy* (indifference) and *ataraxy* (being undisturbed): a state of supreme happiness.

In their ability to participate in the *logos* by means of apathy and ataraxy, all people are, in principle, equal to each other. By comparison, the other more specific characteristics they have, and the specific relations they bring about, lose importance. The Stoics draw no distinction between Romans (Greeks) and barbarians, and no distinction between those who are free and those who are slaves. They were the first to propagate with these ideas a universal human equality in the moral sense. This is well-illustrated by the fact that two of the most important Stoics, Marcus Aurelius and Epictetus, were, respectively, an emperor and a slave. When all accidental and conventional differences fall away, the human community encompasses the whole world. People are not locked up in their own accidental *polis*, but are spiritually part of a *cosmo-polis*.[8] The essence of people is to be citizens of a rational empire, in which the limitations and distinctions which exist in the observable world have no meaning. By relativising these conventions, the Stoics propagate a *natural law*.

The Stoic natural law is nonetheless not completely satisfactory. The fact that people are in principle equal, irrespective of the circumstances in which they find themselves, relieves them of the duty of bringing about social and political changes in reality. That the emperor and the slave as human beings are equal to each other is a nice idea, but it would be even nicer were one to derive the consequence from this idea that such demeaning distinctions should be done away with in reality. However, to want to do this does of course not attest to apathy and ataraxy. The Stoic doctrine is in principle apolitical, whereas politics, as the art of the possible, does not avoid the taking of action, and thus of risks.

Epicurus, who was not a Stoic, realised this all too well. His recommendations do not impose passivity, but even less incite one to engage in disastrous activism:

[7] Isaiah Berlin in his *Two concepts of liberty* (1958) calls this the 'withdrawal to the inner citadel'. When a country has long and unsafe boundaries, the ruler must concentrate on a smaller area which he can keep in his grip; ultimately he digs himself into an impregnable fortress.

[8] Alexander the Great, in the meantime, established a world empire; one can view the Stoic philosophy as a reaction to this.

> We must remember that the future is neither wholly ours nor wholly not ours, so that neither must we count upon it as quite certain to come nor despair of it as quite certain not to come (Epicurus 1994–2009).

The Roman Cicero (106–43 BC), who sympathised with the Stoics, applied their philosophy to law. This is not an inevitable consequence, for the Stoics are basically apolitical. However, a radical aversion to politics is not sustainable, just as it cannot be maintained that we have absolutely no control over external hindrances, but that we do have such control over internal hindrances. Concerning the latter: how can we ever know for sure that we will not be swept away by our desires? If one wants to exclude completely the chance that this will happen, one should commit suicide. Concerning the former: a sensible evaluation of given possibilities and impossibilities, of chances and dangers, as Epicurus suggests to us, is to be commended. This entails some Stoicism: one should not complain about completely unavoidable impediments. One can of course evaluate one's chances incorrectly, but then it is again commendable to react in a stoical way to this. When one wants to exclude the possibility of becoming the victim of circumstances in evaluating one's chances, one should (again) commit suicide.

Cicero assumes that an 'eternal law' exists irrespective of human agency. This eternal law expresses how wisdom rules the world. It governs both non-reasonable (inanimate and animal) nature and reasonable nature: man. Man is governed by means of 'moral laws' and (positive) law, that is, on the basis of intentional lawgiving. Man is capable of this owing to his rational abilities. Knowledge of the normative is, however, made difficult for man because of his physical desires. Moral virtue consists in the complete realisation of reason, as well as an understanding of moral law and law itself. To achieve this, man must, also according to Plato and Aristotle, free himself from his desires and from all interests which are connected to his tangible, physical existence. This can only happen in a community, ruled by positive laws which are derived from nature.

The content of natural law is summed up by Cicero in two main rules. The first rule prohibits disturbing the order of a community; the second prescribes active participation in communal life. The first rule implies respect for existing positive laws. The second rule compels one to contribute as much as possible to the well-being of the human community and to strengthen the bonds of the community through benevolence, generosity, goodness, and justice (these are typical 'republican virtues'). Man is by nature a communal being, so that such actions serve an interest which is shared by all. The first rule is subject to the second, when positive law conflicts too greatly with the common good. Cicero, thus, rejects absolute obedience to law. There is no duty to obey a tyrant who harms the common good of the people.

The scope of human society extends itself increasingly, in the course of history, from the community between man and woman to the family unit (partners and children), from the family unit to the broader family of blood relations, from families to the tribe, from tribes to the state, from the state to the language community. Citizens of a state have many religious, economic, legal and other institutions and customs in common. Language, according to Cicero, however, binds people in the strongest way. The highest community is the *societas humana*, which includes the whole of humanity: the cosmopolitan element in the philosophy of the Stoics.

Cicero's natural-law doctrine had a great influence on classical Roman jurists such as Gaius (130–180 AD) and Ulpianus (ca. 170–228 AD). The first statement of the *Institutes* of Gaius, for example, reads as follows:

> Concerning Civil Law and Natural Law: All peoples who are ruled by laws and customs partly make use of their own laws, and partly have recourse to those which are common to all men; for what every people establishes as law for itself is peculiar to itself, and is called the Civil Law, as being that peculiar to the State; and what natural reason establishes among all men and is observed by all peoples alike, is called the Law of Nations [*ius gentium*], as being the law which all nations employ (Gaius *Institutes* Part 1).

Cicero maintains that all people partake in reason, and that the positive legal rules which appear universally in all legal systems, the *ius gentium*, must, therefore, give expression to natural law.

2.7 The Middle Ages

2.7.1 Introduction

The Greek-Roman civilisation disappeared for the most part in Western Europe with the fall of the Western Roman Empire in the fourth century AD, as a result of attacks from war-mongering Germanic and Slavic tribes. The Middle Ages lasted from 500 to 1500. The Roman state organisation and legal order which had expanded across the whole of the Mediterranean, from the Middle East and North Africa up to England and through the Netherlands, occupied by the Batavians (the Rhine for a long time formed the northern border), fell apart. In the place of the Roman Empire came much more simply organised local national bonds, regulated in terms of customary law.

According to tradition, a kind of direct democracy of free adult men was to be found among a number of Germanic peoples. It would, however, take a long time before an institutionalised democracy, as had existed in classical Athens, would recur in Europe. The latter was, incidentally, already destroyed seven centuries earlier, and replaced by the absolute monarchy of Alexander the Great and his successors. The ethics of the Stoics which was aimed at an inner balance can be explained historically as the result of the impossibility of getting involved in public life in a dictatorship: the exercise of Aristotle's essential freedom in the form of active participation in political life had become perilous. The Roman Empire, after an intervening period as republican class-based state, since the beginning of the Christian era likewise developed into a dictatorial empire. It adopted the highly developed culture of the Greeks, but not the democratic tradition of Athens. On the contrary, the Roman philosopher Cicero remarks scornfully that the Greek democracies were ruled by untrained, impulsive laymen, who knew nothing of matters of state, threw themselves into futile wars, nominated accident-prone persons to government, and banned worthy citizens. The excessive political equality amongst the Greeks, Cicero wrote, led to the total collapse of all the power, wealth and glory they had once possessed. They were, thus, not a good example to the Romans. As indicated already, the Stoics certainly regarded all people as equal from the point of view of supra-sensible universal Reason, but did not attach any political consequences to this. The Stoic Roman emperor Marcus Aurelius, for example, wrote the following:

> *First.* How do I regard my relation to them, and the fact that we were all born for each other: and, turning the argument, that I was born to be their leader, as the ram leads his flock and the bull his herd? (Marcus Aurelius 2006, p. 110)

Even slavery was accepted. On the one hand, the Roman Stoic Seneca contended that 'a slave is a human being and a member of the household':

> Kindly remember that he whom you call your slave sprang from the same stock, is smiled upon by the same skies, and on equal terms with yourself breathes, lives, and dies. It is just as possible for you to see in him a free-born man as for him to see in you a slave (Seneca *Epistles* Volume I XLVII).

Seneca nonetheless does not encourage the master to immediately release his slaves. One must simply treat them in a humane way: do not hit him, allow him to sit with you at the table once in a while.

During the Middle Ages the Roman Catholic Church was the only institution which, from papal Rome, still preserved a general European culture and maintained parts of the classical traditions, including Latin as the European cultural language. Christianity itself was such a tradition: in 313 it was recognised by Emperor Constantine as the official Roman religion. The Christian church based its doctrine on the Old and, especially, the New Testaments. The New Testament describes the life of the legendary Jesus Christ, whence 'Christianity'. Christians believe that he was the son of God who, during the time of the Roman Emperor Augustine, came to free humanity, even though this has not as yet succeeded completely. Like Stoicism, Christianity has a universal tenor: it sees all people equally as creatures of God, and, therefore, as subjects of Christian neighbourly love. For this reason it also fired itself up with missionary zeal in an attempt to convert all non-Christians. Its success appears from the Western way of counting years. Recent estimates indicate that approximately one third of the world population is nominally Christian.

Like Plato, Christians are of the view that the life of people on earth in a mortal body is an inferior intermediate stage in comparison with an eternal existence as immortal pure soul. Christianity, however, does not believe that one's soul returns after one's death to an abstract philosophical realm of Ideas. One is reunited with the divine love of one's Creator, a divinity thought of in a personal sense with an omnipotent will – an inheritance of the individual Jewish God of the Old Testament.

For this reason the Christian worldview is referred to as *voluntaristic*,[9] in contradistinction to classical *rationalism*. God created everyone, to Him one will return. That is, as long as one behaves oneself in the meantime in accordance with His Will: *love your neighbour as you love yourself*; otherwise eternal punishment awaits. It is now one's own responsibility to firmly prepare oneself for heaven. Thus, the human will, too, is regarded as more important than his reason.

In addition, the Roman Church let itself be inspired by classical philosophy. Particularly Aristotle had an important impact on Christian thinking: people attempted to bring faith in line with Aristotle's rational arguments. Important parts of the classical documents found their way back into the West via the Islamic-Arabic civilisation.

The monotheistic religion of Islam was established to the East of the Mediterranean after 616 AD under the leadership of the prophet Muhammad, and is currently, like Christianity, spread around the world. In the Islamic world, 622 AD counts as the year 0. Moses and Jesus are viewed as predecessors of Muhammad. Islam is based on the Qur'an, written by Muhammad, inspired by the Islamic God, Allah. It has an elaborate doctrine of duties.

Two neighbouring gods with a claim to monopoly led to enmity. During the Middle Ages a battle lasting for centuries took place between the Christian West and Islamic East (711: the Arabs attack Spain; 1219: William I of the Netherlands captures the port town of Damiate (on the Nile); 1291: Christians vacate the Holy Land). Initially Arabic culture was much more developed than medieval Western culture; for instance, in the fields of mathematics, medicine and philosophy (Ibn Sina, or Avicenna, 980–1037; Ibn Rushd, or Averroes, 1126–1198). This was due partly to the Greek-Roman heritage, especially Aristotle, as well as its contacts with the Far East. In 1453 Islamic Turks (of non-Arabic, Mongolian origin) conquered Constantinople and with that the East Roman Empire, after which those inhabitants who fled brought a new flood of classical culture which had been preserved to the West. However, whereas Western thinking and life, after the Middle Ages, started to develop freely by separating itself from religion, the free development of thinking in the Arab world, after initially flourishing in Baghdad and Spain, was restrained by religious dogmatism. When the Europeans around 1500 found their own seaway to the Far East, the political battle was won. Since then the West has dominated worldwide. With this we, however, already stand at the beginning of the Modern Era (Chapter 3).

Before it came to this, the Christian church ruled under the leadership of the Pope in the spiritual domain, while local rulers and nobility under the nominal leadership of the German emperor reigned over the secular world. An agriculturally based society was established with a social stratification which reminds one of Plato's class-based state. A hierarchy of clergy, with an exclusive claim to higher wisdom, wielded spiritual power, knights whiled away their time by being brave, and agricultural workers provided for the subsistence of the higher estates. In the feudal

[9]Latin: *voluntas* = will.

system, nobility and the church were the big landowners, while most labourers were as serfs tied to the land. Constitutional law and private law were entangled: rulers and nobility saw their political and judicial powers as a personal, hereditary possession. Frederick II (1194–1250, Holy Roman Emperor and German King) called himself 'Father and Son of Justice', and regarded himself as an independent legal source in addition to customary law. Via a feudal system, relationships of dependency extended from the emperor to the kings and higher nobility, downwards to the lower nobility and their subordinates. The bond between ruler and subordinate was based on personal loyalty. These were mutual, but at the same time asymmetrical, relationships: an exchange of protection from the higher level with services rendered by the lower level. Unconditional obedience was thus out of the question. In the course of time trading towns were established, with artisans and traders. With the urban population as ally, the kings of England and France, as well as other rulers, gradually obtained more central power for themselves at the cost of the nobility. The cities acquired, in return for their support, independent rights, as a result of which they became freed from the feudal system (but the princes would attempt to take the city rights back again once they had acquired power, so that the citizenry also sought support from the nobility): 'city air makes free'.

Individual freedom and equality were, however, still far off. In accordance with the hierarchical division of estates, unequal rights and duties obtained. The individual person was, moreover, not regarded as an autonomous individual, but acquired his identity from his status within an estate or city community. The individual outside the city was bound with his whole person to the duties of the feudal system, which prescribed mutual loyalty and protection. The freedom rights of the Middle Ages were, therefore, not individual rights, but group rights: traditional privileges of an estate or city which were protected against the rising central power of the king. Early collectivist versions of the social contract were used against the absolutist claims of the kings. In contrast with the later philosophical versions of Hobbes and Locke (Chapter 4) these were not philosophical constructions, but real accords. The English *Magna Charta* of 1215, for example, attempted to protect the privileges of the nobility and the cities against the claims of the king. The *Joyeuse Entrée*, granted to Brabant in 1356 and still in operation in 1792, required, among other things, that every duke, when taking office, must confirm the existing privileges, ask the permission of the estates in matters of war and peace, and guarantee an orderly legal process. The Act of Abjuration (*Plakkaat van Verlatinge*) of 1581, which justified the Dutch battle for freedom against Philip II, invoked a right of resistance because Philip had breached the existing group privileges.

On the spiritual level, controlled by the Roman Catholic Church, equal individual freedom rights were similarly out of the question. To be sure, one assumed that all people were created in God's image, and were, therefore, equal in his eyes; in earthly life inequality was, however, justified by means of an appeal to the divine creative order. Hence, Thomas Aquinas defended natural slavery, and saw women simply as an aid to reproduction. He, furthermore, rejected freedom in the sexual domain because God meant sex to be practised exclusively for reproduction, and, moreover, requires monogamous marriage for the sake of the education of future generations.

In this and other areas a battle for the highest authority took place between the spiritual and earthly powers: according to church law, a marriage could not be terminated; the nobility, however, wanted to remarry when a marriage remained childless. Slowly the church realised that it was better to impose its law in a somewhat more diluted form in public life. All non-monogamous, non-heterosexual forms of sex, such as 'sodomy', in accordance with Aquinas's perfectionist legal view, nevertheless had to be prohibited as being *against nature*. Suicide was likewise prohibited, because the individual did not have the right to dispose freely of the life that God had bestowed on him. Freedom of religion was, moreover, rejected. If necessary, people had, in their own interest, to be forced to adopt the proper faith. As Luke 14:15–24 teaches:

> When one of those at the table with him heard this, he said to Jesus, "Blessed is the man who will eat at the feast in the kingdom of God." Jesus replied: "A certain man was preparing a great banquet and invited many guests.... But they all alike began to make excuses...." Then the master told his servant, "Go out to the roads and country lanes and make them come in, so that my house will be full...." (*New International Version* 1984)

Aquinas consequently argued for the death penalty for heresy.

2.7.2 Thomas Aquinas

Since the Middle Ages the whole of Western thinking had been partly controlled by Christianity. Many texts from classical antiquity in addition continued to exercise a great influence. Between the classical and the Christian worldviews a great tension exists, which can be referred to as an opposition between *rationalism* and *voluntarism*. Whereas in the classical worldview the gods were bound to the rational basic order, Christianity emphasised the will of the omnipotent Creator. He could also have created the world differently. Christianity, moreover, placed great emphasis on the individual free will: it is dependent upon the free will of the individual whether or not he conducts himself in accordance with God's will. At the Last Judgment he must personally account for this. Christianity, therefore, emphasised the value of the individual person more strongly than classical rationalism, where the individual was rather regarded as a specimen of a general kind. Herein lies, at the same time, the origin of the modern problem of freedom of will in relation to moral and legal accountability (Section 3.1).

The philosophers of the Middle Ages attempted to reconcile the opposition between the rationalism of the inherited classical texts and Jewish-Christian voluntarism, and emphasised, in one instance, the rational, and, in another, the element of will. This finds expression in the discussion during the Middle Ages about the question whether the good is good because God wills it thus, or whether God cannot will anything other than the good.

Thomas Aquinas (1225–1274) was the greatest of the theologians and philosophers of the Middle Ages. Against the wishes of his noble family he entered the young mendicant order of the Dominicans. He studied theology and philosophy in Naples and Paris, where he went to lecture in 1252. His fame spread quickly, with the consequence that the Pope called him to work at his court, which Aquinas combined with a professoriate at the Dominican college in Rome. In 1258 he again went to Paris, where he became involved in many complex polemics with other theologians and philosophers, but equally with opponents of the mendicant orders. On his way to Lyon, where he would have participated in a council, he was overcome by a sickness of which he died soon after.

Aquinas attempted, like other philosophers of the Middle Ages, to formulate a synthesis between classical (specifically Aristotelian) and Christian thinking. His synthesis boils down to adopting the idea of a rational, purposive and hierarchical foundational order of nature, but views this as a creation out of nothing in accordance with the will of the Christian God.

One of the elements of Aristotle's philosophy which similarly takes a central place with Aquinas, is the notion of purposiveness or teleology. Everything that exists is, according to Aquinas, of its inner essential nature purposive. The natural purpose of everything is the preservation and perfection of its own potentiality. By striving for this purpose, everything that exists fulfils the commands of God. Contrary to animals, which follow their instincts, man must become aware of his purpose and resolutely aspire towards it. Man is created in God's image and thus ultimately oriented towards God.

The teleological element of Aquinas's thinking appears clearly from the following passage in *Summa Theologica*, where he develops his sexual morality:

> Wherefore just as the use of food can be without sin, if it be taken in due manner and order, as required for the welfare of the body, so also the use of venereal acts can be without sin, provided they be performed in due manner and order, in keeping with the end of human procreation.... [T]he sin of lust consists in seeking venereal pleasure not in accordance with right reason. This may happen in two ways.... First, because it is inconsistent with the end of the venereal act. On this way, as hindering the begetting of children, there is the "vice against nature," which attaches to every venereal act from which generation cannot follow; and, as hindering the due upbringing and advancement of the child when born, there is "simple fornication," which is the union of an unmarried man with an unmarried woman. Secondly, the matter wherein the venereal act is consummated may be discordant with right reason in relation to other persons; and this in two ways. First, with regard to the woman, with whom a man has connection, by reason of due honor not being paid to her; and thus there is "incest," which consists in the misuse of a woman who is related by consanguinity or affinity. Secondly, with regard to the person under whose authority the woman is placed: and if she be under the authority of a husband, it is "adultery," if under the authority of her father, it is "seduction," in the absence of violence, and "rape" if violence be employed.... Now it is evident that the upbringing of a human child requires not only the mother's care for his nourishment, but much more the care of his father as guide and guardian, and under whom he progresses in goods both internal and external. Hence human nature rebels against an indeterminate union of the sexes and demands that a man should be united to a determinate woman and should abide with her a long time or even for a whole lifetime.... This union with a certain definite woman is called matrimony; which for the above reason is said to belong to the natural law. Since, however, the union of the sexes is directed to the common good of the whole human race, and common goods depend on the law for their determination... it follows that this union of man and woman, which is called matrimony, is determined by some law (Thomas Aquinas 2008, *Summa Theologica*, Second Part of the Second Part, questions 153 and 154).

The order within which human striving plays itself out is that of the *lex aeterna* (eternal law), the order of creation. Included in this, as part of the eternal law, are the *lex naturalis* (natural law) and the *lex humana* (human law). The eternal law consists of divine wisdom, by which everything is determined. Man is not capable of understanding this completely. To be sure, man can have an understanding of the universally valid natural law which is derived from it. By means of this he has a limited knowledge of good and evil. This understanding does not consist in concrete commands and prohibitions, but in the aims of the natural inclinations. The first natural inclination is self-preservation; the second is the inclination to procreate and bring up children; the third, through which man distinguishes himself from the animal, is what is accorded by reason, such as the inclination to attain knowledge of God and of communal life. From the first inclination, Aquinas derives a right to self-defence, from the third, a duty to strive for knowledge and to not hurt others. Natural law commands love for God and love for man. From this the Ten Commandments can subsequently be derived. All moral commandments and prohibitions are, according to Aquinas, taken up in the Ten Commandments, or implied therein. Human law rests on natural law. Positive law is, in a certain sense, nothing more than an adaptation of natural law to time and place.

The legal thinking of Thomas Aquinas found its expression in the *prima pars secundae partis* (the first part of the second part) of *Summa Theologica*, in the *quaestiones* 90–97. There he defines law as –

> nothing else than an ordinance of reason for the common good, made by him who has care of the community, and promulgated (Thomas Aquinas 2008).

Regarding the elements of this description, we add some comments. What does it mean that human laws have something to do with reason? It means that human laws draw inferences from divine reason, as this makes itself known to human reason via natural law. Without the hint of divine reason, people would arrive at different and mutually conflicting laws, derived from different and mutually conflicting judgments about what is required. Onto human beings as reasonable creatures something, however, radiates from divine reason, and by way of natural law these creatures participate in eternal law. This natural law in broad terms emerges in everyone in the same manner; it cannot change and it cannot be erased from people's hearts. Of course, not all human laws can be derived in detail from natural law and divine law, but this can be said mainly of less important laws, which then at least should not be in conflict with natural law. These less important laws are then not 'inferences' drawn from natural law and divine law, but 'stipulations' of these laws. Reason is here likewise at work, but in a negative sense: it determines what may be entrusted to human law, and what not.

What does it mean when one says that human laws are aimed at the *bonum commune*, the common good? The common good is not simply the sum total of the good of separate individuals. It is the good which is common to all members of a community: valuable matters which are useful and necessary to all, and which can be secured only by way of the community. By means of the common good, individual interest is at the same time advanced, because without the community, people would not have been able to realise their individual goals. Although man does not completely disappear into the community, he is certainly required to sacrifice his property, and eventually even his life, should circumstances demand this. As Aquinas said, the individual person relates himself to the community in the same way in which the imperfect relates itself to the perfect. For this reason law's central function is making people virtuous (for example, moderate and true), so that they subject their passions and sinful inclinations to the perfect community. Criminal law as a result acquires a pedagogical role. With that Thomas Aquinas does not, however, go to the extreme: human law must not attempt to prohibit all possible wickedness, but adapt itself to a certain extent to people's situation. The requirement that human laws be aimed at the common good, places a limit on state power: laws lose their validity and degenerate into false law when they are in conflict with the common good, or when the burdens are not fairly shared across the members of the community. This does not, however, mean that one can then simply cast them aside. In one's inner self one is not bound by such laws, but in one's external conduct one should not give offence and harm the *bonum commune*; and this often requires that one must respect existing laws, even when they are actually 'violations', rather than 'laws', in which case the enforcement of laws is not legal, but an illegitimate act of violence.

Finally, what does it mean that human laws can be promulgated 'by him who has care of the community'? Regarding the nature of the promulgation, Aquinas is terse; he says more about the caring institution. From *Summa Theologica* it is not completely clear whether Aquinas is in favour of a mixed form of government or of the monarchy. The *opusculum* (small work) *De regimine principum ad regem Cypri* (concerning the dominion of the nobles, for the king of Cyprus) provides more certainty in this regard.[10] From the *opusculum* it appears that Aquinas prefers by far the monarchy over other forms of government. One comes across a number of comparisons from which the excellence of the monarchy appears: a king is like the captain of a ship, or like the king (sic) of a bee colony, or like the soul in the body. Monarchical rule deserves preference, because the authority of the king is derived from the authority of God, whose leadership is likewise monarchical. Therefore, the king, too, must adhere to divine law and natural law. This, of course, requires that he must be a virtuous human being in all respects; he must, among other things, excel in prudence and justice. In the case of a king a great power must thus be accompanied by a perfect character. The latter is not without good reason emphasised by Aquinas: a king must certainly be very virtuous, wise, etc, for his regime not to turn into tyranny. A tyrant is someone who does not rule on behalf of the common good, but suppresses others on behalf of himself, consequently exceeding the limits of his own authority. In order to contribute his part in avoiding that rule degenerates

[10]This is an example of a 'mirror for princes', which were popular in the Middle Ages and the Renaissance. A comparison with Machiavelli's *Il Principe* is obvious here. When the prince of Machiavelli rules on behalf of the community, this is simply because he serves his own interest best in the maintenance of his dominion; in most instances repression is an appropriate means. See with regard to Machiavelli Section 3.3.

into tyranny, Aquinas addresses himself in his *De regimine principum* to the king of Cyprus. When he discusses the question, which attitude the subject must adopt in relation to a tyrant, he says expressly that the toleration of a tyrannical regime is mostly to be by far preferred to its overthrow, because then a still greater evil often comes about. In *Summa* he is somewhat less rigid: one may overthrow a tyranny, but one must proceed with the greatest caution.

Aquinas's philosophy has had a major influence. Until today, Catholic thinkers are inspired by him, as well as contemporary popes. In his encyclical letter *Veritatis Splendor* (The Shining of Truth, 1993), John Paul II opposes relativistic pluralism which relies upon subjective conscience or which abides by the diversity of social and cultural contexts. In opposing this he states that every human being in his innermost heart always nostalgically desires absolute truth. Absolute truth points back to God, who provided human beings with an ultimate purpose. Because of original sin human beings are not by their own efforts capable of achieving this true purpose; they must be advised, specifically by the Church, which gives an 'authentic interpretation' of the true purpose in God's sense of human existence. The core of morality can, therefore, not be subjected to the autonomous choice of free human beings, and as little to the rules and forms of democratic decision-making; freedom is subject to truth. The true purpose of human beings has something to do with their nature, which transcends all cultures; it consists in the direction of human action towards God. Certain actions (such as contraception and abortion,[11] euthanasia and suicide) are radically in conflict with the orientation towards God; these actions are absolutely forbidden, irrespective of the eventual good purpose they are stated to serve.[12]

From a legal-philosophical perspective the thinking of Thomas Aquinas is particularly interesting as an example of what we referred to as *naturalistic* natural law (Section 1.2.2.2, where Aristotle's doctrine is announced under this heading). From Aquinas's thinking we can see clearly that naturalism has something ambiguous about it. It can point to all kinds of 'natural inclinations' which man is assumed to share with animals (such as an instinct for survival and a heterosexual orientation). It can likewise point to the reasonable 'nature' of man, by means of which he is to be distinguished from animals (naturalistic and classical-rationalistic natural law

[11] Compare this with the above passage on Aquinas's sexual morality.

[12] In comparison with Locke, who will be discussed in Section 4.2, the Pope allows little space for individual conscience. In his encyclic he contends in some places that the authority of the church does not affect the freedom of conscience of Christians: after all, the doctrinal authority points to the truths which the Christian conscience '*should* already possess by developing them out of the original act of faith'. The word italicised by us raises suspicion. The Pope says that he does not infringe upon the freedom of conscience, because right-thinking Christians *would* agree with the Papal view thereof. But if they do not? Then every form of force can be justified: a variant of: 'forcing them to be free'. The Pope was not an adherent of political liberalism (Section 10.4), although the traditional catholic doctrine of the erring conscience which deserves consideration, could in principle be developed in this direction.

agree with this interpretation, unlike the other naturalistic thinkers who are mentioned in Section 1.2.2.2). That people are 'by nature' aimed at the good, is equally ambiguous: their nature does not prevent them from turning away from their (biological or rational) nature by virtue of their freedom. A natural law, such as that of Thomas Aquinas, calls upon people to 'become' what they already 'are' in essence, and thus shows perfectionistic characteristics. In this respect, too, Aquinas's thinking is interesting: it represents a form of natural-law doctrine with a perfectionistic streak.

2.7.3 End of the Middle Ages

The end of the Middle Ages was announced when Thomist philosophy in terms of cosmic order was overturned. With Aquinas, reason and faith mutually complemented each other. From Aristotle he adopted the idea that reality is organised in a purposive and hierarchical manner, and that this organisation can be recovered via human reason; he, however, views this organisation as created by the will of the Christian God. He consequently describes theology as faith that endeavours to arrive at reason, so that theology and philosophy are complementary. Politics and law have to dwell within the limits drawn by faith and reason.

Duns Scotus (ca. 1266–1308) brought about a breach in this system. He was a very discerning thinker who published much in his short life. He was of the view that Thomas Aquinas had handed theology over to heathen philosophy. Aquinas viewed the supernatural too much as an extension of the natural. The teleological proof of God's existence is, for example, based on this: from the splendid order of nature we can conclude that there is an ordering Creator. But, according to Duns Scotus, with such proof we only demonstrate our own desire for order; we do not step out of nature, and do not approach God. We can only reach God when we open ourselves humbly to his revelation in the Bible, and in the tradition of faith. Beyond that God cannot be known, all the more since God is not an intelligible being, but reveals himself to human beings as absolute freedom.

William of Ockham drew radical theological and epistemological consequences from these ideas, whereas Marsilius of Padua formulated their equally radical legal-philosophical and political consequences.

2.7.3.1 William of Ockham

William of Ockham (ca. 1300 – ca. 1350) was born in Ockham in Southern England. He entered the order of the Franciscans, and studied at Oxford. In 1324 he was called to Avignon by Pope John XXII to account for certain theological statements he had made, and which were denounced by the Pope. In a conflict between the pope and a large section of the Franciscans, he chose the side of the latter, and fled in 1328 from Avignon. He joined emperor Ludwig of Bavaria, with whom Pope John XXII was similarly in conflict. Until his death William of Ockham participated in the dispute about the demarcation between the authority of the emperor and that of the Pope.

The Pope claimed that all power came from God, and that he, as substitute of Christ on earth, therefore, likewise had authority over the emperor. The emperor wanted to see the papal power restricted to spiritual matters. In this he was supported by spiritually inclined monks, such as William of Ockham, who turned himself against a church which concerned itself with worldly matters, surrounding itself with princely beauty and splendour.[13]

Whereas Duns Scotus was still a metaphysical thinker, who regarded reason as capable of penetrating the rational structure of reality (only before God's omnipotence had reason to give way), William of Ockham points to the limits of reason. We can think about everything, but thoughts often do not represent reality. The only knowledge which provides certainty is empirical knowledge, which is related to demonstrable, existing objects. These objects are singular and contingent, so that every attempt to arrive at absolute knowledge is illusory. The general and necessary concepts which, according to the philosophical tradition from Plato via Aristotle to Thomas Aquinas, have truth value are, according to William of Ockham, nothing more than uncertain human constructions. His thinking is, for this reason, referred to as *nominalism*: in so far as human knowledge exceeds the domain of empiricism, it simply contains 'names'; pure mental constructions without truth value; nominalism is opposed to *realism*.[14]

Of God no empirical knowledge is possible, whereas philosophical and theological thought structures can similarly (and obviously) not reach God. Only faith, which stands apart from reason, can approach God, at least when God wants to reveal himself. This is because God is not what the theologians and philosophers have made of him: an authority who manages everything in an orderly way, and who can be known from his organisation of things. God has at his disposal an absolute power, which withdraws itself from every natural theology. All characteristics which were formerly attributed to God (just, good, etc.) melt away in the fire of his inscrutable omnipotence. For morality this has far-reaching consequences. Actions are not good because they are aimed at their natural purposes, as Aristotle and Aquinas supposed. God in his absolute freedom determines what is good, and what bad. What is good today may tomorrow be evil. There is likewise no certainty at all concerning the ultimate destiny of people. Perhaps God will reward the sinners and punish the pious. The believer must humbly bow his head before the unfathomable decrees of God. The omnipotent God is unknowable: voluntarism takes the place of rationalism.

---

[13] William of Baskerville, the main actor in *The Name of the Rose* of Umberto Eco, is the alter ego of William of Ockham; the novel is set in 1327.

[14] 'Realism' is here an answer to the question regarding the reality value of our concepts (Plato is a conceptual realist). This is something different from 'Scandinavian realism', which is discussed in Sections 8.1 and 8.3: law is reduced to the empirical conduct of judges in social reality.

2.7.3.2 Marsilius of Padua

Marsilius of Padua (ca. 1290 – ca. 1343) studied philosophy in Padua, and medicine and theology in Paris. As happened in the case of Ockham, statements of Marsilius were condemned by Pope John XXII. He was even excommunicated. He regularly accompanied the roaming armed forces of the German emperor in Italy, and, a year before Ockham chose this option, found refuge with Ludwig of Bavaria whose personal physician he became. Marsilius wrote only one book, entitled *Defensor pacis* (Defender of peace, 1324). People no doubt thought that Ludwig of Bavaria was to be understood as the defender of peace, but Marsilius's political philosophy had a much wider import: he investigates how an all-powerful state based on the sovereignty of the nation could bring about peace; he regards the pope as one of the most important disturbers of peace, who does not restrict himself to the spiritual (as he should), but (without warrant) concerns himself with the secular as well.

In the domain of theology, Marsilius took the ideas of William of Ockham to their extreme. Faith has nothing to do with reason. The truths which faith contains have for reason an unfathomable, supernatural character. When people follow the divine law, they are rewarded for this in the hereafter. For the contemporary existing world, faith has no meaning at all. In consequence, the actual world becomes the exclusive domain of activity of politics and positive law.

Marsilius gave a thoroughly naturalistic interpretation to the political thought of Aristotle, whom he came to know by way of Ibn Rushd (Averroës). He regarded the state as a living being where all the parts make a unique contribution to the flourishing of the whole. This living being is autonomous, not subject to any external power (such as the pope). On the contrary, in so far as pope and church do not limit themselves to the supernatural, but concern themselves with the natural, they fall completely under the jurisdiction of state authority. The nation as living being must of course be ruled by a legislature which represents the sovereign will of the nation. Human laws have no other origin than the will of the legislature which functions in the name of everyone. Offenders are punished, not because they were immoral or had sinned, but because they had defied the will of the legislature, and by doing so had disturbed the social order. The omnipotent state is the defender of peace.

The thinking of Marsilius was worked out in more detail and in more depth by later thinkers. Both theoreticians of the social contract and adherents of an absolute state authority could rely on him.

2.8 Conclusion

Thus medieval philosophy came to an end. With William of Ockham, rationalism was in the domain of theology replaced by voluntarism; and in the domain of epistemology, realism was replaced by nominalism. Marsilius of Padua completed the demolition work by subjecting the legal-philosophical and political domains to the autonomous will of the sovereign. With him classical natural law was knocked off its pedestal, and the doctrine that would later be called legal positivism, took its place. From what was said above, it appears clearly that the Reformation, which is often viewed as a radical and unexpected breach with the Middle Ages, was prepared for in a number of ways. Luther and Calvin did not fall out of the air.

Chapter 3
The Commencement of the Modern Age

3.1 Introduction

The Modern Age in various ways entails a break with the Middle Ages. It is characterised, among other things, by the emergence of natural science in the 15th and 16th centuries, which led to a worldview that deviated radically from the Christian-Aristotelian outlook of the preceding period. This raised a number of new problems as to the foundation of a duty to obey the law. The most important problem was that the classical idea of the world as a rationally coherent and purposive whole was abandoned in the modern view. Therefore it was no longer evident that human society constituted a moral order with which the individual should identify. Instead, in modern philosophy the individual acquired the central position. A new line of reasoning, therefore, had to be developed to indicate why, and under which conditions, an individual had to subject himself to a legal order.

A number of other developments induced the disintegration of the Catholic worldview of the Middle Ages. In the 16th century the Reformation brought about a break in the religious unity which had existed up until then (Section 3.2). Calvinism, moreover, arrived at a different view of the relation between religion and state. Because of man's sinful nature, government and law would be exceeding their powers should they attempt to force subjects into a morally perfect way of life. One could not expect more from the state than the safeguarding of social order. Protestantism, moreover, strongly emphasised the direct accountability of every human individual towards God. State force to live a good life is then inappropriate.

The Renaissance,[1] which already started flourishing in Italy from the 13th century, similarly regarded the human individual as central, but without religious considerations playing any substantial role (Section 3.3). The ideals of the humanists of the Renaissance concerned the full development of the abilities of each person. This could lead to an amoral attitude to life aimed at the acquisition of power and honour. Machiavelli formulated in *Il Principe* (The Prince, 1513) a realistic political theory: the king should base his rule solely on calculations of power

[1] 'Renaissance' means rebirth, specifically of the pre-Christian classical culture. With this sparkling civilization as model, the 'dark' Middle Ages had to be left behind.

C.W. Maris, F.C.L.M. Jacobs (eds.), *Law, Order and Freedom*, Law and Philosophy Library 94, DOI 10.1007/978-94-007-1457-1_3, © Springer Science+Business Media B.V. 2011

(Section 3.3). In the preceding period state authority had usually been justified with reference to its moral tasks. Machiavelli, however, viewed all moral justifications of state power as mere rhetoric. The classical unity of *politics* and *morality* is thus breached here: power and justice break up into two disconnected phenomena with different spheres of application.

In the Renaissance, trade started to flourish too. In the *economic* domain, as in politics, a separate rationality was developed which was dissociated from moral rationality. In the Middle Ages the doctrine of the 'just price' applied: every object was ascribed its own inherent value, which constituted the benchmark for a correct transfer of property. One could bargain for a high price, but, in doing so, was not allowed to deviate too much from the just price by adding more than 50% to it, and thus disproportionately prejudice the other party. In modern legal thinking the principle of contractual freedom prevails; the determining factor is the intention of the parties. It is, moreover, regarded as economically rational to maximise one's profits, and thus to ask as high a price as possible. The value of an object is determined by supply and demand. Economic efficiency and moral propriety are dissociated.

This businesslike approach to reality arose in interaction with the rise of modern science which entailed an objectification of the process of acquiring knowledge (Section 3.4). The modern pursuit of power and profit requires a realistic knowledge of reality that enables one to make successful calculations for the longer term. Modern natural science provides such knowledge. It attempts to develop an objective view of reality that is not tainted with subjective religious and moral wishes, thus inducing the 'de-enchantment' of the world.

With this approach, the classical unity of the *true* and the *good* is lost. Aristotle and Thomas Aquinas presupposed the existence of a rational natural order which coincides with the morally good. Natural science, however, regards the world as a totality of arbitrary processes that serves no higher purpose. An understanding of these processes enables man to control nature. Science cannot, however, determine the purposes for which he should use his scientific knowledge. In the scientific view, the determination of purposes is dependent upon subjective human choices. According to the ideal of a value-free science, knowledge and morality constitute separate domains.

Modern instrumental rationality was extraordinarily successful, when measured against the aim of maximising knowledge, power and profit. Specialisation in each of these fields significantly increased the efficiency of scientific, political and economic action. Enormous scientific progress occurred because people could freely experiment without being hindered by religious dogma. A combination of objective natural science, search for profits, and struggle for power enabled Western countries to establish trade settlements around the world (think of the invention of the compass and of gunpowder (incidentally invented by the Chinese in the 9th century)). Technological applications of science furthered the control of nature, industrialisation and growth of prosperity, as well as a longer average lifespan to make use of these achievements. New information could be spread quickly thanks to the invention of the printing press.

These developments required the establishment of central states to safeguard co-ordinated trade on a vast scale. (The privileged position of the knights of the Middle Ages had already been undermined: the rise of an assertive class of traders in the cities broke their economic power which had been tied to an agricultural method of production; the invention of gunpowder affected their military advantage. Hence the traditional view of the Middle Ages as a society of estates willed by God lost its potency.) The state had to ensure secure trade routes, guarantee that contracts are complied with, etc. For this purpose the central government had to radically interfere in society by means of law. As a consequence, law became more pragmatic and acquired, in addition to its traditional moral role, increasingly an instrumental function in the ordering of society.

Morality, law, politics, economics, religion and science, as a result, each acquired their own domain, characterised by distinctive purposes and rules. The moral unity of the cosmos which was the standard view in the classical period and the Middle Ages disintegrated in the Modern Age. Even so, many view this modern rationality as a sign of moral progress because it promotes a realistic, consciously chosen way of life. The growing scientific knowledge could lead to *emancipation* from the suppressive superstition of the 'dark' Middle Ages. In the first place, science provides objective knowledge of the causal and consequential relations of natural processes. Therefore, man can control nature in conformity with his own goals. No longer subject to nature's dominance, he can now take an independent stance towards it. Knowledge is power, as Bacon remarked, or *savoir pour prévoir pour pouvoir* (to know in order to foresee in order to control – Comte). In the second place, man acquired internal freedom by exposing the suppressive prejudices and prohibitions of religion and social traditions. He, for example, no longer had to be scared of threats of divine punishment after death. He could emancipate himself from the medieval doctrine that someone's destiny is determined by a society of estates willed by God. Every man could, thus, in future give shape to his life in accordance with his own conscious design.

The moral ideal of modernity thus comes to light in individual *autonomy*. Human dignity consists in taking responsibility for the development of one's own personality. However, if the individual person is a self-legislator, instead of a communal being as in classical philosophy, his obedience to government and law becomes less self-evident. The modern solution to this problem lies in the construction of the social contract. This presupposes that everyone has a shared rational individual interest in a legal order which protects his life and liberty (see Grotius, Section 3.5, as well as Hobbes, Spinoza and Locke, Chapter 4). The ideal of autonomy resulted in the liberal ethics of the 18th-century French Enlightenment: every individual has a right to equal freedom (Chapter 5). Translated into law, this results in the ideal of the democratic constitutional state in which the classical fundamental rights are protected and social fundamental rights are established. *Democracy*: every mature individual must be able to take part in deciding about public matters that affect everyone. The *constitutional state*: to protect individuals against decisions of the majority (which one has to revert to, should complete consensus be absent) as well as of governmental institutions (to which members of society necessarily have to delegate a part of their say). According to the ideal of the constitutional state, all exercises of state power are based on laws, state powers are divided, while the classical fundamental rights protect individual freedom. Social fundamental rights must guarantee that everyone has an equal chance to make use of this freedom.

In this liberal, 'narrow' view of morality, and especially of law, modern ethics fundamentally diverges from the perfectionist 'broad' ethics of the preceding period. Unlike Aristotle's doctrine of virtue, it is not determined in advance how man should develop his personality. And even if the ideal of human perfection were so determined, it would still be each individual's personal responsibility to arrange his or her life in the appropriate manner. Law, therefore, does not have the task of prescribing a virtuous way of life to citizens as with Aristotle. It must simply create the political and social conditions for the equal liberties of everyone.

These modern Enlightenment ideals lay claim to universal validity. In so far as other cultures are not as yet 'enlightened', and have not acquired the scientific way of thinking, they are regarded as 'primitive'. Because of their irrational worldview they find themselves on a lower level of human civilization, comparable with the period of childhood of the individual person. They should in their own interests be 'modernised'.

On closer inspection, however, these parallels between scientific and moral progress become very problematic. This is because in the scientific worldview, knowledge and morality cover two fundamentally different fields, so that the true and the good go their separate ways. The world of science is value-neutral. Science only registers aimless causal processes that explain how things come into being and then perish. To be sure, knowledge of causal relations can be used for means-ends reasoning; but in contrast to the Aristotelian knowledge of final causes, it cannot indicate which ends are proper. Nature thus does not provide any norm, or stated differently, from facts no norms can be derived. In short, the scientific world consists merely of facts; the *evaluation* of these facts is regarded as a subjective matter. If the world itself is without values, are human values then not simply illusions? What kind of independent test can be used to determine their correctness? What happens when different persons advocate opposing moral views? Knowledge is power, but power for what purpose? These kinds of questions can easily lead to moral nihilism.

The Marquis de Sade (1740–1814), for example, objected to the views of the Enlightenment philosophers, arguing that nature, besides constructive tendencies, shows destructive tendencies as well, so that a morality of aggression and *sadism* is as 'natural' as love for one's neighbour (Section 5.4). Another anti-Enlightenment philosopher, Nietzsche (1844–1900), contended that God is dead, so that only an indifferent nature remains from which no values can be derived. 'Will to power' is all there is. Nietzsche rejects the ideal of equality as levelling down the few excellent individuals who can elevate humanity to a higher plane. Egalitarianism is merely based on the resentment of the weak, who use this ideal to empower themselves at the expense of the brilliant elite. The only personal ideal 'beyond good and evil' that remains (exclusive to the Great Individuals) is to live heroically, if necessary at the cost of others. Good is what increases someone's power (see Section 7.5). In our time, Nietzsche's anti-Enlightenment thinking is continued by French *post-modernists* (Section 9.1.4). On closer inspection, then, the scientific way of thinking does not coincide with the emancipation ideal. Because of its value-free character, science cannot provide a foundation for the values of the Enlightenment.

To this can be added that science and human autonomy appear to be mutually exclusive. Science attempts to account for all natural phenomena as the result of causal processes. Everything that happens is, therefore, determined by preceding causes. Should one know all causes, one would in principle be able to predict all events in reality. However, if this applies to human consciousness as well, all human choices are determined in advance by causes, such as biological needs, education or social expectations. They are, thus, in principle predictable. With this determinism, human freedom comes to an end. Taken to its radical conclusion, this view would degrade man from an autonomous 'subject' to a mere 'object', which like all natural processes must be causally determined. On the horizon thus loom spectres of an Orwellian, fully programmed society. Liberal freedom seems to have completely dissolved.

Modern thinking threatens Enlightenment morality in another way as well. It puts all emphasis on the individual, rather than on Aristotelian communal morality. As a consequence, critics contend, all principles of social morality may lose their bearings. Why would an individual not make choices exclusively in his own interest, and disregard all social rules whenever it is to his advantage to do so? Why would he comply with the law when it conflicts with his individual desires? Does modern individualism not in other words undermine social order as such? Representatives of this anti-individualistic counter-current are Rousseau (Section 5.5), Hegel and Marx (Sections 7.3 and 7.4), as well as contemporary communitarians (Section 9.1.2).

In addition, critics of the Enlightenment point to the danger that individuals may misuse the freedom that advocates of liberalism grant them. They argue that the patterns of one-dimensional consumption of most people in modern society do not bear witness to autonomous self-development. For this reason, government should guide citizens to a better mode of life which honours human dignity.

These are the problems for which philosophers of the Modern Age seek answers. Some of those who do not take the modern ideal of autonomy for granted, may still look for the answer in a 'narrow' conception of law and morality, but for different reasons than the advocates of autonomy. They argue that every individual has a strong interest in the general obedience of legal rules, since social order is to the benefit of all. Without organised, peaceful cooperation, life would be miserable and economic and scientific progress would be impossible. This reasoning results in a narrow, but not per se liberal, view of law, because the state should only promote social order and economic interchange, and has no further emancipatory role. This view one finds with Hobbes (Section 4.1), the normative legal positivist Radbruch (Section 1.3) and Weber (Section 9.3.4).

Others argue that a liberal version of narrow morality is the best solution for the modern dilemma of how to live together in spite of deep disagreements in world-views and moral beliefs. In this view, the only way out lies in a procedural ethics of the second order which is aimed at placating substantive moral conflicts of the first order: state and law should allow each person as much freedom as possible to live in accordance with his own norms. The contention is that the state may not impose its own norms of the good life, as these are as contested as all others. Liberal ethics, thus, is designed to enable people to live together peacefully in modern pluralistic societies where moral unanimity is absent. In this manner the Enlightenment values are confirmed via a detour. This political version of liberalism was formulated by John Rawls (Sections 10.5 and 10.6). Critics, however, object that individualistic liberalism provides an insufficient foundation for a communal morality, and will lead to social disintegration. They yearn for the Aristotelian or Thomist ethics of virtue and perfectionist legal morality.

Other adherents of Enlightenment morality want to preserve the ideal of emancipation by disassociating themselves from the pretences of value-free science. They contend that science cannot live up to its pretension of being value-free, because all human knowledge is inevitably based on interpretation which is tainted with human interests. By acknowledging that science is a value-oriented practice, the acquisition of knowledge could still serve the human interest in emancipation. Thus the Enlightenment project could yet be brought to a satisfactory end (Critical Theory, Section 9.3).

3.2 From God's Sovereignty to the People's Sovereignty: Calvinism

In the 16th century, the Christian unity of Europe had collapsed; Roman Catholics, Lutherans and Calvinists came into conflict with each other, sometimes in the same country. The result was a long period of religious wars.

Although the religious convictions of these groups greatly diverged, their views about the proper organisation of society remained similar. In all three groups the authority of Aristotle remained practically unchallenged, although some in addition relied on Plato and Augustine. Because the similarities were so much greater than the differences, we will restrict ourselves here to the political and legal doctrines of only one group. We choose the Calvinists because they exercised the greatest influence on the development of modern ideas – incidentally also on the development of modern capitalism – and because they, moreover, integrated the new ideas of the other two groups.

In one important respect the Protestants – both Lutherans and Calvinists – reverted to an early Christian doctrine which preceded the later thinkers of the Middle Ages: 'pure' natural law, as God intended it for his creation, and as it is taught in the New Testament (the Sermon on the Mount), became unattainable for humans after the fall of man. In its place, owing to an act of divine grace which extends to all people, comes a modified natural law, which is summarised in the Ten Commandments. The latter no longer serve to bring human nature to complete perfection, but only to stem the tide of sin, and hence make man's 'fleeting life' temporarily possible. In Paradise no state existed, no oath, no slavery, no patriarchy, no social inequality, and perhaps no work or private property either. These are all institutions which protect sinful people against each other. This doctrine of *relative natural law* is a predecessor of the conception of a 'narrow morality', specifically in the (Hobbesian) variant of order theory. ('Order' is one of Calvin's favourite terms.)

What distinguishes Calvinism from Lutheranism is the central idea of the absolute sovereignty of God. The believer perceives himself primarily as an instrument to execute the will of God. God's will does not only relate to the acceptance of the Christian message of salvation, but extends to all walks of life. For this reason the believer is active in accomplishing God's will, not only in church, but everywhere outside of it, too. The true believer recognises himself as such by means of this constant participation in God's work. Lutheran humility is not his most important virtue, but the realisation of a divine mission in the world which gives a personal value to him as individual.

The consequence is a characteristic dualistic stance in relation to 'this world': it has no value in itself in comparison with eternal life, but is the domain where the believer must show his true worth as an instrument of divine will. For this reason the believer may not accord value to 'earthly matters' in themselves, but only use them as means. 'In the world, but not of the world' the saying goes. 'Relaxation', a typical Calvinist term, is, for example, allowed only because it makes working more efficient.[2]

That God's will extends to the whole world also has consequences for the relation between church and state. They each have their own task, and are in the exercise of it not dependent on each other. The church strives for the internal acceptance of faith, and uses in this respect only spiritual means. The state strives for the external realisation of God's will, and does this with force. The state, in addition, also enforces the participation of every individual in the administering of the Word and the Sacraments. The church, on the other hand, bears the responsibility for morally correct conduct; it uses in this respect clerical discipline (public admonition, exclusion from the Holy Communion, etc). Hence, church and state work together in Christianising society. The state cannot prescribe laws to the church, but is, on the other hand, not subject to priestly power, only to the will of God as revealed in the Bible.

The state, therefore, serves two purposes: in the first place, maintenance of the true religion; secondly, maintenance of the common good (*salus publica*): order and prosperity. The state, too, is simply an instrument. It must thus strive towards organising itself as efficiently as possible, for which purpose a constitution laid down in writing can be helpful. Governments are bound by natural law; positive law is simply an application thereof, conditioned by historical circumstances.

[2]The important German sociologist Max Weber contended that it is this institution which explains why capitalism developed in Calvinist countries such as the Netherlands, Scotland, and New England. Not only because of a sober, businesslike, planning attitude; but also because continuous, efficient labour is required, whereas the enjoyment of the fruits thereof is suspect: hence comes the hoarding of capital which must repeatedly be invested again.

In a few Swiss city states, Calvinism quickly attained political power. In all other countries to which it spread, it was blocked by a catholic state which attempted to suppress it by means of violence. Because of this, the theory of political duty became of central importance in political thinking. The problem lay in the political point of departure of the protestant doctrine, that is, Romans 13:1: 'Every person must subject himself to the governing authorities, for there is no authority except that which God has established.' This passage does not seem to permit active resistance, only the refusal to obey an order which conflicts with divine law ('passive obedience'). The Lutheran kings in Germany were already confronted with this problem when the German emperor attempted to suppress Lutheranism by military means. The Lutheran jurists formulated the following solution: all governments are instituted by God, therefore not only the Emperor, but also the 'lower magistrates', for example, regional rulers or the councils of free cities. What God categorically prohibited was that a private individual would revolt against a magistrate. However, when a higher authority neglects his duties to God and becomes a tyrant, then there is a duty on the lower authorities, whose task it is to protect the people, to resist the higher authority. The Calvinists extended this doctrine to a certain extent by stating that, owing to God's providence, a special office exists in most countries, to which no positive duties are attached besides preventing the government from exceeding its authority. Such 'ephors' (one who oversees) or 'peoples' tribunals' are in Western European countries the governments of the regions. We see here the hesitant beginnings of the doctrine of separation of powers and of constitutional testing.

This doctrine only granted a right of self-defence, an exception in exceptional circumstances to the normal rule of passive obedience. After 1572 (revolt in Holland and Zeeland, massacre on St Bartholomew's Day of the French Huguenots) in the Netherlands and France a period of permanent civil war started. A stronger justification for resistance against the king became an urgent necessity. For this purpose the Calvinists developed two controversial strategies that would have great influence in the future. The first was an invocation of history: the 'ancient constitution' which had existed since time immemorial. The Calvinist jurists contended that in France the power of the king had always been limited by that of the states (the regions); in the Netherlands it was eventually contended that real sovereignty had always belonged to the States. This argument emphasised the importance of the 'lower magistrates' or 'ephors'. (The higher members of nobility could also count as such: men such as Orange and Egmont.) The second controversial strategy – set out in a document titled *Defence of Freedom against Tyrants*, presumably by Philippe du Plessis Mornay, which appeared in 1579 under the pseudonym Stephanus Junius Brutus – was ironically derived from an important movement in Catholic thinking since the 14th century. This document did not take it for granted that God had subjected man to the government as a remedy for his sinful nature. State power, on the contrary, is granted by an originally free people, and, more specifically, on certain preconditions. If the government does not act in accordance with these conditions, the 'people' can take back the powers that were granted. This theory provides the origin of modern natural law with its characteristic belief in an original position of freedom, the 'state of nature'. The most important difference from a later theory, such as that of John Locke, lies in the view of the concept of the 'people': not the sum total of individuals, but a historically grown community, in which the legal relations between social classes is of central importance. 'Freedom' does not mean that individuals may do whatever they want, but that (in line with Aristotelian thinking) the 'organically' conceived society can function without interruption; collective freedom and order are thus here joined together. The most important relations between people are viewed as having already been in existence in the state of nature. 'Tyranny', therefore, appears particularly in the infringement of historical rights ('privileges') of collective legal subjects, not from the violation of a philosophically constructed, rational, organisational design. At this point the argument of the second strategy leads back to the first.

At the conclusion of the actual state contract the king and the lower magistrates are, therefore, the participants. The magistrates 'represent' the people, not in the sense that they are empowered by individuals to act, but in the sense that they are the only ones who can act in the name of the people. The people are after all thought of with reference to their social segmentation and organisation; as the body can speak only by way of the mouth, the people can speak only by way of their magistrates. The state contract is a mutual oath, whereby the king promises to serve the general interest, and the people through their representatives promise to obey him. In the place of the terminology of the *bonum commune*, the terminology of 'individual rights' sometimes already appears: the task of the king is the protection of the life, liberty and property of his subjects.

In the scholastic tradition, from which the Huguenots derived their theory, two variants of the state contract appeared. Both assume that sovereignty originally belongs to the people. In one variant this sovereignty is irrevocably transferred; in the other, the people remain the owner and simply allow the king as caretaker-manager to exercise their powers. (We will see that the central difference between Hobbes and Locke lies in this distinction.) The Calvinists adopted the second variant. They concluded that the king did not stand above the law – and, therefore, could not be the highest legislature. When the king furthermore breaches natural law or the historical constitution in a systematic way, the contract no longer binds the people. Naturally it is then again the 'ephors' who may, or even *must*, act; private individuals could not claim any right of resistance.

This theory was gradually also accepted by the Dutch rebels revolting against Spanish rule. It can be recognised in William of Orange's *Apology* (1580) and in the *Act of Abjuration* (1581), both written under the influence of, and perhaps co-written by, Philippe de Mornay. According to the Act, 'God did not create the people slaves to their prince, to obey his commands, whether right or wrong, but rather the prince for the sake of the subjects (without which he could be no prince)'.

The endpoint of Calvinist political theorisation is to be found in the work of the Syndic of the city of Emden, Johannes Althusius (1557–1638). He, too, assumes an original position of freedom. All societal structures, families, voluntary associations, communities, and districts, are established by a usually tacitly concluded contract.

This contract regulates the sharing of benefits and burdens. With his contract doctrine, Althusius actually did not at all want to contest the Aristotelian doctrine that living together in communities is natural for people. His point, however, was that in such co-existence, nobody has duties if he does not also have rights: this finds expression in the concept of the contract. In larger communities the contract is not concluded by individuals, but by the constituent smaller communities. The state is the final point in the chain; it is established by means of the association of communities or districts. Its distinguishing characteristic is sovereignty (*majestas*). This sovereignty belongs irrevocably to the state community as collective body.

The powers of the state are actually performed on the basis of a second kind of contract, in which such performance is outsourced to specific persons. The powers themselves are thus not transferred. The reason for this outsourcing lies in achieving as efficiently as possible the purpose of constituting a state – the implementation of natural law as described in the Ten Commandments. When the rulers do not properly fulfil the task entrusted to them, the people, acting by means of its ephors, revoke the assignment and grant it to another.

3.3 Realism and Relativism: The Renaissance

In the Italian city-states of the 15th century, orthodox Christianity had lost all intellectual influence; of importance for the thinking of the Renaissance were the classical authors, especially Plato and the Stoics. Hence the term 'Renaissance': a rebirth of classical antiquity. The cities recruited their high officials from those who were educated in accordance with the ideal of *humanism*, could fluently read and write in Latin, were at home in ancient history and philosophy, could make speeches, and could write theses consistent with the classical model. Political writings from this circle, moreover, indicate a fixed pattern: they glorify the virtues of the ideal ruler and of the ideal citizen.

In reality the power in one city republic after another was usurped by a military dictatorship; the cities wore themselves out through internal party conflict and civil war, and at the start of the 16th century ultimately fell prey to the imperialism of the new absolute rulers of France and Spain. The need arose for the recognition of the realities of political life – corruption, bribery, treason, military blackmail, and political assassination.

The most important figure in this turn towards political realism was Niccolò Machiavelli (1469–1527). Schooled in humanism, and for 15 years a prominent Florentine diplomat, he concerned himself already during his active career with the observation and analysis of the positive and negative qualities of the most important political leaders of his time. On the basis of his notes, after having fallen into disfavour, he wrote *Il Principe* (The Prince, 1513). At first sight this work does not distinguish itself from the prevailing treatises; like these, it wants to investigate which qualities are necessary for political leadership. The aims of political leadership are, first of all: to retain power, but, above all: to attain personal honour. Success in the realisation of these aims depends partly on good fortune, but a great deal of it depends on personal qualities too. More important even: those who have the proper qualities, can in this way influence Fortune in their favour. After all, Fortuna is a woman, and thus not insensitive to genuinely manly qualities. She even likes it to be dealt with firmly.

Machiavelli refers to the qualities needed for success, in line with tradition, as *virtù*. He, however, breaks radically with tradition in the determination of its characteristics. Tradition had firmly established that durable power and honour could never be acquired by way of immoral action. The Good Prince was consequently characterised by the virtues that apply to everyone else: he is wise, just, brave and disciplined; and, additionally, by specific princely virtues: he keeps his word, is magnanimous and generous. Based on his experience of the facts, Machiavelli strongly rejects this moralistic approach. The prince constantly has to deal with opponents who take no notice at all of morality; should he do this himself, he would simply make himself an easy prey for the others. The real *virtù* of the prince is to do resolutely what circumstances require: the good if possible, the bad if it is necessary. And the world unfortunately functions in such a way that it is regularly necessary to act in opposition to truth, love, humaneness and religion. The person who, as commander of the forces, does not want to be 'cruel', relaxes discipline, and by doing this, causes considerably more suffering than one who is prepared to set an example. The prince must, moreover, think of his reputation; not simply because hate and resentment on the part of his subjects threaten his position, but also because honour is ultimately the highest aim. Although he, therefore, cannot always be morally good, he must particularly make sure that he *appears* to be morally good.

In a later work Machiavelli extended his formulation of the problem, and asked the following question: what explains the success and eventual dissolution of states? Athens and especially Rome are in this investigation the big positive examples, the Italian city-states and especially Florence, the negative examples. The primary condition for success appears to be self-government. (Machiavelli calls it 'freedom'. This is likewise the meaning of the term in the title *Defence of Freedom against Tyrants*, and the slogan of the Dutch rebels, *pro religione et libertate*, for religion and liberty. The modern concept of *individual* freedom, however, only appears in modern natural law, for example, with Hobbes and Locke.) To protect their freedom, the citizens of a free state – as is the case with the prince – must have both luck and *virtù*, and the latter again entails the following: they must be prepared to do anything which is necessary, 'good' and 'bad', for the preservation of the state and of freedom. Freedom is lost when citizens withdraw themselves into their private lives, or when they use the power they have obtained in public life, for private purposes. (Note that Machiavelli's 'immorality' certainly does not entail egoism.) In the latter event, corruption, patronage, party conflict, and ultimately tyranny occur. The only way in which to prevent this from happening is through the design of suitable institutions; a successful state is the product of a great legislator. The institutions must not exclude all dissension, specifically that between rich and poor, but must use it precisely in such a way that each group guards over the patriotism of the other, and hence both groups are prevented from obtaining dominance. (This is a theme that returns in the *checks and balances* of the American Constitution.) The institutions must oppose the formation of interest groups, and, therefore, equally the hoarding of private wealth. The ideal is: a rich treasure chest, poor citizens.

In this way Machiavelli gives a new form to the Aristotelian theme that 'the good life' is incomplete without active involvement in the public promotion of the general interest. This *republican* ideal, in contrast with royal absolutism as well as with 'the freedom of the individual', would until the American Revolution remain an important source of inspiration. It, for example, determined the self-esteem of the ruling class in the Dutch Republic, and the idea of 'the true freedom' which prevailed there (that is, the ability to govern without the supervision of a viceroy).

European history of the 16th century – the religious wars, the development of royal absolutism – gave as much impetus to realism as the Italian history of the 15th century. Among the small intellectual elite of humanists, this development increasingly led to the invocation of the classical philosophers of the sceptical school. The new sceptics established, in the first place, that in military and political matters – between the two domains a clear boundary hardly exists – moral considerations in fact do not play any role: in a situation where the profit of the one amounts to the loss of another, and cooperation thus makes no sense, no one is prepared to place unilateral restrictions on himself. Especially where morality would be required most of all, it thus does not exert any influence. The question this poses is whether the validity of moral norms is not simply illusory. The sceptics established, in the second place, that the misery of the religious wars is the consequence of the fact that the different parties adhere without reserve to their mutually contradictory beliefs. In this regard the question arose as to the actual grounds of these convictions, and whether these grounds are sufficient to profess the specific convictions with such force. On closer inspection it appears that the human capacity for knowledge is extremely limited; even our direct observation is often not trustworthy (think here of optical illusions); concerning the physical and moral worlds we can actually know nothing with certainty. People seldom base their opinions, however fanatically they adhere to them, on good grounds. They often simply derive them from their social environment. However, as Michel de Montaigne (1533–1592) remarked in a famous passage in his *Essais*, what kind of truth is it that counts up to the mountain over there, and behind it, is a lie? To be sure, most of these sceptical philosophical thinkers were of the view that some or other form of religious belief is necessary to keep a society together. (Even Machiavelli contended that without religion the undermining influence of self-interest would not be possible to resist.) However, some sceptics even dared to put this into question. A community of atheists was, in their view, conceivable, and at least better than one of fundamentalists.

The sceptics even turned away in disappointment from the republican ideal. The wise man attempts to cut himself loose from all ties and responsibilities, and thinks solely of his self-preservation in a world that is not ruled by wisdom, but by Fortune.

3.4 The Break with Tradition: The Scientific Revolution

At the start of the 17th century a new confidence arose in the human ability to obtain knowledge, based on the success of the emerging natural sciences (the mechanical and astronomical discoveries of Galileo Galilei (1563–1643); the discovery of blood circulation by Harvey (1578–1657)).

This scientific revolution created a new philosophical climate. Especially in France a circle of philosophers originated who, on the one hand, wanted to take seriously the sceptical criticism regarding Aristotelian thinking, and, on the other hand, believed that the emerging physics proved that the sceptical doubt concerning the ability of obtaining reliable knowledge was misplaced.

The first step was to radicalise sceptical doubt. The sceptics established that our senses sometimes cannot be trusted: the stick in the water is straight, but it looks like it is bent. In this instance we can rectify the mistaken observation, but perhaps other observations are mistaken in a way that cannot be rectified. The more fundamental question Galileo raised did not concern the number of mistakes in human observation, but the question to what extent observation can at all tell us something about the world. Our senses are activated by the outside world, and bring about certain impressions in our consciousness, for example, the impression of green grass. It is not only, as the sceptics said, not provable that the grass is green and not red. There is no reason to assume that the grass indeed has a colour; colours, sounds, smells do not exist in the objective world, but only in our subjective experience. In the external world only light vibrations of variable intensity are present, which appear to us as different colours only as a result of processing by our eyes. (The precise explanation is, of course, much more recent than Galileo.) The objective characteristics of reality are only size, form, number, and speed of movement. Each of these characteristics can be measured accurately; the resulting quantitative data lend themselves to mathematical treatment. 'The book of nature', according to Galileo, 'is written in mathematical letters'.

Physics is not, however, concerned with the registration of such measurements; what it comes down to is working out a *theory*, from which the results of observation can be deductively derived: the second and determinate step. Aristotle had formulated a number of laws of movement (for example, that the speed of a falling object is proportional to its weight), and learned people were used to treating these laws as axioms from which they deductively drew a number of conclusions (for example, that movement in a vacuum is impossible). Galileo established by experimentation that these conclusions were incorrect; subsequently he attempted to formulate other laws that could indeed explain the observable facts. Observation is thus essential for science, but not enough. Every separate observation can be misleading; but science can explain theoretically why the observation misleads us (for example, why the stick in the water looks bent), and so clear up the deception. Precisely because of this we draw a distinction between objective and subjective qualities, that is, on the one hand, the characteristics of reality itself, and, on the other, 'characteristics' which only exist in our experience: starting from the objective qualities (light vibrations), we explain the subjective (colours).

With this Galileo rejected as source of scientific knowledge all appeals to authority, of Aristotle as well as of the Bible. (This brought him into violent conflict with the Inquisition.)

The resulting image of the physical world was totally different from that of Aristotle. Aristotle explained natural movement and change as determined by a preceding final aim, analogous to the growth of an acorn into an oak tree or of an embryo into an adult man. This is perhaps still somewhat believable, but less so is his explanation of movement in inanimate nature in accordance with this biological model. Thus, a stone, for example, falls down (and not up) according to Aristotle because it is in search of its natural element, that is, the earth. For the same reason steam rises. According to the Aristotelian view, nature consists of four elements (earth, fire, water and air), which are mixed together. For as long as everything has not yet found its proper place, there will be movement. In short, all natural changes are caused by internal 'final causes', by means of which something realises its essential design. These purposes each have their own value, and, moreover, stand in a value hierarchy in relation to each other. Following from this, everything has the same highest, reasonable and ultimate goal.

Modern natural science states that the movement of inanimate things is caused by accidental, aimless forces which affect them from the outside; in other words, by 'efficient causes' instead of 'final causes'. A stone falling to the earth is thus not the result of an internal aspiration towards an end-goal, but – as Newton (1642–1727) would demonstrate – because of the influence of gravity, which can be formulated in sheer quantitative terms (that is, of the mutual distance between the two bodies and their weight, in this case of the stone and the earth). In the place of Aristotle's qualitative explanation of movement as a result of a specific internal principle of form or essential idea which is different for every kind, Newton developed uniform laws of movement which explain the movement of all kinds of bodies: both the fall of an apple from a tree, and the movement of the heavenly bodies. Newton stated that each body stays in the same state of movement (or in the same state of rest), unless an external force influences it (in contrast with Aristotle, who assumed that a movement ends as soon as something reaches its final goal); and that changes in movement are proportionate to the impact of such a force, as well as to the direction in which the force works. Differing from Aristotle's contentions, there is thus no unique internal cause of movement, and no predetermined direction or ultimate goal of such movement. The direction in which a thing moves is, according to Newton, dependent on the accidental presence of bodies which have an impact on it. In other circumstances the movement could proceed in a totally different direction.

Since natural science rejected final causes or internal essences (or ideas) as explanatory factors, only aimless matter remained of the Aristotelian dichotomy in nature between 'idea' (or 'form') and 'matter' (or 'substance'). Coming into existence, becoming, and perishing are simply rearrangements of matter.

Natural science, by its laws, found that *if* certain causes present themselves, *then* certain consequences would also set in. A person who knows this can make use of it to realise consequences which are desired. However, apart from human intervention, there is nothing which guarantees that everything would move in the right direction.

That a tile falls from the roof and hits the skull of the postman is a convergence of causal processes; no 'sense' or 'meaning' lies behind it. Natural science explains the occurrence of big natural catastrophes, such as floods (for example, with reference to the position of the heavenly bodies), just as competently as the operation of modern machinery, such as steam engines. Nature consists only of blind, normless and aimless processes. Knowledge thereof makes possible technical control of nature for arbitrary aims, good as well as evil.

Hence the hierarchical unity of the world, which Aristotle and Aquinas both presupposed, dissolves. In the place of an 'organic' worldview (analogous to an organic unity) came one that was 'mechanistic' (analogous to a mechanism, such as a clock): things and occurrences do not have a meaningful function in a necessarily coherent, co-ordinated whole, but are just like the cogs and arms of a clock, a combination of separate, measurable parts.

The fundamental insight into the difference between subjective and objective qualities – characteristics which exist only in experience, and characteristics which really belong to things – was acquired, as is often the case with great intellectual innovations, more or less at the same time by different persons independently of each other. Galileo was one of these, the French philosopher René Descartes (1596–1650) another. Descartes, however, went one step further. In our consciousness the things themselves do not appear, but only the impressions which are caused by the impact of the external world on our senses. All of us are thus actually sitting locked up in our own home cinemas, watching the movies of our impressions. When we see green grass, we can, therefore, doubt whether the grass is really green, or whether it indeed has a colour. But who actually guarantees that there is grass? How do we know that a world exists outside of our consciousness, with 'objective characteristics', and not only the movie that we are watching?

Descartes describes his philosophical method in *Discours de la Méthode* (Discourse on Method, 1637). When he discovered that nothing of what is regarded as true knowledge can actually, on good grounds, be accepted (here he thought particularly of the Aristotelian tradition), he decided to investigate whether any of the opinions he holds are completely free of doubt. How does one proceed with such an investigation? Descartes makes a list of all the things which he has until then regarded as true. This list consists of formulations of the following type:

> 'I think that X' (that grass is green, that grass exists, etc).

He subsequently establishes that everything with which he replaces X can be placed in doubt. It is, for example, possible that an evil spirit exists which deludes him with visions of a non-existing world full of green grass (and seemingly conscious co-creatures, too). Nonetheless, according to Descartes, one thing always remains which can absolutely not be placed in doubt, that is, the fact that *I think* that X. What I thus know with absolute certainty is that I myself exist as a thinking being. I can think by myself: perhaps the grass is not green, perhaps it does not exist, etc, but as soon as I think: perhaps I myself do not exist, I realise that this is impossible. I contradict the statement by considering it. *Cogito ergo sum*: I think, therefore I am.

In this reasoning Descartes uses doubt as *method*. In other words, he does not really doubt whether a God exists, or a world as it is described by physics, but for as long as he cannot rigorously prove these opinions, he leaves them temporarily out of account, in search of his unquestionable foundation. As soon as he has found it in 'I think, therefore I am', he proceeds, with the assistance of the acquired insight, to first prove the existence of God (I can represent to myself, in thinking, a wholly perfect being, but the inferior cannot bring forth the superior, therefore I could not have created this idea myself, but must have been given it by this being himself), and subsequently the existence of a world outside of his own consciousness (a perfect being would not systematically mislead me with the delusion of a non-existing external world).

The Cogito is *clair et distinct*: as soon as one considers it, one knows for sure that it is true. This clarity and certainty must, therefore, likewise be the characteristic of all other true knowledge. Disconnected sensory knowledge lacks this characteristic; it is, however, certainly to be found in the mathematically formulated theoretical knowledge of natural science. Differing from Galileo, Descartes is of the view that observation is not essential for scientific knowledge. He regards the central ideas of God, spirit and matter as innate; from the insight into their existence it would, furthermore, be possible to deduce all theoretical knowledge. Characteristic of the philosophy of Descartes and his followers are the onerous demands which they place on scientific proof. Scientific reasoning must by way of fitting inferences (deduction) from unquestionable premises lead to indisputable conclusions. The best example is the way in which Euclid developed his geometry. (Spinoza would for this reason call his main work: *Ethica ordine geometrico demonstrata* (Ethics, proved in a geometrical way).) Descartes' arguments in support of the existence of God and the external world incidentally made much less of an impression than those for the *Cogito*.

The outcome of Descartes' reasoning was that the world is to be regarded as consisting of two totally different things or 'substances'. On the one hand, there is the *res cogitans*, consciousness or thinking, which exists only in time, but not in space. On the other hand, there is *res extensa*, matter, of which the primary characteristic is spatial extension. The ontology of Descartes is, therefore, dualistic, like that of Plato; the only difference is that Descartes does not assume any independently existing rational order external to consciousness. Man himself similarly consists of spirit and body, thought and matter. In the material world movement takes place in accordance with the aimless mechanical laws which science has discovered, including the movement which by means of our senses summons in us the idea of green grass. (Whereas the grass is thus in itself not green at all, but simply a quantity of moving matter of a certain form and size.) The problem is, of course, that this idea belongs to the sphere of thinking: how is it possible that material objects have a causal impact, not only on each other, but also on immaterial consciousness? The different philosophical systems of the 17th and 18th centuries are all, in the first place, attempts to find a more satisfactory answer to this question. According to some (Hobbes), only matter actually exists, according to others (Berkeley), only spirit; and according to Spinoza, spirit and matter are simply manifestations of one underlying reality which he calls 'God'.

3.5 Modern Natural Law: Hugo Grotius

In political philosophy a similar development took place in the first half of the 17th century: the sceptical rejection of the authority of Aristotle was accepted, but scepticism itself was superseded by the finding of new foundations. (Preparatory work had already been done by the scholastic and Calvinist theories of the sovereignty of the people and the state contract.) Classical natural law with its perfectionist ethics, in which political life contributes to the complete realisation of human nature, is abandoned. Instead, the state acquires a much more limited goal. What for the sceptics was a disappointing conclusion: the only thing that remains for man is to secure his self-preservation, became the foundation of a new type of natural law; a political theory built on a narrow ethics.

The pioneering work in this respect was done by Hugo de Groot (1583–1645), known outside of the Netherlands as Grotius. His personal history shows a striking correspondence with that of Machiavelli: a humanistic education (already as a child renowned in Europe for his literary achievements), an important official position (Grand Pensionary of Rotterdam), because of political upheaval he falls into political disfavour and is imprisoned with his patron (Oldenbarnevelt). After having escaped from the castle of *Loevestein* in a book crate, he dedicates himself primarily to his literary and scientific work, with a pension paid by the French king. His main work is *De Iure Belli ac Pacis* (Concerning the law of war and peace, 1625). In *Mare Liberum* (The Free Sea, 1609), Grotius argued that the sea, like the air, belongs to all and is thus free, thereby clearing the way for Dutch colonial trade against the Spanish and Portuguese claims to monopoly. He added to this that since on the open sea jurisdiction is absent, one may start a war to enforce one's rights.

The fundamental legal-philosophical problem that Grotius attempts to solve is that of the binding force of law. Most law is positive law: it is a declaration of the will of an institution – the 'sovereign' – which within a specific territory disposes of the power to enforce its will, if necessary. It is not, however, from this power that law derives its binding force; then law would be nothing but a coercive system. It is rather its binding force which justifies the eventual use of coercion. The question arises, how it is possible for positive law to place us under an obligation.

What Grotius specifically wants to emphasise is that this is a reasonable question. It is not at all self-evident that the declaration of the will of another places us under an obligation. Grotius expresses this proposition as follows: 'by nature' the obligation does not exist. When we describe man in accordance with his essence: gifted with reason, dependent on community, then there is nothing in our description which compels the conclusion that one person should be subjected to the authority of another. We recognise in this the doctrine of the original condition of freedom of Mornay and Althusius: 'by nature' people are free, and, certainly: everyone is equally free, thus also equal, equal in their freedom. Every person is, to start off with, his own sovereign.

If this is the case, there is only one way in which authoritative relations can arise: by way of voluntary subjection. The free man loses his freedom by voluntarily placing himself under the authority of another. Positive law thus ultimately binds us on the basis of an agreement. The subjects of a sovereign promised, or – this addition will become very significant – *must be regarded as having promised*, to obey his commands. However, this simply temporarily displaces the problem: what exactly is an agreement, and why does it bind? (A question which Althusius did not pose.) An agreement, Grotius answers, is a free act of will by means of which we give ourselves reasons to act in a certain way in the future. The binding force of an agreement is thus based on the reasonable insight that compliance with agreements is to be preferred to their violation. Why is this so?

It is such on the basis of natural law. Natural law consists of the rules which apply to us, not because of the will and authority of another, but because we are the way we are, in terms of human nature. This is because man is 'by nature' a communal being. This is, in turn, the case in a double sense: man has an *appetitus societatis*, a natural inclination to live in community. However, even in the event that community does not have this intrinsic meaning for man, then it still has an instrumental meaning: for the fulfilment of his elementary needs man is dependent on the help of others, and at least on their respect.

If community between people is then to be possible, they must be capable of attuning themselves to each other's actions. Unlike ants and bees, this does not happen automatically; man as free and reasonable being must do this consciously, and in accordance with general principles. These principles constitute natural law. One of the essential methods is the following: you declare what you want to do, and subsequently others can thus count on it that you will in fact do it. For this reason agreements are binding. Agreement is the mother of positive law, natural law the grandmother.

A later major representative of modern natural law, Samuel von Pufendorf (1632–1694), summarises this idea, fully in the spirit of Grotius, in the following formulation: duty is to do everything that is necessary for the maintenance of a peaceful community with others. (Hume (Section 6.2) will, for good reason, ask the question why the intermediate step of voluntary subjection via the social contract was necessary. If it is necessary for the maintenance of a peaceful community that political authority exists, does natural law then not directly prescribe that we have to be obedient to it? However, if this is not necessary, why would we agree to obey it? And on what basis would Grotius be allowed to assume that we have done so?) Common sense tells us that the citizen who contravenes positive law for the sake of an immediate benefit, destroys that on which his own abiding benefit depends. Someone who is ready to lay down law and reason will not easily find an ally. (This also applies to the relation between nations.) The social nature of man, moreover, reveals itself in such a way that, in the case of injustice, he can find no peace with himself. Law and (personal) benefit are not in conflict with each other, but ultimately the one cannot be reduced to the other.

A peaceful community with others, according to Grotius, is only possible when people do not cause injury to each other. Everyone thus has, again 'by nature', certain rights: the rights to life, bodily integrity, freedom and honour. Everyone is, precisely for this reason, equally free, because everyone has the same natural rights; and natural law prescribes that these rights must be respected. The emphasis on subjective rights – likewise an invention of the scholasticism of the late Middle Ages – is one of the characteristics of modern natural law, distinguished from the classical conception thereof. The general interest dissolves into that of individuals.

The real foundation of the new ethics is ultimately self-preservation: human life is only possible in community, and life in community is possible only if people respect each other's rights. It is for this reason, according to Grotius, that no society exists in which violence is not prohibited, except as a form of self-defence. This is the minimal objective core of morality. (In contrast with the Aristotelians, the emphasis is on 'minimal'; and in contrast with the sceptics, on 'objective'.)

However, if the natural condition is one of equal rights, how can unequal rights ever be justified? Answer: when it is the result of voluntary agreements by means of which people give shape in more detailed form to their social relations. To promise something entails the renunciation of a right. And this right can then in terms of natural law not again be claimed.

How far can this go? Grotius hesitates in answering this question, but finally sees no bottom line. People can, when it is necessary for their self-preservation and it does not prejudice others, renounce their personal freedom, and make themselves the slaves of another, to whom they then owe absolute obedience. They can, similarly, subject themselves to the unrestricted authority of a king. This is of course not to say that they always do this, but they can. Natural law only requires that rights which have not been renounced, be respected; which rights have been renounced, and which not, is a factual, historical question. In light of the original situation of equal rights, the onus of proof lies on those who claim this authority. Grotius here introduces a maxim which one could refer to as the principle of compassionate interpretation: you may not assume that people have completely renounced their freedom unless it unambiguously appears to be the case. Therefore, Grotius can at the same time acknowledge that in some countries (France, his country of exile) the king rules with absolute authority, *and* insist that his Dutch ancestors had the right of resistance. His theory nevertheless tends towards absolutism. 'Originally' everyone has equal rights, but everyone must also stand up for their rights: defend themselves, punish the infringement of rights, enforce compensation. And it is precisely these powers which individuals at the establishment of a state transfer to their rulers. However, if one no longer has a right of self-defence against the sovereign, then one actually has no right against him at all. (How should one stand one's ground?) Indeed, abuse of power by rulers is a real danger, but a greater danger is civil war, and this is unavoidable if everyone defends his own rights.

The conclusion that no right of resistance exists against the state, was the radical conclusion drawn by Hobbes, the most discerning representative of modern natural law, to which he gave a very unique twist (Section 4.1). We thus see that, probably contrary to what one would have expected, the introduction of the notion of 'natural rights' in political philosophy in the first place leads to the justification of unlimited monarchical power.

The absolute monarchy was, nonetheless, not happy with this, and it never became part of its official ideology. The reason was, that in accordance with this theory the rights of the monarchy were derived from the natural rights of their subjects. In the moral order the individual is most important, and political authority only of secondary importance. Even though authority is absolute, it is nevertheless acquired from individuals, and is aimed at the protection of their rights. The monarch remains a functionary. He, of course, preferred to acquire absolute power directly from God, and to owe only God the duty to serve the general interest. Everyone acknowledges that kings have to act in accordance with natural law. What should, however, be done if they do not comply with their obligations? Hobbes and another proponent of unlimited monarchical power, Robert Filmer (1589–1653), both denied that subjects then have a right of resistance. Hobbes, however, said this because a civil war was for him the greater evil. According to Filmer, God imposes on human beings bad rulers, as well as sickness and accidents, as a kind of trial. The first argument invites critical examination.

Like Hobbes, the third representative of modern natural law whom we will discuss, John Locke, uses all the conceptual instruments of Grotius: the social nature of man; a natural state of equal freedom, in other words, equal rights; the validity of natural law in the natural state which prescribes respect for rights; the voluntary renunciation of rights as the only possibility of arriving at unequal rights; the subjection to state authority as a form of renunciation of rights; the necessity of subjection because of the precariousness of the natural state; the derivation of all the powers of the state from the individual. The only difference is that Locke uses these devices in such a way that state authority is not made absolute, but, instead, bound by limits. With the contract by means of which a civil society is established, people do not give away all their rights. The entire purpose of the contract after all lies in the fact that natural rights are (to a large extent) protected. People should then be able to invoke their rights, also against the state. In this respect Locke returns to the older version of the story, as it was told by Mornay and Althusius.

Apart from Hobbes and Locke, we will in the next chapter pay attention to Spinoza. He, too, was an adherent of modern natural law. In his political philosophy he specifically wanted to show how piety, peace and freedom depend on each other. The contention that societal peace stands in the service of piety and individual freedom, brings him close to Locke. His entirely realistic appraisal of human passions, and his conviction that not so much an appeal to people's good intentions (including that of politicians), but a balance of power, provides the best prospect of decent behaviour, however, makes him resemble Hobbes.

Chapter 4
Hobbes, Locke, and Spinoza

4.1 Hobbes

4.1.1 Life

Thomas Hobbes was born in 1588 in an English rural town, the son of a hardly literate and alcohol addicted church minister. Hobbes Junior was a typical representative of humanism: at secondary school he already translated a Greek tragedy into Latin; both his first and his last publications were translations of a Greek author into English; he, in addition, spoke fluent French and Italian and wrote poetry in almost all these languages. The most distinguished career possibility for a humanist was to enter into the service of a rich aristocratic family as secretary, private teacher, business representative and general adviser. Hobbes entered into this position with the household of the count of Devonshire. A mandatory climax in the education of a gentleman was the *Grand Tour*, a journey through France and Italy, which Hobbes on three occasions undertook with different generations of this family. Such a tour could last up to 5 years, and provided all kinds of opportunities to meet interesting people. In Venice, Hobbes linked up with distinguished representatives of scepticism.

After 1630, Hobbes started, following his employer, to take an increasing interest, first, in the new military technology, and, subsequently, in the new natural science which lay at its basis. He had a meeting with Galileo, and afterwards discovered in Paris the French philosophers in the circle around Descartes. Their project, to achieve a victory over scepticism with the help of physics, fascinated him, and he thought that he could execute this better than Descartes himself. Hobbes realised that the dualism of 'thinking' and 'extension' leads to insoluble problems concerning the relation between the two worlds. From 1637 (the year of *Discours de la Méthode*) he started to set down in writing his philosophical ideas.

In these years the political battle between king and parliament reached a peak. King Charles I prepared for an unpopular war to break up the trade hegemony of the Dutch Republic, and for this purpose raised an unpopular, and, according to many, unlawful tax. Intense discussions concerning the limits of monarchical powers followed. In this situation Hobbes decided to extend his philosophical system

C.W. Maris, F.C.L.M. Jacobs (eds.), *Law, Order and Freedom*, Law and Philosophy Library 94, DOI 10.1007/978-94-007-1457-1_4, © Springer Science+Business Media B.V. 2011

to include a theory concerning state and law, in which he followed Grotius. Many copies of this manuscript, which defended the rights of the king, were distributed in England. When at the end of 1640 the parliamentary party gained the upper hand, Hobbes thought it wise to flee to France. He stayed there throughout the English civil war, in close contact with the Cartesians (also with Descartes himself), and continued with his main philosophical work in three parts, of which the political-philosophical part (*De Cive* (On the citizen, 1651)), was published by the Dutch publisher Elzevier.

This is not, however, the work for which he became famous. After Charles I had been executed and Cromwell had established his military dictatorship, Hobbes wrote in a period of one year a new version of his political philosophy, published it (in 1651) with the title *Leviathan* (a mythical monster from the book of Job in the Bible, which was supposed to represent the power monopoly of the state), and subsequently returned to England. The book is, like the previous one, a defence of the absolute power of the 'sovereign', but the followers of the king nevertheless saw it as a form of treason. For this there were two reasons. The civil war was not only caused by a conflict about political power, but also concerned the relation between state and church. Hobbes chose in this regard the position of Cromwell against that of Charles I: he rejected the existence of an Anglican state church, and argued for a state of affairs where local churches would be independent of central religious organs, such as bishops and synods, but subject to the state. In the second place, Hobbes defended the view that citizens owe obedience to the person or institution which effectively possesses the monopoly of power, whether or not this was obtained by legal means. This legitimation of a usurper was of course welcomed by Cromwell.

When monarchical power was reinstated in 1660, Hobbes was given a hard time by his former friends, although the king himself, Charles II, who had taken a mathematics course with Hobbes in Paris, placed him under his protection. A law which declared atheism a crime, and which was specifically aimed at Hobbes, was rejected at the last moment. It is this whiff of atheism which furthermore explains why the profound influence that Hobbes had on philosophy in the century after him was seldom openly acknowledged. He died in 1679.

4.1.2 Man and World

Hobbes's philosophy elaborates on the discovery – which he alleged to have made independently of Galileo and Descartes – of the difference between subjective and objective qualities. If the impressions in our consciousness are simply the causal product of the activity of our senses, the central question becomes whether there is something in the world outside of consciousness which corresponds with these impressions.

To answer this question, Hobbes conducted a mental experiment which is at least as radical as that of Descartes. Suppose that the whole universe is destroyed, with the exception of one thinking being. This being would continue to watch in his private cinema the movie of his images (memories, fantasies). Would such a being still have a reason to assume that an external world existed or had existed? Yes, Hobbes says, because something that moves – such as the movie of images – must be set in motion by something else. The only things that can move are material objects, or 'bodies'. The only thing that can bring about the movement of a body, is the movement of another body. Thus: an external world with moving bodies exists (or at least existed). And, similarly, the movie of our images, our consciousness, is ultimately nothing but the movement of a body.

Hobbes is thus a materialist. He believes that only one kind of reality exists: material objects; therefore, no Platonic 'ideas', Aristotelian 'substances' or Cartesian 'thinking entities'. The material objects move in accordance with natural laws, by means of which the movement of one body exercises an influence on other bodies. In order to understand the functioning of a complex system, for example, a watch or a solar system, one must proceed as follows. As a start one spreads out in thinking – or if one can, as in the case of a watch, in reality – the parts of which it consists. Of each of the parts one determines how it would move if no external influence at all would impact on it. Then one again joins together the parts one by one, in the course of which one can in each instance explain how, from the independent movements of the separate parts, the dependent movements of the combined parts take place. What would settle the matter would be the fact that the whole system indeed works as could be expected on the basis of one's analysis. (The watch which one first took apart works again; the solar eclipse indeed takes place at the predicted time.)

In this sense human society also is a complex system, and to understand how this system works, one must first analyse it in relation to its parts: human individuals and the way in which they would 'move' independently of each other. This way of proceeding is characteristic of *methodical individualism.*

Human beings are material objects which have in common with other animals and plants that they are alive. What is unique to the movement of 'life'? A coconut that falls from a tree, once it has landed on the ground, comes to rest by itself. Living beings are, however, organised in such a way that they preserve themselves. Life is thus a system of movements – absorption of light, and of food; protection against harmful influences from outside – to which every part must contribute for the continuation of the whole. Hence the organisation of a human individual is likewise aimed at preventing that its *vital motions* stop.

Some partial processes, for example, when a splinter causes a festering wound in the skin, happen involuntarily. In the case of other processes, for example, running away from an attacking terrier, an element of will comes into play. Such movements are aimed at satisfying certain desires. Ultimately such a movement is, however, not different from others: what appears in human consciousness as an object of natural desire – a banana, a bear hide, a sexual partner – are in essence what stimulates the vital movements of the specific individual, and, as a consequence, contributes to his preservation. The programming of the 'material object' is only made *conscious* in desire.

In addition to such desires, the object of which is naturally given, there are others too. People are able to learn from their experiences, and are in this respect specifically influenced by their experiences of pleasure and pain. When a specific state of being is painful, the individual will in future avoid the occurrence of that state. 'Pain' is here nothing but the consciousness of a threat to the vital movements.

However, people are at the same time capable of generalising: they can recognise a state of affairs as one of the same kind which was experienced earlier as painful or pleasurable. They can, furthermore, recognise relations of cause and effect – 'causal' relations. Of this knowledge they make use in performing actions which produce states which were earlier experienced as painful or pleasurable. The ability of generalisation, and the recognition of causal relations, Hobbes calls *reason*, intellect.

Hobbes, thus, describes human beings as characterised by desires and intellect. Desires differ depending on the circumstances. When one has had nothing to drink for a day, thirst becomes one's overwhelming motive; but once the desire has been satisfied, it disappears and is replaced by another. There is, therefore, a continual succession of the most diverse desires.

Based on this description of human nature, Hobbes constructs his doctrine of values, the first part of his ethics. 'Good' and 'bad' always mean good and bad *for someone*; nothing is good or bad in itself. 'Good for me' is usually what fulfils my desires. This is not, however, the most essential definition. Normally my desires are directed at that which promotes my vital movements, but if this is not the case, then my desires themselves are flawed, and their fulfilment is only apparently good, not in reality. Thus it is, for example, possible that I desire something because I unjustifiably think that it will result in something else that is good for me. In this instance the mistake actually lies in my intellect. But it is also possible that I can obtain pleasure from something that actually inhibits my vital movements (see Section 8.2 (psychoanalysis) and 9.4 (deconstruction)); there is then, so to speak, a system defect in my organisation. (Think of someone who gets a kick out of playing Russian roulette, or who suffers from serious depression. Hobbes himself thinks especially of people who are excessively proud or conceited.) The essential definition of 'good for me' is, therefore: what advances my vital movements, what serves my preservation as living being. (With this view Hobbes links up with Grotius.)

This doctrine of value is not, as is often stated, non-cognitivist (the view that moral statements cannot be evaluated as to their truth or falsity): it is a *fact* that it is not good for me to get cirrhosis of the liver; when someone is of the view that it is, then he is mistaken; and if I desire it myself, then it appears that I am seriously disturbed. The doctrine is certainly relativistic: what is good for one (rain for the farmer), can be bad for another (the same rain for a tourist).

4.1.3 The State of Nature

In order to proceed to the second part of his ethics, the normative theory of society, Hobbes still needs two hypotheses, the second of which he incidentally does not explicitly mention.

(1) *People are more or less similar in respect of bodily and spiritual abilities.* Of course, there is a significant difference in physical power and intelligence, in general, but the differences amongst people themselves are small in comparison to that between man and ant, man and mouse, or even man and the primates.
(2) *The world is finite.* From this follows that the objects which people require for the satisfaction of their desires are scarce.

We are now going to put the watch back together again. If people have all kinds of different desires, it can easily happen that two people want the same thing: a banana, a bear hide, or a partner. And from (2) it follows that it would not always be possible for both to satisfy their desires completely without additional costs. When I shoot too many bears, someone else would at least have to look longer to still find one, and perhaps there would be none left. *Scarcity*, in other words, occurs.

When both of us thus strive to obtain a scarce good, then, according to Hobbes, we become 'enemies'; our interests clash, and, therefore, possibly, we ourselves as well.

Something needs to be added to this. The succession of desires is uninterrupted: I, therefore, know that I will in future have desires, but I do not know *which*; I can, after all, not predict which experiences I will have in the meantime. At this point Hobbes introduces a definition:

Power = all the means which someone has at his disposal to satisfy his present *and future* desires.

When I, as a rational being, am capable by my actions of obtaining the means to fulfil my wishes, but I do not as yet know what my wishes will be, then I realise that I will certainly do well should I gain as much power as possible. Wealth is, for example, a form of power, because it enables one to fulfil all kinds of different desires.

However, if everyone not only strives to realise his present desires, but, moreover, to obtain as much power as possible so that he experiences no problems with his future desires, then the possibility of conflict between our interests increases significantly. That empty piece of land: I have no time to build on it now, but it would still be good to permanently have it at my disposal, because who knows, next year I may also have a wife, a child, a slave (or a machine).

As soon as people start living together, the sources of conflict increase. Now hypothesis (1) attains importance, too. If people's capacities diverged radically, conflict would naturally come to an end. The strongest would say to the weakest: you know, if we should fight, I would win. Let us, therefore, skip the fighting. A natural pecking order would thus develop, in terms of which the weakest submit themselves to the wishes of the strongest, and in exchange retain their lives, and perhaps protection. But if everyone is more or less equal – even the strongest must sleep, and can be overpowered by one who is weaker – then no one has to accept defeat in advance; then there is real fighting.

Up until now the fight was about scarce goods which everyone thinks he may in future need. But if one knows that one can at any moment be challenged to fight, one is no longer simply interested in power from the point of view of one's current and future needs, but specifically from the point of view of one's chances in a fight. Then it is not only of importance how much power one has in an absolute sense, but specifically how much power one has in comparison with others. One not only wants to increase one's power, but, more specifically, the difference in power in relation to others. Power becomes a *comparative* good. A form of power which actually has only comparative value is honour or reputation. If people *think* that one is strong, then one is much stronger than when they think that one is weak. They would think twice before they attack one.

If people reach the point where their primary aim is to be stronger than others, it is every man for himself, for that would mean that they would use every chance they get to harm others, even if in an absolute sense they themselves would be worse off.

Hobbes makes explicit here the logic of escalation: once there is a source of conflict, then that conflict has an inherent tendency to extend itself infinitely. Note that Hobbes does not assume an inborn *Will to Power* or aggressive drive (see Sections 7.5 (Nietzsche) and 8.2 (Freud)). His conclusions are not based on a pessimistic view of mankind. That things go wrong in this way, does not happen because people are 'bad' or stupid. Even the most pleasant and peaceful person would, precisely when he uses his brainpower, realise that he must use his opportunities to cause harm to others, whether or not he finds this pleasant: otherwise he would simply be worse off. (An insight that reminds us of Machiavelli.) The conclusion is, that in a state of scarcity an unrestricted war of all against all will develop amongst equal beings.

> In such condition, there is no place for Industry; because the fruit thereof is uncertain: and consequently no Culture of the Earth; no Navigation, nor use of the commodities that may be imported by Sea; no commodious Building; no Instruments of moving, and removing such things as require much force; no Knowledge of the face of the Earth; no account of Time; no Arts; no Letters; no Society; and which is worst of all, continual feare, and danger of violent death; and the life of man, solitary, poore, nasty, brutish, and short (Hobbes 1988, pp. 64–65).

4.1.4 Social Morality

In this situation no unconditional moral norms apply. Suppose that one formulates some absolute norm, for example, a prohibition against torture or the taking of hostages. A situation can arise for anyone in which his position in the balance of power would worsen if he adheres to the norm, and whether such a situation arises only he can judge. Whoever binds himself unconditionally in war to moral norms, penalises himself in relation to a less scrupulous opponent. As every person uses his intellect to see how he can serve the realisation of his desires in the longer term, one cannot reasonably expect of any man that he would accept such impediments. In this sense everyone has an *unrestricted natural freedom*. That I have such a natural freedom does not mean that others have the duty to respect this freedom; it simply means that it makes no sense to prohibit me from doing something. Because, if in my own judgment, I have no reason to hold myself to the prohibition, no one can expect of me that I still do so.

The situation is actually quite remarkable. Our presumption was that people are self-preserving organisms. They strive for things they suppose to be required for their self-preservation; their intellectual reflections stand in the service of this purpose. Now it appears that the rational choices they make in this way bring them into a situation in which everyone's self-preservation is in danger from one moment to the next. Must one not then say: but then the theory does not check out, it leads to a contradiction? The result is certainly remarkable, but not contradictory. Every fisherman has an interest in extending his fishing capacity; but if they all do it, they would empty the sea of fish. On its own, no industry has a sufficient interest in adopting environmental regulations; but if no one does this, in the long run, life and thus production also becomes impossible. We find here a general pattern. In a group of people every member has a choice between two actions: A or B (leave others alone; adhere to the quota; construct purifying installations; pay tax; *or not*). Everyone would prefer that all choose A rather than B, but the worst is to choose A, if the others choose B. If in this situation the whiff of suspicion arises that other group members will choose B, then some group members will choose B because of the fear that he who makes himself a sheep shall be eaten by the wolf; and the greater the number of people that follow their example, the wiser it becomes for the remaining ones to do the same. This is the negative spiral of mistrust which results in the war of all against all.

Luckily this is not the complete story. We are describing what happens in a society without state authority – a 'state of nature' – which is characterised by scarcity, and equality between people. We established the following: everyone there has grounds, every man for himself, to take decisions ('to choose B') which, all decisions taken together, leads to a permanent state of war (an empty sea, an uninhabitable world). However, this is a provisional description, where *the outcome itself has not as yet been taken into consideration*. Suppose that people realise that this will be the outcome. With this they are actually placed before a new choice. No longer the concrete choice of attacking a specific person or not, with the aim of changes in the balance of power which could be expected, but the general strategic choice for or against aggressive conduct, in light of the contribution it makes to the maintenance of the state of nature.

For Hobbes it is totally clear which choice the intellect prescribes: to abstain from aggression, as long as one can count on it that others would do the same; but if one can no longer count on that, to wage war with all means at one's disposal. It is thus a situation in which one has to give up one's natural freedom, because one realises that it is wise to place restrictions on oneself; and that is the state of affairs in which all others do it as well. When people reach the point where they expect each other to conduct themselves in a peaceful manner, then they all have grounds to comply with this expectation, and then it becomes reasonable to expect it from others as well. In that case, Hobbes states that they have obligations. Moral norms thus apply, after all, in the state of nature, but only conditionally: with the proviso of reciprocity. In theory, it would be possible for sensible people to arrive at a state of peaceful anarchy, in which everyone abandons deception and violence in the expectation that all others would also do so.

Given the fact that the fundamental good for individuals is to preserve themselves, the fundamental precept to do everything that guarantees peace, as long as they can hope that others would do the same, applies to them. This fundamental precept Hobbes calls *the law of nature*. All other moral rules (Hobbes summarises fifteen of these: abide by your agreements; in the case of punishment have regard only to future advantage, not to the harm that was done; judge in a fair way, etc) consist in the more detailed elaboration of this precept, and thus all are subject to the same condition of reciprocity. Ethics is the science of cooperative actions which are necessary to guarantee the highest good, that is, peace; and morality is the totality of prescriptions that this science develops.

Such a morality is typically a *narrow morality*. To be sure, as in classical natural law, the doctrine of duty is here derived from the doctrine of value: obligations apply to everyone, because in this way one serves one's own fundamental good. (Kant would say that these are 'hypothetical imperatives' (Section 6.3.1).) However, for one thing, the doctrine of value has become extremely minimal; the foundation of moral norms is not a design of the good life, but simply self-preservation, and then, moreover, simply one's *own* self-preservation. (Even Grotius's *appetitus societatis* dissolves.) At the same time moral rules are restricted to norms for acting cooperatively, specifically for dealing with mutual conflict.

As Hobbes presupposes so little – only the value of self-preservation, and mental insight into the suitable means to ensure this – he believes that he is capable of defeating ethical scepticism, and of establishing a universally valid, albeit minimal morality. The validity of this morality is objectively verifiable. 'The Lawes of Nature are Immutable and Eternall; For Injustice, Ingratitude, Arrogance, Pride, Iniquity, Acception of persons, and the rest, can never be made lawfull. For it can never be that Warre shall preserve life, and Peace destroy it' (Hobbes 1988, p. 82). Moreover, whereas the doctrine of value was still relativistic (what is good for X, is not so for Y), the doctrine of duty is universal: the same basic moral laws apply to everyone. After all, I only have reason to adhere to these if I can expect that you will do the same; then the rule cannot apply only to me, and not to you.

4.1.5 The State

However, if peaceful anarchy is possible, why does it not exist? At this point in his argument Hobbes introduces an additional premise, as the theory would otherwise not be realistic enough: *people usually only use their intellect to a limited extent*.

The consequence is that the state of peaceful anarchy is not stable. Everyone would in fact always have reason to abstain from aggression and corruption, because from the point of view of self-preservation peace has absolute priority. But people sometimes allow themselves, either because of short-term advantage, or because of 'sick' desires, such as revenge and excessive pride, to be swept along, and then still do things which they know will harm their own interest in the long term, or convince themselves that this is not the case. Others are, on more or less justifiable grounds, afraid of this, and in this fear find immediate cause for anticipatory aggression. Hence the downward spiral again takes effect; at a given moment it is beyond dispute that, by still adhering to the prohibition against aggression, one simply makes oneself into an easier prey for others. The war of all against all threatens anew. This time, not because everyone uses his intellect, but because some do not. Short-sightedness is the problem.

But something can, again, be done about this. Persons who have an inclination to contravene the (fundamental) moral precept even though it harms their own fundamental interests, can be prevented from doing so by attaching more inconveniences to the contravention which become operative immediately. Persons who act short-sightedly must be threatened with certain and prompt punishment. The threat can, of course, only be credible when, even though it may still fail, it is carried out irrevocably. This can only happen when the person or institution which carries out the punishment has more power at his or its disposal than that of any other person or association of persons in society. The link between sanction and the contravention of norms is thus only possible in a society if this is coupled with a *monopolisation of power*. Such a monopolist of power, Hobbes calls the 'sovereign'; the society in which he exercises his power, the 'commonwealth'. There can per definition in one commonwealth not be more than one centre of power; if there were to be more than one, the centres of power would not be able to threaten each other successfully with sanctions; and they would then in relation to each other still live in a state of nature, a state of anarchy, not in a commonwealth: if necessary, they resolve their conflicts through fighting, they cannot regulate these by the positing of norms. 'International law' is a contradiction in terms: a legal system can only bind the subjects of one sovereign. 'Separation of powers' is, for the same reasons, impossible.

There is necessarily only one sovereign per commonwealth; and his sovereignty is necessarily unlimited. This applies no less to a democracy than a monarchy. (That Hobbes does not completely exclude state forms other than a monarchy is actually inconsistent: because as soon as more than one person is included in a decision-making procedure, one must, after all, ultimately have the last word concerning the question whether the procedure was properly followed). Suppose that a sovereign were bound by certain obligations, whether or not laid down in a constitution. It only makes sense to speak of an 'obligation' when a norm applies which may not be contravened with impunity. Suppose then, that the sovereign breaches his constitutional obligations. There would then have to be an institution which has the task of punishing the sovereign for this. If the institution was capable of doing so, the so-called 'sovereign' would not really have a monopoly of power, and thus not be the real sovereign.

Hobbes does not deny that a sovereign has moral duties: he must promote the preservation of the life of his subjects, and thus, for example, guarantee to each a minimum level of subsistence; he may not interfere with property relations, and thus, for example, may only tax consumption, not income. However, these duties are not enforceable; if he breaches them, his subjects cannot derive from such breach a right to disobedience or resistance. After all, even in a situation where the sovereign does not respect their property rights, they are still better off than in a state of total war of all against all. Only when the sovereign threatens their life, does their rational self-interest allow them to resist.

4.1.6 The Social Contract

One could couch the reasoning thus far in the form of a story. 'People initially lived in isolation from each other. When they came together, there arose – for the reasons mentioned – a war of all against all. When everyone realised that this could not continue, they came together on a certain day to discuss the situation. They quickly came to the conclusion that peaceful anarchy because of the short-sightedness of people was impossible. For this reason they agreed to the following: Up until then everyone had established for himself which measures were necessary to ensure his self-preservation. Everyone indicated to each other that these decisions would in future, with his agreement, be taken by an Other and all of them designated the same Other for this purpose. The people are from then on, as a result of their mutual agreement, compelled to obey the person or institution authorised by them. They have irrevocably renounced their power to defend themselves to the best of their own insight.'

As a historical account this is of course unsatisfactory. (How did the hostile individuals succeed in all assembling at the same time and have an orderly discussion? Could each person bring his weapons along, and why were these then not used? But most important of all: consistent with the fundamental precept of natural law, everyone only has a duty to act in accordance with his agreements if he can count on it that the other parties to the agreement do the same. How did this trust come about?) Differing from Grotius, Hobbes does not, however, present this as a historical account; he knows quite well that in reality things happen like this only in highly exceptional instances. A commonwealth is, according to him, in reality usually established when one person or a group of persons appropriate for themselves a monopoly of power. How this happens is not relevant either, only *that* it happens. For in this way the basic problem of human society is solved, which otherwise would have led such society to civil war: the problem that conflicts are unavoidable for as long as everyone follows his own judgment concerning what is necessary for the preservation of his life. Because someone who monopolises power is necessary, all subjects have good reason to obey him when he is there. He, after all, ensures that uniform rules apply and are maintained, and in this way prevents chaos. When someone joins the commonwealth, the same reasons immediately apply to him. For this reason one may, according to Hobbes, *assume* that such a person also *promises* to obey the sovereign. In other words, the basis of obedience is not the contract; one infers the existence of a contract because there are grounds for obedience. What is then the sense of the concept of the contract? When one asks someone why he acts decently, then he may perhaps say: it is a kind of agreement that exists between us.

What he means with this is: I do it because I presuppose that the others do it too, and I know that the others do it because they presuppose that *I* do it. The foundation is *reciprocity*.

4.1.7 Law and Morality

Looking back, we find that this line of reasoning is constructed in three phases. In all three the question is posed: what must one, as sensible person, do in a situation of scarcity? Every phase is a correction of, or an addition to, the conclusion of the preceding one. The first answer reads: one must throw oneself into the battle with all one's weapons before one is eliminated oneself. If everyone follows this advice, the result is a war of all against all. Therefore the second answer reads: one must adhere to the moral constitution which prohibits aggression, for as long as one can count on it that others do the same. This answer is not so much mistaken, as irrelevant: for people are too short-sighted to count on it that they will adhere to the constitution, and then the necessary condition for it is not fulfilled. From this follows the third answer: as soon as a person or institution has attained a monopoly of power, one must obey him or it.

Is the third answer an addition to the second, or an alternative thereto? Is morality not superfluous as soon as a state exists with sufficient power to keep in line the smartest criminals? It appears that we can summarise the theory simply as follows: without a state, sensible individuals – about ones who act short-sightedly we do not have to speak here – become involved in a war of all against all; for this reason it is good that a sovereign appears that forces everyone, under the threat of sanction, to keep his hands to himself. Hobbes was indeed understood in this manner previously.

In accordance with this interpretation, the only reason for obeying the state is fear of punishment. One then needs quite a substantial state to guarantee arrest. For this reason the second phase is essential for Hobbes. The most important motive for everyone to adhere to the rules, is that one in this way contributes to the preservation of peaceful interaction with others. This motive would even have been sufficient if there were no people who act short-sightedly. The function of the state is not to create the main motive for obedience, but only the following: to create for some a supplementary motive for obedience, and in this way for others the condition (trust) for the main motive to be sufficient.

Actually, the state thus exists only to support morality, exactly as in classical natural law. (One difference is that it is here only a matter of a narrow morality. Another difference is that Hobbes is not an essentialist; we classified him in Chapter 1 under 'naturalistic natural law'.) But suppose that a difference of opinion arises concerning the interpretation of morality: what exactly are 'Injustice, Ingratitude, Arrogance, Pride, Iniquity, Acception of persons'? In such an instance the sovereign must determine which interpretation is proper, because the sovereign must punish the contravention (and a separation of powers is impossible). One cannot now say that the sovereign is obliged to take account of certain limits to interpretation, because we have already shown that the sovereign can have no enforceable duties. Everyone, thus, has grounds to regard the rules which the sovereign determines as the correct interpretation of morality, because the only other alternative is for one to stick to one's own interpretation. But if everyone adopted his own interpretation of the rules, then we would have no rules at all. This was exactly the problem that the sovereign had to solve.

For this reason only the sovereign has the right to interpret natural law. And whoever, according to Hobbes, interprets the law authoritatively, establishes it.

With this we have arrived at Hobbes's conception of law: law consists of the commands of the sovereign. Law is, on the one hand, dependent on morality. It requires obedience on the basis of the foundational moral principle to be peaceful as long as everyone else does the same. At the same time, law replaces morality as regards content: the sovereign establishes authoritatively what the foundational principle exactly entails.

In his political theory, Hobbes, just like the sceptics and Grotius before him, bids perfectionism farewell. The aim of the state is not to bring man to the complete realisation of his nature, to advance certain virtues, etc, but only to stem the tide of conflicts which flow forth from the diverging wishes of people in a finite world. The state does not serve the good life, but only the minimal condition for the good life: peace. (The relative natural law of Lutherans and Calvinists can be regarded as an intermediate step in this development; see Section 3.2.)

At the same time his theory is not liberal, as little as that of Grotius. He does not say, 'and once the condition is fulfilled, everyone is free within the allocated limits to realise the good life as he himself views it'. The power of the sovereign is unlimited. If the sovereign prescribes a specific mode of life, then this is obligatory. This is not so because it would be just, but because peace is attainable only by means of obedience.

Peace is, thus, the only ideal which man secures by establishing a state institution; all other ideals are only realisable in so far as the sovereign allows room for them. Law itself only serves 'order', the prevention of a war of all against all. In its substance, law is not bound to any value at all: what the sovereign commands is law, irrespective of its content. It is, however, a precept of natural law to obey the sovereign.

The legal doctrine of Hobbes deviates as much from classical natural law (Section 1.2.2.1) as from the descriptive legal positivism of people like Bentham and Austin (Section 1.2.3.1). The latter are in agreement with Hobbes in so far as he says that everything the sovereign commands is law, and that there is no further moral criterion for the validity of law. They, however, conclude from this that something can be legally valid law, when it is morally completely unacceptable and does not deserve to be obeyed. For them there are two questions: what does law require, and what does morality require? The answers to these questions do not at all coincide. For Hobbes, on the other hand, there is only one question and *one* answer. There is always a moral reason to obey law, irrespective of its content: the preservation of peace as highest good. Hobbes is the characteristic representative of *order theory*; he is a normative legal positivist.

4.1.8 Commentary

In a kind of *Post Scriptum*, Hobbes himself formulates the most important objection that can be raised against his theory. (We will not discuss the reasons he mentions to overcome this objection.)

Think back to the example of overfishing. If everyone catches too many (B), I have no reason to adhere on my own to the quota (A): the fish stock would hardly be depleted less quickly and I would become poor more quickly. If I use my intellect, I would, however, rather prefer that everyone chooses A than B. Up to this point, Hobbes's story tallies. Posit now the unlikely scenario: that all other fishermen suddenly adhere to the Brussels guidelines. Hobbes says that in such an instance it would also be sensible for me to do so, but this does not necessarily follow. Reasoning – like Hobbes – from the perspective of my own interest, I not only have no reason to be the first to adhere to the rules, but as little reason to be the last to adhere to the rules.

Certainly, my own self-preservation is served with the transformation from general aggression to general peace, but all the same it would be still more advantageous for me to be the only one to withdraw myself from the prohibition on aggression. Irrespective of how much I desire peace, it is for me personally never advantageous to be peace-loving, not only when the others are aggressive, but also when they are peace-loving. And this, of course, applies to everyone. But if this is the case, then Hobbes's meticulous three-phase construction falls apart. For as long as every person simply thinks of survival based on his own interest, he cannot accept the fundamental *law of nature*, and the only possible way of making him abandon aggression is to force him to do so. The absolute police state, therefore.

If one wants to avoid this conclusion, one must be prepared to attribute to the people *in the state of nature* other motives on the basis of which they could accept the *law of nature*. History shows that problems, such as over-fishing and environmental pollution, are sometimes solved, however difficult it may be to do so: in the Middle Ages there was poor relief, and today, there is social welfare. In introducing this, states fulfil an essential function, without falling into an absolute police state (De Swaan 1988), and this is precisely the function that Hobbes prescribes. The most important problem is not that no one is prepared to contribute something except if force is used, but that everyone is scared that others do not contribute enough. Most people are willing to cooperate, as long as others also bear part of the burden, and do not parasitise. They are apparently prepared, even without force, to acknowledge moral duties *which cannot be reduced to their own interest.*

If we are allowed to make this addition to the premises, we can also correct the conclusion partially. Typical for Hobbes is his thinking in terms of social order: the commands of the sovereign require obedience, irrespective of their content. This is because everything is better than the state of nature with its war of all against all. However, if moral duties, which are irreducible to one's own interest, prevail in the state of nature, and people are to a certain extent willing to take these duties seriously, then our view of the state of nature need not be that dismal. And when our view of the state of nature is less dismal, an absolute state is likewise less necessary.

In that event we can place *qualitative* demands on the commonwealth, and ask of the sovereign that he guarantees these demands, and thus respect them, too. This is because the logic of the theory is to the effect that the commonwealth must always involve *progress* in relation to the state of nature.

We will see how the theory of Hobbes is corrected on both these points by John Locke. The result is *liberalism.*

4.2 Locke

4.2.1 Life

Around 1680 England experienced anew one of the high points in the lengthy battle for power between king and parliament. Charles II was childless; his successor was his brother James. The latter was, however, Catholic. Large groups in the House of Commons (representatives of medium-sized property owners and of the City of London) attempted by any means to exclude him from the succession. The leader of this opposition was the Earl of Shaftesbury; the circle around him would later become known as the *Whigs*. Shaftesbury's family doctor, as well as personal friend and adviser on economic, political and educational matters – again the typical position of a humanist in an aristocratic household – was the philosopher John Locke (1632–1704). He played an active role in these intrigues. Shaftesbury finally lost his suit and had to flee to Amsterdam, where he died soon after. Locke followed him into exile. For other conspirators a harsher destiny awaited. Algernon Sidney was executed, among other things because a manuscript was found in his house in which he had contested the theories of Robert Filmer. Locke, thus, did not flee for nothing: he had produced a similar polemical manuscript. According to Filmer, the court ideologue of the Stuarts, the king derived his power directly from God. He could, therefore, not be deposed by the people; as little could his legal successor to the throne be excluded.

During Locke's 6 year stay in the Dutch Republic, the tide turned. James II circumvented parliament, and, because of the measures he adopted in favour of Catholics, resistance against him grew. In the end it was not only the *Whigs* who wanted to dethrone him; representatives of the *Tories*, adherents of the notion of the divine authority of the king, also belonged to the delegation who went to request his son-in-law, the Dutch stadtholder William III, to intervene. In 1688 the *Glorious Revolution* took place; William and Mary became king and queen of England, after having signed a *Declaration of Rights* which confirmed the triumph of the parliamentary party. Locke returned with the ship that brought Princess Mary to England, and again took up his position as an influential political adviser behind the scenes. Again it was with the political leader of the *Whigs*, now Lord Somers, with whom he closely aligned himself. In 1690 he published the book *Two Treatises of Government* that he had written in opposition to Filmer. A large part of the manuscript had incidentally been lost for unknown reasons. He reworked it somewhat in light of the changing circumstances: now it had to serve as a theoretical foundation for the right of Mary and William to the throne. In reality, Locke, however, still had oppositional intentions: he thought that much more drastic constitutional changes were necessary than those contained in the *Declaration of Rights*, to prevent the abuse of monarchical power in the future, as happened under the Stuarts. These views were still not popular, certainly not with William. Locke, therefore, published the book anonymously, and guarded his secret carefully. Only in his will did he confirm his authorship.

In the first of the two treatises, Filmer's views were refuted point by point with a great display of Biblical knowledge; the second set out Locke's own theory. He linked up with the doctrine of Grotius that people as such, independently of any state organisation, had rights. As we saw, Grotius used this idea mainly to underpin royal absolutism. The disadvantages of anarchy would be so great that people would necessarily come to the realization that there is only one way in which to make life tolerable: by jointly transferring their rights to a State. Locke is the philosopher who made the theory of 'natural' rights subservient to liberal politics. In the case of Locke too, the state is based on an agreement aimed at obviating the drawbacks of anarchy. However, with the agreement, people do not transfer all their rights; on the contrary, the logic of the agreement is precisely to be found in the guarantee of the original and inalienable rights to life, liberty and property. The purpose of the state is the protection of the individual rights of its citizens. When a government systematically violates these rights, it loses all authority. Citizens may then revolt and establish a government which better fulfils its purpose. According to Locke, they had done this in the case of the *Glorious Revolution*, and that was what king William III had difficulty in accepting.

4.2.2 Law in the State of Nature

Like his predecessors, Locke starts his argument with a description of the state of nature. The question immediately arises as to what he means with this notion: an initial situation of anarchy which actually once existed in the mists of time? This Locke indeed believes, but the historical interpretation is not essential for his argument. One could reconstruct this as follows. Question: what justifies the existence of a state? To answer this question we start off by thinking away the state. Suppose no state existed, which reasons could people then have to institute it? This argument thus primarily has the sense of a thought experiment.

The main point for Locke then is: if the state falls away, all rights which people can enforce against each other do not fall away. Not all rights are legal-positive rights; not all rights are dependent on (human) authority. People may not kill, mutilate, or enslave each other, whether or not a state exists to enforce this. If they were simply not allowed to do this because a government had prohibited it, then the authority of the prohibition itself could be based only on power. Then there would be no distinction between a legal and an illegal government, and the question concerning the basis of the legitimacy of the state would be meaningless. This distinction between legal and illegal can be made only because criteria of legitimacy exist: moral precepts which apply independently of the existence of the state. These precepts combined, Locke calls (very traditionally) 'natural law'. It is, thus, actually not law at all, in the sense of a totality of rules that is posited by a specific earthly authority. It is rather a morality: a totality of norms which applies to everyone all along; not derived from any authority, but itself the basis of all authority.

Natural law itself is theologically founded by Locke: it consists of norms which apply to people because they were created by God for a specific reason. God did not create anything with the intention of destroying it or damaging it: for this reason every person has an inalienable right to life, bodily integrity, and freedom.

The right to property, likewise, belongs to the fundamental rights. The existence of property relations thus cannot be a product of positive law either, but precedes it as norm and foundation. At the same time Locke does not, however, want to assume that property was granted by God (as Filmer, for example, claimed). He, therefore, adopts a similar kind of reasoning as in relation to the state: let us, to start off with, think away all private property. In the original position everything is shared by all people. In other words: the earth is still undivided, no one has a specific claim to specific objects, no one may exclude another from the use of any object.

This situation cannot continue to exist, not even for a day. Because even to eat one fruit from a tree, one must appropriate the fruit for oneself, withdraw it from the possible use of others. The fruit must, thus, be removed from the communal property. If this was not allowed, or if it was allowed only with the permission of all co-owners, everyone would quickly starve. This cannot be God's intention for his creation.

Locke's problem is, therefore, not actually to justify the existence of private property as institution, but to indicate how a rightful distribution of (original) property is established. If one starts off with an undivided nature, where do the first concrete property claims come from?

Locke's famous answer to this question is: by way of labour. What happened between the moment upon which I encountered the fruit on the tree in undivided property, and the moment upon which I rightfully consumed it? I plucked the fruit from the tree, and in this way performed labour. No single part of nature is in its natural state suitable for human use; everything must be processed. Nature viewed in itself thus actually has no value, only nature processed by people. Labour is the source of all value. If I would, therefore, appropriate something for myself which was made by another, I would actually be parasitising on his effort. On the other hand, by removing something from the undivided property by means of labour, I do not per se have to disadvantage someone else. I only do this when, after my appropriation, not enough remains of nature for others to cultivate.

From this argument follows the so-called *proviso* of Locke, which still plays an important role in political philosophy (Nozick, Section 10.7). Everyone may transform from the communal property of nature into private property anything with which he can 'combine his labour', on condition that he leaves to others *enough and as good*. The important question is, of course, whether this condition could be fulfilled in England in the year 1689, or in the world at the present time.

4.2.3 The Formation of the Political Community

We have seen up to this point that everyone in the state of nature has the right to life, bodily integrity, personal freedom, and fairly acquired property. What must one do if someone else wants to infringe one's rights? Then one has the right to protect oneself, to punish the transgressor of natural law, and claim, as well as enforce, compensation for the harm suffered. If one did not have these rights, the other natural rights would not mean much. One only has the right to something if one does not have to accept it when someone else takes it away from one.

However, if everyone had the rights to self-protection, punishment and damages, various things threaten to go wrong in the state of nature:

- A difference in opinion can easily arise concerning the interpretation of natural law. My cows broke loose and caused damage to your grass: how much compensation do I owe you? According to Locke, there is always a clear answer to such questions, but people do not always see it, and tend to calculate in their own favour.
- For the same reasons, a difference of opinion will arise concerning the proper punishment. If you are the victim, you would tend to find a punishment too severe to be reasonable; if you are the perpetrator, one that is too light. And the imposition of an unreasonably severe punishment, of course, equally amounts to an infringement of rights, which itself would call for punishment. Hence feuds are set in motion.
- Lastly, it would indeed not be easy to execute a punishment, irrespective of how fair it is, in the case of criminal law which is left to the parties concerned.

These are, thus, the *inconveniences of the state of nature*. What could we (continuing the thought experiment) do about this? According to Locke, people will decide to transfer the rights that cause problems to the 'political community': a cooperative association of everyone who within a specific area regularly deals with each other. One does not transfer all one's rights. Indeed, the purpose of the transfer is precisely to enable one to enjoy one's fundamental rights in a more stable way; the task of the political community is, therefore, to guarantee the fundamental rights. The rights which are transferred are those of self-defence, punishment, and the enforcement of compensation. The political community acquires three tasks which correspond to the three 'inconveniences of the state of nature':

- The community must interpret natural law, thus explicitly and in detail determine the rights of everyone. (The community, therefore, does not *grant* rights.) This happens in the form of positive legal rules.

- The community must determine a reasonable penalty.
- And it must take responsibility for the execution of the penalty so determined.

In this analysis a distinction can clearly be recognised between legislative, judicial and executive powers. Montesquieu's famous thesis concerning the separation of powers (Section 5.2) was inspired by Locke. The judicial power is, however, mostly not sharply distinguished by Locke from the legislative: both involve the interpretation of natural law.

The political community as a whole must take a decision concerning these matters. However, it is in practice not workable that everyone should have to go to all meetings. For this reason the members of the political community will decide to assign the exercise of their powers to a special organ: the government. Actually there is only one decision that the community as such (by a majority of votes) must take; thereafter everyone can go home, and the government governs. It, however, continues doing so in the name of the political community, and not by virtue of an inherent power. All governmental authority is based on delegation.

4.2.4 Limits of Power

Locke derives his doctrine of resistance from the idea that governmental authority is based on delegation. There are three types of limits to governmental authority:

(1) The first limit is constituted by the basic rights to life, bodily integrity and freedom. If the government violates these, it loses its authority. The government cannot deny these rights, because they are inalienable (as we saw, Grotius contended that citizens transferred these rights to the state). No one can give away what he does not have himself, and no one has the power to alienate his basic rights.

(2) The right to property is, of course, not an inalienable right. But in this respect Locke invokes the following precept (derived from Grotius): when people transfer their rights, they do this to improve their position. But people do not have any reason to transfer the total package of their property rights to the government; on the contrary, they instituted the government precisely to have their property rights, among other things, better protected. We may, therefore, not assume that these rights have been alienated, unless it has been done expressly. A government, thus, similarly loses its authority should it take away the property of its citizens.

(3) If the political community institutes a government by way of delegation, then it can, and usually would, do so subject to certain conditions. These conditions do not follow, like points (1) and (2), directly from natural law, but will be based on insights which the political community acquired the hard way in the course of history. One cannot trust rulers completely, as little in fact as one can trust other people: certain guarantees are, therefore, necessary for the proper

functioning of government, especially against the abuse of its powers. Important 'constitutional' requirements for Locke are the following:

- *The rule of law.* The executive power may do nothing for which the legislative power has not expressly granted the power. Wherever law ends, tyranny begins' (Locke 2003, p. 189).
- The closely related principle of the separation of powers (derived from Locke by Montesquieu and by the leaders of the American Revolution): whoever possesses the executive power may not at the same time hold the legislative power (because then the principle of the rule of law would easily become a dead letter).

Authority is granted to the government subject to certain conditions. If the government thus exceeds these limits, it loses its authority. According to Locke, one cannot, when citizens resist abuse of state power, say that they 'revolt', because actually it is the government which revolts. Where authority disappears, no government exists any longer, only private persons who attempt to suppress other private persons. The latter can then simply exercise their natural right to self-defence.

Such a situation nonetheless does not entail a return to the state of nature. The government has certainly disappeared, but not the political community. A general assembly can then again meet to delegate governmental authority to new persons or institutions. This is incidentally the proper moment to change a constitution, or even more correctly: it is the only moment when this can happen. Citizens have learnt a lesson from what went wrong previously, and to prevent this in future, construct new guarantees. Governmental authority is then granted under new conditions. This was, according to Locke, the situation in 1688–1689. And it was precisely because of the implications of further constitutional reforms that William III and his Ministers rejected this interpretation.

In Locke's political thinking the conception of the neutral state emerges for the first time. The state must guarantee to its citizens the undisturbed enjoyment of their rights; what they, for example, do with their property is not the state's concern at all, as long as they do not infringe the rights of others. This idea (in the *Second Treatise*) is, similarly, central in the *Letter concerning Toleration* which Locke wrote during the time of his exile in the Netherlands (addressed to the protestant professor Philippus van Limborch of Amsterdam). The letter was published in 1689, again anonymously.

Locke summarises the theory of the *Second Treatise* as follows: 'The commonwealth seems to me to be a society of men constituted only for the procuring, preserving, and advancing their own civil interests. Civil interest I call life, liberty, health, and indolency of body; and the possession of outward things, such as money, lands, houses, furniture, and the like' (Locke 2003, p. 218). The task of the civil magistrate is only to serve the fair possession of these goods: by enacting laws which apply equally to all, and by punishing the violation of the rights of another. The welfare of the soul cannot, however, belong to his legal authority.

This is, in the first place, because no one can deny responsibility for the care of his own eternal soul. Whatever one's creed, and whatever the form of external worship one performs, only the conviction of the heart counts before God. However, nobody can have faith based on the instruction of another, even if he wants to. The magistrate has means of coercion at his disposal, but these cannot bring about any faith. For this reason nobody's soul can be saved by external force. In the end everyone has to be left to himself and to his own conscience.

In the second place, however, even supposing that it was possible to convert souls by means of the sword, it would still not be desirable. To which church should the state lend its power of prosecution? To the orthodox church of course; but every church regards itself as orthodox, and there is no judge on earth who can resolve this dispute with the required authority; certainly not the civil magistrate, 'either at Constantinople or elsewhere upon earth'.

Given all the differences in opinion amongst rulers regarding religion, the narrow road leading to heaven would be accessible to only a few people, and, for the people of most countries, not at all: the accident of one's birth would then determine one's eternal salvation. There is only one true religion; when a person does not follow his own intellect and conscience, how great is then the chance that he will find it? Suppose he is sick and there is only one remedy, but no one agrees about what it is. Is it then the task of the magistrate to prescribe the remedy; is it safe for the sick person to follow such a prescription? Can a magistrate ever give a guarantee for the kingdom of heaven? What every person should himself evaluate seriously cannot be regarded as the unique possession of specific kinds of people. Kings have more power than others, but not for this reason more knowledge, and certainly not concerning religious matters.

Locke argues here, in fact, for a separation between a public domain where the state has certain responsibilities, and a private domain, where every person must find his own way towards eternal or temporary happiness. With the above arguments, he seeks to substantiate why religion must belong to the private domain. The same arguments apply to scientific views, as well as to views regarding the good life. That Locke wishes to point in this direction appears clearly from his affirmative description of what belongs to the public domain.

The argument in favour of tolerance is not based on scepticism. It is not because no truth exists in the domain of religion, that everyone should be allowed to go his own way. If no truth existed, then it would not be so problematic to follow the command of the king. Precisely because it is so important to find the one right medicine, one cannot be prepared to follow the instructions of another whose judgment one cannot absolutely trust.

The most important insight of Locke is that state organs have a delegated power, and, therefore, only have a claim to obedience for as long as they properly fulfil their functions. Positive law which claims to have authority must comply with certain moral demands. (Positive law is 'only' an interpretation of natural law.)

That law has to comply with moral demands in order to claim authority, was already acknowledged in classical natural law (Aristotle, Aquinas). The formulation of the demands is, however, completely different in modern natural law. Classical natural law regards it as the task of the state to design the ideal community. Politics must contribute to realising the good life for everyone in society. If the state neglects this task, its law loses its legal nature; then it becomes a form of sheer power. According to the modern 'Lockean' natural law, the state must only create the conditions under which individuals can autonomously give form to their own lives.[1] The most important condition is that others respect their private domain, and this is precisely what the state attempts to guarantee. If the state neglects this task, for example, by imposing on individuals a certain conception of the ideal community, then its law loses its legal character: then it is no longer law, but coercion.

The design of the state institution must be aimed at keeping the government within the limits of its task. We saw above the proposals which Locke submits in this regard. Parliamentary democracy does not here stand at the forefront; it is far more essential that all governmental action must be covered by laws which were established lawfully, are generally formulated, and promulgated publicly. Locke is the philosopher of freedom rights and the rule of law, not of democracy. As such, he has had a greater influence than any other modern philosopher, perhaps with the exception of Marx. Of this, incidentally, little could be noticed during his lifetime. Even in the first half of the 18th century, modern natural law was restricted to being the ideology of a small group of radicals. In the second half of that century this, however, changed. In a number of movements which struggled for radical change, a similar development can be detected: first, people argued for a 'return' to the 'ancient constitution', generally interpreted in a rather unhistorical way. (We saw this theme appear with the Huguenots, the French Calvinists.) After some time the discourse of natural rights and the social contract entered the scene. The *founding fathers* of the American Revolution wrote their declarations and constitutional drafts in terms directly derived from Locke, and the same goes for the ideological leaders of the Dutch Patriotic movement. During the French revolution, too, the traces of Locke are no less clear than those of Rousseau (Section 5.5).

4.2.5 Grounds and Limits of Reliable Knowledge

As we pointed out, Locke's doctrine of tolerance is not based on scepticism. In certain areas, according to him, the truth is, in principle, attainable. This is so in principle only, because in fact people mostly allow themselves to be influenced by the fashion of the day, and believe what they want to believe. In doing this they overestimate the human faculty of cognition, and think they can know things which people cannot know.

[1]Because Locke bases his argument on theological premises, it still shows some relation to the natural law of the Middle Ages, but one can also understand his theory without this. We, therefore, did not classify him in Chapter 1 under classical natural law, but under 'naturalistic' natural law; human beings develop best in a society based on freedom and equality.

The search for truth within the limits of human possibility is a task which God imposed on human beings, and the fulfilment of this task can be the object of moral evaluation. Locke undertakes his enquiry 'into the origin, certainty, and extent of human knowledge, together with the grounds and degrees of belief, opinion and assent', not out of curiosity, but as foundation for an *ethics for the attainment of knowledge*. This approach is characteristic of the developing Enlightenment thinking. In the final instance, each individual is *responsible* for the excellence of his views: for this reason we have to determine the extent to which this excellence can be improved. In his main philosophical work – *An Essay concerning human understanding* (published in 1690, but not anonymously) – Locke aims at showing the way in which the attainment of secure knowledge is possible, and why it is that most people so seldom tread this path. What specifically interests him is, on the one hand, moral and religious knowledge, and, on the other hand, scientific knowledge. This is because it is in the case of these kinds of knowledge that people are often blind with regard to the shortcomings of their way of thinking: the religious fanatics who are 100% sure of their conflicting interpretations of obscure Biblical texts; the clergy who refused to look through Galileo's telescope because they already knew from Aristotle what the universe looked like.

Locke, like Galileo, Descartes and Hobbes before him, starts from the distinction between the external and internal worlds. What is given to us initially is simply the content of our own consciousness. Such content of consciousness Locke refers to as *ideas*. These are partially of objects in the external world, and partially a result of the operation of the mind itself.

Descartes was of the view that the human spirit disposes of certain inborn ideas, but Locke contests this. With small children one after all finds no abstract concepts; whoever is colour blind since birth never forms the concept of 'colour'; and the notion of God, which Descartes found in his own spirit, is in many nations completely unknown. From such data Locke concludes that the human spirit is at birth still an unwritten page. Content arrives in two ways in the mind. The ideas of objects in the external world come into being because our senses are stimulated by these objects: by means of them we acquire ideas, such as 'yellow', 'hot', 'bitter', 'hard'. (The hardness of a stone is what one experiences when one attempts to push through it; not how a physicist interprets the experience.) The ideas due to the operation of the mind come into being by way of introspection; because of this we establish that we observe, think, doubt, reason, and want. These two sources of *ideas* Locke calls *sensation* and *reflection*, but both are forms of observation. All knowledge, thus, starts with observation. The products of such observation are 'singular ideas'. One cannot be in doubt that one finds these contents in one's consciousness; they are simply given. Locke thus subscribes to Descartes's adage: what I know for sure is '*that* I think' and '*what* I think'.

But subsequently the mind starts working with the material by forming by means of comparison and combination, 'combined ideas'. This happens, as a start, with the idea of a concrete thing, which exists separately from all other things through the course of time (has an own 'identity'), and which combines more than one characteristic in itself. Next, general concepts are formed through generalisation and abstraction from sensory experiences. After we have, for example, had a series of perceptions of blue, we note the similarity between the singular ideas, leading to the formation of the general concept, 'blue'.[2] Finally, the mind constructs theories with the assistance of these general concepts which explain the different observations. These theories require from us that we distinguish between the contents of consciousness which do, and which do not, portray reality: objective and subjective characteristics. (Locke speaks of 'primary' and 'secondary' qualities.) The objective world is that of physics: bodies in movement.

All these operations of the mind are subject to error, precisely because the mind is active and not purely receptive. In many instances, in the case of scientific theories, for example, no certain, but only probable knowledge can be attained: then the ethics of the attainment of knowledge requires that one must attribute to one's convictions no higher degree of probability than they possess in fact. (This is the claim which is sinned against most often.) Both concept and theory formation must link up with sensory observation. The senses and the mind are arranged consistent with practical purposes: survival and orientation in the world. Our faculty of cognition is able to provide us with the information we need for these purposes: the insight into causes and consequences, which makes it possible to obtain power over our own environment, and in this way improve our destiny. Man nonetheless, due to pride, strives to penetrate into the hidden causes and the essential nature of things. Such perfect and all-embracing knowledge is, however, unattainable. (Using the terminology of Plato: we are sentenced to life in the cave.) Therefore, (according to Locke) we will, for example, never know whether a rectangle can exist with the surface area equal to that of a circle, nor whether purely material objects have consciousness. Attempts to nonetheless attain such knowledge can lead only to disappointment, and usually result in people going to the opposite extreme. When we stay within our possibilities, we undoubtedly stand stronger against scepticism: it is enough for a seaman when he knows that his plumb line is long enough to indicate dangerous areas, even if it is too short to gauge all the depths of the ocean.

That we cannot be completely sure of many of our views is a reason for humility and tolerance. According to Locke, we can certainly be sure of the existence of God and the validity of natural law. He, however, never systematically set out his arguments in support of this thesis, despite the frequent insistences of friend and foe, probably because he himself was (rightfully) never completely satisfied with them. When he makes the acceptance of this thesis into a precondition for the followers of aberrant convictions to be tolerated, this is incidentally not because the thesis would be possible to prove. One must accept natural law because it is the foundation of a harmonious society. And for the same reason one must accept the existence of God: atheists cannot take their oath of fidelity seriously, because they do not believe in the

[2]With this empiricist theory of knowledge Locke stands in direct opposition to the rationalism of Plato, according to whom general concepts, such as 'blue', precede particular perceptions of separate blue things, and enable us to recognise the things *as* blue.

sanctions which accompany such an oath. In this respect Locke suddenly appears to, after all, think in a very 'Hobbesian' way: the final reason for the required trust in others is their self-interest. One can, in other words, trust and live in a community with only those who fear eternal damnation, and who, therefore, refrain from certain conduct in their own interest, which is somewhat similar to what we find in Hobbes.

4.3 Spinoza

4.3.1 Life

Baruch (Benedict) de Spinoza was one of the greatest Dutch philosophers. He was a contemporary of Locke; both were born in 1632. His father was a Portuguese-Jewish merchant who, after some roaming around, settled in Amsterdam, where Baruch was born. His father had an important role in the Portuguese-Jewish community. After his death in 1654, Baruch continued the business with his brother. Already in his youth, Spinoza distanced himself from traditional Judaism; he spent much time with non-Jews and, moreover, learnt Latin, the language of most of his publications. Because of his unorthodox views he was excommunicated in 1656. He successively went to live in Ouderkerk, Rijnsburg, Voorburg and The Hague. He earned money by grinding lenses. In 1673 he received an invitation to become professor in Heidelberg, but, not wanting to lose his freedom, he declined the position. During his life he only published a few books, including his *Tractatus Theologico-Politicus* (Theological-Political Treatise), which was published anonymously in 1670 by a fictitious publisher in Hamburg. As was the case with his other works, his main work, *Ethica*, was published posthumously. Spinoza died in 1677.

Spinoza gives a headstrong answer to the central question of political liberalism: how should the government deal with the plurality of worldviews? The societal diagnosis he gives, and the solution he posits, are instructive and deviate in interesting respects from those of Locke. We will focus here on Spinoza's *Tractatus Theologico-Politicus*.

4.3.2 Pluralism and Tolerance

Spinoza was surprised by the fact that followers of Christianity, who preach love, joy, peace and moderation, oppose their fellow-Christians, as well as the followers of other religions, with vindictive hate. Their faith is seemingly overrun by fear about the uncertainty of their destiny, so that they search for a semi-certainty in some or other superstition, with the related pomp and circumstance. That such superstition flows from fear and uncertainty they seek to hide from themselves by constructing a dogmatic system around it, which they protect with fire and sword. The matter becomes worse when despots take advantage of these fears, and when they seek to bring their subjects under their control by making all of them march under the banner of such superstition. Then not only political freedom is destroyed, but also piety; because piety can, according to Spinoza, only thrive when people are allowed to establish for themselves what the truth is. In resisting this state of affairs, Spinoza sets himself the task of showing that the granting of freedom not only does not harm public peace, but that freedom is essential for the thriving of piety and for securing public peace. Spinoza's manuscript for this reason is called 'Theological-Political': it shows that in both domains freedom is not only not harmful, but even advantageous, and that political freedom is, moreover, beneficial to religion, and religious freedom is conducive to politics. Spinoza's political liberalism is his answer to ideological pluralism.

How can the fear about the uncertainty of destiny be conquered? Some people can do so by way of philosophical insight, according to which everything that happens necessarily happens in this specific way, and must be understood as a manifestation of the will of the only God, who is equated with the rationality of Nature.[3] Most people are not capable of this insight; a personal God has, nevertheless, been revealed to them, who is merciful and just and who calls on people to be obedient and show neighbourly love. When they follow this call, their inclination to superstitious fear disappears, and they will furthermore obey the laws of the state which serve to guarantee peace, not out of fear of punishment, but because of an inner urging – which promotes public peace. Spinoza in this way draws a distinction between the core of revealed faith, which can, and must, be adhered to by all (described by him as the acknowledgement that God is merciful and just, and that he calls people to obedience and neighbourly love), and those aspects concerning which everyone can, and is, allowed to develop their own ideas. The core does not consist simply of a moral message; it supposes a doctrinal content, albeit of modest scope. When believers practise neighbourly love out of obedience to the merciful and just God, whom they want to serve and love, then it presupposes minimally that they accept that God exists, that he provides everything, that he is omnipotent, that it is his will that the good enjoy prosperity and the bad are lost for all eternity, as well as that our salvation depends exclusively on his grace. To the aspects of faith concerning which everyone can, and may, develop his own ideas, the biggest part belongs to the doctrinal content of faith, concerning which theologians lock horns with each other, and because of which adherents of the different religions oppose each other; the discord loses its highly explosive character when all acknowledge that these matters do not touch the core of faith, and can thus be left to the opinion of every person.

4.3.3 Commentary

Spinoza's theological-political recommendations did not have many adherents. Believers regarded Spinoza as a heretic. The Jews of his community reproached him for rejecting the idea that the Jews are God's elected people (according to Spinoza,

[3]One can see here that Spinoza's thinking shows some relation to that of the Stoics, Section 2.6.

this did not belong to the doctrinal core of revealed religion). Jews *and* Christians frequently suspected him of being an atheist, because of his denial of the divine origin of the Bible and of divine providence. The Christian rulers of the Dutch Republic found him to be a suspect figure because of his uncertain religious identity (he drew as easily from the Jewish as from the Christian tradition, and, moreover, perceived in many other religions a core of truth). Spinoza's pleas for political freedom also increased the mistrust of political rulers.

Spinoza indeed anticipated all these reactions by publishing his book anonymously. Perhaps he did not actually want to address his book to believers and politicians. He did not without reason write the book in Latin, and he mentions in his preface that he addresses himself to philosophical readers, and, in addition, asks the rest of humanity to leave the book unread. What could be the reason for these statements? Spinoza does not only articulate the viewpoint of believers, but also gives an explanation of belief, and this explanation can be termed 'functionalist': revealed religion is aimed at bringing people to obedience, and doctrinal belief-contents are legitimised because of the useful role they play in relation to this goal. This functionalist explanation, from the external viewpoint of an observer, stands in tension with the internal perspective of a believer. Perhaps Spinoza realised that his explanation of belief, therefore, at the same time leads to its unmasking, which for non-philosophical readers would have an effect contrary to that which he had wanted to achieve: whoever realises that faith is only true faith when it leads to moral repentance, undermines all epistemic pretensions of faith; a faith freed in this way from its foundations not only makes no contribution to the stability of the political order, but even undermines it.

At any rate, Spinoza's plea for a pluralism of worldviews cannot engender enthusiasm on the part of the adherents of diverse worldviews, because they are asked to reduce the full richness of their worldview to a pitiable remainder which is declared to be its core. It is not surprising that Spinoza was accused of heresy and of atheism. He attempted to overcome the pluralism in worldviews by showing that at their core all worldviews boil down to the same: a monism lies at the basis of this pluralism. The contention that a kind of highest common factor is shared by all worldviews, cannot but lead to resistance on the part of genuine adherents of these worldviews. They are not taken seriously. We can even say that Spinoza does not take pluralism quite seriously. This has the consequence that his plea for tolerance is somewhat ambivalent.

4.4 Conclusion: Hobbes and Locke

With the theories of Hobbes and Locke modern legal philosophy developed two different versions of the social-contract model as legitimation of state and law. They both put the individual at the centre of their political theory. The social contract serves here as metaphor for the view that an individual is bound to a central authority only if he could have voluntarily agreed to it. In the case of both, this leads to a narrow account of morality and law. The difference between Hobbes and Locke lies primarily in the fact that Hobbes bases his argument on a completely amoral point of view: the self-interest of the individual man in light of his instinct for survival. Locke, on the other hand, takes a moral perspective: the *right* to freedom of an individual. These different points of departure lead to dissimilar views of the role of the state. Locke arrives at a liberal state which has to protect in a neutral manner the freedom and property rights of everyone. Hobbes propagates an absolutist state, aimed at the maintenance of order to make it possible to live together in peace. Later kindred spirits added to this that obligatory legal rules, such as those in relation to property, are not only to the benefit of all because they prevent the 'war of all against all', but also because they increase the prosperity of everyone by making possible cooperation and the division of labour.

An immanent objection against the theory of Hobbes goes as follows: sheer rational self-interest provides an insufficient basis for a general duty of obedience to law, and must, therefore, be supplemented by moral presuppositions. A moral objection: Hobbes's absolutist state conflicts with the ideal of human emancipation. The first objection is created by the problem of the parasite. Hobbes and his followers mistakenly assume that social order and cooperative undertakings for mutual benefit are threatened only by short-sightedness. They are actually threatened also by the rational 'parasite' or 'sponger' who profits from the efforts of others through egotistical calculation. The problem arises, in particular, from the fact that there are instances in which it is impossible to exclude people who do not contribute to the fruits of cooperation, from enjoying them. This is specifically the case with so-called 'public goods', such as a canal, public security, and a clean environment. In this sense a system of property rules is a public good, too: everyone has an interest in others adhering to these rules, but not in themselves doing so. If this is the case, then, in addition to self-interest (Hobbes's point of departure), moral grounds such as trustworthiness and *fairness* (not to want to profit from others), are necessary, in addition, not only to stabilise 'conventions', but also to develop them. This point can be further illustrated with the following example. Two farmers each cultivate crops which ripen at different times, and which neither of them can harvest entirely in time without assistance. Both thus have an interest in helping each other. Suppose that farmer A volunteers of his own accord to give farmer B his assistance: then B will afterwards not abandon A either, because he knows that A would otherwise not be back the next year. In this way the convention of mutual assistance arises by virtue of the anticipation of fitting reciprocation. The convention to make good one's promises arises in exactly the same way. Suppose that A offers to help B, if B promises to subsequently help him too. Then B still has an extra reason to turn up: because otherwise A would never trust him again when he (B) promises something. Thus, the binding force of promises can be explained on the basis of a convention rooted in self-interest. But suppose that A and B know that B is going on pension the next year, and thus would no longer need A's assistance. If the convention is based on self-interest (as Hobbes implies), A will know that B will no longer help him, and thus A will, to start off with, not help B. (And because both know this, they would abandon each other the year before that, and so on.) Situations, therefore, exist where self-interest is sufficient to make one adhere to a convention (for example, to drive on the right or left side of the road) as well as situations in which this is *not* so (for example, in the case of the production of public goods). In the second case (where B is about to go on pension) conventions only develop when parties, already to begin with, can mutually ascribe motives to each other, other than self-interest, specifically moral considerations, such as loyalty.[4]

It appears that Locke is able to overcome both the immanent and moral objections against Hobbes. In the first place, he does not start from rational self-interest, but from the mutual respect for each other's freedom rights. Nevertheless, his line of reasoning does not fail if rational self-interest in fact leads to disobedience of the law. The egoist, who violates another person's freedom and property rights, simply acts improperly. In the second place, Locke overcomes the moral objection against Hobbes because his freedom ideal guarantees human emancipation.

But Hobbes could respond to this by saying that an illegitimate dogma lies at the basis of this solution. Locke bases his principle of freedom on a divine creation plan, but the theological argument applies solely to believers. To be convincing to everyone, Locke would have to supplement his theory with an argument, such as that contained in Chapter 1. This argument would proceed as follows: a political theory which is based solely on the human instinct for survival, and which places all the emphasis on social order, offers a miserable view of human life; man can only develop himself in a free society. Locke could add to this that a revised version of Hobbes's doctrine would similarly leave room for liberalism: if one can assume that, even without state coercion, spontaneous cooperation on the basis of a sense of loyalty is possible, the state does not have to assume such an absolutist character, and within the state association there is latitude for free individual development. However, in Chapter 1 it was indicated that concerning specific ideals of human perfection, much less unanimity exists than concerning the necessity of peacefully living together. The liberal ideal of autonomy is also strongly contested. This comes to the fore in the philosophy of the 18th-century French Enlightenment. Here the ideal of equal freedom was worked out in more detail, while Rousseau in the same period formulated serious objections against liberal individualism.

[4]A hypothetical alternative would be that the obedience of everyone is enforced in a totalitarian police state. But in reality it is impossible to guard everyone continually, including the guardians themselves.

Chapter 5
Eighteenth-Century French Enlightenment

5.1 Enlightenment, Freedom, Equality and Fraternity

5.1.1 Enlightenment Through Science

The Enlightenment has provided the spiritual foundation of the modern constitutional state. The motto of the Enlightenment could have been: *theory and practice go hand in hand* (*theoria cum praxi*).[1] Or, stated differently, scientific knowledge of nature, man and society leads to Enlightenment because its practical application would make an end to unhappiness caused by ignorance.

The views of Hobbes, Locke and their kindred spirits had a great influence on the philosophers of the 18th-century French Enlightenment. The confidence in modern science of thinkers such as Montesquieu, Diderot, Voltaire and Beccaria,[2] was moreover inspired by the unprecedented success of modern physics, specifically the mechanics of Newton. Theology had to give up its place of honour to philosophy, and even more so to the exact sciences. The factual, empirical reality of man and society became prominent. Reality was no longer interpreted teleologically (as having an ultimate purpose and as valuable in itself). The Aristotelian 'organic' portrayal of man and world which had an influence reaching into the Renaissance, made way for neutral, 'value-free', and mechanical notions of man, society and reality in general. Realistic knowledge would lead to emancipation.

This belief in progress appeared from the immense undertaking which led to the *Encyclopédie, ou dictionaire raisonné des sciences, des arts et des métiers, par une société de gens de lettres* ... (Paris, 1751–1780, seventeen volumes text, eleven volumes illustration, five supplements and a two-volume register, a monument of 18th-century learning and printing). Under the guidance of Diderot, many Enlightenment philosophers contributed to the *Encyclopédie*.[3] The *Encyclopédistes*

[1] This was stated by Leibniz, who prepared the way for the Enlightenment, but whose thinking will not be dealt with here.

[2] An Italian, but who became famous by virtue of the French Enlightenment.

[3] Montesquieu and Rousseau were also contributors, although Montesquieu refused to write about democracy and despotism. He restricted his contribution to a section on taste. Rousseau wrote the section on music, and thus kept a similar distance from his regular subjects, politics and law.

C.W. Maris, F.C.L.M. Jacobs (eds.), *Law, Order and Freedom*, Law and Philosophy Library 94, DOI 10.1007/978-94-007-1457-1_5, attempted to interpret and unify the science of the day. In the *Prospectus* for the *Encyclopédie* (1750), Diderot wrote:

> The purpose of the encyclopaedic summary of everything that belongs to the fields of science, art and craft, is to show their mutual connections, to determine more accurately, with the assistance of these connections, the underlying principles and bring to light their consequences more clearly; to show the distant and closer connections of the things which nature consists of and which have occupied man. . .and to provide a general examination of the efforts of the human spirit in all fields through the ages.

Our understanding of the Enlightenment is not made easier by the self-imposed, as well as enforced, censure of 18th-century France and Europe. The *Encyclopédie* was, for example, repeatedly banned, also under pressure from the Jesuits (until they were in turn banned in 1765), and the text was badly battered by the conservative printer. Only a small part of Diderot's original texts survived. As for Montesquieu and Rousseau, it can likewise no longer be determined to what extent they restrained themselves out of fear for the authorities. It was, however, precisely against this lack of freedom that the project of the Enlightenment was aimed.

The Enlightenment expected that modern science would free human reason from traditional and religious superstition. It was believed that, on the basis of scientific knowledge, society could be 'modernised'. Scientific insight could, more specifically, lead to emancipation by unmasking suppressive ideologies, such as the belief that state authority is willed by God. Free from prejudices and irrational fears, political, legal, and personal decisions could in future be taken on purely reasonable and empirical grounds. Teleological worldviews made way for the 'causal' worldview of modern science. Man and society had to become just as transparent in the long term as the scientifically explained processes in inanimate nature. More science would equally mean more power over reality, particularly more possibilities to change social reality for the good.

The academic optimism of the *lumières* (the 'lights' of the Enlightenment) stood out in stark contrast to social reality. Differing from England, in France an absolute monarchy ruled, which was supported by feudal relationships reminiscent of the division of estates of the Middle Ages. The largest section of the population lived in appalling circumstances. Around the middle of the 18th century everywhere in France dying people could be found on the roads. Ever since the 30 Years War the peasant population of France was the poorest in Europe. This was, among other things, because of exploitation by an aristocratic and clerical elite who made little contribution to the economy. From this situation the population could now be emancipated, thanks to the new ideas of the Enlighteners.

The scientific orientation of the Enlightenment, however, has a dark side, too. The *facts* of science after all do not lead straightforwardly to *norms* of humanity. The science of human phenomena can be used against people as well. This occurs with Sade and others: sadism as inversion of enlightened humanity (Section 5.4).

5.1.2 Legal Philosophy of the Enlightenment

At the time of the Enlightenment the spiritual and material foundations of the modern constitutional state were established. Of central importance was the rejection of divine authority, both in respect of the truth of science and the authority of politics and law. In its place came the ideal of human autonomy: every person is equally responsible for his own life. With this, monarchy lost its traditional ground of justification. In terms of the new view, government should serve the people, not the other way around. The Enlightenment philosophers thus arrived at a radical critical stance vis-à-vis existing political and social relationships: the French absolute monarchy and feudal division of estates with their inequality and lack of freedom were in blatant conflict with human dignity. The political and legal philosophy of the French Enlightenment showed two different responses to this social exploitation: a liberal response, with Montesquieu (Section 5.2) and his kindred spirits, and a perfectionist response, with Rousseau (Section 5.5). Both would become prominent in philosophy and science, and in addition acquire a significant historical influence.

The liberal Enlightenment philosophers articulated the ideals of freedom and equality in association with rights and separation of powers. The estate-based society had to be replaced by a democracy in which everyone could participate in equal freedom. The freedom of citizens had to be protected by a threefold division of state power. The legislative power belongs to the people, who, as the highest authority, establish a legislative assembly. Thus, laws are an expression of the general interest, or at least of the will of the majority. The (preparation and) execution of laws had to be left to the administrative power. The judge decides in disputes concerning the implementation of general laws.

This constitution implies a distinction between personal and public morality or first and second-order morality. Morality of the first order determines the private lives of individual people. Morality of the second order is provided by the principles, rules and laws of the constitution: these must create an order in which everyone can live equally in accordance with his personal, moral views of the first order. The fundamental rights thus protect the personal domain of life, particularly against the highest authority of the state, whether or not this is the people themselves. The public, second-order morality stands in a neutral relation to individual, 'private' views of first-order morality. Individuals are precisely for this reason the highest legislators, because their lives and their (diverse) first-order moralities constitute the final value.

The question remains, how the second-order morality should be enforced. Even if the monopoly of power of the state is legitimate, this does not as yet validate the establishment of criminal law. Beccaria was the first to sketch a criminal law of which not vengeance and retaliation, but the prevention of criminal acts, is the central rationale; and in which criminal procedure does not only serve to detect and punish, but also to protect the fundamental rights of citizens and suspects against the prosecuting authority (Section 5.3).

In contrast to the 'scientific' optimism of Montesquieu, Beccaria and other *lumières*, stands the social criticism of Rousseau. Modern science, for him, entails alienation rather than liberation. Rousseau made an in-depth enquiry into the alienating interplay between people and their cultures: made by people, but at the same time by far transcending individuals, alienating and threatening them. In his view, individual negative freedom to live according to a first-order morality is illusory, as long as the 'authenticity' of individual life plans is destroyed by the sham civilizations of the Modern Age which have deviated from 'true nature'. In this Rousseau saw nothing more than palpable wealth for some, grinding poverty for others, and spiritual poverty for everyone. The ideals of the liberal constitutional state, too, were for him nothing more than products of degeneration, far removed from the authentic human being: individual negative freedom leads to egoism. In its place Rousseau posits the ideal of human development in a community which is based on the ideals of equality and fraternity.

With this, Rousseau is the first great critic of the liberal separation of first- and second-order morality, the distinction to which his contemporary Montesquieu, with his view of the separation of powers, contributed so much. In his criticism of liberal individual freedom he moreover posits a 'broad' morality of the good life of the natural person as against the 'narrow' morality of liberal conceptions. For him, therefore, *essential freedom* is at stake. For this reason Rousseau could make the paradoxical statement that people can be forced to be free.

5.2 The Liberal Enlightenment: Montesquieu's Separation of Powers

5.2.1 Montesquieu

Charles-Louis de Secondat (1689–1755) (only later known as the *baron de la Brède et de Montesquieu*) was an aristocrat and president of the Parliament of Bordeaux. His wealth, titles and positions were acquired by inheritance from an uncle and with the money of his wife. In other respects, too, Montesquieu was no stranger to ambition and a certain opportunism. He deserted his wife and left his castle to make his name in the world (and, in addition, to gather material for his books). His entry into the *Académie Française* in 1728 was not without difficulty. He was regarded as a niggard: guests complained about the bad receptions at the castle; he was without mercy towards the smallest debtors, slack in relation to creditors; even for the wedding feast of his daughter he appears to have been skimpy. (Psychologists would suggest that Montesquieu remained caught in an early phase of his childhood, where 'having' was more important than living, and a lack of self-respect had to be compensated for by means of possessions and vanity. Montesquieu's childhood and character would have been as formative of his moderate liberal-bourgeois views as those of Rousseau were of his social criticism; see Section 5.5.1.)

Montesquieu published an anonymous erotic satire of Louis XV, as well as the work for which he became famous: *De l'esprit des lois* (The Spirit of Laws, 1748). He worked on this book for 17 years. It is a treasure-chest of historical and sociological material: perhaps not in all respects equally meticulous, but often entertaining and highly original. Revolutionary it is not. For the same reason it was fashionable at a time when the moderate, but no less aristocratic, class-state model of England served as an example not only for Montesquieu.

Montesquieu nonetheless expressed himself very critically regarding the irrational, feudal and superstitious morality and customs of his time. In his *Lettres persanes* (Persian Letters, published anonymously in 1721) he masqueraded as two Persian nobles, who as surprised foreigners describe what happens in France and Europe. The King of France was presented as an unfathomable magician, with a minister who was 12 years old, a mistress of 80 and endowed with the remarkable ability of making people kill each other without having a quarrel.[4] The pope is presented as an idol who is customarily fumigated, and who succeeds in making people believe that three is actually *one*. Not without reason does Montesquieu make others speak, while his criticism is not overt: freedom of expression did not exist.

5.2.2 The Spirit of Laws

In *De l'esprit des lois*, the most important work of Montesquieu, the emphasis is not placed on an ideal political and juridical order, valid for all times and places. The subtitle of the book consequently reads: *Du rapport que les lois doivent avoir avec la constitution de chaque gouvernement, les mœrs, le climat, la religion, le commerce, etc.*: concerning the relation which laws must have with the legal orders of all states, with morality and customs, the weather, faith, trade, etc. That is why the original edition of *De l'esprit des lois* contained a map of Europe and Asia Minor.

Montesquieu attempted to investigate the origin and meaning of laws in different states by means of a historical enquiry. He followed a very different approach to that of Plato and his followers. The latter assumed abstract, metaphysical and/or normative-ethical concepts and ideal laws, as a standard for existing legal orders and states. (The social contract doctrines of Hobbes and Locke, which are in other respects so different, have a similar abstract character). In contrast to these, Montesquieu used empirical-scientific methods that take environmental, cultural and historical differences into account. He stated that the rules which apply to politics and the law must not be approached like principles of reason, but like the laws of natural science. The laws of the legal order can be understood only in the light of political reality. Reality is dependent on time, nation, culture and natural conditions, and thus always different.

Montesquieu gave the most varied examples of this important insight, even though these appear at times quite far-fetched. Especially the climate and the unfavourable influence of heat caught his attention. In a chapter entitled: 'That in the Countries of the South there is a Natural Inequality between the Two Sexes' he

[4]An allusion to the massive wars and their unwilling victims among both serfs and citizens which troubled the 18th century. Later Voltaire would expose the madness thereof, likewise satirically, in *Candide ou l'optimisme* and in his story *Micromegas*, in which the insanity of warmongering humanity is assessed from the point of view of a giant, with reference to the death of millions for the sake of a piece of ground as large as a stamp.

describes how in northern regions the equality of the sexes is a result of the cold, in which womanly beauty is better preserved and because of which women, at a later age, marry men of the same age. But in warm countries, women already marry on their eighth or ninth birthday, and they are discarded by the time that they are 20. By then the heat has destroyed their beauty and their husband looks for another wife. In this way polygamy (or, more precisely, 'polygyny') is explained. Great heat likewise has an unfavourable influence on men. *En passant* the domination of China by the Manchurian emperors from the north is explained by the simple fact that great heat destroys the strength and courage of people, and that it is simply colder in the north of China. A related and constantly recurring theme is the connection between slavery and the tropics. Only people in the milder to cold climates have the strength and the courage to fight for their freedom. The condition of the soil is of great importance for the political and social order, too. Asia is always dominated by large-scale despotism, because the land is flat, the rivers are easily navigable, and the mountains are not too high or too cold. In such regions only the slavery of the whole population is appropriate, whereas in Europe the condition of the soil allows for no central authority, so that the spirit of independence and freedom could be established.

Good legislation is, therefore, in Montesquieu's view, not a product of philosophical thinking about universal state ideals, but a practical and harmonious solution to diverse social and political problems. Laws never apply unconditionally, but only in a specific society at a specific time. So as to not lose himself completely in an infinite variation of place and time, Montesquieu arrives at three foundational political principles. A despotically governed state is ruled by fear, a republic is supported by virtue, and a monarchy is based on honour. Stability is only possible when laws reflect social conditions. Montesquieu opts for a republic, because it furthers such reflection. He rightly connects the republican constitution with virtue: to be sure, the welfare of the republic not only depends on the reasonableness of the government, but also on the virtue of citizens. If the citizens do not have a warm heart for the republic (the public good), it is doomed to failure.

5.2.3 Separation of Powers

Montesquieu contends that in every state model, legislation should be the highest authority. He became famous for the notion of separation of powers.[5] Legislative, executive and judicial power must each be exercised by independent organs to counteract the danger of absolutism. The executive power must be bound by the laws of parliament, as guarantee of the freedom and property of citizens against the arbitrary

[5]Montesquieu was undoubtedly influenced by the parliamentary system in England, and possibly, in addition, by the separation of legislative and executive powers which is found in Locke's *Two Treatises of Government* (Section 4.2).

exercise of power by the state. As a result of the corrupt and class-based judicial decisions of pre-revolutionary France, Montesquieu granted an independent, but nonetheless very limited role to the judicial power. Here, too, the legislative authority thus has the final say. The right of the individual to freedom and personal development is guaranteed only when a constitutional order and separation of powers discourage the monopolisation and abuse of power. The separation and restriction of the powers of the state, as proposed by Montesquieu, have been adopted in all modern democracies.

Montesquieu did not systematically work out the separation of powers in *De l'esprit des lois*. Was this out of fear of the authorities? His preface does not without reason start with a song of praise to the political order of the then existing France. The 'separation of powers according to Montesquieu' nonetheless became one of the most influential ideas of the Enlightenment.

A truly democratic or republican separation of powers implies the following: the highest authority belongs to the people. The people can govern only by way of elected legislators. The legislative assembly, therefore, has no other task than promoting the interests of citizens. For this purpose general laws applicable to all are enacted.

The execution (and preparation) of laws is the task of the executive power, the administration. The latter is thus subject to the legislative power; the state branch has no other task but to ensure that laws are actualised and remain as such. Differing from the legislature, the administration makes no other contribution than a purely administrative one: it should select the measures which are most suitable to achieve the purpose of the law.

Like the administration, the judge is bound by the law, but in a different way. The judge decides in disputes concerning the application of law between citizens, and in criminal law between citizens and the state. Citizens can submit disputes to a judge about rights *in rem*, contracts, torts, and other matters which are regulated by law. The judge does not adjudicate on the basis of the general interest or the will of the majority in the legislature, but on the basis of the equal application of the given law to all citizens.

In this classical view of the separation of powers, the role of the judge is limited. He does nothing but apply the given law. As such, he acts as the guarantor of the equal application of laws, and thus protects the citizens against arbitrariness. The judge in criminal matters assesses the legality of sanctions and other measures that the administration wants to impose on disobedient citizens. Other forms of judicial protection against the government did not as yet exist in the 18th century. The contemporary judge has a much greater power in relation to the legislature and the administration. In some countries he tests laws against (unwritten) legal principles, and in others against the explicit provisions of a Constitution or international treaties such as the European Convention on Human Rights. In legal systems that allow for judicial review, the judiciary protects the citizen's individual rights against infringements by the democratic majority or policies pertaining to general well-being. Criticism in certain countries of contemporary practices is well-known: the democratic legitimacy of (complex and excessive) legislation is questioned, the administration (officialdom) is reproached for their factual omnipotence, and judges are accused of fulfilling a quasi-legislative role. But irrespective of how much has changed, until today 'the spirit of Montesquieu' has persisted.

The principle of the separation of powers illustrates the substantially different tasks of the three state powers. The sovereignty of the people as legislature is unlimited here, as long as the legislature adheres to the rules of separation of powers. The administration is completely subordinate, and the judge makes no other contribution but applying the words of the legislature to the facts of the case. But Montesquieu would have been no pioneering sociologist and psychologist if he did not emphasise the importance of the separation of powers as factual guarantee against state absolutism. Even if the legislature in principle has the final word, only the factual existence of a distribution of powers across many people in different social positions can prevent abuse of powers. In the United States and in other legal orders the importance of the balancing and control of state powers has acquired more or less official status as the doctrine of *checks and balances*.

This can be ensured also by means of a spreading of powers: different organs have powers within the same state function. Hence, legislation is the task of government *and* the representatives of the people, which is different from a strict *separation* of powers (one organ for each separate state function). Because of the blurring of the distribution of state functions in many contemporary legal orders (for example, the judiciary which exercises a quasi-legislative function), this variant of the separation of powers becomes more prominent.

5.2.4 Montesquieu as Moderate Liberal

Montesquieu was a liberal, but not because of his adherence to absolute principles. 'Freedom has its roots in the soil', he wrote in *De l'esprit des lois*. According to him, freedom is more likely in mountainous areas and on islands (the Switzerland and England of his time), than on fertile plains. Islands and mountainous regions can more easily be defended against foreign oppressors, and require more diligence, thrift and independence from the individual. Peace and order, furthermore, contribute to individual freedom. These are better guaranteed by a constitutional state and separation of powers (at the time of Montesquieu only to be found in England and Switzerland) than by a monarchy or despotism.

Freedom is, according to Montesquieu, nothing more than the right to do what laws permit. This is a much more restricted view of freedom than that of Locke (as well as of Mill in the 19th century), who described freedom as the absence of interference by others. In accordance with Locke's concept of freedom, laws always amount to restrictions of personal liberty, because laws are interferences by the state in the life of citizens. Such a limitation is only permissible in the name of the very same freedom, specifically to combat an infringement of the equal freedom of others. In the 19th century, Mill formulated in this spirit the *harm principle*: the state may interfere with someone's freedom only to prevent that another is harmed (Chapter 7). With this formulation the liberal imposes a fundamental limit on the legislature. With Montesquieu, the scope of the private domain is more a question of chance: people are free within the scope which the state grants them in its discretion. His view concerning (negative) freedom is rather an expression of the principle of the formal constitutional state: the state may not arbitrarily, without preceding law, interfere in someone's life.

To be sure, Montesquieu in general subscribed to moderate views. He was certainly no revolutionary. In *De l'esprit des lois* he even writes:

> It is a capital maxim that the manners and customs of a despotic empire ought never to be changed; for nothing would more speedily produce a revolution. The reason is that in these states there are no laws, that is, none that can be properly called so; there are only manners and customs; and if you overturn these you overturn all (Montesquieu 2005, p. 368).

Montesquieu seemingly regards facts about human beings and society, as well as existing morals and customs, as alterable, but not as givens which can be changed at will by human interference. For this reason, too, he wants legislation to be based on empirical scientific enquiry into human and social circumstances.

Differing from Rousseau, Montesquieu did not engage in fundamental human and societal criticism. His narrow morality had a conservative character. (After the French Revolution, Robespierre apparently said about Montesquieu that he was nothing more than a weak-hearted, dogmatic and prejudiced *parlementaire*, and definitely no *bon républicain*, and that he, as a good revolutionary, would certainly have made Montesquieu a head shorter.)

5.2.5 Commentary

The most well-known criticism of Montesquieu concerns the conservative character of his views about law and the state. Good legislation is, according to Montesquieu, not based on metaphysical or normative-ethical principles, but on factually given circumstances. This view rather leads to the adjustment of the law to these circumstances, than to radical change. This adjustment fits in with Montesquieu's aristocratic position and perhaps also with his character. Conservatism, however, seems not to have been the most appropriate response to the wrongs of 18th-century Europe.

The question, moreover, is: how can laws which *prescribe* what people should do, be derived from empirical-scientific descriptions and explanations of the *existence* of human and societal conditions? Hume, a contemporary of Montesquieu, denied that this is possible: from an 'is', no 'ought' can be derived (Section 6.2). The laws of a legal order differ in kind from the laws of science (as John Stuart Mill repeated in the 19th century). Scientific laws are descriptions and explanations of reality as it is, the laws of a legal order prescribe what people must do, and aim precisely at *changing* reality.

Natural law, which claims to be an expression of the true law that prescribes what should be contained in any positive legal order, is, therefore, usually not based on empirical facts. Plato grounds natural law in a metaphysical realm of Ideas. Aristotle assumed a metaphysical unity of descriptive natural laws and normative principles: natural laws would give expression to the immanent development which is to the benefit of reality. Others sought the foundations of natural law in the will of God. Empirical facts, on the other hand, cannot be the source of legal morality. Montesquieu, as one of the pioneers of the empirical science of legal sociology, can provide no firm foundation for natural law with this empirical enquiry. A part of his work consists of descriptions and explanations of the connection between law and existing morals and customs. His normative standpoint, such as the prescription of a separation of powers, cannot be based on these descriptions.

Yet, empirical facts such as those propounded by Montesquieu may be useful as a realistic framework for normative deliberation. *Ought implies can*: refrain from implementing values that cannot possibly work in the actual world. Moreover, Montesquieu's sociological descriptions of the diverse legal systems may be read as an attempt to evade censorship of explicit political statements. His picture of the English constitution may conceal an implicit criticism of French royal absolutism. After all, the French climate is more akin to that of its neighbour Britain than to Eastern sultriness. So, why despotism? Would a liberal constitution not better match the French environment? Facts, then, can still be relevant to norms, although they cannot justify them.

The next question is whether Montesquieu's descriptions are accurate. *De l'esprit des lois* pours out onto the reader a real shipload of exotic facts and suggestions. Some of these are treasures, whereas others appear more like small mirrors and beads. The old Romans did everything better; principles of Turkish criminal law should be imported into Europe; in Japan everything is subject to the death penalty, which prevents criminal law there from functioning; and in China people are only robbed and not murdered because the Chinese authorities are clever enough to cut up into small pieces only those who rob *and* murder. *Épater le bourgeois* (to shock the people) is something in which Montesquieu found delight. In fact, very little of his description of the English legal system was accurate, but English contemporaries were full of praise for the clarity of his arguments, and remarked that Montesquieu had a better conception of them than they themselves had.

5.3 Enlightenment of Criminal Law

5.3.1 Monopoly of Power and Criminal Law

The European administration of criminal justice in the 18th century was, in terms of contemporary standards, cruel and inhuman. Without a codified criminal law, legal certainty was, even on paper, difficult to find. 'Confessions' were obtained by means of not particularly gentle bodily coercion. Presumptions of innocence did not apply, and in the secret criminal procedures that were followed they would have made little sense. The most diverse earthly and spiritual 'authorities' had extensive powers of sanction. The catalogue of executed punishments offered a true cabinet of horrors.

During the old times of absolute state power, abuses, such as the *lettres de cachet* (blank orders of the French king to detain people, which could be bought with money, and which could be arbitrarily filled in), could still be explained on the basis of the omnipotence of the king, subject to no control. Both Montesquieu's separation of powers and the doctrine of the social contract, however, stand in tension with treating citizens in an arbitrary manner in criminal matters.

The separation of powers entails that the administration responsible for criminal justice is bound by the word of the legislature, the law. In terms of the law the judge in criminal matters must ensure that the rights of citizens are not violated. Fundamental in this respect are the boundaries of the social contract. The power monopoly of the state should protect citizens' rights against murder and manslaughter. This does not fit in well with a right of the state to revert to murder, manslaughter, and abuse in the form of an unrestricted criminal law.

However, with these outlines of the social contract and the separation of powers, the institution of criminal law is not as yet completely established. Beccaria became famous for his elaboration of enlightened principles of criminal law. He was the first to plead for a purely preventative administration of criminal justice. Punishment for him serves no other purpose than the confirmation of the social contract and the general welfare. 'The greatest happiness for the greatest number' as the goal of society and the state was expressed for the first time by Beccaria. Later this principle would become famous through Bentham (see Section 7.2).

5.3.2 Cesare Beccaria

Cesare Bonesana Beccaria (1738–1794) was not only a criminal law scholar, but also an economist. As aristocratic descendant he had a university education and joined a Milanese circle which was known as 'the academy of fists': a society devoted to far-reaching social transformation. Partly because of this he was influenced by Montesquieu, Diderot and Hume. As professor and civil servant, Beccaria concerned himself primarily with economics, in relation to which he advocated moderate liberal views. The book on account of which he instantly became famous (*Dei delitti e delle pene*, or On Crimes and Punishments, published anonymously in 1764) is probably partly the work of the brothers Ferri (the life and soul of the society of fists), who brought him into contact with criminal law. His societal position could have contributed to the fact that his extremely cutting criticism of the then existing administration of criminal justice was not banned, and quickly became generally accepted, more particularly in the circles of the French Enlightenment. Voltaire wrote a eulogising preface to one of the six reprints which appeared in one and a half years, and it was quickly translated into all European languages. The 18th-century codifications of criminal law, and with that the contemporary administration of criminal justice are unimaginable without his work.

5.3.3 Criminal Law According to Beccaria

The last chapter of *Dei delitti e delle pene* consists of nothing more than the following recommendation:

> From what I have written results the following general theorem, of considerable utility, though not conformable to custom, the common legislator of nations:
>
> That a punishment may not be an act of violence, of one, or of many, against a private member of society, it should be public, immediate, and necessary, the least possible in the case given, proportioned to the crime, and determined by the laws (Beccaria 2004, p. 64).

Nowadays this is so self-evident that one can easily forget how revolutionary it was in the 18th century. Beccaria's book can be read as a contemporary exposition of the principles of criminal law. Many of the wrongs against which he objected have disappeared in modern constitutional states. Torture to coerce 'confessions', no longer exists in civilised criminal law systems. However, other wrongs criticised by him, such as the long lapse of time between the commission of the crime and the imposition of punishment, abuse of detention to serve as punishment, criminal law judges creating law, as well as arbitrariness in sentences, still characterise the contemporary administration of criminal justice. He specifically criticised the privileges which certain classes enjoy in criminal matters. Officially these privileges have been abolished, but even in modern constitutional states it is still a striking phenomenon that more poor than rich people are in jail, whereas nothing indicates that poor people commit more crimes.

The principle of Beccaria's criminal law is prevention. Punishment may, according to him, serve no other purpose than the protection of the general welfare. In his interpretation of the social contract, criminal law is founded on the endorsement of citizens. They have given up as much of their freedom as is necessary to give all others sufficient reason to defend this freedom. This is connected to Beccaria's standard of 'the greatest happiness for the greatest number'. In the first chapter of his *Dei delitti e delle pene* he emphasises this point as follows:

> If we look into history we shall find that laws, which are, or ought to be, conventions between men in a state of freedom, have been, for the most part, the work of the passions of a few, or the consequences of a fortuitous or temporary necessity; not dictated by a cool examiner of human nature, who knew how to collect in one point the actions of a multitude, and had this only end in view, the greatest happiness of the greatest number (Beccaria 2004, p. 3).

In Chapter 2, however, an exposition follows of the social contract as basis of state authority and criminal law. How are these two points of departure to be reconciled? In other words, how does the greatest benefit for the greatest number fit in with the protection of fundamental rights as the central idea of the social contract? Beccaria attempted to resolve this problem by making the greatest happiness of the greatest number into the essence of the contract. Here his 'calculating' view of man and society already comes to the fore. The contracting parties would also be aiming to organise society in such a way that makes everyone as happy as possible, which would include individual freedom rights. They give up a component of their personal freedom for the sake of the general welfare, Beccaria states. Hence, society had to become an oiled machine, in which the strengths of individual interest merge as well as possible with the general interest. Beccaria appeals to Rousseau (Section 5.5), but his views actually fit in better with those of Hobbes and Locke. Rousseau makes use of the social contract as an allegory for the social nature of man and clearly not as justification for a communal state based on the rational endorsement of calculating individuals. The latter was Beccaria's view.

Criminal law is, therefore, interpreted 'instrumentally' by Beccaria, both in terms of the social contract and the general welfare. The contract does not justify measures which are more painful than are necessary for the protection of everybody's freedom. Stated differently, punishment as deterrence is based on the calculation of the benefit to the general interest. Serious crimes do not as such justify severe punishments, but only if these severe punishments would be necessary to sufficiently prevent those crimes. Beccaria writes in Chapter 6 of his *Dei delitti e delle pene*:

> It is not only the common interest of mankind that crimes should not be committed, but that crimes of every kind should be less frequent, in proportion to the evil they produce to society. Therefore the means made use of by the legislature to prevent crimes should be more powerful in proportion as they are destructive of the public safety and happiness, and as the inducements to commit them are stronger. Therefore there ought to be a fixed proportion between crimes and punishments.
>
> ...
>
> That force which continually impels us to our own private interest, like gravity, acts incessantly, unless it meets with an obstacle to oppose it. The effects of this force are the confused series of human actions. Punishments, which I would call political obstacles, prevent the fatal effects of private interest, without destroying the impelling cause, which is that sensibility inseparable from man. The legislator acts, in this case, like a skilful architect, who endeavours to counteract the force of gravity by combining the circumstances which may contribute to the strength of his edifice (Beccaria 2004, pp. 9–10).

Beccaria (2004, p. 9) regarded this as 'one of those palpable truths which though evident to the meanest capacity, yet by a combination of circumstances, are only known to a few thinking men in every nation, and in every age'. The quasi-mechanistic, almost scientific, approach to criminal law as *social engineering* cannot be better and more beautifully expressed. In this respect Beccaria is a typical representative of the optimism of the scientific Enlightenment.

The application of punishments as 'obstacles of social-political nature' is, according to Beccaria, not to be determined on the basis of intent and fault. The deterrent effect would, after all, disappear if punishment is, because of the absence of fault, not imposed on facts which, because of their external characteristics, are punishable. Moreover, good intentions can have evil consequences, and 'wicked intent can, viewed socially, bring about the happiest consequences'.

Beccaria was, moreover, the first to publicly turn against the death penalty. Whatever else citizens may have transferred to the state with the social contract, the right over life and death was not included. Otherwise the social contract would have no meaning at all. It after all serves to safeguard the quality of life of citizens.

Beccaria ruled out torture as a means to coerce 'confessions', just as corporal punishment. Imprisonment is sufficient, and minor transgressions must be threatened only with a fine.

According to Beccaria, all of this must be laid down in clear laws. Codification is a necessary condition for the reasonable administration of criminal justice. Citizens must be able to know what is punishable and what not, if there is to be legal certainty, and if punishment is to have a deterrent effect as a well-known prospect. Codification is at any rate the only way by which to exclude arbitrariness in criminal law. The task of the criminal law judge does not go beyond establishing whether or not the accused has contravened the law.

Beccaria is, similarly, the pioneer of the modern law of criminal procedure. Criminal proceedings, according to him, not only serve the purpose of punishment as deterrent, but also the protection of the accused, and with that the interests of all citizens. In criminal procedure Beccaria does not, therefore, deviate from the notion of utility on which his whole criminal law is based. Moreover, the ratio of prohibitions, such as that against torture to force the making of desired statements, is not only legal protection of the suspects, but also the rationality of criminal law as deterrent for the purpose of prevention. Punishment of criminal acts which are not established in a way that is acceptable to all does not work, but simply sows unrest and fear.

In criminal procedure Beccaria turns specifically against the abuse of coercive measures. The prosecuting authorities may not detain any suspect unless there are sufficient grounds for the suspicion of such person. If there are reasons to arrest someone, then coercive measures, such as detention, may serve no other purposes than procedural ones. Coercive measures are not punishments, because the latter can be declared only by a judge after the impartial investigation of the case. The separation of powers is here of great importance: see Section 5.3.5.

5.3.4 Instrumental Criminal Law and Individual Justice

Beccaria's founding of criminal law on the consent of citizens is not very convincing. In the first place, the same arguments apply here which are generally raised against the social contract: such a contract was never actually concluded, and a hypothetical contract cannot be binding. Such objections apply even more so to criminal law, because of its far-reaching consequences for citizens. The consent can, in the second place, just as little be said to have been implicitly given by the offender, in the fashion of 'volenti non fit iniuria' ('whoever willed it himself is not done any injustice'). A person who knows that punishment is a consequence of crime and still commits a crime, would in terms of this reasoning himself have taken the punishment to boot as an 'impediment of a socio-political nature'. However, on the basis of this principle, the death penalty in the event of damage to property can similarly be justified. Even if the state provides citizens with a free choice, the quality of such choice is co-determined by the options from which the choice can be made. A third interpretation, in terms of which the consent of citizens about criminal law is obtained by way of democratic legislation, is the least implausible. However, even democracy can trample underfoot the rights of suspects and citizens in a criminal law system which, apart from democratic legitimacy, has no other reasonable foundation. The only way that the social contract may still work as a hypothesis is by viewing it as a metaphor for reciprocity: each citizen has good reasons to agree with its conditions, provided all others do the same. But the utilitarian reasons proposed by Beccaria are not good enough.

Beccaria's endorsement of prevention as the only goal of criminal justice runs into problems as well. Small violations can occur so often that they amount to a serious wrong. Severe punishment could make an end to this, but is this just? Beccaria states that the seriousness of the punishable fact is determined by the harm to society, and that the harm is determinative for the punishment. In this hides an unexpected ambiguity. For example: a single act of tax evasion does not cause serious harm, and does not, therefore, legitimate a severe punishment. For the concrete consequences of such a singular fact it does not matter much whether or not others evade tax as well. However, if many people evade tax, the social harm is certainly serious, and it does appear legitimate to impose severe punishments: light sentences seemingly do not work well enough. Severe punishment of serious wrongs committed by means of many recurrent small violations can, taken as a whole, be effective, but are for this reason still not just in a retributive sense. The individual perpetrator does not have to take the blame for the consequences of the crimes of (many) others. Even if Beccaria did not intend such a result, his criminal law theory does not exclude this possibility.

Fair punishment, moreover, needs to correspond not only with the seriousness of the delict, but also with the degree of fault. Beccaria attaches no importance to intent and fault for punishability. From a preventative, deterrent viewpoint this is understandable, but here, too, calculated rationality stands in opposition to justice. Beccaria stated that telescopes and quadrants are not necessary to see the enlightening quality of his model of criminal law. This shows that the quasi-mechanistic balancing of social interests stands at a loss in relation to the conflicting notion of justice which in this context requires the legal protection of individuals *against* the general interest.

Many scholars of criminal law since Beccaria have resisted a purely preventative system of criminal justice, with an appeal to the notion of justice as retaliation. Then punishment does not amount to *social engineering*, that is, deterrence as a calculated expression of social welfare, but to retribution. This retribution is irrational, in the sense that it cannot be justified on the basis of any calculation of welfare. Retribution nevertheless amounts to justice if understood in a certain sense: it is 'making good again' of what went wrong, by making the perpetrator suffer in a similar manner the wrong of his crime. This can detract from 'the greatest happiness for the greatest number'. From Hegel (Section 7.3) originates the seeming contradiction that offenders are precisely because of the punishment viewed as full human beings (they are held personally responsible for their acts), whereas in a preventative system of criminal justice they are nothing but instruments of the public good.

Moreover, to this very day, it is contended that punishment as a preventive measure is irrational because the administration of criminal justice is not effective. Even if no objection could be raised against the prevention of punishable facts to promote the general welfare as a general principle of criminal law, then the question remains whether criminal justice fulfils this purpose. Not only abolitionists (advocates of the replacement of criminal justice by alternative measures against crime, such as mediation), but others, too, state that the sum total of all the consequences of criminal justice probably adds up to a negative balance. Stated differently, the prevention of the suffering caused by crimes by means of the preventative system of criminal justice does not weigh up against the suffering caused by punishment, specifically imprisonment.

Should retribution then be the foundation? But how does one justify the reproduction of suffering that has already occurred? Moreover, modern criminal procedure since the 18th century contains elements which do not fit well with the idea of punishment as retribution. The principle of expediency provides that those suspected of punishable facts can escape prosecution if this is required by the general interest. This is an instrumental principle, falling within the scope of the idea of the administration of criminal justice as prevention in the promotion of the general interest. The principle of retribution requires that every guilty perpetrator has to be punished. This likewise applies to the possibility (existing in practically all modern constitutional states) of suspended sentences, which makes sense from a preventative perspective, but which is not reconcilable with the notion of retribution.

Unified theories are attempts to make prevention and retribution coincide. The successes of the two approaches would be able to solve the individual problems of each theory *and* bring about more unity in the domain of criminal law. Hence, punishability could be determined with reference to standards of retribution, whereas sentencing could depend on social benefit. Such attempts at reconciliation disregard the fact that important problems in each of the two approaches cannot be resolved in this way. For example, sentences which are based on the social benefit of deterrence remain disproportionate to the seriousness of the individual punishable fact; and retribution can appear obligatory for punishable facts where no danger at all exists of repetition. This problem may be solved by a further fusion of retribution and prevention in the assessment of the penalty. On the one hand, the sanction should not be more severe than is required for prevention; on the other hand, it should not exceed what is proportionate to the seriousness of the crime, as retributive justice demands. Beccaria also has been regarded as one of these unifiers. His book must, however, be placed unread on the rack to force it to have such an import.

5.3.5 Separation of Powers and Codification

Criminal law is a textbook example of the importance of the principle of separation of powers. The legislature determines in general terms which facts are punishable and which punishments are appropriate (substantive criminal law), as well as the way in which criminal law may, and must, be maintained (criminal procedure). The executive power prosecutes and punishes crimes, the judge sees to it that the law is complied with in this regard.

Punishment is the worst thing that can happen to the citizen through the agency of the state. Even if corporal punishment and the death penalty are prohibited, the consequences of imprisonment and arrest are in general serious and irreversible. Arrested citizens run the risk of stigmatisation for life. Judicial supervision of the prosecuting authorities is therefore important. For this reason, already since the 18th century the principle applies that lengthy limitations of freedom, for example through temporary detention, must be approved by an (examining) judge or magistrate. The restriction of freedom may, furthermore, not amount to punishment. Coercive measures during the procedure may serve only to promote the administration of justice, for example, to prevent the suspect from fleeing or interference with the obtaining of evidence. Punishment may be imposed only when a judge or magistrate has decided about the legality of the claim of the prosecuting authorities. The petition to punish is partly determined by appropriateness. It is after all the task of the prosecuting authorities to represent the public interest.

For the protection of the accused and, as a consequence, of all citizens against the state, the judge or magistrate (in some countries a jury fulfils certain of these functions) has at least three tasks. He must evaluate the evidence; determine whether the proven facts amount to an offence in terms of legislation or the common law; and determine an appropriate punishment. The independent judge stands above the (unequal) dispute between the prosecuting authorities and the accused. He can, however, be impartial only if he can appeal to the law as guarantee against arbitrariness. The codification of criminal law and criminal procedure, already pleaded for by Beccaria, is, therefore, closely connected with the important notion of separation of powers.

This applies equally to other domains of law. The great codifications in Continental Europe in the 18th century were not only intended to provide legal certainty to well-intentioned citizens. Statutory law has to ensure that disputes between citizens and the state in criminal law, and amongst citizens themselves in private law, are resolved on the basis of a law knowable by all, and not by virtue of the political preferences of the judge. Nevertheless, codification in criminal law is much more important than codification in other legal domains, on account of the principle 'no punishment without preceding law'. In order to protect the individual citizens against the overwhelming power of the state, criminal law requires a strict application of the principle of legality.

5.4 Natural Law, Enlightened Science and Cruel Arbitrariness

We said before that the laws of the legal order and of morality cannot be equated with the laws of nature. The equation is an Aristotelian inheritance, in respect of which some philosophers of the Enlightenment are less modern than it appears. This plays a role with Beccaria as well. The Enlightenment in general deals poorly with the relation between value-free empirical science and normative views of political and personal life, including, specifically, fundamental rights. The Enlightenment philosophers expected that progress in scientific knowledge would similarly bring about social and moral progress. However, science and normative views are categorically separated. Empirical science can at most show which means lead to the achievement of specific goals, so that man can improve his control over the world. Natural science summarises causes and effects in general laws: in the event of cause a, then always consequence b. The causes can be utilised as means: a person who aims at b, must do a. Technology is 'reverse' natural science. Viewed thus, the industrial revolution which started at the end of the 18th century is not conceivable without the physics of Newton.

The *Encyclopédie* is permeated by optimism about the application of the new science. It is the first major work in which science and technology, theoretical knowledge and practical crafts and arts, were brought together in a unity. The optimism was partly justified. Never before had people succeeded in having such complete control over nature. All the same, empirical science can determine only the means for a predetermined goal. The goals as such must have other grounds. Scientific knowledge can, moreover, be utilised for very diverse purposes, both good and bad. Medical knowledge makes it possible to heal people, but also to wage bacterial war. In so far as the Enlightenment philosophers invoke empirical scientific ideals, the underpinning of their emancipation ethics remains at risk.

This also appears from the ease with which some 18th-century philosophers could overturn existing moral views by applying the materialistic worldview of natural science to human beings. De La Mettrie, for example, contested in *L'homme machine* (Man, the Machine, 1747) the traditional dualism of body and soul. He denied that apart from matter, that is, the object of natural science, an incorporeal reason exists. The spiritual side of human beings is not something independent, separate from the body. Human thinking is, according to him, a natural physical process: man is nothing more than a machine. On account of this materialistic portrayal of mankind he viewed religion as meaningless, just like the moral feelings of guilt and remorse that would belong to the same category. De La Mettrie developed an ethics of unlimited pursuit of individual pleasure. This can, from the point of view of traditional ethics, have immoral consequences: I sacrifice you for my pleasure – this radical conclusion was, in as many words, drawn by Sade. However, on closer inspection, even this alternative ethics cannot be founded on an empirical view of man, irrespective of how materialistic it is: from the fact that man pursues pleasure it does not follow that he should do it.

The same applies to the theory of the infamous Marquis de Sade. Sade took the materialistic view of man and world to its logical conclusion, with the intention of overturning all traditional Christian values. In his arrogance man believes unfairly that with his reason he stands above matter, maintained Sade. Nature, including man, is, in his view, simply a meaningless coming into existence and demise of matter. Constructive activities are, therefore, as 'natural' as destructive ones. To murder someone, for nature simply means that its matter is being rearranged. Why then not give nature a helping hand? Because of this, Sade recommends an ethics which has since then become known as *sadism*: torturing, burning, killing, as long as the perpetrator experiences enjoyment in doing so. Empirical nature, after all, shows that the strong utilise the weak for their own pleasure. For sadism, however, the same applies as for the pleasure morality of De La Mettrie: it is as much founded on a one-sided selection from a totality of natural phenomena as its converse, the neighbourly love of Christians and the equality ideal of the Enlightenment philosophers.

In this modern amoral view nature includes everything that is observable. Therefore, it does not provide any standard with which to choose one observable phenomenon rather than another. From an ethical perspective, out of nature everything and, therefore, nothing can be derived. This affects the foundations of the Enlightenment belief in progress, as progress in science does not entail moral progress. This tension between emancipation and nihilism likewise dominates the contemporary discussion concerning *postmodernism*, which raises the question whether the project of progress of the Enlightenment still has a chance of success (modernism), or whether it is ultimately doomed to fail (postmodernism, see Section 9.1.4).

5.5 Rousseau: Nostalgia for Natural Security

5.5.1 Rousseau's Life and Work

Criticism of the Enlightenment with a less nihilistic import was developed by Rousseau. Rousseau, too, firmly contested the belief that reason and science bring about progress for humanity. Rousseau was a highly original thinker. He cannot really be compared with his predecessors and contemporaries. He led a restless and adventurous life, continually fleeing from real or supposed enemies. His life and many of his (often autobiographical) writings create the impression that he felt nowhere at home. His criticism of society partly stems from this, even though the plausibility of the critique cannot be evaluated in terms of his character. Rousseau was not an academic philosopher. By virtue of birth and character he did not belong to the *beau monde* (fashionable society) that he hated so much. The concept of 'alienation', which is so important for modern political and moral philosophy, Rousseau experienced personally.

Jean-Jacques Rousseau (1712–1778) lost his mother a few days after his birth in Geneva. He was brought up by an aunt and by his volatile father. He never had the benefit of much formal education. After a series of unpleasant dealings with employers and other unhappy adventures, Rousseau fled from Geneva. The protection and friendship of Madame de Warens had a great influence on his life, but he continued to lead a nomadic and restless life. He, nonetheless, in 1743 became the secretary of the French ambassador in Venice. This, too, did not last long, because, after a quarrel with his employer, he had to leave. Ending up in Paris, he started a relationship with the illiterate Thérèse Levasseur, with whom he appears to have conceived five children. They all ended up in an orphanage. In the meantime Rousseau met important *lumières*, such as Diderot and d'Alembert, who ensured that Rousseau could write for the *Encyclopédie* about music.

Rousseau's literary career started in 1750, with the award-winning *Discours sur les sciences et les arts*. His opera, *Le devin du village* (the fortune-teller of the town), was performed in the presence of Louis XV. Rousseau, however, did not want to be introduced to the king, and consequently forfeited his chances of money and honour at court. After various meanderings he settled down, from 1756, in a country house of another rich French female friend. Until 1762 he wrote there his most important books, including *Emile* and *Du contrat social.*

Rousseau increasingly started to have quarrels, even with the *Encyclopédistes*. His books were banned, and eventually he ended up in England as guest of the philosopher David Hume. Again, Rousseau did not bear it for long, and this was definitely not the fault of his kind-hearted host. He fled once more and eventually arrived in Paris. At the end of his life his work became increasingly autobiographical. In his attempts at self-analysis, the tragic gift for paranoia reappears. A feeling of security was never set aside for Rousseau. This plays an important role in his political work as well. The life and work of Rousseau were determined by a desire for natural security. (Perhaps Rousseau would have written nothing of importance if his mother had been there for him.)

5.5.2 Feeling Versus Reason: The 'Natural' and the 'Civilized' Person

Rousseau disliked rationalism and the individualistic liberties of the Enlightenment. Nonetheless, he was a passionate advocate of the freedom of man, freedom from the frequently inhumane power structures of the society of his time. His conception of freedom is, however, different from that of the liberal Enlightenment. In his two most important books, *Du contrat social* (The Social Contract, 1754/1762) and *Emile ou de l'éducation* (Emile, or On Education, 1762), he states that freedom does not entail *not being obstructed by others* (an individualistic, egoistic view), but *living in natural conditions, together with other people, in a world which is suitable for human beings*. In other words, Rousseau advocates man's *essential freedom*, rather than the negative liberty of liberalism.

Rousseau's thinking is strongly influenced by the idea that culture and civilization are not merely good for human beings. Cultural products, such as science and art, can after all be employed for bad purposes as well. In Rousseau's view, man has increasingly strayed from his natural existence, as his social environment is increasingly determined by culture. In a society in which one can become rich at the expense of others, the natural inclinations of man have degenerated into unrestrained greed and desire. By contrast, in Rousseau's view man has a good nature. Man in his natural state finds the suffering of others abhorrent. He, moreover, has *amour de soi*, self-love, which according to Rousseau constitutes the essence of human existence. However, in 'civilized' societies the *amour de soi* has degenerated into *amour propre*, empty vanity. In their natural state people are free and equal. This comes to an end as soon as, together with society, private property comes into existence. This results in economic and social inequality. Legislation is introduced to maintain discrepancies in property ownership. Jealousy and an egotistical drive for possessions are the consequences.

Rousseau did not contend that his natural man ever really existed. His criticism of the society of his time was not of a historical nature. His idea of the natural man is a reconstruction: who is the man who hides behind this illusory culture, the crass differences in income and power, the abuse of reason, and the fine arts of modern times? According to Rousseau, man is not by nature the way Hobbes had sketched him: in the first place a rational individual who is in search of his own advantage, if necessary at the cost of others. Egoism is not the most natural tendency of man, but an invention of the modern, rationalistic science which dissects everything into individual and other elementary particles. By nature man is not primarily a rational being, but a being with feelings, with real self-love, self-respect and natural sympathy for others. This self-respect is destroyed by a culture of ostentatious display of money and power of the few that contrasts with the poverty and suffering of the many. The rich suffer because of this as well: they think they are better off, but their supposed self-respect is just as inauthentic as their relations with their subordinates. In his satirical narrative *Candide ou l'optimisme* (Candide, or, Optimism, 1759) Rousseau's contemporary, Voltaire, expressed this as follows:

> [I]n the cities, where people appear to live in peace, and the arts flourish, men are devoured by more envy, worry, and dissatisfaction than all the scourges of a city under siege. Secret sorrows are more cruel even than public tribulations (Voltaire 2006, p. 53).

Rousseau thought that the education of young people could give rise to a more natural, authentic society. Indeed, one of his well-known books deals with education: *Emile ou de l'éducation*. According to Rousseau, education should serve as a counterweight to the alienating elements of modern society. Children should not be exposed to the wisdom of books, but must through personal experience learn to know their place and their abilities in natural reality. Rousseau is one of the first scholars of modern times who emphasised the fundamental importance of childhood. If children are given the opportunity to find their place in the world on the basis of their personal experience, they will develop a natural feeling of compassion for, and unity with, other people. Education must recreate the conditions of natural man in the 'civilized', and in many respects degenerate, modern society. Against the rationalistic fashion of his time, Rousseau made it clear that children are much more than beings with an inborn reason. His insight that the circumstances of early childhood have a substantial influence on later life, was revolutionary as well. The social and political importance of education became increasingly clear in subsequent centuries, for example in the psychology of Freud (Section 8.2).

5.5.3 Politics, Law and State

The title of Rousseau's most well-known work, *Du contrat social*, makes one suspect that he was an adherent of the doctrine of the social contract such as one finds with Hobbes and Locke. His view on law and the state is, however, quite different from classical contract theory, which seeks to explain why citizens must obey governments, as well as what justifies the existence of governments and of state coercion. In Rousseau's view, Hobbes explains this as follows: Life in an unorganised 'society' of individuals is 'nasty, brutish and short'. The natural egoism of the individual drives him to serve his own interests at the cost of others. He can, however, in turn become the victim of still stronger individuals. People, therefore, out of personal interest reach an agreement, leading to the establishment of a power monopoly, a state. Hobbes thus bases his contract theory (according to Rousseau) on a modern, individualistic portrayal of mankind. The individual is by nature free, and is primarily led by rational self-interest. By nature he is not bound by social obligations. For this reason he can only by virtue of agreement be obliged to obey the state.

Rousseau's views of the state are far removed from this individualistic and egoistic point of view. According to him, egoism is not a natural inclination of man, but a product of 'civilization'. His view of the state is the opposite of that of Hobbes and his kindred spirits. According to Rousseau, it is precisely modern society which corresponds to the nasty, brutish and short life that Hobbes wrongly ascribes to the state of nature, degenerate as it is because of extreme inequalities in power, status and wealth. Classical contract theory reversed the order of things. According to Rousseau, man's natural way of life, not as yet degenerated by culture, is his ideal state. Modern societies and states are not legal institutions called into being by means of agreement to promote individual interests, but the means of power of the few at the cost of the many which are not consciously willed by anyone.

Rousseau specifically turns against the atomism and individualism of his predecessors. Philosophers like Hobbes and Locke assume that societies and states do not add or subtract anything substantially to or from individuals. In their views of the social contract, states are nothing more than external and accidental means for the protection of individual interests. Viewed historically, different states have arisen from the most diverse causes and backgrounds which may be illegitimate from the perspective of the social contract. Yet the justification for states, according to contract theory, is based exclusively on the shared self-interest of all individuals.

Rousseau contends that man is essentially a communal being. By nature, man lives in his family, in a secure environment, without any fundamental differences in views and goals. By virtue of the recognition of his fellow human beings, man can be himself. Rousseau extends this image of the happy family to society as a whole. A society is not an arbitrary gathering of (more or less) reasonable individuals, but an authentic community with shared backgrounds in language and other forms of culture. People find their identity in their life with other human beings.

Here again Rousseau's distaste for narrow rationalism with its emphasis on rational self-interest shows itself. People are primarily beings of feeling, aimed at, derived from, and shared with, their fellow human beings. They derive *amour de soi*, positive self-love and self-respect, from the natural sympathy of others. One can only have self-respect if one is respected by others. Modern individualism, then, does not portray the true nature of man, but, conversely, shows his alienation from natural society. In the ideal community no distinction between society and the state exists.

This distinction was essential for Rousseau's rationalistic and contractualist predecessors. In their view, society (the totality of human and social relations) is legally and politically of no relevance, and the state (the juridical-political organisation of social life) is nothing more than an arbitrary means to guarantee individual interests. Rousseau, however, maintained that, in a good society, state authority must merge with the natural authority of the community. This is what he meant by his 'social contract': by virtue of proper deliberation between all members of society the common will comes to light, the *volonté générale* of the community. 'Each of us puts in common his person and all his powers under the supreme direction of the general will; and in our corporate capacity we receive each member as indivisible part of the whole', he writes (Rousseau 1986, p. 16). The social contract is thus for Rousseau a metaphor. In the first place, it is not a contract in the sense of a consensus *ad idem* between individuals, but an expression of the *volonté générale*. In the second place, actually existing states are not in fact based on the sovereignty of the people.

Rousseau draws a strict distinction between the *volonté générale* (general will), the will which everyone forms from the general, societal point of view, with an eye to the general welfare, and the *volonté de tous* (will of all), the highest common factor of conflicting individual interests. The individualistic contract theory is based upon the *volonté de tous*. According to Rousseau, people would adopt the viewpoint of the *volonté générale* when they had an equal voice in the state. State and community merge in the ideal society. Actually there is then no real state, for the people themselves are the sovereign. (Rousseau was probably influenced by his experiences in Geneva, then a city-state with a direct democracy.)

Rousseau had a different view of democracy than rationalistic and individualistic political thinkers. Democracy is for him not a mechanism to determine the interests of the majority (*volonté de tous*) as a kind of sum total and compromise of arbitrary individual interests. It is a fundamental form of human relationship. Through proper deliberation the true interests of the individual and of society must be expressed and realised: the *volonté générale*. Everyone will be in agreement with this, because everyone forms part of the community, and likewise of the general will. When the condition is fulfilled that everyone votes from the shared point of view, then, in the event of a lack of unanimity, the majority can decide. Then the minority will recognise that they have been mistaken.

Rousseau uses his idea of the ideal society to evaluate actual states. Obviously, in large societies a direct democracy is not possible. The distaste of Rousseau for modern civilization is related to his misgivings about large states. Such states he distinguished from societies. Actually, the distinction should not exist, but modern states do not have much success with the *volonté générale* so that it would be misleading to equate them with societies, and even less so with the true society of people. Nonetheless, they should as much as possible approximate the spirit of the *volonté générale*.

Rousseau, however, does not attach any revolutionary consequences to the deviation of most actual states from his ideal of community. He rather emphasises the importance of education, which would lead to a better man, and thus to a better society and state. Rousseau expects that after a revolution the same wrongs would occur again sooner or later. Attempts to transform society on the basis of scientific rationality, moreover, would result in an even greater suppression of spontaneous, instinctive human nature.

Rousseau's communal theory stresses the dependence of individuals on societal bonds. This is of course not to say that Rousseau agreed with the societies of his time, because these were based on oppressive inequality instead of brotherly equality. Revolutions, however, often lead to the temporary destruction of social institutions. People are much more dependent on these institutions than they think. An example: corn traders and other exploiters were during the French revolution violently removed from the scene. This, however, meant that storage, transport, and the sale of corn and other means of life, also came to a standstill. As a result an inestimable number of people died of starvation. By wiping out the exploiters the people unconsciously signed their own death warrants.

5.5.4 Commentary

In the individualistic liberal tradition the freedom of the individual means the absence of coercion by others. Individuals are free to do what they want, as long as they do not harm other people. They themselves must decide what they do with their own freedom. The liberal theory of the social contract is closely related to this 'negative' view of freedom. Individuals conclude an agreement so as to ensure that they can do and leave what they want, without being obstructed by other people. The state must then guarantee that citizens respect the freedom of their co-citizens. The social criticism of Rousseau is in direct opposition to this view of freedom. In his view, people mistakenly think that they are free when they choose to do hard and exhausting work to accumulate material riches. Actually this makes them slaves of their culture, where material riches serve as the criterion for the respect accorded to others in light of the absence of authentic foundations of self-respect. In this 'development' of culture people have acquired all kinds of unnatural and selfish desires and inclinations that destroy their natural freedom.

Freedom is not only externally directed, but has an internal aspect as well. People cannot be free as long as they have arbitrary goals, desires and inclinations. In Rousseau's view, true freedom means having proper, human goals, in harmony with the social nature of man. The true, essential freedom of man entails living in accordance with the *volonté générale*, free from unnatural selfish inclinations. People are free when they are in agreement with each other, and when they have found true harmony with nature.

This view of freedom as living in accordance with one's true nature appears convincing at first sight. Is an appeal to the 'true nature' or 'essence' of human beings not, however, based on a subjective, normatively tainted selection from the totality of human nature? This may explain how it is possible that Rousseau and Hobbes can propound such completely opposing views of human nature. Is the *volonté générale*, the 'general welfare', indeed something objective? Rousseau does not make it clear what the 'true will' of human beings entails. Neither does he escape from the difficulty of modern thinking: from the facts of man and society, such as man's natural state, norms and ideals cannot be derived. The *volonté générale,* then, entails something arbitrary.

Anarchists have just as convincingly appealed to Rousseau as have adherents of totalitarian regimes. Anarchists often allege that suspension of the state would bring to light the authentic human being. In Rousseau's footsteps they assume that man is good by nature. If only people were freed from suppression by state and society, they would act in a humane way, thereby exposing the superfluity of government. In *Du contrat social* Rousseau, however, tends towards a moderate totalitarian view, rather than to anarchism. He fears that, should the state disappear, the right of the strongest will fill the vacuum, so that the consequences of human egoism will be far worse in anarchy than in the state. Rousseau does not expect people to suddenly reacquire their natural goodness as soon as the state vanishes.

By means of his ideal state, Rousseau wants to steer society and culture in the right direction, back towards natural harmony. He holds the paradoxical view that people can be forced to be free. 'True freedom' requires a way of life based upon authentic aspirations that strongly diverge from the preferences that most people hold on to in their actual lives, such as their desire for personal enrichment at the cost of others. The state, as expression of the *volonté générale*, must, if necessary by force, ensure that people return to their natural existence and rediscover their true freedom. Rousseau's essentialist ideal of freedom, then, runs the risk of turning into totalitarianism.

5.6 French Revolution: The Declaration of the Rights of Man and of the Citizen

Montesquieu's and Rousseau's opposition to revolutionary change did not prevent the occurrence of violent upheaval at the end of the 18th century. Unlike the situation in England, French political life had not gradually adapted itself to the new circumstances. The middle class had acquired great economic power, but this was not translated into political and social rights. Because of maladministration by the king, the national debt had grown enormously. Attempts to convince the nobility and the priests to pay taxes were rejected as a violation of ancient privileges. The middle class was disgruntled because now they were saddled with all the taxes. In the end, in 1789, the Estates General was convened for the first time in a long while. Half of the representatives supported the Third Estate, but because voting took place per estate, they nonetheless were in a minority. For this reason the Third Estate separated from the rest. They named themselves the National Assembly, and swore not to adjourn until France had a constitution. When the king prepared to take action against them, a popular revolt broke out on 14 July, which spilled over to the rural areas where peasants killed many of the nobility. In the same year the liberal *Déclaration des Droits de l'Homme et du Citoyen* (Declaration of the Rights of Man and of the Citizen) was promulgated. In 1791 the Constitution was adopted, and in 1792 the First French Republic was instituted. The king lost his head on the guillotine.[6]

That philosophy can influence social reality was shown when the privileges of the monarchy and the nobility were replaced by the *Déclaration*: the Enlightenment ideals were now actually incorporated in the French Constitution. Although both Rousseau and Montesquieu had rejected the right to revolt, the revolutionaries adopted many of their other ideas. Indeed, the *Déclaration* consisted of a mixture of a liberal constitutional state (à la Montesquieu) and democracy (à la Rousseau).

According to article 1 all men are free and equal in rights (social distinctions are allowed, but exclusively for the sake of the general welfare). According to article 2, the goal of the state is to maintain the natural rights of man, that is, freedom and property. Article 4 gives a liberal definition of freedom: the ability to do everything which does not harm others. Article 5 implies limited government based on the rule of law: the state may only infringe someone's freedom on the basis of a law; and such a law may be enacted only to prevent social harm. Article 16 requires separation of powers as the guarantee of fundamental rights. The protection of natural rights is proclaimed in article 10 (freedom of opinion), article 11 (freedom of expression) and article 17 (protection of property). These articles imply a liberal constitutional state in the sense of Locke and Montesquieu. Beccaria, too, could have been the author of a part of the *Déclaration*. Article 7 prohibits criminal prosecution, arrest, and detention outside of the law. In terms of article 8, the law provides for no other punishments than those that are strictly and clearly necessary. In the same article the principle of legality is laid down: no punishment without a preceding and properly promulgated law. Article 9 prescribes the presumption of innocence, and prohibits coercive measures that are not strictly necessary for the trial of the suspect. These articles replaced the arbitrariness of the criminal law of the pre-revolutionary absolutist state with the rule of law of the constitutional state, at least on paper.

Democracy à la Rousseau is prescribed by article 3 (sovereignty belongs to the people) and article 6 (legislation is the expression of the general will; all citizens have the right to participate personally or by means of their legislators in the enactment of legislation; and have an equal right of access to official positions). Differing from what one finds in Rousseau, the sovereignty of the people is limited by the rule of law: articles 3 and 6 are contextualised by articles 2 and 16, which define the purpose of state and law as the protection of the inalienable human rights of article 1. The same is expressly stipulated in the Preamble to the *Déclaration*:

[6] A recently invented, very effective mechanism, which replaced the imperfect handiwork of the former executioner. The guillotine had humane intentions because the executioner sometimes chopped inaccurately. The effectiveness of this new execution mechanism, however, also encouraged an increase in death penalties, as the next few years would illustrate.

> The Representatives of the French people, organized in the National Assembly, considering that ignorance, forgetfulness, or contempt of the rights of man are the sole causes of public miseries and the corruption of governments, have resolved to set forth in a solemn declaration the natural, inalienable, and sacred rights of man, so that. . .the acts of the legislative power and those of the executive power, may at each moment be compared with the aim of every political institution.

Irrespective of its grand name, the *Déclaration des Droits de l'Homme et du Citoyen* in fact had a limited import. It was primarily a declaration of the freedom rights of the well-off male middle class in opposition to monarchical despotism and the privileges of the traditional estates. Equal rights for women were brushed aside. Social fundamental rights were absent. The draft of the *Déclaration Jacobine* of 1793, which included socio-economic rights, such as the right to work, to payment in the case of labour incapacity, and to education, never came into effect.

Moreover, of the freedom rights of the middle class, little soon remained in revolutionary practice. The reality of the French revolution was far removed from the spirit of the Enlightenment. The horrors that the Parisian revolutionaries indulged in, in the name of the good cause, against real and supposed opponents from reactionary *and* revolutionary circles, are well-known. Less well-known are other brutalities which the anti-revolutionary arguments of Montesquieu and Rousseau had warned against.[7] In Vendée and other parts of France (catholic) revolts against the (secular) revolution were suppressed without mercy.[8] In the name of the revolution and against the exploiters, traditional trading structures in rural areas were destroyed, as a consequence of which countless numbers of people died of starvation. The poor became the victims of the complete devaluation of the *assignat*, the paper money of the Revolution.

The contradictions of the Enlightenment came to the fore most clearly during the rule of Robespierre and his kindred spirits in the reign of terror of 1793. The sadistic side of the Enlightenment was confirmed in a horrific and absurd way. In the name of the good cause Robespierre protected the people by playing rival parties off against each other in order to destroy them. In the meantime, upper limits were laid down for prices and salaries, the decimal system and the Republican calendar were introduced, starting with the year one, as well as a Religion of the Supreme Being (which replaced a Religion of Reason which had been introduced earlier).[9] The ideals of the

---

[7]The famous conservative Burke wrote in *Reflections on the Revolution in France* (1790): The French revolution is a 'strange chaos of levity and ferocity' (1982, p. 92), and amounts to a disregard of the value of the historically grown, extremely complex interaction of forces on which the institutions of society are based.

[8]Around the time of the celebration of the bicentenary of the French revolution in 1989, public conflicts broke out concerning the disappearance from official historiography of what has been termed the first genocide in modern European history. In Vendée, for example, the populations of whole regions were eradicated by drowning them in tightly sealed river boats. According to current estimates, more than a million people met their deaths in these cleansings, which matches the deaths due to famine.

[9]This was based on the pragmatic consideration that the people require religious rituals, even if these do not have any truth value.

Enlightenment had acquired a violent relentlessness. The idea of social engineering of a pliable society was promoted at any cost, as if, with the revolutionary calendar, human history likewise made a new start. Rousseau's ideal of the *volonté générale* degenerated into the exoneration of arbitrary violence against anything which did not seem to fit. In the *Déclaration* the general interest and fundamental rights were still posited on an equal footing, but in practice a still more utopian 'general interest' was implemented at the cost of the fundamental rights of 'opponents of progress': the revolutionary elite set themselves up as the true representatives of the general will of the people, who should not be hindered by constitutional limitations.[10] With the removal and death of Robespierre in 1794, the French revolution had actually run its course. Soon it was time again for monarchical despotism. After a coup d'état in 1799, Napoleon crowned himself Emperor in 1804, and when he was defeated in 1815, a restoration of the pre-revolutionary monarchism took place.

The *Déclaration* nonetheless continued to exercise a great influence as the model of an ideal constitution. Later in the 19th century the liberal fundamental rights and constitutional bodies were taken up anew in the French Constitution, and positivised in the constitutions of most other Western European countries. In the United States of America, after a war of independence against the colonial motherland England, a liberal constitution had been introduced as early as 1787.

5.7 Continuation of the Enlightenment

Napoleon is reported to have said about Rousseau and other intellectuals of the Enlightenment, that the Bourbons (the French kings) should have looked better after their inkpots had they wanted to stay in power. The historical influence of the Enlightenment is indeed significant. Not only the French *Déclaration* and the *Declaration of Independence* of the United States embraced the ideas of the Enlightenment. All modern constitutional states rest on a separation of powers à la Montesquieu. Other characteristics of modern constitutions likewise found their first expression in the Enlightenment. Human rights and fundamental rights were extensively discussed in the *Encyclopédie*. The idea of the social contract has been interpreted differently, but always from the basic idea that a government can derive its authority solely from the consent of the citizens. Only in a democracy is this consensus guaranteed.

The dark side of the French revolution, on the other hand, was inspired by the 'horrible simplifications' of radical Enlightenment philosophers. Think, for example, of Robespierre's elimination of supposed opponents of progress. Around the middle of the 18th century two camps had emerged in the French Enlightenment. Some thinkers were imbued with the statement of Francis Bacon that reality is much

[10]The Cambodia of Pol Pot's *Khmer Rouge* is the most recent in a long chain of repetitions of the deadly utopianism of the Reign of Terror, as well as of the violent paranoia of the defenders of the revolution against the countless enemies and traitors in their own ranks of the 'true society'.

more complex than the human mind can ever grasp. Therefore they had moderate views about the pliability of society. Montesquieu and Rousseau consequently rejected revolution. The moderates were opposed by 'horrible simplifiers' such as De La Mettrie and Holbach. De La Mettrie's idea that everything could be reduced to plain empirical science incited the revolutionaries to radical social engineering. The revolutionary zeal at the end of the 18th century was infused with the idea that, once ancient superstition and ancient morals and customs had been eradicated by science, the 'enlightened' life could be established by means of a radical methodical approach. Robespierre's terror was thus inspired by the radical revolutionary logic that the emancipation of humanity requires the elimination of all human individuals who stand in its way (in the view of the revolutionary vanguard): a physical version of *Ockham's razor*. Political radicalism cost many human lives, also in later revolutions. In reaction, Kant, as Montesquieu before him, would caution that revolutions may induce the beginning of the end of everything (Section 6.4.1). A century later Popper pleaded in the same vein for gradual social evolution rather than radical revolution (Section 8.4).

Modern science did not make politics, law and personal life easier. To be sure, it did provide a new technology that would bring about the industrial revolution and greatly increased man's control of nature. However, as said earlier, technology cannot set its own goals. As a consequence, modern Enlightenment philosophy exhibits a split nature, the progress of amoral science having a dynamic different to the liberal ethics of emancipation. The progress of science cannot underpin apparently reasonable political and moral ideas, such as the ideal of individual autonomy. Montesquieu attempted to reform law on a scientific basis, but was not sufficiently aware of the fact that his normative recommendations could not have empirical foundations.

The narrow morality of political liberalism seems to fit in best with this dilemma, as some Enlightenment philosophers endorsed in the footsteps of Locke. Since a comprehensive ideal of the good life cannot be derived from empirical science, everyone must be free to choose his own norms and values. The enlightened person is aware of the scientific facts of life, and will be able to obtain happiness by the selection of the appropriate means for the achievement of his goals. The liberal Enlightenment, for this reason, draws a principled distinction between the public domain ruled by the state, and the private domain of individual citizens.

Rousseau advocated different views, which had a significant influence on 19th-century philosophers such as Hegel and Marx (Sections 7.3 and 7.4). Both deny that human existence is determined merely by reason. Like Rousseau, they do not draw a rigorous distinction between man, society and state. Both assume that individuals are in continuous interaction with their culture, society and state. The individual must be understood in terms of his social, cultural and political environment, which in turn is determined by individual actions. The interaction, or dialectic, of parts and wholes in the case of Marx clearly ties in with the ideas of Rousseau: Marx similarly states that modern man is the victim of his social circumstances. Only a 'return' to a natural way of life can bring true man to light. Differing from Rousseau, Marx saw a revolutionary end to capitalist society as the only solution. In Rousseau's times there was yet no industrial revolution, no proletariat, and no modern large-scale capitalism, as one finds in the 19th century. This also explains the differences in view between Rousseau and Marx.

Rousseau had a major impact on contemporary *communitarianism* (Section 9.1.2). The communitarian critique of the liberal state emphasises the importance of communities and the supporting role of traditions. Many modern communitarians give the impression of being conservative, by agreeing with Rousseau that man and society cannot be fashioned in accordance with rational prescriptions. More so than Rousseau, they emphasise the importance of tradition, and thus of history, as decisive for individuals and their communities. On the other hand, they share Rousseau's criticism of the liberal separation between society and state. This separation characterises the ahistorical construction of the liberal state in terms of a (hypothetical) contract, in which government and state are viewed as a 'service centre'. At any rate, like Rousseau, contemporary communitarians reject the instrumental view of man and society. Man is more than a compilation of goals and means, which can, in keeping with enlightened rules, be joined together and realised. The state is more than a means for the realisation of the goals of an individual. This is too narrow a view of rationality. True citizenship presupposes identification with society, both for Rousseau and for contemporary communitarians. In other words, 'essential freedom', in the sense of human fulfilment within a community, is more important than liberal 'negative freedom'.

With Beccaria the revolution in criminal law commenced, even though it is not as yet completed. Criminal law, although greatly improved by virtue of the Enlightenment, remains controversial. None of the usual justifications of the administration of criminal justice appears acceptable without reservation. The limits of the rational Enlightenment appear most clearly in this indispensable coping stone of the legal order – the stopgap of criminal law. Rational deterrent theories, such as that of Beccaria, appear insufficiently just and insufficiently implementable. Not only from a philosophical perspective is it unsatisfactory to simply claim that the modern constitutional state cannot maintain itself without criminal law.[11]

Undeniably the Enlightenment has, at least on paper, brought about the victory of freedom, equality and fraternity. Without the concepts and the theories whence it derives, modern constitutional democracy is inconceivable. However, the optimism of the Enlightenment concerning liberation by means of science has in the meantime been dashed. 'Theory and practice go hand in hand' has lost its original sparkle. Hamann, a great critic of the Enlightenment, wrote: 'Think less and live more'.[12]

[11]A radical critique of the Enlightenment reforms under the influence of Beccaria and kindred spirits like Bentham was voiced in the 20th century by Michel Foucault in *Surveiller et punir: Naissance de la prison* (Discipline and Punish: The Birth of the Prison, 1975). According to Foucault, these reforms were simply the result of contingent changes in society in the 18th century which called for a different form of economic calculation from that which had preceded it.

[12]In a letter to Herder, 18 May 1765; see Berlin (2000, p. 255).

Chapter 6
The Synthesis of Kant

6.1 Introduction

As a supporter of the Enlightenment, the German philosopher Immanuel Kant (1724–1804) attempted to design a grand synthesis of the two Enlightenment ideals, scientific and moral progress: He defined the Enlightenment as follows:

> *Enlightenment is man's emergence from his self-incurred immaturity....* The motto of enlightenment is therefore: *Sapere aude*! Have courage to use your *own* understanding! (Kant 1991, p. 54)

Kant realised that these two ideals stand in tension with each other because empirical science is value-free or amoral: no norms ensue from facts. Moreover, if one can explain everything causally, human consciousness included, what then remains of human freedom? To this problem, Kant's philosophical studies of human reason attempt to provide a solution, which had a great impact on philosophy after him.

Kant was a real hero of the spirit. His knowledge was extensive, but originating almost completely from the library. Without ever having travelled, he could tell gripping stories of foreign nations and their customs. Great events did not occur in his life; as a bachelor he was primarily married to his books. With rigorous self-discipline, he dedicated his whole life to philosophy and to science. After his philosophical studies he spent some time as tutor with families from the nobility. From the age of 30 until his death he worked at the Prussian University of Königsberg. There he lectured on a broad spectrum of subjects: philosophy, theology, physics, geography, anthropology, ethics and natural law. His most well-known works are *Kritik der reinen Vernunft* (Critique of Pure Reason, 1781), *Kritik der praktischen Vernunft* (Critique of Practical Reason, 1788) and *Kritik der Urteilskraft* (Critique of Judgment, 1790), which made him famous already during his lifetime. As a liberal, Kant praised the French Revolution, but condemned the succeeding terror.

As the extract above shows, the highest value of man, in Kant's view, lies in his ability of self-legislation. From this portrayal of mankind he deduced a liberal constitution of the state, based on arguments that are also to be found with Locke (Section 4.2). This appears among other things from *Über den Gemeinspruch* (On the Common Saying, 1793), in which Kant responds to the French Revolution.

C.W. Maris, F.C.L.M. Jacobs (eds.), *Law, Order and Freedom*, Law and Philosophy Library 94, DOI 10.1007/978-94-007-1457-1_6, © Springer Science+Business Media B.V. 2011

He subscribes there to the principle of equal freedom as foundation for the state. The restraint imposed by state and law on the autonomous individual is based on a social contract. Unlike Locke, Kant does not see the social contract as a historical or implicit agreement. It is a *hypothetical* contract: a metaphor for the demand that the state must be organised in such a way that it *could* be willed by all free, rational individuals. According to Kant, everyone could agree to a state that protects the rights to the freedom and property of everyone against infringements by others. Because of human autonomy, laws may relate only to the external political and social relations between citizens. Internal matters, such as a philosophy of life, should, on the other hand, remain free from state interference. As autonomous beings legal subjects must be able to establish for themselves what is good for the welfare of their souls.

> No-one can compel me to be happy in accordance with his conception of the welfare of others, for each may seek his happiness in whatever way he sees fit, so long as he does not infringe upon the freedom of others to pursue a similar end (Kant 1991, p. 74).

The government, moreover, does not possess any special authority in the spiritual domain: 'Caesar is not superior to the grammarians.' In short:

> *Right* is the restriction of each individual's freedom so that it harmonizes with the freedom of everyone else (in so far as this is possible within the terms of a general law) (Kant 1991, p. 73).

This does not mean that the individual, in Kant's view, may arbitrarily make use of the negative freedom with which the law leaves him. For private life Kant develops a perfectionist ethics: self-legislation means that you must make *good* use of your freedom. This is, however, pre-eminently a personal responsibility. Should the state force you to act correctly, the act would as a consequence lose its moral character.

How, then, does one establish what the good entails? Modern science cannot furnish such moral knowledge: from facts no norms can be derived. Because of its value-neutral character, science is not capable of providing a foundation for the liberal principles of freedom and equality. Because such principles are nowhere objectively observable, from the perspective of empirical science one should actually regard them as subjective human ideals. But if they are simply subjective, they can make no claim to universal validity. Kant was acutely aware of the fact that the two most important ideals of the Enlightenment, scientific progress and moral emancipation, are in tension with each other. He realised specifically the extent to which science directly threatens the ideal of individual autonomy. Because it wants to explain everything causally, including human thinking and conduct, it leaves no room for free human choices. According to science man is pre-determined by fixed natural laws, not by *self*-legislation.

Kant, nonetheless, attempted to reconcile the two Enlightenment ideals with each other. In doing this he does not fall back onto the classical metaphysical unity of the True and the Good (Chapter 2), because as modern Enlightenment philosopher he rejects the possibility of knowledge of an invisible higher reality, such as Plato's realm of Ideas or the Christian kingdom of God. Modern natural science is, in his view, the only source of reliable knowledge of reality. Kant looked for a more modest solution by allocating to each of science and ethics their own domain: of, respectively, *theoretical reason* and *practical reason.*

In this regard his analysis differs from that of the empiricists (Section 6.2). According to the empiricist model of knowledge, sensuous impressions provide the source of all knowledge: the stream of loose empirical observations is through generalisation organised into general categories. Groups of impressions that are akin are generalised into general concepts, such as 'tree' or 'person'. Likewise, the causal relations between groups of phenomena are inventoried by the generalisation of observations. When one observes that two groups of sensory phenomena with great regularity follow upon each other, one concludes that the first is the cause of the second. If knowledge commences thus, the empiricists say, then judgments about knowledge must be controllable with reference to empirical observation. One should be able to analyse complex judgments of knowledge by means of simpler judgments which refer directly to observable reality, such as 'this wooden door is brown'. Judgments that cannot be tested in this way, such as 'God is great', 'the soul is immortal' or 'lying is bad', can be disposed of as metaphysical fantasy. The rationalistic view of philosophers like Plato that true knowledge is based exclusively on reason is, in this view, a chimera.

However, if an adherent of the Enlightenment takes seriously the empiricist criterion of knowledge, he loses his two ideals. He would, in the first place, have to acknowledge that his ideal of moral emancipation is based on fantasy. In the second place, natural science would similarly fall from its pedestal, whereas the success of this same science is the very source of inspiration for the empiricists. Indeed, two fundamental characteristics of a scientific law in the form, 'whenever x occurs, this causes y', cannot be derived from observation. *Causes* are not observable: in fact, one only experiences that y always follows *after* x. Moreover, the *whenever* cannot be derived from empirical experience: natural laws claim to apply to the past and future, but one's experience relates only to the relations between x and y that occurred in the past. Actually, in empirical observation only successive, disconnected impressions occur. The organisation of these impressions is the work of consciousness, and must, therefore, strictly speaking, be banished to the same fantasy world as metaphysical judgments about the First Cause or the Eternal (that is, god). This would mean the end of science.

As it happens, Kant saves *both* science *and* morality by fully acknowledging, contrary to empiricism, the constructing role of human consciousness. It is human reason that makes scientific knowledge possible by organising the chaos of observations into general categories and causal relations. Reason, in other words, precedes observation, and, therefore, does not itself have to be justified with reference to empirical observation. Up to this point Kant goes in the direction of rationalism. At the same time Kant accords to reason more modest capacities than the classical rationalists: one cannot exclusively by way of thinking, separate from empirical reality, arrive at knowledge of the world. In brief, human consciousness provides the structure, that is, organises the empirical phenomena into general concepts as well as into relations of causal regularity; sensory experience provides the content or material of knowledge. In accordance with the ideal of natural science, judgments about such content must, therefore, be testable against empirical observation; up to this point Kant agrees with the empiricists. Metaphysical judgments concerning non-observable notions, such as God, do not furnish any knowledge.

By means of this manoeuvre Kant succeeded in saving the scientific ideal of the Enlightenment, but at a price. If scientific knowledge is partly based on the constructions of human consciousness, it has only relative value. It only furnishes knowledge of reality as it appears to our consciousness, not of reality in itself as it exists separate from observation and human organisation. This, however, also has an important advantage: with the same manoeuvre with which Kant relativises the validity of science, he secures a space for ethics. The causal relations into which science organises reality are after all likewise a human construction. Reality as such may look quite different. Whether this is the case we cannot possibly know. In Kant's view, we, however, do have an indication that there is more, that is, a moral reality.

This indication is to be found in our moral consciousness (Section 6.3). Our conscience speaks to us in the form of *unconditional* precepts: 'Thou shalt!' You should not lie or kill, also not, or especially not, when it would be in your own interest. 'Unconditionally' in other words means: irrespective of the empirical circumstances. Kant, therefore, believes that moral consciousness does not allow itself to be explained empirically. Take, for example, the causal, empirical explanation of Hobbes's natural law (Section 4.1). According to Hobbes, individual human conduct and thinking are caused by the natural urge to survive. This pursuit motivates individuals to institute a peaceful legal order via a social contract with foundational rules, such as 'you may not kill'. The duty of obedience of individuals to a rule such as this thus applies only conditionally: only in so far as this assists them to survive. Therefore, in the state of nature killing is allowed. As a result, however, Hobbes cannot explain why one has the awareness that killing is *never* good (except in self-defence). In his empirical theory of morality the moral motive is, at most, *one* of the many conflicting inclinations, not a moral law that stands above all others.

Kant concludes from this that human reason entails two forms of judgment. Via our *theoretical reason* we construct a scientific, causal-explanatory worldview. Apart from this, we can also via our *practical reason* establish how, irrespective of our empirical selfish motives, we should act in the world. In our scientific reality we create order by way of explanatory *natural laws*, whereas in the moral world we are guided by the *moral law* as this finds expression in our conscience. We can accordingly view our conduct in two ways. When we view things from a scientific perspective we assume that all our conduct is determined by a complex of preceding causes: by education, friends, mood, etc. From the perspective of this deterministic viewpoint it is difficult to hold someone accountable for his actions: he could after all not have done otherwise. Such a causal explanation is, however, simply an organisation which we impose upon the world, and, therefore, does not exclude other possibilities. When we subject our conduct to a moral law, such as 'you may not lie', we assume that we *can* also act in terms of it, even if moral truth works out badly for us. In other words, if we adopt the moral point of view, we assume that we are *free* to choose the good as well as the bad, and that we are responsible for the choice.

The next step is to ask what exactly the moral law entails. Because Kant rejects metaphysics, he cannot consult traditional morality which appeals to God's Ten Commandments, or the ethics of Plato's ideal state. The only thing that we can know about the Moral Law, in Kant's view, is the form in which it appears to our moral consciousness: as an unconditional and universally valid law or precept (*Categorical Imperative*). Still, this provides a sufficient basis on which to subject moral views to a formal, critical test: can you will that the reason you give for a specific action should also serve as a general law which regulates the actions of every person in such circumstances? This test is called the *principle of universalisability*. Suppose that, being in a bad mood, I stab someone to death in a dark alley. On being asked about it I, lacking conscience, give as reason: 'I killed him because he bothered me.' You cannot generalise (*universalise*) this reason into a universal law, a generally valid reason for the actions of everyone: 'everyone may always kill all others who bother him.' Everyone, including you yourself, can then become the next victim. Ultimately no one will remain, so that the general law is annulled. My reason can be justified only from the point of view of *my* personal inclinations. However, a law applies irrespective of the person concerned.

This equality before the moral law Kant also expresses as follows: you may never use other human beings merely as a means for your own ends; you must always also view them as autonomous beings with their own ends. In this way his formal test, in addition, acquires a more specific substantial content: all people are of equal value. As in the case of the conflict between freedom and causality, Kant's separation of the scientific and the moral points of view enables a synthesis in the conflict between empirical inequality and moral equality: although all people as empirically observable individuals have different characteristics, as moral, autonomous persons they have an equal value.

According to Kant's natural-law doctrine, law is derived from this general ethics (Section 6.4). In their substance, law and morality overlap, because the core of law must consist of moral rules that are necessary for peaceful co-existence. These are the same rules that were identified by Locke: respect each other's bodily integrity as well as property and freedom rights (Section 4.2). The function of law is to make it possible for people to live together, and law is, therefore, a necessary condition for the further moral perfection of human beings, as is required by ethics. This is why Kant regards coercion as necessary to maintain legal order, although from a general ethical point of view it deprives action of its moral character. For this reason state coercion must remain restricted to the minimum: it must, in terms of the social contract, merely align the negative freedom of one person with the equal freedom of all others. Kant's liberal, narrow state morality thus stands in the service of a perfectionist, broad personal morality.

6.2 Theory of Knowledge: Synthesis of Empiricism and Rationalism

Kant wrote his great work on theoretical knowledge, the *Critique of Pure Reason*, only at the age of 56. When he started with philosophy he was, like many of his contemporaries, a faithful follower of Leibniz and Wolff, thinkers who had elaborated on the rationalism of Descartes. Like Descartes (Section 3.4) these rationalists were of the view that all knowledge stems from human reason. They rejected the senses as an unreliable source of knowledge. At a certain moment, Kant, however, came into contact with the empiricism and scepticism of Hume, who rejected rational knowledge as an indemonstrable illusion. After he had digested Hume, Kant arrived at his synthesis of the two movements. For purposes of a proper understanding of Kant's theory of knowledge, we first give some attention to Hume.

6.2.1 The Influence of the Empiricism of Hume

The Scottish philosopher David Hume (1711–1776) wrote his primary work, *A Treatise of Human Nature,* when he was only in his twenties. Because the book was for the most part met with a lack of understanding, he dedicated a great part of his life to give an elaboration of the main aspects of his thinking in a more accessible and less offensive way.

Hume, like Locke, revolts against the rationalistic theory of knowledge of Descartes. General concepts are not inherent to reason, but come into being by way of generalisation and abstraction from sensory experience. Hume refines Locke's description of the content of consciousness (see Section 4.2.5) in various respects. He, for instance, draws a distinction between *impressions* and *ideas*. The image that I have of a chestnut tree at the moment that I actually observe it ('impression') is stronger and more vivid than when I later recall it in my mind's eye (recalling or imagining as 'idea'). *Ideas* are faded copies of earlier *impressions*. We suppose that this happens because the chestnut tree in the first instance, together with the light and our eyes, is an antecedent in the causal process by means of which the impression comes into being. Hume does not, however, want to start from indemonstrable suppositions; he wants to stick to that which is given to our consciousness, and that is the powerful and vivid image of the tree, not the tree itself.

Hume develops, just like Locke, an empiricist epistemology: general concepts come into being by means of generalisation from sensory observations. Sensory impressions, for example the colour black, can leave behind a 'simple idea', a copy in the memory or imagination. From the material of such simple ideas, 'combined ideas' can subsequently be formed. Hence the concept 'coal' is a combination of the simple empirical characteristics hard, black, etc. Hume uses this investigation into the *origins* of our ideas to arrive at a *criterion of legitimation* for claims concerning knowledge. One must in the following way verify whether claims of knowledge in an assertion are justified. One must first take apart the combined ideas of the assertion to arrive at the constitutive simple ideas. After this analysis one must verify whether all elements of the assertion refer unambiguously to sensory givens. If not, then one has to do with pseudo-knowledge. Metaphysical assertions, such as 'God has the shape of a sphere', can, for example, not be tested against empirical observation, assertions, such as 'it rained on 21 August 2008 in Edinburgh', can.

In addition, Hume also regards as justified, knowledge of the relations between ideas, such as that of mathematics and logic, although these do not stem from sensory experience. This kind of knowledge is, however, only concerned with the ideas themselves, not with the reality outside of the ideas. Thus,'2+2=4', or 'it rains or it does not rain' (formally expressed as 'either p, or not-p') are fully determined by the content of the concepts that are used (in the last instance, by the concepts 'or' and 'not'). This appears from the fact that their denial ('it rains *and* it doesn't rain') results in a contradiction. The judgment 'it rains or it does not rain' is *necessarily* true, irrespective of whether it rains in reality.

Judgments that pretend to concern reality, but that are based merely on reasoning about ideas, such as 'God', which cannot be established by sensory observation, do not, on the other hand, furnish any knowledge.

> If we take in our hand any volume; of divinity or school metaphysics, for instance; let us ask, *Does it contain any abstract reasoning concerning quantity or number?* No. *Does it contain any experimental reasoning concerning matter of fact and existence?* No. Commit it then to the flames: for it can contain nothing but sophistry and illusion (Hume 2007, p. 144).

However, suppose that the book in question is Newton's *Principia Mathematica*. This classical work on natural science contains many causal laws. The compound ideas of causality and regularity do not, however, comply with Hume's test. In our observation only the following is given: a billiard ball comes rolling across the billiard table, it touches another ball, it comes to a standstill, and the other one starts rolling. Irrespective of how many times we have observed this, it is never sufficient to be able to say that the movement of the first ball *causes* that of the second, only that the movement of the second regularly follows on that of the first. Something like a separate 'cause' is not given in the observation. When we say that the first movement causes the second, we do not only mean that the second follows regularly, but also that it *necessarily* follows upon the first. The idea of necessity is, however, misplaced here: one can easily imagine, without contradiction, that the second ball does *not* start moving (like the billiard table, when a ball hits its cushion). Therefore, Hume decides, we must replace the idea of causation with (or interpret it as) that of 'regular succession'. Tested against Hume's empiricist criterion of knowledge, the laws of natural science, however, encounter a second problem. Regular succession only relates to the past: we have exclusively observed that up until now the one has followed upon the other; our observations, thus, do not prove that the same would occur the next time around. A general law: 'given circumstances O, if a, then also b', always exceeds experience. It is simply an assumption that the sun will rise again tomorrow. 'Induction' (deciding on a general law based on a number of particular examples) is actually an invalid type of reasoning. Science, moreover, assumes that it describes and explains a reality of material things outside of human consciousness. However, as already indicated, this assumption cannot be empirically proven either: actually we only observe *pictures* of reality, not reality itself. Consistent with Hume's empiricist criterion of knowledge one may, thus, not assume that material things exist outside of our consciousness which cause our sensory impressions, and that these things are connected by causal relations of regularity.

Thus Hume is confronted with the question whether convictions that cannot be abandoned by human beings, can actually be justified. The universal causal laws of Newton's natural science lose their foundation in Hume's epistemology, whereas natural science is regarded as the very model of reliable knowledge. In general, every intelligent anticipation of future occurrences by human beings is based on observations of the past – plus the assumption that the established regularity will continue. All knowledge deriving from observation is, furthermore, based on the examination of what is given to us in our consciousness – plus the assumption that these data are generated by external objects. In both instances the assumption can never be justified. When properly considered, the senses actually provide us with no certain knowledge, but only a stream of separate, incoherent, observations, Hume sceptically concludes.

In practice, things nevertheless work better than could be expected. People are programmed in line with inductive reasoning; a child who once burnt himself by the fireplace, will not do so a second time. (And thus not reason: 'From one example, one may not draw general conclusions; that my sister-in-law cannot drive, after all does not prove that all women are bad drivers.') If this was not the case, the human race would long ago have ceased to exist: it is, therefore, a *useful* custom. (Note that the previous sentence implies inductive reasoning, too.)

6.2.2 Kant's Epistemology

The work of Hume made clear to Kant that reason, the human capacity of thinking, can never serve as the only basis for knowledge and science. With Hume, Kant is convinced that the content of all knowledge and science must be derived from observable reality. Reason on its own leads to unverifiable thought constructions. The rationalism of Descartes (Section 3.4) is, therefore, untenable. On the other hand, Kant regards the sceptical conclusions that Hume draws from his empiricism as too radical. In his view there is specifically *one* indisputable example of certain knowledge: natural science. Never before has a theoretical system after all been so successful in the explanation and prediction of occurrences in reality. At the same time Kant is of the view that objective moral knowledge still is possible.

> Two things fill the mind with ever new and increasing admiration and reverence, the more often and more steadily one reflects on them: *the starry heavens above me and the moral law within me* (Kant 1977, p. 133).

On this basis, Kant arrives at a position between empiricism and rationalism.

Kant confirms that in the scientific worldview no place exists for an objective ethics, and, equally, not for human freedom and rationality, because the world of natural science consists of causally determined, aimless and amoral processes. As Hume had indicated, an unbridgeable gap exists between the domains of 'is' and 'ought'. Through his synthesis of empiricism and rationalism Kant nonetheless wants to recognise natural science as the source of universally valid knowledge, and at the same time securely posit an objective ethics as well as the rationality and freedom of man. Kant attempts to give to each of natural science and ethics its own space, by making a sharp distinction between, on the one hand, the domain of empirically observable nature, and, on the other, of rationality and freedom. In the first-mentioned domain, natural laws apply, in the second, moral laws. This division plays an important role both in his epistemology and in his ethics. He formulates his epistemology, which concerns the possibility of scientific knowledge, in his *Critique of Pure Reason*. The possibility of an objective ethics is dealt with in his *Grundlegung zur Metaphysik der Sitten* (Groundwork of the Metaphysics of Morals, 1785) and in his *Critique of Practical Reason*.

In contrast with the scepticism of Hume which undermines the claims to knowledge of natural science, Kant is convinced that natural science provides irrefutably certain knowledge; he regards Newton's natural science as *the* example of objective knowledge. Kant concludes from this that Hume's empiricist epistemology cannot be completely accurate: the non-empirical part of our knowledge must stem from a source other than the senses. Kant's question, therefore, becomes: how is this knowledge possible? What are its conditions of possibility?

In answering this question Kant draws a distinction between three types of judgment: *synthetic* judgments a priori, *synthetic* judgments *a posteriori*, and *analytical* judgments *a priori*. Synthetic judgments a priori furnish us with new knowledge by combining the data of our experience with each other ('synthesising'); but they, in addition, contain 'a priori' elements, preceding all experience, specifically because of their generalising character. 'All events have causes' is one example of a synthetic judgment a priori: it provides knowledge which is certain, independent of all experience. Concrete knowledge of the world, for example, concerning which causes bring about which events, are on the other hand, still synthetic a posteriori: their accuracy appears only after ('posterior') empirical observation. An example of a synthetic judgment a posteriori is: 'In Amsterdam a Royal Palace is to be found.' The truth of this judgment can be established only with reference to empirical experience. It is not fixed a priori. The correctness of analytical judgments, on the other hand, simply follows from the meaning of the concepts used – thus detached from experience. For this reason an analytical judgment is likewise always a priori: its correctness is independent of what occurs in reality. This form of a priori knowledge only provides insight into our concepts.

Should Hume have used this terminology, then he would, in contrast with Kant, have said that synthetic judgments a priori – judgments which provide knowledge independently of sensory observation – cannot be reduced to empirical experience and are, therefore, senseless. What is indeed meaningful is the other kind of a priori judgments, the analytical, which exclusively express relations between ideas and do not furnish any knowledge of reality. Judgments concerning reality are in terms of Hume's empiricist epistemology always synthetically a posteriori. This would, however, undermine the claims of natural science.

To this, Kant responds with the statement that our reason also plays a role in the knowledge of natural science: it provides the formal a priori structure with which we organise the multitude of our sensory impressions. Kant links up with Hume's conclusion that the senses as such provide nothing more than an incoherent stream of perceptions. He adds to this that reason brings about an objective order and unity in these perceptions. Reason orders the chaos of perceptions into coherent things and events in space and time, and discerns causal relations between them. 'Space', 'time' and 'causality' are, therefore, not themselves empirical data, but are preceding, organising principles of our minds, which structure sensory givens.

Kant nonetheless does not regard these principles as subjective in Hume's sense: they indeed form a substantial part of our knowledge. Kant contends this with the statement that their general validity must necessarily be presupposed, because they belong to the conditions of possibility of natural science. Should one not recognise them as basic elements of our knowledge, natural science would be impossible; but natural science specifically provides certain knowledge; therefore, these principles of the mind must also be objective. In Kant's view, Hume's empiricist theory of knowledge is, therefore, too limited.

This does not mean that Kant in the end reverts to rationalism. He rejects the rationalist assertion that the mind can completely on its own arrive at true knowledge. Mere rational reasoning, according to Kant, leads to contradiction and indemonstrable thought constructions. Assertions concerning a non-observable world of Ideas, or concerning God, are based on unfounded speculation. Our knowledge is limited to the world that we observe via our senses, albeit that our mind provides in this respect the formal structure. The role of reason limits itself to the organisation of the raw material that the senses provide.

Knowledge, therefore, neither stems directly from reason as the rationalists contended, nor exclusively from the senses as the empiricists maintained, but from cooperation between them.

This, however, also means that natural science only has a limited validity. It is, after all, partly the product of the structuring activity of our own consciousness. The above-mentioned organisational principles constitute, so to speak, glasses that we can never take off. How the world is in itself, disconnected from these principles, we can, therefore, never know. We only know the world as it appears to us, or as Kant says, the 'phenomenal world'.[1] Reality as such, which he refers to as the *Ding an sich* or 'noumenal world' (ideal world), lies beyond out reach.

The validity of natural science is thus indeed universal, but limited to the world as it appears to us via our consciousness. Hence Kant provides space for an objective

[1]Phenomenon = something as it appears to us.

ethics in addition to an objective science. Science after all leaves open the *possibility* that the world-in-itself is indeed rational, purposive and valuable. The world of natural science only shows blind, amoral processes, which have no aim, but are determined by the causal impact of accidental external forces. 'Causality' is, however, an organising principle of the human mind. For this reason causal natural laws apply to the world only in so far as *man* organises it. This leaves open the possibility that the world as it really is, is not causally determined, but has a rational and moral character. Perhaps it does have a purpose and is valuable. According to Kant's epistemology, we can, however, have no knowledge of such an eventual moral world. Substantive knowledge separate from sensory experience, is after all beyond our reach. Kant nonetheless contends that there is an indication that the world as it really is indeed has such a moral and rational character: we experience a moral awareness that prescribes conduct of an impartial nature to us. According to Kant, this cannot be causally explained (for example, on the basis of our instinct for survival). Therefore, this awareness must refer to a non-causally determined moral sphere, although this is not knowable to us any further.

Kant's theory thus amounts to saying that natural science does indeed produce generally valid knowledge, but that this only relates to what he refers to as the phenomenal reality: the world as it appears in our organising mind. Our mind specifically organises sensory perceptions *from the viewpoint of causality*: everything that happens has a cause. Phenomenal reality does not limit itself to external nature; internal nature, for example someone's character, is also determined by general causal laws. But irrespective of the extent to which empirical reality is causally determined, in Kant's view this does not affect the fact that people make themselves and others accountable for their actions. The 'person', in the sense of the responsible subject, escapes from the causal laws of natural science; when one puts it like this, one adopts the viewpoint of freedom and responsibility.

6.3 Ethics

6.3.1 The Categorical Imperative

In his *Groundwork of the Metaphysics of Morals* Kant starts with a description of moral actions: what does someone do who acts morally; in which way do moral actions distinguish themselves from other forms of action? A person who acts morally, according to Kant, obeys an absolute precept, for example: 'do not steal', even if stealing has all kinds of benefits. Differing from what Hobbes contends, moral consciousness is disconnected from calculation on the basis of rational self-interest.

Kant analyses moral consciousness in terms of a 'good will', which cannot stem from the empirical, causally determined world. An example may explain this notion. Suppose that I want to return to the owner a book I borrowed from him. He seems to have absconded from his apartment so that my intentions cannot be carried out.

According to Kant this does not devalue at all the purity of my motive; the world does not morally regress because of this incident. Suppose, on the other hand, that I want to go and steal a rare book. I go to the bookshop where I recently saw it being displayed. It appears to no longer be there, and I cannot carry out my intentions. In this instance I exhibit an evil resolve and the world, from a moral point of view, has experienced harm, even though on the face of it nothing happened. For the goodness of the good will it does not matter whether the act actually succeeds; for the badness of the evil will it does not matter whether the act actually fails. Does the good will, therefore, not have to pursue results? It does indeed: when I intend to give back a borrowed book, I must at the same time (attempt to) do it: this result must be intended. But when external circumstances have the consequence that my intentions fail, this does not negatively affect my moral intent. It is the same with bad intent: when the intended result is not achieved, it does not change the bad will into something good.

After his analysis of the good will, Kant articulates the moral motivation in different terminology: someone who acts in a moral way does not act on the basis of 'inclinations', but on that of 'duty'. How is this to be understood? Kant gives some examples: (1) most people like being alive and do not have the inclination to commit suicide; (2) some people are plagued by bad luck and entertain the desire of making an end to their lives; (3) many people are by nature friendly and tend to bring pleasure to others; (4) some people are so preoccupied with their own misery that they cannot bring themselves to have any interest in the fate of others. These are all causally determined 'inclinations' and they are, according to Kant, morally neutral: people find these in themselves and can do nothing about the fact that they are like this; these are givens, in the same way as rain and sunshine are givens. But in contrast to the weather, these inclinations do form the object of a moral judgment: one can distance oneself from them, and ask oneself whether it is a good thing to give free rein to these inclinations. Someone who, on the basis of such a consideration, does not seek to exercise control over inclinations 1 and 3, but does so in relation to inclinations 2 and 4, acts by definition not 'based on inclination', but 'out of duty'.

The question then arises what exactly 'duty' means. Kant analyses the notion with the assistance of two new terms, *autonomy* and *heteronomy* (self-legislation and legislation by others, or, less literally but more precisely, rational self-determination and causal determination by external and internal forces). Inclinations are heteronomous: they force themselves onto people; when you do nothing about them, they drag you along. They belong to the causally determined world. Duty is autonomous: after one has distanced oneself from the given inclinations and subjected them to a moral judgment, one either endorses or rejects them deliberately and voluntarily. They belong to a non-causally determined sphere of free, rational choice. What duty entails can similarly be expressed as follows: inclinations are directed at things (I want to stay alive, or rather not; I want to bring pleasure to others, or rather not), whereas duty is directed at the inclinations: 'Can I really will my inclinations? If not, then it is my duty to distance myself from them.' Stated somewhat more formally, inclinations are preferences of the first order (they relate to things external to themselves); the sense of duty is a preference of the second order (it relates to the preferences of the first order). By way of the preferences of the first order, people are defined (heteronomy), whereas the preferences of the second order prescribe the law for the preferences of the first order (and are, therefore, autonomous). Not all preferences of the second order are, however, autonomous preferences. Suppose that each time when I want to consume a portion of chips, the spirit of my deceased father whispers to me that I should refrain from doing so. 'I only want to do what my father allows me to do' is then a heteronomous preference of the second order. Also, my ranking of preferences may again be determined by my heteronomous inclinations. Kant's sense of duty acquires an autonomous character because the given preferences (and, thus, also the given preferences of the second order) are subjected to a *moral* judgment. How does this happen?

In order to subject the given inclinations to a moral judgment, one must first express them in words, in relation to which Kant introduces the term *maxim*. Maxims are subjective principles of action; they give expression to elements of what one could call someone's personal way of life. I, for example, stand before the choice of giving back borrowed money or not. Then I either act according to the rule: 'I give back borrowed money', or according to the rule: 'I only give back borrowed money if the owner would treat me very badly should I keep the money.' Kant at this point proposes a thought experiment: only those rules are morally justified that you can will as *universal* rules for everyone in similar circumstances. From an egotistical perspective the second rule is perhaps the best. The moral perspective, which attests to rationality and impartiality, however, produces a different outcome: which one of the two rules can I will as a *general* law that is universally observed? Only the first rule, because I cannot will that borrowed goods in general never be given back (including when I myself am the lender). In the balancing of a rule, such as 'I never kill others' against 'I kill others when it comes to it', things are even clearer. As general rule for everyone the latter rule would have the consequence that ultimately no one remains to observe the rule. In the case of general observation, this rule would thus annul itself. In short, as a general rule, it is not even conceivable.

Maxims are thus subjected to a moral judgment. A person who answers the call of moral judgments, complies with what Kant calls the *categorical imperative*, an unconditional rule which often goes against one's own interests. He formulates it as follows: 'Act only according to maxims of which you can at the same time will that they become a general law.' Kant opposes this categorical imperative to *hypothetical imperatives* or conditional rules. These are rules of the following type: *if* you want to achieve this, *then* you must do that (if you want to boil an egg, you have to heat the water to 100°C (or 212°F)). Such prescriptions are conditional, because their execution depends on the desire of someone to pursue the given aim: they take their point of departure in given inclinations, and do not subject these to a moral judgment. Morality, in Kant's view, consists, by contrast, of rules that apply absolutely. You should not steal, even if you strongly want to do this. Morality, moreover, provides *universal* rules or imperatives: everyone who finds himself in the same situation should act in the same way. Via moral consciousness, man hence gives to himself laws of a generally valid and unconditional import.

How must the categorical imperative be understood? It is often interpreted as follows. After one has formulated a maxim (for example, the maxim that one does not have to give back borrowed money), one attempts to imagine everyone acting in accordance with such a maxim. If one can think and/or will the situation that would then occur, the maxim is morally allowed; if not, it is prohibited. However, a situation in which no one gives back borrowed money, and in which, therefore, after some time no money is lent out anymore, can very well be *thought* without contradiction, in so far as there is nothing contradictory about a society that does not make use of money. Furthermore, that I would not *will* such a situation in which no money is lent out, would only be the case when I, for example, have an irregular income so that I sometimes have to borrow money. But if I am a wealthy person, I would have no objection at all to a world in which no money is lent.

When one adopts this interpretation of Kant's categorical imperative, the imperative ultimately rests on a conviction on the part of Kant that some institutions, such as money and property, are of great social importance. The problem is that this interpretation makes of Kant a utilitarian: he assumes the social utility of various institutions, and calls actions morally justified when they support these useful institutions, whereas actions that endanger useful institutions are immoral. In this way, nothing remains of the autonomy of moral judgment. Morality must then adjust itself to social utility in the 'phenomenal' world.

It is, thus, better to interpret Kant's categorical imperative as follows: the contradiction in thinking or willing does not lie *in* the imagined general practice, but *between* the imagined general practice and my intention to *continue* my action with its *original* aim within this practice. If no one returns borrowed money, I equally cannot call on others to lend me money; it is inconceivable that in a situation in which everyone knows that no one gives back borrowed money, *I* would succeed in borrowing money from someone. I can thus only act with success in accordance with my maxim not to give back borrowed money, when (most) others do *not* act according to the maxim. This means that I parasitise in these circumstances on an existing practice upheld by the actions of others. But with what right do I grant myself certain benefits that I at the same time cannot extend to everyone? Evidently I am not acting on the basis of a moral motive, but of 'inclination': I simply stand in a special relation to myself. The categorical imperative prohibits making exceptions to general rules to the advantage of persons with whom one has a special affective relationship (oneself or those one likes), to the detriment of others to whom this does not apply. Interpreted thus, the categorical imperative is a maxim of the second order: a *meta-maxim*: 'I only want to act in accordance with maxims that can be generalised.' Because of this, Kant's ethics is referred to as 'formal': the moral value of people's actions is not determined by their 'substance', because it leads to an objective that is considered good, but by its 'form', because the underlying maxims can be generalised or are *universalisable*.

The categorical imperative, presented in this formal way ('Act only according to maxims of which you can at the same time will that they become a general law'), is formulated by Kant in a less formal manner as well: 'Never use others merely as a means for your own ends, but also respect them as persons with their own ends.' In this formulation the moral motive finds very clear expression. An example in criminal law: one might punish people simply because this has a preventative effect on the actions of others. When someone messes in the street, you could give the person a very severe punishment, for instance the death penalty, so that other people would in future also refrain from doing so. Thus one could serve the general interest at the cost of one individual (the severely punished polluter). The ethics of Kant prohibits this because then one person is used as a means for the welfare of others.

When we attempt to express this formulation of the categorical imperative as a meta-maxim, we arrive at something like this: 'I only want to act according to maxims which are compatible with the respect of all people as equals.' Kant's thought experiment gives expression to the unity and equality of all people from a moral perspective: we place ourselves in the position of others as if we ourselves were those other people. Thought of as empirical, 'phenomenal' people, we are all very different. All individuals in observable reality, moreover, have their own subjective inclinations and preferences, which result in strong mutual tensions. The categorical imperative wants to show how we can annul these differences: as 'noumenal' rational beings we are all equally subjects of the same moral law. For this reason we may never use other people merely as instruments for our own ends, but we must always respect them also as fellow human beings, that is, as ends in themselves.

On the basis of the (variedly expressed) categorical imperative we can establish which rules that regulate our actions are morally just, and which not. In Kant's view, the correct rules form a coherent whole, which because of their rational character apply always and everywhere. However diverging human lives and cultures may be, fundamental rules, such as that people may not be abused and murdered, that promises should be kept, that damage should be compensated, and that need should be alleviated, apply universally. The general realisation of such rules, where people respect each other as ends in themselves, in the sense explained, would lead to what Kant calls the *Reich der Zwecke* (Kingdom of Ends). This is the ideal society in which all people are fully rational, are treated as ends in themselves and in which they can realise their personal ends in harmony. In the Kingdom of Ends we would be really free, free from the unwanted interference of others, and free to do what we ourselves want to. The Kingdom of Ends appears to exist only in our moral imagination, as a far-removed ideal. It has no empirical reality: in time and space it appears inconceivable. My actual life is largely determined by empirical conflicts with other people (and with reality). In the ideal, but conceivable, Kingdom of Ends, the conflicts with other people are, however, suspended. Kant does not say that we can imagine the historical realisation of this *Reich*, but that we should nonetheless pursue it, by controlling our desires and by acting as if we live in such Kingdom.

Kant's Kingdom of Ends thus appears to be a liberal version of the Aristotelian ideal of social harmony, supplementing Aristotle's social ethics with individual autonomy and its associated negative freedom rights. This liberal twist does not imply that Kant is a supporter of a narrow morality in the private domain as well. His emphasis on the purity of the moral intention fits in badly with this. Kant's ethics is summarised by himself somewhere as follows: *You must strive for the perfection of yourself and the happiness of others*. This implies *essential freedom*: freedom *from* selfish tendencies *for the sake of* moral rationality and impartiality. At stake is, therefore, a perfectionist ethics which the individual imposes on himself – which, however, in the public, political and social spheres leads to a non-perfectionist, liberal, 'narrow' morality, to which people enjoin each other. In public life only 'negative freedom' applies.

That social and political morality cannot be perfectionist, can, in keeping with Kant, easily be illustrated. Suppose that people would have the duty to bring each other to moral perfection (and that this task is carried out by the government), then the success of the intention would at the same time entail its failure. After all, if people under the pressure of others or out of fear of punishment by the state adhere to morality, they would not be acting with a purely moral motive. People cannot lay hold of the autonomous moral will of others, nor can the state. For this reason only the duties that people impose upon themselves can have a perfectionist nature; the social duties to which people subject each other, are non-perfectionist: they only relate to external conduct. We can even say that Kant does not perceive of social morality as perfectionist in order to create space for individuals to live a life of perfection without state coercion. This comes to the fore most clearly in Kant's legal philosophy (Section 6.4).

6.3.2 Kant's Deontological Ethics Versus Utilitarianism

On account of his clear separation of the domains of the factual and the normative, Kant opposes every form of ethics that seeks its foundation in empirical nature. Kant rejects specifically the normative ethics of *utilitarianism*, which is based on the factual human pursuit of pleasure.[2] As criterion for the moral goodness of an action, utilitarianism holds that it must contribute optimally to the greatest happiness of the greatest number. This means that the determination of the proper action in a concrete case is not fixed a priori, but depends on ends-means calculations. One must, for example, attempt to estimate to what extent the telling of a lie or of the truth would cause happiness.

[2] Utilitarianism is discussed in detail in Section 7.2. Here we view it from a Kantian perspective.

In Kant's view, this is in complete conflict with the nature of ethics. Ethics after all manifests itself to us in the form of unconditional universal precepts, or as a categorical imperative. 'Thou shalt not lie' is, for example, an absolute principle of such fundamental importance that it applies irrespective of the consequences. The universal import of the rule implies that its validity cannot be dependent on changing empirical circumstances, such as human happiness. Furthermore, the utilitarian criterion 'The greatest happiness of the greatest number' can in the case of conflicting interests lead to the choice of actions that advance the happiness of a great majority at the cost of a minority or an individual person. Imagine, for example, that the happiness of 90% of the population would be greatly enhanced by keeping 10% unemployed. According to utilitarianism, one would have to actually do this, because comparatively the unhappiness of the minority is much smaller. Measured against Kant's categorical imperative, however, this would be pre-eminently immoral: one uses some persons merely as means for the happiness of others.

Kant, moreover, contends against the utilitarian consequentialist ethics that this would lead to great uncertainty. We after all possess only deficient knowledge of nature. Calculations to establish which conduct would bring about maximal happiness are, therefore, based on expectations that are too disputable.

Utilitarianism is, moreover, in conflict with the law-like character of ethics. If one had to keep account of all changing circumstances, one would continually have to make exceptions to moral rules. The categorical imperative, on the other hand, applies absolutely, without exception or internal contradiction. In Kant's view, real moral conflicts do not exist. They are simply incorrect applications of the categorical imperative, which can be attributed to irrational factors, such as our empirical inclinations and desires.

6.4 Legal Philosophy

6.4.1 Law and Ethics

Kant's legal philosophy flows directly from his ethics. He regards law as a central subdivision of ethics, which has the specific function of making human co-existence possible. He is, therefore, an adherent of the doctrine of natural law, albeit that he interprets it in his own way. Man lives in communities, in relationships of mutual dependence and influence. Only in a more or less ordered community – and thus not in a Hobbesian 'state of nature' where everyone is about to kill each other – can people realise their ends. The existence of a community is ensured through *law*, which, according to Kant, consists of an application of the categorical imperative to the extent necessary for social co-existence. Examples of necessary rules are: do not kill, do not steal, comply with agreements.

Suppose that it was permissible to kill people when you feel like it. Should everyone accept this as a general rule, society would disappear. Not only can you not will this; you cannot even imagine a society like that. Another example: when people comply with agreements only when it is to their own advantage, the whole institution of agreements would disappear, and together with it the reasonable mutual expectations that people must have of each other if they want to live together.

Ethics in its totality consists, in brief, of general rules which emanate from the categorical imperative, and which one imposes on oneself. *Law* consists of the general rules which are, moreover, essential for society, and which people impose on each other. All other duties that emanate from the categorical imperative are purely moral in nature, and not juridical. The non-legal part of ethics is not constitutive of the existence of society, but simply determines what a *good* society would look like.

This constitutive role of law in creating an orderly society requires that law must be actually operative in social life, thus in the 'phenomenal world'. Law is so important that it must be enforced by the state, by means of concrete sanctions in observable reality. Because of its organising social function, law directs itself primarily at the factual conduct of legal subjects, whereas ethics essentially is concerned with a proper, pure mental attitude. Stated somewhat differently, law restricts itself to *legality*. It is sufficient when one's external conduct is correct, even if one's motives are improper. Ethics, by contrast, is essentially concerned with *morality*, or with pure motives. For Kant, the actual consequences of actions are less important in the case of ethical duties which are not also legal duties. When I have sincerely done my best to help someone in need, then I have likewise done my moral duty, even if I have not succeeded in my intentions. We simply do not have complete control over the circumstances under which we act. Legal duties are, by contrast, so clear and so important for society that they must without qualification be complied with, irrespective of people's intentions.

According to Kant, law consists not only of constitutive rules that follow directly from the categorical imperative, but also of other positive rules which the state has promulgated. Indirectly these also follow from the categorical imperative because societal order requires just as much that the state regulates a number of specific matters in greater detail (for example, right-of-way rules).

Kant emphasises the empirical aspect of law also in the following way. In its content, positive law can deviate greatly from the ideal, natural law that follows from the categorical imperative. In Kant's view, such law is indeed immoral, but it nevertheless falls within the concept of 'law' – in contrast to the traditional natural-law doctrine, which denies to very unjust law the status of law in the true sense. Kant even states explicitly that bad positive law must always be obeyed.

He derives this absolute duty of obedience from the legal part of the categorical imperative, consisting of the rules which are necessary for social life, and which create the possibilities for the further development of a morally good life. These are so important that they must be established and maintained by the state through uniform laws. Law would lose its ordering function if every individual could establish for himself whether positive laws are just or not, in other words, whether they comply with the categorical imperative. When each citizen can interpret the law in his own way, everyone takes the law into his own hands, which will result in social chaos. Measured against the categorical imperative, such a society one cannot will. Hence Kant gives absolute priority to order and legal certainty on account of the categorical imperative, in comparison with justice which is derived extra-legally from the same categorical imperative.

With this Kant comes close to Hobbes's absolutist theory of the state. Unlike Hobbes, Kant, however, does assume the existence of an objective moral standard against which positive law can be tested: the categorical imperative obliges the government on its part to formulate positive law in accordance with the general moral law. According to Kant, government is in this respect, however, solely accountable to its own conscience. Citizens have no legal right of resistance when the state nonetheless adopts immoral law. They may only in legal and peaceful ways attempt to replace this with law which is morally more just.

Kant consequently arrives at a paradoxical relation to revolution: there can never be a moral duty, and even less so a legal duty, to overthrow state authority. But once a revolution has succeeded, the new sovereign should, consistent with the same order argument, again be obeyed unconditionally. Kant was certainly enthusiastic about the French revolution, but not because of the violent overthrow of the monarchy. His enthusiasm concerned the new liberal constitution which complied in various respects with the categorical imperative. Here again, Kant proved to be a supporter of the ideals of the Enlightenment.

6.4.2 Social Contract

Kant presented his liberal legal philosophy also in terms of a hypothetical social contract. As a requirement of practical reason, Kant formulates the *bürgerliche Verfassung*, the civil constitution, through which the community is ruled by law, in the form of a *pactum sociale*, a social contract. He presents this social contract as an agreement where people commit themselves to a community or a communal purpose. The first duty of everyone is to create and maintain a civil state. Here people have the right to be protected by enforceable state laws.

In its most ideal, moral form, law consists of rules that guarantee everyone's freedom in so far as this is reconcilable with the *equal* freedom of all others. If the state nevertheless limits one's freedom more than is necessary, one must still obey because of the absolute duty of obedience mentioned before. 'Freedom' here refers to what Kant calls *negative freedom*: being able to do what one wants to, free from the interference of others. In the space which law should leave open, we are thus free in the negative sense: we may do what we want to. In Kant's view, however, this is only freedom in the legal domain. In the moral domain, in our conscience, we should act in accordance with the non-legal, perfectionist part of the categorical imperative. Here action attains moral value only by virtue of the good intentions of the actor. Good conduct because of external coercion would negate all authentic moral quality. It is for this reason that Kant favours maximal freedom in the domain of law, which is after all enforced by sanctions. This freedom may be limited only by laws that protect the equal freedom of everyone. Since laws which limit freedom in this way emanate from the categorical imperative, and thus from our reason and our freedom, we are, in obeying the state, still autonomous, or self-legislating.

In Kant's view, the civil constitution must be regulated by a triad of principles that are related to the Enlightenment ideals. The first principle entails everyone's individual freedom as a human being. Within constitutional limits everyone must be able to act as he wishes, and be happy in his own way. The state has no right to make people 'happy against their will' (anti-paternalism).

The second principle is that of everyone's equality as subject of the law. This entails that everyone has an equal right to legal protection against others and the state, or equality before the law. Although Kant viewed all people equally as autonomous persons in moral respect, he did not advocate substantive equality in a legal sense. In the empirical-legal sphere of social life he simply advocated formal equality before the law. As classical liberal he rejected feudal estate privileges: all positions had to be accessible to everyone on the basis of their personal merit. But since the talents of different people vary considerably, the formal principle of equality does not exclude socio-economic inequality:

> Thus. . .the one must obey the other, (as the child its parents or the wife her husband), the one serves (the labourer) while the other pays, etc (Kant 1991, p. 75).

In the same vein Kant also rejected equal political rights. The legislative power must be determined solely by people who occupy an *independent* position:

> The only natural qualification required by a citizen (apart, of course, from being an adult male) is that he must be his *own master* (*sui iuris*) (Kant 1991, p. 78).

And these are men who are independent of others because they have some possessions. Only they comply with the requirement of maturity.

The third principle is that of everyone's independence as a citizen. With this Kant refers to the original contract by virtue of which the community is established. This hypothetical contract obliges the state to legislate in such a way that its laws could have had its origin in the general will of the people. Although Kant rejects a general right to vote, the legislature thus has to serve the general interest. These three principles lie at the foundation of the state.

This 'general will of the people' refers, just like the 'original contract', to Reason, the rational noumenal aspect of all people. Kant's social contract does not refer to an actual agreement, but expresses the idea of general validity. Viewed practically, its import is to bind the legislature to the hypothetical general will of rational people.

6.4.3 International Law

As we saw in the preceding discussion, the central function of the state is to protect the freedom of citizens. This has consequences for international law as well, for a state cannot succeed in this task when in their mutual relations states each go their own way. Therefore, the principles of freedom and equality should also obtain validity in international relations. In line with the immanent logic that determines the civil constitution, international violence must be monopolised by a supra-national institution. A league of nations must ensure that states do not violate their mutually adopted agreements, and that appeal is possible when they disagree about the correct interpretation of international treaties. Wars must be banned by the league of nations. With these ideas Kant was the first philosopher to advocate an international legal order of which the United Nations nowadays constitutes a weak shadow.

According to Kant, international law not only determines the relations between states, but also the way one state deals with the subjects of another state. Foreigners may not be treated as enemies or be robbed of their possessions or their freedom. When someone wants to settle abroad permanently, a more detailed agreement must be established; one has no appeal to a right to world citizenship that would allow one to settle anywhere permanently. From this follows that colonial practices are impermissible. This is evident when the inhabitants of one country take possession of another country for economic reasons. Kant moreover objects to paternalistic colonial practices such as a civilization offensive for the sake of the colonised (as propagated by Douwes Dekker/Max Havelaar, see Chapter 1). He phrases this objection by analogy to his argument against revolutions: one may not use illegal means in order to bring about a better legal condition.

6.5 The Separation of 'Is' and 'Ought' and a Narrow Social Morality

Kant's *Critique of Practical Reason*, which concerns moral knowledge, shows important parallels with his *Critique of Pure Reason*, which concerns theoretical knowledge. In both instances he accords a decisive role to reason, but at the same time limits its role to providing a formal structure.

There is, however, also a fundamental difference between moral and theoretical knowledge. Meaningful theoretical knowledge comes about through the cooperation between the senses and reason; theoretical knowledge without a foundation in experience loses itself in meaningless speculation. Each of these two sources of knowledge (senses and reason) separately has too little to offer. Things are different in the case of moral knowledge. According to Kant, the empirical plays no role here at all. Kant, therefore, restrains himself from formulating substantive moral norms, such as the Ten Commandments. His *categorical imperative* entails a critical formal test which judges conduct by its acceptability from a supra-personal, impartial point of view. Reason here provides, independently of sensory experience, in itself a sufficient anchor. Ethics consist simply of the form of a universal law, of an unconditional, universally valid precept.

This difference is a consequence of Kant's endorsement of the worldview of natural science: facts do not have any normative value. Kant concludes from this that morality must have its source in a totally unique sphere of reasonableness. For this reason it bears a formal character. Reason alone can after all provide us with no substantial knowledge. All our substantial aims stem from our empirical lives: they derive from our needs, desires and inclinations. For this reason they lack any moral character: what we actually desire does not have to coincide with what is morally desirable. Only by testing our desires against the rational moral law does it appear whether they are morally acceptable. In Kant's view, there is consequently a fundamental gulf between is and ought, that is, between facts and norms.

In this respect Kant's ethics differ radically from that of Aristotle (Section 2.5). In the worldview of Aristotle, reality clearly has a normative and rational character. Because of this the essential purposes which one comes across in reality are similarly normative in nature. There is no separation between facts and norms; to know reality likewise means to know the good. Greek rational ontology assumes a natural unity of the True and the Good.

This teleological metaphysics is abandoned in the worldview of modern natural science. Nature is regarded here as value-free and irrational. Therefore, Kant must place his ethics in a radically different domain. Hence he arrives at a dualistic worldview: on the one hand there is amoral, causally determined nature, on the other hand the rational domain of human ethics. The latter domain, Kant can no longer find in the external irrational world. For this reason he situates it in human consciousness which stands against the rest of nature. Thus man, in accordance with the modern worldview of Kant, acquires the role of autonomous self-legislator. At the same time man is the legislator of external nature, as scientific causal laws are human constructions, by means of which man acquires a hold on the empirical world. This stands in contrast with Greek ontology, which regards rationality and norms as present in the world, demanding of man to conform to it. Here nature plays the role of legislator.

Kant reproaches the rationalistic ethics that preceded him, of defending a highest good which stands external to human beings, for example, by deriving a standard of perfection from the design of nature. In Kant's view, the autonomous ability of self-legislation corresponds much better with the unique moral responsibility of human beings.

The modern worldview also leads Kant to a limitation of perfectionism. Because human rationality can no longer find any anchor in an eternal rational nature, its capacity becomes significantly smaller: all it can still do is to bind subjective maxims to moral conditions. Kant does not search for human perfection in an all-round development of abilities, but simply in internal 'good will'. The good will is internalised to such an extent that one cannot with certainty state of any person that he is of good will. In comparison with Greek ethics, Kant's view of the perfect way of life is considerably restricted. Only the good will 'shines like a jewel', Kant says somewhere, whereas in Greek ethics the whole human being, and even the cosmos, is in essence a perfectly structured jewel.[3]

Since man has been proclaimed as self-legislator because of his unique reasonableness, individual autonomy attains a central status. In legal philosophy this

[3]Greek: *kosmos* = both *order* and *jewel*.

means that the government must ideally grant its subjects as much freedom as possible to determine their own lives. This stands in sharp contrast with Plato, where the state must force its subjects to live a morally perfect life (Section 2.4). Kant's social morality, which culminates in his legal philosophy, is a 'narrow', liberal, non-perfectionist morality.

Kant's narrow social ethics deviates in a number of fundamental respects from the ethics of Hobbes, although there are important agreements between them (Section 4.1). The agreements are especially to be found in their legal views. Kant and Hobbes see the law as a means to maintain social order, and, therefore, (almost) never allow for revolt. Law, according to both of them, consists of the rules that are necessary for a peaceful social order. They both contend this by means of the idea of a social contract.

For the rest, Kant stands closer to Locke's liberalism. His legal viewpoint is based on the extra-legal, moral value of autonomy, and not like Hobbes's legal theory, simply on the desire to survive and to lead a life of pleasure. In order to further moral autonomy, the law must guarantee individual freedom. Hobbes's state, in contrast, allows no basic liberties, because this would threaten the legal order. Kant, who tests positive law against an extra-legal morality, would call law immoral if it violates freedom. But, just like Hobbes, he would on the basis of the order argument then still require obedience. In contrast with Hobbes, Kant would, however, regard it as obligatory to change illiberal law via legal means.

6.6 Commentary

Kant's philosophy has been the subject of much criticism; we limit ourselves here to a few critical comments on his ethics and his legal philosophy.

In the first place, criticism of what can be referred to as Kant's 'moral narcissism'. If the only thing which can unconditionally be called good is the good will, then people are encouraged to preoccupy themselves with the purity of their motives, and to leave it at that. This can lead to the navel gazing of what Hegel has called the *schöne Seele* (beautiful soul): someone who rejoices in his own excellence, and, therefore, does not want to dirty his hands with worldly matters. This moral narcissism can affect all human relations. When I only help someone because the maxim 'I never help anyone' is not universalisable, then all things considered, the object of my care is not the person who seeks help, but my maxim. To do good to someone is then not directly a morally valuable act, but only indirectly. This approach could impoverish human relations.

In the second place, Kant's ethics radiates an ungrounded optimism. In his view every moral problem can be solved by applying the universalisability test. Its application requires no specific philosophical competence: every person has the required abilities; what is more, especially simpler people can do it best. The problem is, however, that an act can be described in different ways. In terms of one description it is possibly universalisable, in terms of the other, it is not. (A related joke: 'May

I pray while I eat?' Answer: yes. 'May I eat while I pray?' Answer: no.) Kant's example of a person who, on the run from a killer, seeks shelter with me is notorious. The killer knocks on my door, and asks whether I saw the person passing. According to Kant I should not lie in this situation; lying is forbidden under all circumstances. But why could my act of not telling the truth not instead be described as 'To mislead someone who threatens the rights of another so that his evil intent is defeated'? Kant makes absolute *one* description of the act in question, not allowing for any nuance: lying is forbidden under all circumstances, full stop. Kant's optimism consequently easily leads to legalism and rigidity. Many moral dilemmas cannot be solved by applying a formula to them, and whoever thinks that he can do so, becomes a literalist who passes by the complexities of moral dilemmas.

In the third place, one can question Kant's unconditional prohibition of revolt. The prevailing order must always be obeyed, and preferred above the uncertainty of a new order brought about via a revolution, irrespective of how unjust the existing order is. In this respect Kant sides with Hobbes against Locke. But why should this actually be the case? Why may the obedience to a legal authority not have a conditional character? The maxim 'If the ruling regime violates elementary human rights and encourages people to report their own family members to the police, I attempt to bring about a revolt', does not, when generalised, have to lead to chaos. Moreover, when governments are aware of the fact that the obedience of citizens is conditional, the chance is greater that no chaotic abuses will occur.

In the fourth place, and tying in with the previous point: Kant's somewhat schizophrenic relation vis-à-vis revolution is surprising. You may not participate in it; it is a kind of natural catastrophe which simply occurs, and which you have to allow to take its course. But if something good arises out of it, it is a welcome bonus. Thus a dualism arises between the amoral world history and the moral conduct of individuals: it is never morally justified for individuals to participate in revolutions, which nevertheless still happen, and then, even when not willed, can bring about moral progress. The moral actor consequently becomes a spectator who does not want to participate in the dirty work of others, but who afterwards wants to profit from it. Is this not a form of parasitising – something which Kant's ethics prohibits?

The previous point of critique relates to Kant's dualism between moral actor and actor in natural life. This ties in with his dualistic distinction between the spheres of the reasonable (the sphere of freedom) and the empirical (the sphere of causality). Our fifth critical remark relates to this. Kant might contend unjustly that non-egotistical human conduct cannot be explained in an empirical way. Hume's invocation of the ability for sympathy (or rather empathy) may present a satisfactory explanation (see also the discussion of Freud in Section 8.2). According to Hume, the impartial character of our moral consciousness is the consequence of a process of socialisation, by which we learn to imagine ourselves in the shoes of another, and take account of his views and interests. By means of this process the general suprapersonal rules are established which are necessary for co-existence. In contending this, Hume does not have to divide up the world into two spheres, the causally determined and the moral. With him, morality is a part of man's psychology and of social life. With Kant, the bridging of the spheres of freedom and causality is difficult to imagine. Nevertheless, ethics requires that man turn his rational moral considerations into action. But every time this happens, free will would break into the causal chain of empirical events. And then the principle that everything in nature is causally determined would no longer be valid. Descartes produced God in order to bridge the gap between the spiritual and the material. But according to Kant, rationalistic evidence of the existence of God exceeds the limits of the human capacity for knowledge.

To solve this problem one could interpret Kant's philosophy in terms of the 'two-aspect theory'. One would then not assume that man really consists of two completely dissimilar substances (a spiritual and a physical, or noumenal and phenomenal). According to this interpretation, there are just two different *points of view* regarding the same thing. On the one hand, we can regard ourselves as a branch of empirical nature. Then we regard our feelings, tendencies and motives as completely causally determined, and thus in principle predictable. This is the viewpoint of Hume and of modern empirical psychology. In general, this interpretation is characteristic of the objectifying spectator perspective of empirical science. This interpretation of human conduct leaves no space for freedom of choice and moral responsibility.

The same human actions can, however, also be viewed differently, from the viewpoint of the participant. From the point of view of the acting person himself his choices appear to still be free: he can reason for himself which conduct deserves preference, weigh up reasons in favour of and against it, etc. In our daily lives it is very difficult to see ourselves as completely unfree. We, moreover, do not regard other people as automatons or animals led by their instincts, but appeal to their responsibility. From this point of view human actions are not blind, determined, natural events: it could also have been different had the 'actor' willed it.

The two-aspect theory makes no pronouncement about what reality is like. We can, after all, only know how it *appears* to us. And according to the two-aspect doctrine it appears in the above-mentioned two ways, dependent on the perspective that one adopts: the scientific or the moral. (In daily life – and in criminal law judgments – these perspectives, moreover, frequently cross each other.) By interpreting the two-aspect doctrine methodologically, the problem which the ontological interpretation of Kant's ethics brings about is avoided, that is, that man really consists of two radically different 'substances', with the interaction being a mystery.[4] With his two-aspect theory Kant wants to escape from both empiricism and rationalism. In doing this he creates space for ethics outside of the domain that is occupied by natural science.

[4]To escape from such dualism, some writers adopt a reductive approach: they reduce the one aspect to the other. According to August Comte (1789–1857), everything, also man, can be explained causally; the idea of the autonomous man who makes his own history is illusory; Comte's empiricism sees through this illusion. A rationalist, such as Sartre (1905–1980), does exactly the opposite: the true man is the absolutely free man; it is a form of bad faith when one, in an extension of science, subscribes to the view that man is causally determined.

Methodologically interpreted, the two-aspect theory nonetheless retains something unsatisfactory. Both points of view, after all, exclude each other. This inconsistency gives to both perspectives an *as if* character: as soon as one adopts the one point of view, it is difficult to still take the other seriously.

To conclude, we add some brief points of criticism. Kant invokes the unequal maturity of empirical human individuals to legitimise unequal substantive rights. Against this, social-democratic critics have contended that it gives women and labourers few chances to develop their maturity – an important difference compared to children (who are immature as such). Communitarians have opposed Kant's vision that autonomy constitutes man's moral essence: this is based on an unjustifiable metaphysical worldview, because people would be primarily communal beings (see Section 9.1.2). Forceful criticism has also been expressed against Kant's respect for empirical science, among others by Hegel (Section 7.3) and Habermas (Section 9.3).

Nonetheless, Kant's philosophical heritage is large. In the domain of epistemology, it is nowadays generally accepted that human consciousness plays an important constitutive role in the formation of knowledge. In contemporary ethics new variants of the procedural principle of universalisability have been developed (see Hare, Section 8.3.2; Habermas, Section 9.3; Rawls, Section 10.5).

Chapter 7
Nineteenth Century

7.1 Introduction

7.1.1 General Developments

In the 19th century the tendency towards the scientification and objectification of social life, as well as towards moral emancipation in a liberal direction, continued under the influence of two revolutions, the French and the Industrial. The political changes at the end of the 18th century were ushered in by the *French Revolution* with its principles of freedom, equality and brotherhood (moral emancipation), and the ensuing dictatorial regime of Napoleon with its efficient organisation of the central state (objectification). By the end of the 19th century, Western European societies had taken the political form of national constitutional states founded on liberal ideas. Furthermore, an *Industrial Revolution* took place on the economic terrain: applied science led to technical innovations, such as the steam engine, which in the second half of the 18th century resulted in England in large-scale industrial production concentrated in factory cities, which were populated by large numbers of labourers. After 1815 the Industrial Revolution caught on in continental Europe. This was coupled with market expansion through an increasingly drastic colonisation of the non-Western world, which reached its peak at the end of the 19th century. Traditionally isolated countries like China and Japan, too, were by military intervention forced to open their borders to Western trade (in China, especially for the importation of opium). This enormous colonial expansion was, apart from economic motives, also stimulated by a political race for world domination between the European national states. In philosophy these fast-changing social and economic relationships were reflected in a more detailed elaboration, as well as fundamental criticism, of liberal principles.

The political changes in the different Western European countries showed greater parallels than in preceding periods. The development since the 16th century did show general trends, but it still took on very divergent forms. Almost everywhere central monarchies were established (in Germany and Italy incidentally only in the form of small principalities). As a result the nobility of the Middle Ages partly lost their power. The kings obtained absolute power. Unrestricted by any constitution,

C.W. Maris, F.C.L.M. Jacobs (eds.), *Law, Order and Freedom*, Law and Philosophy Library 94, DOI 10.1007/978-94-007-1457-1_7, © Springer Science+Business Media B.V. 2011

they stood above the law. The nobility still enjoyed extensive privileges compared to the upcoming class of shop-keeping and trading citizens in the cities and peasants in rural areas. The central state protected its own economy by means of import duties, import bans and export subsidies (mercantilism). The Republic of the United Netherlands was a notable exception: its structure was that of a decentralised federation which was ruled by the urban patricians in a relatively un-authoritarian way. In England a liberalising process commenced at an early stage: in 1689, under the influence of Locke's liberalism, individual freedom rights and a modest form of parliamentary legislation were introduced. Thanks to these relatively peaceful reforms a stable society with a free market was established, which provided fertile soil for personal initiative and economic growth. It was for these reasons that the industrial revolution started here. The economist Adam Smith advocated the withdrawal of the state from the market and international free trade: when one leaves economic interchange to the free play of supply and demand and to individual initiative, this would lead to an increase in general welfare. In continental Europe political liberalisation still had to wait another century. A radicalised version of the English (unwritten) constitution was nonetheless propagated by the French Enlightenment philosophers as an alternative to the ruling absolute monarchy and aristocratic privileges.

Inspired by Locke, as well as economic self-interest, England's American colonies, after a revolt in 1783, separated themselves from the motherland, as the United States of America. The American *Declaration of Independence*, cited in Chapter 1, granted citizens inalienable fundamental rights: the right to life, freedom and to the pursuit of happiness. In France, the ideal of the liberal state was after the Revolution of 1789 translated into positive law. The French then attempted to export their revolutionary achievements by conquering the surrounding non-liberal countries, meanwhile seeking the support of local revolutionaries. The Dutchman Van der Capellen tot den Pol wrote in 1781 in *Aan het volk van Nederland. Het democratisch manifest* (To the People of the Netherlands. The Democratic Manifesto), that the Dutch had to regain their original democratic freedom rights as they were practised in the old days by the Batavians: 'Take up your weapons, elect those you must obey.' In consequence, in 1795 the Netherlands was under French leadership transformed into the constitutional Batavian Republic. The ancient noble privileges were abolished.

The French Revolution, however, devoured its own children and ended in terror. Dogmatic revolutionaries executed competing revolutionaries with deviating views, until they themselves lost their heads on the guillotine. The foreign wars subsequently brought a general onto the political stage, Napoleon, who, after a coup d'état in 1799, crowned himself as emperor in 1804 and set aside the liberal constitution. Napoleon specialised in large scale wars of conquest against the rest of Europe: England, Austria and Russia. Local representatives of the bourgeoisie, in Germany, among others, Goethe and Hegel, praised Napoleon's victories in the hope that this would lead to the modernisation of society. In order to wage his wars efficiently Napoleon indeed brought about modernisation, but in a different way than was hoped for by liberals. The institutions of the central state were developed to great heights. In the interest of his army, based on conscription, the whole nation was provided with family names and registered. In this way taxes could be levied more efficiently too. The state bureaucracy increased proportionally. The diverse legal fields were each unified by the first national codifications, which served as models for codification in other European states. These codifications, furthermore, promoted an increasing differentiation of law into separate areas, such as private law, constitutional law, and criminal law.

Of the liberal principles in the Code Civil of 1804 two elements were safeguarded that were of particular importance for modern economic interaction: all citizens were equal before the law, and their right to property was inviolable. In the sphere of private law, codification thus increased legal certainty. This relative independence of law from political power was a major step forward, as the codifier Portalis (2004) wrote in the *Preliminary Address on the first draft of the Civil Code* (21 January 1801):

> In despotic States, where the prince is owner of all the land, where all commerce is carried out on behalf of the head of State and for his profit, where individuals have neither freedom, nor will, nor property, there are more judges and hangmen than laws. But wherever citizens have property to protect and defend, wherever they have political and civil rights, wherever honour counts for something, a certain number of laws are needed to confront all situations.

However, apart from the freedom to promote one's interest in the market place, no liberties were granted during Napoleon's dictatorship. Individual freedom in private law did not coincide with constitutional political freedoms.

Codification of criminal law similarly provided the citizen with some protection against the state, in particular, against arbitrary arrest and conviction: in the future, prosecution should take place only on the basis of a pre-determined, public specification of criminal offences. For a liberal this is not sufficient. In the first place, nothing is yet said about the content of criminal offences: criminal laws can be politically tainted, for example, by prohibiting free expression. Liberals, therefore, advocate additional constitutional protection against the legislature by means of constitutional freedom rights. Moreover, making criminal law uniform can further a more efficient exercise of governmental power, at the expense of individual freedom. Napoleon's government thus posited the two tendencies of the modernisation process in opposition to each other. It promoted rational control by the central government at the cost of moral emancipation: in political respect citizens were no longer free and equal individuals, but instruments of the national state in its pursuit of power.

After Napoleon had met his Waterloo in 1815, the victorious monarchical states decided at the Congress of Vienna in favour of a *Restoration* of the pre-revolutionary monarchies. From this moment onwards political developments in large parts of Western Europe proceeded along parallel lines for a long time. The Netherlands, too, turned into a kingdom under the Oranges, who were previously only stadtholders. William I ruled as an enlightened despot. The Constitution of 1815 nonetheless granted a number of basic rights: freedom of the press, protection of property, and the right of petition. The powerful bourgeoisie, however, did not let themselves be held back for long. In 1848 everywhere in Europe new revolts broke out, after which little by little increasingly liberal constitutions were introduced. In the Netherlands, William II of necessity became a liberal within 24 hours. The class privileges were abolished for the second time. The constitutional amendment of 1848 introduced suffrage for the Second Chamber to all citizens who pay taxes, thereby granting voting rights to all well-off male citizens, approximately 2.5% of the population. The argument in favour of granting political power exclusively to the rich was that persons who were economically independent have experience in running their affairs in a rational way. All others did not possess the independence and capacity for oversight required in matters of state. The people's representatives acquired the right of amendment, and the executive power, under the leadership of the king, would in future be accountable to them. Furthermore, the right of association and assembly, freedom of education, and secrecy of the post, were introduced as new basic rights.

The *Industrial Revolution* was made possible by technical applications of modern science. Newton's mechanics and thermodynamics led to the invention of the steam engine: thanks to the artificial generation of energy, textile and steel could be mechanically produced on a large scale. Moreover, raw materials and the new mass products could be transferred over much greater distances due to the steam-powered trains and ships. Farm labour and industry diminished in importance; peasants and manual workers joined the growing masses of factory workers in the new factory cities.

Because of these developments the landed gentry finally lost their social importance as well. Their remaining privileges appeared increasingly arbitrary, and were for the most part abolished. In the second half of the 19th century, capitalist citizens, by means of an appeal to freedom and equality, took over the leading position on all fronts. The freedom of property and contract in the 19th-century minimal state allowed them to increase their market share. Thanks to tax-based suffrage they acquired influence in government.

However, from the point of view of the new 'fourth class' – the poor workers – these rights of the third class appeared like new arbitrary privileges, which were difficult to reconcile with the principle of *equal* freedom. Owing to the industrial revolution the production and national income of countries, such as England, had indeed increased significantly, but this progress was to a great extent cancelled out by the population explosion (which again tied in with the improved ability of producing essential food, storing it, and transporting it to places where it was needed). The oversupply of labour led to very low wages, especially in the first half of the century. In such circumstances labourers had little profit from the formal legal freedoms: in their case the free market of supply and demand of labour implied that from their childhood onwards they had to put themselves out for hire for a hunger wage. Without any labour protection, they had to survive lengthy working days, in extremely unhealthy circumstances, as bolts in a numbing factory device. They lived in miserable circumstances. When they could not look after themselves, they were dependent on charity; the government did not provide for social legislation. As a result, life expectancy and quality of life were initially very low. Only after 1840 did wages and living conditions improve.

Slave labour in the colonies was even more miserable. There workers were not persons, but things: legal property of the exploiters, who often subjected them to cruel corporal punishments. Slaves did not even have formal freedom rights: they could not move about freely, say what they thought, or get married.

During this period, progress in technical and economic rationality was, therefore, only very partially accompanied by moral emancipation: the principles of freedom and equality were interpreted one-sidedly in the interests of the new wealthy. Moral ideas, however, have a logic of their own which rises above partial interests. Once one has publicly declared that all people are free and equal, one finds oneself in a compromising position if one subsequently grants rights exclusively to one particular group. The middle class attempted to justify their privileges by asserting that the reasoning abilities of women, workers and non-Europeans were not sufficiently developed to live an autonomous life. As in the case of children, such immature people as a matter of course did not deserve full rights. A similar argument is to be found with Kant (Chapter 6). However, this reasoning cannot be maintained once it, for example, appears that women can actually study just as well as men, and that it is precisely *because of* their exclusion from academic studies that they are kept ignorant. With such objections, strong protests were immediately raised against the one-sided interpretation of liberalism. In 1791, a non-official *Declaration of the Rights of Woman and the Female Citizen* criticised the domination by men, with the argument that women possess the same intellectual abilities. Article 1: 'Woman is born free and lives equal to man in her rights. Social distinctions can be based only on the common utility.' In 1793, in France, a constitution was drafted which included socio-economic rights, such as the right to work, to benefits in the case of labour disability, and to education, which, however, never came into effect. The *Encyclopédie* had already condemned slavery as incompatible with the equal freedom that all people have by nature. After the French Revolution, the *Société des Amis des Noirs* (the Association of Friends of Blacks) advocated the abolition of colonial slavery, but this ran into economic objections. After a slave revolt in 1791 the first black state was established in Haiti. The revolutionary government only in 1794 abolished slavery in the *Code Noir*, but shortly thereafter all liberal rights were repealed.

In the course of the 19th and 20th centuries these inconsistencies were slowly but surely remedied, for both humanitarian and opportunistic reasons. At the start of the 18th century, European countries first abolished slave trade, and by the middle of the century slavery itself, as well. The Netherlands followed in the rear, proceeding to free slaves only in the 1860s: *keti koti!* (as the Surinamese say: chains broken). In the United States a civil war against the Southern States was necessary to make this happen (1861–1865). The European powers nonetheless strictly maintained political power in their colonies. Through the vast expansion of colonial empires the indigenous inequality and lack of freedom were replaced worldwide by colonial domination, as appears from the *Max Havelaar* conflict with which this book commences. Only deep into the 20th century, after the Second World War, did colonial oppression come to an end. Meanwhile in Europe, partly under pressure of labour movements, a start had been made with social legislation. In England child labour under the age of nine was already prohibited in 1833; in the Netherlands a law against child labour was enacted in 1874. Voting rights were gradually expanded, too. In the Netherlands general suffrage was introduced in 1917, so that women and labourers also attained a political voice.

7.1.2 Liberalism and Utilitarianism

In philosophy these political and socio-economic changes evoked divergent responses. Liberalism was further elaborated upon by philosophers such as John Stuart Mill (1806–1873). In *On Liberty* (1859) Mill formulated the famous *harm principle*:

> That principle is, that the sole end for which mankind are warranted, individually or collectively, in interfering with the liberty of action of any of their number, is self-protection. That the only purpose for which power can be rightfully exercised over any member of a civilized community, against his will, is to prevent harm to others. His own good, either physical or moral, is not sufficient warrant. He cannot rightfully be compelled to do or forbear because it will be better for him to do so, because it will make him happier, because, in the opinion of others, to do so would be wise, or even right (Mill 1982, p. 68).

Briefly summarised: freedom, unless harm to others. Mill defines freedom as the ability of the individual to strive towards his own good in his own manner. The government should refrain from *moralism* (forcing citizens to act or refrain from acting because it regards this as morally just) and *paternalism* (forcing citizens to act or refrain from acting because it regards this to be in their own interest, thus to prevent them from harming themselves).

Mill bases this liberal principle on a mixture of liberal and utilitarian grounds. Liberal is his emphasis on the value of individual autonomy and self-development. Every individual must, therefore, be free in his thinking and feelings, in the expression of his thoughts, in living in accordance with his own objectives, and in entering into agreements with other individuals. In addition Mill argues, in accordance with the utilitarian principle that something is good when it leads to optimal general welfare, that individual freedom promotes the welfare of the individual, and of society as a whole. In the first place, freedom increases the happiness of the individual himself, because it allows him to live according to his own preferences. Conformism, on the other hand, disfigures you; your life is bound like the feet of a Chinese woman. On the social level individual freedom promotes new initiatives and an increase in knowledge. Non-conformist geniuses must, therefore, be given as much space as possible. Mill does not advocate asocial individualism or selfish indifference towards others either, because no one lives in isolation. Yet, social virtues must be instilled by means of education, not force. Liberalism simply wants to enable everyone to establish his own views in the face of traditions and social morality.

In Mill's view, political decision-making also requires freedom of thought and of opinion. Public policy requires an open critical debate, because every government is fallible. Without open public deliberation a government cannot know whether its view is the right one: even if it is right, it would not know why. Political participation in a representative democracy furthermore promotes personal growth. However, according to Mill, democracy works only when citizens are well-informed and educated, and when they are tolerant of deviating views and modes of life. Mill, moreover, wanted to tie the democratic legislature to fundamental freedom rights, in order to prevent tyranny of the majority over non-conformist individuals. Mill also opposed the subordination of women. Although initially a supporter of the free market and the corresponding minimal state, towards the end of his life he advocated the adoption of social legislation. Nevertheless, Mill argued, everyone should, in as far as possible, remain responsible for his own fate.

Mill thus combined liberalism with *utilitarianism*, which was mentioned earlier in the chapter on Kant (Section 6.3.2). It is discussed in more detail in Section 7.2, where on closer inspection it turns out to hardly be reconcilable with liberalism.

Utilitarian ethics has, after Mill, remained prominent in the English-speaking world. But here, too, it has in the last few decades been harshly criticised because its consequences can crush the liberal ideal of individual autonomy and freedom. In its intention, utilitarianism nonetheless tallies with the Enlightenment: it wants to improve the world by a rational, scientific approach to society and law. In ethics the utilitarians reject the traditional Aristotelian and Christian metaphysics: there are no invisible higher ends or values in nature. Therefore, it is irrational to sacrifice your life for a Christian ethics that deludes you with the promise of an illusory life in heaven after death. One should emancipate oneself from such superstitions.

From the perspective of man the only remaining value that can be empirically established is his earthly pursuit of a happy life – Hobbes started from a similar empirical basis.[1] Good is then what makes man's happiness as great as possible. Besides *happiness*, utilitarians also speak of *utility*.[2] How to find happiness is a personal matter that one can establish only for oneself; the objective criterion to judge different ways of life is the result and ultimate purpose of all human activities, the experience of happiness.[3] According to the founder of utilitarianism, Jeremy Bentham (1748–1832), one can quantify the happiness that an action brings about: by calculating the number of those who are happy as well as the duration and intensity of their feelings of happiness. An act is good when

[1] See Chapter 4; see also the minimal natural law of Hart, Chapter 1.

[2] Latin: *utilitas* = utility; from there the name Utilitarianism.

[3] Nietzsche (Section 7.5) in this regard famously remarked in *The Twilight of the Idols* (2004, p. 4): 'Man does not strive after happiness; the Englishman only does so.'

it optimises the total happiness of all people involved. This emphasis on quantity instead of quality corresponds with the approach in natural science, which deals with mathematically calculable relations between phenomena, and which rejects pre-scientific assumptions of *qualities* in nature as one finds in Aristotelian metaphysics.

A problem, however, now arises: my happiness can conflict with your happiness; what is useful for society as a whole can clash with what is useful for me. In the event of scarcity, what I acquire is subtracted from what others have. My happiness increases when I steal your money, whereas your happiness decreases. The utilitarian solution: since the world is not harmonious, you must unfortunately choose the least bad, *the greatest happiness of the greatest number*. When you want to bake an egg you have to break the shell: one sometimes has to sacrifice the happiness of an individual or of a minority in order to increase the total happiness. Bentham expected that this quantifying approach would lead to a rationalisation of social life so that the general welfare would increase. For this purpose the capricious and unpredictable English judge-made law had to be replaced by codification.

Evidently this utilitarian approach respects no essential private sphere within which the citizen is free from the interference of others: when it comes down to it, the individual has to adapt himself to what general utility requires. The total happiness of the majority may even benefit from the slave labour of a minority. Because of this totalitarian emphasis on general utility, on closer inspection utilitarianism fits in better with the tendency towards rational efficiency of modern science, than with the moral emancipation which the liberal Enlightenment thinkers had in mind. Mill's utilitarian justification of liberal freedom appears to rest on an unhappy marriage between two irreconcilable ideas. In certain circumstances censorship may promote general happiness better than freedom of speech; or extensive social discipline may have greater utility than nonconformist freedom. Mill attempts to escape from this dilemma by giving a *qualitative* definition of happiness: intellectual and moral pleasures are superior to physical pleasures. However, when one replaces quantity with quality one takes the heart out of the utilitarian approach (see Section 7.2). The utilitarian sacrifice of the individual person to an anonymous overall utility is the most severe point of criticism. In line with this, the liberal legal philosopher Dworkin has pointed out that utilitarianism is actually an ill-considered elaboration of the equality principle. The assumption is after all that everyone's happiness has the same weight (different from under feudalism). However, then one may not cancel out the happiness of an individual for the sake of the majority on the basis of considerations of efficiency. On the contrary, the individual should be protected by fundamental rights against measures that promote the general welfare. To speak with Kant: every individual human being is an end in himself.

7.1.3 German Historical School

In its turn, liberalism has been subjected to severe criticism, precisely because of its emphasis on individual freedom. Critics from the left and the right oppose liberal individualism, because they regard man, following Rousseau, as a communal being.

According to them, the community precedes the individual, both in time and in value. For this reason the individual has duties to, rather than rights against, his society, and such duties do not follow from his free choice. Left and right, however, advocate different ideals of community. Conservatives hanker for the good old times of the pre-revolutionary hierarchical society. In contrast, communists, such as Karl Marx, yearn for a much more radical social egalitarianism: the French revolution did not bring about the socio-economic equality which brotherly cooperation requires.

Conservatives point warningly to the terror in which the French revolution had ended. This would prove that one cannot reform society according to a rationalistic blueprint. Liberals like Locke would unjustifiably adhere to an abstract view of human beings: a fictitious rational individual who, detached from social relations, arranges his life in a completely independent way. Taking such atomistic individuals for real, liberal philosophers consequently construct an ideal society via the model of a social contract which is just as fictive. In reality each man is born in a society; he develops his ideals and views of reality within traditions which are passed on to him by society. On his own he would hardly be able to develop above the level of an animal. Liberal philosophy overestimates the rationality of man: the realisation of abstract schemes leads in practice to all kinds of unanticipated and undesirable consequences. Hence, the pursuit of freedom of the French revolution undermined the traditional associations which are necessary to keep a society together, with unbridled egoism and abuse of power as consequences. It is better to adhere to ancient traditions in which the life experience of generations is stored up, according to the conservative critique (which is in recent times continued by *communitarians*, such as MacIntyre: see Section 9.1.2).

This applies to law as well. The English conservative Edmund Burke opposed the French *Declaration of the Rights of Man and of the Citizen* in his *Reflections on the Revolution in France* (1790). Such so-called universal human rights explode in one blow all the legal customs which have developed through the ages, with societal normlessness as a consequence. In the same conservative spirit, the *Historical Legal School*, under the leadership of Friedrich Karl von Savigny (1799–1861), opposed the proposals to codify German private law using as model the recent civil codes of France and Austria, which held themselves to be realisations of natural law. According to the Historical School, the idea of an eternally valid rational natural law is an illusion. You cannot in the abstract construe an ideal legal system that would accord with human nature as such, independent of all historical development. The true living law, according to Savigny, one does not find in law books: the only authentic legal source is the organically grown customary law that differs in keeping with the needs of each society.

With this relativistic legal doctrine the Historical School comes close to the view of Montesquieu. According to Savigny, however, the content of law does not depend on natural causes, such as climate, but on cultural factors: law is an expression of the character of a people. To be sure, in more complex legal societies law is developed further by legal specialists, but they are ultimately the technical mouthpiece of the *spirit of the people*. If you want to proceed towards codification, then this should be done not by the importation of legal systems which are foreign to the people, but by starting from a thorough knowledge of one's own legal history. Against codification as such it is contended that this would place a brake on the spontaneous development of the living law. Partly because of this criticism, a general civil code was introduced in Germany only in 1900.

In the spirit of Savigny, German historicists threw themselves into the study of old Germanic law.[4] The more dogmatic movement of *Begriffsjurisprudenz* concentrated on the analytical effect of legal concepts that supposedly had their source in people's customary law. Under the influence of attacks on natural-law doctrine other legal scholars arrived at the equally relativistic *legal positivism* that, however, accorded an independent, and even decisive, role to the central state: law is what the government enacts as such (see Section 1.2.3). In the 19th century this movement initially assumed the form of *legislative positivism* or *legalism*: the judge must be guided by law, as Montesquieu had already prescribed. With this the legalists did not, however, mean that the judge may not at all interpret the words of the law. He must indeed only interpret the *legislation*, because in accordance with the ideal of separation of powers, creation of law is reserved for the legislature. As codifications aged, this respect for legislation declined, with the consequence that in the 20th century, legal positivism acknowledges judicial decisions as an independent legal source.

7.1.4 Hegel

In philosophy too, there was criticism of rationalism and the liberal ideal of equal individual freedom of the Enlightenment, as well as its undesirable consequences for law. In this chapter three critics will be discussed in detail: the German philosophers Hegel (Section 7.3), Marx (Section 7.4) and Nietzsche (Section 7.5).

Unlike Locke and Mill, George Friedrich Wilhelm Hegel (1770–1831; *Grundlinien der Philosophie des Rechts* (Elements of the Philosophy of Right, 1821)) did not see the state as an agent in the service of the free development of individual citizens. He regarded the state, more in line with the view of Rousseau, as an institution in which all partial interests are raised to a higher level, as a supra-partial legal and moral entity. This is not to say that states always have this form in reality, but in Hegel's view it ideally is their purpose.

Hegel, moreover, opposes the abstract rationalism that is characteristic of Enlightenment philosophers, such as Kant. Kant attempted to overcome Hume's scepticism with his thesis that the human faculty of cognition organises reality by means of a fixed rational structure. Hegel, in opposition to this, contends that human

[4]From the same romantic anti-rationalist idealising of a unique people's spirit, the legal historian and language expert Grimm collected traditional fairy tales that had been handed down orally through the generations. Strangely, Savigny himself saw Roman law as an ideal model, which stirred a conflict among German legal scholars between the Romanists and Germanists.

reason does not stand outside of changing reality, but that it partakes in it: it develops itself through interaction with its changing environment. Hegel emphasises, like the Historical School, the historical development in which society, law, state and human thinking continually take on new forms. Every nation develops its own social and moral character, although Hegel nonetheless detects in the course of history an increasing rationality. Via successive generations, human thinking, step by step, comes increasingly to greater insight, which is reflected in the form of society. Hegel calls this the *objective spirit*: just like a novel or a law forms a meaningful entity which rises above the subjective intention of the author, individual ideas are objectified and institutionalised by subsequent generations: they are elevated into larger thought patterns, interpreted anew, and developed further. In this way great cultural traditions and social institutions in the fields of morality, art, religion and philosophy are established, by means of which man puts his spiritual stamp on the world. Cultural institutions have an independent development consistent with their own rules ('objective spirit'): they form the human individual, rather than the individual forming them.

This also applies to legal evolution: law is a cultural product, which slowly and falteringly in the course of time assumes a rational character. With this view Hegel opposes, on the one hand, the rationalistic expectation of Enlightenment philosophers that one can, through the codification of an abstract reasonable natural law, construct a completely new ideal society. Look, for example, at the way in which the French revolution ended in terror. On the other hand, Hegel likewise opposed the radical historical relativism of the Historical School: according to the Historical School, particular legal traditions are all we have. Hegel adopts a dynamic position between historical relativism and rationalistic universalism.

Legal evolution commenced with unwritten customary law, in accordance with the view of the Historical School. The first human societies were held together by informal rules and solidarity, as in a family. In a later phase of human evolution, customary law is gradually codified into law books. In modern civil society with its extensive division of labour, citizens interact with each other in a more impersonal, more economically-oriented way than in less commercialised societies. By means of general rules modern law must regulate economic exchange, the mutual satisfaction of needs and labour relations. For this purpose legislation focuses on subjective rights which guarantee that individuals can live their lives as independent persons: property and contract law, as well as the protection of these rights by criminal law. The central legal principle reads thus: be a person and respect others as persons as well. The modern legal order, then, on the one hand, is the product of a historical social development. On the other hand, however, one can reconstruct it retroactively as a rational system of rights and duties which is necessary in the given circumstances, as Hobbes, Locke and Kant did with their theories of the social contract.

The liberal contract doctrine of Locke and Kant leads to a separation between the public domain, ruled by the narrow morality of law, and the private domain, where the individual is responsible for his perfection as a moral person. According to Kant, the legal order wants to prevent the infringement of legal interests, whereas morality requires much more, specifically a pure intention. Therefore, the domains of *legality* (law) and of perfectionist *morality* stand apart. This liberal ideal of negative freedom for public life is described as follows by Kant: a general law should guarantee that the caprice of one can coincide with the caprice of another. Hegel rejects this, arguing that the consequences of negative freedom without positive realisation are shown by the derailment of the French Revolution into terror and chaos. True freedom is not subjective freedom of choice but identification with one's reasonable person: rational organisation of one's feelings and emotions. An individual can impossibly achieve this on his own, without the guidance of state and law. Hegel opposes the liberal ideal of the autonomous individual. When he posits freedom as a central principle, he refers to metaphysical *essential freedom*: one is free when one identifies oneself with the rational course of history.

Thanks to the emergence of the state, the initial separation between law and morality, between the just and the good, can, in Hegel's view, be overcome: they are assembled in a higher moral community in which individual life has been absorbed. The state provides an amalgamation of the solidarity of family life and the objectivity of economic exchange, now extended to all legal subjects. All specific interests acquire a balanced place in a greater organic whole. In this way man finds his higher reasonable destiny and his true freedom. Therefore, each individual has the duty to act as a subject of the state community.

Hegel's approach thus corresponds far more with the *volonté générale* (general will) of Rousseau than with the individualistic negative liberty rights and political participation rights of liberalism. In order to contain the arbitrariness of individual negative freedom, in constitutional law Hegel advocates a mixture of a constitutional monarchy and a corporative estate system. In this arrangement, king, nobility and guilds play a supra-partial role in the interests of everyone. Hegel's ideal state does not entail liberal political participation rights. Hegelian freedom means that the individual voluntarily accepts the rational decisions of state organs. The state is not at the service of its citizens, as the liberal doctrine of the social contract presupposes. Citizens are at the service of the state, a supra-personal moral power in which not the individual, but humanity, attains perfection.

In Hegel's view, this development towards rationality is guided by a metaphysical Absolute Spirit, a dynamised rational God-figure or Platonic Idea. The rational development of the Absolute Spirit involves a kind of spiritual self-therapy in which human thinking serves as sounding board. Hegel depicts this dynamic development of the Spirit as *dialectical*, that is, in the form of a dialogue of statement and counter-statement. Every human position is one-sided, because thinking attempts to grasp the changing and flowing reality by means of fixed concepts. However, because of the human desire for perfection, such an imperfect thesis leads to an anti-thesis, which, however, mirrors the one-sidedness of the thesis. From this clash between thesis and anti-thesis a deeper insight subsequently arises, which yet again involves a new one-sidedness, after which history repeats itself on a higher level. Hence thinking, via a three-fold succession of thesis, anti-thesis and synthesis, becomes increasingly reasonable, until it ultimately arrives at perfect (self-)consciousness. According to Hegel, the ideal state is a manifestation of this Absolute Spirit.

7.1.5 Marx

Karl Marx (1818–1883) turned Hegel upside down. He adopted Hegel's historical model of development via oppositions. According to Marx, however, not intellectual oppositions are decisive, but economic ones. Man primarily survives by cultivating nature in cooperation with his fellow men. Unlike animals that merely react to their natural environment, man uses his labour to construct his own environment. Human thinking stands in the service of these communal productive activities. The manner in which labour is divided is decisive for social relations and cultural institutions, such as law, morality, religion and philosophy. Even Hegel's 'Absolute Spirit' is, therefore, man's handiwork. Philosophy does not have a theoretical significance, but primarily a practical one. In this vein Marx's own philosophy does not primarily want to interpret the world, but rather change it. In his *Manifesto of the Communist Party* (1848) he calls for an overthrow of the capitalist order.

Human relations are, according to Marx, inherently discordant because of an unequal division of labour. In classical antiquity, physical labour was performed by slaves, whereas the proceeds flowed to the free citizens. The Middle Ages showed a similar kind of opposition between the peasantry and noble landed gentry. In his own time a *class conflict* was taking place between factory workers and capitalist owners, described by Marx in *Das Kapital* (*Capital*, 1867). The economic position someone occupies in such a conflict of interests determines his preference of legal rules. The ruling classes transform the legal and moral ideology which serves their interests best into positive law. They attempt to instil their ideology in others as if it presents objective universal values. However, changes in the *forces of production*, raw materials, implements and labour techniques can catch up with such social hierarchies, or rather, asymmetrical *production relations*.

Marx regards the idea that the liberal legal order is based on a universal rational human nature as misleading. In reality liberalism is simply an expression of the self-interest of the bourgeoisie. The absolute right to property, for instance, does not provide any guarantee against anti-social abuse of this right at the expense of others. On closer inspection it is simply the right of the strongest in disguise. This inhuman legal order can be abolished only through a revolution of the proletariat, who form the large majority and who have nothing to lose. Just as the bourgeoisie abolished the feudal estates, the workers must in their turn abolish the capitalist class society. Marx's writings intend to bring the working class to this liberating revolutionary insight. The proletariat, who are already used to not owning anything and surviving in solidarity, will after the communist revolution abolish all private property. In future everyone works happily ever after in the fraternal community of a classless society. Everyone contributes according to ability and receives according to need. Law now only has the task of co-ordinating the labour process. More is not necessary, because all social conflicts finally belong to the past. Therefore, unlike Hegel's contention, a truly human society can get along quite well without the state.

Marx attempts in his communist philosophy to combine the two main ideals of the Enlightenment: scientific objectivity and moral emancipation. He does not present communist society as a moral utopia, but as an objective scientific fact:

as the necessary endpoint of a historical process of economic conflicts. At the same time this end of history coincides with an emancipated, truly human society. Marx's communist ideal, however, dismisses the individualistic liberal interpretation of the Enlightenment principles: emancipation leads to equality and fraternity rather than to freedom and equality. Like Hegel, he defines freedom as *essential freedom*: only in the community can one find one's true destiny as a human being.

Marx's scientific predictions did not come true. In industrialised Western Europe, the revolutions of 1848 resulted in gradual reforms in a liberal direction. In agrarian Eastern Europe no factory proletariat was present. It was there, against Marx's expectations, that in the decades after the Russian Revolution of 1917 communist societies were established, but these did not result in moral emancipation in Marx's sense. Instead, the 'dictatorship of the proletariat', that Marx thought necessary during a stage of transition, turned into a lasting dictatorship of the communist parties. The communist experiment ended some 70 years later when its production forces were outmatched in a competition with the liberal Western world. Marx's criticism of 19th-century capitalism indeed contributed to improving the position of Western European workers, thanks to social legislation. Liberalism thus appears to be more elastic and less class-bound than Marx thought, partly through an incorporation of Marx's critique. Stated differently, the internal contradiction which Marx pointed to in bourgeois liberals – between the ideal of equality and factual exploitation – liberalism itself partly cancelled out, without destroying itself. According to neo-Marxists this accommodation, however, does not go far enough. It simply entails *repressive tolerance* on the part of the ruling classes: concessions are made to those who are suppressed, in order to all the better sustain the suppression.

7.1.6 Nietzsche

On the contrary, in the view of Friedrich Nietzsche (1844–1900), such concessions go much too far: the social democracies of the 20th century, Nietzsche would likely have said, lead to extreme equalisation which prevents all human development. Nietzsche reacts not only against liberalism, but also against communism, as well as against Enlightenment philosophy and the whole of rationalistic Western thinking since Plato. You must not think but *live*, Nietzsche thought, filled with romantic passion.

Like Hegel and Marx, Nietzsche does not view man as a rational being, but rather as a creative actor who, in his struggle for life, makes a mark on his environment. In Nietzsche's view, however, the subject of these creative activities is not the human community, but an individual genius, the 'superman' (*Übermensch* – with which Nietzsche does not refer to the blond noble German which the Nazis would glorify in the following century). Such unique geniuses constitute the apex of human culture. The masses, on the other hand, show only a blank conformism. Out of jealousy they attempt to pull down everyone who stands out above them. Communism represents such an attempt at stultifying equalisation. Nietzsche likewise condemns the equal freedom rights of liberalism, since people are not at all equally rational autonomous beings. Far from being *rational*, they are driven by a tempestuous amoral *will to power*. They are not *autonomous*, because the majority consists of a fearful herd. Only the superman is capable of self-legislation, of creating his own unique mode of life. Overflowing with energy, he deploys his abundant will to power; the masses attempt to acquire power in a negative manner by hiding in a safe collective, in order, from this position, to belittle those who are great.

In line with this elitist division of humanity, Nietzsche distinguishes between a *master morality* and a *slave morality*. The slavish majority seeks protection against the powerful through weak values, such as neighbourly love, compassion and equality. Nietzsche rejects this slave morality as being hostile to life, because it attempts to restrain the aggressive vitality of the strongest. The supermen stand above such inferior values; they are after all their own legislators. With them virtues, such as a strong will, bravery and creative power, constitute the basis for the subjection of the world to their will to power.

Nietzsche's political philosophy shows great similarity with Plato's totalitarian class-state. The masses must through diligent labour provide the material conditions for the full development of the supermen, who as artist-tyrants subject society to their will. The hell of Marx is thus the paradise of Nietzsche.

Nietzsche voiced a romantic, artistic protest against the tendency to uniformity and social discipline. Just like Marx, Darwin and Freud, he shattered the human pretension of rationality: so-called reasonable arguments conceal an underlying power play. Nietzsche still exercises a great influence, specifically on *postmodernism* (Section 9.1.4) and on *deconstruction* (Sections 9.1.7 and 9.5). As political philosophy, however, his views are not plausible. The modern state and legal order require complex bureaucratic organisations that do not match the vitality of creative geniuses.

7.2 Utilitarianism

7.2.1 Introduction

Utilitarianism has been of great importance for legal philosophy. It measures the rightness of human action against its useful consequences. More specifically, 'the greatest happiness of the greatest number of people' constitutes the criterion for just action. A number of variants of utilitarianism have been invented. We limit ourselves to the two variants which were elaborated in more detail by Jeremy Bentham and John Stuart Mill. Bentham regards happiness, the final goal of human action, only in quantitative terms. Mill gives it a qualitative turn. The first is non-perfectionist: in order to compare one action with another, it suffices to see which produces the most pleasure. One of the remarkable aspects of Mill's ethics is that he appears to make a switchover from a non-perfectionist to a perfectionist form of utilitarianism.

As a consequence it shows some correspondence with Aristotle's ideal of human perfection.

Although Mill came after Hegel, we discuss his utilitarianism in relation to that of Bentham, who preceded Hegel.

7.2.2 Jeremy Bentham

Utilitarianism was founded by Jeremy Bentham (1748–1832). Bentham studied law, but he was very critical of the legal system of his time. Therefore, he did not want to become a legal professional. He preferred to transform society by means of the reform and rationalisation of law. As such he was at the centre of a socio-political movement, known as the 'Philosophical Radicals'. Bentham's criticism of the *common law* related specifically to the unpredictability of the judgments of judges, who followed their middle-class prejudices. As a consequence, conduct which hardly caused any harm (for instance 'immoral' sexual behaviour) was punished harshly, whereas conduct with detrimental consequences was often barely punished or not at all. Whoever allows himself to be led by his prejudices as if they were eternal moral laws, disregards the consequences of his conduct. According to Bentham, this is an irrational way of proceeding. Therefore, the legal system should be codified on the basis of an uncontroversial and clearly applicable moral principle that sees to the consequences of actions. In *An Introduction to the Principles of Morals and Legislation* (written and printed in 1780, but only published in 1789), he presented the principle of utility, which he described as follows:

> By the principle of utility is meant that principle which approves or disapproves of every action whatsoever, according to the tendency it appears to have to augment or diminish the happiness of the party whose interest is in question: or, what is the same thing in other words, to promote or to oppose that happiness (Bentham 2005, p. 2).

The principle of utility evaluates *actions* in relation to their consequences. Motives and intentions (so much emphasised by Kant, see Section 6.3) are only of an indirect interest: these are evaluated with reference to their consequences for conduct. The emphasis does not lie on a ('liberal') fencing off of everyone's free domain of action. Bentham's utilitarianism makes individual freedom subject to social utility. Actions are either *approved* of or *disapproved* of, in relation to their *tendency*: do they, or do they not, promote happiness? This can actually be established only afterwards; nonetheless, it must be estimated beforehand what chance an action has to promote happiness; this is its 'tendency'. *Happiness* is, for Bentham, equated with 'pleasure' and opposed to 'pain', and is understood in quantitative terms. By taking account of factors, such as intensity, duration, (un-)certainty and 'extension' (in other words, the number of persons whose interests are at stake), one can determine the 'value' of each act. An easy sum (the 'hedonic calculus')[5] then determines which conduct is commanded.

---

[5]Greek: *hèdonè* = pleasure.

By means of this criterion for good conduct, utilitarian ethics raises itself above egoism: from an impartial point of view, and recognising that everyone's happiness has equal value, it provides a supra-personal criterion with which to solve conflicts of interest. It thus requires of the individual to take due account of others. People do not automatically tend to adopt the best utilitarian action. According to Bentham, people are after all by nature egoistic. Therefore, a system of rewards and punishments ('political sanction') must bring them on the right track. For criminal law, Bentham designed the model of the modern panopticon.[6] The prisoners, locked up in cells on the inside of a circular building, are under continuous surveillance from a central point in the middle of the building. The criminal then internalises the all-seeing, punishing look of the state in his own consciousness, so that this asocial personality is transformed into a disciplined citizen. As a consequence, the general welfare increases.

Bentham exercised a significant influence on the father of the most famous utilitarian, John Stuart Mill, and actively participated in the education of the young John Stuart.

7.2.3 John Stuart Mill

John Stuart Mill lived from 1806 to 1873. He never went to school, but obtained an extraordinarily multi-faceted and intensive education from his father, James Mill, which he later supplemented with self-study and contacts with scholars of his time. He was active in many fields, writing about the economy, the emancipation of women, and especially about philosophy. As a philosopher he acquired fame because of his ethics and his social philosophy, but proved his abilities as well as a logical thinker, as a metaphysician and (in spite of his atheism) as a philosopher of religion. From 1823 he worked at the East Indian Company. Because certain of his ideas about the Company were badly received, he resigned in 1858. In 1865 he was elected as Member of Parliament, but in the election of 1868 again defeated. After having lost his office, he still lived for a few years, a period during which many people, mostly without success, tried to approach him for advice. Of significant influence on his person and his work was Harriet Taylor, whom he met in 1831. He maintained a relationship with her for many years, until, after the death of her husband in 1852, they got married. Their relationship resulted in many joint activities, including matters of a scientific nature and of public interest. Harriet died in 1855, when she was staying with Mill in Avignon. So as to be able to often visit her grave, he bought a house in Avignon, and for the rest of his life stayed alternately in Avignon and London.

Mill was confronted with the utilitarianism of Bentham ever since he was young, and he embraced it enthusiastically. In 1826 he, however, suffered from severe depression for months on end, which he recounted in detail in his *Autobiography*

[6] Greek: *panopticon* = all-seeing

(1873). The experience made clear to him that, although he was intellectually attracted to Bentham's thinking, his emotional life remained untouched; he had become 'a sheer reasoning machine'. He, therefore, started with a revision of Bentham's utilitarianism, so as to correct its one-sided emphasis on the quantitative. This ultimately resulted in his *Utilitarianism* (1861). His relationship with Harriet Taylor contributed significantly to his critique of Bentham's utilitarianism. He regarded her as a genius, as the inspiration of all his ideas. Under her influence Mill developed an emancipatory outlook on women, which made him years ahead of his time. The inspiration of Harriet Taylor, according to Mill himself, manifests itself strongly in *On Liberty* (1859; see Section 7.1.2 for more about this book), which he moreover dedicated to her. Even more clearly than in *Utilitarianism*, he distanced himself here from the utilitarianism of Bentham. *On Liberty*, together with Locke's *Two Treatises on Government*, laid the foundation of political liberalism; it can be regarded as one of the classical works on ethics and political philosophy.

7.2.4 Mill's Utilitarianism

Mill in his *Utilitarianism* agrees with Bentham that the various forms of pleasure show many differences. It, for example, makes a difference whether one experiences pleasure by listening to music or by the exercise of power. However, Mill adds to Bentham by saying that pleasures can not only quantitatively but also qualitatively be compared with each other. It is even very well possible that a quantitatively smaller pleasure may be chosen above a quantitatively greater pleasure, because it is qualitatively better. Mill consequently speaks about 'low' and 'contemptuous' goals, which, for example, compare unfavourably with the 'loftiness of spiritual pleasure'. In sharp contrast to the statement of Bentham that poetry is of the same value as a silly children's game when they produce the same pleasure, Mill contends: 'It is better to be a human being dissatisfied than a pig satisfied; better to be Socrates dissatisfied than a fool satisfied.'

This is a significant turn, although Mill makes it appear as if the introduction of qualitative differences simply involves an improvement on Bentham's calculus. However, Bentham introduced his calculus precisely to establish objectively what the value is of 'pleasure' and 'pain'; for this purpose he distinguishes between its divergent quantifiable 'dimensions'. It is only *quantification*, according to him, which makes it possible to escape from the arbitrariness of qualifications. And now Mill appears on the scene to propose an improvement on Bentham's utilitarianism: one must not only take account of quantities, but even more so of qualities. This correction in fact explodes the whole calculus.

If the calculus is in fact done away with, how does one determine which forms of pleasure are to be chosen above other forms? Mill adopts a practical solution: he introduces an imaginary tribunal, consisting of experienced people, who have to determine which forms of pleasure deserve preference. It is not surprising that this tribunal would prefer 'spiritual' and 'moral' pleasures above sheer 'animal' pleasures (which Mill preferred personally too: the tribunal, evidently, is himself).

Mill regards altruism as one of the greatest human pleasures. People experience the happiness of the community to which they belong as their own pleasure. They have a psychological disposition to have empathy for other people's fortune and misfortune. This natural feeling constitutes the psychological condition for the acceptance of the principle of utility. The 'political sanction' which is central for Bentham, thus takes a subordinate position with Mill. This is easy to understand. Because Mill is of the view that people are by nature socially motivated (a disposition which is developed especially through education), everyone would gladly accept the judgment of the competent judges, who accurately give expression to the general interest.

One can imagine that in a perfect world complete harmony exists between 'individual interest' and 'general interest': motivated by his communal feeling, everyone makes a contribution to the happiness of others, so that ultimately everyone benefits and no one lacks anything. In such happy circumstances the maximising of total happiness means, at the same time, the maximising of everyone's individual happiness. There is hardly any difference between 'egoism' and 'social consciousness': someone who finds pleasure in belonging to a group and in making his co-members happy, does no wrong to himself. On the contrary, here morality and rational self-interest coincide.

How are things, however, in less favourable circumstances? It may occur that maximising of total happiness is possible only if some *sacrifice* their interests for the sake of the interests of the group. Mill has great respect for the virtue and self-sacrifice that a hero or martyr displays in such circumstances. In his view, no one is happier than the martyr when he sacrifices his life in the interests of the group. Jesus of Nazareth is the perfect incarnation of this utilitarian morality.

This sounds very nice. To understand its import we should note that utilitarianism is not primarily about the personal domain, but a social morality with political consequences. A social morality furnishes the rules which people must adhere to in their mutual interaction, and which they may, if necessary, enforce against each other. A personal morality is something to which people can, and must, commit *themselves*; it does not contain any instructions as to the claims that people can make on each other.[7]

Before we evaluate the strength of utilitarianism as a social and political doctrine, we should first view the story of the competent judge and his value scale from the perspective of a personal morality. One can imagine an individual contemplating how he will arrange his life. He goes for advice to someone who is regarded as competent. This person advises the following: you must suppress your animal inclinations and cultivate yourself; and you must especially develop your 'social

[7] With Kant we encountered both: his doctrine of virtue entails a personal morality, his legal doctrine a social morality.

feelings': in extreme circumstances you must be prepared to sacrifice your own interests for the interests of the group.

Who can be regarded as 'competent'? Mill says: those persons with a 'noble character' and a 'cultured mind' who from their own experience know the different forms of pleasure between which a choice has to be made. Here, however, a problem arises. How can a person with a 'noble character' and a 'cultured mind' from his own experience know the perspective of a 'pig'? Such a person views a pig in advance from a noble perspective, so that the judgment has already been made; and the pig does not even have the possibility of challenging the decision. It is a mystery what Mill *means* when he writes:

> And if the fool, or the pig, is of a different opinion, it is because they only know their own side of the question. The other party to the comparison knows both sides (Mill 2002, p. 10).

Perhaps Mill would acknowledge that a comparison between 'lower' and 'higher' forms of pleasure in advance benefits the higher forms. From the perspective of the personal sphere of life, this is unproblematic. The experience of the adviser taught him that he can recommend the passage from lower to higher forms of pleasure to everyone, because it shows that people who travel along a difficult road, look back on their life with greater satisfaction than when they simply chase after their own pleasures. If the student wants to follow him on this road, he can himself test the value of his advice. If needs be, he can always fall back on his enjoyable pig's life.

Things change when one relates Mill's text to a social-political doctrine; when the judging agency is not simply an *adviser* whom one has chosen oneself, but a *judge* who contributes his share to a social scheme which ensures general happiness. Mill aims at something like this with his social ethics. When the 'sum total of happiness' requires this, individual happiness must, if needs be, be sacrificed to the happiness of the group, or even of humanity. Political authorities protect the general interest, and they have 'political sanctions' at their disposal to see that the subjects who lack insight into what the general interest requires and may overestimate their partial interests, toe the line. Mill might regret this application of the 'political sanction', for it would have been much nicer if people, thanks to their education, voluntarily learn to subject their individual interests to the group interest. However, if it cannot be otherwise, the maximizing of everyone's happiness must be enforced legally and politically.

Who appoints the competent judges, the persons who, in the name of everyone, must establish the content of real happiness? How does one select them? General elections would not really achieve much; at least 'pigs' should have no right to vote. Only those who are good themselves can appoint the judges. The self-aware elite, then, choose in the name of everyone how social life will be organised. Everyone is, under certain circumstances, encouraged to sacrifice their own lower happiness to the higher happiness of their group, or even of humanity. Mill's theory consequently has an immanent tendency towards moral tyranny.

By now it should be clear that utilitarianism is an example of a *teleological* ethics.[8] A teleological ethics defines the morally 'just' as what promotes the 'good'. Under 'good' is to be understood matters of intrinsic value, which, therefore, could be the *goal* of human conduct. Utilitarianism is *consequentialist*, too: it judges actions according to their consequences. Utilitarianism more specifically judges actions by their 'utility', defined as the ability of maximizing the happiness of everyone concerned. It is, therefore, eudemonistic (aimed at happiness) and maximalist (as much happiness as possible for as many people as possible). The equation which teleological theories make between the 'good' and the 'just' are rejected by *deontological* theories,[9] of which Kant is the great spokesperson (Chapter 6). There the 'just' constitutes an absolute pre-condition for the 'good', for the goals people may set for themselves. One's duty to act justly is unconditional: one *should* not lie, irrespective of the consequences.

7.2.5 Mill's Liberalism

To find a tendency towards moral tyranny with Mill, even if it is unintentional, is astonishing, since Mill was one of the primary advocates of political liberalism. The government should protect the freedom of citizens, while keeping itself aloof from their ways of life. Likewise, Mill in his *On Liberty* discusses the question of the extent to which state and society may coerce an individual. He applies this question specifically to a democratic society. At first sight one would tend to say that, once tyranny has given way to democracy, the exercise of state coercion is no longer problematic: in a democracy the people themselves, after all, impose coercive measures, and this is unproblematic. Mill, however, contends in direct contrast to this, that in a democracy, too, unfair coercion can be imposed by majorities violating the freedom of minorities or individuals. This can occur, at the level of politics, in the establishment of laws and the accompanying formal sanctions. It can likewise occur at the level of society, when individuals are placed under social pressure to conform to what the majority finds appropriate. According to Mill, the social coercion of informal sanctions is often worse than coercion via laws. In order to protect freedom, formal and informal coercive measures must be kept within limits. The limits must, furthermore, be independent of the accidental preferences of the majority: even a friendly majority still constitutes a potential danger. Mill then proposes a principle that indicates the limits within which people may meddle with other people's affairs. This is the *harm principle* (see Section 7.1.2).

We will not attempt here to answer the question how Mill could reconcile utilitarianism with political liberalism. Perhaps this can be explained psychologically. Viewed objectively, it remains somewhat of a mystery.

[8] Greek: *telos* = purpose.

[9] Greek: *deon* = what one should do.

7.2.6 Commentary

Until the 1960s, utilitarianism was prevalent in political ethics in the English-speaking world. Afterwards it was increasingly subjected to criticism, specifically by theories that reject its maximalism (we must strive for the greatest happiness) and its universalism (we must strive toward the happiness of all). In so far as these theories posit individual freedom and the right to assume special obligations (for example in relation to friends and family members), they maintain that such freedom and obligations may not be sacrificed to enforced social responsibility. In this respect the Mill of *On Liberty* was often played off against the Mill of *Utilitarianism*. However, frequently the liberal-utilitarian thought-complex as a whole was exposed. The 'communitarians', in opposition to the utilitarian combination of individualism and universalism, advocate the traditional values of specific communities from which people derive their identities (see Section 9.1.2). Here, we discuss only *one* essential question which everyone must pose to himself, who, on the one hand, incorporates social interests into his ethical theory, but, on the other hand, recognises its differential division of costs and benefits among those concerned. This question concerns the problematic relation between *collective* goods and *individual* rights. Directed at utilitarianism, it reads as follows: can an aggregate principle (where only the sum total of all enjoyments is relevant)[10] do justice to the distributive principle of justice (where the division among the relevant persons is relevant)?

This question is, for example, contained in the criticism that the liberal John Rawls in *A Theory of Justice* (1971) levels against utilitarianism.[11] Rawls states that utilitarianism extends the principle of rational choice (where one individual divides the means available to him in an optimal way among the goals established by him) to society as a whole: how can the scarce means for the satisfaction of needs be distributed in such a way that the total level of satisfaction is maximised? Consequently, many persons are fused into one person. In the same way in which one individual, in order to maximise his happiness, can decide to suffer pain today in the dentist's chair so as not to have to suffer much worse toothache tomorrow, the utilitarian legislature can decide to sacrifice the happiness of a few for the sake of the many, so that the total happiness can be maximised. According to Rawls, utilitarianism, therefore, does not take seriously the distinction between persons, or to express it in a Kantian way: some are merely treated as means at the service of others.[12]

What this can lead to was spelt out by the English philosopher John Harris in his book *Violence and Responsibility* (1980) with the notion of a *survival lottery*. In a hospital Y and Z are close to death; Y can be saved only if he gets a new heart, and

---

[10] An aggregate is the addition or collection of units.

[11] For more about Rawls, see Sections 10.5 and 10.6.

[12] In this criticism of Rawls one recognises the critique formulated in Section 6.3.2 regarding utilitarianism from the point of view of a deontological ethics.

Z, if he obtains new lungs. But no donor is available. Y and Z, however, point to B, a healthy person who has a good heart and excellent lungs. Should B be killed, and his heart transplanted into Y and his lungs into Z, only *one* person dies and not two. What are we waiting for? Someone who thinks in a utilitarian way has no choice but to support Y and Z.[13] The fact that most people recoil at this conclusion demonstrates that they do not think in a utilitarian way, or at least not in a purely utilitarian way. They are not simply after the maximization of happiness, where the chosen means in principle justify the ends. This goal may be strived for only if a number of other moral pre-conditions are complied with, such as that no one may merely be used as means for the advancement of the happiness of others. This leads to a rejection of the *survival lottery*, as well as of other practices, such as slavery.

This criticism was worked out in a different way by the English philosopher Bernard Williams, in his *A Critique of Utilitarianism* (1973). He puts on the stage a certain Jim who somewhere in a South American town encounters a group of twenty Indians standing against a wall. A white person is on the point of having them shot dead. However, in honour of the unexpected visitor, he makes him an offer: if Jim shoots one Indian of his choice, the other nineteen will be spared. If Jim were a utilitarian, he would accept the offer. Many would, however, hesitate and say: if I do not accept, twenty Indians would indeed be killed, but this is not my responsibility, but that of the guy over there. I am not prepared to stain my hands in the way he wants. A utilitarian, who takes account only of the total happiness that is produced by human action, would not understand this at all. Such a non-consequential motive (where the expected consequences are not decisive, but the way in which responsibilities are allocated) would to him appear irrational.

The events sketched by Harris and Williams can be viewed from the perspective of both the 'perpetrators' and the 'victims'. The first occupy centre stage in the expositions of Harris and Williams: here the utilitarian is a kind of director of total happiness. The second would come to the fore when B would ask himself if he has the duty to give his heart and lungs to X and Y, or when one of the twenty Indians steps forward and offers to be shot by Jim. In the first case, a non-utilitarianist would say: people do not have the *right* to treat others as mere means for the sake of total happiness. In the second case: people do not have the *duty* to allow themselves to be treated as mere means for the sake of total happiness. Of course, we would all admire B and the one Indian, but we do so because they would be doing more than can be morally expected of them. Whoever requires that others must regard themselves as mere producers of the happiness of everyone, does not take seriously the distinction between persons (to quote Rawls). He denies them the right to give shape to their own lives in their own way (within limits which are determined by the equal rights of others to an autonomous life). Within the limits of justice everyone may do what he wants, even live a life which is regarded as 'immoral' by others.

---

[13] In order to prevent people from diddling each other out of bodyparts in an *ad hoc* fashion, Harris consequently develops an ingenious lottery which determines whose turn it is to give up bodyparts, the *survival lottery*.

It will not have escaped the reader that the criticism of utilitarianism as just formulated is partly inspired by the other work of Mill that we briefly discussed, *On Liberty*. This work is a landmark in the history of liberalism. Liberalism can be summarised in line with the last phrase of the previous section: within the limits drawn by justice, everyone may do what he wants, even living a life that others regard as 'immoral'. Mill's version of this reads as follows: everyone may do as he wants, provided he does not *harm* others.

7.3 Hegel

7.3.1 Introduction

George Friedrich Wilhelm Hegel (1770–1831) was, as a young student of theology at the Tübinger Stift, friends with the poet Hölderlin and the somewhat younger Schelling, who would later be a famous philosopher himself, and, to a greater or lesser extent, Hegel's rival. This group was taken with the ideas of the Enlightenment, and hoped that the spirit of ancient Greece would revive in the Christian Germany, but now at a higher level. Hegel had a somewhat difficult career. In 1806, when Napoleon was doing battle at Jena, Hegel was an unpaid university lecturer there. He could only just leave the city in time, taking with him the manuscript of his first major work: the *Phänomenologie des Geistes* (Phenomenology of Spirit), which was published soon thereafter. Despite the misery of war, Hegel was very impressed with Napoleon who brought a modern order to Germany. In a letter he said that he saw at Jena the *Weltseele zu Pferde* (the World Soul on horseback). Alexander the Great, Caesar and Napoleon are for Hegel individuals whose passions are used by Reason to achieve a great objective in history. They themselves were probably pursuing other goals, but Reason often works behind the backs of individuals. After the battle at Jena, Hegel worked as editor of a newspaper, and as rector of a gymnasium. During this period he wrote his *Wissenschaft der Logik* (The Science of Logic) and acquired great fame as a philosopher. He got married in 1811 and had two sons. In 1816 he became professor of philosophy in Heidelberg and in 1818 in Berlin where he died in 1831, presumably because of cholera. In Berlin Hegel became very influential because of the way in which he connected his philosophical system, history of philosophy and state theory into a coherent whole. After his death an ideological struggle commenced between right-Hegelians, who emphasised the importance of state and religion, and left-Hegelians, who increasingly converted their religious criticism into societal criticism. From the circle of the latter came Feuerbach and Marx (Section 7.4).

7.3.2 Hegel and Liberalism

Hegel was convinced that the principle of the Modern Age was the realisation of freedom. In Hegel's view, the insight that freedom and rationality in essence are the same, and that the generality of the moral law could merge with the absolute value of individual subjectivity, already found expression in an abstract manner in the Kantian concept of autonomy. Hegel wanted to establish, in modern concepts, a synthesis of the fundamental principles of the Greek and German-Christian spirit. Yet, he also had an eye for the negative dimensions of this process of the 'coming to itself of reason'. Negativity had to be understood as a necessary moment in the development of freedom as a whole: without resistance and conflict the subjective side of freedom cannot realise itself. In order to understand the positivity of the negative, particular events had to be viewed from the broad perspective of the whole process. Hegel built his entire life on a philosophical system which claimed to understand reality in its totality as the development of a reasonable principle. In 1817 he published his *Enzyklopädie der philosophischen Wissenschaften* (Encyclopedia of the Philosophical Sciences), in which he set out the whole of his philosophy as a dialectical, conceptually constructed system. The legal philosophy of Hegel was, as philosophy of 'the objective spirit', already present in concise form in the *Enzyklopädie*.

In 1818 the liberal Minister of Education, Altenstein, managed to procure Hegel for the Berlin University. In the busy period of 1819 Hegel's *Grundlinien der Philosophie des Rechts* (Elements of the Philosophy of Right) was finalised. In the 18th century, Prussia became one of the most powerful German principalities with a strongly centralised form of government. This kingdom relied, on the one hand, on a large army, consisting of countrymen, for the most part serfs of great landowners (the *Junkers*), but in political respect it was managed by a class of officials who directly served the king. In the Napoleonic period those in favour of reform gained great influence. This led to the abolition of serfdom and servitude, as well as the establishment of the University. After the Congress of Vienna the kingdom found itself in more restorative waters, but officials favouring reform continued to exercise an influence within government. Measured against Prussian standards Hegel clearly belonged to the reformers, and he was certainly not called to Berlin as philosopher of the restoration. In so far as the political principles of liberalism implied the freedom and emancipation of the individual, Hegel continued to endorse and defend these. He was, however, a strong opponent of the idea that society consists simply of individuals. Only by being part of an ethical community which through its traditions, laws and institutions is the expression and representation of a supra-individual will, can the freedom of individuals acquire an ethical substance, according to Hegel.

Radical-liberal ideas were widespread among German students, and were frequently connected with strong feelings of nationalism. With his criticism of liberal individualism and by emphasising that the state is not founded on emotion but on reason, Hegel for the most part had a moderating influence on his students. After the murder of the conservative writer Kotzebue by a student (Karl Ludwig Sand) in 1819, and on the instigation of Metternich, the German government imposed strict limitations on freedom at universities, including censorship. A Berlin professor of law was, for instance, dismissed because he had expressed himself in positive terms about the student in a letter of condolence to his mother. Hegel persistently defended these measures. In the Preface to the *Elements* he strongly criticised the 'coarseness' of the views of his former colleague, Fries, from Jena. The latter was dismissed in 1819 because he had a few years earlier, at the politically turbulent 'Wartburg festival' of nationalist student associations, enthusiastically argued in favour of the voice of the people, and for something which we might in today's terms call 'grassroots democracy'. However, in the *Burschenschaften* (student fraternities) radical-liberal thinking went hand in hand with fanatical nationalism and anti-Semitism. Hegel's criticism appears rather to have been aimed at this fanaticism than at the liberal notions that they invoked. Hegel incidentally, in turn, experienced a great deal of criticism because of his attitude. He reacted to this by requesting the government to keep the criticism of his person out of the public sphere through censorship – he was after all a state official.

Because of this it does not come as a surprise that the generation after Hegel viewed his political philosophy as a legitimation of the Prussian state. This point of view, in turn, had the consequence that some regarded the *Elements of the Philosophy of Right* as a conservative turn in which Hegel would have abandoned his more liberal principles. Hegel, indeed, very expressly states that philosophy has to develop the concept of the state in conformity with how it *really* is. The state is, in his view, in itself a reasonable reality; it is the highest manifestation of the 'objective spirit'. The concept of the state can, therefore, not lie *outside* of it as a normative ideal which philosophy presents from an external perspective. If philosophy adopts such an attitude towards the state, it does not rise above the viewpoint of subjective views, feelings and an invocation of morality without substantial content. Philosophy is concerned with reality because – as Hegel dares to express it in his Preface – 'What is rational is real; and what is real is rational.' It would, however, be incorrect to conclude that Hegel in the *Elements* posits the concept of the *Prussian* state. According to Hegel, such a limitation to *one* specific state would be philosophically impossible.

7.3.3 Legal Philosophy as Philosophy of the Spirit

Hegel regretted the fact that he did not have the time to publish his legal philosophy completely in the dialectical form of the philosophical idea. He was of the view that the philosophical structure and argumentation would be clear enough to those who knew his *Logic*. In this he was somewhat mistaken, because there are major interpretive problems, specifically in so far as its completeness is concerned, as well as the way in which this publication has to be fitted into the whole system. Therefore, something more must be said about the content of the philosophical system as a whole in order to understand the purport of Hegel's legal philosophy.

Hegel's system consists broadly of three parts: logic, natural philosophy and the philosophy of the spirit. In the *logic*, Hegel clarifies the meaning of the fundamental (philosophical) concepts, as these evolve systematically out of each other and in opposition to each other (thus dialectically). In the *natural philosophy*, he shows that nature must ultimately be understood as something external, which is not capable of bringing forth the inner unity and reality of the spirit. We consequently cannot understand the spirit on the basis of concepts which are derived from natural science. (In legal philosophy this insight leads to criticism of all forms of natural-law philosophy which try to derive law from a supposed natural state of man, or from his natural desires.)

The philosophy of the *spirit* consists of the philosophy of the subjective, the objective, and the absolute spirit. The *absolute spirit* is religion as well as art and philosophy, because they bring to expression and conceptualise the essence of religion. Legal philosophy belongs to the domain of the objective spirit. The *objective spirit* can be described as the objective reality to which the spirit relates itself as 'its own world'; and which, therefore, does not, like nature, belong to a 'different order of being' than the spirit. Considered concretely, it is the human world, to which man as bodily spirit belongs with other people, and which, moreover, exists only because of people and their history. One can similarly describe the 'objective spirit' with the modern terminology of 'cultural and social environment', provided that one understands these as the objective reality within which man lives and by which he is defined, and not as an object of his consciousness; the subjective 'world of experience' would, with Hegel, belong to the sphere of the *subjective spirit*.

In Hegel's view, the philosophy of the objective spirit, to which the state belongs, has, like the philosophy of the subjective spirit, to do with the spirit in its transient manner of existence. The subjective spirit can be described as the spirit in so far as it comes to 'awakening' and development in the actions and consciousness of individual subjects. The subjective spirit is the domain of philosophical anthropology and psychology. In human individuals the spirit can realise itself only in a limited way. In their way of living individuals are still subject to natural necessities and contingencies of time and place. During his lifetime, each individual evolves increasingly into a unique subject, but he can do this only by sharing in communal life. One cannot say either that each individual has to exist as such. To be sure, the multitude of particular individuals belong essentially to the spirit, but none of these individuals are, as specimen of the human species, an essential manifestation of the spirit. The individual as such, disconnected from his concrete relations with others and society, is, for Hegel, merely numerically to be distinguished from others. Such individuality hardly has any meaning for the spirit. Something similar applies to the objective spirit. The manifestations of the objective spirit are families, social institutions, states. According to Hegel, these particular manifestations are ways of being of the spirit, which are to be understood from the idea of the spirit itself and in this sense have a necessary existence. They exist as law and as freedom of the spirit. However, here, too, the spirit exists as a variety of families, states, and the like. Every family and every state does have a right of existence, but their individuality – as simply one of the many – is nonetheless external to the concept of their being, that is, of none of them can it be said that they necessarily have to be there. Philosophy attempts to understand what is necessary, and cannot, therefore, have the essence of a particular, historically existing state as its object, nor can it legitimise or found an individual state. States affirm themselves in reality, in their conduct towards their citizens, and in the battles and agreements with each other. The 'last judgment' regarding a specific state does not accrue to philosophy, but completes itself in history: the *Weltgeschichte* (world history) is the *Weltgericht* (world court).

7.3.4 Law, Morality and Ethics

Legal philosophy with Hegel consists of three parts:

A. abstract law
B. morality
C. ethics.

The originality and complexity of this division can be explained by means of a comparison with the *Metaphysik der Sitten* (Metaphysics of Morals) of Immanuel Kant, which covers the same field, and which is split into two parts, that is, legal doctrine, on the one hand, and the doctrine of virtue or morality, on the other (Sections 6.3 and 6.4). In legal doctrine, Kant attempts to derive from purely reasonable principles the rules and duties which should apply to all human interaction. The central idea is that individuals, for the sake of their own freedom, have the right to limit each other's freedom if this occurs in terms of a general law which equally applies to everyone. A reasonable natural law is, in Kant's view, based on this principle, which for the sake of its own efficiency requires state authority. Both the existence of the state and of the constitution ought to be based solely and exclusively on the principles of law, which can regulate only the external relations between human individuals. The state and legislation should, therefore, not concern themselves with the *forum internum* or the inner motivations of individuals. The human character, individual life plans, and the convictions of people belong to their private domain. The norms and values which apply here are a matter of conscience and inner inspiration. Legislation which would prescribe moral values or which would attempt to make society good and happy in keeping with moral standards, would degenerate into despotism.

In this Kantian concept of *morality*, according to Hegel, the ideas of subjectivity and of the moral autonomy of the individual come to the fore, which were acknowledged for the first time in Christianity, but only came to full realisation in modern society. Alongside this principle Kant posited the law as an external sphere for individuals, the sphere of *legality* within which they only figure as abstract individuals, and within which only the formal generality of law counts. According to Hegel, concrete individuals do not, however, only as abstract persons form part of a family, a state, and the other institutions of society. The legal relationships of Kant's concept of law are not relationships of concrete subjects with each other, but relations concerning property and mutual relations with regard to things, as they are laid down in agreements (treaties). Hegel is, therefore, a harsh critic of Kant in so far as the latter specifically views marriage, family relations, and the state, simply as institutions of 'abstract' law. Every view which bases marriage or the state on a contract robs these communities of their specific ethical content, and reduces the fullness of the concrete and living human community within which individuals can, for the first time, realise a true subjectivity, to relations of abstract legal persons. For these reasons Hegel makes the philosophy of the human community into an autonomous part of legal philosophy, under the title of *ethics*.

Legal philosophy as a whole is thus supplemented with a socio-political philosophy which ties in with the classical philosophical tradition of Plato, and especially Aristotle. The modern distinction between legality and morality is recognised by Hegel as a fundamental principle. In abstract law the essence of the legal concept as well as the generality of law, which belong to everyone without distinction, are of central importance. As a person every man has a right to *property*, to distinguish him as owner from the things that can be possessed. Slavery denies the universal character of this distinction between person and object, and is, therefore, in conflict with the idea of law itself. However, the abstract general principles of law cannot solve the problems which arise from the fact that people appropriate for themselves specific things, and thus exclude others and end up in legal conflicts with them. In the absence of a positive legal order the abstract legal principles necessarily turn into injustice, because the 'individual will', at the end of the day, posits itself as the law. The extent to which an individual will can be a good will, is the problem of morality. In morality the core of the problem is the subjectivity and singularity of individual persons, as well as the relation between the particularity of the subject, on the one hand, and the generality of 'the law' and 'the good', on the other. However, only in a concrete, ethical community can an objective legal order come into existence, in which a higher authority counts as law. In themselves legality and morality are, therefore, simply abstract principles, on which *real* law cannot be founded. Hegel continues by reproaching the individualistic liberalism of his contemporaries who do not understand that these principles attain reality only in a living community. The philosophy of 'ethics' must consequently return to modern society the idea of a true community, which it risks losing under liberalism.

In so far as abstract law can be described as 'the law of the person' and morality as 'the law of subjectivity', ethics can be described as 'the law of the community'. Law should not be understood here only in the sense of legality, but also as 'the good of the community'. Ethical communities are, for Hegel, a goal in themselves, and have as such a right in relation to the individual. Here the subject is for the first time confronted with substantial rights and duties, and only here can the individual arrive at a concrete, worthy, life plan. Ethics is 'in accordance with the necessity of the concept' to be distinguished on three levels of communal life, that is, the family, (civil) society, and the state.

7.3.5 State and Society

Only in the Modern Age have state and society, each for itself and in distinction from each other, acquired a separate mode of existence. The distinction between the political and the socio-economical is, according to Hegel, the work of the Idea, the self-realisation of the concept. The emancipation of civil society, with its individualism, its emphasis on self-interest and economic profit, its oppositions between public and private, and between legality and morality, appears as the phase of dissension. Civil society would more likely be a Hobbesian war of all against all, should it be isolated from ethics as a whole. In such social relations, abstract right would not be able to establish a legal community. It is, therefore, a misconception to regard society simply as a contract between individuals for a better co-ordination of their interests. Because society factually nonetheless functions as a unity, Hegel attempts to show that the narrow idea of the rule of law – as it is conceived of in liberal political philosophy and economy as *civil society* and *bürgerliche Gesellschaft* – is not the true successor to the classical state. Modern society, ruled by economic interests, can continue to exist and be understood as something good and legal only because it is supported by a greater inner unity. The diversity within civil society must be understood as an element of freedom within a modern state form, which brings about a *unity* of the will by means of (higher) principles of essential freedom. Without the state, civil society would, according to Hegel, simply amount to the *loss* of ethics.

Hegel regards civil society as the layer of society into which family relations have been dissolved, and in which individuals interact with each other, everyone for himself, as an autonomous entity of needs and aspirations. It is, on the one hand, the system of individual entrepreneurship; on the other, it is also of universal dependence, because individuals, in order to realise their own goals, must take account of the goals of others, and in this way are dependent on each other's support. This calculation-based interdependence of interests, familiar to us especially in the economic sphere, forms its own institutions. It furthermore, thanks to law and morality, brings about a more or less *external* unity of association, as it is specifically expressed in theoretical, liberal views of the state. Hegel calls this the 'external state', or the 'state of need and of the understanding' (a state that is rationally instrumental to human needs); the latter can at most be an *abstract* state, thought completely from the perspective of the principles of legality. If this were, however, the only principle that holds the state together, the latter would long ago have dissolved. According to Hegel, the strength of the modern state lies precisely in the fact that it gives complete scope to the principle of individuality, and nonetheless does not destroy itself due to self-interest. The actual state exists on the basis of an 'inner' tie between the citizen and the state, which because of this unites them into an inner unity. The constitutional monarchy is, for Hegel, the modern form of government in which this highly developed unity of generality and individuality is realised.

7.3.6 Constitutional Law

According to Hegel, the modern state must reasonably – 'in accordance with the necessity of the concept' – be segmented into three distinct powers, that is, legislative power, governmental power, and monarchical (or sovereign) power. Hegel, with this move, distinguishes himself from the classical liberal theory of the *trias politica* or separation of powers. In accordance with the latter doctrine, the state consists of three powers: the legislative power or sovereignty, the executive power or government, and the judicial power. Hegel retains the legislative and executive powers, but he replaces the judicial power with monarchical power, which he also identifies as sovereign power. The general views of the legislature can never in the final instance establish what has to happen here and now. The judiciary and the administration of justice are, according to Hegel, not political state organs, but institutions of civil society. Monarchical power takes the position of the conclusion, the final act of will, but simultaneously is as such the embodiment of the unity and autonomy of the state as a whole. For this reason Hegel allocates sovereignty to the monarchical power.

Another important distinction in relation to the *trias politica* doctrine is that Hegel does not emphasise the *separation* of powers, but the organic unity of the three powers. The notion of separation of powers is, in his view, inspired by the citizens' fear of state power, whereas the principle of inner differentiation expresses the rationality of the constitution. None of the powers, therefore, operates, according to Hegel, independently of the others. And it is precisely in monarchical power that the three powers combine themselves into a unity. The monarchical power does not only have the particular constitutional function of final decision-making organ, but also guarantees that the decision-making procedure completes itself as a unity. In this sense it, moreover, encompasses the legislative and executive powers and combines the three powers in itself.

As distinctive power, monarchical power is, by Hegel, thought of in terms of a constitutional monarchy, where the monarch in fact just 'puts the dot on the i' or the signature underneath political decisions, after all segments of society have had the chance of extensively deliberating and bringing to the fore their interests and diverse points of view. In monarchical power all the emphasis lies on the *individual* character of the last moment of choice, of the will which prevails as such, the moment of decision, which, according to Hegel, must at the same time exist as an individual act of will. General decision-making procedures cannot deprive man of this highest moment of personal and responsible choice. In the state, however, only *one* person can bring the final moment to actuality. The French revolution ended in a reign of terror because it propagated too abstract a concept of autonomy, in which every individual will in principle had to count as sovereign will. In that case, the autonomy of the one is the destruction of that of the other.

In the chapter on civil society Hegel advances that civil society necessarily – 'in accordance with the nature of the concept' – is segmented into three estates, that is, (1) of farm labourers and landowners, (2) of industry, and (3) of those who serve the general interest, that is, the bureaucracy, magistracy, and the like. Individuals belong, partly by accident (inherited estate and inherited nobility, for example) and partly by own choice, to one of those estates, and develop only because of this a certain particularity. Citizens should, according to Hegel, by virtue of this *particularity* be involved in state activities; thus not like the monarch by virtue of their person as such, but by virtue of more specific capacities, their 'role in society'. Unlike citizens, who according to their particular place and capacity make a contribution to the state community, the head of state simply exercises the functions of the human being as such, and in that way represents everyone. One actually does not have to have any specific qualities for such a function. This is one of the reasons why Hegel wants to withdraw the choice of head of state from competitive conflict, and has no problems with a hereditary monarchy.

The third estate, also referred to by Hegel as the 'middle estate' and 'general estate', is characterised by its intellectual education and cultural formation (*Bildung*). In order to dedicate themselves to 'general matters' the members of this estate must, by means of their wealth or a state income, be relieved of the need for direct work. The administration of justice, police (which specifically includes welfare) and corporations are controlled by officials who are appointed partly by some form of election and partly by directions of the government. In this way the middle class 'mediates' between the particular interests of civil society and its organisations, on the one hand, and the government, on the other. The government itself is likewise constituted by officials. In principle everyone who has the qualities required is eligible for such functions. In this respect, too, one can speak of a 'general' class. From the many suitable candidates the monarchical power makes its appointments, by virtue of its own insight and pleasure. In this way, according to Hegel, the citizens in the bureaucracy are directly, and yet through the monarch, involved in government. This prevents the formation of a more or less independent aristocracy in state matters.

Because the third estate already has a share in government, it does not have to be represented more specifically at the level of the legislative power. Hegel was not in favour of democratic elections because this would again scatter the people into separate individuals. The traditional division of constitutions into monarchy, aristocracy and democracy, Hegel (like Kant) incidentally finds to be of little philosophical importance. The division simply says something about the number of individuals who are directly involved in decision-making, but nothing about the internal structure of the state, and about the way in which citizens are involved with the community as a whole and with the general interest. It is, therefore, not appropriate for characterising the constitution of states. Just like Aristotle, Hegel emphasises that monarchical, aristocratic and democratic aspects must in different places within the state organisation be given their due. The third estate, or the bureaucracy, represents as it were the democratic principle of equality within Hegel's view of the state. In the second estate, a kind of apolitical idea of democratic freedom is moreover at work, which we currently associate with individual property rights, free entrepreneurship, pluralism, advancing one's own interests, and freedom of contract and of association. These kinds of democratic freedoms must, according to Hegel, be embedded, supported and structured by the interests of family and state, and cannot be privatised or constitute the basic principles of a free, sovereign state. Posited in an absolute sense and disconnected from communal life, they would undermine every form of ethical life. Hegel is not a real opponent of the idea of the sovereignty of the people, although the people without a head of state and without government are simply an amorphous mass of atoms and thus no real nation.

Monarchical power and government, according to Hegel, constitute part of the legislative power, but the first two estates are also represented. Hegel again sees the representatives of the estates as fulfilling a mediating role, now between the government and the 'people dissolved into individuals', to which the third estate can, therefore, not belong. The representation of the estates is divided into two houses. The one is for the 'estate whose ethicality is natural, and whose basis is family life and the possession of land'; the members sit there because of their birth. The second house is for the 'private sector', as the class of industry, consisting of artisans, manufacturers and traders, is called. Their representation must be based on the corporative organisations. Hegel stands here at the cradle of the corporatist view of the state.

Hegel does not want a right to vote for individuals, because the organic structure, which civil society has acquired precisely as a kind of foreshadowing of the state, would get lost, and individuals would in their abstract capacity come to stand in opposition to the state. The corporations are already partially controlled by the government, and now the representatives of the corporations must with the government via deliberation and decision-making about the most general matters (legislation in its most general sense) bring the people and government to a unity. The bureaucracy already does this in its own way, and so too the monarch, as representative of the personality principle. By virtue of the bond between the first house and the monarch (in accordance with natural principle and birth) and of the second house with the government, Hegel again ascribes a mediating function to the separation of the two houses.

7.3.7 Commentary

The range of thought of Hegel's political philosophy has had an enormous influence on the political thinking of the 19th and 20th centuries, especially, but not only, via Marx. Because Hegel has often been defended against Marx's criticism, and passes as authority in the refutation of both socialism and liberalism, Hegelianism has acquired somewhat conservative connotations. Some advocates of liberalism, such as Karl Popper (Section 8.4), view Hegel as a forerunner of fascism. Fascism, however, strives toward an identity of state and society, whereas Hegel favours the distinction between them in modern society as an essential condition for preventing state absolutism and totalitarianism, and for preventing individualism from turning into terror.

Hegel's criticism of the liberal idea that the ideal state is the result of a contract between free individuals is still highly current. According to the critics, it is inconceivable that such a contract can create a legal order which has adequate force and authority. Hegel rejects the Hobbesian legal order as a form of law which is based merely on power and fear of the violence of the state of nature or of the power of the monarch. This submission of subjective freedom to unrestricted monarchical caprice can turn into the highest injustice. In this sense Hegel agrees with Locke's criticism of Hobbes. However, in Hegel's view, Locke's contract theory is philosophically untenable as well. By regarding the relation between monarch and the people as a contractual relation, no state or political unity can be constituted: the sovereignty of the will of the state is instead suspended. Hegel was nonetheless too quick to regard all social-contract theorists as the same. He was consequently not fully alive to Rousseau's distinction between 'the will of all' and 'the general will', and with this the entirely unique character of Rousseau's idea of the *Contrat Social*. Nonetheless, Hegel's criticism of the abstract and individualistic character of Rousseau's concept of will, remains important. For Hegel, as was pointed out, individuality has meaning only in so far as it actualises itself as subjective spirit in an objective form. The unique and subjective character of the individual can and must not be negated. The interests of the individual can, therefore, not so straightforwardly be turned into the single will of 'the' community. The absolutist character of Rousseau's direct democracy, which does not leave any space for personal views, shows that a truly general will cannot be established in the form of an ahistorical and totally unfettered contract. Not the idea of a community, but only the concrete historical community in which the individual participates from the time of his birth, can guarantee the rights of the individual. Philosophy must not desire to construct a state, but, in the concrete state, attempt to extract its legal principles.

Because of his criticism of diverse forms of individualistic liberalism, Hegel remains an important source of inspiration for communitarians (Section 9.1.2). It is, moreover, clear that he is one of the most radical defenders of freedom, understood as *essential freedom*. Essential freedom does not apply only to the private domain, but is a form of *Ethics*, a shared and public form of life; the only way in which individual happiness, family and social welfare as well as the political autonomy of a people combine into an actual possibility. Hegel realised that philosophers who conceive the realisation of freedom, likewise are children of their times. However, the idea that essential freedom had to be realised in a strongly corporatist manner at the political level was even in Hegel's time not self-evident. Corporatism[14] is itself only a specific point of view on what is the best way in politics to deal with social conflicts. It, for example, denies the importance of the class struggle at the level of the constitution, attempts to reconcile class oppositions via socio-political structures, and, therefore, opposes the formation of parties which would lead to political polarisation.

One can have objections against corporatism from different points of view, none of which are imperative philosophically either. Socialism and liberalism appear to be political ideologies which can be defended quite well, and which in democratic pluralism can, alongside corporatism, serve as the basis of party formation. The resistance against the corporatist elaboration of politics from a more rigorous

[14]Corporative state: the state is not organised on the basis of individual participation, but on the basis of corporations, bodies which represent functional groups, such as employers and employees.

liberal view on freedom, is, however, something different from the tendency of economic liberalism to reduce the state to a system of mere negative freedom rights. Against this reduction (of economic liberalism), Hegel's criticism of the *Not- und Verstandesstaat* (state of need and of the understanding) indeed provides meticulous and decisive arguments. A state like this does not give any due to the principles on which it is itself based, and that can be elucidated only through a more specific understanding of what the political order entails. The same argument can be levelled against Marx's criticism of Hegel's view of the state.

According to Marx, the development of modern society would in principle have made the political state superfluous, but the capitalist class would still have a need for the state as a veiled system of suppression. Hegel would, however, have revived the state as a political-ethical community. Hegel's attempts to reconcile and mediate the oppositions within the state in complex consultative structures, is interpreted by Marx as a contradiction in Hegel's view of the state. Thus, Marxism and economic liberalism coincide, albeit from completely different backgrounds, in the marginalisation of the state. In both approaches politics is essentially viewed as a mere form of socio-economic policy making, where the question of state interference or state abstinence becomes the central theme, and liberalism is increasingly identified with capitalism. In so far as the fundamental political significance of the distinction between state and society is not recognised, socialism and economic liberalism both have few political-philosophical arguments with which to defend the state against national-socialist ideas which would (similarly) want state and society to coincide.

Hegel's notion of the distinction between civil society and the political state makes it very clear that the state cannot be reduced to a means to realise specific social ends. The state must establish the ends. But how can it do this, how can a political will be established there, and whence does the state acquire the right to enforce its will? In Hegel's political philosophy this question is of central importance, and he makes it clear that an answer to these questions cannot be of a merely abstract-intellectual nature. A state is rooted in the history, as well as the specific traditions and societal structures, of a concrete human community. Hegel's notion of the ethical character of the community (*Sittlichkeit*) can make a substantial contribution in preventing democracy from becoming a kind of self-evident and merely abstract decision-making procedure, and from being reduced to a mere means for the regulation of socio-economic issues without further concerning itself with its own legitimacy.

To conclude, a brief remark about Hegel's idea of the 'general class'. The views which Hegel developed concerning officialdom, bureaucracy and government were undoubtedly modern for his time. The fact that modern parliaments and political parties are to a great degree bureaucratised fits in well with Hegel's description. The strong emphasis he places on the duty of the official to make the general interest his specific concern, and his idea that in the attitude of officials the corporate spirit and patriotism of the citizen is alive par excellence, today perhaps appears somewhat old-fashioned and moralising. One would nonetheless even today formally expect of both the official and the people's representative an attitude towards the state which extends beyond that of the ordinary citizen. We do not expect from every citizen that he should continuously concern himself with matters of the public interest, or that he should participate in organs which are burdened with their formulation. A political elite in some or other way comes into existence, which concerns itself professionally with politics, and it is certainly of great importance that this group does not merely operate on the basis of self-interest and private opinions. Marx's criticism of the bureaucratic spirit is nonetheless itself still very modern. In almost cynical terminology he characterises the 'spiritualism' of the bureaucracy as a coarse materialism which continuously attempts to strengthen and increase its own power in society by legitimating itself through the general interest. Hegel did not take account of the fact that the emancipation of the bureaucracy into a kind of fourth power could impede the development of the democratic principle. The dualism of parliament and government, of which Hegel would certainly have been no supporter, constitutes an attempt to resist this danger.

7.4 Marx

7.4.1 Introduction

One of the most influential philosophers of the 19th century was Karl Marx (1818–1883), writer of, among other things, the *Manifest der Kommunistischen Partei* (Manifesto of the Communist Party, 1848, with Friedrich Engels) and *Das Kapital* (Capital, 1867). Marx attempted to bring about a unity between the two ideals of the Enlightenment: scientific progress and moral emancipation. His ideas not only had an influence on philosophy, but also a worldwide effect on political practice. This in accordance with Marx's statement, which likewise adorns his grave: 'Philosophers have only *interpreted* the world in various ways; the point, however, is to *change* it.' The French revolution of 1789, according to Marx, brought about too little change. Specifically, the working class was still suppressed. He, therefore, proposed a new, communist revolution which had to establish a truly human society.

Because of his radical political views, Marx did not have any prospect of an academic career at one of the German universities, where the local rulers applied strict censorship. To obtain a position as a purely interpreting philosopher he, therefore, did not stand much of a chance. Because of the reactions of the authorities against his revolutionary writings and political action, Marx thought it necessary to emigrate from Prussia to France and subsequently to London. He spent a great part of his life in the enormous library of the British Museum, working on his communist philosophy. As an intellectual coming from the middle class, he himself had little contact with the working class. Raddatz ends his Marx biography with the following account of a discussion Marx once had:

> 'I cannot imagine you in an equalising time, because your preferences and habits are after all entirely aristocratic' – 'I can't either', Marx answered. 'These times will come, but we must then be gone.' (Raddatz 1975, p. 56; our translation)

Although Marx aimed at intensifying the self-consciousness of workers, his writings were understandable only to fellow intellectuals. He had a preference for fierce polemics and was extremely intolerant towards dissidents. However, Marx was indeed a man of action in the sense that he led the International Labour Organisation, and showed up where revolutions were taking place. Shortly before the French February revolution of 1848 against the constitutional monarchy he published the *Manifesto of the Communist Party* with the ominous opening sentence: 'A spectre is haunting Europe – the spectre of communism' and the famous final sentence: 'Working Men of All Countries, Unite!' When this revolution took place Marx immediately returned to Paris, where the socialist provisional government made him an honorary citizen of France. As soon as the revolution spread to Germany in March, Marx settled in Cologne to propagate communism from there through publications and party formation. This was in vain. With the elections in France in April 1848 the socialist government was again voted out by the majority of voters from the rural areas. In the German principalities and in Austria democratic concessions were extracted, but the monarchs retained their authority over the army and the instruments of government. In 1849 the Prussian army restored the old order and Marx disappointedly withdrew to the British Library.

Marx thus actively pursued political change, but during his lifetime he did not experience any successful communist revolution. The revolutions of 1848 rather led to a gradual political evolution in a liberal direction. As workers' revolt they were, however, a failure. Marx spoke of a victory of the bourgeoisie over the proletariat. Socialist criticism of the one-sided nature of liberal freedom rights nonetheless eventually gained influence. In the last decades of the 19th century a start was made with social legislation in several European countries, which increasingly limited market freedom.

Only in 1917 did the Russian revolution bring about a radical upheaval in the name of Marx. In European countries, such as the Netherlands, general voting rights were then quickly introduced to prevent more radical changes. The question, however, is whether Marx would have been satisfied with the results of the communist revolution. The new Russian government carried out a simplified 'vulgar Marxism', and the 'real existing socialism' in Eastern Europe, Asia and South America made itself guilty of merciless abuse of authority which left little of the human dignity which Marx expected from communism.

7.4.2 Historical Materialism

The change which Marx's philosophy aspired towards was the emancipation of the fourth class, the workers, or the *proletariat*. When this last exploited group had obtained its rightful position, he expected that a harmonious, dignified society would come into being, governed by true freedom, equality and fraternity. In this respect Marx further elaborated on the emancipatory ideals of the Enlightenment. He, however, vehemently opposed the liberal interpretation of these ideals by most

Enlightenment philosophers, which after the French revolution were positivised in the *Declaration of the Rights of Man and of the Citizen.* He saw individual freedom rights as an expression of the self-interest of the third class, or bourgeoisie. He argued that the liberal freedom of the market led to the right of the economically strongest and to the exploitation of the economically weak groups in society, more specifically the working class. The Revolution, thus, did not fulfil its promise of equality and fraternity in the spirit of Rousseau. It simply abolished the privileges of the nobility in favour of the new wealthy, the merchant citizens.

During Marx's lifetime the working class increased greatly in number because of an economical-cultural upheaval which had taken place around the same period as the political French revolution. It is metaphorically referred to as the *industrial revolution.* In England this started in the second half of the 18th century, continental Europe followed somewhat later. Improved techniques made large-scale mechanical production possible, which stimulated the shift in working activity from rural areas to the city. Thanks to the steam engine, manufacturers were no longer dependent on natural energy resources; they established factory cities where great concentrations of industrial workers gathered, having moved away from the rural areas. Improved communication through steam trains, steam boats and the telegraph created a global market for the new mass products (through which all local cultures are swept away, Marx already warned). Liberal market freedom meant that labourers were paid in keeping with the law of supply and demand. In the case of an oversupply of labour, the wage was often too low to live on. Socialists challenged this as capitalist exploitation. They invoked Locke's statement that *labour* is the source of all value (Section 4.2). The profit which the capitalist bourgeoisie made was thus actually based on theft. In the same spirit, Marx appointed himself as champion of the exploited workers. Labour, he stated, is characteristic of man. Animals simply preserve themselves; a man does more: he makes the surrounding world his own by systematically cultivating it and in this way giving a human character to the non-human. As a consequence man finds his true destiny in work. This goal is, however, frustrated when the capitalist appropriates the products of the worker and sells them at a profit to third parties.

Unlike the idealistic 'utopian socialists' before him, Marx wanted to formulate a strictly *scientific* form of socialism. He, therefore, connected the emancipatory aspect of the Enlightenment with its other side, its scientific outlook. Marx specifically made a connection with economic science, developed in parallel with the industrial revolution by the Scottish philosopher Adam Smith in *The Wealth of Nations* of 1776. In this book Smith described the process of the division of labour and of specialisation, as well as the free market which, according to the author, would through a harmonious interaction of all individual interests lead to optimal general welfare. In line with the historical tendency of the 19th century, Marx added an evolutionary perspective to this, which he derived from Hegel: humanity has developed itself through a process of thousands of years, towards ever higher forms of civilization. Marx called his combination of historical and economic explanation *historical materialism*: the history of humanity is, in his view, determined by material, and more specifically, economic factors.[15] Marx thus turned Hegel's philosophy on its head:

> In direct contrast to German philosophy which descends from heaven to earth, here it is a matter of ascending from earth to heaven.... It is not consciousness that determines life, but life that determines consciousness (Marx and Engels 1998, p. 42).

Whereas Hegel as philosophical 'idealist' saw the spiritual life in religion, art, and especially philosophy as the driving force behind human development, Marx contended that the material circumstances of life are decisive, also for human thinking. As the Marxist Bertold Brecht would later say: 'Food comes first, then morals.' The primary goals of man are to acquire sufficient food, drink, and shelter. When this is provided for, man in addition persistently acquires novel needs, and searches for the means with which to satisfy them.

However, in circumstances of scarcity, as Hobbes had already pointed out, this leads to a struggle for life. Marx sees society as fundamentally conflictual. In the initial phase of humanity (up to this point Marx agrees with Rousseau) man still lived in a natural community where everyone shared everything with the members of his group: a primitive kind of communism. Social development has, however, spoiled this state of nature: in a more complex society, people specialise in diverse branches of the labour process. One becomes a baker, the other a butcher, the third, a shopkeeper. This, moreover, means that they must acquire products which they do not produce themselves, through exchange with others. As a neutral means of exchange, money is introduced, which one can hoard more easily than natural products. In this way inequality comes about: henceforth groups of possessors and the powerless oppose each other in a bitter battle.

Alluding to Hegel's dialectic, Marx likewise speaks of *dialectic materialism*: pushed on by oppositions, humanity develops into increasingly higher levels of life. But, again, in Marxism the point is not a clash of ideas, but between groups with contrasting economic interests, such as the nobility, capitalists, and workers. Such groups do have conflicting ideas, but these are derived from their economic position. Capitalists consequently regard the doctrine of the free market with its individual rights as holy, whereas labourers highly estimate solidarity. The position someone adopts in such a conflict of interests, similarly determines which legal rules he would favour. In 19th-century England the landowning nobility

[15] As already said in Chapter 5, *materialism* in philosophy has a different meaning than in everyday communication. A philosophical materialist is not someone who always seeks material advantage, but an adherent of a specific ontology: he is of the view that reality is of a material nature. This in opposition to philosophical *idealists*, such as Plato and Thomas Aquinas, according to whom the essence of reality is of a spiritual nature. Materialists deny that the human mind is an immaterial substance. Consequently, according to Hobbes and the Enlightenment philosopher De La Mettrie, man, including his consciousness, consists of small material parts, atoms. In Marx's version of materialism, wholly lifeless matter is not central, but matter which undergoes active human cultivation. According to Marx, human thinking is not the expression of an independent spiritual sphere, but a reflection of the human mode of economic production.

advocated legal prohibitions on the importation of corn to protect their own corn production. The capitalist entrepreneurs were in favour of the free market because with the importation of cheap grain from abroad their labourers could survive on lower wages. Marx calls such subjective convictions, inspired by self-interest, but nonetheless experienced as objectively just: *ideology*. According to him the material *substructure* constitutes the basis of the spiritual *superstructure*: law, religion, art, philosophy are all by-products of economic development (although they, according to Marx, subsequently in their turn exercise an influence on the economy). Because the ruling classes hold political power, they can frequently through indoctrination impose on the powerless an ideology which justifies their position in universal moral and legal terms. 'The class which has the means of material production at its disposal, consequently also controls the means of mental production' (Marx and Engels 1998, p. 67). This is precisely what the third class attempted to do with its liberal morality. The suppressed class will nonetheless likewise develop its counter-ideology.

Marx's materialistic view thus subscribes to Montesquieu's thesis that human life is determined by material circumstances (Section 5.2). Montesquieu pointed, for example, to the influence of climate on the legal system: in warm countries, such as in Northern Africa, women become barren quickly, so that polygamy is common there; people there are more warm-blooded and hot-headed, too, so that a strong authoritarian government has to keep them under control; this in contradistinction to the phlegmatic English who, thanks to their cool climate and spirit, can allow themselves a democracy. Marx argues against this observation that it does not explain how dramatic social changes can occur while the climate stays the same. His version of materialism grants man a more active role vis-à-vis nature: the way in which people manufacture things out of nature is decisive. The different phases of human history are characterised by specific means of production, which are derived from what Marx calls *forces of production*: the existing natural raw materials, the available equipment and labour techniques. Such ways of production at the same time have repercussions for social relations, or for *relationships of production*. In this way the agrarian manner of production of the Middle Ages coincides with an opposition between the owners of land, the nobility, and agricultural labourers, often serfs who were bound to the land. When the forces of production change, for example, because of the invention of new equipment, such as the steam engine, social relations often lag behind. Hence, agriculture after the Middle Ages increasingly became of lesser importance because of the rise of industrial production and trade. The large landowners, the traditional nobility, nonetheless still hung on for a long time to their privileges and political power, although the middle class had in the meantime acquired economic power. Such a tension between forces of production and relations of production then leads to a crisis, such as the French revolution, where the third estate (or rather class) claimed the political and legal rights which coincided with their power over the means of production.

7.4.3 Class Struggle

Marx describes the history of humanity in terms of *class struggles*: all historical periods are characterised by a tension between a class of possessors of the forces of production and a class of persons who work in their service.[16] These social conflicts lead to more highly developed forms of society, but subsequently, on this higher level, similar conflicts appear with new groups being exploited. Hence a successive development of social systems occurs, that is, slavery (Greek and Roman period), feudal estate society (Middle Ages) and capitalism (in Marx's time). In the course of time, workers become more independent, in accordance with the greater skill which the more complex production techniques require of them. A 19th-century labourer is nonetheless, according to Marx, not freer than a Greek slave. He, after all, out of necessity has to hand over his labour and thus himself to the capitalist factory owner, who on his part contributes no labour, but only capital.

In the capitalist system of production of the 19th century the struggle is thus between the working class and the class of the owners of capital. Unlike the classical liberal economists, Marx did not see the merger between capital and labour in a factory as a functional, harmonious division of labour, but as a fundamental conflict. In the liberal view of economics, all economic players act on the basis of rational self-interest; but as if steered by an invisible hand, without anyone consciously striving for it, the mechanism of the free market ensures that the total result of all individual acts benefits everyone's interests. In order to make a profit, someone takes the initiative to invest his money in a new factory. In so doing, he at the same time creates new work opportunities, so that workers benefit from this as well. Under the strain of competition with other entrepreneurs who similarly strive to make a profit, the manufacturer attempts to improve his product and at the same time sell it as cheaply as possible. Hence his offer coincides exactly with social demand. Thanks to their wage, workers can also profit from the production. The pursuit of profit of the entrepreneur, in other words, creates economic growth, which would not have existed without the market, and at the same time brings gains for people around him.

However, Marx interpreted the relation between capital and labour in terms of conflicting interests: due to their superior strength, capitalist entrepreneurs can make their employees work for a hunger wage, under miserable working conditions, without time off, and without allowing them any share in the profit or any say in the operational management. And, to be sure, in the first decades of the Industrial Revolution, factory workers were captured in a merciless economic regime. The minimal state of that period protected only the rights to property and freedom, from which the working class derived very little profit.

[16] Marx describes the social stratification not in the traditional terminology of 'estates', but in terms of 'classes'. *Classes* are defined on the basis of their economic position. The traditional *estates*, in the Middle Ages, for example, the clergy, the nobility and the citizenry, are defined in accordance with their social function and status. Because money, in the period of capitalism, becomes decisive, the opposition between estates is explicitly defined as class oppositions.

Marx argued that workers had the fullest right to the product of their labour, whereas the capitalist can make no claim to it at all. He based this argument on a radicalisation of Locke's statement that property originally comes into being as a result of the cultivation by someone of a part of nature (Section 4.2): labour is, according to him, the only activity which creates value. Capital, on the other hand, Marx wrote in *Capital*, 'is dead labour which, vampire-like, lives only by sucking living labour' (Marx 1992, p. 342). The capitalist violates the natural relation between producer and product: he appropriates the product for himself, and sells it at a profit to a third party. This profit consists of the difference between the labour wage and the return on the product. The producing worker should actually have the right to the profit as he has, after all, performed the labour. The capitalist, however, pays him only what the working force is worth on the labour market: the total wage which is required to keep him alive. Because capitalists control the means of production, they can force workers to work the whole day for such a low wage – the English factory law of 1850 allowed a 6-day working week with an average working day of 10 hours, but the legal maximum was often exceeded by shortening the breaks; working life often already started in childhood. The factory owner puts what Marx calls *surplus value* in his own pocket without doing anything further to deserve it.

Following Rousseau and Hegel, Marx sees such social inequality not only as an injustice, but also as a fundamental violation of the workers' humanity. Capitalism brings about four forms of *alienation*. In the first place, the producer is not the owner of his own products; his product, which should be a reflection of himself, is foreign to him. More generally, products which are actually only meant to provide for the necessities of life, now lead a life of their own. Means, such as money and other consumer goods, become an aim in themselves – Marx speaks of 'commodity fetishism'. Instead of a truly human life, people now only pursue wealth and ever more goods. Secondly, man is alienated from the labour process: as a result of work segmentation he is now only a cog in the whole production process, so that, unlike the artisan in the Middle Ages, he cannot even envisage the end-product on which he is working. As a supplement of the machine, he now performs only stultifying, monotonous labour. Because each worker concerns himself only with a separate part of the production process, he, thirdly, becomes alienated from his co-workers. Finally, he is alienated from himself, because he cannot fully develop his abilities.

Marx expected that the class struggle between the proletariat and the capitalists would be the final one in human history. The proletariat would be victorious, after which the true humanity of original communism would return. This victory he describes as a historically necessary outcome of the dialectical course of history: capitalism, because of its inner contradictions, already contains the germs of its own destruction. Because of market competition, capitalists cannot mutually reach solidarity, although trade in the industrial period has become so complex that it requires central organisation. The complex production process requires the close cooperation of all participants, and thus appeals to the notion of communal property. In the contest between entrepreneurs the weakest drop out, so that capital is amassed by an increasingly smaller group. To keep ahead of their competitors, the entrepreneurs introduce new machines – because, if they should employ more workers, the price of labour would rise and surplus value would decrease. However, only the largest businesses can permit themselves to do this, and consume the smaller ones. The small middle class becomes part of the proletariat. The growing working class, concentrated in factory cities, are, on the contrary, dependent on solidarity because they have to work under increasingly miserable conditions. Marx mentions here a newspaper report on 'death through overworking'. Because of mechanisation a part of the working force becomes superfluous, so that the supply of labour increases and wages drop. Pressured in this way, workers organise themselves in trade unions and political parties. They then form a well-disciplined majority. The proletarian majority thus actually already has the power in hand, if it was not for the liberal ideology of capitalism which prevents the workers from recognising this power as something which legitimately belongs to them. When the working class becomes conscious of this material and spiritual oppression under the influence of Marx's critical writings, they will through a revolution establish the classless society:

> Centralisation of the means of production and socialisation of labour at last reach a point at which they become incompatible with their capitalist integument. This integument is burst asunder. The knell of capitalist private property sounds. The expropriators are expropriated (Marx 1992, p. 929).

Things must, all the same, still at first be set right via a 'dictatorship of the proletariat', through progressive taxation, expropriation, abolition of the right of succession, as well as a state monopoly on the financing of capital, means of communication and transport, and education. But then humanity has arrived at its true destination.

Thanks to modern techniques of production, in the future communist society there would be no scarcity, and, after the disappearance of alienation, its members would no longer develop any insatiable artificial needs. Since all capitalistic division of labour has been suspended, everybody can develop himself to the full:

> For as soon as the division of labour comes into being, each man has a particular, exclusive sphere of activity, which is forced upon him and from which he cannot escape. He is a hunter, a fisherman, a shepherd, or a critical critic, and must remain so if he does not want to lose his means of livelihood; whereas in communist society, where nobody has one exclusive sphere of activity but each can become accomplished in any branch he wishes, society regulates the general production and thus makes it possible for me to do one thing today and another tomorrow, to hunt in the morning, fish in the afternoon, rear cattle in the evening, criticise after dinner, just as I have a mind, without ever becoming hunter, fisherman, shepherd or critic (Marx and Engels 1998, p. 53).

Especially the possibility of rearing cattle at night appears enticing. One can now live together in harmony, property is in future communal. Everyone contributes according to ability and receives according to need. After the restoration of the original human solidarity, at the same time the necessity for a state and legal system to control social conflicts disappears. They retain only a co-ordinating function. The critical self-reflection of Marx's practical philosophy is, therefore, no longer necessary: 'philosophy's sublation by its realisation'.

7.4.4 Marx, Liberal Human Rights and the State

Marx explicitly turned against the liberal freedom rights of the French *Declaration of the Rights of Man and of the Citizen* because they brought about unjust material inequality and disruptive social conflicts. In *Zur Judenfrage* (On the Jewish Question, 1843) he argued that the so-called 'human rights' are actually not the rights of humanity as a whole at all, but exclusively favour the members of bourgeois society. They after all guarantee only equality in the formal-legal sense, and not material equality. What use does one have for equal freedom rights and the right to property when one has nothing to eat? From a political point of view, Marx did detect progress in comparison with feudal society: the political participation rights of the *Declaration* provided the prospect of joint state management by all people. However, in his view such political changes were not revolutionary enough: unaccompanied by *social* improvements, they did not do justice to the social nature of man.

Political rights had a disappointingly abstract character because the liberal view of the state consciously dissociates politics from social life. The liberal freedom rights after all imply a far-reaching separation between the public and the private domains: the state must withdraw so that everyone can establish for himself what to believe and how to use his property. According to Marx, however, extensive individual freedom has inhumane consequences. Modern society is no longer held together by the traditional bonds of feudalism (which did not as yet imply the separation between the private and public spheres). Since these traditional braking mechanisms on egoism have disappeared, only separate individuals remain who see their fellow human beings as mere means for their own goals. This results in an economic war of all against all, in which the powerful capitalist bourgeois can exploit the weaker working class. Equality in the field of politics thus does not entail socio-economic equality. In short, the political emancipation which the *Declaration* proclaims is inadequate for general human emancipation. (Vice versa, the liberal separation between the private and the public domains leads to alienation in politics: the state frees itself from everyday life, and appears to the individual as a strange external force.)

This one-sided individualistic character, Marx maintains, shows itself in the diverse 'human rights' of the *Declaration*. *Freedom of religion*, for example, implies that individuals in their private lives remain imprisoned by the chains of religion. Moreover, since everyone locks himself up in his own convictions, it leads to the spiritual separation of people. The *Declaration* furthermore defines *freedom* as: one may do everything which does not harm others. At stake is thus the selfish freedom of the isolated individual, who is separated from all others by a legal barrier. As a consequence one learns to see one's fellow man primarily as a bothersome limitation on one's own freedom. The *property right* is in the French Constitution of 1793 described as a right to enjoy one's possessions as one wishes. Here, too, we find a notion of freedom as individual arbitrariness, completely separate from the interests of others.

All these freedom rights in fact merely reflect the need of the greedy bourgeoisie for unrestricted economic trade, Marx argues. Nevertheless, many unjustifiably claim that they are *universal* human rights. Once bourgeois society has come into existence, one tends to liken the asocial bourgeois individual to the 'natural' man as he really is when one thinks away the state. This is, for example, shown in Locke's representation of man in the 'state of nature', with his individual 'natural rights'. But, in fact, only bourgeois individuals are portrayed, who are alienated from their true social nature as a consequence of capitalism.

Marx wants to counter this alienation by extending communal political authority to social life, specifically by abolishing private property. The bourgeois separation between the individual private sphere and the political sphere is then neutralised. According to Marx, this can be accomplished only by overthrowing the state, which is, after all, established to protect individual civil rights.

With these ideas Marx opposes Hegel's idealisation of the state, which he directly attacks in his *Zur Kritik der Hegelschen Rechtsphilosophie* (A Contribution to the Critique of Hegel's Philosophy of Right, 1843). Hegel saw civil society as the sphere where people can satisfy their conflicting material needs. In his view the state lifts civil society to a higher plane where all conflicting interests are reconciled with each other in a rational manner. The suppressive Prussian state was, in Marx's view, the model for Hegel's ideal impartial state: the desired impartiality is, Hegel argues, achieved via three state institutions which set themselves apart from the particular interests that control social life. In the first place, the king, who acquires his position on the basis of a right to succession and not because of any particular social bond. For this reason, according to Hegel, he stands above the parties. Secondly, the state bureaucracy, which forms an unattached 'general class' whose viewpoint coincides with the general interest. In the third place, the state assembly which, through its representation of the estates, provides a guarantee of neutrality: the higher chamber consists of aristocrats who are so wealthy that they do not represent any specific political interest; the lower chamber is constituted by guilds, which represent the tradesmen on the basis of an objectified professional interest. Consequently the state can guide the members of civil society via legislation to a higher level of general humanity.

Marx accuses Hegel of idealising the actual state by analysing it uncritically from the perspective of a metaphysical ideal of the state. Because of this, Hegel regards the real as rational, concealing all actual irrationalities of the state. Viewed incisively, Hegel's metaphysics is itself an ideological reflection of historical interests instead of objective truth: it legitimises the irrational Prussian state by representing it as reasonable. In reality the bureaucracy is not at all impartial, but an instrument of the powerful. The king represents the power of a single individual. The nobility and the guilds are interest groups with outmoded privileges dating back to the Middle Ages. Marx concluded that the representation of estates should be replaced by a democratic government, based on a general right to vote. A truly democratic government represents the whole of society, so that the liberal separation between the political life of the state and the individual lives of the citizens in society is dissolved. Then a true community would flourish: a Rousseau-like harmonious society where all oppositions between community and individual have disappeared and everything is jointly owned. Because the general interest and particular interests coincide, the liberal defensive or negative freedom rights, including the right to property, are completely superfluous. The state plays no further role as a *political* institution, and restricts itself to the requisite central coordination of the labour process.

7.4.5 Marx and Freedom

Marx thus emphasises the last two of the three Enlightenment principles of freedom, equality and fraternity. He attaches a non-liberal meaning to the principle of freedom. This can be illustrated with reference to the formula of the freedom principle from Chapter 1:

X is free from Y to Z

Unlike the liberals, Marx does not regard the autonomous individual as the subject (X) of freedom, but man as member of a community. In so far as restrictions (Y) are concerned, he does not only think of positive restrictions like the classical liberals of his time do: the presence of something that stands in the way of achieving goal Z. The *absence* of means to achieve goal Z, such as the lack of food, income, education, and health, similarly qualify as restrictions of freedom. The later social-democratic liberalism adopted this criticism, contending that the state must accommodate such needs by means of social fundamental rights. Marx further argues that someone can suffer from *internal* restrictions, too, such as a 'false consciousness': as a consequence of ideological indoctrination by the powerful a person can be alienated from his true interests. The preferences which he himself expresses can thus hinder his free development as man. Classical liberals would, on the other hand, simply accept someone's actual preferences, at least in the political discussion. At stake is thus the freedom of each person to establish his own goals (Z). Marx, however, defines Z from the point of view of the true destiny of man, which does not have to coincide with someone's factual wishes. Only Marx's philosophy after all unveils what true humanity entails.

Marx, in short, is concerned with *essential freedom* rather than liberal freedom of choice. You are not free when you do what you want, but when you choose what befits your true nature. This essential nature is not autonomous individuality, as metaphysical liberals like Locke think, but fraternal, communal, creative labour with the other members of one's community. The image of the free, autonomous and rational individual is a metaphysical projection; in reality, in his thoughts and actions each individual is influenced by the membership of his socio-economic class (for as long as the class struggle continues) or of human society as a whole (in the future classless society).

The liberal state with its classical freedom rights is regarded as one of the obstacles in the achievement of Z. For this reason the proletariat, as actual bearer of Z, must overthrow the state. Via a temporary dictatorship of the proletariat it must guide the rest of the population to Z: they must force them to be free. After that a spontaneous, total, and true freedom prevails once and for all.

7.4.6 Marx's Normative Views

7.4.6.1 Introduction

Marx had the pretence of designing a historical-scientific theory which (in keeping with the 19th-century ideal of value-free science) does not contain any normative elements. The proletariat, according to Marx, does not have morality on its side, but history. Morality is through and through a historically determined phenomenon which must itself be accounted for. He regards value judgments more specifically as ideological justifications of class interests. In the preceding elaboration of Marx's thinking we have, nonetheless, used many normatively laden terms. Marx does so regularly as well, but, because it does not fit in with his scientific ideal, he does not reflect on the various possible ways of providing normative criticism. In what follows we, therefore, want to systematise Marx's normative views. In the first place, capitalism is inefficient: because of specific relations of production not all forces of production can be fully developed. This we do not discuss any further. In the second place, capitalism is alienating. This is discussed in Section 7.4.6.2. In the third place, capitalism is unjust, in the sense that the distribution of money and goods does not occur here as it should. This will be discussed in Section 7.4.6.3.

7.4.6.2 Alienation

In one specific respect people are, in Marx's view, not alienated: even under capitalism they are still human beings. What does Marx's anthropology entail? He develops its constituents persistently within the framework of the man/animal distinction (which distinction he invariably exaggerates). Elements of this anthropology are the following: human beings possess self-consciousness; they do not act instinctively but intentionally; their language does not consist only of signals but also of abstract concepts; they make use of tools and produce these, too; on diverse levels they cooperate with each other.

In which respects are human beings then alienated from themselves in capitalism? Marx is more explicit in his criticism than in the depiction of his alternative: he more frequently explains what alienation entails than what the absence of alienation would consist of. Because he does not analyse the latter, he similarly does not concern himself with the question whether an unalienated humanity can exist in reality. In the rest of this section we will look, first, at what this state of alienation consists of (a), next, at what an unalienated humanity would entail (b), and, finally, we will ask whether this unalienated humanity can be realised (c).

(a) People are, in general, alienated from *themselves* and from *each other*, when their *needs* and *possibilities* become fixated, appear in isolation from each other, lead an independent existence, in short: are not integrated into the person as a whole, or if the needs and possibilities of one person bring him into conflict with those of other persons.

People are alienated from their *needs* when a lopsided need (for example, of material consumption or an obsessive need for money or status) dominates their whole life. What makes such a need lopsided? From the examples Marx gives we can reconstruct a variety of possibilities. The first possibility: a certain desire cannot be explained from the point of view of a fundamental need; for example, all kinds of artificial needs which arise from the fact that people want to imitate each other (fashion), or fetishism. Second possibility: certain needs cannot be satisfied and be subjected to the law of diminishing returns;[17] for example, the need for even more money, or for drugs, or the need for security. Third possibility: the pursuit of the satisfaction of a need frustrates itself; the need to make an impression results precisely in a rotten impression (macho conduct). Fourth possibility: there are needs which can be satisfied only if those of others are frustrated, such as the need for positional goods (goods which people want because, and for as long as, others do not have them – a very expensive and famous painting, for example). One can think here, too, of the need of capitalists to produce surplus value, which, according to Marx, must have the consequence that not only workers are alienated from their individual and social needs, but the capitalists themselves, too: their desire for even more money is, par excellence, an example of a lopsided need.

People are alienated from their *possibilities* when none, or only a small number, of their productive and creative abilities can be developed. This can again assume different forms. In the first place, no possibilities are developed: for example, work at a conveyor belt. In the second place: only certain possibilities are developed, as a result of which they hypertrophy (grow excessively), at the cost of others which atrophy; Marx gives the example of a painter who under capitalism only paints (compare, too, the fairy tale in which one woman has a large thumb, the other a large tongue, and the third, a large under-lip); division of labour is the general denominator of this. One can, thirdly, think here of the *cognitive alienation* from which people suffer in capitalism. They can harbour the illusion of what Marx characterises as 'fetishism': they wrongly think that commodities, money and capital have characteristics in themselves as a result of which they can be exchanged for other goods: that money entails real wealth, that capital has a kind of inherent capacity of producing more capital. (Fetishism conceals underlying social processes, some of an exploitative nature.) People can, in the fourth place, be *ideologically seized* by morality, religion, political ideas or philosophical theories. Reasoning in this vein, morality may suggest a unity of interests, and proclaim its values of freedom,

---

[17]The law of diminishing returns provides that output falls when a certain point is reached in relation to input. With some needs this point of equilibrium is, in other words, never reached, at least not in the eyes of the beholder.

equality and fraternity. These values are said to be embodied in laws and political institutions. However, nothing of this is to be encountered in actual social life, or in the sphere of labour, production and consumption. What morality preaches is, therefore, nothing more than an illusion. How can it then exist and have authority? Because actual social life requires illusions. Because the ideal is not realised in everyday life, one 'realises' it 'in the idea'. Because paradise is unattainable, people console themselves with the illusion of it. A danger hides in this contentment. The illusion replaces reality; it functions as an outlet for the energy of discontent. Ideologies, on the one hand, mirror existing alienation, and, on the other hand, thus consolidate themselves. This manifests itself in what may be called *moral alienation*, a form of ideological alienation: workers *and* capitalists think that workers receive, to be sure, a low, yet just, wage for the labour performed, because they are all of the view that the means of production are the rightful property of the capitalists, and as such deserve respect. (When one unmasks this moral alienation by ideology critique, this part of Marx's normative theory turns into a weapon in the class struggle.)

In his criticism of alienation Marx does not explicitly draw a distinction between 'objective' and 'subjective' alienation. In the case of objective alienation the feeling of meaninglessness is lacking. In the case of subjective alienation one specifically has a feeling of meaninglessness. This distinction is nonetheless of great importance for the question of how one can pass from capitalism to communism. One cannot say, as Marx indeed does, that the objective need for the removal of alienation as such will actually bring it about. It is very well possible that the existence of objective alienation without subjective alienation can make people *hold on* to capitalism. Someone who realises this can then force people toward communism, against their will but for their own good: here we have the germ of the vanguard function of the communist party, which harmed socialism so greatly. Only alienation which is experienced as such can motivate people towards social change. This experience must then be based on an anthropological theory which is accepted as true, which expounds the characteristics of an unalienated human existence, as the basis of a normative theory which criticises alienated forms of human existence. In short: Marx must, whether or not he wants to admit this, develop a normative theory which makes an essential contribution to the overthrow of capitalism and the establishment of communism.

(b) We can trace what, according to Marx, *unalienated human existence* entails when we look at the optimal relationship between human needs and human possibilities. Needs are at first physical needs. In their satisfaction, these give rise to new needs, both in 'depth' and in 'breadth': the fulfilled need for bread can raise the need for steak, and the fulfilled need for food can raise the need for a good book, etc. Human needs develop in depth and in breadth under the influence of the cognitive, creative and productive capacities of human beings (which are, after all, primarily aimed at making possible the satisfaction of needs). The dynamism of needs, however, at the same time takes possession of the evolution of the creative capacities themselves. Because of this, labour can, apart from an extrinsic good, become an intrinsic good as well:[18] one can develop a need for labour as such. And this, too, can occur in breadth and in depth: one wants to refine one's creative activities, and start new activities, etc.[19] Here Marx's ideal of unalienated human existence comes to the fore: 'the development of the rich individuality which is as all-sided in its production as in its consumption' (Marx 1993, p. 325). Incidentally, according to many texts, the emphasis lies rather on the productive than on the consumptive side: Marx has a marked preference for active needs (such as the need for the creation of art, and the writing of a book) above passive needs (such as the need for the enjoyment of art, and the reading of a book). And, we can add to this: everyone's all-round and sophisticated production, concurrent with the active satisfaction of his needs, is not only good for himself, but for all other people, too, for humanity as a whole.

(c) Against Marx's optimism about the possibility of *realising* unalienated human existence, we want to raise a few points of criticism.

In the first place, Marx's excessive emphasis on the importance of production and active consumption is 'parasitical' of passive forms of consumption. The writing of books becomes senseless when there are no readers.

In the second place: creative people can indeed be appreciated by humanity as a whole (for example, Vincent van Gogh). However, the fact that creativity constitutes the highest value in communism can be frustrating for many individuals who lack these capacities. Moreover, there can be no successful philosophers when they have not been preceded by a great number of minor or even failed philosophers. That creativity is good for humanity as a whole, therefore, does not automatically imply that it is good for everyone individually: the frustration of failed individuals is a necessary condition for the full development of human talents. This can give rise to feelings of jealousy, and it cannot be expected that these will be absent under communism.

It can, thirdly, not be expected that people will achieve optimal self-fulfilment, for example as lawyers or philosophers, when they do not relinquish many other ways of improving themselves: growth 'in depth' cannot go together with growth 'in breadth' – however much Marx may think so ('to hunt in the morning, fish in the afternoon, rear cattle in the evening, criticise after dinner'). Whoever wants to develop certain abilities, must allow them to hypertrophy. People may, in a certain sense, become obsessed with them, and one must allow others to atrophy: compromises are, therefore, necessary – something to which Marx is blind in his depiction of the ideal communist society.

This hypertrophying has, fourthly, as consequence that very creative people are often very displeased with their achievements – however much others praise them.

---

[18]Extrinsic good: something that serves only as a means; intrinsic good: something that constitutes a goal in itself.

[19]Marx's view on the place of work within communism is incidentally not that clear: on the one hand, he states that work is the primary need in life; on the other hand, work there becomes superfluous, and man realises himself beyond labour.

This is the counterpart of the earlier mentioned jealousy: those who are unproductive are jealous of the productive ones, those who can do so much; and those who are productive, of those who are unproductive, who need to do so little. Specifically those people who are supposed to be very happy, are in this sense very unhappy, both in their creative periods, and when with old age their creativity decreases. In this respect, too, Marx's ideal society is unrealistic.

In the fifth place: to this can be added that Marx actually has no eye for the finite nature of life: for the fact that people will die, that their abilities in the course of their lives decrease, that they can become sick or have accidents, etc.

Marx's ideal society is, all in all, based on psychological premises which are the outcome of *wishful thinking*.

7.4.6.3 Is Capitalism Unjust?

Concerning the question whether Marx has a normative theory of justice there are diverse views, and all these views can invoke Marx's texts in support.

According to some he has no theory of justice at all, in fidelity with his Hegelian conviction that nice ideals do not determine history: 'Communism is for us not a *state of affairs* which is to be established, an *ideal* to which reality [will] have to adjust itself. We call communism the *real* movement which abolishes the present state of things.' (Marx and Engels 1998, p. 57) A kind of objective necessity determines the course of history, and the only issue is to grasp it scientifically.

In the view of others, Marx has no theory of justice in the sense that there would be absolutely valid norms of justice. Yet, he does have such a theory in the sense that a certain conception of justice suits a specific mode of production. Justice is consequently something completely relative: if it is in general true that the ideas of the ruling class are the prevailing ideas, then a particular idea of justice prevails under capitalism, something like: property must be respected and contracts must be honoured; or perhaps: everyone contributes according to free choice and receives according to contribution. In socialism a second theory of justice would then be present, that is: everyone contributes according to capability and receives according to contribution; and in communism again a third: everyone contributes according to capability and receives according to need. See the following scheme.

Contribute according to \ **Receive according to**	need	contribution
capability	communism	socialism
choice	utopianism	capitalism

(This, for example, means: in communism everyone receives according to need, and everyone contributes according to ability. In socialism everyone receives what he has contributed. The latter is for Marx a transitional situation, where goading still is required. In the ideal communist society everyone receives according to need.) Can these three ways of understanding Marx's theory of justice be brought into synthesis? Perhaps this is possible, without having to do too much violence to the texts.

According to still others, Marx is of the view that 'justice' in all its variants is something which suits the societal types which precede communism. As soon as people in communism can realise their full potential together with others, a conception of justice is no longer required; justice is transcended.

Let us enquire into the notion that 'Everyone contributes according to choice and receives according to contribution', which we just characterised as 'capitalist': in capitalism the capitalist is rewarded for the fact that he unites workers and makes their cooperation productive, whereas the workers are rewarded for the work they do. This is not, however, simply a neutral formulation of an objective fact. On the contrary, the class perspective of the *capitalist* finds expression here, the capitalist having an interest that the workers share this view. In opposition to this stands the viewpoint of the *working class*: the workers do not obtain what they deserve; they are denied their 'surplus value'; they are exploited. How must one view this dispute?

One can, in the first place, say that this is not a rational discussion, but simply a reflection of the real conflicts of interest of the participants. It, therefore, does not make any sense to approach the views of the capitalists and of the workers rationally, to discuss their respective pro's and con's; one must simply choose sides for the one or the other class, and in this way promote its interests; if one's party wins, new ideas will prevail. This is an application of the Hegelian model.

The social struggle is, nonetheless, waged under the banner of conceptions of justice. What does the fact that capitalists and workers believe that their interpretation of 'Everyone contributes according to choice and receives according to contribution' is the correct one, contribute to their cause? One could say: in so far as the parties have more confidence in the justice of their cause, they will actually mobilise more for the sake of it, and the chances become greater that their party will be victorious. Belief in a conception of justice is consequently likened to a force of nature, which strengthens already-existing natural forces. Some of Marx's texts support this interpretation. There is nonetheless something strange about it, as will appear from the subsequent discussion.

A Marxist is likely to say: 'It is in the interest of workers to believe that capitalism is unjust, because that belief strengthens their anti-capitalist struggle.' Is this a reason for workers to believe that capitalism is unjust? This is not the case, as an analogous example may show. It appears that men in general do better in society than women because they believe that their success depends on themselves, and that their failures are a result of their social environment, whereas women often believe the contrary: they attribute their failures to themselves and their successes to others. The 'male' belief makes one active: one mobilises against one's surroundings and this increases one's social chances, whereas the 'female' belief makes one passive: one wants to toady to one's surroundings and this decreases one's social chances. Nonetheless, the fact that it is in one's interest to believe that success is attributed to oneself and failure to the environment, is not a reason to actually believe it. One must 'really' believe in it. Now, this may be a weak example, because it concerns purely psychological attitudes, which can be manipulated. (Stuttering is caused by the fear that you will stutter again; when you believe that you will not do it again, you will not; all kinds of training are based on the internalising of such beliefs.) A better example would be the following: an advocate who believes in the innocence of his client will defend him more vigorously; nonetheless, the insight that belief in the innocence of a client makes one more combative, is no reason to believe in this innocence; for that purpose, objective indications are required which are not easy to manipulate psychologically. Continuing the argument in the same vein, we could say that Marx not only had the conviction that belief in the justice of the proletarian struggle advances their cause, but certainly believed in its justice too.

This we indeed find in his *Kritik des Gothaer Programms* (Critique of the Gotha Programme). Here Marx discusses the principle that 'Everyone contributes according to ability and receives according to contribution', which in the socialist transitional society constitutes the guiding principle. He has rational objections against it, making it unsuitable as guiding principle for the communist society: not everyone has an equal ability to perform productive labour, which means that some would benefit and others be prejudiced in terms of this principle. In other words, the equal right to share according to an equal standard during this transitional phase, still amounts to inequality. Here Marx actually develops a non-relative conception of justice: if everyone had the same abilities, the above guiding principle would be defensible. This conception of justice at the same time gives Marx the possibility of criticising capitalism, specifically the principle that 'everyone contributes according to choice, and receives according to contribution'. This is actually unjust in a two-fold sense: in the first place, it assumes that everyone has the same possibilities of choice, whereas this is already contradicted by the unequal division of abilities; secondly, capitalism does not apply its guiding principle in a consistent manner, because the surplus value that capitalists appropriate for themselves, does not entail a reward for their contribution, but is based purely on the exploitation of workers.

In other words, Marx's relativistic conceptions of justice are based on a non-relativistic conception of justice.

Conceptions of justice are nonetheless of secondary importance in Marx's normative theory. A person who thinks in terms of justice, according to Marx, regards people as beings with different preferences and ideals. As a consequence, in a world of scarcity they enter into conflict with each other. A system of rights and duties must, therefore, be introduced, guaranteed by the state. Someone who thinks in terms of rights and duties regards people, then, as beings who are in competition with each other, or even as beings who are hostile to each other. However, scarcity is largely artificial: all kinds of preferences are imposed upon people. Essentially, people have only a limited number of fundamental needs (more specifically, to realise their own potential through productive labour). This need they can satisfy only in cooperation with each other. Once the technological level is high enough, the essential needs *can* all be satisfied. From then on structural conflicts can be avoided. A society is possible in which the self-realising activity of each leads to the enrichment of the lives of all. Now it is no longer necessary to speak in terms of justice and morality. Speaking like this is a symptom of the fact that people in capitalism are alienated from each other. Similarly, human rights are no longer necessary. When one proclaims individual human rights, one has to concede that one individual must be protected against others. This is, however, only the case in an antagonistic society where the means of production are in the hands of individuals. In a socialised economy, human rights are superfluous, and the whole of law, and actually the state as well, lose their raison d'être.

This view of morality, then, is reconcilable with the fact that Marx, in the transitional period from capitalism to socialism and from socialism to communism, makes use of moral terminology. And thus we have indicated that the three notions of justice that one finds with Marx are reconcilable with each other.

The question then remains: is this normative theory of Marx plausible? More specifically, is Marx right when he says that capitalism is based on exploitation, and that it, therefore, does damage to its own conception of justice? And when he says that a form of society is conceivable in which individual interest and general interest are harmonised, so that no conception of justice is required any longer? We want to address both of these questions briefly.

(1) Is capitalism based on exploitation? We do not want to contend that this is *not* the case, but simply indicate that exploitation is more complex than Marx appears to think, and that further theorising is, therefore, necessary. Suppose that we live in a socialist society, where the means of production are socialised and everyone contributes according to ability and receives according to contribution. There are, therefore, differences in income because people differ in abilities. Suppose now, that one of the more capable people has in the course of time saved enough money to establish a small business, and suppose that this is not prohibited. Certain means of production thus belong to him and not to the community. He subsequently recruits workers and offers them a higher wage than they receive at state companies; he is capable of doing this because his business is run more efficiently than state companies. This wage does not, however, coincide exactly with the contribution of each person. In his company 'surplus value' is, therefore, produced in the strict sense of the term, and our socialist-capitalist puts this in his own pocket. Is this a form of exploitation? The answer is not self-evident. The workers in this capitalist island in the ocean of state companies receive a higher wage than any state company can offer. They are, therefore, not forced to sell their labour, or otherwise be punished with impoverishment. If all those involved agree to this arrangement, nothing much can be said against this form of 'exploitation'. In short: Marx's

statement that every form of production and unequal distribution of surplus value is unjust requires fine-tuning. This requires more normative theorising than Marx displayed.

(2) Can it ever be expected that individual interest and general interest are in harmony with each other, so that disputes and discussions about the just share of everyone become superfluous? We want to raise one argument against this here. In communism everyone contributes according to ability and receives according to need. This does not mean that everyone does the same and receives the same; uniform equality is no virtue of communist society, Marx warrants time after time. Everyone has the same chance to realise himself, and people do this in diverse ways. For this self-realisation material goods are often necessary, and indeed in different quantities. Somebody who wants to read poetry requires fewer goods than someone who wants to produce an action film: this latter preference is *more expensive* than the first. It cannot be expected that a society would ever have enough material means so that everyone attains the unlimited opportunity to satisfy his expensive preferences. Must one then assume that in communism, in direct contrast with capitalism and socialism, people will live together so harmoniously that such expensive preferences will not arise? This is unlikely. It would indeed be necessary to have social discussions about the question of who acquires what for which purpose: precisely the kind of question that is in need of a normative theory of justice.

To summarise: Marx has every reason to develop a theory of justice. In his texts, however, this only appears in a rudimentary and contestable form. Therefore Marx's views need to be developed in more detail.

7.4.7 Commentary

Marx's philosophy as a whole is currently regarded as one-sided. On the other hand, important parts of his theory have now become widely accepted. First the criticism.

Marx's combination of science and moral emancipation leads, as already indicated, to problems because of the pretence of science that it is value-free: it simply states how reality is; how reality should be, it can, on the other hand, not objectively establish; normative statements are in the empiricist view based on subjective assessment. According to this separation between values and facts, Marx himself regards moral statements as utterances of the subjective ideology of the group to whom the speaker belongs. However, what is then the status of his support for the struggle of the proletariat against capitalism: 'Working men of all countries, unite!'? Do workers win the class struggle because historical laws make this unavoidable? In that case, human history is nothing but a power struggle, so that, viewed morally, it does not matter who wins. Or does Marx, nonetheless, imply that the proletariat are fighting a *just* struggle?

On closer inspection the problem is even more complicated because Marx views human knowledge as such as an instrument with which man appropriates the world.

Science is then, just like other products of the human spirit, determined by the biased perspective that the scientist adopts in the production process. This relativising of the objectivity of science at the same time strikes back at Marx's own scientific work: it interprets the particular point of view of the proletariat, and can, therefore, make no claim to objective truth. Even more so because Marx himself belongs to the middle class.

From a scientific viewpoint the belief that Marx shares with Hegel is curious: that the historical process necessarily comes to rest at an optimal destination and that this End of History is imminent. This view reminds one rather of the teleological metaphysics of Aristotle (Section 2.5) than the aimless, amoral processes which are described in the natural science of Galileo and Newton (Section 3.4).

In fact, this teleological part of Marx's doctrine has in the meantime been falsified by history. The German revolution of 1848, which he himself witnessed, failed, and in the 1860s he waited in vain for the crisis of capitalism. During the First World War the proletariat of all countries fought against each other in their various national armies, instead of uniting themselves in an international labour movement against international capitalism, as Marx would have hoped. The reason for this is that Marx left out of account one function of the national state: the state is not only an internal means of the powerful class to keep down the powerless, but it at the same time constitutes a defensive unit against external attackers. Because of this the nationalistic feelings of the workers could gain the upper hand over their cosmopolitan class solidarity.

In the meantime, instead of less, increasingly more capitalists have emerged because workers themselves started participating in civil society and the democratic liberal constitutional state. Contrary to what Marx predicted, capitalism thus did not progressively marginalise itself into a state of misery. The American vehicle manufacturer Henry Ford, for example, realised that if he gave his workers higher wages, they, too, could buy his cars.

Communist revolutions mainly succeeded in pre-industrial, agrarian, feudal countries, such as Russia and China, precisely where Marx did not predict that they would occur. In these countries, 'actually existing socialism' led to the opposite of a humane society. The dictatorship of the proletariat became an excuse for merciless suppression of the population. The weak performance of the communist state economies at the same time showed that the free market and self-interest are indispensable motors of economic production, and should, therefore, at least not be completely eliminated. Communism is especially concerned with distribution, not with production. However, if nothing is produced, there is nothing to distribute. Where communist regimes have not already disappeared, they are not taken seriously by most people.

From the above a moral danger of Marx's doctrine also appears. Marx assumes that those who are suppressed are not aware of their own true interests as a consequence of indoctrination. An intellectual vanguard that does have this insight must inspire the exploited masses to participate in a violent upheaval and temporarily establish the dictatorship of the proletariat. As Popper (Section 8.4) later remarked, after his experience with the dictatorships of Stalin and Hitler, this claim to vanguardism invites the same abuse that threatens in Plato's ideal state: everyone can claim that he represents true humanity and *essential freedom*, and then enforce his will with rhetoric and violence. This in fact happened in countries where communism was imported. Because, according to Marxist theory, no opposing interests any longer exist in post-revolutionary society, the internal control mechanisms which are built into Western democratic constitutional states were declared to be superfluous in these countries. The consequence was a totalitarian regime which prescribed in the smallest detail what everyone has to do and think. Popper, therefore, pleads for the more realistic view that power mostly corrupts. One must control the rulers through constitutional institutions, such as individual human rights and separation of powers, including an independent judicial power.

Marx unjustly debunked liberal human rights as merely a means of power of the bourgeoisie. They were indeed after the French revolution interpreted and positivised in a biased manner. However, the underlying ideal of equal freedom has a broader import: the lack of socio-economic means of existence can restrict one's freedom (negative restrictions), too. Consequently the very liberal ideal of freedom supplies the working class with an argument with which to claim social fundamental rights against the middle class on the basis of the latter's own liberal ideals. Marx would nonetheless have been justified in remarking that fraternity is then still not guaranteed.

Another contemporary moral reproach against Marx is that he views nature merely as an object of human cultivation. After the end of the class struggle, a new relation of exploitation would, therefore, come about, now between man and non-human nature, which people nowadays want to counteract by according rights to animals, plants, as well as rainforests.

Despite this criticism, parts of Marx's philosophy in a less radical form are incorporated into the received worldview. His undermining of the belief in human rationality has had a great influence: that material circumstances and social status exercise a great influence on human thinking is generally acknowledged (although Marx exaggerated its economic aspect). From a political perspective, his criticism of the exploitation of the weaker groups was one of the reasons for the establishment of social fundamental rights and of the welfare state. Consequently, Marx's prediction of the ruin of capitalism has perhaps not come true because of its influence as a self-denying prophecy.

In the course of the 20th century, workers, too, have through redistribution and democratisation become active participants in capitalism, although not quite in the way Marx would have wanted. Neo-Marxists see these developments as part of the strategy of capitalists to tame the final class struggle predicted by Marx by means of sweeteners. Workers, their criticism goes, have acquired only some say in their working conditions, but they still do not have any substantial say in their own products. Other social critics often do support Marx's Rousseau-like accusation against the one-dimensional urge of consumption which characterises contemporary society.

7.5 Nietzsche

7.5.1 Introduction

Friedrich Nietzsche (1844–1900) was an even more radical critic of his time than Marx. He wanted to 'philosophise with a hammer'. Nietzsche rejects the Enlightenment as such, and repudiates both its ideal of scientific progress and of moral emancipation. He even calls himself an 'immoralist'. His alternative has a heroic-aesthetic rather than a political import: the individual must live grandiosely and vigorously, against the stream of conformism. Equality and brotherhood à la Marx, Nietzsche finds despicable because of its equalising effect. Christianity and rationalistic Greek philosophy likewise do not pass muster because they want to place the whole of life into a straightjacket. It is not reason which characterises man, but his domineering *will to power*. Nietzsche looks for inspiration in pre-Socratic philosophy, with Heraclitus as exemplary hero: 'War is the father of all things.' Nietzsche: 'War and courage have achieved greater things than neighbourly love.' In addition, he was a great admirer of Wagner's theatrical operas. His philosophical style is similarly imbued with the dramatic:

> Of all writings I love only that which is written with blood. Write with blood: and you will discover that blood is spirit (Nietzsche 2003a, p. 67).

To Nietzsche's most famous works belong the poetic *Also sprach Zarathustra* (Thus spoke Zarathustra, 1883–1885) and *Jenseits von Gut und Böse* (Beyond Good and Evil, 1886) as well as *Genealogie der Moral* (Genealogy of Morals, 1887).

Nietzsche opposed everything which he absorbed during his education. His father was a church minister. He died when Nietzsche was 5 years old, and the young Nietzsche was thereafter brought up by his mother and sisters in accordance with protestant virtue. Hence Nietzsche grew up as a good-natured child dreaming of a courageous virile life detached from God and conventional virtue. His development progressed according to the three stages of the human spirit as he described them in *Zarathustra*. During childhood, one at first conforms to the authority of one's teachers: like a camel one is burdened with the values of another person. Then one acquires like a proud lion a distinct sphere of freedom *from* external authority. And, finally, one creates one's own identity by realising freedom as freedom *toward* self-constituted goals and values. After studying classical languages, Nietzsche, at only the age of 24, became a professor at Basel, but because of his bad health, retired just 10 years later. After this his writings became increasingly idiosyncratic. During his lifetime he received little attention. Nietzsche withdrew further into the loneliness of his own thoughts, becoming insane in 1889. He died in 1900. In the 20th century his fame became increasingly great, and at present, too, he is a much-read author. His work has a fragmentary character, but interpreters nonetheless detect coherence in them.

Nietzsche's first publication, *Die Geburt der Tragödie aus dem Geiste der Musik* (The Birth of Tragedy: Out of the Spirit of Music, 1871), is a study of Greek culture which was strongly influenced by his own preoccupations. Nietzsche detects two contradictory tendencies in Greek culture. Classical architecture and sculpture are known for their balanced, symmetrical and rigid construction. This emphasis on measure and order is similarly characteristic of the rationalist philosophy of Plato. Nietzsche calls this tendency *Apollonian*, after the Greek sun god Apollo. However, in Nietzsche's view, this emphasis on harmonious order is so strong specifically to provide a counterweight to an opposing tendency which is as characteristic of the Greeks: a vital tendency towards ecstasy and intoxication which come to expression, above all, in dancing and music. Nietzsche baptises this tendency *Dionysian*, after Dionysus, the god of wine, chaos and fertility. Plato indeed presents his rational state order as a means to rein in the chaotic animal drives of the irrational masses (see Section 2.4). Platonic justice means that everything takes its right place in the cosmic order, so that reason rules over emotion. Art forms, such as tragedy and poetry, are forbidden in Plato's ideal state, because they have too much of an effect on the emotions. In the same spirit, Aristotle's ethics always opts for the balanced, golden mean between two irrational extremes (for example bravery between cowardice and recklessness). Nietzsche rejects this excessive emphasis of rationalism on controlling and moderating the drives as hostile to life, just like the rationalistic preference for the spirit over the body. He accords the primary role to the passionate Dionysian archaic drive, the motor of all life and creative power. Reality is not a rational order of eternal Ideas, but a stream of energy which in a process of coming into being and passing away, always creates new forms and then destroys them again. Only after this does Apollonian stylising come to the fore. In this way, Nietzsche writes, Greek tragedy is born from the spirit of Dionysian music. Wagner's music he sees as a contemporary example of such compelling art. In a similar way, all great individuals must give creative form to their life energy.

The way in which Nietzsche paints his historical study in keeping with his own view of life corresponds with his idea of the role of historiography. Nietzsche dismisses the historicist tendency of 19th-century philosophy, as it appears, among others, in Hegel and Marx. A man should not see himself as part of an inescapable historical process, because this hinders his own development. Instead of allowing oneself to be dictated to by the past, one must opt for the present. Historiography is allowed, but it must stand in the service of actual life. There is, therefore, nothing wrong with projecting one's own idea of life onto the past, as Nietzsche does in his historical study of Greek tragedy.

The same applies to all forms of knowledge: knowledge stands in the service of the development of one's life, or the *will to power*. Contrary to the rationalist view, objective truth does not exist. The rationalistic view of knowledge is based on a false idealisation of the human ability of obtaining knowledge, as if this is an independent reasonable institution which provides access to an objective reality. This philosophical self-deception derives from the human need for a safe, conveniently arranged world with an external standard which provides certainty. In reality, human conduct and knowledge is for the greatest part determined instinctively. Human consciousness is an instrument with which to control the environment: in the first place, to survive, and additionally, to arrange it according to one's own viewpoint.

One, therefore, always makes one's observations from a specific, interested point of view, and interprets the world from the perspective of one's own values. Insight into a higher metaphysical truth is, therefore, not possible. The same goes for objective, empirical knowledge: all one knows is that external stimuli touch one's senses, then awaken an image in one's consciousness, which one subsequently designates with abstract concepts. Whether human conceptual constructions correspond with an external world which caused the stimuli, one cannot possibly know. It is always from within the framework of one's own conceptual constructions that one organises the sensory impressions.

Like Kant, Nietzsche, therefore, does not see human knowledge as a faithful reflection of an external rational or material reality, but as a construction of human consciousness. However, whereas Kant regards the structures by means of which consciousness organises experience, as a fixed, rational order, in Nietzsche's view they change in keeping with the viewpoint of the observer.

Up to this point Nietzsche's perspectivist view of knowledge comes very close to Marx's relativism: according to both, knowledge is a changing product of human practices. However, according to Marx's political philosophy someone's perspective is determined by the position which his economic group occupies, whereas Nietzsche, more aesthetically orientated, sees knowledge as a highly personal creation. This fits in with his artistic view of human life: the point is to design one's own vital forces in an authentic manner. Nietzsche consequently expressed his philosophy in poetic images rather than with conclusive argumentative reasoning.

7.5.2 Beyond Good and Evil

Nietzsche's emphasis on self-determination only partly coincides with the emphasis of the Enlightenment on individual autonomy. The Enlightenment philosophers regard all people equally as self-legislators. Nietzsche, on the other hand, is radically elitist: in his view, only certain individuals possess sufficient independence and creative power to arrange their lives fully in keeping with their own standards. The masses stay behind like a camel weighed down by the burden of moral tradition. However, it is precisely creative individuals around whom everything turns. By way of evolution, all species have developed themselves into higher life forms, except for man. Now man, too, has to exceed himself by becoming a superman (*Übermensch*).

> What is the ape to men? A laughingstock or a painful embarrassment. And just so shall man be to the Superman: a laughingstock or a painful embarrassment (Nietzsche 2003a, pp. 41–42).

Nietzsche did not have biological or racial evolution in mind (like the Nazi's in the 20th century), but a cultural jump ahead of genial individuals. The Enlightenment ideal of equality simply amounts to an equalising brake on the creative individuals who strive toward Nietzsche's superman ideal.

In keeping with Nietzsche's phasing of the development of human thinking, he had to first free himself from the prevailing morality before he could design his own ideal of life. The moral tradition, after all, constitutes a pressing burden for those who want to fully cultivate themselves. Christianity adopts a hostile attitude towards life: it condemns bodily sensuality and exchanges earthly life for a supposed eternal life in the hereafter. Plato's rationalistic ethics is similarly driven by the fear of fully surrendering to life. With their equalising trends Christian neighbourly love and the humanistic ideals of the Enlightenment turn themselves against unique individuals. Likewise, Kant's formal categorical imperative with its universalisability criterion treats individuals as equals. It is, therefore, high time for the re-valuation of all values.

Thanks to his criticism of metaphysics, Nietzsche can free himself from these moral chains: knowledge of a higher world of Platonic ideas or the Christian God appears to be impossible. In fact, such representations are simply human projections, inspired by the need for certainty. Thus: *God is dead.* With this all supra-sensuous moral values at the same time come to ruin, unmasked as human creations: it is man who has inserted values into the world.

The neighbourly love of Christianity and the principles of equality and brotherhood of the Enlightenment, Nietzsche rejects as inferior, vindictive fabrications of the weak masses, aimed at keeping the strong under their control: a 'slave morality'. Nietzsche points to the fact that the first Christians were Roman slaves: out of revenge they wanted to degrade their masters to their own despicable level. At present the mediocre majority, because of its fearful herd mentality, strives toward conformity and equalisation. In Nietzsche's view, Christian neighbourly love, therefore, does not represent an objective morality, but flows forth from the interests of the inferior masses.[20] What else is to be expected of a weakling than fearfully squeaking that one must turn the other cheek when hit? As soon as the strong recognises this precept he has lost his superior power: in future he will suffer from a paralysing bad conscience when he uses force. And indeed, since the 'all too many' thanks to such egalitarian principles rule modern society, it degenerates into impotent decadency and uniformity. Against this nauseating bourgeois mentality, Nietzsche turns his cultural criticism. His *genealogy of morals* (as one of his book titles reads) exposes the amoral origin of the prevailing morality, founded on vile group interests, thus undermining its claim to objective authority. Freed from this burden, one can then choose one's own life ideal, which does not have to be objective, universally valid, or impartial – such pretence is, after all, always false. Although Nietzsche calls himself an 'immoralist' he does formulate an alternative view of the good life. It is simply not a *morally* good life in the current sense, for Nietzsche's ideal of life finds itself *beyond good and evil* (the title of another of his books).

After God's death a world remains without unity, purpose or meaning. Individual existence itself takes place in a moral void, without any metaphysical connection with a cosmic order. At first this insight can lead to despair. However, strong spirits accept life as it is and make the best of it. Overflowing with the joy of life they

[20]See the analogous criticism of the Sophists in Section 2.3.2.

expand their vital forces, their will to power. Nietzsche refers to the heroic morality of the aristocratic warlords of the pre-classical Greek period who are described in Homer's *Iliad*. Full of pride the powerful then took what they could obtain. They did not pursue equality and neighbourly love; on the contrary, they wanted to distinguish themselves from others by courage and fame. They lived 'beyond good and evil': in their pre-moral egocentric world, that was called 'good' which served their personal development, and 'bad', what obstructed it. Modern decadent 'slave morality', on the other hand, restricts the individual lust for life by testing it against universal standards which would be good for everyone. In the post-moral world the issue is to proceed anew beyond good and evil, and to re-capture the 'master morality'. Now, as then, Nietzsche says, one must distinguish oneself by means of courage and willpower, which is set aside only for an elite of excelling individuals. He nonetheless gives a more cultural turn to the ancient martial chivalrous morality: heroes of the spirit, such as Goethe, can make their creative mark on the world, too.

One must 'become what one is', or fully develop one's personal possibilities. With this Nietzsche does not want to defend a purely individualistic ethics. He develops a perfectionistic moral viewpoint for personal life which is based on a hierarchical order between high and low lifestyles: one must develop a superhuman character. However, what exactly a perfect mode of life entails he leaves open, because this will depend on the specific individual. Every individual must, moreover, from out of all his contradictory impulses create his own unique form of life, so that one cannot in advance in general establish what human excellence entails. Nietzsche does indicate a few basic virtues of which every noble person is in need, to perfect his will to power. In the first place, one must overflow with a lust for life. One can allow others to share in this abundance, not because it is a duty of justice (because then one would recognise an objective value superior to oneself), but because one gives something of oneself to the world:

> But how could I be just from the very heart? How can I give everyone what is his? Let this suffice me: I give everyone what is mine (Nietzsche 2003a, p. 94).

Nietzsche calls this the 'giving virtue'. Due to this generous attitude the superman, too, can act justly and with mercy towards the weak, irrespective of whether they are useful or harmful to him. The will to power, therefore, does not per se lead to blood and mayhem. Other instrumental virtues are courage, willpower, harshness towards oneself and others, honesty in relation to oneself, and creativity. Proceeding from this basic personality one must find the mode of life which suits one best, so as to perfect one's personality in this specific manner. Consequently, 'one becomes who one is'.

7.5.3 The Nietzschean State: Artist-Tyrants

Which state ideal fits best with Nietzsche's superman ethics? Nietzsche does not concern himself much with political issues, and his cursory remarks in this domain are ambiguous. As can be expected, Nietzsche revolts expressly against the Hegelian view that the state forms the highest goal of man: 'the state where universal slow suicide is called – life' (Nietzsche 2003a, p. 77). State control of universities, for example, creates cautious, subservient philosophers, like Kant, instead of free, creative spirits. Nietzsche regards culture as much more important than the state, and for the development of an elevated culture one needs creative supermen. One would then expect him to prefer an anarchic, Hobbesian state of nature in which the law of the strongest applies. And Nietzsche (2003a, p. 78) indeed expresses himself in this vein:

> There, where the state *ceases* – look there, my brothers. Do you not see it: the rainbow and the bridges to the Superman?

One could, however, likewise expect a Nietzschean state which is organised in such a way that it provides a fertile breeding ground for geniuses. This train of thought is also to be found with Nietzsche: a totalitarian state in which the masses of the 'all too many' slavishly serve the noble elite. As in the case of Plato, this state is hierarchically based on three classes. However, the elite does not govern in the best interests of all, in the name of an objective idea of justice as in Plato. It rather resembles the selfish tyranny which Plato rejects with abhorrence: the state exists merely in the interests of the rulers. Nietzsche's artist-tyrants each strive for their own perfection as supermen. The other two classes must create the conditions for this: the third class, consisting of the amorphous masses, performs all professional activities, and hence provides for the material needs of the nobility. A second class consisting of people who excel in physical strength ensures that this happens in an orderly manner, by maintaining the law. The masses do not only obey state authority because of coercion, but primarily on account of religious respect and custom. They, after all, have a greater need for the support of metaphysical and religious illusions than for freedom of thinking. In view of this, the elite will, therefore, uphold the traditions, which the supermen themselves realise are illusions. They benefit more from such a subservient state than from total chaos. The rulers therefore enact legislation to make the masses toe the line.

The rulers themselves, of course, are above the law. The superman after all is his own legislator:

> Are you a new strength and a new right? A first motion? A self-propelling wheel? Can you also compel stars to revolve about you? (Nietzsche 2003a, p. 88)

The tyrants are thus free *from* state power *to* self-legislation, and shape their subjects consistent with their will. Nietzsche rejects the doctrine of the social contract:

> He who can command, he who is a master by "nature," he who comes on the scene forceful in deed and gesture – what has he to do with contracts? (Nietzsche 2003b, p. 58)

Because of an exalted sense of dignity the master can nonetheless voluntarily keep his word. Nietzsche does think that it makes sense for the masters to agree among themselves, out of mutual respect for their equal power, that they will refrain from violence and exploitation. However, this could never be a general foundational principle of society as a whole.[21] Elsewhere Nietzsche indeed suggests that the rulers have a positive duty to spare their subjects, that is, based on rational self-interest: otherwise these subjects cannot fulfil their serving function. Even then the relation between master and servant is utterly asymmetrical:

> The *inequality* of rights is the very condition of there being rights at all (Nietzsche 2004, p. 128).

So-called scientific theories which predict a future society without exploitation, such as that of Marx, are, therefore, without any foundation. It would entail a denial of life.

> [L]ife itself is *essentially* appropriation, injury, overpowering of what is alien and weaker; suppression, hardness, imposition of own forms, incorporation and at least, at its mildest, exploitation (Nietzsche 1989, p. 203).

Moreover, in Nietzsche's view, this suppressive class state can similarly be defended from the point of view of Aristotle's definition of distributive justice: does not Aristotle maintain that one must treat equal cases equally, and *un*equal cases unequally (see Section 2.5.3)?

7.5.4 Commentary

Nietzsche was a great critic of culture, an astute psychologist, and a compelling writer. He can be grouped together with the great 19th-century demolishers of the exalted human self-image. Just like Darwin, Marx and Freud, he showed that the self-understanding of man as a being who distinguishes himself fundamentally from the rest of nature through his rational or godlike essence, is based on arrogance. In fact, human rationality is nothing more than a thin veneer of civilization on a fundamentally irrational, instinctive foundation. Nietzsche's critical analysis of the traditional virtues exposed a great deal of hypocrisy. His romantic protest against conformism and social equalisation is still pertinent. His perspectivist view of knowledge has a significant influence on contemporary philosophy. Specifically the *postmodern* movement views in Nietzsche's footsteps claims to theoretical and moral knowledge as statements reflecting power (see Section 9.1.4).

Nietzsche shows an extreme possibility of what one can opt for in a world without higher values. His relativistic approach to knowledge and morality, however, bites its own tail: according to Nietzsche himself, it can be true only for him and his kindred spirits. (Viewed psychologically his ideal is, however, based on an inversion: Nietzsche wanted at all costs to become what he was *not*. He did not succeed

[21] Incidentally, Hobbes similarly teaches that the sovereign does not himself participate in the social contract, albeit that, in so far as his conscience is concerned, he is bound thereby; see Section 4.1.

in developing his life as a joyful manifestation of greatness. His own courage was restricted to the writing table where he attempted to drown his weakness on paper.)

Nietzsche's ideal of life is plausible, at least within a restricted domain. Highly personal creativity and a non-conformist mode of life are first and foremost suitable for the relatively free and elitist sphere of the arts and sciences. There conformism is the most annoying, and an experimental attitude the most fertile. This sphere not only constitutes a social niche for nonconformists, but also provides a useful sanctuary for experimentation to which the rest of society owes much of its dynamism and design.

However, for the rest, Nietzsche's heroism and praise of the strong individual fits in badly with the complexity of modern society where each individual is bound to others by many relations of dependence. The modern weapons of destruction strip physical warfare of all chivalry (if indeed there ever was anything like this). Because of occupational specialisation one can no longer expect cultural and physical excellence to go hand in hand, as it was still possible with Renaissance geniuses like Leon Battista Alberti. Cultural celebrities, such as Einstein or Madonna, can still within their specialised areas make a mark on their environment, but they are not rulers who open new horizons on all fronts. Overpowering political rulers, such as Hitler, Stalin or Mao, are, on the other hand, cultural barbarians. (Nietzsche was unjustly annexed by the national-socialists. He did not with his *Übermensch* target the blond Germanic race: his ideal was individualistic, not collectivist; he regarded French culture as much higher than German culture, and despised anti-Semites.) Although talents can vary enormously per individual, no one can in all areas of life stand out above the rest. For this reason it is better that the diverse, specialised elites remain divided in separated spheres of justice, and that the political elite be subjected to democratic control.

This commentary gives a bourgeois, liberal turn to Nietzsche's romantic hero worship. Creative individuals must indeed acquire as much space as possible outside of the political sphere. The government can, because of the social importance of experimentation, even create additional free space for the arts and sciences. However, in the public sphere this freedom may not affect the freedom of other citizens. To guarantee equal individual freedom, everyone must have equal rights to political participation. Hence, Nietzsche's vitalism is taken over in sterilised form in the liberal legal order. Mill, too, after all, campaigns for nonconformist individuals, on condition that they have been made harmless, as required by his harm principle.

Chapter 8
Twentieth Century: 1900–1945

8.1 Introduction

8.1.1 General Developments

In the Western world, the 20th century was the stage for a continuation of the combined action of the two conflicting tendencies which are associated with the scientific worldview: the nihilistic-objectifying and the emancipatory. The first tendency found expression in a far-reaching rationalisation of social life under the influence of the pursuit of efficiency, characteristic of both natural science and the capitalist economy. This technological approach did not limit itself to the control of inanimate nature, but increasingly directed itself at human life. The consequence was the progressive arrangement of social life in accordance with means-ends rationality under the influence of two processes which had already been established in previous centuries, but now started to control the whole of society: in addition to growing industrialisation, an extensive bureaucratisation process occurred which led to the far-reaching regulation of social life by the state. The role of law was increased in proportion, with the consequence that the minimal state of the 19th century quickly belonged to the past.

Bureaucracy has a tendency towards technological rationality, because it is characterised by the separation of public position and person (in contrast with feudalism) as well as by functioning in accordance with standard rules. The advantage of this is that it furthers the efficiency of state action. Many, however, see in this a disadvantage, because they fear that it will lead to a standardisation and dehumanisation of social life. People would then merely be used as means towards anonymous state ends, and be regarded as objects to be manipulated. According to this criticism, all of this is the consequence of the instrumental approach of the natural sciences, aimed at the control of the causal processes of inanimate nature, to a domain where it is not at home: human life.

The process of modernisation developed along different lines depending on historical and social circumstances. In the whole of Europe, the United States, Australia and parts of Asia a process of economic and political rationalisation occurred, which led to enormous growth of industry and trade, to the centralisation of power,

C.W. Maris, F.C.L.M. Jacobs (eds.), *Law, Order and Freedom*, Law and Philosophy Library 94, DOI 10.1007/978-94-007-1457-1_8, © Springer Science+Business Media B.V. 2011

bureaucratisation, and uniform legal systems. In Russia and China this was, however, accompanied by a communist polity; in Germany, Italy and Japan by a fascist state; and in the rest of Western Europe and in the United States by a liberal constitution. The precondition for development in the liberal sense was the existence of an economically independent city bourgeoisie, having sprung up as a consequence of free capitalist trade and the demolition of feudalism. In other countries modernisation was imposed by the state, so that the traditional, authoritarian forms of government remained in place.

In Germany and Japan the nobility (and the peasantry) had mainly retained their influence, so that the bourgeoisie was too weak to enforce political liberalism. In Germany capitalistic development was imposed late in the 19th century from above by members of the traditional elite, such as Bismarck. In the 1930s this authoritarian state form, via an unstable, intermediate democratic phase, led to populist fascism. 'The people are everything, you are nothing', was a characteristic maxim. With the help of modern techniques, political opponents were mercilessly eliminated; internal 'enemies of the people' were murdered by the millions in concentration and annihilation camps. Against external enemies, the Second World War was started in 1939.

Russia and China followed a third route. In these countries an agrarian mode of production had dominated since ancient times, led by centralised imperial bureaucracies which fended off external influences. Trade with foreign barbarians was regarded as despicable in China. Here no independent city-dwelling bourgeoisie came about. Ultimately the governments were forced to implement economic reforms so as not to be swept away by foreign countries. This was greatly resisted by the conservative rural population. In Russia, in 1917, the communists made use of this situation to grab power via a revolution. For the sake of convenience the communist leaders decided that the 'dictatorship of the proletariat', which Marx had predicted as a transitional phase, for the time being had to remain in place. This meant, in fact, that the Party appropriated to itself an absolute monopoly of political and economic power, as the only legitimate representative of the people. Since the people themselves were supposed to be in power, separation of powers and freedom rights were superfluous. An individual who opposed the politics of the party was per definition wrong. Every invocation of individual freedom rights against the state was regarded as the expression of criminal, petit-bourgeois egoism. Individuals mainly had duties in relation to their community. Private property was replaced by collective ownership, centrally controlled by the communist government. Obedient to Marxist dogmatism, the new rulers enforced speedy industrialisation by means of the traditional centralised bureaucracy. In this collective process of modernisation, the Soviet dictator, Stalin, caused the death of millions of peasants.

In the bourgeois, liberal countries the tendency towards rationalisation was tied to a process of emancipation which increasingly included larger sectors of the population, in accordance with the ideals of freedom, equality, democracy, the rule of law and human rights. For example, since 1919 all adults in the Netherlands have an active right to vote. The fourth class thus now had a say, too, as well as the second sex. This tendency towards equal sharing of political power was, especially after the Second World War, in Western Europe supported by a more equal distribution of socio-economic goods, among other things, owing to the rise of the welfare state. In the United States the New Deal had, in reaction to the economic Depression, already in the 30s brought relief to the poor, although American social security never took the extensive form of care from the cradle to the grave that characterises Europe. The extreme emphasis of 19th-century liberalism on the principle of freedom was consequently rectified by means of more equality and less freedom in the economic domain. Even though in the last decades of the century the welfare provisions in Europe and America have been reduced for economic reasons, it is now generally accepted that unequal social starting conditions impede an equal use of freedom.

In international relations, too, a liberalising tendency occurred. The large fascist states were, after their defeat in the Second World War, from 1945 transformed into democratic constitutional states (in bureaucratic Japan, however, mainly as a formality), and absorbed into the liberal Western world of their victors. In the same period the sphere of influence of Russia, the other victor of the Second World War, extended itself to Central Europe, where communist vassal regimes were installed. The communist countries were referred to jointly as the 'Second World'. However, towards the end of the 1980s the European communist dictatorships, too, collapsed because of their weak economic performance, without liberal constitutions, however, being established everywhere in their place. Moreover, after the Second World War an increasing emphasis was placed on human rights. These were laid down in the *Universal Declaration of Human Rights* (1948) and a number of international treaties. In recent times positive law in European countries is increasingly tested against the European Convention of Human Rights (1950). Towards the end of the century it was accepted in international law that the Security Council of the United Nations can authorise humanitarian intervention against rogue states that systematically violate the basic human rights of their own citizens, for instance in the case of genocide. In 2002 the International Criminal Court was established in The Hague for the prosecution of crimes against humanity, genocide and war crimes.

It is, however, controversial whether there has really been progress in conformity with the Enlightenment ethics. The objectification process that is inherent in the scientific approach after all led to two worldwide wars, the last of which was ended by means of an atom bomb, and to the large-scale violation of the environment. Critics, furthermore, often point to the fact that far-reaching state interference has indeed had the consequence that everyone's basic needs are provided for, but that this was paid for by the extensive control of everyday life. The welfare state, for example, guarantees a basic income, but this requires extensive bureaucratic control of personal life: does the social security recipient have hidden earnings? does he live with someone? is he not on holiday for too long? This disciplining process, moreover, would have a negative influence on human consciousness. People have to learn more and more self-control, as they have to take account of an enormous variety of rules in all areas of their life. This tendency would have deprived human life of much of its spontaneity. Other critics complain that the welfare state promotes an egotistical consumption drive. It would furthermore undermine the sense of social responsibility, by granting the citizen too many rights without accompanying duties.

Doubts about the Enlightenment ideals were, moreover, raised under the influence of developments in the non-Western 'Third World'. As a consequence of the decolonisation process non-Western cultures laid claim to an equal status. Because of the large-scale migration of inhabitants of the former colonies to the former colonising countries, Western legal orders now also need to take account of the deviating lifestyles of cultural minorities. Consequently, the self-evidence of Western cultural superiority has been questioned. The idea that Western civilisation constitutes a higher phase in human evolution, whereas non-Western cultures still find themselves in a primitive stage, has greatly lost its force. In its place many argue in favour of cultural relativism, which assumes the equal value of all cultures.[1] This tendency has been strengthened by the economic success of Japan, China and other Asian countries around the turn of the millennium, which combine a modern economy with a non-individualistic way of life.

Because the moral conceptions of different cultures diverge greatly, cultural relativism can lead to ethical relativism: the diverse moral views of all cultures are similarly of equal value. This would mean that cultures where inequality and lack of freedom are regarded as morally appropriate have an equal voice vis-à-vis Western culture with its Enlightenment values. The values of freedom, equality, democracy and human rights can then make no claim to universal validity, and can no longer be regarded as the culminating point in a process of moral progress of human civilisation. They are then simply a time- and place-bound product of Western culture.

8.1.2 Developments in Philosophy and Related Fields

These developments left their mark on the philosophy of the 20th century. Some philosophical currents continued the emphasis of the Enlightenment on the close connection between scientific progress and moral emancipation in a liberal sense. Other currents were less optimistic, stressing the irrational side of mankind.

In 1900 an influential publication set the tone of the latter view. At the turn of the century Sigmund Freud introduced his method of psychoanalysis to the world with the publication of *Die Traumdeutung* (The Interpretation of Dreams), which left an equally significant imprint on the general as well as philosophical thinking of that century (Section 8.2). With this method access could be gained to the human

[1] See the Max Havelaar discussion at the beginning of this book.

unconscious, a dimension of the mind which led Freud to the conclusion that the modernist belief in the foundational nature of human consciousness is an illusion. Consciousness is only a derived effect of the more primary unconscious where the sexual and aggressive drives play a dominant role. The forces in the unconscious, according to Freud, are always at work, and their operation can most clearly be seen in dreams. Freud's insights opened the way not only towards a reconstruction of the narratives of patients, but also towards a radically revised understanding of all human practices, institutions and texts. Freud at the same time shared the Enlightenment belief in moral progress, for example, in his comparison of 'primitives' and 'savages' with children and neurotics. They are, according to Freud, (still) dominated to a great extent by their unconscious drives, as compared to mature, Western man who has learned to suppress these drives as a consequence of the development of reason. The contribution Freud made to legal philosophy lies, amongst others, in the attempt he made to understand the origins of law with reference to the forces at play in the unconscious. This is related, but at the same time stands in stark contrast, to the attempts by Grotius (Section 3.5), Hobbes (Section 4.1), Locke (Section 4.2), Kant (Chapter 6), and Rawls (Section 10.5) to find the origins of law and the state in the conscious decision of legal subjects. Based on an analysis of totems (the guardian spirit of a clan in the form of an animal, plant or inanimate object) and taboos in 'primitive' societies, Freud came to the conclusion that the origins of law lie in the Oedipus complex (a murderous intent of a boy against his father, and a desire for his mother, sublimated in moral conscience in the form of strict prohibitions on murder, incest and the like), which he views as a universal characteristic of man. Freud's views in this respect were partly based on the studies of anthropologists towards the end of the 19th and the beginning of the 20th centuries. Later anthropologists, however, cast serious doubts on the universality of the institution of the totem, which in turn places a question mark behind Freud's hypothesis of the universality of the Oedipus complex, as well as the progressive moral development of man.

A tension can be detected in Freud's texts between a belief, on the one hand, that the Oedipus complex in the unconscious constitutes the energising force leading to the establishment of law, religion and morality, and, on the other hand, the attempt to explain the development of consciousness and everything that goes along with it, with reference to a death drive which precedes the unconscious. The notion of a death drive was hypothesised by Freud to explain the peculiar feature of the repetition of unpleasant experiences in the mental lives of some people, in contrast with his earlier thesis that the pleasure principle prevails in the psyche. This drive Freud similarly viewed as a universal characteristic of man as well as of other organisms, which necessarily has to be 'repressed' in order for life to proceed. The more complex the organism, the more elaborate the detours that eventually returns it to death. Although the notion of a death drive took on increasing importance in Freud's later thinking, he did not work out in detail the implications of this thesis for his earlier reflections on the origins of law, morality and religion. Jacques Derrida attempts to do this by means of what he refers to as 'deconstruction' (Sections 9.1.7 and Section 9.5).

In logical positivism (Section 8.3), which similarly developed in the first half of the 20th century, the optimistic belief in progress which characterised Enlightenment philosophy dominated: as a consequence of the growth of scientific knowledge, moral emancipation would come about too.[2] In their manifesto of 1929, *Scientific Worldview*, the logical positivists expressed their concern about a revival of metaphysical and theological thinking, behind which they suspected a conservative, anti-Enlightenment attitude that sought to call a halt to the liberalisation and socialisation of society. This attitude is no longer suitable in the Modern Age, the positivists contended. As a consequence of the objectivisation of economic and social relations, people nowadays have become more down to earth. They look for their knowledge in sensory experience, and for their morality in worldly happiness: 'The scientific worldview serves life, and life receives it.' In the first place, the individual can, thanks to modern science, realistically determine his own goals. Furthermore, socio-economic relations can now be controlled as well, owing to the practical application of the new social sciences, such as sociology and economics. This 'social technique' enables the democratic central state to adjust the negative aspects of the free market: state intervention in the market can prevent economic recessions and rectify unjustified differences in income. Such a socio-economic emancipatory programme implied a substantial extension of the 19th-century minimal state, which guaranteed only negative freedom rights. In accordance with this social version of liberalism, the state, moreover, had to counteract the absence of the material conditions for equal freedom (or 'negative impediments', see Section 1.4). Here, in brief, the contours of the social-democratic welfare state are sketched.

With their name the logical positivists indicate that they regard empirical science as the model for all knowledge: 'positivism' implies that they take the positive (given) empirical phenomena as criteria for valid knowledge; 'logical' refers to the neutral, mathematical language in which science organises statements regarding such observations, in order to strip them of all subjective influence. Statements which claim to provide knowledge are, according to them, meaningful only if one can verify them, or test them against objective phenomena which are observable by everyone. Metaphysical statements about non-observable conceptions, such as God, gnomes, Hegel's Absolute Spirit, witches, the people's spirit, unicorns, or Plato's Ideas, are by contrast, because of their unverifiability, meaningless: concerning things unobservable one can fantasise as much as one likes, but one actually does not know what one is talking about. Such thought constructions are rather expressions of someone's subjective feelings; it is wonderful if one can bring them to expression in poetry or music, but they have no place in an objective argument. Their initial kindred spirit Wittgenstein (2007, p. 89) expressed it thus (albeit with a somewhat different, mystical intention): 'What we cannot speak about we must pass over in silence'. As an extension of this scientific worldview, the logical positivists propagated their emancipatory ideals, such as the rational reform of the state in a

[2]Logical Positivism is thus a general philosophical movement, not to be confused with legal-philosophical legal positivism, see Chapter 1.

liberal way, the socialisation of economic relations, and the unification of humanity as a whole.

It, however, soon appeared that the positivist belief in progress was too optimistic in three respects, which will be discussed below. In the first place, scientific knowledge and moral emancipation on closer inspection do not coincide as seamlessly as the logical positivists had hoped in their naïve optimism. Secondly, the ideal of objectivity of empirical science is likewise untenable: sensory observation itself is a matter of interpretation. Thirdly, the actual political and social developments in the 1930s and 1940s provided unprecedented evidence of an aggressive moral regress in an anti-liberal and anti-democratic direction. In Germany, the fascist and racist Nazi movement came to power, started a worldwide war, and committed large-scale genocide. In Russia, after the communist revolution of 1917, a terrorist dictatorship developed under Lenin and Stalin, which cost millions of lives.

(1) That the scientific ideal of the logical positivists has no logical relation to their moral and political ideals comes to the fore when one applies its verification criterion to liberal statements, such as 'all people are free and equal'. Empirical experience after all shows that people in reality are not always free, nor equal in all respects. Such normative statements, in brief, cannot be verified via sensory experience, and are, therefore, according to the epistemology of logical positivism, as meaningless as statements about gods, goddesses and mermaids.

Later kindred spirits of the logical positivists, such as Stevenson and Hare, who concentrated on a value-free analysis of moral language, concluded in this mode that normative concepts such as 'good' or 'just' primarily have an emotive or prescriptive meaning, rather than a descriptive import. Normative statements aim at guiding someone's actions. The content one ascribes to such prescriptions ultimately depends on one's personal attitude, so that there is no rational way of settling differences between moral views. According to some, moral debate is, therefore, mostly rhetorical persuasion in the spirit of the Sophists (see Chapter 2).

This value-free analysis of normative language nonetheless still provides some possibility for a rational moral debate (Section 8.2.2). In the first place, an apparent difference in moral views can be based on disagreement about empirical facts, which can be resolved on the basis of the empirical criterion of knowledge. Secondly, the parties to the discussion may share a background value, on the basis of which they can settle their moral dispute. Thirdly, with his moral statements a speaker claims to express more than just his personal preference, that is, he claims to posit a generally valid prescription. When I say that all people must be free, I mean that everyone should think this, and likewise act in accordance with this idea. In a political debate I will attempt to support this with arguments. According to Hare, I can never give decisive arguments in this respect to a person with a fundamentally different attitude to life. However, owing to the general claim of my statement, it does have consequences for me: when I soon thereafter argue in favour of slavery, I am being inconsistent. Because of their claim to universal validity, moral statements prohibit one from making an exception for oneself. And because nobody wants to be a slave himself, Hare contends, nobody can logically preach a slave morality (in the style of Aristotle, not in the style of Nietzsche; on which, see below). Hare consequently develops a formal, immanent test for the tenability of moral judgments, even though they are not objectively verifiable: does the judgment concerning a specific instance allow itself to be universalised for all instances which are similar in relevant respects, including the hypothetical instance that one would oneself be in the disadvantageous position? This universalisability test shows similarities with that of Kant's Categorical Imperative (see Section 6.3.1; compare, likewise, the universalisability test of Habermas, Section 9.3, and Rawls, Section 10.5): It forces one to view the matter from an impartial point of view.

There is, however, an important difference. Kant's test presupposes that all people are equal in dignity, so that one cannot merely use others as a means for one's own ends. He bases this on his metaphysical conception of man: all people are autonomous persons. With Hare, by contrast, all substantive moral assumptions are absent, because these can in terms of his empiricist criterion of knowledge not be proved objectively. Therefore, his universalisability test is much more permissive. A Nietzschean (see Section 7.5) would be able to defend his elitist arrangement of masters and slaves as universal morality on the basis of his assumption that the elite and the masses are in the relevant respects fundamentally dissimilar: that a herdsman has to play the role of a servant, therefore, does not mean that a superman must likewise be able to see himself as a slave. If one regards the empiricist criterion of knowledge as decisive, the possibility of settling moral disputes is thus very limited. Liberal values, such as equality and freedom, cannot be proved to those who think differently. Progress in empirical science, then, does not necessarily coincide with moral emancipation.

In this completely value-free version, empiricist philosophy was elaborated on by *Legal Realism*, which aims at scientifically mapping the law as a social reality. The realists rejected the natural-law doctrine as non-verifiable metaphysics, as well as every invocation of objective values, such as justice. This movement flourished especially in the United States and Scandinavia. According to the American realists, law can be reduced to the factual conduct of judges. If one wants to know what the law prescribes in a specific instance, one must predict what the judgment of the judiciary will be in this case. In this realistic view the normative character of the law (the legal rule) is thus interpreted as a social fact (the judgment of a judge), which the legal scientist must map out from a value-free perspective: as a matter of fact, the American judge judges that slavery is not permissible. Or, in a hard case about which jurisprudence is not yet clear, one has to predict how the judge will probably decide, in the light of the relevant empirical material, such as laws, precedents, the preferences of the judges, etc.

The Scandinavian Realists looked at the law rather as a supra-personal social system. The function of the law is, in their view, to realise social order by means of the central establishment of norms. This occurs through the interplay of four factors in the relation between state and legal subjects, which is based on power and authority. An authoritative central institution establishes general norms (1); if necessary, it maintains these by means of force (2); legal subjects mostly obey the legal rules owing to a combination of unselfishness and self-interest: via education a normative consciousness has been instilled in them that they should observe the general norms, even when this conflicts with their self-interest (3); this is supported by fear of sanctions (4). Apart from formal laws, customary law as well as unwritten principles of reasonableness and fairness play a role, too.

This realistic view of the law is akin to the sociological description of the legal positivist Hart who similarly points to the interplay between external coercion and internal acceptance of the power of the legal authorities (see Section 1.2.3.2). This acceptance is, according to Scandinavian Realism, nothing more than a social-psychic reality: it is a social fact that legal subjects, because of a process of socialisation, experience their legal system (inter)subjectively as valid law. Concerning objective justice, science cannot make any pronouncement, because normative statements simply express the subjective preferences of the speaker; legal norms are expressions of the ruling ideology in a legal culture. Empirical legal science can, on the basis of an investigation of the actual consequences of legislation on society, indicate by which legal means the legislature can realise its aims in the most efficient manner. The selection of the aims is, however, an extra-scientific, political affair.

(2) However, if this is the case, critics of the positivistic scientific ideal argue, then the applied science or 'social technique' from which the positivists expect moral progress, can equally be used for amoral or immoral purposes. Amoral: by raising science to the one beneficial institution, one cultivates a purely instrumental way of thinking. State and law become mere instruments in the control of social life; individuals are subordinated to an anonymous bureaucracy. Control replaces individual autonomy. Immoral: in the 1930s and 1940s the Nazi regime made extremely effective use of modern applied science in committing mass murder and waging a total war.

In the first half of the 20th century sharp criticism was in this fashion voiced against the scientific ideal of the positivists: empirical science, according to critics, provides only an impoverished technocratic thinking, which can give no account of the meaning reality has for man. Adherents of *Phenomenology* and *Existentialism*, such as Husserl and Heidegger,[3] contend that the phenomena which appear in human experience are determined by the intentions of the perceptive consciousness. In this view, philosophy must give an analysis of reality as it appears to human consciousness, our 'life-world'. Everyday experience is not value-free; people inevitably view the world from the perspective of value-laden goals. Even so-called value-free science has a specific goal – control of the environment – and is, therefore, just one of the many human cognitive activities.

According to Heidegger, man distinguishes himself from other living beings because he is aware of his existence. On the one hand, he is determined by the world as he encounters it, and, on the other hand, he must design his own life by cultivating his environment and making it his own. He, however, experiences the

[3] Heidegger himself denied that he was an existentialist, and there are clear differences between his thinking and that of Jean-Paul Sartre, one of the most famous French existentialists.

relative indeterminacy as terrifying, especially because he realises that his life ends in death. He thus has the responsibility of making something of his life within a short period. Because of a fear of death many people tend to deny this finiteness and responsibility, and seek refuge in a superficial, conformist mode of life. The positivistic limitation of human knowledge to the fixed categories of science, likewise testify to fear of the elusive richness of life. Philosophy as well as poetry must behind the veil of science and conformism observe life itself.

Related to this view of man as a meaning- and value-giving being, is the approach of *hermeneutics*, or the doctrine of the interpretation of the meaning of human action and its products (Section 8.5). Hermeneutics seeks to understand human intentions, while natural science explains natural events by determining their causes. One can study inanimate nature quite well by means of the observation of external regularities, such as the orbits of the sun and the moon. However, the actions of human beings one can only situate when one knows their motives, ideals and values, and such contents of consciousness are not empirically observable. Take the following example. On the hallstand of a restaurant hang a row of overcoats. I take my worn coat even though next to it a much better one is hanging. You can understand my conduct only if you know that I have an awareness of the notion of property, and that I respect the difference between what is mine and what is yours. As the legal positivist Hart expresses it: my actions are guided by a rule which I accept as appropriate. From the two coats themselves the difference between what is mine and what is yours cannot be seen, neither can it be seen from my empirically observable exterior: I am motivated by an internal consciousness of norms. When I *do* put on the other coat, I am likewise led by a motive, possibly the desire to look presentable.

The idea of an observing, value-free natural science undermines Aristotle's teleological worldview, which ascribes to all natural phenomena an immanent purpose: according to natural science the world consists of blind processes without a final goal. Hermeneutical human science contends, in opposition to this, that human practices clearly demonstrate an orientation towards a goal. These goals are, however, cultural, not natural. Hence, Hart views the legal order as a system of norms which is based on the value which people attach to their own survival. The rules of Hart's 'minimal natural law', such as not to kill and not to steal, serve this goal (see Section 1.2.3.2).

A scholar in the human sciences cannot observe another man's intentions, but because he is himself equally a human being, he does know his own intentions. By analogy he can reconstruct similar contents of consciousness from the utterances of the persons whom he investigates. Hermeneutics not only concerns the psychological understanding of concrete human actions, but especially the interpretation of the meaning of impersonal human utterances, such as legislative texts, or of cultural practices, such as religion or literature, which have a specific sense or value for the participants.

The goal of the human sciences is, therefore, more practical and normative than the objective-explanatory natural sciences: they strive towards increasing one's insight into one's own life practice by taking note of other human practices or cultural utterances.

According to the legal theory of Paul Scholten (Section 8.5) and other hermeneutic scholars, such as Ronald Dworkin (Section 1.2.3.3), legal science has a similar practical-normative character. The practising lawyer and the legal scholar aim, in a hermeneutic manner, at deriving jurisprudential guidelines for the conduct of legal subjects from authoritative legislative texts and earlier judgments. This presupposes that lawyer and legal subjects participate in the same normative legal order, and accept the basic assumptions of its legal practice. However, modern positive law is so complex that non-specialists can impossibly take it in at a glance. For lawyers the law is similarly not always clear. Often the law first has to be interpreted before it can be applied to a specific case. According to Scholten, the judge then develops with his mind's eye, and by going back and forth between the specific case and general rules, an intuitive insight into the right answer. Scholten, as a Christian, presupposes that God helps the judge to find this answer. In retrospect, the judge legitimates his legal finding by anchoring it in an acceptable way in the law.

Dworkin advocates a more rational hermeneutic approach to hard cases. As a first step, the ideal judge brings more coherence to the set of unsettled laws and precedents. For this purpose he constructs a limited number of unwritten principles which one must presuppose, should one wish for the specific laws and jurisprudence to cohere in a meaningful way. For instance, he can in separate legal fields, such as the (American) law of sale and lease as well as labour law, characterised by protection of weak parties, such as the tenant and the employee, presuppose the existence of an implicit substantive principle: the principle of equality. Subsequently the judge derives from these general implicit principles the right interpretation for the specific hard case.

A value-free empirical legal science would never be able to replace this normative communicative practice of social-scientific and legal understanding, goes the criticism of hermeneutic scholars against the logical positivists. It can indicate means-ends relationships only. It thus leaves people empty-handed who are wondering how to arrange their personal and social lives.

(3) This reproach against the logical positivists is supported by the very same empirical reality from which the positivists derive their truth claims: history shows that science, because of its amoral character, can as equally lead to immoral practices as to moral progress. The political developments in the first half of the 20th century in fact demonstrated the concurrence of extremely modern, applied science and unprecedented moral regress. Rhetorical and physical violence replaced moral rationality and equal freedom. In the *Gay Twenties* after the First World War things momentarily appeared to go in the democratic direction. However, in financial respect the belief in progress was undermined by the worldwide stock-market crash of 1929, which in one fell swoop destroyed fortunes and ushered in a protracted economic depression. Because of rapid social modernisation many had, moreover, lost their traditional foothold. In Germany people sought help in a strong Leader, Hitler, who in 1933 in a democratic manner, but equally by means of terror, came to power, and subsequently established a national-socialist, totalitarian, racist, state. (He called it 'national' and 'socialist' because the national state lay claim to

encompass all of the people.) National-socialism was based on a caricatured mixture of the legal-historical 'people's spirit' and Nietzsche's 'will to power': the German people had to internally purify its Germanic body and spirit from foreign, especially Jewish, infection, and externally conquer 'living space' from the inferior Slavic race. Fellow Germanic peoples, such as the Dutch and Scandinavians, were supposed to exultantly join in all of this. Hitler combined this pre-modern racial mysticism with an extremely modern, centrally organised use of technology in transportation, communication, weaponry, and mass murder, as a result of which he could deploy the German masses for his goals with unprecedented efficiency, and annihilate his political and racial enemies in concentration camps. In 1939 he started the Second World War, which initially proceeded surprisingly successfully for Germany and its allies, Italy and Japan. Within a short period most of Central and Western Europe, with the exception of Great Britain, was conquered. The Netherlands was overpowered in 5 days and lost the Dutch East Indies to Japan. However, when Russia and the United States became involved in the war, the tide turned. In 1945 Germany capitulated. Japan was brought to its knees with a sophisticated scientific invention, the atom bomb.

The ideal of scientific progress can, nonetheless, in an indirect manner be presented as a model for moral emancipation. During the Second World War, a kindred spirit of logical positivism, the Austrian Karl Popper, who as a Jew fled from the Nazis to Australia, wrote a philosophical study against the despotic regimes of Hitler and Stalin, *The Open Society and its Enemies* (Section 8.3.2). Popper (1902–1994) gave his criticism the philosophical appearance of an attack on the totalitarian state ideals of Plato, Hegel and Marx.

With an appeal to the epistemological model of empirical science, Popper opposed the metaphysics behind Plato's ideal of an elitist government by philosopher-kings (Section 2.4). According to Plato, philosophers have to take the political lead, because only they possess supra-partial wisdom: they have an exclusive insight into supra-sensory rational Ideas, such as the True, Good and Beautiful. However, in Popper's scientific model of knowledge such metaphysical claims to absolutely valid knowledge cannot be proved. Human knowledge is necessarily restricted to past experience, and, thus, in principle fallible. This similarly applies to scientific knowledge: natural scientific laws take the form of universally valid regularities in the style of '*always* when x, then y', but in fact an empirical phenomenon can occur tomorrow which negates this law. The claim to certain, all-encompassing knowledge of philosophers such as Plato and Marx, is, therefore, unfounded, and dangerous in practice: the elite who think that they possess all wisdom regard themselves as infallible and close themselves off from criticism. Intolerantly they force others to follow their totalitarian plans, which subsequently mostly fail in practice. Moreover, experience shows that power tends to corrupt. One must, therefore, not entrust rulers with all power if one wants them to rule impartially.

As alternative, Popper pleads for an open society, based on the liberal principles of freedom and equality. If knowledge does not stem from a higher metaphysical source, but from human experience, it is in principle accessible to everybody.

Although people vary in their mental capacities, nobody rises so high above the rest in all domains of knowledge that one should entrust him exclusively with state power. Therefore, all should have a say in governmental policy via a representative democracy. Freedom rights are necessary for an open critical debate, by means of which the plans of the fallible rulers can be tested for their tenability. Only in this way can one learn from one's mistakes. Separation of powers is required to prevent abuse of power.

Popper acknowledges that he cannot ground his liberal state ideal in empirical science, since norms cannot be derived from empirical facts. However, from the success of science one can by analogy draw lessons for other social domains: just as fallible scientific knowledge progresses by way of methodical, critical testing, political decision-making leads to the best results when it is exposed to public debate. In brief, experience teaches that democracy, understood as organised mistrust, provides the best guarantee of social progress.

8.2 Psychoanalysis

8.2.1 Introduction

Sigmund Freud (1856–1939) is known as the father of psychoanalysis. An understanding of his thinking concerning the unconscious is essential to comprehend much of 20th-century philosophy which via France influenced the rest of the world. Although Freud probably would have denied being a philosopher, his meta-psychology and reflections on culture engage in important respects with the concerns of the philosophers who have been discussed thus far, so that Freud indeed deserves attention here. Freud first contemplated becoming a lawyer, but then decided to rather study medicine and eventually specialised in nervous diseases. It is during this time that he came to the conclusion that some 'ailments', specifically those of neurotic patients,[4] cannot be explained simply with reference to physical factors, and realised that these cannot be treated effectively with the then existing techniques. His first book on the topic, *Die Traumdeutung* (The Interpretation of Dreams, 1900), posits the notion of unconscious mental processes as the primary cause of dreams. Freud's investigation is already anticipated by Plato (Section 2.4), who in the *Republic* notes that '[o]ur dreams make it clear that there is a dangerous, wild, and lawless form of desire in everyone, even in those of us who seem to be entirely moderate or measured' (Plato 1997, p. 1181). According to Freud, dreams are a result of the weakening during sleep of the control which is usually exercised

[4]Greek: *neuron* = nerves, and *osis* = thrust, push, resulting in an abnormal condition. The term is nowadays mostly used to refer to mild mental disorders, such as hysteria (any kind of frenzied emotional state), anxiety, depression, obsession, compulsion, hypochondria, and phobia. Neurosis is usually distinguished from psychosis (a serious mental illness, such as hallucination, delusion and schizophrenia) and from mental problems that are regarded as having a physical cause (such as epilepsy or Parkinson's disease).

by the *ego* in waking hours over unconscious mental processes. Freud furthermore asserts that dreams, in spite of the seeming irrationality of their manifest content (the dream as recalled), have a 'meaning' if account is taken of their latent content (the thoughts that lie behind the dream). In *Zur Psychopathologie des Alltagsleben* (The Psychopathology of Everyday Life, 1901) and *Der Witz und seine Beziehung zum Unbewussten* (Jokes and their relation to the Unconscious, 1905), Freud further emphasises the fact that everyone is affected by their unconscious. The operation of the unconscious can be detected in everyday life in, for example, slips of the tongue and forgetting certain things. The laughter evoked by a joke is caused by the link between that joke and the unconscious. A joke dares to say out loud (for example, by alluding to sex or by invoking wordplay) what is usually suppressed, thereby satisfying an instinct, causing pleasure, or a discharge of energy, by means of laughter. The lack of control of unconscious mental processes makes all people neurotic to a certain extent, although not everyone suffers to the same degree from neurosis. The so-called Oedipus complex became increasingly central to the thinking of Freud as the cause of most neuroses and, as we will see below, is likewise relied on by Freud to explain the development of law, morality and religion.

Sophocles's drama *Oedipus Rex* (ca 420 BC), tells the story of Oedipus, the son of Laius and Jocasta, the King and Queen of Thebes in Greece. Laius was told earlier by an oracle that should he have a son, he will grow up to kill his father. To avoid this, after the birth of Oedipus, Jocasta gave instructions to a servant for Oedipus to be killed. Oedipus, however, survived this attempt on his life, and was eventually adopted by the King and Queen of Corinth who were childless. Many years later, after having heard that he was adopted and upon trying to find out the truth from an oracle, he was told that he will kill his father and have sex with his mother. To prevent this from happening he left Corinth. On his way to Thebes he entered into a dispute about the right of way with a stranger. This led to Oedipus killing the stranger, who, it later turned out, was his father Laius. When Oedipus later solved the riddle of the Sphinx which saved Thebes from her curse, he was made King of Thebes and was given Jocasta, his mother, as wife. Their sexual union led to the birth of four children. When he later found out the truth, Oedipus stabbed out his own eyes and left Thebes, with his daughter, Antigone, guiding him. Jocasta hanged herself.

According to Freud, an Oedipus complex develops between the ages of three to five in all children. A little boy at this age desires his mother sexually. He sees his father as a threat to this desire and, like Oedipus, desires to kill his father to be with his mother. Because of the fear of castration (resulting from a threat, usually uttered by a caregiver), the symbolic substitute of which is blindness, in combination with having seen that girls are 'castrated' (lacking a penis), as well as the realisation that his desire cannot be satisfied, the boy, in the case of 'normal' development, destroys his Oedipus complex, and through the formation of the *super-ego*, or conscience, introjects the authority of the parents along with the prohibition of incest. In the case of girls, the mother is similarly the first love-object. After a realisation that the mother is castrated, and believing the mother to be responsible for her (the girl's) own castration, a girl turns away from her mother in hostility, towards her father as love-object. Her penis envy, which Freud describes as 'unappeasable', makes her want a baby as a gift from her father as a substitute. She then in a sense takes the place of her mother, by desiring her father. Because a girl does not have the fear of castration that is found in boys, a girl does not have the same motivation as a boy to overcome the Oedipus complex, Freud asserts. According to Freud, girls remain in this complex for a long time and if they overcome it, do so incompletely.

After initially exploring with hypnosis, Freud concluded that neurotics can best be 'cured' by allowing them to talk to the psychoanalyst by saying anything that enters their mind (free association), thereby circumventing the censorship that is usually imposed by the ego on the unconscious. (Habermas (Sections 1.2.2.3, Section 9.1.5, and Section 9.3) incidentally sees a correspondence between this effort of psychoanalysis to undo repression and his own theory's attempt to achieve emancipation by way of the resolution of distorted communication in society as a whole.) It is important to note from the start that Freud uses the term 'unconscious' in a number of senses in describing psychic life. It is firstly used in a *descriptive* sense, referring to everything that is not conscious or that one is not aware of at a certain point in time. Used in this sense, latent memories, too, are unconscious. It is secondly used in a *dynamic* sense to refer to the unconscious proper, and in order to distinguish it from the preconscious. Memories in the preconscious, as we will see, can relatively easily be recalled, whereas those in the unconscious proper can be recalled only with difficulty or not at all. This is because of repression which incidentally can likewise occur in relation to the preconscious. The unconscious in this sense is so to speak 'active behind the scenes'. Thirdly, it is used in a *systemic* sense when partitioning the mind topographically or structurally. The systemic unconscious is where the primary process in the mental apparatus is situated, and would later be referred to by Freud, following Nietzsche (Section 7.5), as the *id*, or the animal instincts. A fourth, *economic* 'sense' of the unconscious can be distinguished, which paradoxically undermines the notion of the unconscious itself (see Section 9.5). Freud relies specifically on this perspective in seeking to understand the relation between *Eros* (sexual desire) and *Thanatos* (the death drive), and he speaks in this regard in 'economic' terms of the free flow and binding of energy in relation to, respectively, the primary and secondary mental processes.

8.2.2 The Mental Apparatus

In order to understand Freud's reflections on the origins of law, morality and religion, it is necessary to enquire briefly into his model of the mental apparatus. In his book, *Das Ich und das Es* (The Ego and the Id, 1923), Freud divides the mental apparatus topographically into the ego, the id and the super-ego, and in doing so abandons, because of its ambiguity, the use of the term 'the unconscious', except in its descriptive sense. The three realms, regions or provinces of the mental apparatus do not all occupy the same 'space'. The *id* occupies a space which is much larger than that of the ego or the preconscious. According to Freud, the development of the ego from out of the id involves a later development, brought about by the demands of the external world that are placed on the perceptual system. We can even go as far as saying that the ego is the representative in the mind of the real external world. In the id the primary instincts are at work, and all mental processes take place unconsciously. This is the 'place' which, in Nietzsche's words, is beyond good and evil (Section 7.5.2), as the id knows no morality and no judgments of value. Freud describes it as 'the great reservoir of libido'. Consciousness, which is characteristic of the *ego*, is furthermore only a small part of psychic life, and of a passing nature. With the development of the ego (from out of the id), a portion of the contents of the id is taken up in the ego, whereas another portion stays behind – the unconscious proper. A part of the ego is, therefore, likewise unconscious, to be distinguished from the preconscious portion of the ego. In the development of the psyche, certain experiences of the ego are, furthermore, for defensive reasons repressed and pushed into the id. The unconscious portion of the ego is, according to Freud, for example, to be seen in the resistance of the ego (in collaboration with the super-ego) in analysis, more specifically in refusing to concern itself with what has been repressed. This resistance is something patients are often unaware of.

In addition to the ego and the id, Freud identified a *super-ego*. The ego, as we saw, is formed out of the id and at the same time attains its energy from the id. The way in which the ego concentrates its energy on objects is a result of the instinctual demands of the id. This, moreover, explains the formation of the super-ego. Apart from a conscious portion, it has, like the ego, an unconscious portion, and in this respect it has an intimate relation with the id. The parent, as we saw above, is first desired as a sexual object (this happens with boys, too, in relation to their fathers before the Oedipus complex sets in). When the child is obliged to give up on this object it compensates itself by setting the object up in the ego or by intensifying its identification with it. The installation of the super-ego is thus a result of a successful identification with a parental figure. The super-ego is consequently an heir to the Oedipus complex and involves more precisely a repression of the Oedipus complex. This explains the function of the super-ego as a critical, observing and prohibiting agency which continually confronts the ego in instances where it seeks to comply with the demands of the id. By means of the super-ego, that which is the lowest or most 'primitive' part of mental life has thus, by turning it into an ideal, been transformed into that which is the most valued. Whereas unpleasure is the consequence of abstention due to inhibiting forces in the external world, compliance with the wishes of the super-ego leads to pleasure. Other figures that take the place of the parents, such as teachers or other ideal models, similarly inform the super-ego, although these figures are not incorporated or introjected[5] like the early parental figures. The formation of a child's super-ego is furthermore determined by its relation not with the parents themselves, but with the super-ego of the parents. This is the way in which tradition and culture are passed on from one generation to the next.

[5]Freud does not draw a strict distinction between these notions, something which would later be done by the Hungarian-French psychoanalysts Nicolas Abraham and Maria Torok.

Freud, thus, to a certain extent, agrees with both Kant (Chapter 6) and with Hegel (Sections 7.1.4 and Section 7.3) regarding the way in which morality is formed: with Kant, in so far as this is determined by the super-ego; and with Hegel, in so far as the super-ego is not simply of an individual nature, but determined by tradition. As we will see later, the notion of the super-ego, in addition to its important role in relation to morality, likewise explains the formation of a social sense and of religion.

The ego can thus be said to have three 'masters': reality, the id, and the super-ego. In his *New Introductory Lectures* Freud describes as follows the difficult task the ego has of satisfying these 'severe' masters:

> Thus the ego, driven by the id, confined by the super-ego, repulsed by reality, struggles to master its economic task of bringing about harmony among the forces and influences working in and upon it; and we can understand how it is that so often we cannot suppress a cry: 'Life is not easy!' (volume XXII, p. 78)

The different parts of the mental personality are, furthermore, not sharply distinguished from each other, but rather melt into one another. The development of the different parts, moreover, takes place in different ways in different persons. From the above it should be clear that that which is conscious does not simply coincide with the ego, nor that which is repressed, with the id.

8.2.3 The Functioning of the Mind

In light of the main themes of this book, Freud's contemplations on the workings of the mind are of particular interest to us. This of course ties in with the topographical picture of the mind presented above. In the philosophical theories we have discussed thus far, mention has often been made of the (untamed) instincts, or what Kant refers to as inclinations, which we can now locate in the id, and which Freud from an economic perspective refers to as the primary process because of its relation to the discharge of energy. The notions of logic, rationality and common sense, which entail a secondary, inhibitory process, we can locate in the ego. The ego is, moreover, where the perceptual system introduces the notion of time, in comparison with the id which has no relation to time. The notion of conscience or the moral law in Kant, and which Plato refers to as 'shame', we can locate in the super-ego. Freud could more specifically be said to reduce Kant's notion of moral consciousness to the sphere of empirically observable reality or the phenomenal world, seeing that it reflects the influence and judgments of one's parents, grandparents and ancestors, and is, therefore, in a way, causally determined. The objectivity that Kant ascribes to the supra-sensory, rational moral law which speaks to us unconditionally via our conscience is hence unmasked as an illusion. (Freud incidentally agrees with the utilitarians that the seeking of happiness, or what Freud refers to as the pleasure principle, dominates in the mental apparatus, and he did not fail to link this to genital love as the prototype of all happiness; he, however, expressed some doubt regarding the dominance of the pleasure principle in mental life in *Beyond the Pleasure Principle*.) With Kant we saw the synthesis of the views of empiricism that mental processes are preceded by empirical observation and of rationalism that empirical observation is preceded by certain ideas in the mind. Freud, as an empirical scientist, seeks to go beyond Kant's answer that the mind structures the way in which empirical observation takes place. Psychoanalysis, in Freud's view, enables us to answer the question as to what drives us to interact with objects, and at the same time how it comes about that the mind structures this interaction in a specific way. The instigator of both empirical observation and of rational thinking is to be found in the unconscious. Freud, in other words, contends that the ego and the super-ego are only secondary effects of a more primary process to be found in the id. The id is, in other words, the locomotive energy of the psychic system. For the purpose of instinctual satisfaction it brings the organism into motion. The only contact the id, however, has with the external world is by way of the ego. According to Freud, the ego has acquired the task of representing the external world to the id. This is so because without the ego's 'reality-testing' (which includes the laying down of accurate pictures in the memory traces) the id would have destroyed the organism in its attempt to satisfy the instincts. To understand this we have to investigate the phases through which a psychical act goes from the unconscious to consciousness.

According to Freud, thought relies on the mnemic residues of experience. Where are these residues to be found in the mental apparatus? As we saw above, the perceptual-conscious system forms the surface of the mental apparatus, the contact that exists between an organism and the external world. In the latter respect it produces perceptions of excitations of the sense organs that come from the external world. The excitatory processes leave no traces within the perceptual system itself, as it would otherwise not be able to remain open to new receptions of stimuli. The perceptual system thus has no memory. The excitation is instead transferred to the other (mnemic) systems lying within the mental apparatus (adjacent to the preconscious system) and leaves traces behind there. In his *Notiz über den 'Wunderblock'* (Note on the 'Mystic Writing Pad', 1925), Freud illustrated this manner of functioning with reference to a writing pad consisting of a celluloid sheet, thin waxed paper, and a clay or wax slab. The celluloid sheet of the writing pad can be written on with a sharp instrument without the need for ink. The celluloid sheet can furthermore be lifted from the slab to remove the markings and, like the perception-consciousness system, does not itself retain any permanent traces. The wax slab, like the unconscious, permanently preserves all the inscriptions that have been made on the celluloid cover. This registration of an event is, according to Freud, registered in different ways or in keeping with different methods of classification: in one mnemic system, for example, according to simultaneity in time, and in another, according to relations of similarity. In so far as relations of similarity, or what could be termed 'chains of association', are concerned, some dream-images are, for example, about things which sound the same, such as *kilo*metre and *kilo*gramme. In a descriptive sense, all memories are unconscious. Whereas events registered in the preconscious system are generally accessible to consciousness, those registered in the system unconscious or id, are as a rule inaccessible to consciousness. This is so because in the unconscious system, thing-cathexes[6] of objects take place. Unconscious presentations are, therefore, only of things, whereas in the preconscious system, the thing-presentation is hyper-cathected by being linked to the word-presentations that correspond with it. Word-presentations are thus residues of memories which at one time were perceptions – words that were heard or read. Freud elsewhere nonetheless affirms the possibility that some memories may be destroyed in the normal course of things, and thus will not be subject to recollection by any means. (This will be referred to again in our discussion of Derrida in Section 9.5).

Repression (involving a withdrawal of cathexis) can in light of the above be said to involve the refusal to translate into words that which is attached to an object. Should a presentation not be put into words, it will remain in the unconscious in a state of repression, hence the importance of the talking cure. Repression can, moreover, be described as involving a process of censorship of psychical acts coming from the unconscious. If it passes the test, the psychical act goes through to the preconscious system from where it can become part of consciousness. In the preconscious stage it is not, however, as yet conscious, it is simply capable of becoming conscious. This enables us to define the activity of thought or rationality as the postponement between a need, or what the id desires, and an action. By means of thought, the ego tones down the seeking for pleasure in the id, by testing these desires against reality. For conscious thinking to occur, excitation of the perceptual-conscious system must, therefore, flow from the interior of the mental apparatus. In his *Entwurf einer Psychologie* (Project for a Scientific Psychology, 1895, published posthumously in 1950) Freud contends that this is indicated by the fact that qualities (conscious sensations) cannot originate in the external world as there one finds only masses in motion (see Hobbes in Section 4.1.2). Memory is similarly without quality. Something else must, therefore, give rise to an idea becoming preconscious (for a thing to be connected to a word), and consequently for conscious sensations to arise. It is as a result of contact between the different systems, as Freud explains in the *Note on the 'Mystic Writing Pad'*, that consciousness arises, and this contact consists of cathectic (or libidinal) innervations. Consciousness is extinguished every time the cathexes are withdrawn, resulting in the coming to a standstill of the entire system. This 'something else' is unpleasant (a heightening of tension) and is aimed at what is pleasant (a lowering of tension). The activity of (conscious) thinking thus involves the making of a connecting link between unconscious thought-processes and that which Freud, in *Der Mann Moses und die monotheistische Religion* (Moses and Monotheism, 1939), refers to as the 'mnemic residues of visual and auditory perceptions along the path of the function of speech'. By means of the interposition of word-presentations, internal thought-processes are, in other words, made into perceptions. For this reason the 'inexplicable' phenomenon of consciousness arises in the perceptual system, *instead of* the memory traces.

[6] *Cathexis* = attachment of an amount of psychical energy to an idea, object, etc.

The process of thought can be clearly illustrated by what happens in dreams (and hallucinations). In the case of dreams, a retrogressive movement (already commented on by Hobbes in his *Leviathan*) takes place from mnemic systems towards the perceptual-conscious system (the ego), for example, in visual images. This is so because dreams are made from memories, some of which were registered shortly before the dream, and others which date from childhood. Something similar happens in thinking, the only difference being the absence of a hallucinatory revival of perceptual images. Unconscious thinking is, in other words, and as already noted, as active in the day as at night, although it is mostly not strong enough to make itself perceptible during the day because of the censorship of the ego. The similarity between the processes taking place in dreams and wakeful life can be better understood when, as Freud points out in *The Interpretation of Dreams*, we recognise a dream –

> as a *form of expression* of impulses which are under the pressure of resistance during the day but which have been able to find reinforcement during the night from deep-lying sources of excitation (volume V, p. 614).

8.2.4 The Origin of Law, Morality and Religion

In a number of publications Freud attempted to tease out the implications of his 'discovery' of the structure of mental functioning and the Oedipus complex in individuals, to society as a whole. Freud, in other words, contends that the same mental structures as identified in individuals are to be found in societies, with 'primitive' societies corresponding with the mental functioning to be found in infants, and more 'civilized' societies corresponding with the mental functioning of adults. These contentions have, of course, not remained uncontroversial. According to Freud, unconscious (suppressed) memory-traces of past experiences are retained not only in individuals, but also in groups, such as a community or a nation. (Some have understood this as an expression of Lamarckian views on the inheritance of acquired traits, but Freud need not be understood thus.) For Freud, this, for example, explains the notions of totem and taboo, in what we will refer to here as 'archaic' communities (see Section 1.2.1.2), as a first attempt at religion, as well as the other large-scale manifestations of religion, for example, Judaism, Christianity and Islam. In *Totem und Tabu* (Totem and Taboo, 1913) Freud enquires into 'totemism', with reference to some of the anthropological studies of the time which followed an evolutionary approach to social phenomena. In accordance with the version of totemism which Freud adopts, a totem (originally an animal, but later also plants, or natural phenomena, such as rain or water) is used to distinguish one clan from others, and has important implications for sexual relations. In its original form, according to Freud, the totem animal is worshipped as the progenitor and protector of the clan, and may not be harmed or killed by members of the clan. The totem animal is, nonetheless, killed once a year during a special ceremony, where all the men of the clan tear it apart and consume it raw. As part of the ceremony all the members dress in the likeness of the totem and imitate it in sound and movement, thus stressing their identity with the totem. After the consumption of the totem animal, its death is mourned, followed by licentious festivities. To try to explain this institution, as well as the fact that many of the archaic communities still observed at the time consist of bands of males in totemic clans while concerning themselves primarily with the prohibition of two crimes (murder and incest), Freud posits an event which shows some correspondence with the notions of the state of nature to be found in philosophers, such as Hobbes (Section 4.1), Locke (Section 4.2), Rousseau (Section 5.5), and Marx (Section 7.4). In *Moses and Monotheism* Freud points out that this event took place over thousands of years and was repeated numerous times. In the beginning stages of mankind, Freud contends, mankind lived in small hordes with a jealous, primal father in each instance ruling over such horde. The father had exclusive possession of all the women in the horde. If a son would invoke his father's jealousy, he would be killed, castrated or driven from the horde. The sons, fearing, honouring, and at the same time hating, the primal father (as is the case with male children in contemporary society), deprived by him from having their sexual desires fulfilled by their mother(s) and sisters, one day rose against him, killed, and consumed him. Either because none of the brothers was strong enough to take the place of the primal father, or because if one of them were, it led to new battles, they eventually realised that the previous position of a single leader is no longer tenable. For the sake of peace with one another, they therefore decided on the institution of a (totemic) community of brothers, a kind of 'social contract' by means of which incest and murder (of the totem animal) were prohibited.

In this development lies the commencement of social, moral and religious obligations, according to Freud. The institution of the totem (the totem being a substitute for the father) and the totem prohibitions served a number of purposes: (1) a covenant between the sons and the totem (the totem granting them everything they could wish for, and they in turn respecting its life); (2) making amends for the murder of the primal father out of a feeling of guilt; (3) an attempt at self-justification: if the primal father had treated them the way the totem treats them, they would never have killed him; as well as (4) making it possible to forget the event which lies at the origin of the totem. This is so because after the murder the feelings of affection they had for him turned into remorse. The dead father consequently became stronger than he had been before. The father was, in other words, internalised by way of the super-ego, as explained above in the case of individuals. The special nature of the totem festivities point to the fact that the killing of the father is both prohibited (as a rule), and yet the occasion for joyful celebration.[7] Freud indicates that the institution of the totem was likely to have been preceded (during the period when there was no leader strong enough to take the place of the primal father) by, and perhaps even existed alongside, a period of gynaecocracy (government by women), with women deities developing towards the end of this period as a compensation for taking power away from women. Men thus gradually started re-asserting themselves, first by means of the totem prohibitions, and then through the further development of religion. They,

[7] We saw a similar ambivalence in Section 6.4.1 in Kant's estimation of revolutions.

moreover, slowly came to institute themselves as the heads of smaller families. At a later stage the primal father was re-introduced in a different form by means of the notion of a god who stands in some relation with an animal; male gods in the form of sons who appear together with great mothers; thereafter, by the idea of supreme deities; and later, the idea of one father-God; and in Christianity, the idea of God's son having atoned for the sins of the brothers (for killing the father), becoming God himself. All religions, Freud contends, are attempts at solving the problem of remorse for, as well as satisfaction concerning the triumph of, the killing of the father. There are, moreover, clear similarities between Christian Holy Communion and the totem meal, involving the symbolic drinking of blood and the eating of flesh. At the basis of every religion, Freud contends, lies a longing for the father. The bond between brothers that made possible the killing of the father, Freud suggests, was possibly based on homosexual feelings and acts. These social fraternal feelings, furthermore, continued to have a profound effect on the further development of society, as, for example, expressed in the general prohibition of the murder of any member of the clan, thereby extending the prohibition on the killing of the totem in accordance with the tie of blood; and later, to all members of society.

Did Freud believe that the killing of a primal father actually once occurred, or is it a hypothesis as with Hobbes (Section 4.1)? According to Freud, the archaic mind is similar to that of neurotics who do not draw a rigid distinction between thoughts and actual events. The Oedipus complex, as we saw, is for Freud the primary cause of neurosis. This is so because of the similarly ambivalent attitude sons have towards their father, loving and admiring him, and at the same time hating and desiring to kill him as an obstacle to their craving for power and their sexual desires. This complex, in other words, lies at the foundation of totem and taboo as well as of society, whether or not an actual murder of the pre-historic father occurred.

In an exchange of letters with Albert Einstein, *Warum Krieg?* (Why War?, 1933) Freud similarly explains the institution of law as a development which flowed from the initial domination of the strongest. Without referring expressly to his theory of the primal horde in *Totem and Taboo*, Freud expresses the view that at some point a realisation occurred that the unity of a number of weaker men was more advantageous than domination by one who is the strongest. This new order was called 'law' in comparison with the violence of the one individual. Right, law or justice is, in other words, the might or violence of the community. This new order can be kept in place only by means of an organisation of the community, the issuing of regulations, and the establishment of institutions which enforce these laws (by resorting to violence) against anyone rebelling against them. This organisation leads to emotional ties between the members of the community which serve as the source of its strength. Matters are, however, not that simple as a community never consists only of people of equal strength. Differences exist between men and women, parents and children, and slaves and masters. Because of power imbalances, struggles, civil wars or revolutions will occur within a community as a result of attempts by the oppressed groups to achieve greater equality with the dominant ones or to rule over them. Because of the necessities of living together, relative peace within a community is possible. This is not, however, the case between different communities, races, nations or empires. A society structured to ensure peace between members of the community is, like Hobbes (Section 4.1) proposes, in other words, no guarantee against wars with other nations or groupings. Wars sometimes lead to the establishment of greater unities which can ensure peace for a certain period of time between the united groups, which then often fall apart again. Freud expresses his scepticism that it would ever, or at least in the near future, be possible to unite all the peoples of the world through an idea (such as the League of Nations, which was established in Freud's time) to ensure permanent peace. Freud explains this with reference to his theory of the drives. He distinguishes here between the erotic or sexual drive, the aim of which is to preserve and unite, on the one hand, and the destructive or aggressive drive which seeks to destroy and kill, on the other. Both these drives are essential to life, and the one never operates completely without the other. Freud finds the origin of the destructive drive in what he refers to in *Beyond the Pleasure Principle* as a death drive that is at work in every organism, and which seeks to make life return to its original inorganic state. (In a sense, tying in with what was said towards the end of Section 4.1.2, Freud contends that we are all 'seriously disturbed', although some of us succeed in 'repressing' this better than others. The 'existence' of such a drive clearly has the potential of complicating the principle that stands central in many philosophies of law, for example, in the theories of Hart (Section 1.2.3.2), Grotius (Section 3.5), and Hobbes (Section 4.1.5), and which are themselves based on the assumption of the primacy of an instinct or inclination, that is, of self-preservation. We will return to this in Section 9.5.) The German philosopher Schopenhauer (1788–1860) similarly expressed the view that the actual purpose of life is death. When this death drive is turned outwards by means of certain organs, it finds expression in the destruction of extraneous objects, and serves to preserve the life of the organism. Some part of the death drive, however, at the same time operates within the organism, causing it to turn the destructive instinct towards itself. It is, therefore, according to Freud, impossible to get rid completely of man's aggressive impulses. They are in a sense more 'natural' than the effort to prevent them from finding expression. The only way in which war can to some extent be combated is in an indirect way: by encouraging emotional ties between men via the opposing drive, Eros. This can be done through relations that are similar to those towards a love object, and/or by means of identification by sharing important interests. The evolution of culture which finds expression in the displacement of instinctual aims and the limitation of instinctual impulses, according to Freud, inevitably leads to a resistance to war, although this in itself threatens the survival of the human race as it, in turn, leads to the impairment of the sexual function.

The notion of equality can, in Freud's view, be explained equally well at the level of individual psychology. In *Massenpsychologie und Ich-Analyse* (Group Psychology and the Analysis of the Ego, 1921) Freud explains the notion of justice or equal treatment for all with reference to individual mental life which is on a par with the story of the primal horde recounted above. According to Freud, these ideas, which some would call a herd instinct, are not something with which children are born. These ideas arise from the family relationship where the older child is confronted with the birth of younger siblings. The birth of a younger sibling evokes feelings of envy and the wish to destroy or in some other way neutralise the rival(s). However, a realisation that this hostile attitude is ultimately not in his own interest, as well as the observation that the other children are loved by the parents as much as he himself is, leads to identification with the other children. A communal or group feeling is consequently developed, and even more so, at school. This forced identification or reaction-formation results in the imposition of the demand for equal treatment: if I cannot be the favourite (any longer), nobody else should be either. What was originally envy is hence replaced by a group feeling or spirit. Freud consequently explains social justice as follows:

> Social justice means that we deny ourselves many things so that others may have to do without them as well, or, what is the same thing, may not be able to ask for them. This demand for equality is the root of social conscience and the sense of duty (volume XVIII, p. 121).

The exception to this demand of equality is the leader, who has to be superior to the members of the group. Freud compares the leader of the group who loves no one but himself, and others only in so far as they serve his needs, with Nietzsche's 'superman' (Section 7.5.2). Viewed from the perspective of group psychology, the father of the primal horde, by inhibiting the sexual desires of the sons, as we saw, forced them into emotional ties with himself and with each other. Freud in this way provides an explanation of the origins of the Enlightenment ideals of equality (or equal freedom), and brotherhood.

8.2.5 Commentary

To conclude, a few points of criticism that have been raised against Freud, and then, finally, an assessment. Many psychoanalysts have not accepted Freud's idea of a death drive, and his views on the universality of the Oedipus complex have been questioned. This has also been the case with many of his other theories. As can be expected, those who adopt a strictly scientific view (such as Popper in Section 8.4) have contended that Freud's theories do not qualify as such as they are not falsifiable (a similar contention can be made in terms of the position adopted by logical positivism, discussed in Section 8.3). Freud's theories are from this point of view of a 'metaphysical' nature. To this it can be responded that Freud specifically tries to investigate what made the development of scientific thinking possible, or what motivates people to form a society and start thinking in a scientific way: a sublimation of libidinal instincts, as we saw. To contend that these views are not 'scientific' in Popper's sense, is perhaps to put the cart before the horse. This does not, however, mean that Freud's theories amount to wild speculations. Although he rigidly held fast to many views, he changed many others because of their failure to account for mental 'reality' as he observed it. The fact that something is not strictly speaking 'science' in terms of Popper's definition (or in terms of the criterion of logical positivism) furthermore does not necessarily make it metaphysical, if one views metaphysics as Heidegger and Derrida do (Section 9.5).[8] Marxists have termed Freud's psychoanalysis a 'bourgeois science' (Freud incidentally regarded Marx's view on the sole importance of economic motives as somewhat restrictive, and communism's belief in harmony amongst men once capitalism is abolished as naïve). In relation to human nature and the origin of law, Freud undoubtedly probed more deeply than anyone before him. Anthropologists have, nevertheless, mostly reacted with scepticism to Freud's theories about the universal and originary nature of totemism as well as his story of the primal horde, at least in so far as the latter involves (or may involve) a claim to historical truth. Those who believe in the equal value of all cultures (see Section 9.2) have understandably accused Freud of Western cultural arrogance; and those with a religious bent have, as understandably, not found Freud's views on religion very attractive. Feminists have found many objectionable things in Freud's writings, for example, the notion of penis envy and a resulting inferiority complex which Freud identified in women, his view that women have a weaker super-ego than men, that they are more narcissistic than men, have little of a sense of justice, are more jealous than men, are weaker in their social interests, and have a lesser capacity than men of sublimating their instincts.

Why should one then, despite all these criticisms, still take note of Freud? Freud, as we saw, provides us with an explanation of the origins of the institutions and laws we have in society, as well as of the differences between societies. This explanation, as we moreover saw, is intimately related to a view of human nature, that is, that unconscious processes which are similar in all individuals and nations are fundamental to humanity. This structure is quite different from the ones we have encountered before. Freud saw his task, in line with the ideals of the Enlightenment, as opening the eyes of humanity to the important influence of unconscious mental factors, and especially of sexuality, in everyday life. In this respect he undoubtedly succeeded: his writings have had an enormous impact on intellectual life in the 20th century, and which is bound to continue in years to come. The French psychoanalyst Jacques Lacan (1901–1981) and the Algerian-French philosopher Jacques Derrida (Section 9.5) are probably the most important thinkers who have, in markedly different ways, sought, after his death, to develop further Freud's thinking. To conclude, Freud was sceptical, especially in the later part of his life, of the possibility of effecting lasting changes in neurotics by means of psychoanalysis, as well as of curing humanity as a whole from its illusions, the most important of which is religion. The demands placed upon the ego by the super-ego, the id and reality, as well as those impossible demands which society's super-ego by way of culture places on its members, make discontent a lasting feature of humanity. Freud's sceptical optimism for the individual is expressed in the famous maxim: '*Wo Es war soll Ich werden*' (where id was, there ego shall be); and of humanity, that hopefully one day the

[8] In terms of Derrida's understanding of metaphysics, Freud's thinking none the less shows many signs of still belonging to metaphysics, as is, for example, illustrated by the oppositional categories he employs, such as Eros and Thanatos.

ideal will be reached of 'a community of men who had subordinated their instinctual life to the dictatorship of reason' (*Why War?*). In spite of his emphasis on the unconscious, Freud, unlike Nietzsche, still believed in the rationality of science.

8.3 Logical Positivism

8.3.1 Scientific Progress

Logical positivism, which views natural science as the model for all human knowledge, recognises claims to knowledge as meaningful only when they can be tested against sensory ('positive') data. Thus, logical positivism follows in the steps of the earlier positivism which was formulated by the 19th-century philosopher Comte (1794–1857). According to Comte, human thinking has evolved from subjective, phantasy-laden 'magical' thinking to objective scientific knowledge. Primitive people still possess little knowledge, and, therefore, interpret the world by analogy to themselves. They represent all things, similarly to man, as having a soul, in accordance with the animistic belief in spirits: every tree, every river is ruled by its own spirit. This magical way of thinking makes sense in a period when scientific control of nature is not as yet possible: it at least gives primitive man the idea that he can influence his environment, for example, by pleading to the spirits by means of sacrificial rituals to let it rain, or by reading the future from the stars. In the evolution of human thinking still greater abstraction and generalisation subsequently takes place. When astrologers study the stars to determine Destiny, they at the same time fortuitously gather real empirical knowledge concerning the orbit of planets and the relation of the sun and the moon to the earth. Hence, irrational astrology is in the long term converted into the realistic science of astronomy. Before it reaches this point humanity first has to go through an intermediate phase. In the second 'metaphysical' phase, events in the world are still presented as purposive (analogous to human intentional action), but now under the influence of abstract forces, such as Aristotle's final causes, Hegel's 'Absolute Spirit', 'God', or 'Nature'. In the scientific or 'positive' third stage of evolution, this teleological outlook is finally replaced by a worldview that is based on objective observation, and thus presents the world as it is.

This rationalisation of human thinking, according to Comte, does not take place simultaneously in all areas. First, during the 16th century, the natural science of Galileo and Newton emerged, which enabled man to control inanimate nature (and led to an industrial way of production). The systematic scientific approach to the more complex phenomena of human social life only occurred in the time of Comte, who is himself regarded as the father of sociology. Thanks to this new science of human relations, Comte expected that people would in future likewise be able to arrange social life according to rational planning. Thanks to economic developments, the modern society of his time already showed significant moral progress in comparison with the militaristic, chivalrous culture of the Middle Ages. Because of the industrial division of labour and expansion of the market, people had become more dependent on each other. When one needs others in the longer term, people will treat each other with greater care, and feel responsibility towards the whole network of social relations. Comte did notice that the drastic increase in labour specialisation had actually induced narrow-mindedness and group egoism. However, this deficiency could, he believed, in future be addressed by means of better social organisation on the basis of the growing knowledge of social science: specialisation must be compensated for by means of integration at the central level of the state, so that a general feeling of solidarity can come into existence.[9]

Logical positivism stems from a group of philosophers and scientists, such as Carnap, Schlick and Neurath, who in the 1920s and 1930s regularly met in Vienna (*Wiener Kreis*). In 1929 they published a manifesto with the title *Wissenschaftliche Weltauffassung: Der Wiener Kreis* (Scientific Worldview: The Vienna Circle), in which they set out their philosophical programme. Their programme was of a mixed epistemological and ethical nature. Following in the footsteps of the Enlightenment and Comte's positivism they expected that scientific progress would lead to moral emancipation.

In the first place, the logical positivists propagated the empiricist ideal of scientific knowledge as a model for all knowledge, including that of human life (*Unified Science*). The logical positivists added the term 'logical' to 'positivism', because they emphasised logic and language, and specifically analysed the language of science. According to the logical positivists, a knowledge claim concerning reality is meaningful only if it complies with the *verification criterion*: it must be provable on the basis of sensory observation, which in principle can be accomplished by everyone. An assertion of knowledge must in all its elements and relations provide a symbolic reflection of empirical reality. For this reason all claims of knowledge must be capable of analysis into simple statements of observation which refer directly to the simplest observable characteristics of reality, such as 'This is red'. In this way scientific language has direct contact with reality, so that subjective distortion and interpretation are excluded.

All metaphysical contentions concerning a non-observable 'higher' world behind empirical phenomena, such as 'God has the shape of a sphere' or 'The movement of things is the result of final causes', are, on the contrary, not verifiable. The metaphysical thinker cannot with reference to reality make clear what concepts, such as 'God' or 'final cause', mean, and thus his utterances are meaningless from the perspective of knowledge.

In the second place, logical positivists intended to promote the emancipatory ideals of the Enlightenment with the assistance of objective scientific knowledge. After the First World War hope momentarily grew of a more humane society. (The positivist Neurath participated in the short-lived soviet-style Republic of Bavaria.)

[9]Comte subsequently arrived at a hierarchical, illiberal, ideal of society in which spiritual power would rest with scientists and worldly power with bankers.

However, after 1919 an authoritarian reaction set in, partly justified by means of traditional theological and metaphysical (neo-Kantian and neo-Hegelian) authoritarian thinking. The Vienna Circle wanted to oppose this by means of the scientific approach, both in a theoretical and a political sense. The logical positivists hoped for a rational improvement of society by unmasking metaphysical prejudices and ideologies (for example, that the government obtains its authority from God). In so doing, power asymmetries would diminish, and individual maturity would increase. All individuals would be able, in a situation of freedom and equality, to arrive at rational choices on the basis of unbiased factual knowledge.

The social sciences would, moreover, enable a better control of social relations, in the service of the equal happiness of all citizens. Thanks to the growth of science, Neurath contended, in modern times social conditions can be realised which in earlier times appeared to be fantastic utopias: 'utopianism as science'. In the Greek myth, Daedalus could escape from the Labyrinth by flying away with self-made wings. Nowadays we have learned through methodical scientific research how one can really fly. In the same way, social utopias can now be realised, too, with the assistance of applied social science, or 'social technique'. To attain that goal, the social technician must map out all the characteristics of human consciousness, such as curiosity and fidelity to tradition, ambition, egoism, and myopia. (Freud's analysis of the unconscious partly had a similar intent.) In his study of human beings the scientist must, in brief, view everything that characterises them and determines their socio-economic actions, in the same way as an engineer determines the elasticity of iron, resistance against copper fractures, the colour of glass, and such like. With the help of this knowledge, the state, which had during the First World War rationalised its organisation to wage war more efficiently, could now deploy its institutions for peaceful purposes, Neurath maintained.

In this way the central state would use economic and statistical knowledge to regulate socio-economic life more efficiently and more humanely. The unregulated free market had led to unjustifiable inequalities in income, and to uncontrollable catastrophes, such as the stock market crash of 1929 and the economic Depression of the 1930s. State regulation of the economy on a scientific and democratic basis had to prevent this in future.[10] The democratic state, moreover, had to socialise economic relations. With this Neurath did not aim at complete equalisation, but, among other things, at bringing wages in line with performance. In all of this the state could delegate its regulatory power to consultative bodies of employers, employees and consumers. Within industries, democratisation likewise had to take place, but the economic operational management had to stay in the hands of expert entrepreneurs. In brief, Neurath developed as a scientifically sound utopia the model of a social democracy, which after the Second World War would be realised in the

[10]The economist Keynes argued during this time in favour of the cushioning of economic recession by way of active state intervention in the market: state expenditure on public works would stimulate the economy and as a result increase the general welfare; Hitler's state in the 1930s indeed stimulated the German economy through large-scale state investment in the war industry and road construction, but this is not quite what Neurath had in mind.

Western European welfare states (albeit in more moderate form, without the central harmonisation of production and consumption).

8.3.2 Ethics

The Enlightenment ideals of logical positivism, however, on closer inspection stand in tension with its empiricist model of knowledge: measured against the verification criterion, moral utterances are as meaningless as metaphysical ones, because a moral term, such as 'good', cannot be reduced to observable characteristics of reality. The statement 'Suffering is bad' grammatically has the same form as 'This apple is green', but it does not furnish any verifiable, objective knowledge. A kindred spirit of the positivists, Bertrand Russell, therefore regards moral statements as the expression of subjective desires:

> When a man says "this is good in itself," he *seems* to be making a statement, just as much as if he had said, "this is square". . . . I think what the man really means is "I wish everybody to desire this" (Russell 1997, p. 235).

Someone who contends that 'It is just that all people be treated equally' therefore does not say something objective, but simply expresses a personal preference. He actually says something like 'Hurrah for Equality!'. Adherents of the scientific model of knowledge can at most establish the value-free fact *that* some people express such moral preferences – and that other people have opposing preferences.

According to this meta-ethical non-cognitivism in the case of moral disputes, no objective test exists with which to establish who is right.[11] One can only attempt to convince one another by rhetorical means. Logical positivism must, therefore, acknowledge that its own moral Enlightenment ideals of freedom and equality are not justifiable. The statement 'all people are free and equal' does not correspond with empirical reality. The actual social division of labour is specifically based on the diverse capacities of different people. Individual freedom from moralising interference by the state or fellow men is, moreover, as a matter of historical fact, the exception rather than the rule. Such a moral statement, therefore, does not attempt to describe empirical reality – indeed, if everyone was already free and equal, it would not make any moral sense. It aims at formulating a normative measure against which to test reality. If reality deviates from this standard, so much the worse for the facts. However, according to the verification test of logical positivism, these and similar normative statements lack solid ground. One can just as well, like Plato and Nietzsche, from the fact of human inequalities, conclude that there should be *un*equal rights and duties. In the empiricist view, both normative positions, in favour of moral equality *and* of inequality, say more about the speaker than about reality: these are subjective expressions of his attitude towards life.

[11] *Meta-ethics*: the a-normative analysis of normative ethics: Which types of ethics exist? What is the function of ethical concepts? How can ethical points of view be justified? *Non-cognitivism*: the thesis that knowledge (cognition) is not possible.

Whether scientific knowledge will really be used in favour of emancipation thus is an open question. The only emancipation of which logical positivism is capable on the basis of its own verification criterion is the unmasking of ideologies which appeal to an incorrect account of the empirical facts (such as a racist state ideal, based on an incorrect biological racial theory). It can likewise reject ideologies which are justified by invoking non-verifiable phenomena (such as: the Japanese emperor has to be obeyed because he is of divine descent). However, positivists are not capable of grounding any alternative social ideal in its own right.

Thus, all that remains is the nihilistic-objectifying tendency of modern science. Scientific knowledge can furnish means-ends relations, but according to the scientific ideal of knowledge the establishment of goals is based on irrational decisions. The 'social technique' of applied social science, therefore, is at risk of leading to the instrumental control of society by an anonymous state bureaucracy. Should this be the case, state and law may equalise citizens, but will show little respect for their individual freedom.

Later linguistic philosophers of kindred spirit have modified the thesis that moral language is meaningless. They support the view of meta-ethical non-cognitivism that ethical statements do not furnish any knowledge, but in the final instance are based upon subjective valuation. Yet, they still regard moral language as meaningful and partly susceptible to rational argumentation. In their view, language which furnishes no knowledge can nonetheless be meaningful. Commands, for example, have an inherent meaning even though they do not have the sense of describing reality.

According to the linguistic philosopher Stevenson, moral statements are similar to commands: one expresses an emotional attitude with them, and attempts simultaneously to have others adopt the same attitude. Stevenson calls this the 'emotional meaning' of moral judgments.

By attaching the pseudo-objective moral concept 'good' to an element of reality which is emotionally preferred by the speaker, he is, according to Stevenson, making use of a *persuasive definition*: moral terms possess a suggestive, emotional force which reflects on a particular element of reality, and suggests that the addressee similarly approves emotionally of that element (in the same way as 'whitening power' in an advertisement for toothpaste). As an example of the persuasive use of suggestive, normatively laden terms, Stevenson points to the Marxist interpretation of the concept of 'value'. Early economists like Adam Smith gave a purely technical, value-free description of this notion: 'value' is what is added to something by means of labour. However, because the word 'value' in everyday language use has a peculiarly emotional meaning, Proudhon could later make persuasive use of Smith's definition: what an object costs more than its value (according to Smith's definition, consisting of the costs in labour time and expenses) constitutes theft. In the same way, Marx's view that only labour can create value and that interest and profit, therefore, constitute theft, is a suggestive conclusion from a definition intended as value-free, made possible by the emotional meaning which the word 'value' possesses in everyday language use.

According to Stevenson, in the case of moral disputes rational discussion is, nonetheless, possible within certain limits. In the first place, certain moral disputes are on closer inspection based on a disagreement about facts which can indeed be settled empirically. Suppose that the parties to the discussion, because of like-minded emotions, all agree to a persuasive definition of what amounts to 'good', such as: 'good is what promotes peaceful co-existence', and are thus in agreement about the *normative* meaning of 'good'. On the basis of this presupposition, currently almost everyone in Western culture, including liberals, agree that the state has to instil in citizens certain basic virtues which are necessary for peaceful social relations, such as respect for mine and thine. The argument in favour of a responsibility of the state to make citizens virtuous in a broader sense, which is in some of these countries made by Christian Democrats, is, however, controversial. They advocate this view with the argument that citizens have become amoral and egotistical after the demise of the influence of the church and other traditional bonds. Opponents can falsify this Christian-Democratic moral appeal on the grounds of sociological research showing that the greatest majority of citizens actually still adhere to the ideal of a virtuous, monogamous family, and subscribe to the existing democratic legal order.

Secondly, the parties to the discussion may share a deeper value on the basis of which they can settle their moral dispute at a more concrete level. Suppose that I argue in favour of absolute freedom of expression, whereas my opponent wants to prohibit racist statements. To his question why I am so much in favour of freedom, I answer as an authentic liberal: it follows from my ideal of individual autonomy; to develop their own life ideals, people must be free to collect information and to express their views. – But I am in favour of autonomy *too*, says my opponent, and thus also in favour of free speech; but the very same autonomy ideal implies that this freedom ends when one's statements deny the equal autonomy of others by excluding them as inferior beings. – You are right again, I may concede.[12]

However, a substantive dispute concerning basic moral values, for example, whether one should privilege individual autonomy or communal traditions, is based on differences in the mind-sets of the parties to the discussion, and these cannot be resolved rationally. Whenever such a moral disagreement arises, Stevenson contends, only irrational persuasion or war remains. This confirms that the ideals of freedom and equality cannot be objectively proved to opponents of the Enlightenment.

The linguistic philosopher Hare extrapolated the full implications of Stevenson's analysis of the use of moral language. Hare supports Stevenson's statement that moral language primarily has a prescriptive character, and does not describe objective norms. He, however, contests Stevenson's view that the language of morals is simply suggestive and rhetorical: it entails a claim of impartiality which rises

[12]However, I *could* also argue that racist actions must be prohibited, but that racist speech can be better opposed by counter-arguments.

above mere subjective arbitrariness. For this reason Hare sees more possibilities for rationality in ethics.[13]

Hare belongs to a later generation of linguistic philosophers who, just like the logical positivists before them, concentrated on linguistic analysis because it is by means of language that people orient themselves in the world and conceptualise reality. Like Stevenson, they did not, however, limit themselves to scientific language; they also attempted to analyse the meaning of other types of language use, such as moral language. Hare thus diverges in many respects from the empiricist programme of the logical positivists. His non-cognitivist meta-ethics, nonetheless, remains related to it. Hare does not regard moral statements as reports of knowledge, because they primarily reflect the subjective attitude of the speaker.

Hare nonetheless criticises Stevenson for too closely associating moral statements with expressions of subjective emotion. In fact, the speaker has a different intention. When someone says: 'It is good that you are generous towards X', he does not wish to express only his personal preference. Otherwise he would rather have said: 'I *find* it good'. His '*is* good' means that all people should subscribe to the principle of generosity in general, not only in this specific case, but in all similar cases. The speaker thus intends to dispense a prescription with universal implications.

In Hare's non-cognitivist view, the specific content which a speaker gives to moral terms like 'good' is not fixed beforehand; an openness which is absent in judgments concerning facts. One cannot, for example, equally well say 'The earth is square' and 'The earth is round'. The empirical facts only allow for the second description. But one can with equal right say 'Human equality is good' and 'Human inequality is good'. It depends on one's attitude to life which specific moral position one chooses, and this may vary per person. Yet, the universal purport of moral statements does make rational criticism possible in retrospect. It imposes a logical limitation on irrational arbitrariness: logically, a moral judgment is acceptable only when it complies with its own universal claims. The test for this is whether the speaker would accept his statement in all circumstances which are the same in relevant respects. He can, therefore, not make an exception for himself. If Aristotle states that slavery is good, he would then have to accept that he *himself* can end up in the position of a slave. He would, on the other hand, logically contradict himself if he should say: 'Slavery is good, except for me'. The *universalisability criterion* will, according to Hare, disqualify a great number of lopsided moral judgments. Few people would after all want to be a slave themselves. For sure, it is possible that someone finds slavery such an important good that he would even accept this arrangement if he himself complied with the criteria of a slave. But someone like this is disqualified by Hare as a 'fanatic', and would in fact seldom be found.

Hare recognises, on the other hand, that rational moral criticism has its limits. In moral disputes where all conflicting views have passed the universalisability test,

[13] Hare's later work, where he converts to utilitarianism, will not be considered here.

no further rational discussion is possible. When two speakers pronounce contradictory moral prescriptions, for example, in favour of, and against, human equality, and if both are prepared to accept the consequences of their own prescription were they to find themselves in the position of the others involved, then no further criteria are available to settle their dispute. Here two persons with opposing mentalities simply confront each other. The possibility of rational argumentation in ethics is, therefore, greater in Hare's view than in Stevenson's, but still very limited.

The rationality of Hare's ethics is even more reduced because of a difficulty which he does not sufficiently realise. Hare's universalisability criterion entails that the speaker must accept the same moral judgment in all instances which are similar to each other in *relevant* respects. This emphasis on 'relevant' is necessary, because situations are almost never completely identical. Thus, it first has to be established what is regarded as 'relevant'. Because of this, infinite chances of evasion arise, as one can always allege that there is a relevant difference between two situations. One could even deny that all *human beings* as such are similar in relevant respects. Someone who, like Plato, Aristotle or Nietzsche, presumes that different categories of people are unequal in kind, may simply refuse to put himself in the position of others whom he regards as inferior. Nietzsche, for instance, contended that intelligent, courageous, and authentic people are of a superior class, who stand high above the masses of the 'all too many' and, therefore, have to rule over the masses (see Section 7.5). A Nietzschean superman would deny that herd-people are similar to him in the relevant respects and, therefore, he does not have to imagine how he would feel should he himself be in their position. A cow after all does not have to place itself in the position of the grass that it eats. (Or, if it did, it would have no problem in conceding: 'Of course, *if* I were grass, I should be eaten.') Hare thus mistakenly supposes that every speaker, as a human being, is interchangeable with all other human beings who are involved, and, therefore, has to place himself in their position. Under the mask of a neutral analysis of the meaning of moral language use, he smuggles in a contested substantive norm of human equality. Plato, Aristotle and Nietzsche would not have to accept it.

This shows that Hare's meta-ethics is not capable of grounding the Enlightenment value of equality. The same applies to the principle of freedom. Someone who does not care much about his personal liberties can very well propagate an unfree mode of life as universal norm.

Finally, Hare has no arguments against those who themselves refrain from making moral statements. His universalisability criterion merely provides a retrospective critical test, which can be applied only after a speaker has used moral terminology. He can then be required to be consistent. However, Hare's analysis of moral language allows for a complete rejection of morality as such. According to Hare, moral statements do not refer to something objective. They are just the expression of someone's mental 'disposition'. Why, then, would I take any interest in such prescriptions? Why be moral? This also applies to the moral prescriptions which emerge from my own mental disposition. Suppose that my moral consciousness prohibits me from engaging in all kinds of egotistical enjoyments. Why would I then not consistently choose in favour of my egotistical inclinations without further justifying them in moral terms? My conscience after all does not, as Kant assumed, refer to some rational moral law; my moral dispositions can be explained as a result of socialisation, and are thus not of a higher order than my other empirical dispositions. I find myself confronted by an internal conflict between two psychical inclinations – in Freudian terms, between my ego and my super-ego. I only live once, thus why would I not be egocentric? Morality is for the simple-minded.

Hare's invocation of the universalisability criterion is characteristic of modern ethics. One recognises it in different terms in Kant's categorical imperative,[14] as well as in the ethics of Habermas (Section 9.3) and Rawls (Sections 10.5 and 10.6). It indicates that, since in the Modern Age no self-evident agreement exists concerning the content of moral values, ethics falls back onto a more *formal* standard, which expresses the impartial character of moral decision-making. For this reason the universalisability criterion requires of one to distance oneself from one's egocentric perspective, and reconsider one's viewpoint from a general point of view. Hare's version of this approach operates unsatisfactorily as a critical test, because the selection of acceptable moral judgments depends strongly on the psychological fact whether a subjective speaker would regard something as acceptable for himself should he find himself in the position of the others who are involved. In the next two chapters it will be discussed whether versions of the universalisability criterion that take the form of an intersubjective deliberation procedure (Habermas) or a hypothetical social contract (Rawls), can produce more satisfactory results.

8.3.3 Law

For *legal science* the requirement of empirical verifiability in its most radical form implies that the legal scientist should restrict himself to statements about the externally observable conduct of legal subjects. Legal science would thus have to take the form of a kind of legal sociology that describes the law in the manner of the legal philosopher Austin (Section 1.2.3.1): The highest authority proclaims commands; the conduct of the majority mostly coincides with these commands; and if not, coercion follows.

Legal science would by contrast lose its status as *science* as soon as it makes normative statements about non-observable matters, such as 'reasonableness and fairness', 'good faith', 'equality', 'tort/delict', 'illegality' or 'fault'. These are unverifiable and, therefore, meaningless statements, which have nothing to do with objective knowledge. References to supposed objective, metaphysical moral values, such as justice, as with Plato, or an eternally valid natural law as with Thomas Aquinas, are completely unwarranted.

[14] Or unconditional command: A rule of conduct counts as moral only when it is acceptable as *universal law*, see Section 6.2.

The verifiability criterion would thus require a legal science that radically differs from jurisprudence as it is typically taught today at law schools. Contemporary academic legal studies are not aimed at the objective registration of observable facts, but at normative argumentation about the best solution for legal problems in light of the positive legal order. This appears from scholarly articles in law journals and commentaries on decisions of the courts. In these publications the legal scholar usually performs a similar kind of normative activity as the judge, albeit in a more systematic manner, and sometimes also with a critical attitude towards positive law. From the perspective of unified science, this practice is not 'science' at all, but rather a skill, or 'legal scholarship'.

In keeping with the ideal of unified science, an empirical approach to law was in the 20th century developed by American and Scandinavian *Realism*. The *American Realists* focused on the empirical conduct of judges: law is what the judge actually says it is. The judge indeed consults the legal texts, but it is his interpretation that settles the matter. When the view of the judge in a hard case is unclear, the legal scientist must predict what the outcome of the interpretation will be. In this realistic approach the legal scientist must then in a value-free manner take stock of the norms which the judge in fact proclaims, for example: it is an empirical fact that judges condemn murder and punish it harshly.

With this approach the American Realists place themselves in opposition to the views of legal formalism which dominated 19th-century legal science: the judge must simply apply the general rule of the law to the specific case. To be sure, as the Realists themselves recognised, legal sources such as legislation and precedent, play a role as a backdrop to the judicial decision. Ultimately, however, the judge establishes how these are to be applied: one does not find the law in books, but in judicial action. The judge is, furthermore, influenced by his own view of the general welfare and his highly personal preferences, political prejudices and mood of the day: Does he like blonde women? Does he dislike men with beards? Is he a Catholic? Is he altruistic? The legal scientist must take account of all the legal and non-legal stimuli to describe and explain legal reality.

The *Scandinavian* variant of Realism gives a more systematic description of law as a subsystem of society as a whole, and also gives a better account of law's normative side. According to the Scandinavian Realists their American congeners disregard the institutional embeddedness of judicial power: they do not realise that the judicial institution is in its turn determined by rules of competence, so that the person of the judge is not all-decisive. Moreover, the Americans can also not explain why the authority of the judiciary is generally accepted.

This realistic picture of the law is akin to the sociological description of the legal positivist Hart, who similarly points to the interplay between external coercion and internal acceptance of the rules of the legal authorities (see Section 1.2.3.2). Much earlier than Hart, the Scandinavian legal realists opposed the view of Austin's legal positivism (Section 1.2.3.1) that custom and coercion alone are sufficient to explain why most citizens generally obey the law: the general public must also have the subjective conviction that it is *appropriate* to obey the law. This acceptance, according to Scandinavian Realism (and Hart), does not point to an objective morality or to natural law – something like that is after all unverifiable. It reflects the psychical fact that most legal subjects possess a 'legal consciousness', a moral-legal sense of justice which is established by means of socialisation and education within a legal culture.[15] Such psychological facts subsequently lead to changes in social reality. Legal-moral assertions, such as 'This car is my property' or 'He is my heir', have actual social consequences, because within a legal community they invoke in a suggestive manner representations of appropriate action, and legal subjects will subsequently act accordingly. In this respect the realistic explanation of the operation of legal terms corresponds with Stevenson's analysis of moral language.

According to Realism, law on the other hand distinguishes itself from morality through its ordering function, which requires central legislation and its enforcement. As a consequence, law has taken the shape of a social institution which is based on the interaction of four factors. The legal order consists, first, of a system of coercive sanctions. This system of coercion is bound up, secondly, with a mental attitude of legal subjects, that is, self-interest, stimulated by fear of sanction. In the third place, an authoritative public institution exists to establish general norms, and which derives its authority from a fourth factor: an unselfish normative consciousness (formed through education) requiring subjects to obey these legal norms. The content of the law is not only determined by central legislation and judicial decisions, but also by customary law and non-positivised principles, such as fairness.

Realistic legal theory leads to a non-cognitivist view of the normative legal discussions that typically take place in legal practice and in academic legal scholarship. In the case of disputes about the right answer in hard cases where positive law is unclear, no generally valid standard exists. Criticism invoking natural law is based on subjective preferences.[16]

In an extension of this view, Hans Albert, a follower of Popper (Section 8.4), scornfully compared normal legal science with theology: it views laws and precedents as authoritative sources of legal reasoning, in the same way as traditional theology uncritically builds upon religious dogmas, such as the existence of God or the validity of the Ten Commandments. Legal scholarship, just like theology, is based on an irrational *revelationist* model of knowledge: the belief that one

---

[15] Scandinavian Realism, moreover, takes account – in this respect it is less strict than Logical Positivism – of psychic phenomena which are not directly verifiable, such as moral consciousness. The existence of the contents of consciousness is indeed not directly observable by the senses, but can, according to the Realists, be verified indirectly. A hypothesis, such as that a person has the intention of renting a house, can, for example, be verified by observing his external conduct.

[16] Subjective rights, such as the right to property, exist only in a social sense: as the mutual expectations of legal subjects, derived from the central regulatory process and coercion. 'Natural rights' or non-positivised human rights are simply figments of the imagination, from which a suggestive rhetorical force can none the less go forth.

must obtain the truth from the utterances of institutions which are clothed with indisputable authority to solve the problems in question.

The empiricist ideal of Realism and of Albert requires that legal science abandon all normative positions. In this way it may be more objective than traditional legal scholarship, but this has to be paid for by a loss in practical usefulness. Science after all provides no normative guidelines to legal practice. Albert points out that empirical science can, on the other hand, assist in means-ends calculations. Just as in the case of normative legal scholarship, public goals must be established elsewhere – in the political domain. Subsequently the legal scientist can, by means of applied science, indicate which rules or interpretation is functional if one wants to attain these goals. 'Legal technology' can even do this much better than dogmatic legal science, because it focuses on the empirical relation between law and its social environment. It can in this way screen the efficiency of the whole legal system, and confront it with more effective ways to attain its goals.

8.4 Critical Rationalism

8.4.1 Popper

Critical rationalism improved on some of the weaknesses of logical positivism, but nonetheless remains closely related to it with its empiricist criterion of science and correspondence theory of truth. Critical rationalism is now considered as the standard approach in scientific practice, at least in the natural sciences.

The founder of critical rationalism is Karl Popper (1902–1994), who in the 1930s attended gatherings of the *Vienna Circle* and then already criticised a number of deficiencies in logical positivism. According to Popper, logical positivism with its empiricist criterion of verification makes the same mistake as the rationalistic theory of knowledge, which the positivists themselves reject as unverifiable: rationalists *and* positivists search erroneously for a certain foundation for all knowledge. Rationalism searches for this foundation in what is a priori self-evident to reason. Logical positivists regard this as speculative, because what appears self-evident in the eyes of rationalists often turns out to be completely subjective. Instead, they posit sensory observation as the certain foundation. They regard empirical data as objective, because these are directly verifiable by everyone.

However, this empirical basis likewise appears on closer inspection to be less certain and objective than the positivists claimed. According to Popper, even the simplest statements of observation, such as 'This is red', require interpretation. When I, for example, in an ostensive (demonstrative) definition point to a red piece of paper, the addressee must already understand that I am referring to the colour, and not to the shape or to the material. Popper, therefore, speaks of a 'searchlight' view of observation: observation is led by a selective viewpoint which places the spotlight on aspects of reality that are regarded as relevant. What counts as a 'fact' is not objectively given, but turns out to be dependent on human conventions.

Popper nonetheless retains the principle of empirical verification as delimitation of the domain of scientific knowledge, as well as the correspondence theory of truth: a theory is true when it corresponds to external reality. The conventional nature of scientific facts does not detract from this, because people in general do not disagree about which facts are relevant for scientific testing. According to Popper, in the scientific forum such a degree of consensus actually exists regarding what counts as empirical facts, so that these can nevertheless serve as an intersubjective test for the truth of theories.

On the other hand, the character of empirical testing diverges from positivism because of Popper's objections to the positivist principle of verification. The most important objection is that the verification criterion prohibits universal statements of regularity such as '*always* if x, then y', whereas this precisely constitutes the core of natural science.[17] The reason for this lies in the 'induction problem': a finite number of observations are insufficient to verify universal statements concerning an infinite number of cases. Such universal statements relate to all future cases, and these are per definition not as yet confirmed by observation. The logical positivist, therefore, has to reject the scientific laws of nature as senseless, whereas he specifically regards natural science as *the* example of objective knowledge. To escape from this outcome, Popper introduces a *falsification criterion* in the place of the verification criterion of the logical positivists. The falsification criterion only posits the negative claim, that from scientific statements concrete predictions can be derived regarding possible observations which can refute the statement as *un*true. Because of this, universal statements are again permissible. The statement 'All ravens are black' can, for example, not be fully verified, but it can be annulled by the observation of a white raven. By contrast, all statements which cannot be falsified by means of empirical observation, fall outside the domain of science. Popper incidentally does not regard forms of knowledge which are not falsifiable, such as myths, Plato's metaphysics, Marxism, or psychoanalysis, as completely senseless. They can provide a useful heuristic strategy to invent scientific hypotheses. They only do not themselves furnish any objective knowledge. In this respect, Popper distinguishes between the *context of discovery* where anything goes, and the *context of justification* that has to comply with strict methodological standards. That the empirical basis provides a less objective standard than logical positivism contended does not detract from the essential difference between such pre-scientific theories and real science. Although the falsifiable fact is based on human interpretation, and is, therefore, not identical to reality-in-itself, a scientific theory at the moment of falsification indeed touches 'something' in reality. Reality thus provides resistance against all wild speculation. This gives Popper the confidence that it is possible to come still closer to the truth, even if we can never reach it completely.

[17]The same problem is pointed to in the discussion of Kant's doctrine of knowledge (Section 6.2).

Because it appears impossible to posit universal scientific statements with complete certainty by way of empirical observation, Popper regards these as hypotheses. Such hypotheses can be regarded as true only *provisionally*, that is, for as long as they have not been falsified.

8.4.2 The Open Society and Its Enemies

Popper posits the requirement of negative empirical verification for both the natural and the human sciences. Critical rationalism thus subscribes to the ideal of the unity of the scientific method of logical positivism. What is not empirically falsifiable, falls outside the domain of scientific knowledge.

This, moreover, means that *ethical* and *legal-normative* statements cannot make any claim to the status of objective science. Normative judgments can after all not be refuted by way of observation of facts. Popper thus subscribes to the empiricist dualism of the logical positivists and Hume between factual and normative statements: statements about facts provide objective knowledge; but normative judgments are ultimately based on an irrational subjective decision, which cannot be grounded any further. Science can at most provide the most efficient means, after the irrational choice in favour of a normative purpose has been made.

Popper did, however, work out the implications of his doctrine regarding the uncertainty and provisional nature of all human knowledge for the normative domain of political decisions. *The Open Society and its Enemies*, which he wrote in Australia after having fled Austria when it was under Nazi rule, is a pamphlet against the Nazi dictatorship. Popper moulds it in the form of an attack on theories of philosophers, like Plato, Hegel and Marx, who defend a totalitarian state. Popper contends that in politics, just as in science, one should acknowledge the fundamental fallibility of all human convictions and compensate for this by being open to criticism. Only thus can one learn from one's mistakes. This results in a liberal view of state and law, in accordance with the Enlightenment ideals.

Popper recommends two precautions. In the first place, one must not attempt to improve society as a whole in one fell swoop in accordance with a blueprint of the ideal society – as propagated by Plato and Marx. Because of our deficient knowledge we cannot predict the real consequences of such a utopian ideal so that there is a good chance that the result could be even worse than the current situation. (Notorious for example, is the anti-sparrow war which Mao later in the century imposed on the whole of communist China. All sparrows had to be killed because they ate the seeds in the fields. Unfortunately, after the sparrows were exterminated, caterpillars could increase their numbers without hindrance into a new plague that destroyed the harvest.) Popper argues in favour of an evolutionary cautiousness instead of revolutionary rashness: do not start completely anew, but fix the worst abuses on the basis of experience. In addition he propagates a kind of negative utilitarianism: one cannot know which social institution leads to the greatest happiness for the greatest number, but it is clear where the greatest suffering occurs. One, therefore, has to concentrate on the removal of this.

Secondly, Popper advocates an *open society* where decisions are taken by means of critical democratic deliberation about desirable social developments. Against Plato's authoritarian state ideal, he contends that no person can ever possess the infallible knowledge which Plato ascribes to the philosopher-kings. On the basis of his falsification criterion Popper recognises only knowledge of the sensory observable world, which in Plato's view too consists of provisional and changing 'opinions'. Plato's appeal to a higher form of knowledge, located in an unchanging world of Ideas, Popper regards as indemonstrable and unscientific. Thus only empirical knowledge remains. The latter, as Popper contended in his polemic with the logical positivists, can never be certain, and always has a provisional character. Progress in knowledge, according to Popper, takes place only by way of the progressive falsification of untrue theories. For this reason in society, too, an open and critical climate should exist, in which all views are tested against experience, so that man can learn from his mistakes. Popper argues on this basis, in contrast with Plato, for an 'open society' where freedom of expression rules. Because there is no elite who possess all wisdom, a democratic constitution should give everyone an equal vote in decisions about the organisation of society. According to Popper, history illustrates that the state should be arranged in such a way that the authorities are under constant critical control. Absolute, authoritarian state institutions have in almost all instances led to abuse of power, however much the rulers have argued that control is not necessary because they embody 'the people', 'the proletariat', or 'the general will', in brief, the general interest. Democracy, then, must, in Popper's view, not be viewed in terms of delegated trust, but as organised distrust. Popper's theory about the essential fallibility of human knowledge that moreover exclusively refers to the empirical world, consequently results in a normative plea for the rule of law, democracy, equality, and freedom rights.

Popper nevertheless retains the distinction between objective factual knowledge and subjective moral positions: in the case of normative discussions about the best way of organising the state, an external empirical test, which *can* settle scientific disputes, is lacking. For this reason Popper concedes that his own choice for an open, critical society is indeed based on argumentation (rather than on empirical facts), but that the acceptance of these arguments ultimately amounts to an irrational decision.

8.4.3 Commentary

Logical positivism and the related movements in meta-ethics and legal philosophy must pay for their ideal of scientific objectivity with the loss of rational ways to settle fundamental normative disputes. This involves the risk that the objectives of the individual, the community, the state and the law are surrendered to a blind political power play, as some Sophists have it. Moreover, traditional legal science degenerates into an irrational practice. The expectation of the positivists that they could unite the two ideals of the Enlightenment – scientific progress and moral emancipation – thus ends in failure because of the amoral character of empirical science. The positivists, moreover, overestimated the objectivity of scientific knowledge, because sensory observation always rests on interpretation.

Popper's critical rationalism addresses the second, and partly the first, objection. Popper does give an account of the interpretive character of science, but retains its empirical foundation. His scientific doctrine, therefore, similarly leaves no room for a rational foundation of normative positions. He does, however, give reasons in favour of a liberal constitution in presenting his scientific model to the political domain by way of analogy. In the domain of law, Popper's follower Albert arrives only at an instrumental 'legal technique', which itself cannot provide any objectives. However, in combination with Popper's liberal basic values, this applied empirical legal science does open up certain possibilities.

Critics, however, contend that causal-explanatory science is as such unsuited to give an account of human life, since the latter is characterised by having meaning and value for the actors (Section 8.5). Causal-explanatory science moreover denies non-empirical, but nonetheless meaningful ways in which to arrive at reasonable solutions for normative problems, including hard legal cases. The mode of conflict resolution by way of impartial arbitration which has been developed in legal practice could indeed serve as model for moral discussion in general, states Habermas (Section 9.3).

8.5 Hermeneutics

8.5.1 The Practical Meaning of Understanding

Logical positivism and critical rationalism both propagate the ideal of a unified science in accordance with the model of natural science. Opponents object that this model has fundamental shortcomings in relation to human conduct. For this reason the social sciences require a unique method of their own, that of interpretive understanding or *hermeneutics*.[18]

As regards human life, hermeneutics wants to restore the Aristotelian teleological model at the expense of the causal model of natural science. According to hermeneutics *human* activities are indeed determined by normative objectives and not by efficient causes, such as the aimless, mechanical processes of inanimate nature. Unlike Aristotle, hermeneutics restricts this teleological model to the cultural world. Hence, according to Hart, the legal order is at the service of the common human urge to survive (see Section 1.2.3.2). This is more than a neutral, empirical fact, Hart contends. From an objective viewpoint it is indeed immaterial whether people live or die, but from the viewpoint of man himself, his survival has a special value which affects his entire interpretation of reality. From this perspective he

[18]The doctrine of understanding, interpretation; derived from the Greek God Hermes and the Greek verb 'hermeneuein'. Hermes is presented as messenger of the gods. He had to make divine truth clear to the limited understanding of mortals. The verb means reporting, making clear.

classifies the world in value-laden concepts which determine his conduct: herb and weed, healthy and sick, rain and sunshine, order and chaos, conduct and misconduct, freedom and harm; in brief, things which one either has to cherish or avoid. Only by gaining insight into this tendency, which is also to be found in legal practice, can one understand the meaning of legal institutions, such as property, contract and penal sanctions. This insight can subsequently serve to provide *reasons* to legal subjects for honouring these institutions.

Hermeneutics was initially developed under the inspiration of legal scholarship. Consequently, due to the reception of the codifications of Roman law of the sixth century AD in 13th-century Italy, the need arose for a method to make authoritative legal texts from an earlier historical period via interpretation applicable to a totally different kind of society. Later on, hermeneutics was extended from textual interpretation to a method with which to interpret human action in general. The most sophisticated version was formulated by Hans-Georg Gadamer (1900–2002) in *Wahrheit und Methode* (Truth and Method, 1960).

The point of departure of hermeneutics is that human life and its cultural products (such as legal texts) show a meaningful coherence. Unlike inanimate nature, man is not determined by causes, but guided by reasons or rules. In other words, human beings themselves give meaning to their lives, and this cannot be registered by means of external observation in accordance with the model of natural science. It must be understood from the 'inside'. The human scientist is capable of this because he is himself also a meaning-giving being.

It, for example, makes little sense if you should observe this text in accordance with the scientific method simply as an empirical observer from the outside. The observation of the black characters on the white surface, which together constitute this sentence, in itself does not provide any insight into the meaning of the sentence. You nevertheless understood the sentence. This is possible because you *interpreted* the characters as letters that belong to the English language, which together form words, which in turn are signs for concepts. These concepts are, moreover, so polysemic that they acquire their specific meaning only in connection with the text as a whole (and the larger cultural environment). The reader must, therefore, also take account of the symbolic coherence of the whole. In brief, he can interpret his perceptions only from a preceding understanding of the English language and culture.

The same applies to the understanding of all human action. People after all act on the basis of a meaning-laden interpretation of reality. People orient themselves in social reality, specifically in relation to each other, via shared, normatively-laden concepts (which do not at all comply with the requirement of value-free language use of natural science). Concepts such as 'man', 'woman', 'child', 'adult', 'judge' and 'suspect', are, for example, laden with normative expectations concerning the proper exercise of a social role, in accordance with social rules which are determined by the practices of the specific society. What these rules contain cannot be established by the observation of external conduct. The empirical observer can after all only register external regularities, but not the *reasons* why people act in this way. Someone who without any foreknowledge observes the external conduct of adults in a democracy, would, for example, indeed be able to establish that most of them, once every four or five years, enter a large building, and there colour a space on a piece of paper. He would, however, never be able to understand the meaning of this conduct (voting for Parliament or the President) on the basis of these empirical data. To understand this, he would have to know which ideas regarding representative democracy, political programmes, etc, lead people to such actions. The social scientist must, therefore, first acquire the normatively laden interpretation of reality on the basis of which the members of a society act, if he wants to gain an understanding of social reality.

The legal positivist Hart (Section 1.2.3.2) made the same contention about legal science. Hart opposed the earlier legal positivism of Austin, according to whom the obedience of legal subjects to positive law is caused by pressure from state sanctions and custom. According to Hart, customs, or externally observable regularities of conduct, do not provide a sufficient explanation. Austin denies the internal, normative aspect of law: most legal subjects obey the law because they accept it as appropriate. As Hart expresses it: at stake is not a custom, but a *rule*. One must, therefore, first understand this non-empirically observable state of consciousness before one can understand the conduct of legal subjects. That a normative legal consciousness like this indeed motivates others' actions one can indirectly derive from their external conduct: one must presuppose the existence of such a motive when someone criticises others (or himself) because of the contravention of a law. Through this combination of intention and external conduct, human conduct acquires its meaning.

In the place of the neutral observation of observable facts, hermeneutics, therefore, posits *understanding* (*Verstehen*) by means of the interpretation of symbolic connections. The interpreter is, according to hermeneutics, moreover not capable of neutral observation, because he himself necessarily interprets from the perspective of his own traditionally determined pre-understanding (*Vorverständnis*). Interpretation of a text, for example, presupposes command of a language. The interpreter has acquired a language via a learning process which, however, differs depending on the social situation and historical period. As a consequence of this, every person is caught in local traditions. Therefore, every reader initially approaches a foreign text with questions from his own interpretive framework. Only gradually does he replace his provisional interpretation on the basis of his own prejudices by a growing insight into what was initially foreign to him. The original pre-understanding is then changed through confrontation with the text, and this makes it possible to posit new questions. The most important recent defender of hermeneutics, Gadamer, regards complete understanding of the original meaning as impossible. In his view, at most a 'fusion of horizons' takes place.

This furthermore means that knowledge without prejudices is not possible. Gadamer does not attach a negative meaning to the term 'prejudice'. He makes a distinction between blind and justified prejudices. The second kind consists of interpretations which have been refined by taking account of alternatives. Authority and tradition, according to Gadamer, similarly play an important role in the selection of the better prejudices. But again: it is not a matter of blind obedience to authorities, but of recognising the better insight of the expert; and not of the irrational, dead ballast of the past, but of living, working traditions. Hence, for the legal interpretation of a legislative text it is of great importance how the text has been interpreted on previous occasions, especially by the highest court in a specific legal order.

The understanding of social science also deviates fundamentally from the method of analysis of component parts of classical natural science (applied by Hobbes to social phenomena, such as human society – see Section 4.1.2). The parts of a text, for example, the separate words, after all acquire their specific meaning only in relation to the text as a whole. On the other hand, one cannot understand the whole without first having read all the parts. The interpretation process which is connected with this is referred to as the *hermeneutic circle*: the glance of the reader roams during the reading, as it were, constantly backwards and forwards between the parts and the whole of the text until he understands it as a coherent whole.

Hermeneutics does not regard objective descriptive and explanatory knowledge as the central aim of social sciences like sociology, cultural anthropology or history. Their import is rather of a *practical* nature: increasing insight into one's own situation by taking account of models of life which stem from other sources. The interpretation is regarded as successful when the interpreter is able to put his newly obtained insights into practice in his own environment. According to Gadamer, the comparative interpretation of different models of life cannot provide any universal standards for the good life. One can at most establish that the one mode of living is *different* from the other, but not that it is *better*.

In the same way, models of conduct which are to be found in more recent sources of one's own culture can be interpreted to serve as a guideline for practical orientation. Interpretation of such recent sources is characteristic of contemporary judicial decisions and legal science where authoritative legal texts, in light of the jurisprudence and the commentary of legal experts, are applied to actual legal practice.

The above in fact amounts to a methodical explanation of the process of cultural transfer. Via language every new generation learns to interpret its environment in accordance with the worldview of its culture. This worldview is not an objective representation of the world, as logical positivism requires, but a tainted narrative: it does not contain any objective judgments, but constitutes a totality of 'pre-judgments'. It is nevertheless the warehouse of the solidified experience of all previous generations. Man, moreover, has no other anchor with which to orientate himself in his environment. Because the living conditions of human beings change continuously, the traditional authoritative stories must be adapted continuously to new situations by means of interpretation, as in the case of the reception of Roman law texts since the 13th century.

In brief, in the view of hermeneutics, because of their practical import the human sciences are not satisfied with the value-free distance of the natural scientist. There is little space for an external observer in this field. The issue at stake is precisely the *participation* of a symbolic being, the researcher, in a symbolic order. The goal is unification through the 'fusion of horizons': one must make the interpretations of others, *one's own*. Communication takes the place of calm registration. For this reason it is said that the subject-object model of the natural sciences must be replaced in the human sciences by a subject-subject model. The criterion for truth is no longer the match of a theory with reality, as is the case with the correspondence theory, but intersubjective agreement about the most appropriate interpretation, as required by the consensus theory of truth.

Such a participatory understanding moreover has a practical, *normative* significance. The interpretation stands in the service of the life and practices of the interpreter and his audience. For this reason hermeneutics links up especially well with contemporary legal science.

8.5.2 Hermeneutics and Legal Science

As indicated in Sections 8.1, 8.3, and 8.4, contemporary legal science falls short of the empiricist requirements that logical positivism and critical rationalism pose for knowledge and science. The empiricist model of knowledge requires the scientist to adopt a neutral position by taking the perspective of a value-free observer. The accepted view of legal science ties in more closely with hermeneutics. The legal scholar Paul Scholten (1875–1946), an early Dutch precursor of Dworkin's view that the right legal answer is to be found by a rational construction of immanent legal principles (Section 1.2.3.3), demands exactly the opposite of neutral distance:

> The science of positive law is always the science of a specific positive law in a specific country. It is itself determined historically and nationally.... This implies something else. Only someone who partakes in law can work on it; only the Dutch can process Dutch positive law (Scholten 1949, p. 437).

Scholten's legal scientist is, therefore, an active participant in the same legal order which he studies. This is connected with a second characteristic of contemporary legal science, which empiricism strictly prohibits: its normative character. Legal science, as viewed by Scholten, is ultimately aimed at the formulation of normative statements, because it constitutes an extension of legal practice: it aims at giving direction to legal decision-making, with justice as ultimate objective. This normative function can be performed well only by a member of the legal order: 'only he who feels himself responsible for the application, may express a judgment about it' (ibid).

Scholten stated all of this in an address in which he defended the scientific character of contemporary legal science against the claims of empirical 'unified science'. Measured against the ideal of knowledge of natural science, the traditional academic study of law is, as mentioned before, simply a pseudo-science. Consequently, the German legal scholar, Von Kirchmann, as early as 1848 spoke about *Die Wertlosigkeit der Jurisprudenz als Wissenschaft* (The worthlessness of jurisprudence as a science). In contrast, in his address Scholten opposes the monopolistic claims of empirical science. He points to other human sciences, such as linguistics and historiography, which like legal science do not formulate any causal regularities but establish connections of another kind.

Although Scholten does not use the typical terminology of hermeneutics, his view of legal interpretation is closely connected to it. This is not strange because hermeneutics was originally developed under the influence of legal science.[19]

Scholten subsequently enquires in detail into the resemblances and differences between natural and legal science. The similarities are summarised in five points: both kinds of science regard all data as objectively as possible; both are governed by logic, specifically by the principle of non-contradiction, which brings about a consistent unity between statements; both strive towards simplification, by reducing the diversity of specific ideas to a smaller number of general ideas; both analyse and classify data by means of the construction of concepts; and, finally, both disciplines make their findings intersubjectively verifiable by reconstructing them into a coherent argument which refers to experience and which is accessible to everyone. On the basis of these methodological similarities Scholten concludes that both natural science and legal science equally qualify as 'science' in the full sense of the term.

For the rest, however, the two disciplines have a completely different character. In the first place, natural science is aimed at truth. Legal science, on the other hand, has justice as its ultimate objective, even though it also relies on factual knowledge of the historical and social context within which law is applied: 'law and legal science strive towards value-judgments, which are dependent on judgments concerning reality'.

Legal science differs, in the second place, from natural science because of its greater freedom of interpretation. The verification principle of logical positivism is aimed at reducing the interpretive space, by binding theory-construction to elementary statements of observation and logical construction. Legal science, in Scholten's view, however requires a different interpretive *method*, because of the specific nature of its *object*: it after all does not take ordinary sensory observation as its point of departure, but complex polysemic social circumstances, in combination with texts, constructed in non-formalised language.

In contrast with the artificial language of the natural sciences, argues Scholten, legal language by its very nature cannot be analysed into simple component parts: law forms a coherent whole, in which the separate legal rules and jurisprudential statements acquire their meaning because of their place and interaction in the system as a whole. Furthermore, legal rules can only be understood in their social context and in relation to the concrete cases to which they apply. Reciprocally social circumstances must be interpreted in accordance with their legal relevance. In every new case it may be unclear whether it is similar enough to the paradigmatic case envisaged by legislation, with the consequence that it has to be treated analogously, or that it differs so much therefrom that it should be decided *a contrario*. What is

---

[19] An explicit application of hermeneutics to jurisprudence has, for example, been formulated by Josef Esser and Karl Larenz.

at stake in legal interpretation is relating abstract rules to concrete cases. In this, Scholten's view of legal science is closely related to hermeneutics.

With this approach Scholten also rejects *legal formalism*. According to the formalist view, the legal interpreter can arrive at a legal decision via purely logical, deductive reasoning, by directly subsuming the concrete case without any interpretation under the given legal rules. However, according to Scholten, this is impossible because of the polysemic nature of legal reality.

Scholten describes the method of interpretation of legal science as follows:

> It interprets legal rules. What does this mean? It attempts to summarise the unwritten rules into specific formulas; it explains the authoritatively prescribed rule; attempts to ascertain its scope of application by investigating its history and purpose, by fitting the rule into the rest of the system, by analysing the words employed, or by moulding the rules in a different way, so that they are ready for application to cases which have occurred or which are anticipated. The interpretation always takes place from a specific idea: the background of the law, its logical form, its quality of justice, towards a specific objective: the application, the transposition of law to real life. It fills up the skeleton of the law or other authoritative rules with new statements, which it regards as included in the existing ones. And at the same time it 'construes' the law (Scholten 1949, p. 457).

Scholten here mentions a number of traditional interpretive methods of legal science, successively, the historical, teleological, systematic and grammatical. He does not, however, provide a meta-method to choose between these alternative ways of interpretation. The legal scientist can thus go in many different directions. He can in other words get close to the right answer in hard cases by making explicit the immanent general principles that express the common purpose of relevant laws. However, this still does not unequivocally lead to a 'right' solution.

Scholten subsequently limits this interpretive space by invoking a Christian conception of law: law stands in the sign of a God-given idea of justice, of which the jurist can have knowledge through his conscience. The idea of justice must continuously serve as the decisive guide for legal interpretation. Scholten, however, acknowledges that this idea is one of the most polysemic legal elements. In his Calvinist view it resides in our legal consciousness, but because of our sinful nature, we have only a limited insight into it. Therefore, the normative conclusions of legal argumentation necessarily require an evaluative leap, since they cannot be directly derived from the legal rules and social circumstances.

As a consequence of this freedom in legal interpretation, the very personal characteristics of the scientist which natural science attempts to eliminate, play a prominent role in legal science. Scholten attaches much importance to the interpretive intuition of the jurist:

> The history of legal science mentions the names of men who reasoned in a pointed way and thought logically, and whose work was nonetheless sterile or harmful, because they lacked intuition, because they sometimes simply did not ask the question of the justice of their statement – a question which a proper judge *cannot* avoid (Scholten 1949, p. 458).

In the natural sciences, by contrast, the observer should as much as possible detach himself from his personal peculiarities. Here, objectivity must appear from the interchangeability of scholars.

Scholten's legal scientist, in brief, does not maintain a neutral distance from positive law, but practises the same normative activity as the judge: legal interpretation. Scholten subsequently distinguishes *within* the viewpoint of the participant in legal practice between different levels of abstraction. The least abstract is everyday reality which has to be regulated by law. Positive law itself, as formulated by the legislature and the judge, is more abstract: it stands at a distance from empirical reality, by organising it into general legal concepts. This abstraction is required because legal order makes use of general rules. Moreover, because of its ordering function, law requires concepts of a much more precise definition than the polysemic everyday use of language. Legal science has a still higher level of abstraction: it develops the concepts of positive law into a systematic, logical, balanced hierarchy of rules. Because positive law itself is already systematic in design, the academic systematising activity is a direct extension of legal practice. Legal practice and legal science, moreover, serve the same normative objective: finding the proper solution for legal cases. There is, therefore, no fundamental difference between them.

In opposition to the neutral distance and value-free character of natural science, Scholten thus emphasises the normative involvement of legal science, in accordance with the hermeneutical view of science. The legal scientist must not only be able to identify himself with the objectives and normative views of the participants of a specific legal community. His involvement, moreover, appears from his normative proposals for the desirable development of the legal order. This lack of distance and neutrality of legal science goes along with a diminished verifiability of its claims.

The hermeneutical approach is also akin to the view of law of Dworkin (Section 1.2.3.3). As with Scholten, Dworkin's legal theory is based on an analysis of the interpretive activity of the judge. The judge, according to Dworkin, tackles hard cases via an interpretation of the spirit of the legal order as a whole, against the background of the prevailing political and moral ideals. Dworkin's model for judicial interpretation is more specific than Scholten's view, and leaves less freedom of interpretation to the judge: the judge must deduce a number of fundamental moral principles from the positive law as a whole, which can justify a major part of it as a coherent system. These immanent principles of positive law must then serve as guideline for decisions in hard cases. Unlike Scholten, Dworkin believes that in this way an ideal judge can find the right answer. The resemblance with hermeneutics is clear: legal texts must be read as a coherent whole, which in turn acquires its meaning from an understanding of the cultural context. This legal interpretation subsequently serves as guideline for a social practice.

8.5.3 Commentary

Measured against the empiricist model of knowledge of the logical positivists and the critical rationalists, the normative activity of most law schools in the world today is unscientific. On the other hand, this legal practice can maintain its status as 'science' in the view of science adopted by hermeneutics. As an alternative to the approach of natural science, in the domain of human life, hermeneutics proposes the criterion of intersubjective consensus. This leads to the question whether this criterion is sufficient for the settlement of moral and legal disputes. Does it provide the lawyer with a way out in hard cases where the law mumbles under its breath? Is it adequate for the legitimation of a liberal constitution, based on the values of freedom, equality, democracy and the rule of law?

In our Post-Metaphysical Age the practising lawyer cannot reasonably appeal to a suprasensory natural law, or a divine intuition à la Paul Scholten. Legal positivism provides him with as little of an anchor, as appears from Chapter 1: according to Hart he is faced with normative problems which cannot be resolved by simply invoking positive law. If judicial interpretation wishes to avoid ending up in arbitrariness, rational extra-legal standards must be supplied.

Hermeneutics appears to be insufficiently capable of this. This movement starts from the assumption that all human practices, including their standards of rationality, are historically and culturally determined. When conflicting practices clash with each other, one can only ascertain that the one differs from the others, not that one of them is better. This leads to ethical relativism: the consensus stops as soon as fundamental disagreements occur. Legal subjects who accept the moral principles of their legal system may within this framework arrive at a consensus regarding specific legal disputes, by means of Dworkin's constructivist hermeneutics.[20] However, where cultures clash, basic agreement cannot be attained because independent critical standards are lacking. In a liberal legal order Dworkin's method leads to equal individual rights, in a fascist state, to the total subjection of the individual. More generally, from the hermeneutic point of view, the Enlightenment ideals as a typical product of modern Western culture have only limited validity. If one assumes with hermeneutic scholars that both metaphysical and empirical objectivity is impossible because knowledge is necessarily based on human interpretation, it becomes difficult to establish standards for the right interpretation. These are after all themselves again based on interpretation.

[20]See however the criticism of Critical Legal Studies that the legal system may be too incoherent for this, in Section 1.2.3.4.

Chapter 9
Twentieth Century: 1945–2000

9.1 Introduction

9.1.1 Political and Philosophical Developments

After the victory over national-socialism in 1945, it was smooth sailing for the liberal ideals of the logical positivists and of Popper, at least in the Western world where after the reconstruction of Western Europe, unprecedented economic growth took place. Later in the century this growth obtained a new impulse through the *electronic revolution*. Western countries combined a relatively free-market economy with political liberalism, in addition to which Europe developed a far more extensive social welfare state than the United States. The positivistic hope for a united humanity came closer through the *Universal Declaration of Human Rights*, which was adopted by the United Nations in 1948 to, in future, prevent terror, such as that of the Nazis. Would humanity then indeed be able to learn from its experiences, as Popper hoped? In the processes at Nuremberg and Tokyo, German and Japanese leaders were condemned on the basis of newly formulated, international law crimes against humanity and against peace. Colonial exploitation came to an end because Western European powers were so weakened by the Second World War that they were forced to grant independence to their most important colonies. The moral conviction that colonialism involves illegitimate oppression also played a role in this.

Already in the 1950s, however, a non-violent cold war arose between the main victors of the Second World War, the United States and the Soviet Union, through which the world fell apart into two power blocks. But towards the end of the century, communism surrendered, battle-weary. In Eastern Europe communism was replaced by parliamentary systems (some of which still tended to authoritarian rule, most notably Russia). Around the turn of the millennium many European countries had joined economic and political forces in the European Union, in terms of the Charter of Fundamental Rights of the European Union and the European Convention on Human Rights. By then, the United States was by far the most powerful country in the world. The dictatorship in communist China opened the door to capitalism,

C.W. Maris, F.C.L.M. Jacobs (eds.), *Law, Order and Freedom*, Law and Philosophy Library 94, DOI 10.1007/978-94-007-1457-1_9, © Springer Science+Business Media B.V. 2011

which led to huge economic growth; the party leaders are still holding on to political power, but as a convincing ideology communism has had its day.

As a result of the decolonisation process, in addition to the liberal First World and the communist Second World, a Third World of independent, but often dictatorially governed, former colonies came into being.[1] Initially many of the Third World countries played the two power blocks off against each other. After the fall of communism this kind of politics was no longer effective, and these countries became more dependent on the West. Countries that were socialist in name, confessed to capitalism, but continued having difficulties with the political freedoms of liberalism. A number of authoritarianly governed Asian countries, such as Japan, Taiwan and other 'Asian tigers', later joined by China and India, developed advanced industries and experienced strong economic growth in the last decennia. Based on their successes, these countries started to proclaim themselves as being superior to Western liberal societies, also in respect of morality: their traditional communal morality was far preferable to the Western emphasis on individual rights, which would lead to selfishness, drug abuse, free sex, divorce, and social disintegration. Chinese intellectuals, also in 'Communist' China, in this respect often refer to the philosophical tradition of K'ung Fu-tzu or Confucius (551–479 BC), who proposed an ideal state in accordance with the hierarchically constructed, communal model of the patriarchal family.

In Western (legal) philosophy these developments were accompanied by a further elaboration of the ideals of the Enlightenment, as well as of the fundamental criticism thereof. Criticism of the idealisation of scientific thinking by phenomenology and hermeneutics (Section 8.5) was continued by existentialism (Sartre), Critical Theory (Adorno, Habermas, see Sections 9.1.5 and 9.3), later analytical linguistic philosophy (Wittgenstein, see Sections 9.1.3 and 9.2), communitarianism (MacIntyre, Section 9.1.2), neo-Aristotelianism (Nussbaum, Section 9.1.6), (post-) structuralism (Foucault), postmodernism (Lyotard, Section 9.1.4), and deconstruction (Derrida, Sections 9.1.7 and 9.5). These movements maintain that knowledge which limits itself to empirical data (that is, what can be observed only from an external point of view), cannot succeed in accounting for substantial aspects of human existence. Whereas Foucault and Derrida enquire into the structures which determine our understanding without us being aware of them, the other movements contend that human existence can be understood only from the 'inside out', that is, from the perspective of the meaning that human beings give to the world. Moreover, knowledge, scientific knowledge included, is, according to this criticism, always based on human interpretation. Science cannot possibly be value-free because it is itself a human activity which has its basis in everyday human existence, thus in normatively laden human interests. For this reason these movements oppose the

[1] Nowadays it is more politically correct to speak of countries in terms of their level of development.

empiricist subject-object model of knowledge (a subject observing from a neutral position an object that requires explanation), the correspondence theory of truth (a theory is true if it corresponds to the objective facts), as well as the contrast between, on the one hand, objective assertions of fact and, on the other, subjective, normative assertions. Some of these theories adopt *intersubjective consensus* as the criterion of true knowledge. As already came to the fore with hermeneutics (Section 8.5), this anti-empiricist view clears the way for normative-practical reasoning in law and ethics.

The critics of scientific thinking, however, differ from each other as to whether their epistemological alternatives give better support to the liberal Enlightenment ideals than scientific empiricism. Wittgenstein's follower Winch (Section 9.2) and MacIntyre (Section 9.1.2) deny that the emancipation ideal of the Enlightenment has universal validity. With hermeneutics they tend towards historical and cultural relativism: moral values and other ideals of life can be understood only from within the culture in which they have their origin. When one imposes so-called rational, universally valid ways of life onto another culture from the outside, this would lead to social disintegration.

Others reject the scientism of the Enlightenment, but defend its liberal ethics (Habermas, Lyotard). Habermas strongly advocates the emancipation ideal of the Enlightenment as universal model for the whole of humanity (Sections 9.1.5 and 9.3). Other champions of liberalism, such as Rawls, adopt a more modest position (Sections 10.5 and Section 10.6). They recognise that the portrayal of man as an autonomous individual by Locke and Kant is based on indemonstrable metaphysics, and thus has no universal validity. They nevertheless see liberal freedom rights as the best political solution for modern plural societies, in which people have to cooperate in spite of their conflicting ideals of life.

A third position, adopted by Derrida (Sections 9.1.7 and 9.5), is that the Enlightenment ideals need to be radically re-thought. Freud's death drive plays an important role in this respect. This does not lead to a rejection of a liberal ethics, but to the positing of an unconditional standard of self-sacrifice in relation to which this ethics needs to be transformed.

9.1.2 Communitarianism

The conservative criticism of liberal human rights (see Section 7.1.3) is continued in the second half of the 20th century by proponents of *communitarianism*, such as MacIntyre, who view traditional communal values as being threatened by the modern emphasis on individual autonomy. MacIntyre denies the existence of unwritten, universal human rights: 'there are no such rights, and belief in them is one with belief in witches and in unicorns' (MacIntyre 2007, p. 69). They are arbitrary thought-constructions that belong to the rhetoric of liberal ideology. Rights can, according to MacIntyre, only exist within the framework of a system of rules that has grown historically in a specific social situation. They thus differ per culture, and cannot possibly be attributed to man as such.

For the same reasons MacIntyre turns against the idea of human autonomy which lies at the basis of human rights. The idea of an independent 'I' is likewise pure fiction. Think of Descartes (Section 3.4). He thought that he could question all truths that have been passed down, in order to subsequently find a totally new, indubitable truth which makes a start in his own thinking: *I think, therefore I am*. An individual cannot, however, possibly think completely independently from point zero, MacIntyre objects. MacIntyre, moreover, regards it as impossible to place everything in doubt at the same time: doubt always arises in a historical context, and is formulated in a language which is based on communal traditions. Just as little can one establish completely independently what a good way of life entails for oneself. Everyone derives his identity from social roles, such as man, woman, family member, employee, citizen, etc, which in turn are determined by the practices and traditions of the society in which one lives. In contrast with the suggestion of the liberal social-contract model then, social associations also do not rest on the voluntary agreement of the individuals concerned: every person, from childhood on, willy-nilly grows up within them. To these roles, virtues are attached which determine how one could perfectly fulfil them. A traditional society, moreover, has general ideals of life which combine the diverse social roles into a unity.

In modern society such communal traditions have regrettably fallen away, MacIntyre sombrely concludes. Because of this, society has sunk deeply into a moral crisis and social disintegration. The Enlightenment propagates liberation from traditional bonds; in fact, this has not led to *autonomy*, but to *anomy* (normlessness). MacIntyre does not expect any good from the attempts of the Enlightenment philosophers to replace traditional virtue ethics with a universal liberal ethics. Liberalism moves away from communal traditions and substantive life ideals so that the classical freedom rights simply offer an empty concept of freedom. Because of this, society fragments into separate individuals, who have lost all anchors which could have given direction to their lives. In this way liberal human rights in reality simply lead to individual caprice. In addition, liberalism causes social fragmentation through its strict separation of state and society: there is no longer a relation between one's role in the public and in the private spheres.

MacIntyre moreover points to the tension within modernism between the ideal of an objective value-free science, on the one hand, and the moral ideal of individual emancipation, on the other: because in the scientific worldview nature contains no values, moral ideals can no longer be legitimised. Modern disenchanted culture consequently lacks a rational criterion with which to settle moral disputes. Ethics is reduced to a matter of subjective emotions. All that remains is the boundless Self, completely separated from the moral definitions which traditional societies derive from their inherited personality ideals. The modern individual no longer has any reason to take account of others as soon as this clashes with his self-interest.

Because science renders agreement on moral values impossible, and can only provide knowledge concerning causal relations, MacIntyre complains, modern man takes his refuge in pragmatic means-ends calculations: people see each other, as well as social and political institutions, simply as instruments for their own purposes. Social relations then degenerate into mutual manipulation. This can take on two undesirable forms: unrestricted egoistic caprice, or totalitarian bureaucratic control. In short, one can only hope that the shore stops the ship of the Enlightenment, so that people can find the way back to warm communal values.

9.1.3 Philosophy of Language and Cultural Relativism

The value of cultural traditions is, similarly, defended against the belief in progress of the Enlightenment by adherents of cultural relativism, who want to defend the authentic cultures of non-Western thinking against the imposing Western lifestyle. Spokespersons for this view are to be found among cultural anthropologists and philosophers, such as Peter Winch (Section 9.2). Winch adopts the view that all theoretical and moral views are culturally determined. As a consequence an invocation of universal human rights is impossible since views concerning human nature differ along with culture. In this view both the claim to objectivity of empirical science and the claim to universal validity of liberal emancipation ethics dissolve. Each cultural way of life has its own unique value.

In a normative extension of this relativist view, a collective right to cultural identity is argued for. The more specific rights that are associated with this, such as the right to self-determination of peoples, the right to national resources, and cultural rights, are currently referred to as *third generation human rights*. Such group rights can clash with the two earlier generations of human rights – the classical and the social – because in many cultures the principles of freedom and equality are not recognised. The right to one's own culture played an important role in the decolonisation process which took place after the Second World War. The former colonies invoked it to underline their own identity as against their former Western occupying powers, who had partly justified their actions with an appeal to the Enlightenment ideals: thanks to colonisation, immature primitive nations could be educated so as to reach the level of civilisation of the enlightened motherland (see the Max Havelaar fragment with which this book opens). The right to the self-determination of every people is, for instance, laid down in the *African Charter on Human and Peoples' Rights* of 1981 – but what counts as a 'people' is controversial: the inhabitants of the earlier colonial territories or the pre-colonial tribal units.[2]

In the former Second World, the tension around questions of ethnic and cultural identity has increased since the 1990s after the disintegration of the communist regimes. In the First World, the political and economic unification of Western Europe raised a new need to protect the separate cultural identity of different nations (in so far as this is not in conflict with the human rights of the European Convention).

[2] Art 27 of the International Covenant on Civil and Political Rights of the United Nations of 1966 recognises the right to an own identity of ethnic, religious or linguistic peoples or minorities. Art 5 settles the generational conflict between first and third generation human rights by making group rights subject to liberal freedom rights: the right to individual freedom may not be cast aside through the invocation of communal values which do not recognise individual autonomy.

In addition, an argument is raised in favour of group rights for cultural minorities in Europe coming from the Third World. It is controversial to what extent these immigrant groups may retain their own identity. In the prevailing view they, at the very least, have to adapt themselves to Western constitutional values, but according to radical relativists such an adaptation would already go too far.

The cultural and ethical relativism of Winch is based on the philosophy of language of the later Wittgenstein (Section 9.2). Like MacIntyre, Wittgenstein states that people derive their view of the world from cultural traditions – the form of life – of the community within which they are brought up. According to Wittgenstein's linguistic philosophy such traditions are handed down via language. In its conceptual organisation, language constitutes a worldview from which people interpret the world (and which is differentiated in various 'language games' that are associated with diverse social practices, for instance those of religion, science, ethics or law). Such a linguistic worldview functions like glasses which one cannot take off. It can itself not be tested against empirical facts, because it also determines what one views as 'fact', 'meaningful', 'rational', and 'true'. Logical positivism thus incorrectly states that empirical verifiability constitutes an objective criterion for meaningful statements. Because of the lack of independent objective standards by which to test worldviews one cannot even say that a scientifically oriented culture provides better knowledge than cultures with a magical worldview. In contrast with what Enlightenment philosophers hoped for, science, therefore, does not per se lead to cognitive progress.

In the footsteps of Wittgenstein, Winch arrives at a relativistic view of moral knowledge: what counts as morally just is dependent upon the moral practice of a culture. The identity of a person, too, is fully determined by his communal traditions, so that it is impossible to settle intercultural moral conflicts with an appeal to human nature. As a consequence, liberal human rights cannot make any claim of universality vis-à-vis cultures that reject individual autonomy, freedom and equality (a conclusion which Winch does not explicitly state). Individual freedom rights are a typical product of Western culture. In this way Winch decides in favour of normative relativism: one must respect the value of each culture. Someone who wants to impose human rights on other cultures thus makes himself guilty of spiritual colonialism. As Wittgenstein remarked, 'Think what happens when missionaries convert natives' (Wittgenstein 2003, par. 612).

9.1.4 Postmodernism

The modernising project of the Enlightenment has recently been criticised by the movement of *postmodernism*. Under the influence of Nietzsche's perspectivism (Section 7.5) postmodernism is even more relativistic than the cultural relativism of Winch: even a culture does not constitute a unity, but entails a great diversity of conflicting viewpoints. Postmodernists view this plurality positively as a breeding ground for creativity: it is not identity which is worth striving for, but *difference*.

Claims to cultural identity induce stifling conformism where everything which deviates from the standard is excluded and suppressed. This applies to the moral ideals of the Enlightenment as well: because they claim universal validity, they mould reality into an oppressive, normative straitjacket. In the present age, all-encompassing Grand Narratives have lost their appeal, such as that of modernisation through Enlightenment. The modernist belief in progress is in any event no longer credible after the Second World War and the Holocaust. Therefore, this movement playfully calls itself *post*-modernism.

The French postmodernist Lyotard states under inspiration of Wittgenstein that the diversity of 'language games' does not allow for universal values, such as those of the Enlightenment. One can, for example, not ground these values in scientific knowledge. Prescriptive and descriptive statements after all belong to different language games which are irreducible to each other. Moreover, within science increasing specialisation leads to extreme fragmentation: a jurist, an economist, and a biologist can hardly understand each other. The social theatre is split up into divergent stage plays, leading to clashes of conflicting patterns of expectation. An officer storms ahead with the command, *I am attacking, follow me!* Perhaps the soldiers will rush ahead behind him. They can, however, just as well exclaim *bravo!* from the trenches and treat the hero to civilised applause. There is no universal rule which makes one response better than another.

Lyotard pinpoints such justification problems with a legal metaphor. In a legal dispute (French: *litige*) a conflict can be settled through the invocation of law. The law then serves as the shared paradigm of judgment for the arguments of the parties. A legal system, however, only permits arguments which are relevant in terms of existing legal categories. An appeal to moral principles which do not fit into the system would thus not be recognised by the judge. When a judge convicts someone who rejects the existing positive law as unjust, this would, according to Lyotard, therefore amount to an injustice. Since in such an instance a shared standard is lacking, one should not speak of a legal dispute, but rather of a discord (French: *différend*) or battle. The judge who employs the state's monopoly over violence is then the real criminal.

In general, conflicts can be settled only between parties who share the same dialogical paradigm with common criteria. By contrast, one does an injustice to another person when one imposes one's own frame of reference upon him. Universally valid judgments are consequently impossible. If the emancipation ideal of the Enlightenment is nevertheless imposed universally, this leads to destructive cultural equalisation. In this respect Lyotard's view is similar to Macintyre's conservative criticism of the Enlightenment ideals and Winch's culturally relativistic defence of non-Western cultures. Lyotard, however, has no nostalgia for the homogeneity of pre-modern societies. Instead, postmodernists welcome social diversity. He therefore expects the most from a plurality of subcultures. Along this way Lyotard still arrives at a liberal conclusion: individual freedom rights provide the best constitutional guarantee of social diversity.

9.1.5 Critical Theory

Other adherents of the consensus model of theoretical and moral truth advocate the emancipation ideal of the Enlightenment. Philosophers of *Critical Theory*, such as Habermas and Apel, invoke a theory of language which is related to Wittgenstein's linguistic philosophy, but arrive at a universalistic ethics (Section 9.3). They share Wittgenstein's criticism of the scientific model of knowledge: scientific language is embedded in a variety of other meaningful linguistic practices. They, however, oppose the relativistic consequences which Winch and Lyotard draw from the philosophy of language. According to Habermas and Apel, diverse language genres have a common purport which coincides fully with the modernising project of the Enlightenment: they are in essence aimed at the emancipation of humanity, which must find institutional expression in a democratic constitutional state with human rights.

Man orientates himself in the world especially via language, Habermas and Apel contend, and is, therefore, above all a communicative being. Communication also takes place between successive generations: in the process of education the accumulated experience of all preceding generations is passed on via the traditions of a culture, thus establishing the intersubjective conceptual understanding which is required for social interaction. Up to this point, Apel and Habermas subscribe to the views of Winch and MacIntyre. But as the name indicates, their Critical Theory distinguishes itself from the hermeneutical approach and from linguistic philosophy because of its critical dimension. Via *ideology criticism* à la Marx (Section 7.4) one can expose the oppressive character of existing traditions. Language, which enables man to abstract from the given situation, can help him to find a better way of life by looking up new information and by standing at a distance from existing traditions in a critical discussion. Such emancipation can, however, only take place in an open communication society where everyone can freely exchange arguments.

In actuality such a critical, open argumentation will often be hindered by traditional ideologies which legitimise the prevailing power relations, as Marx had already pointed out. Through indoctrination the powerful establish a general acceptance of the current social order, which is then also endorsed by the oppressed groups. In such circumstances space for criticism hardly exists. According to Habermas and Apel, one should try to subvert such ideologies: one has to strive for a society free from power asymmetries where everyone can freely and on equal footing participate in public deliberation. This emancipation ideal is already implied in everyday communication. After all, in the long term communication can succeed only when it complies with a number of conditions: the partners must be able to trust in each other's honesty and truthfulness. Communication thus has an emancipatory import, even though this often remains hidden in actual exchanges. Therefore, Habermas and Apel conclude, the essential nature of communication requires of man to strive for an *ideal communication society* which leads to a rational consensus on the basis of open argumentation.

This ideal of open communication supposes a democratic constitutional state that is based on the principles of freedom and equality, and that includes the classical and social human rights. Within this constitutional framework, society must be organised via public decision-making based on rational consensus: only those arguments are taken account of which are acceptable to all participants. With this universalisability criterion, Habermas ties in with Kant (Section 6.3). Non-ideal societies should be emancipated in this direction.

9.1.6 Neo-Aristotelian Natural Law

The hermeneutic approach has also resulted in a non-metaphysical version of Aristotelian natural law, notably with John Finnis (1980) and Martha Nussbaum (1992).[3] In the hermeneutic tradition, Nussbaum maintains that knowledge of reality depends on human interpretation. In this way she also rejects metaphysical natural law because it claims an indemonstrable insight into the essential nature of man. Nevertheless, Nussbaum asserts that universally valid assertions concerning human nature are possible. Although cultures differ significantly in their interpretations of reality, we do recognise others worldwide *as* human beings. Via self-interpretation we can indicate a number of distinctive characteristics which define 'man'. Nussbaum calls this *internal essentialism*, in distinction to the 'external essentialism' of Aristotle's metaphysics (see Section 2.5). For the rest, she ties in closely with the Aristotelian worldview: if one knows which traits characterise human life, one likewise knows what is *good* for human flourishing. Subsequently one can construct a universal *natural law* which contains rules for a society in which human nature can thrive. Nussbaum's version of natural law thus distinguishes itself, on the one hand, from classical natural law: the normative element is not inherent in external nature, but flows from the internal human perspective. On the other hand, she stands at a distance from empirical science through her normatively guided hermeneutic approach: a strict separation between description and valuation is both impossible and undesirable.

In the latter respect she agrees with the hermeneutic element in the 'minimal natural law' of Hart. As was indicated in Section 1.2.3.2, Hart, as legal positivist, rejects classical natural law, as being based on the indemonstrable metaphysical presupposition that nature exhibits a rational orientation to final ends. According to this metaphysical essentialism, distinct, inherent purposes would be hiding in all things, which coincide with the perfection of their essential nature. In opposition to this, Hart endorses the view of modern, value-free science that natural processes are determined by blind causal laws without any higher purpose. Biological organisms do show an orientation to inherent ends, such as the aspiration to stay alive, but

[3]Nussbaum diverges from the natural-law tradition in that she develops a theory of social justice as a standard for law, without, however, making it part of the definition of 'law'.

such instinctive tendencies can be explained causally. Hart bases his empirical, minimal natural law on the human instinct of survival: any human society requires that one should respect each other person's bodily integrity and properties, and that one should observe agreements. As appears from Section 8.5, Hart adds a hermeneutic element to this empirical view of law. *Human* life indeed shows a normative purposeful orientation: man can intentionally set ends for himself, resulting from his evaluative interpretations of his environment and himself. People do not only instinctively seek to survive. As a starting point, almost everyone values his own life. This appears from the manner in which people interpret the world, as well as what they regard as good and bad: health versus sickness, vitamins versus toxins, skilful versus unskilful, etc. Therefore, Hart's doctrine of minimal natural law also provides a *reason* for keeping to these basic rules: they assist one in attaining one's most basic aim, staying alive. Hart, however, does not extend his natural law beyond this minimal content because people have very different interpretations regarding what the *good* life entails. In contrast, Nussbaum asserts that from an internal viewpoint far more universal human characteristics can be identified, from which one can derive a view of the good life as well as a perfectionistic natural law. She, therefore, speaks of a 'broad theory of the good' in contrast to the 'narrow theory' of liberalism (which restricts itself to the ideal of equal freedom, and in this respect in its turn is somewhat broader than Hart's minimum natural law).

Via self-interpretation as a human being, Nussbaum arrives at a list of ten characteristics, which are necessary for a truly *human* life, and indicate the conditions for human flourishing: (1) mortality: therefore everyone must be in the position to live a fully human life until his natural end; (2) bodily needs (hunger, thirst, sex, and movement): one must have sufficient means for a healthy life, as well as sufficient food, shelter, opportunity for sexual satisfaction, and the possibility of moving around; (3) the ability to experience pleasure and pain: unnecessary suffering must be avoided, and the conditions must be present for pleasurable experiences; (4) affectionate bonds during childhood (through which one learns how to deal with mutual relationships): everyone must have the opportunity of attaching himself to others; (5) social needs (life in family relationships as well as wider social relationships): it must thus be possible to live in such relationships, as well as in relationships of mutual affection and care; (6) solidarity with the natural environment: people must live in harmony with surrounding nature; (7) humour and play: there must be sufficient opportunity for playing and laughing; (8) individuality: everyone should have the possibility of living a distinct life in a self-chosen environment; (9) the cognitive ability to observe, to think and imagine: every person must be able to use these faculties; (10) practical reasonableness (the ability of designing one's life plan): every person must be capable of critical reflection concerning life.

These characteristics are irreducible to each other, and are all necessary for a flourishing human life. Yet, Nussbaum, agreeing here with Aristotle, regards man's social nature (5) and practical reasonableness (10) as his most essential characteristics: they provide coherence as well as a specifically human character to the rest. To be sure, there will be no complete intercultural unanimity concerning this list, but Nussbaum expects that she could nevertheless count on a broad, overlapping consensus.

For legal philosophy, Nussbaum's list implies that the creation of the material and social conditions for a good life in conformity with the ten listed characteristics is a central task of government. But, in accordance with the 'subsidiarity principle', the state only has a role in those areas where people cannot do better themselves. According to Nussbaum, this requires a democratic constitutional and welfare state with freedom rights and social rights, which appears very similar to the 'narrow' state ideal of liberalism. At first sight one would not expect this in light of Nussbaum's neo-Aristotelian perfectionism: she advocates an ideal of the good life which emphasises man's social side. From a similarly essentialist concept of man, Aristotle defines 'freedom' as *essential freedom*: a citizen is free if he actively participates in political life, and in this way shares in the rational fashioning of his community. From this it could follow that the state must, for their own benefit, force citizens to take part in politics, so that very little freedom of choice (*negative freedom*) remains for them. Nussbaum, however, reasons differently: although not all lifestyles are equally valuable, the state must nonetheless guarantee the classical freedom rights out of respect for everyone's practical reasonableness (10) and because of his right to a distinct individuality (8). It may not *force* citizens to live the good life when they actually give preference to an unreasonable existence. From this follow the classical liberal negative freedom rights, an important deviation from Aristotle. This flows particularly from Nussbaum's modern, individualistic characteristic (8) with which she adopts a position in-between communitarianism and liberalism.

Because of the vulnerability and neediness of all people (1–7), Nussbaum's just state furthermore has a caring function, entailing fundamental social rights. However, here a difference can be detected between Nussbaum's perfectionist ethics and a liberal social-democracy. Social democrats concentrate on the redistribution of material goods, such as income and fortune, in order to provide everyone with a socio-economic basic existence, but allow individuals to choose the life style for which they want to employ these goods. In Nussbaum's view, such redistribution must occur in light of her 'broad' ideals of functioning well as a human being. Here the state is thus not as neutral as liberals would want.[4] In this way, the state may, because of characteristics (7) and (9), promote elitist 'higher' cultural goods via subsidies, even when many citizens see no point in them, and they would have disappeared in the free market. Think of opera and poetry. The state only acts here in a facilitating role. In contrast with Aristotle's or Plato's perfectionist state, it must for the rest grant full cultural freedom to individual citizens.[5] Nussbaum's just state only

[4]Nussbaum develops her political philosophy specifically via a polemic with the liberalism of John Rawls; see Sections 10.5 and Section 10.6.

[5]Such activities are, moreover, also worthy of protection for a liberal state because of the benefit that the arts and the sciences, as semi-public goods, have in the long term for society as a whole; see the commentary on Nietzsche, Section 7.5.

guarantees the possibility to visit the opera, but does not *force* anyone to actually do so.

Just like the 'ideal communication society' of Critical Theory, Nussbaum's universalistic natural-law doctrine opposes the cultural relativism of Winch and traditionalistic communitarians: in many illiberal cultures the state institutions and traditional social bonds should undergo a fundamental change. A legal system which does not recognise individual freedom rights or favours unjust social relations constitutes an impermissible hindrance to human flourishing. As examples of unacceptable cultural traditions Nussbaum mentions the unequal relations between Japanese men and women, and purification prescriptions which impede the freedom of menstruating women in India.

In comparison with the procedural natural law of Critical Theory, Nussbaum's 'broad' natural law provides extensive moral substance. This makes her theory more vulnerable to the relativist objection that she wrongly presents her partial moral intuitions as universal truths. Specifically regarding the importance of an individual private sphere, and thus of freedom rights, views so strongly diverge that an overlapping consensus may actually be out of reach.

9.1.7 Deconstruction

The emancipation ideal of the Enlightenment is also advocated by *deconstruction*, with the French philosopher Jacques Derrida as its major spokesperson (Section 9.5). As with almost all characterisations of deconstruction, this statement cannot be made without qualification.[6] To understand something of Derrida's view of the Enlightenment and the relevance of his thinking for legal philosophy, it is necessary to first say something in brief about (1) the 'metaphysics of presence' which, according to Derrida, characterises Western philosophy, and which he seeks to challenge; (2) his neologism, the 'notion' of *différance*, the genealogy of which Derrida traces back to, amongst others, Nietzsche (Section 7.5), Freud (Section 8.2), and Heidegger (Section 8.1.2); as well as (3) deconstruction. According to Derrida, the notion of a metaphysics of presence involves the setting up of a hierarchical opposition, such as that between good/evil, pure/impure, proper/improper, meaning/nonsense, essential/accidental, original/imitation, normal/abnormal, speech/writing, nature/culture, literal/metaphorical, and reason/madness, where the first term serves as foundation or as a form of 'presence', with the second term representing a 'fall' from presence which is, moreover, to be understood in terms of the first term. In Western philosophy Plato's Ideas, God as creator, the self-presence of the cogito, consciousness, subjectivity, the belief in a reality that is directly accessible to the senses, have all played an important role in grounding the above oppositional structure. Derrida then

[6]This also motivates the use of quotation marks in relation to some concepts in this section as well as in Section 9.5 below. The reason for such qualification will appear from the discussion.

proceeds to enquire into that which made the construction of these hierarchies possible in the first place. As we will see, 'desire' plays an important role here, which returns us to Freud (Section 8.2).

Freud's thinking in relation to the economic conception of the unconscious and the notion of the death drive can assist us in understanding certain aspects of the 'notion' of *différance*,[7] which plays an important role throughout Derrida's thinking. *Différance* is, according to Derrida, more 'originary' than the desire for presence which has characterised Western philosophy up until now. The notion of *différance* alludes more specifically to the restrictive movement or relation between the desire for presence and the desire for death, which Western philosophy has always attempted to exclude. Freud's notion of the death drive, as we saw, refers to a 'desire' which characterises all living organisms. It refers to a (never present) force without economy, aiming at an expenditure without reserve, in discord with, and differing from, the economic forces in the psyche. In other words, for life to continue, the fulfilment of the one desire (for death, the different, the absolutely other) necessarily has to be postponed or deferred. Freud explains this process by way of what he refers to as the 'conservative drives' which seek to preserve life. In metaphysics this conserving movement has resulted in a constant search for presence. Life and all its artefacts, including language, can therefore be said to ultimately amount to the repetition of this structure of deferral or postponement of the desire for death. The structure or 'stricture' of *différance* is relied on by Derrida to exceed in a certain way the metaphysics of presence. The 'stricture' of *différance* has the consequence that the oppositional structure informed by the desire for presence becomes destabilized, as the desire for presence necessarily stands in a *differantial* relation with a desire for radical absence. This, moreover, places a question mark behind the foundational value of all ideas of origin, such as, for example, to be found in the modern notion of subjectivity as well as of the ideals posited by such a subject.

In light of the above, *deconstruction* can be described as the 'attempt' to overcome the metaphysics of presence, including its hierarchical oppositions and ideas of origin, by pointing to the operation of *différance* in all structures.

In the legal and political context the desire for death is translated by Derrida into absolute hospitality or the closely related 'concepts' of justice, the gift, forgiveness, and the democracy to come. Because of the functioning of *différance*, all these concepts, however, acquire a different 'meaning' to that which has prevailed in the Western tradition up until now. In the tradition these concepts have mostly been given a restricted economic meaning, ensuring a return to the subject in an individual or collective sense, for example, in the notion of democracy as self-government. In their deconstructed 'sense' these concepts allow for no return to the self, and provide for a general instead of a restricted economy. Derrida consequently calls,

---

[7] *Différance* combines the French *différence* (difference) and *différer* (to differ, to postpone, to defer). The 'a' in *différance* cannot be expressed in speech (it sounds the same as *différence*), but only in writing.

somewhat like the prophets of the Old Testament, but perhaps more radically so, for an 'affirmation' of the desire for death and its related 'concepts', as the only way in which to exceed the well-nigh inescapably self-preserving nature of law, politics and ethics. In the legal context, because law is also structured with reference to *différance*, decision makers, such as judges (as well as political office-bearers), are now required to suspend the law and affirm justice in this unconditional sense. This, for example, means the complete suspension of the restricted economic interests of the nation-state as they appear, for instance, in matters involving the way in which poverty in the world should be addressed, matters of immigration, and the treatment of animals. A judge must, in other words, no longer simply calculate with reference to rules, principles or ideals (which ultimately serve the collective subject), but must go beyond these in giving effect to unconditional justice, or what Derrida also refers to as 'the impossible'. This does not mean that all calculation, rules, principles and ideals must be abandoned in the taking of a decision. In order to survive (the other side of *différance*), these restrictions are necessarily required, but then only after the judge has given himself (as representative of the collective subject) over to the impossible decision. The notion of *différance* as well as the implications for law just stipulated, explain why Derrida, differing from most of the (legal) philosophers discussed in this book, does not attempt to spell out how society should be re-structured in light of his thinking. This is because such re-structuring will always again amount to a restriction of absolute hospitality. This can be frustrating for those who seek ethical guidance from his texts or practical guidelines as to the preferred institution of society or else for the best political policies to adopt. This does not, however, mean that deconstruction does not concern itself with these matters, as we will see in the more detailed discussion below (Section 9.5).

9.1.8 Intersubjectivity and Politics

The opposition to the Enlightenment's idealisation of natural science leads to an alternative model of knowledge that is endorsed by most of the philosophical approaches mentioned above: knowledge is the product of the intersubjective process of making sense of reality. Consensus then becomes the criterion for theoretical and moral knowledge. This leads to a problem as soon as basic agreement between cultures, groups or individuals is lacking: there are then no shared standards with which to settle differences in opinion. Communitarians, such as MacIntyre, and philosophers of language, such as Winch, welcome this: it confirms the importance of shared traditions in communal life. Such relativists, however, stand with empty hands when cultures or subcultures come into conflict as worldwide communication increases and cultures become increasingly plural. Relativists, furthermore, have no criterion with which to criticise oppressive cultures; on the contrary, one has to respect these as much as the others. As Finkielkraut ironically expresses it:

> But what if a culture teaches people to inflict corporal punishment on delinquents, to reject barren women, to kill adulterous women, to consider the testimony of one man the same as the testimony of two women, to give a sister only half as much inheritance as her brother, to

> perform female circumcision, to forbid mixed marriages and permit polygamy? To love our neighbour must we respect these customs? If the answer is yes, we seem to be saying that the serf should be able to benefit from the knout, that to deprive her of this would mutilate her being, threaten her dignity as a person, give evidence, in other words, of our racism (Finkielkraut 1995, p. 105).

Habermas's Critical Theory attempts to escape this problem via a criterion of *rational* consensus which implies a confirmation of the liberal Enlightenment ideals. Habermas derives this from the same intersubjective character of human communication that Winch invokes. The weakness of his solution, however, lies precisely here. Critical Theory presupposes without justification that all forms of language have *one* essential characteristic in common, that is, that all communication is aimed at argumentation. There are after all many non-argumentative forms of communication which have nothing to do with the exchange of true and honest arguments. Literature is based on fiction, the language of advertising on suggestion, and the language of diplomacy on deception. Euphemistic language use, moreover, appears to be as indispensable for social interaction as truthful communication. In many non-Western cultures, telling the truth is regarded as very unrefined. The emancipation ideal of Apel and Habermas is then a typically Western invention which does not follow from the communicative nature of man as such. Because of this, this ideal cannot substantiate its claim to universal validity.

How must one then solve the problems of a pluralistic societal and world order? The political liberalism of John Rawls (Sections 10.5 and Section 10.6) attempts to do this. In this chapter a more detailed discussion of the linguistic philosophy of Wittgenstein and Winch (Section 9.2), the Critical Theory of Habermas (Section 9.3), and the deconstruction of Derrida (Section 9.5) will be undertaken.

9.2 The Philosophy of Ordinary Language

9.2.1 Linguistic Philosophy

The philosophy of language, or analytical philosophy, which has its origin in the Anglo-Saxon world, was in its early stages during the first half of the 20th century closely related to logical positivism (Section 8.3). Later on this movement moved away from the emphasis on the language of natural science of the logical positivists, and developed in the direction of hermeneutics (Section 8.5). Its adherents then concentrated on the clarification of ordinary language use, instead of artificial scientific language. For this reason it is referred to as 'philosophy of ordinary language' or 'linguistic philosophy'. Now, moral language use was no longer regarded as meaningless, but as having a distinct rationality of its own.

Ludwig Wittgenstein (1889–1951) played an important role in both stages. His *Tractatus Logico-Philosophicus* (1921) advocated an empiricist theory of knowledge and was one of the inspirational sources for the logical positivists. In a later period Wittgenstein criticised, in his posthumously published *Philosophische*

Untersuchungen (*Philosophical Investigations*, 1953), his original defence of the exclusive meaningfulness of empirically verifiable assertions. There he argues that one cannot formulate simple assertions of observation which refer unambiguously, and without the mediation of interpretation, to observable facts. In his view, an ostensive (demonstrative) definition, where a word, by pointing to a thing, is directly related to reality, is impossible. Suppose that someone attempts to teach his language to a foreigner. He says the word 'white' while pointing to a piece of paper. From these actions the foreigner can impossibly determine precisely which part of reality is meant: the colour? the form? the material? Even a simple statement, such as 'This is white', presupposes an insight into what 'colour' entails. Stated somewhat differently, one always observes a thing *as* something (in this case, as colour). Therefore, one is interpreting right from the start, with the consequence that the neutral observation of empirically given facts is impossible. Such an interpretation is, according to the later view of Wittgenstein, not a matter of individual caprice. It is determined by the conceptual structure of the language with which someone has grown up. Science, therefore, has no direct contact with reality, but only through the mediation of language traditions. The symbols of artificial scientific language, too, must in the end be defined by the concepts of colloquial speech in order to be understandable to scientists. In brief, scientific language does not provide unique access to the world. Something precedes it: the conceptual relations which are contained in the rules of our everyday use of language.

Because of this, the claim to priority of scientific language is unfounded. The later Wittgenstein consequently contends that science is only *one* of many meaningful linguistic *activities*. In addition to empirical description, one can with language also command, ask, act on stage, etc. Giving ethical prescriptions now regains its status as a meaningful activity as well. Wittgenstein refers to such linguistic activities and all other types of symbolic action as *language games*. Every language game has its own sense and its own rules. Taken together, these language games express the culture of the members, of their *form of life*. Such a form of life implies a worldview consisting of both factual and normative beliefs. The inherited language of a culture provides the inescapable paradigm by way of which one orientates oneself in the world, thus also of scientific practice.

The practice of science is therefore regarded as a conventionally determined activity of a scientific community. The correspondence criterion of truth is replaced by the consensus criterion: a theory is true when it is in line with the conventions the community of scientists agrees with. Such conventions, and not empirical reality, determine what is regarded as 'fact', 'knowledge', 'true', and 'rational'. These scientific conventions are, in their turn, based on a traditionally grown consensus regarding the language rules of a society. (They are thus not intentionally formulated arrangements.)

The foundational rules of our language provide a 'synthetic a priori' framework: they constitute the pre-given worldview within which we organise our knowledge. For instance, the statement that the world consists of material things (and not of spirits) is not verifiable, thus not true or untrue. The foundational rules constitute the inherited framework of all our further assertions concerning the world, in this example specifically concerning concrete material things, such as 'This is my hand' (or this chair, or that house). Linguistic philosophy thus confirms Kant's anti-empiricist statement that our knowledge is the result of human constructions (Section 6.2). However, unlike Kant, Wittgenstein does not assume a universally valid, rational, organisational scheme. The fundamental concepts of a worldview are based on historically grown traditions. They are thus subject to change and, moreover, differ per culture.

This view of science relativises the positivist statement that natural science has an exclusive monopoly over knowledge. It opens the possibility of a variety of other kinds of sciences in addition to empirical natural science, for example, hermeneutics and jurisprudence. The natural and human sciences can, in this view, after all be regarded as different language games, each practised by a separate scientific community. In each of these scientific forums a distinct view applies concerning object, method and truth. Ethics as well acquires the status of a meaningful activity which is determined by its own rules.[8]

9.2.2 Linguistic Philosophy and Ethical Relativism

In the linguistic philosophy of Wittgenstein the making of ethical statements thus regains its status as a meaningful activity. Wittgenstein's version of linguistic philosophy, however, inclines towards ethical relativism. It after all presupposes that all knowledge is determined by the conceptual framework of the language of a particular culture or 'form of life'. This constitutes a worldview, an interpretive scheme through which we organise our knowledge. Because this worldview also determines what counts as fact, rational, and good, no independent objective standard exists by which to test the accuracy of a worldview as such. A language game has no foundation apart from itself. 'It is not reasonable (or unreasonable). It is there – like our life' (Wittgenstein 2003, par. 559). When different cultures with divergent worldviews have conflicting normative ideologies, there is, in Wittgenstein's view, no independent, supra-cultural moral standard by which to settle moral disputes. His linguistic philosophy, therefore, regards moral criticism of existing life forms on the basis of external standards as impossible. It even denies expressly that this belongs to the task of philosophy. Philosophy has as its sole task the clarification of the rules of the given language games through conceptual analysis. This can occur only by taking one's point of departure in the concepts and other types of language use of the participants of a language game. The later linguistic philosophy thus links up with the internal, normative, participant viewpoint of language users. As Wittgenstein (2009, par. 124) remarked: 'Philosophy ... leaves everything as it is'.

[8] Hare's analysis of moral language use exhibits similar features: the import of moral language is, according to Hare, the furnishing of prescriptions for conduct with a universal pretence; to the rules of the moral language game, therefore, belong that the speaker must take this pretence seriously; on the basis of this one can subject his normative statement to the universalisability criterion – see Section 8.3.2.

This coincides with the statement of the hermeneutic philosopher Gadamer that an enquiry aiming at 'understanding' can establish only that a foreign way of life is different, but not that is it better or worse. The researcher himself is after all, in his turn, determined by his own cultural horizon.

Peter Winch elaborated Wittgenstein's 'language-game' theory into a cultural and ethical *relativism*: every culture has its own traditional conceptual organisation, thus its own worldview and form of life, which determines what counts as 'fact', 'good and bad', or 'rational'. In the moral domain one has to distinguish between three types of cultural relativism, which cannot be reduced to each other, but to all three of which Winch subscribes. *Descriptive relativism* establishes that different cultures in fact recognise divergent values. Such descriptions of cultures belong to the domain of cultural anthropology. *Epistemological relativism* denies, moreover, that a supra-cultural standard exists with which to settle value conflicts between different cultures. This expresses a philosophical view on the possibility of knowledge. Finally, *normative relativism* states that different cultures each have a right to their own form of life. This is an ethical-philosophical conclusion. The statement that different cultures adhere to diverse views is in itself not as yet sufficient to arrive at epistemological relativism. It is after all possible that, viewed from an objective or intersubjective point of view, one of these cultures is simply wrong. In this way, someone who believes in the objectivity of natural science would insist that thunder and lightning can be better explained as a consequence of collisions between atoms than through the Germanic doctrine that the god Donar (Thor) throws his hammer. If Plato's theory of knowledge and morality was correct, the modern, Western, liberal-democratic culture would, viewed objectively, be immoral. Wittgenstein's theory however includes the additional epistemological thesis that supra-cultural objectivity is impossible. In his view of knowledge there are no objective standards which can serve as external test for the correctness of a worldview, because such criteria themselves can in turn only be established from within a worldview.

The remaining criterion for the correctness of a belief, then, is the consensus within a culture concerning the interpretive framework with which its members organise the world. For this reason external criticism of a culture on the basis of universally valid standards is impossible. A culture in which language use is, for example, permeated by magical concepts and a belief in spirits, is therefore not inferior to Western culture with its scientific belief that nature consists of aimless and inanimate material objects and forces. According to Wittgenstein, each worldview ultimately constitutes a mythology, also that of science. What one regards as good reasons for one's actions is thus fully determined by one's confidence in the worldview of one's culture. A farmer who wants to know whether it is going to rain will in a scientific culture be guided by meteorology, in a magical culture by an oracle. The one belief is not more rational or more objective than the other. When two cultures are irreconcilable, its respective members cannot but regard each other as crazy. As there is no shared foundation for an exchange of arguments, only rhetorical persuasion remains. Following in the footsteps of Wittgenstein, Winch opposes the traditional Western view that Western culture entails a higher phase in the development of human civilization in comparison with non-Western 'primitive' cultures.

Winch rejects the idea that a universal progress of humanity has taken place from a primitive childish way of thinking to a more mature rational-scientific attitude, as the evolution theory of Comte implies (Section 8.3). According to this theory of progress, man in primitive societies is caught within irrational prejudices and superstitious fears. He projects his own human consciousness onto nature: he depicts inanimate things as animated and, therefore, believes that spirits lurk behind everything. The Christian belief in *one* single God is a more abstract version of this. An even more abstract form of this mechanism of projection is provided by the metaphysics of Plato and Aristotle who assume the existence of non-observable ideas behind, or final causes within nature. Through objective scientific thinking in the more highly developed cultures, man would be able to escape from such superstitions and arrive at an independent, rational standpoint in relation to life. According to Winch, this theory of cultural evolution is, however, itself based on a prejudice of Western culture which unjustly accords to itself a monopoly over rationality. Winch wants to protect non-Western cultures against such spiritual colonialism, and points to the distinct value and rationality of every culture.

Winch's cultural relativism is supported by the relativistic movement in cultural anthropology which set in since 1900. This movement opposes the self-confidence with which people in the West regard their own culture as superior. Accordingly, Ruth Benedict contends in *Patterns of Culture* (1934) that the ideals of the good life vary greatly in accordance with culture. The Hopi Indians in the south-west of the United States, for example, regard a moderate, controlled way of life as ideal, whereas the Dobu in the south of New Guinea favour an aggressive attitude. A person in Dobu society who lives in accordance with the Western ideal of neighbourly love would be regarded as a maladjusted lunatic.[9] According to Benedict, man at birth has a wide variety of dispositions that he may develop when growing up. In contrast with animals, his conduct is only to a small extent determined by heredity and instinct. In the cultural traditions of a society a particular set of characteristics is selected from this reservoir, which represent the ideal personality of that culture. Under the influence of education and social pressure the members of this society will then adopt the culturally desirable characteristics. Because each culture in this way makes its own selection from the totality of human possibilities, according to Benedict no single culture possesses universally valid standards by which to criticise the life ideals of other cultures.

On the basis of this descriptive and epistemological relativism, Benedict advocates normative relativism: all cultures are of an equal value; therefore one has to respect the differences between them. That is why Benedict and a number of her colleagues opposed the claim to universality of the *Universal Declaration of Human*

[9]Later critics incidentally contended that Benedict had over-exaggerated these differences.

Rights of 1948. The so-called universal rights are, according to her, nothing more than a one-sided product of the individualistic Western culture. If the Universal Declaration should be implemented universally, it would lead to a worldwide identity crisis because the greatest part of humanity can then no longer live in keeping with their own traditions. This would go against the findings of cultural anthropology that people can develop their personality only via their own cultures. For this reason a person is only really free when he lives in accordance with the view of freedom of his society, according to Benedict. In a truly universal declaration of human rights one would, therefore, have to replace the Western ideal of individual autonomy with the collective right of cultural autonomy.

In itself the relativism of Benedict and Winch is well intended. By emphasising the distinct value of other cultures they seek to resist the Western spiritual domination of the world, through which many non-Western life styles are sidelined. For this reason they argue in favour of the right of each culture to its own way of life. This normative relativism nevertheless runs into a number of difficulties. In the first place, it is inconsistent with Winch's normative conclusion that all cultures must be respected. This conclusion, after all, itself presupposes a *universal* value of mutual respect, which is in conflict with relativism: many cultures do not recognise the value of tolerance. Winch can thus at most argue for tolerance as a partisan value. Or else, an inverse contradiction may arise here: cultures with a relativistic tolerant view must indeed regard themselves as superior to cultures which are convinced of being absolutely in the right.

A second objection against relativism is that it provides no solution when different cultures come into conflict with each other. Such conflicts inevitably occur because the worldwide communication between cultures is becoming increasingly intensive. This objection comes clearly to the fore in a society with cultural minorities who endorse values that deviate fundamentally from those of the dominant culture. How should one, for example, in a democratic constitutional state deal with minorities who are in favour of the inequality between men and women, or who have no understanding of the importance of freedom of expression, or who regard killing because of violated honour as a moral duty?

As a solution to such value pluralism, liberalism, as a political ethics of the second order, is often proposed. Political liberalism allows optimal freedom for everyone to live in accordance with his morality of the first order in so far as it does not affect the equal freedom of others (see Section 1.4, and the political liberalism of Rawls, Section 10.5). But if one accepts this solution, ethical relativism is on closer inspection not the endpoint. It appears to involve a universal ethics: liberalism. Critics therefore object that liberal freedom is unacceptable for cultures with an ethics of absolute claims. A culture with a Platonic perfectionist ethics would, for example, regard the tolerance of dissenters as reprehensible, and would, therefore, not be prepared to accept liberal tolerance. Plato would as little accept the liberal thesis that a way of life has moral value only when it is chosen voluntarily. He after all rejects the autonomy ideal because he regards most people as incapable of making independent rational choices. For a clash with an intolerant culture, relativism provides no solution. Only war then remains.

To conclude, a third objection: from the perspective of the emancipation ideal it is objectionable that Winch's relativism respects cultural ideologies which are fundamentally in conflict with the values of freedom, equality, brotherhood, democracy, the rule of law, and human rights. Ethical relativism, in other words, undermines the ideal of progress of the Enlightenment. In accordance with Enlightenment philosophy, authoritarian or anti-egalitarian cultures should be emancipated. However, according to relativism, the Enlightenment values are themselves culturally determined so that they can make no claim to universal validity. In Winch's view, Multatuli's Max Havelaar was therefore wrong in attempting to break down the hierarchy of the prevailing Indonesian customary law on the basis of his Western ideal of equality. The call of Ayatollah Khomeini for censorship (and religious murder) was in this relativist view as rational as the Western notion of freedom of expression. Cultures in which women are denied a role in public life have an equal value to cultures which prohibit sexism in their constitutions. The presumption of the Enlightenment that it entails moral progress of human civilization is nullified through this approach.

One can of course respond that a lack of freedom and equality is not so bad as long as this is accepted by the members of illiberal societies. Perhaps the Enlightenment values *are* not universally desirable. Critics of relativism, however, contend that the general acceptance of cultural values does not count for much, because such a consensus is often the outcome of indoctrination. The powerful frequently succeed in making the powerless believe in an ideology which justifies their inferior status. For example, in many non-white countries which used to be Western colonies, the ideals of whiteness still dominate. In the West most women for many centuries accepted their domestic function without much protest as 'natural'. According to this criticism one should break through such oppressive consensus by way of ideology criticism in the interest of the oppressed. This is specifically the viewpoint of Critical Theory which, just like Wittgenstein, places the emphasis on the importance of communication through language, but from this, instead of ethical relativism, derives a universal ideal of emancipation.

9.3 Critical Theory

9.3.1 Neo-Marxism

The initially Neo-Marxist inspired, but later social-democratic and liberal-oriented Critical Theory (Bloch, Lukács, members of the German *Frankfurter Schule*, such as Adorno, Marcuse, Habermas and Apel) developed a critical theory of society in opposition to the dominant scientific, technological way of thinking of capitalist society. The critical theorists state that scientific thinking has lost its original association with the emancipatory Enlightenment ideals of freedom, equality, and fraternity. Empirical science now simply provides 'instrumental rationality' (knowledge of the means with which to achieve a goal), but regards moral and political questions about the goals themselves as rationally unanswerable. This instrumental scientific approach currently dominates not only the whole labour process, but has also infiltrated all other areas of human life. Through this objectification ('colonisation of the life world') social life has been dehumanised ('alienated' from its original humanity).

The Neo-Marxists acknowledge that, unlike Marx predicted, no revolution has taken place against the capitalist system (see Section 7.4). Technology developed massively after Marx, but so did the ability of capitalism to adapt itself. This happened, among other things, through active state intervention via social legislation that removed the sharp edges of capitalism, while at the same time maintaining the free market. Because of this, workers, according to Critical Theory, still lack an essential right: the right to a say in operational management. In the capitalist system this has remained in the hands of the providers of capital and of managers. As a consequence, the largest section of the population has no say in the determination of a fundamental part of their own destiny. They are still being disposed of as if they were sheer economic objects, on the basis of the economic utility of their labour. Neo-Marxists for this reason regard the welfare state as a sweetener. The 'proletariat' is currently, moreover, in all kinds of ways ideologically bound to the existing production relations, by means of increases in wages that promote their consumption. The need for consumption is furthermore manipulated by advertising and incentives of social status. In this way the members of capitalist society are, according to Neo-Marxism, alienated from their true human needs. Marcuse speaks of a 'one-dimensional man'.

Critical Theory attempts to promote emancipation from this alienation by alerting people to the dehumanising functioning of capitalism as well as scientific thinking. It wants to make people aware of the fact that the social system with all its inequalities is not an inescapable natural occurrence, but constructed by people (albeit not purposefully). It can, therefore, likewise be changed by people. When man acquires insight into his ability of self-mastery, he can arrive at a more humane society, in which everyone cooperates in freedom, equality, and fraternity.

9.3.2 The Interest in Emancipation

The critical philosophers Habermas and Apel do not oppose natural science, provided it restricts itself to the terrain of inanimate nature. There it has indeed contributed to a useful increase in knowledge. They only reject its claims in areas where it is inadequate, such as human social life. The latter requires a distinct manner of attaining knowledge.

Habermas distinguishes three specific ways in which man relates to his environment. These three attitudes determine the perspective from which he acquires his knowledge. With these correspond three 'knowledge interests': (1) In relation to external non-human nature, man adopts a technological attitude: he *exploits* it via his labour. (2) This he does in cooperation with other people with whom he lives together in a community. The relation with his fellow men is of a *communicative* nature: people can gear their activities to one another by means of a shared colloquial language, which is rooted in the traditions of their culture. (3) Finally, man has a relation with himself. The individual must adapt himself to communal life. For this purpose he has to develop a personality in which his egocentric, instinctive desires are brought into line with the demands of the prevailing social relations. According to Habermas and Apel, three types of knowledge, each characterised by a distinct human interest, correspond with these three types of relation.

(1) Natural science aims at controlling external nature. It is dominated by a *technological interest in knowledge*. Through knowledge of the causes, man can after all co-determine the course of nature. In this model of knowledge, the 'subject' stands in opposition to the 'object'. One should not, however, attempt to use this method in other fields. Because of its 'scientistic reduction' of human life to causal regularities, in the humanities it can provide no insight into specifically human relations. There it plays into the hands of an impoverished, technocratic and manipulative view of man and society. This approach leads to a view of people as sheer objects, controllable by causal knowledge, instead of as fellow human beings with whom one cooperates towards a shared purpose.

(2) Hermeneutic social science provides interpretive knowledge through which one learns to orientate oneself within communal traditions. The human sciences are aimed at the understanding of human life forms. Here a *practical interest in knowledge* plays a role: the knowledge of the social sciences provides guidelines for the better design of one's own life. In the place of the subject-object model of natural science, the communicative subject-subject model comes to the fore. In other words, the test for true knowledge of social relations is not correspondence with facts, but intersubjective understanding: has the enquirer understood the motives of the acting persons in such a way that they themselves agree with his interpretation of their way of life?

This second form of knowledge thus incorporates hermeneutics as well as linguistic philosophy into the Critical Theory of Habermas and Apel. As indicated, according to these two movements a universal ethics is impossible, because one always remains caught within one's cultural traditions. This is, however, unacceptable to Habermas and Apel because they regard many of these traditions as oppressive. One often grows up in a society which is dominated by traditions that were formed under the influence of great social inequalities and power asymmetries. Again and again the dominant groups succeed in shaping the worldview of all members of society in accordance with their own interests. In this way, capitalists will attempt to justify their power with the ideology that humanity as a whole is better off with free competition: the principle of the free market would guarantee high-quality production for prices that are as low as possible, from which everyone benefits. If the capitalists succeed in making everyone believe in this ideology, the underlying power structure acquires an anonymous, apparently objective force, which determines human conduct as if it is an inescapable natural law: economic laws simply are like this.

The biased character of such an oppressive ideology can, according to Critical Theory, not be unmasked by the hermeneutic approach of the humanities. In keeping with its communicative import, hermeneutics attempts to understand human action from the internal perspective of the insights and values of the members of a society. However, according to Critical Theory such values can be in conflict with the true human needs of a society. Through indoctrination, women themselves can, for example, come to believe that they are inferior to men. The approach to understanding hermeneutics can, as Gadamer acknowledges, not provide an independent standard for criticism of a society. It can at most establish that one society is different from another, not that it is better. Habermas and Apel, however, state that man can transcend the limitations of such traditions by means of a critical social science.

(3) In the third place, there is an *emancipatory interest in knowledge* which leads to the *critical social science* which is characteristic of the Critical approach. This third interest in knowledge is based on the human ability of increasing self-awareness. People can realise that their own personalities have been deformed by oppressive ideologies, and on the basis of this 'emancipatory knowledge' adopt an autonomous, self-chosen way of life. The criticism of ideologies of critical social science must promote this self-awareness by unmasking the dominant power system – in the same way as, in personal life, Freudian psychotherapy may help an individual to free himself of neurotic obsessions by exposing their origin. It then shows that the generally accepted social convictions have no objective foundation, but serve as a covert justification for economic power relations. Critical social science can, for example, attempt to show that the free market principle in fact plays into the hands of egoism instead of cooperation and solidarity, and ultimately is in the interests of only the powerful. On the basis of this insight one can subsequently strive for a shared say in the production process aiming at everyone's interests. In this way critical social science stands under the sign of the 'emancipatory interest in knowledge'.

9.3.3 The Ideal Communication Society

From this view on the ways of acquiring human knowledge, Habermas and Apel derive a universal ethics of emancipation. They contend that of the three knowledge interests, the aspiration towards emancipation constitutes the essential characteristic of man. For this reason, every person has the duty to strive towards an emancipated society, controlled by the principles of freedom, equality, and fraternity. Habermas and Apel substantiate this with reference to the intersubjective, communicative character of human knowledge and culture.

Because the attainment of knowledge, in the view of Habermas and Apel, is guided by specific human interests, they reject the positivist claim that empirical science provides a value-free objective version of reality. Natural science is, according to Critical Theory, determined by the human need to control the environment, or by a 'technological knowledge interest'. Empirical science, therefore, observes reality in a selective manner: it limits itself to the aspects which lend themselves to causal control. (For this reason, the method of natural science is not sufficient for social life.) It follows that the empiricist separation between objective judgments concerning facts, on the one hand, and subjective normative judgments, on the other hand, is untenable. Every form of knowledge is determined by a human need, and, therefore, has a normative import. Habermas and Apel conclude that knowledge must overtly be placed in the service of human interests, that is, of the emancipatory interest.

Apel invokes in addition an argument that has a natural-law flavour: the emancipatory aspiration constitutes the essential nature of man, and is, therefore, a universal norm for all people. Apel contends that intersubjective communication through language constitutes the essence of human life, and that the fundamental significance of all communication consists in a free and unprejudiced exchange of ideas and arguments. Therefore all people should strive towards emancipation on the way to an 'ideal communication society' in which freedom and equality prevail. Communication is, in Apel's view, an essential characteristic of man because the whole of human culture is based on language. Animals live in accordance with fixed, instinctively determined patterns of conduct. Man can, however, to a certain extent stand at a distance from his immediate environment. He can gather knowledge of the surrounding world, and on that basis adapt his environment to his needs. This is possible through language. With language, reality can be organised into general concepts which make it possible to speak abstractly *about* reality, instead of living immediately *in* it. Language, according to Apel, is not an individual issue, but an intersubjective means of communication which constitutes the expression of a long cultural tradition. Via language the experiences of many generations can be safeguarded and passed on so that human culture can evolve continuously. People thus orientate themselves in relation to their natural environment and in relation to each other via the shared language traditions of their culture, or via intersubjective communication.

Up to this point, Apel's contention corresponds with that of the hermeneutists and linguistic philosophers. This contention could lead to the conclusion that man, due to a lack of natural instincts, has no other way to orient himself but his cultural traditions. This would mean that all moral standards are culturally determined. One can then through the study of foreign cultures indeed broaden one's own horizon. However, because one always interprets from within one's own cultural traditions, one is not capable of formulating an objective, supra-cultural standard in order to establish which life form is the best.

Apel, however, adds to this that the central immanent purpose of human communication consists of transcending the restrictions of the dominant cultural traditions. Apel specifically argues that the core of the idea of human communication lies in the unrestricted and honest transfer of information, thus in free *argumentation*. In everyday communication, open argumentation is, however, often distorted because the parties manipulate the discussion for reasons of self-interest. Where the linguistic traditions are determined by the interests of the powerful, all communication is from the very start tainted by a suppressive ideology. Because of this, one can in everyday life hardly speak of real communication in the sense of an open and free exchange of ideas and arguments. This ideal form of communication is, in Apel's view, nevertheless presupposed in every actual communication. Lying would, for example, have no effect when parties to a discussion do not assume that people mostly speak the truth. Indoctrination often no longer succeeds when one becomes aware of the manipulation. Therefore, the purpose of communication implies that parties to a discussion are honest and make true and understandable statements. If statements are placed in doubt, one must be able to defend them with arguments. If necessary, the whole cultural interpretive framework of a society must be subjected to discussion.

Since the ability of ideal communication constitutes the essence of man as communicative being, he must, according to Critical Theory, strive towards eliminating influences which distort this ideal. In Apel's view, the aspiration towards an *ideal communication society* is contained in the essential nature of human communication, that is, a society in which everyone can equally join the discussion in a free exchange of ideas. This societal ideal implies freedom of expression, political freedoms, equality in social conditions (thus the classical and social fundamental rights), as well as a democratic decision-making procedure.

In democratic deliberation about the further design of society, moreover, only those claims and needs should be recognised which can be justified intersubjectively, in other words, all claims which are in harmony with the claims and needs of all others. This is Habermas's version of the universalisability principle which he regards as a consequence of the ideal of impartiality that characterises moral discussion. Unlike Hare (Section 8.3.2), but similar to Kant (Section 6.3), Habermas does not limit the application of the universalisability principle to the normative statements of an individual speaker. He applies it to the imaginary community of all potential participants in moral communication as a whole. From this follows a universal duty placed on all people to eliminate unequal social power relations which distort ideal communication.

Contrary to the hermeneutists and the linguistic philosophers, in this way Apel derives a universal standard from the communicative nature of man with which to measure divergent cultural value systems. He regards cultures that are designed in conformity with the emancipatory ethic of the Enlightenment as superior, because only there can man flourish in accordance with his true nature. Societies which deviate from this, for example, because of a caste system or the unequal position of women or a capitalist economy, must be brought in line with this societal ideal. Contrary to Winch, Apel thus propagates the ideal of progress of the Enlightenment as universal test for the value of cultures.

Apel's invocation of a human 'essential nature' makes one think of the metaphysical, essentialist natural law of Aristotle and Thomas Aquinas (Sections 2.5 and Section 2.7.2). The difference is that these arrive at a broad ethics, whereas Habermas and Apel argue for an ethics that retains an intermediate position between perfectionism and liberalism. The reason for the difference lies in their divergent views of knowledge. According to Aristotle and Thomas Aquinas, objective knowledge of (a higher, spiritual) nature is possible. This includes knowledge of an objective ideal of human perfection, thus a perfectionistic, broad ethics. Apel and Habermas reject such claims to objectivity because human interpretation necessarily plays a fundamental role in the attainment of knowledge. What is regarded as knowledge is, therefore, dependent on human consensus. Their ethics consequently does not follow from knowledge of the content of nature, but is based on a *procedure* for the achievement of rational consensus. Morally just is everything that is acceptable to all. To the conditions of this procedure belong that all parties to the discussion must arrive at their point of view in equal freedom, thus without having been forced into a specific way of life. The criterion of intersubjectivity in this way leads to a liberal, procedural ethics, in conformity with the Enlightenment ideals.

The emancipatory ethics of Critical Theory, however, also shows perfectionistic features. It after all does not accept all actual preferences that individuals have as basis for the formation of a free consensus. Desires that are in conflict with 'true humanity' must first be unmasked. Critical Theory thus adopts an ideal of human perfection: that of the emancipated, 'truly free' man. Yet, this does not imply a perfectionist *political* theory. As long as the ideal communication society has not as yet been achieved, most critical theorists want to present their liberating insights via open, rational argumentation in accordance with a liberal democratic decision-making procedure. In this, they adhere to a form of political liberalism. However, some more radical adherents of this movement contend that indoctrinated people are not open to rational argumentation. Therefore, strategic means may be used in addition in order to bring them to proper insight. In so far as Critical Theory in this way, following in the footsteps of Rousseau, wants to 'force people to be free' its political theory is perfectionist rather than liberal.

9.3.4 Legal Philosophy

Habermas has worked out the implications of his moral philosophy for law in the form of a modern natural-law doctrine. Contemporary Western law, in Habermas's view, has an inherently moral import, in which it shows a close relationship with his procedural ethics: law aims to solve social conflicts by an impartial procedure. The impartial character of law appears, among other things, from the institution of the impartial judge and from procedural rules concerning the allocation of the onus of proof, the hearing of all parties, and the judicial duty of justification. This presumption of supra-partiality one can subsequently adopt as a moral standard for the legitimation of actual legal decisions: can these indeed be defended from all possible points of view? Laws and decisions must, in other words, be tested in the imaginary decision-making procedure of Habermas's ideal communication society.

Habermas places this *procedural* natural-law theory in opposition to the classical metaphysical natural-law doctrine and to legal positivism. In his view, the metaphysical natural-law theory has lost its foundation through the 'disenchantment' of the world since the 17th century under the influence of natural science and modern economics. Law, economy and politics in this way separated themselves from traditional religious values. Previously the law enacted by the state derived its legitimacy from the assumption of natural law that it was an elaboration of eternal values. Because faith in this metaphysical foundation has fallen away, *only* state law remains. This is reflected in Austin's legal positivism, which depicts law as the enforceable commands of the sovereign (Section 1.2.3.1). Austin's legal theory is, however, too simplistic because his definition does not distinguish between law and politics (power). The successive theory of Hart gives a better account of the typical structure of positive law as a hierarchy of norms: the state is in its enactment of rules itself bound by secondary, power-conferring rules (Section 1.2.3.2). Hart's legal doctrine is similarly legal positivist because what counts as law is exclusively characterised by formal criteria that rule its establishment, and not by substantive moral demands. Since according to legal positivism all rules count as law that are enacted as such by the government in the formally correct way, the question arises whence law can derive its legitimacy.

Habermas opposes the thesis of normative legal positivism which equates the *legality* of law with *legitimacy*: law which has been established in the correct manner should be obeyed. A standard argument for this equation goes that only then legal certainty, and thus social order, is safely secured. According to the sociologist Max Weber, owing to a number of formal characteristics, positive law possesses a distinct rationality which provides sufficient reason for obeying it. Positive law constitutes a well-organised system of laws which is formulated in a general, supra-personal form. Thus it can guide social interaction and state organisation into orderly trajectories which run according to generally known, calculable patterns of expectation. Through private law institutions, such as property and contract, law makes organised economic exchange possible. Rules of public law that assign authority regulate the power relations in political life. Positive law in this way provides a framework within which the citizen can lead a regular and calculable life according to his own values.[10] This gives modern law its specifically formal 'legal authority', a legitimacy that is no longer based on a moral foundation, as in traditional societies.

Habermas, however, contends that the legitimacy of law cannot be based upon a legalistic foundation. He points out that current law no longer complies with the formal characteristics which Weber ascribed to it in the first half of the 20th century. Since then law has been 'de-formalised': it no longer constitutes a closed system of commands and prohibitions which can be identified by the way in which it comes into effect, but an open system in which account is taken of social consequences and moral considerations. For example, in the second half of the 20th century in Western Europe a welfare state has been established which is based primarily on regulatory law in the service of political purposes such as redistribution. Moral values which have been positivised in constitutions play an increasingly important role in judicial decisions. In the terminology of Dworkin: instead of by *rules*, law is increasingly governed by *principles* (Section 1.2.3.3). Because of this 'materialisation' of law a strict separation between law and morality is no longer possible. Nowadays, legal

---

[10] Weber regards such values as the result of irrational subjective preferences, because of which no generally valid moral demands can be made of law.

certainty is only one of the principles which the law serves. The property right as such, for example, only makes interferences with someone's property calculable. In the contemporary view of property, the principle of legal certainty must be balanced against the principle of equal chances for everyone which may require redistribution by the state. This is not guaranteed by the general and abstract form which characterises law in Weber's view. This form only provides for formal equality before the law, or impersonal application of existing legal categories, but not for material equality in economic and political life. For this reason, the 19th-century absolute right to property was in the course of the 20th century increasingly relativised.

According to Habermas, positive law consequently can no longer derive its legitimacy exclusively from its legality, as normative legal positivism claims. Then again, because of the decline of metaphysics and religion, the self-evident, generally shared moral traditions which of old used to serve as test for legitimacy no longer exist. Exit classical natural law. Instead, Habermas arrives at a formal version of natural law: the test for the appropriateness of legal rules is whether they can be the result of an impartial decision-making process. In support of this he points to an inner association between law and morality which is of a *procedural* nature: the law functions as an impartial arbitrator, which is formalised in the institution of the impartial judge, the principle of hearing both sides, and the judicial duty of justification. Legislation in contemporary Western culture is, moreover, established via a democratic decision-making process which is based on the idea of the free and equal participation of all citizens in the political and legal order. Habermas's procedural justice is, therefore, immanent *in* legal reality. Law has an inner relation with this procedural morality.

Just like the legal positivists, Habermas, therefore, bases the legitimacy of law on formal criteria. These criteria, however, do not refer to the legality of law, but to a more abstract characteristic with a moral import: the procedures concerning the impartial settling of disputes. In other words, the ability to solve conflicts in accordance with fixed rules (that is, legal certainty as stressed by normative legal positivism) does not provide a sufficient foundation for legitimacy; in addition, the law must solve such conflicts in a specific *neutral* manner, as is implied in the very nature of positive law. Only because law professes to stand beyond the parties can it legitimise a general duty of obedience, not simply by providing certainty and order.

The ideal of impartiality takes on different forms in the divergent legal procedures of decision-making. At the level of legislation where the formulation of general rules and principles is involved, this leads to the *universalisability criterion*: only those decisions are legitimate with which all involved may agree to in a free discussion on an equal footing. At the concrete level of judicial decisions this leads to the *adequacy criterion*: a judgment is legitimate when the judge has taken account of all aspects of the case. The form of government which complies best with these criteria is the democratic constitutional state. According to Habermas, the ideal of procedural justice was also contained in earlier forms of modern natural law, specifically in the social-contract model of Hobbes and Kant. The metaphor of the social contract indicates that the social order and the legal order must comply with values to which all citizens could agree.

In Habermas's view, then, law amounts to an extension of his general procedural ethics. This is not to say that law and procedural morality fully coincide. The most important difference lies in the positivised, institutionalised character of law which would provide an efficient societal order. In concrete instances, the outcome of the imaginary decision-making procedure of Habermas's procedural ethics is uncertain, because the universalisability criterion is formulated very broadly. Judicial decision-making is, on the contrary, not imaginary, but positivised. Here, the criterion of impartiality has assumed the concrete form of the independent judge and democratic legislature that make concrete decisions. Law is, in brief, based on positive legislative and judicial procedures, as a result of which a great number of rules are fixed beforehand, in order to make the conduct of citizens predictable. Law, moreover, supplements this through the possibility of using force against unwilling citizens. Law furthermore does not only consist of positivised moral principles, but is also an instrument for political policy.

Habermas realises that actual legal practice in the Western world does not comply with this ideal of law. Many democratic decisions do not result from reasonable argumentation, but from compromises between power factions. Citizens are often satisfied as long as their material interests are attended to, and decline further participation in the political debate. Therefore, in actuality, laws will not be equally acceptable to all. Judges moreover often insufficiently motivate the way in which they apply such laws. Their decisions are co-determined by social prejudices and partial interests. Nevertheless, Habermas contends that the fact that they are in such instances confronted with criticism regarding their *judicial* function, proves that the impartiality ideal nonetheless constitutes the core of the legal institution, even if positive law in actuality to a great extent does not comply with it. Morality, therefore, on the one hand, constitutes a substantial part of legal reality, and, on the other hand, provides the basis for a critical legal theory in relation to positive law.

In a very unjust legal order citizens may have a right to revolt. In a democracy, they have the more moderate right to 'civil disobedience' when the government violates their basic rights. They may take refuge in illegal acts in order to symbolically protest against specific unjust, for instance, racist laws. At the same time they should explicitly express their acceptance of the legitimacy of the legal order in general: their illegal actions should be in the open, non-violent, and related to the wrong in question. Exemplary are the actions of Martin Luther King. In line with Habermas's philosophy of language, the aim of civil disobedience is primarily communicative, giving a sign to the democratic majority to reopen the discussion about the legitimacy of the laws in question.

9.4 Commentary: Intersubjectivity and Universal Ethics

Critical Theory takes its point of departure in the same emphasis on intersubjective consensus as hermeneutics and linguistic philosophy. All these movements assume that knowledge is tainted by human interpretation. Objectivity in the sense of correspondence with objective reality is, therefore, an illusion. This is superseded by the consensus criterion of truth: an interpretation is correct if it is met with a general consensus.

Philosophers of language and hermeneutists recognise that different cultures diverge in their interpretive frameworks. For this reason they advocate cultural and normative relativism. Morally good is what is accepted as such within a culture. In opposition to this, Habermas and Apel state that an *actual* consensus does not have to be the final word. It is often based on prejudices and power inequalities which can and must be transcended. The communicative essential nature of man imposes an obligation to strive for a *rational* consensus, based on a free and equal exchange of information. In the place of the criterion of factual acceptance by all those involved, they posit the criterion of *acceptability* for all in the hypothetical ideal circumstance of rational communication.

It is, however, very doubtful whether the claim to universality of this emancipation ethics can persist. Apel contends that it is a universal duty of all people to strive for an 'ideal communication society'. He bases this on the argument that all people are essentially communicative beings, and that communication is in essence argumentation which is free from power asymmetries. This reasoning, however, appears to be based on an unfounded essentialism. Even if one accepts that man is in his essence a cultural and thus communicative being, Apel's next step remains debatable: his equation of communication with argumentation. Apel is indeed correct with his statement that *argumentation* is aimed at unprejudiced, and honest discussion on an equal footing. *Communication*, however, also includes other, non-argumentative uses of language which are expressions of power, such as commands, or strategic persuasion, like advertising language and the language of diplomacy. Language can by means of its symbolic character refer to things which are *not* present, and is, therefore, pre-eminently suited for lies and manipulation.

Apel's emphasis on the informative and argumentative character of language appears to be strongly determined by culture. The language use of many Eastern cultures is rather aimed at the achievement of social harmony and the prevention of loss of face than the furnishing of objective knowledge. The aspiration to provide objective information is perhaps a specific characteristic only of the scientifically oriented Western culture. For that matter, without the constant use of euphemisms, social interaction in the West would probably also quickly come to an end. In Nietzsche's view, the whole of language is since its origin permeated by unequal power relations:

> The masters' right of giving names goes so far that it is permissible to look upon language itself as the expression of the power of the masters: they say 'this *is* that, and that,' they seal finally every object and every event with a sound, and thereby at the same time take possession of it (Nietzsche 2003b, p. 11)

In brief, even if man is in essence a communicative being, it does not follow that all people are characterised by an inherent pursuit of emancipation. When one assumes that intersubjective consensus is decisive for man, one can establish that the lives of all people are dominated by shared cultural traditions. However, these traditions contain many divergent forms of communication. Human culture and language are as much characterised by a pursuit of power as of emancipation. The designation of *one* of these aspects as *the* human essence is based on an unfounded essentialism. One cannot, therefore, derive a universal emancipation ethics from the communicative nature of man. With this we are back with the thesis of the hermeneutists and the language philosophers that historically grown cultural traditions constitute the horizon of human life. The emphasis on the intersubjective character of human culture then leads to cultural and ethical relativism, with all its problems.

The same applies to Habermas's natural-law theory. This is primarily inspired by the form that law has recently taken in Western culture: that of the democratic constitutional and welfare state. In contrast, in authoritarian states with great social inequalities and a lack of freedom it is much less self-evident that Habermas's procedural justice is contained in legal reality. When the judge has an impartial role there, this would at most consist in an impersonal application of the prevailing authoritarian principles.

The problems of relativism become even greater when one assumes that cultures are not homogenous, because within one culture divergent subcultures exist with mutually irreconcilable moral views. Individual members of a culture can moreover give a new twist to dominant ideals. In such instances the internal consensus is shattered. It is then conceivable that, even within a single culture, universal moral standards can no longer be formulated, because no single moral view is generally accepted. In comparison with the moral non-cognitivism of the empiricists, the cultural relativism of Winch has the advantage that it at least allows for moral consensus within a single culture. But this view appears to be no longer tenable in a pluralistic society. The criterion of intersubjective consensus, then, provides no solution.

Two approaches which seek to address the problems inherent in Critical Theory, as well as the problems of relativism, will be discussed in the next section and in the final chapter. Deconstruction seeks to do this by enquiring, among other things, into the philosophical and political implications of Freud's thinking. In this way a certain 'standard' is invented against which the plurality of political views in society can be measured. Political liberalism (Sections 10.4 and Section 10.6) seeks the solution in a narrow liberal ethics. In the absence of generally shared substantive standards, everyone must observe the rules which are necessary for peaceful and fair social interaction. For the rest, tolerance and freedom should prevail.

9.5 Deconstruction

9.5.1 Psychoanalysis Radicalised

Jacques Derrida (1930–2004) in the 1960s gave the French word 'deconstruction', which was largely unknown at the time, a new impetus in his attempt to overcome the metaphysics of presence which, according to him, has characterised Western philosophy since its commencement. Derrida is known for his 'deconstructive' readings of the texts of philosophers and other writers, including some of those who have been discussed thus far, such as Plato, Aristotle, Rousseau, Kant, Hegel, Marx, Nietzsche, Husserl, Freud and Heidegger. Some of his readings are also of novelists, such as Jean Genet, Maurice Blanchot, Franz Kafka, Edgar Allan Poe, Francis Ponge and James Joyce.[11] To have some conception of what deconstruction entails, it is necessary to first elaborate somewhat on what Derrida understands by the notion of a 'metaphysics of presence', as well as the 'notion' of *différance*, which according to him to a certain extent exceeds metaphysics.

According to Derrida, one of the primary features of the *metaphysics of presence* is the hierarchical opposition that it imposes in relation to different terms, such as life/death, original/imitation, normal/abnormal, interior/exterior, infinite/finite, good/evil, reason/madness, and speech/writing. The latter distinction is, amongst others, to be observed in the texts of Plato (Section 2.4). In the *Phaedrus*, by mouth of Socrates, Plato, for example, shows his aversion to writing, indicating instead his preference for the living, breathing purity of speech. Writing is described by Plato as a fallen kind of speech, a mere aid, dangerous and secondary to living memory, as corrupting originary meaning, as dead or empty repetition, and as dead and rigid knowledge. The typical strategy of metaphysics is illustrated here, that is, to take as its point of departure what is regarded as pure and present, and thereafter to consider deviations from such presence as secondary effects. This positing of a presence is derived from a belief in the existence of an original foundation, for example, Plato's Ideas, God as Creator, modern man as subject, or reality. Metaphysics thus constantly erects a structure which in its essential features shows a remarkable similarity across the different ages. Why does this happen? According to Derrida, this is due to a persistent desire for presence, which at the same time reveals the way in which metaphysics views death. A specific strain in the thinking of Freud (Section 8.2) plays an important role here. Derrida, it could be said, seeks to 'analyse' Western philosophy in a way which corresponds to a certain extent with Freud's analysis of his patients and of the structures of law, morality and religion. As we saw earlier, Freud's thinking concerning the unconscious mostly centres on the Oedipus complex which he regards as the nuclear complex of the neuroses. The Oedipus complex, according to Freud, has furthermore had a determining influence on the development of law, morality and religion. Freud's notion of the death drive, upon which he elaborates in *Jenseits des Lustprinzips* (literally: Beyond the Principle of Lust), however, stands in tension with this finding. The death drive, in Freud's view, could explain the observation that patients tend to repeat unpleasant experiences, for example, in analyses and in dreams. The death drive, Freud contends, is a feature of all organisms, and life itself simply amounts to a detour with the ultimate aim of death. This detour is somewhat paradoxically determined by the sole wish of an

[11]In *Force of Law* (Derrida 2002, pp. 230–298), Derrida, for example, refers to both Kafka and Blanchot. The law and literature movement relies somewhat similarly on literary texts, either in general or in so far as they specifically deal with law, in order to critically reflect on law. Another approach is to view law from a literary perspective, in other words, as itself being a form of literature. Derrida's readings tend to focus on the insight these authors show into man's relation with death.

organism, which is to die in its own fashion, to die its own death or to die 'properly'. In his reading of Freud's text, Derrida shows that death and sexual desire are very closely related, so that these two forces do not stand in opposition to each other, as one often finds in readings of Freud (that is, *Eros* versus *Thanatos* – a typical metaphysical opposition), but that the death drive effectively amounts to a desire for absolute sexual pleasure or final orgasm. This 'desire beyond desire', which will henceforth be referred to as a 'desire for death', exceeds and precedes the unconscious in Derrida's reading of Freud. Viewed thus, the Oedipus complex must itself involve a dissimulation[12] of the desire for death, Derrida contends. The Oedipus complex is, in other words, only one of the possible effects, more precisely, one of the strictest possible effects, of the desire for death. In light of this understanding of the Oedipus complex, Freud's contentions in relation to law, religion and morality, require reconsideration. These products of humanity, it now appears, are not simply reflections of the Oedipus complex. Viewed more rigorously in light of Freud's own insights in relation to death, they entail a dissimulation of the desire for death. In other words, law, morality and religion in the final analysis amount to a search for presence, a restriction of the desire for death. Nietzsche's notion of the will to power (Section 7.5) can consequently, using the terminology of Freud and Derrida, be explained as an expression of the search for presence, or the 'binding' of the desire for an absolute powerlessness.[13] The desire for death can similarly be expressed in the language of Hobbes, who, as we saw earlier (Section 4.1), insists on the characteristic of self-preservation in all living beings: The self-preservation which necessarily accompanies life can now be said to amount to a 'binding' of the desire for death, the latter entailing a complete abandonment of the self. The notion of a desire for death can furthermore explain the reason for the observations of Locke (Section 4.2) and Rousseau (Section 5.5) that self-preservation is not the only characteristic of human beings: the 'altruism' that they identify, it now appears, is made possible by a similar 'binding' of the desire for death, the latter entailing an 'altruism' which exceeds itself in self-destruction.

In the above analysis the 'notion' of *différance* has already been touched on. The binding or dissimulation that is, in Derrida's view, at stake in the relation between the desire for presence and the desire for death, gives expression to *différance*. This 'notion' which, according to Derrida, is not a 'word' or a 'concept' in the strict sense, can be explained as the postponement (deferral) of the desire for death (the different, the absolutely other) until death. This 'notion' and the relation between forces which it describes can be explained further with reference to Freud's dynamic conception of the psyche (Section 8.2.2), which, as we saw, effectively constitutes an economy of forces. In contrast, the desire for death involves a general economy, an aneconomy, or a pure loss of expenditure. Instead of a mnemic system

[12]Latin: *dissimulare* = to simulate, feign, disguise or conceal by pretence.

[13]It is, therefore, not surprising that Derrida's reading of Nietzsche is somewhat different from the reading in Section 7.5. According to Derrida, Nietzsche's texts also at certain points exceed metaphysics.

(Section 8.2.3), the desire for death entails the annihilation of memory, or forgetfulness. It, in other words, does not involve the recalling of some 'thing' in the psychoanalytical situation, at least not in the same way in which the Oedipus complex can be recalled. For this reason Derrida also refers to the desire for death as an unanalysed, illegible remainder. It, moreover, finds 'expression' in that 'spot' of a dream which, as Freud notes in *The Interpretation of Dreams*, is unplumbable: 'a navel, as it were, that is its point of contact with the unknown' (Freud volume IV 111 fn 1). This 'forgetfulness', by means of dissimulation, leaves traces in language and culture, as we will, for example, see below in the concepts of hospitality and the gift. *Différance* thus clearly plays a role similar to that of the 'origin' in metaphysical thinking, but at the same time subverts it. To distinguish it from the metaphysical conception of origin, Derrida refers to it in terms of a pre- or non-origin which 'precedes' the origin of metaphysics. Since Descartes, philosophy has, for example, been constructed on the basis of the full presence of the subject of consciousness to itself. Freud and Derrida contend that this is an illusion. A certain kind of dislocation from self-present experience always takes place. For Freud, this happens through the unconscious. For Derrida, even more radically, consciousness always has to pass through death in order to arrive at itself. In recalling oneself to oneself, as, for example, happens in thinking, one is, in other words, placed in relation to the (forgotten) memory of death. It is precisely the 'relation' we have to death that enables us to relate to ourselves, to others, and to things, Derrida contends.

According to Derrida, *différance* is constantly at work, and one can see its operation in his *deconstruction* of the texts of the philosophers and other writers referred to above. What is often the focus of attention in Derrida's readings is some seeming contradiction in the text(s) of the writer concerned. Plato, for example, in the *Phaedrus*, not only denigrates writing, but points to its necessity, value and importance. At times the focus in Derrida's deconstructive readings is a text which is treated with suspicion or contempt by commentators, for example, because it is regarded as a 'lesser', 'earlier' or 'immature' work of the specific philosopher concerned. Taking again the example of Plato's *Phaedrus*: it has been regarded as either the work of a young, immature Plato or an old Plato, close to senility. Because of the desire for death, texts are, according to Derrida, not completely dominated by the intentions of their authors. Texts are 'heterogeneous' or marked by tensions, and they tend to 'repress' this desire in dealing with the main thesis. In other words, the author will usually attempt to impose a restricted economy on the text in contrast with the general economy implied by the desire for death. By rigorously analysing this 'repressed' desire and its relation to the rest of the text, Derrida shows that what was 'repressed' actually makes the text possible and exceeds the restricted economy of the text. The notion of *différance*, in other words, lies behind this peculiar 'hermeneutics' of Derrida.

The operation of deconstruction can also be explained with reference to Derrida's analysis of 'ethical' concepts in some of his texts. The concept of the gift, for example, as it finds expression in different cultures, always involves some kind of (expectation of a) return. Yet, as Derrida points out, the concept itself seems to imply something which exceeds economy: a gift should not expect a return, because if a return is expected it no longer, strictly speaking, constitutes a gift. The concept of the gift, in other words, implies the giving of some 'thing' without expecting any return to the self, an absolute expenditure, therefore, without economy. Something similar can be said of hospitality. A hospitality which is restricted, which imposes limits on the guests who may enter or on their behaviour, does not do justice to the concept of hospitality. Derrida, therefore, contrasts absolute hospitality, which would impose no limits on the hospitality that is being offered, with restricted hospitality. The notions of 'meaning' and 'sense' are strictly speaking no longer applicable here, because the gift and hospitality as understood thus entail a meaninglessness, which must now be understood as an 'essential' part of the structure of these erstwhile concepts. The effects of *différance* can, in other words, be detected in traditional metaphysical concepts; it can in a sense be said to 'haunt' these concepts. The metaphysical understanding of concepts such as these is, in Derrida's view, dominated by the idea of presence to the self of consciousness. They, in other words, especially since Descartes (Section 3.4), reflect a belief in a subject, both in an individual and in a collective sense, which is fully present to itself. Actions of such a subject (such as the giving of a gift or offering hospitality) are consequently also understood in terms of a restricted economy or as characterised by a return to the self. A constitution that is enacted is, for example, traditionally understood as the expression of a fully conscious act of a people and/or their delegates which returns to itself, that is, in terms of the notion of democracy as self-government. The concepts of freedom, equality, and fraternity are traditionally understood in a similar manner.[14] If the 'subject' is, however, 'constituted' by a desire for death, all politico-legal concepts implicitly also give expression to this relation. In Derrida's later texts, the notion of the desire for death is then also translated into a quasi-transcendental ethics and politics through an analysis of, amongst others, justice, the gift, hospitality, forgiveness, friendship and democracy. Derrida can be said to 're-conceptualise' these concepts so as to give expression to the desire for death.

9.5.2 Legal Philosophy

The above should make it easier to understand Derrida's reflections on justice and law, as set out in his essay 'Force of Law: The "Mystical Foundation of Authority"' (Derrida 2002, pp. 230–298). The notion of *différance* clearly influences Derrida's

[14]Derrida would possibly contend that the conceptual schema invoked in Section 1.4 places the bearer or the conscious subject (X), whether individual (liberalism) or collective (perfectionism), at the centre of the enquiry whereas by virtue of the thinking of Freud in relation to the unconscious (Section 8.2) and Heidegger on Being (Section 8.1.2) the subject has been displaced from the foundational position it has occupied since modernity. Deconstruction thus cannot easily be made to fit into this conceptual schema, unless we no longer hear it as a propositional statement describing the state of being of a subject, but as a promise of the 'freedom' of the subject (X) from the restrictions (Y) which life and it goals (Z) inevitably impose on him. Freedom is here to be understood in terms of the Freudian death drive.

description of justice as an experience of the impossible, a certain madness, a responsibility without limits, a responsibility before memory, a heteronomy, as well as a certain desire. These are all in a sense synonyms for the desire for death. This also appears from his description of justice as a –

> demand of gift without exchange, without circulation, and without rules, without reason and without economic circularity, without calculation and without rules, without reason and without theoretical rationality, in the sense of regulating mastery (Derrida 2002, p. 254).

One could regard justice as described here as a 'higher law' which provides a 'measure' for positive law. Justice, in other words, in a certain way transcends positive law and serves as a measure for it. Why, and in which way, do we refer to justice as a higher law? At this point we need to return to Kant, and especially to the point made earlier as to the consequences of Freud's thinking regarding the super-ego for the categorical imperative (Section 8.2.3). We saw above that Derrida reads Freud's *Beyond the Pleasure Principle* as saying that the Oedipus complex is itself formed through a dissimulation of the death drive. This means that behind our (culturally influenced) 'conscience' lies a more 'radical' demand of which the categorical imperative is actually a dissimulation. The demand, to paraphrase Freud, is to the following effect: 'No longer desire to die your own death'. Like Kant's conception of the categorical imperative, this higher law has a non-causal, unconditional and supra-sensory nature, but cannot be said to depend on cultural influence or individual make-up. Although there are resemblances between this 'higher law' and the tradition of natural-law thinking, there are important differences too. The 'foundation' of this higher law is not the essence of man (Section 1.2), but his 'an-essence'. Through this 'notion' of justice Derrida could, furthermore, be said to radically revise the thinking in relation to the state of nature of, for example, Grotius, Hobbes, Locke, Rousseau, and, to a certain extent, Freud. Man, since his inception, finds himself within the tension between a desire for death and a desire for presence or for certainty. The different forms which law or legal systems have assumed through the ages are simply varied expressions of the dissimulation of the desire for death. This dissimulation of absolute desire itself constitutes a 'law', which Derrida expresses with the neologism *différance*, which, as we saw, points to the inevitable deferral or postponement of the desire for death in the life of any organism or organisation. Derrida's notion of justice is, as we saw, no less universal than Kant's categorical imperative, although its practical implementation is less absolute as, in accordance with *différance*, a negotiation is always required between the unconditional and the conditional in concrete circumstances. Differing from the categorical imperative, it, moreover, exceeds rationality, as it involves, in accordance with the desire for death, a certain kind of 'madness'.

Some of Derrida's further contentions in 'Force of Law' are the following. The founding act of a state is neither legal nor illegal, but becomes legal only retrospectively. For this reason Derrida describes law as a groundless power, violence, and force (see also Freud in Section 8.2.4 above). In the United States Declaration of Independence, for example, the delegates of the people gave themselves the power to adopt the Declaration in the name of *the people* of the United States, who of course actually came into existence only *after* the coming into effect of the Declaration. The founding of law in addition always is accompanied by a 'repression' or dissimulation of self-destruction which threatens at such a moment (see also Section 5.5.3 on the French revolution). The founding of a state thus involves an 'overcoming' or 'repression' of the Freudian desire for self-destruction of the nation (the subject in a collective sense). According to Derrida, justice in the above 'sense' is posed and 'repressed' at the moment of the revolutionary founding of law, as well as in its conservation or enforcement. The desire for self-destruction is, in other words, not something that ceases with the founding of a nation, but continually threatens to destroy it. Derrida furthermore agrees with Walter Benjamin in his *Critique of Violence* that the institution of law does not take place with the aim of eradicating violence, but of monopolising it. Law's primary interest as a consequence lies in preserving itself (see similarly Hart and Hobbes in Sections 1.2.3.2 and 4.1). This does not, however, mean that justice stands opposed to law, because law requires justice and justice requires law, and, as Kant emphasises, also force, in order to be effective (Section 6.4.1). Justice and law, therefore, stand in a continual tension with each other, in the same way in which the desire for death continues to operate in the 'life' of any individual organism. Law, similar to life, ultimately amounts to a postponement of death. This makes the question 'what is law?' with which we started (Section 1.2.1), somewhat out of place in Derrida's thinking. As one can see from the above, law, according to Derrida, has no essence; no pure inside distinguished from an outside: it exceeds itself in a desire for self-destruction.

In Derrida's description of what happens in a court case in 'Force of Law', there are certain resonances with Lyotard's description referred to earlier (Section 9.1.4), but this should not lead to the conclusion that Derrida adopts a relativistic approach. According to Derrida, justice requires that the law not simply be followed, but that it be suspended and in each case be re-invented. A judge is, in other words, required to give effect to justice, whilst at the same time calculating with laws and rules. The judge has to negotiate a relation between law and justice which comes as close as possible to justice. As we saw above, justice requires the absence of calculation and of reason, and involves a certain madness. What this entails can be explained with reference to Derrida's thinking on hospitality, in the context of the long-running European debate on immigration and refugees. Here we return to the tension between absolute hospitality and restricted hospitality referred to earlier. Absolute hospitality, according to Derrida, would demand an unlimited opening of all borders (and of the home), whereas restricted hospitality refers to the legal (and personal) limitations that, for the sake of survival, are necessarily placed on absolute hospitality. These restrictions usually relate to the possibility of integration and the contribution that the person concerned can make to society. Law, in other words, involves a calculation, as well as the imposition of all kinds of restrictions on those who may or may not visit a specific country or region, as well as for how long they are permitted to stay and what they may and may not do. Absolute hospitality or justice, on the other hand, requires that there be no such limitations. If a judge (or a legislature) is, therefore, to do justice in the case of (economic) refugees, there must be a recognition that the limits that law imposes ultimately have no foundation. (The existing inhabitants of a 'country' are such as a result of invasion, occupation, murder and robbery, often in the long forgotten past.) Everyone should be welcomed without exception. In Europe this evokes images of masses of poor African and Asian immigrants streaming into the region, of the current inhabitants ultimately losing their majority status, as well as their culture, their language, their religion, their identity, their rights, their homes, and even their lives. Absolute hospitality and justice as described by Derrida clearly entail a hyper-ethics and hyper-politics which can only with disastrous consequences be given effect to in law or politics (or on a personal, ethical level). This realisation does not, however, in the least mitigate the demand which deconstruction seeks to affirm. What is required on a politico-legal level is inevitably a negotiation between justice and law, between absolute and restricted hospitality; a negotiation which furthermore (should one in politico-legal decisions follow deconstruction's affirmation of the impossible) will have to come as close as possible to absolute hospitality.

Deconstruction, therefore, in a sense re-introduces the notion of a 'shared standard' which can be 'invoked' in politico-legal debates, even in the case where there are vast differences in points of view between persons and cultures. As appears from, amongst others, Derrida's own advocacy for the abolition of apartheid and of the death penalty, as well as for the recognition of partnerships that go beyond the heterosexual norm, this 'shared standard' is not one which facilitates compromise, but instead provides a 'foundation' for a 'left' politics within a democratic constitutional state. The support which Derrida expresses for democracy stems from the fact that the institution of democracy, in comparison with other state ideals, comes closest to the 'idea' of absolute hospitality or of justice. This is so because the concept of democracy in principle opens itself to its own complete transformation. Derrida similarly expresses himself in favour of human rights (especially on an international level) because of the tension which these rights introduce in relation to the notion of the sovereignty of the nation-state. The same 'radical' openness' that characterises the concept of democracy is to be found in the classical fundamental rights, for example, freedom of expression and freedom of assembly. Nevertheless, Derrida does not simply call for the protection of existing democracies and of human rights, but for a 'democracy to come', and for going beyond the notion of rights (which are inherently tied to the notion of subjectivity and to human beings). This should again be understood in light of Derrida's thinking on *différance* and the demands which the latter imposes. Derrida does not seek in his texts to provide details as to the ideal structure of society, but instead seeks to show whence these structures derive. Through an 'affirmation' of this pre-origin, an opening is created for the transformation of society.

9.5.3 Commentary

To conclude, a brief discussion of some of the responses to Derrida's thinking. The following can be mentioned here: (1) accusations of an alleged lack of intellectual rigour, by Habermas; (2) allegations of a tension in Derrida's thinking between that of a serious quasi-metaphysical philosopher and a private ironist, by Richard Rorty; (3) accusations of inconsistency and failure, in Derrida's attempt to exceed metaphysics; (4) expressions of doubt as to the practical relevance of Derrida's thinking, again by Rorty; (5) attempts to associate Derrida with Nazism and/or relativism; and (6) appropriation, by those who are in general sympathetic to his thinking.

In so far as (1) is concerned, in *Der philosophische Diskurs der Moderne* (The Philosophical Discourse of Modernity, 1985) Habermas (Sections 1.2.2.3, 9.1.5 and 9.3), who, as we saw, adopts only a few of Freud's ideas in relation to therapy, accused Derrida of getting caught in a performative contradiction, of asserting the primacy of rhetoric over logic and of levelling the genre distinction between philosophy and literature. In response, Derrida commented on the strangeness of the fact that Habermas, who is known as the philosopher of consensus, dialogue and discussion, can attribute these incorrect claims to him, by primarily relying on secondary texts in his attempt to understand and criticise his thinking. There is, for example, no claim in Derrida's texts (as Habermas asserts, relying on Culler) that any understanding is a misunderstanding or that any interpretation is a false interpretation. Derrida also never rejects the importance of logical arguments, although, as we saw, he does extend the notion of logic in conformity with Freud's thinking on the unconscious. What thus appears to be no more than rhetoric, as well as the wordplay and sexual allusions one finds in Derrida's texts, are, as we saw, not simply informed by frivolity, but by the need for philosophy to take seriously the insights of Freud. The third claim, in relation to literature and philosophy, stems from the fact that Derrida thinks that a number of 'novelists', such as Blanchot and Kafka, have succeeded better than many philosophers in exceeding metaphysics by their reflections on death and desire. His reliance on literature can, therefore, more accurately be described as part of an attempt to exceed Western philosophy (that is, metaphysics), rather than as an attempt at levelling the genre distinction between philosophy and literature. The 'intellectual' animosity evident from Habermas's comments on Derrida, and the latter's response thereto, were, incidentally, later brought to an end by them cooperating on a number of projects, such as a plea for a common European foreign policy (which they found absent during the invasion of Iraq in 2003), even though they remained far apart philosophically. This cooperation is not difficult to understand in light of the discussion above of the concern for emancipation from oppression that these thinkers share (Section 9.1.5).

Richard Rorty (2) has a greater appreciation for Derrida's work than many other philosophers, but nevertheless has a problem with the so-called quasi-transcendental nature of Derrida's thinking, that is, the seeking for conditions of possibility in a Kantian style. He also pokes fun at aspects of Derrida's philosophical thinking, noting for example that

> all that supposedly deep stuff about the primordiality of the trace in Derrida's earlier work looks like a young philosophy professor, still a bit unsure of himself, making quasi-professional noises (Critchley et al 1996, p. 41).

Rorty can identify better with what he views as the playful, highly imaginative irony that characterises the later work, in which Derrida abandons all attempts to present a non-metaphysical alternative to the metaphysical texts he deconstructs. However, as a pragmatist, Rorty asserts that Derrida's philosophy consequently has no political relevancy, because political philosophy presupposes intersubjective argumentation, which is absent in Derrida's non-propositional texts. In this view, Derrida's 'ethical turn' would imply both an inconsistent return to his former transcendentalism and a political philosophy that lacks argumentative underpinning. Rorty's reading of Derrida as a private ironist, and the view that he takes the doctrine that 'all awareness is a linguistic affair' to its extreme, is not, however, convincing. Through a more rigorous reading of Derrida's texts it is easy to show that even in his seemingly playful, self-referential texts, something more serious is always at stake, as Derrida has also repeatedly confirmed in interviews. Such a reading will show that Derrida always concerns himself with pointing to the conditions of possibility of the text he is reading, and that the notion of 'play' in his texts and his own 'playing' are closely tied to the desire for death.

Connected to the previous point is the view that is sometimes expressed (3) that the 'indeconstructables', such as justice and absolute hospitality, which Derrida invokes, simply entail another form of metaphysics. In other words, Derrida's so-called ethical turn in the late 1980s involves a nostalgic return to a quasi-metaphysical approach. Derrida seemingly believes, so the argument goes, that something absolute hides behind the textual constructions he is deconstructing, and that from this certain ethical consequences necessarily follow. It could be pointed out in defence of Derrida, however, that the conditions of possibility which he posits do not serve the function of providing a fixed foundation as in, for example, the thinking of Kant, Husserl and Heidegger, but instead relate to an abyss, which testifies in a radical way to the absence of foundations in the midst of a continuous seeking for foundations. This 'structure' characterises all Derrida's work, so that one cannot speak of an inconsistency or 'ethical turn' in his texts. The sceptic can still argue that Derrida's assumptions are especially problematic in his ethical and political texts where he translates the highly debatable existence of a 'desire for death' into a duty of absolute hospitality. Even assuming that a desire for death can be said to 'exist' in some or other way, this would still not turn it into a norm. An adequate response to these questions would require a detailed discussion of Heidegger's analysis of the question of Being in the attempt to overcome metaphysics, as well as of Derrida's deconstruction of Heidegger in so far as the latter still remains attached to metaphysics. The ultimate line of defence, that is, that Derrida does not so much pose duties, but rather a 'duty beyond duty', is nevertheless not likely to convince all sceptics.

As indicated above under point (2), because of his adherence to pragmatism and his consequent dismissal of 'transcendental' philosophical thinking, Rorty (4) views Derrida's thinking as not politically consequential, at least not directly and immediately. For Rorty, real politics is about finding solutions to opposing viewpoints, for which one does not need 'deep' philosophical reflection. As with the previous point, it is difficult to resolve this debate in a few words. A brief response would be, that avoiding deep philosophical reflection in political matters has the almost inevitable consequence that philosophical (and thus, for Derrida, necessarily metaphysical) concepts, such as democracy, justice and rights, are engaged with, based on a number of assumptions as to their unproblematic nature. Engaging in such reflection could arguably also have immediate, rather than long term, consequences, as indicated earlier. For those seeking 'practical' guidelines to resolve political conflicts, this approach is nevertheless likely to remain too abstract, even when one takes account of some of Derrida's comments in interviews about immigration and how this relates to the notion of absolute hospitality. The idea of a re-situated subject who is no longer in complete control of his own fate is, again for understandable reasons, unattractive to pragmatists.

The response in relation to Derrida's alleged association with Nazism and/or with relativism (5) can be briefly addressed within the context of the 'scandal' surrounding deconstruction, when a prominent adherent of deconstruction and a close associate of Derrida in the United States, Paul de Man, was found to have written articles, some of them with anti-Semitic overtones, for a pro-Nazi newspaper in his native Belgium from 1940 to 1942. For some this 'scandal', together with Derrida's frequent invocation of Heidegger, made it clear that deconstruction is logically associated with Nazism. Another response was that deconstruction with its supposed (moral) relativism (even the Holocaust can be said to simply be a 'text') made it impossible to criticise something like Nazism. Derrida countered these charges by stressing that deconstruction makes it possible precisely to investigate the conditions of totalitarianism in all its forms (which does not mean equating them) in order to free oneself therefrom as far as possible. It seeks to break with the desire for roots which finds perhaps its strongest expression in Nazism, but which is a fundamental feature of all metaphysical discourse.

In so far as (6) is concerned, Derrida's thinking is often appropriated in such a way as to tone down its 'revolutionary' nature, and in this way make it easier to 'consume' or incorporate it into existing institutions. This happens frequently, also in legal philosophy when Derrida is presented as a political liberal or a postmodernist. In the end, very little remains of Derrida's 'revolutionary' thinking when he is read in these ways. These interpretations are again partly a result of the complexity of Derrida's texts (some would say, their convoluted nature), a feature (amongst others) which is bound to result, at least for the foreseeable future, in its remaining a discourse on the margins, also in political and legal philosophy. The political liberalism of Rawls, which will be discussed in the next chapter, has thus far found much greater acceptance, at least in the Western world.

Chapter 10
Conclusion: Law, Order and Freedom

10.1 Introduction

In the preceding chapters a variety of central themes can be singled out. The *first* central theme is of an epistemological nature: is it possible to present a conclusive argument in favour of a specific constellation of law, order and freedom, or are such conceptions based on irrational choices, accidental conventions, or dominant power relations? The *second* central theme concerns the possibility of a legal morality, that is, of specific moral criteria for the validity of law. Traditionally this has been formulated as the question of whether a necessary relation exists between law and morality. This question is answered in the affirmative by the natural-law doctrine, in a large variety of interpretations, whereas legal positivism answers this question in the negative, also in various ways. The *third* central theme concerns the nature of the morality that lies at the basis of law. Is this a 'broad', perfectionist morality, which controls all domains of human life, imposing an ideal mode of life on everyone? Or should legal morality rather have a 'narrow', liberal character, confining itself to ensuring that human society proceeds in a more or less peaceful and fair fashion?

It is clear that these central themes interfere with each other. Someone who adopts the non-cognitivist view that decisive arguments cannot be presented for any specific normative conviction, cannot argue in favour of a necessary relation between law and morality. And someone who denies the existence of a necessary relation between law and morality cannot engage himself with the question whether law is based on a broad or a narrow morality. This interference does not, however, have to be ill-fated. Even when no definitive answer can be given to the epistemological question, much still remains to be said about the relation between law and morality. In practice it is quite possible to live with relative certainties. One does not have to be able to provide a conclusive argument in favour of the preference for matrimony over other forms of cohabitation before entering into a marriage. It is like this in science and philosophy, too: a theory can create adequate order in the chaos, even when definitive proof is absent. Perhaps the striving towards definitive proof, or the regret about its unattainability, is an infantile need. Within certain margins of epistemological uncertainty, there is scope for many arguments,

C.W. Maris, F.C.L.M. Jacobs (eds.), *Law, Order and Freedom*, Law and Philosophy Library 94, DOI 10.1007/978-94-007-1457-1_10, for example, about the relation between law and morality, as well as for the preference for a narrow morality over a broad morality. This likewise occurred in the preceding chapters. Nevertheless, a tolerant attitude towards the (un-)verifiability of theories may not tempt one to neglect the central epistemological questions. When fundamental disputes arise as to whether a narrow morality is to be preferred over a broad one, either between or within cultures, everyone is ultimately confronted by the question whether such controversies can be settled in a rational way at all.

The interference between these central themes specifically does not have to have any fatal consequences for adherents of a liberal morality. Liberals do not have to become dejected by the thought that conclusive arguments in favour of a specific constellation of law, order and freedom may be lacking. A narrow morality is after all a morality of the second order, which is reconcilable with the verifiability *and* the unverifiability of morals of the first order. Of importance is only that people find themselves to be fundamentally at odds concerning the moralities of the first order. One can reach this insight along various routes. Even when a specific faction would support the only correct view (but how can someone know this for sure?), other factions can still actually disagree with this. If the privileged faction imposes its view on the rest, at best an armed peace will get under way which in case of a real or supposed shift in the power balance will degenerate into war; and this is what a narrow meta-morality seeks to avoid most of all. It is sufficient that all factions recognise the fragility of their political power. Or suppose that another faction is in the right with its radical scepticism concerning the force of reason. In this case narrow morality commands them as non-cognitivists to tolerate other parties that are irrational enough to believe in reason. The notion of a narrow morality is, then, not primarily a philosophical thesis which pretends to be true or untrue, but a practical political morality which may or may not fulfil its pacifying function with success.

For the sake of simplicity, the interference between the three central themes could be reduced to an opposition of two views. One may attempt the following construction. Adherents of the possibility of conclusive arguments (let us call them 'cognitivists') are also of the view that a necessary relation exists between law and morality (cognitivists thus embrace natural law), and identify natural law with a broad morality. Sceptics (non-cognitivists), on the other hand, advocate the separation of law and morality (thus embracing legal positivism), and argue in favour of a narrow morality that at least resists the escalation of conflict. In the second section this construction is scrutinised in the light of its relation with law, order and freedom. In the third section we demonstrate that this construction is too simplistic, after which, in Sections 10.4, 10.5, 10.6, and 10.7, the complex connection between law, order and freedom in a liberal morality, as well as the perfectionist critique, will be analysed. The eighth section discusses the decisive question whether a liberal morality can claim universal validity. In the last two sections some remaining questions are answered and conclusions drawn.

10.2 Cognitivist and Non-cognitivist Views on Law, Order and Freedom

Classical Greek-Roman and Christian metaphysics assumes that a higher spiritual world lies hidden behind the observable, material world. In this view the empirical world as such is too unsettled, too discordant and too imperfect so as to derive objective norms from. This imperfection is compensated for by the underlying perfect order, which constitutes an ideal model for empirical reality, and brings about unity in the disharmony of everyday life. This worldview thus takes for granted the unity of 'is' and 'ought': objective norms are contained within (the higher or deeper domain of) reality.

Man himself would stand at the cutting edge of these two worlds: in bodily respect he belongs to the imperfect empirical world; by means of his spirit he has a share in the higher spiritual reality. Through the latter he can attain insight into a more perfect mode of life, and guide his inferior side in that direction. In the everyday life of man acute conflicts frequently occur between his immediate bodily needs, and what he rationally regards as the best way of action; or between his egoistic and social inclinations. Idealistic ontology provides a standard for the resolution of such conflicts. It organises the contradictions of the empirical world into a hierarchical unity, where the lower aspects (the individual and the physical) stand in the service of the higher (the social and the rational). Viewed in terms of freedom (Section 1.4), this metaphysical worldview advocates *essential freedom*, or freedom from internal impediments such as weakness of will or irrational inclinations.

This metaphysics leads to a natural-law doctrine which is based on a perfectionist, broad ethics that prescribes a fixed pattern of the good life to man, both in the personal domain (an individual virtue ethics) and the political domain (a perfectionist political philosophy). The state must, if necessary, enforce this ideal way of life by legal means. With Plato, Aristotle and Thomas Aquinas the content of this broad ethics stands at right angles to the modern values of freedom, equality, democracy, and human rights.

This perfectionist ethics has no place for individual freedom, classical fundamental rights and democracy, because nature objectively prescribes what the proper way of life entails. Unrestricted individual freedom would mean nothing else than the freedom to lead an improper life. It would come into conflict with the rational self which constitutes the essence of human beings, or with the aims that are central to human nature, thus with his *essential freedom*. The state must by means of law force the individual towards the right way of life, freedom rights being regarded as depraved. This approach also conflicts with the decision-making process of democracy where every opinion counts, even if it is inaccurate from an objective point of view, and where a quantitative criterion (the majority vote) is ultimately decisive.

In this (perfectionist) view, law does not serve to create order in an earlier chaos. It must copy the pre-given, universal and just cosmological order, which requires that people be respected in accordance with their status in this order. This can lead both to a rejection and an acceptance of the equality principle. Plato and Aristotle argue in favour of the unequal treatment of different categories of people, because they possess different degrees of rationality. The class of free men is characterised by their independence from others and their full participation in political life; they rule over the class of slaves, who lack those characteristics. In contrast, the Stoics favour universal human equality because all people are reasonable beings who are free when they follow their rational nature (without however translating this metaphysical ideal into political and social equality).

This claim of ethics to objectivity and universal validity becomes fragile in the Modern Age; this development was anticipated by the Greek Sophists who denied any higher cosmic order and considered law and morality as mere conventions. In so far as modern philosophy is dominated by the empiricist ideal of knowledge that stems from natural science, it concludes that *only* an empirical world exists. In the scientific view this world consists of aimless and competing causal processes. In the human body, for example, constructive tendencies struggle with destructive ones (such as the division of cancer cells). The survival instinct of the lion conflicts with the drive for survival of the lamb. Different human individuals can have contrary interests, too. Within the life of one individual, instinct and intellect can compete with each other, as well as egoistic and social inclinations. According to empirical science, these inclinations are all equally 'natural'. A higher reality that could rank such conflicting inclinations or interests is regarded as unverifiable. The scientist can establish only that such conflicting phenomena actually exist, and that now the one is the strongest and then again the other. A choice in favour of one of them is based on a subjective evaluation.

Because no norms can be derived from the empirical world, most empiricists tend towards a non-cognitivist meta-ethics: one can speak objectively about observable facts, since disputes about facts can be settled on the basis of an objective standard: empirical observation. The normative statements of law and morality, on the other hand, are purely subjective. Normative disagreements between different people originate in differences in their personal attitude to life.

The dissolution of metaphysics in modern times leads to a fragmentation of what used to be seen as a coherent unity: norm and reality no longer coincide, but stem from two different domains: respectively, from the subjective, inner world of man and the objective, external world. Society and individual no longer constitute a natural harmony; even within a single individual, conflicting inclinations fight for priority; and there may be as many conflicting moral views as there are individuals. According to the empiricists, every metaphysical ontology that nonetheless assumes an underlying unity, is based on human projection, fed by the human longing for a more perfect world than the actual one.

Evidently this view does not allow for a necessary relation between law and morality as the natural-law doctrine has it. From here non-cognitivists can take two paths.

First, they can proclaim something like the 'right' of the strongest. This was done by certain Sophists, and by Nietzsche who elaborated this idea to its radical, nihilist consequences. Nietzsche claims that 'God is dead', so that nature no longer implies higher values or goals, but only efforts to survive and power play. On this basis, he positions himself 'beyond good and evil', advocating an individualistic ideal of life that is based on the 'will to power' and aims at a heroic life for an elite of 'supermen'. Nietzsche's superman glorifies struggle, in revolt against conformity with social traditions, and particularly with the prevailing principles of human equality and democracy. In this view no rational coherence can be constructed between law, order and freedom. Every law that restricts the spontaneity and superiority of the strongest (their 'freedom'), is reprehensible; laws that support them are superfluous, and would be counter-productive (the superior person who knows that the state will support him in his superiority becomes lax and lazy, so that he loses his superiority). Consequently the acknowledgement that objective moral knowledge is impossible can directly result in war. After all, disputes about the right way of life cannot be settled by way of generally valid standards.

In the second place, the non-cognitivist can make a virtue of necessity by solving the conflicts in a peaceful way. A narrow ethics presents an alternative, which may be based on ethical non-cognitivism in combination with the insight that human beings cannot do without social cooperation. A representative of this approach is Hobbes.[1] Hobbes's narrow ethics is not based on a moral value, such as autonomy, but simply on everyone's shared interest in survival. This is symbolised by the representation of the social contract, which contains all norms that are required for an orderly society. Indeed, Hobbes's ethics is grounded in the very desire to prevent war that he assumes all people share. Clinging to subjective moral convictions, Hobbes cautions, leads to more war and may thus end in death.

In Hobbes's world the metaphysical harmony of classical and Christian metaphysics is totally absent. All that remains are conflicting individual aspirations, without any organic bond. Nonetheless Hobbes still perceives some minimal harmony and unity: everyone's self-interest points in the same direction of a shared social order, because survival on one's own has very little chance of success. Via this detour Hobbes still arrives at generally valid public norms: a minimal narrow ethics that consists of rules which are required for a peaceful social order.

Hobbes's ethics thus only guarantees *order*, as well as the legal rules that are required for this purpose, such as mutual respect for life, property, and agreements. It is not possible to underpin further rules that guarantee a *just* social order. Hobbes's

[1]In our version of Hobbes (Section 4.1) we incidentally neglected somewhat the non-cognitivist interpretation of Hobbes's philosophy. Hobbes's laws of nature can be understood as universal laws which impose themselves on those who want to survive in a situation of scarcity and competition. Problems between people then do not exist at a cognitive level, but testify to a lack of co-ordination.

ethics does not require that the legal order guarantees *freedom*. Hobbes rejects individual freedom, because he fears that every infraction of absolute state power will trigger chaos. His narrow ethics, therefore, leads to normative legal positivism: it is the sovereign who must specify what the law entails. Subjects who disagree with his decisions nevertheless do well to conform with them in order to avoid chaos. In this way, non-cognitivism leads to a minimal morality, which is positivised in law by an absolute sovereign with unlimited power. Hobbes's narrow morality is not a liberal morality at all: law does not serve freedom, but order. In the same spirit, the young Radbruch arrives at normative legal positivism. What 'justice' entails cannot be established in an objective way, Radbruch argues, therefore it is the state that must co-ordinate social interaction with general legal rules. In this way, at least legal certainty and order are guaranteed.[2]

10.3 Complications

Can we really draw a line from cognitivism (1a) via natural law (2a) to a broad morality (3a); and from non-cognitivism (1b) via legal positivism (2b) to a narrow morality (3b)? Certain philosophers fit in well with this scheme. In relation to the first line, the previous section pointed to Plato, Aristotle and Thomas Aquinas, and in relation to the second, to Hobbes and the young Radbruch. However, this is a one-sided selection from the authors discussed in this book: on the one hand, the metaphysical perfectionists, on the other hand, the non-cognitivist and anti-perfectionist advocates of social order as the highest good. Law and order with that have nicely come into their own, but what has happened to the value of freedom? How do Locke, Kant and Hegel fit into this scheme?

Let us first look at Locke. In his way he is a cognitivist: the laws of nature are anchored in the will of God, who imposes Himself on human beings (1a). Locke is, moreover, an adherent of natural law: the laws of nature are a set of rational rules that exist independently of the state. They are not derived from any human authority, but are themselves the basis of all human authority. Positive law should be based upon natural law (2a). Locke nevertheless adheres to a narrow, non-perfectionist legal morality, in particular a liberal morality, which expressly requires that the state adopt a neutral position towards the diverse moral views of citizens. It must restrict itself to creating the conditions for all ways of life that the citizens may choose (3b).

How can Locke breach our scheme and arrive from cognitivism (1a) via natural law (2a), at a narrow morality (3b)? This can be easily understood. Locke was convinced that faith, to which all are called, cannot be imposed; and that imposed faith

[2]It incidentally goes without saying that a narrow morality can take on liberal features. Social order is already possible when a state conducts itself in a reserved manner. A liberal order is possible because it is in everyone's interest to retain as much freedom as is compatible with peaceful social interaction. Liberal variants of the non-cognitivist narrow ethics therefore argue in favour of a much less extensive state and law, restricted to the maintenance of public order, and which beyond that allows as much individual freedom as possible.

leads only to hypocrisy and contempt for God. A church is, according to him, 'a voluntary society of men, joining themselves together of their own accord in order to the public worshipping of God' (Locke 2003, p. 220). From this it follows that the state must hold itself aloof, restricting itself to the protection of a narrow morality. Law, to be sure, guarantees order, but this is only for the sake of freedom. This liberal morality and its associated tolerance are not based on any value-scepticism; on the contrary, the very respect for values, which must be embraced in freedom, forces tolerance upon the state. A state that does not respect the natural liberty rights of its citizens breaks the social contract, so that the subjects are free to revolt against the unjust laws.

Something similar we find with Kant. Can Kant's ethics be called cognitivist? Not in the sense of theoretical reason: in this sense ethics makes no cognitive claims. However, in the sense of practical reason it certainly does: morality is characterised by a unique form of rationality, to which one must adapt one's inclinations. In the ethical domain Kant is thus after all a cognitivist (1a). Kant defends natural law: the basic features of positive law are derived from morality and its categorical imperative (2a). He finally draws a distinction between individual ethics, on the one hand, and social and legal ethics, on the other hand. Individual ethics has a perfectionist character: it concerns the purity of the moral intention (similar to Locke's sincere devotion to God). Kant's socio-political ethics is, however, liberal: the value of individual autonomy requires that the state adopt a neutral position (3b). Just as with Locke, Kantian law serves to protect freedom, precisely because the perfection of man lies in his self-legislation. Unlike Locke, out of fear for social chaos Kant prohibits every kind of resistance against the state, even if it violates all basic rights of liberal natural law. Law and order thus take priority over freedom. In this respect Kant's narrow ethics leads to normative legal positivism in accordance with the view of Hobbes (2b). This is strange, and our schema enables us to show precisely where the shoe pinches, as will appear below.

Finally, how are things with Hegel? One can for sure call him a cognitivist, even though he disagrees with the idea of an epistemology that precedes understanding (you can similarly not learn to swim on dry land, says Hegel). True epistemology implies metaphysics: it unfolds the rational core of reality (1a). Hegel is an adherent of natural law in the sense that natural rights are connected with the nature of human existence and human society. Positive law simply follows upon what occurs in other domains in a historical period, specifically in morality and ethics. Hegel disagrees with the idea of social engineering, the instrumental use of law for aims that are not imbedded in the prevailing moral traditions (2a). But which kind of natural law is advocated by Hegel? He welcomes the fact that in the Modern Age freedom rights have been accorded to everyone. In this respect he appears to be an adherent of a liberal natural law à la Locke and Kant. On the other hand, Hegel condemns liberal natural law as 'abstract', as it situates people in civil society where they merely pursue their private interests. People find their true destiny in 'ethics', which turns them into citizens of the state: not private interests, but the general interest of the political community, should concern them. However, unlike classical natural law, Hegel denies any supra-historical standard against which the actually dominant morality can be tested. Because of this, Hegel's natural law acquires some characteristics of normative legal positivism: people do not have the right to distance themselves from the prevailing ethics of their society (and when philosophers devise better worlds, this is a form of useless conceit) (2b). We arrive at the same ambivalence when we finally ask the question whether Hegel is an adherent of a broad or a narrow ethics. Both elements of liberalism (tying in with Locke) and anti-liberal perfectionism (tying in with Plato's *Republic*) can be found in Hegel's philosophy. His emphasis on individual freedom of conscience, for example, ties in with the first, but his demand that the state should watch over the true freedom of citizens, turns him into a perfectionist (3a and 3b). The complications which come to light when we attempt to force Hegel's thinking into our scheme, show an ambiguity that is difficult to comprehend: he is a liberal and a perfectionist in one. In this respect his approach is close to that of Rousseau, whose concept of liberty consists of perfectionist 'essential freedom', rather than of liberal 'negative freedom'.

Which lesson can we draw from this? Locke, Kant and Hegel distinguish themselves from philosophers like Plato, Aristotle and Thomas Aquinas, by stressing that freedom is essential for human identity. Let us, therefore, call them *metaphysical* liberals: one of the essential characteristics of man is that he is called to freedom and the pursuit of his own reasonable insights. This can lead to a distinct liberal political and legal philosophy (Locke and Kant). It can also lead to an obscure amalgam of modern and classical ideas (Hegel). In its consistent forms, metaphysical liberalism thus leads to a liberal philosophy of politics and law (1a, 2a and 3b).

However, metaphysical liberalism is controversial. It is subject to the same difficulties as all metaphysical ideas: how is it to be proven to dissenters? Why is liberal metaphysics better than the metaphysical systems of Plato or Thomas Aquinas? If metaphysical liberalism would be the only road to liberal politics, things appear bleak. In that case, its politics will be accepted only by people who share its metaphysical presuppositions. Is it possible to arrive at a liberal political philosophy without the heavy burden of metaphysical liberalism?

In the next two sections an explicitly non-metaphysical version of liberalism will be scrutinised: *political liberalism*, which limits itself to articulating the conditions for the peaceful cooperation of persons with conflicting worldviews. It is, therefore, exclusively a practical theory of the political domain, not a metaphysical doctrine of the nature of man.

10.4 A Liberal View of the Relation Between Law, Order and Freedom

Political liberalism, with its original focus on religious freedom, was the child to which the religious wars laboriously gave birth. Those wars had in their turn been stimulated by the pacifying arrangement of *Cuius regio, eius religio*[3] of rulers who

[3] 'Whose region, his religion', a provision of the religious peace of Augsburg, 1555.

were confronted with a fragmented faith community. This religious fragmentation had its origin in the Reformation, which had delivered the decisive blow to the preceding spiritual unity of the Middle Ages that was based on the merged paradigms of Aristotelianism and Catholicism, interpretations of a cosmic order that allocates an innate place to all and everyone. After political liberalism had embraced freedom of religion, this freedom extended itself to other domains: the state should not concern itself with the way in which people flesh out their own lives, as long as one person's freedom is reconcilable with that of others. This is the only way to maintain peace. Political liberalism is *political* in so far as it aims at a practical social goal: the maintenance of peace. Political liberalism is *liberal* because it regards the guarantee of freedom rights as a necessary means to achieve this purpose.

To be sure, metaphysical liberals, such as Locke and Kant, likewise regard freedom rights as a means to achieve the objective of peace. But that is not all. In addition, their freedom rights have a metaphysical foundation: they are founded on a view of the essence of man, that is, his identity as self-legislator. No doubt metaphysical liberals will also accept liberalism in the political field. On their part, however, political liberals distance themselves from their metaphysical brothers, because they want to persuade persons with other, non-liberal conceptions of man, to embrace political liberalism as well.

What does political liberalism imply? A political liberal will say that law should promote the freedom of all. This can be expressed in morally laden terms: liberal morality is a public morality designed to guide the autonomous development of the personal moralities of all citizens along an orderly course. 'Personal morality' includes the views of an individual of the goods that make life intrinsically valuable, and the way he and others should thus arrange their lives. The latter shows that personal morality has a social aspect as well: it also refers to the way of life of others. That in modern societies such conceptions of the 'good life' strongly diverge is an undeniable social fact. Some people adhere to metaphysical liberalism, others are plain libertines, a third group longs for a heroic life, a fourth wants to serve God. Obviously these ideals can lead to serious social conflicts. 'Public morality' indicates the limits within which an individual can give shape to his personal morality, taking account of the equal right of everyone else to follow *their* personal moralities. Therefore, it can be called a morality of the second order, or a 'meta-morality', that is, a meta-personal morality: a morality that formulates the necessary political conditions for the personal moralities of all citizens.

Of personal morality, little can be said which is generally valid (although many may feel a need for this). In this book we nevertheless came across philosophies that take this step: the Stoics, Kant, and maybe also Nietzsche. Of public morality, more can be said. We stated that public morality, according to liberals, provides the limits within which people can follow their diverse personal moralities. This may seem problematic because views of public morality diverge just as much as those of personal morality. Some want more freedom, if necessary at the cost of equality; others prefer more equality, if necessary at the cost of freedom, to mention a few. Here we arrive at an impasse: the means that should solve the problem is itself equally problematical.

Political liberalism has devised a solution to this meta-problem: 'procedural liberalism'. When we cannot straightforwardly arrive at a consensus, we may still agree on a *procedure* that solves the conflict in an acceptable way. We can appoint an arbiter, or institute majority rule, however qualified, and the like. Here we arrive at the domain of politics in the acute sense of that word (political theory as moral theory of a non-ideal world). When political action in accordance with just procedures results in positive laws, these are procedurally justified.

Has morality disappeared from the scene as a consequence of this political move? Is the cohesion of modern societies ensured only because everyone accepts the outcomes of the political and legal procedures on prudential grounds (otherwise social peace would be in danger)? This is not the case. The procedural justification is equally defensible from the perspective of public morality, and citizens are prepared to accept the procedures on moral grounds as well. After all, when the unity of morality has fragmented, and the views on the good life of citizens diverge, then one of the main functions of political morality is to respect this diversity. Therefore, liberal political morality focuses on safeguarding fundamental rights that allow individuals to devote themselves to projects that might otherwise conflict with the ethical ideals of others. This moral meta-value has its incarnation in a unique moral attitude, that of *tolerance*.

Another focus is to be found in the demand that people respect the laws that result from the democratic rules of the game. Legislation often produces collective goods, for instance, penal law, that offers an optimal combination of extensive security for all citizens, on the one hand, and a modest regime of sanctions that protects suspects and criminals, on the other hand. It requires a process of give and take to establish which package of collective goods of what scope is adequate; if political negotiations do not lead to a unanimous outcome, voting takes place: *the requirement of accepting fair compromises is, therefore, a central element of liberal political morality; as well as the requirement that everyone must contribute his part to fund the package of collective goods that is democratically chosen.*

A final point of focus of liberal-political morality concerns the independence of the judiciary. Thanks to the separation of the judicial and the executive powers, the latter can be subjected to judicial decisions that protect citizens. The fact that Western governments accept the verdicts of independent judges demonstrates that their political system is not primarily based on the monopoly of power of the state, but on its intent to win the trust of its citizens: they can ensure that the state will not abuse its authority.[4] Moreover, the implementation of democratic legislation requires the loyal cooperation of everyone, because laws are compromises between opposing political views. Someone who contravenes a law destroys the compromise. In order to avoid the threat of escalating conflicts that would harm everyone, the interpretation of the law should be assigned to an impartial institution. An independent judiciary safeguards the compromises that are agreed upon. Although it is

[4]This is where the crucial difference lies between Hobbes and Locke.

fallible, their judgment must be respected as a final decision: *the preparedness to do so is the shibboleth of all who respect liberal political morality.*

The political-liberal view of law can be summarised in the thesis that, in a world of discordant and mutually incompatible ideals, law is an indispensable instrument of public morality that guarantees everyone the free development of their personal ideals. In this view, the function of law is not to impose a particular personal morality (a particular realisation of 'true freedom') upon all citizens. So far, then, legal positivism is correct in its separation of law and morality. On the other hand, the view that law is an indispensable instrument of public morality agrees with the association of law and morality of natural law. (Note that 'natural law' here is not a theory concerning the nature of law, but a theory of *how* law should be.)

Another observation is called for here. When it is useful to rely on a tripartite of personal morality, public morality, and law, the liberal restraint in the imposition of a specific morality can be viewed in another light. Politics in the specialised sense of the word (the institutions in a specific community that establish and sanction the public rules which people should observe in their interactions) may not directly concern itself with someone's private morality: agreed. It is not, however, self-evident that liberal politics has nothing to say about the education of people into mature citizens who should in the public sphere respect public morality. The liberal state has a task in civic education, for instance, by broadcasting television spots that warn against prejudices and racial discrimination; by encouraging people to vote in elections; or by seeing that public schools give courses on constitutional values. If citizens are not able to lead a personal life and develop the accompanying personal morality, the state must ensure that the necessary conditions for personal autonomy are realised. Does this not make the ideal of liberal autonomy self-contradictory, in the sense that 'people are forced to be free?' No: autonomy is a meta-ideal here, an ideal of the second order, which can be realised by every individual citizen in his own way. The only things to be enforced by the state are the conditions that are indispensable for the exercise of autonomy.

Liberalism, then, is anti-perfectionist in the domain of political morality: in this sphere it supports negative individual freedom. This is reconcilable with perfectionism in the domain of individual morality. An exemplary combination of these two elements is to be found with the metaphysical liberals Locke and Kant: human perfection consists of the exercise of autonomy and in following one's personal, reasonable insights in one's private life; politics should trump this with negative freedom rights. All the same, political liberals who reject metaphysical liberalism can endorse a completely different view of personal morality, for example, that freedom is an illusion, or that the essence of man consists in the pursuit of pleasure, or that man has to conform to a cosmic rationality.

A last observation: the familiar opposition between natural law and legal positivism is refined in the liberal view. The question whether a necessary relation obtains between law and morality is split up into the question whether a necessary relation exists between law and *public* morality (answer: yes), and the question whether a necessary relation holds between law and *personal* morality (answer: no).

10.5 An Example: Rawls's Theory of Justice

In the preceding section an ideal-typical description was given of the liberal view on the relation between law, order and freedom, and with that, between law and morality. To concretise this somewhat, we provide in this section the main outlines of the theory of Rawls, who in the 20th century gave a new momentum to political liberalism.

In *A Theory of Justice* (1971) John Rawls (1921–2002) arrives, on the basis of a social contract procedure, at a theory of justice which implies a narrow ethics. Rawls starts with the moderate non-cognitivist statement that everyone, to be sure, has a sense of justice, but that regarding the content of the concept of justice nothing more is fixed than that all people should be treated as equals. For the further realisation of this he takes refuge in an imaginary deliberation procedure which has to guarantee that its outcomes actually take equal account of all interests. Rawls for this purpose invokes a conception of the social contract which is characteristic of the modern view of a narrow ethics. The social contract is a metaphor for the criterion of universalisability or acceptability to all, which is meant to compensate for the lack of an objective, generally valid ethics: right are those principles with which everyone could reasonably agree. Rawls does not refer to the actual consensus which exists in a society, because that may be based on one-sided interests, and thus does not guarantee justice. At stake is a rational consensus in a hypothetical situation of impartiality, as the idea of justice requires. To articulate the nature of justice, Rawls formulates a number of specific procedural conditions with which the imaginary contractual deliberation has to comply. The parties to the discussion must specifically be ignorant of the specific personality and the particular position that they will have in the society to be designed. This guarantees that no one can calculate in his personal favour. After all, you can become anyone in the future society. Thus, everyone is forced to take equal account of the interests of all possible social positions.

Rawls states that all rational people in this hypothetical contractual deliberation will mutually agree to the following two principles: (1) equal freedom rights (the classical fundamental rights) and rights to political participation; (2) equal distribution of socio-economic goods, unless an unequal distribution is to the benefit of all, or, if that is impossible, of those who are the least advantaged; these inequalities must furthermore be linked with social positions that are open to anyone. The further realisation of these principles must occur via democratic deliberation. If legislation by the democratic majority, however, seriously violates the fundamental individual rights of Rawls's first principle of justice, *civil disobedience* may be a legitimate way to protest against such unjust laws. Thus, Rawls arrives at a narrow liberal ethics.

The narrow nature of his ethics, moreover, appears clearly from the argument that leads to the first principle. In opposition to the idea of a broad, perfectionist ethics Rawls contends that there is no generally valid moral norm for the perfect life, or at least that reasonable people will disagree about what should count as such. Therefore, the further determination of the best way of life remains open during the contractual deliberation. In the course of this process nobody knows who he will be in the future society, neither which ideal of the good life he will prefer. Everyone thus has an interest in designing an open society that provides maximum space for all possible ideals of the good life. That is why everyone chooses in favour of the classical liberties that guarantee freedom of opinion and expression. Whatever ideals one may turn out to have in the future society, one will be able to live in accordance with them, provided one does not frustrate the equal freedom rights of others. In short, according to Rawls, a just state should confine itself to the distribution of 'primary goods', neutral instrumental goods, such as liberties and money, which everyone needs for the pursuit of his personal ideals. Hence, Rawls's ethics likewise ties in with the liberal autonomy-ideal of the Enlightenment.

In *A Theory of Justice* Rawls invokes the Kantian concept of autonomy. In later publications, such as *Political Liberalism* (1993), Rawls distances himself from Kant, in that he does not want to defend an all-encompassing metaphysical liberalism but only a more moderate, political version of liberalism. He thus deliberately bypasses metaphysical, natural-law controversies because these will lead to an escalation of conflicts rather than to peaceful cooperation. The only way to pacify ideological controversies in a plural society in a fair way is to agree to disagree. Therefore Rawls simply seeks to elaborate further on the ruling political traditions in the modern Western world, which already imply the basics of his narrow political morality. What does he mean with his non-metaphysical, but 'political', concept of autonomy?

It boils down to the following. When you ask people what they want to achieve in their lives, the answer will almost never be that they wish to be autonomous. At best, a person who tries to escape from prison, or who wants to emigrate from an oppressive country, will in anticipation of his move declare that freedom is his highest value. In normal circumstances, however, people pursue a happy relationship, an interesting career, and the like. Only in very special circumstances are people interested in the more abstract question whether they are free. This is the case, in the first place, when they suffer from a lack of freedom, like the prisoner mentioned above. In the second place (and this Rawls emphasises), when they realise that they are dependent on others for the exercise of their freedom, and that these others have an equally great interest in freedom. In such circumstances they have a good reason to arrive at an arrangement which does justice to all interests, given the fact that what some want can be incompatible with the preferences of others. Whoever considers this political question has exceeded the level of his private existence (including what we have called a personal morality), and has assumed a public identity (related to what we have called a public morality, which is a morality of the second order). This has important consequences.

In the first place: as private persons, people are emotionally and affectively bound to other persons and to particular values; they cannot, and will not, easily give up their loyalty to these. They feel that their position in life is strongly determined by what they did and experienced in the past, and that they have only a slim chance of radically changing it. However, as public persons they assume that everyone is rational, in the sense that he can design a life plan for himself and, if required, review it. (Rawls defines *rationality* in this context as the competence to establish one's own ideals of life.) In some respects, this is really the case: people can deliberately plan their lives, or change direction, but this happens rarely. In real life, 'rationality' only plays a major role at moments that one is confronted with existential choices: on these occasions a person may indeed redefine his ideals. In this uncontested weak sense, individual autonomy is an empirical phenomenon that any theory of justice should take into account. But more often people just react to the possibilities that present themselves, and lack the desire of rationalising the course of their lives. Nevertheless, they all act *as if* they are all free and rational. Why the masquerade? It expresses the view that nobody has the right to interfere in the life of another person because he holds him for someone who lacks rationality or true freedom. The fiction that everyone is free and rational expresses nothing else than that people are prepared to respect each other's existential decisions, however irrational they may appear. Its aim is to protect persons who are contented with their way of life, and thus feel free from interference by others who think that the former are determined by oppressive or irrational forces.

In the second place: as private persons, people are hardly interested in the question which negative and positive duties people exactly have vis-à-vis each other, and where these come from. Usually, they attempt to live lives that are satisfying to themselves and their inner circle. In doing so they are willing to observe certain limits. Yet their main concern is not the determination and safeguarding of such limits, but their own life within this domain, and this they all know of each other. Yet, as public persons they assume that everyone is involved in political agreements about the rules that all should mutually respect. They moreover assume that nobody wants that these rules stem from the dominant power relations. On the contrary, such power relations should be subjected to rules, in the construction of which everyone is involved. Here, too, a fiction is at play, the fiction that everyone is reasonable – in this context Rawls defines *reasonableness* as the competence to equally respect the interests of all fellow-citizens. For instance, it is assumed that people cast their vote in elections in order to serve the general interest, whereas in reality most may vote for the party that optimally promotes their personal interests or for an appealing party leader.[5]

The ideal of freedom, then, merely requires that people allow each other maximal space within which each can arrange his own life as he likes, however irrational it may appear to the outside world, provided he likewise gives maximal space to others. Consequently, in the public domain, the ideals of *rationality* and *reasonableness* prevail as the characteristics of citizens, although to a great extent these have a fictional character. The purpose of the fiction is to enable people to adhere to their own ideals in their private domain. *Rationality* and *reasonableness* hence imply a unique ideal of freedom. Unlike other conceptions of freedom it is an ideal of the second order, which is compatible with a variety of divergent ideals of the

[5]Rawls, of course, does not require that everyone participate in public deliberation, still less that they find their highest fulfilment in politics. This would be in conflict with the requirement to respect everyone as free. Rawls consequently distances himself from the political ideal of Plato and Aristotle, according to whom true freedom consists in political participation.

first order. In relation to these ideals of life, the ideal of freedom of Rawls's Political Liberalism takes a neutral stance. Yet it does not legitimate *all* moralities of the first order, since it rules out intolerant *(unreasonable)* ideals that do not respect the ideals of others. In so far as ideals clash, liberal freedom requires that such conflicts be solved according to political procedures that are acceptable to everyone.

Rawls introduces the idea of *public reason* to indicate that the use of state force should be justified only by reasons that are *public*, i.e. understandable and acceptable to all. This rules out arguments that only have private appeal, as being derived from a particular religious or metaphysical worldview. In a modern open society, a plurality of diverging worldviews will arise, about the truth of which one may reasonably disagree. It would be *un*reasonable, then, to enforce one of those views upon people of different persuasions. Therefore, the state should be neutral in ideological respect, simultaneously giving each individual maximal liberty to follow his own ideals in his private life.

10.6 A Liberal Law of Peoples

Under the influence of rapidly increasing globalisation, in *The Law of Peoples* (1999) Rawls discusses whether his liberal principles of justice apply in international relations. In *Political Liberalism* he maintained that his theory of justice is primarily designed to pacify ideological conflicts within Western democracies; it articulates the dominant liberal consensus, which has emerged from the learning process that Western peoples have gone through since the European religious wars. Nowadays most citizens agree upon its tolerant principles, in an 'overlapping consensus' that is supported by the major prevailing 'comprehensive' views of life. Not only metaphysical liberals will support political liberalism; modern Christians will embrace tolerance as well since they recognise that religious faith is an internal affair that should not be enforced. It would seem to follow, then, that a similar moral consensus is not to be expected outside the Western world. In other words, liberal rights are not necessarily *human* rights. Recall that Rawls has bracketed the assumption of his former metaphysical liberalism that individual autonomy constitutes the essence of all human beings (which does not imply that he has renounced his conviction that liberal states are morally superior to illiberal ones; the bracketing is primarily meant to pacify ideological struggles by excluding deeply contested metaphysical views from the political debate). Still, Rawls argues that a set of "urgent" basic rights should be implemented worldwide, albeit not the full catalogue of liberties of his first principle of justice. As for his second principle, in Rawls's view redistribution of socio-economic goods is not a universal requirement at all. According to him, it only applies within a liberal state – and even here political liberals may reasonably disagree about the extent to which the state should interfere with the free market.

The full catalogue of what is commonly known as human rights will only be acceptable to liberal peoples, Rawls admits. They will be willing to establish a second, international social contract with each other in order to protect the liberal rights that govern their constitution according to the national social contract. On this basis they will respect each other's sovereignty. Still, a core of the fundamental rights that figure in Rawls's first principle may also be acceptable to non-liberal, yet 'decent', societies. Rawls thinks of non-democratic hierarchical societies that do not recognise all its inhabitants as free and equal persons, for instance, on the grounds of a state religion. Nevertheless, these societies are *decent* in that they are peaceful. All groups are consulted in the process of public decision-making, and the humanity of its members is recognised. The latter is secured by basic human rights, in particular, to life and personal integrity, to freedom from slavery, to liberty of conscience, and to equality before the law. These are, according to Rawls, truly *human* rights because they constitute the minimal requirements for social cooperation. By contrast, political rights and full religious freedom may be lacking. Rawls expects that liberal and decent societies may side as allies to protect their common decency against 'outlaw states', dictatorships that tend to aggressive warfare, and violate the basic human rights of their own citizens. As outlaws, these states have no claim to sovereignty. In the ultimate case, such as ethnocide, humanitarian intervention is allowed in order to protect the victims against their dictators. According to Rawls's law of peoples just war is either a war in self-defence, or one to intervene in the name of basic human rights.

Both liberal and decent peoples accept a duty of economic and other humanitarian assistance to 'burdened societies' that live in conditions which are too poor to build a decent political system meeting the basic needs of all inhabitants. Rawls denies that well-ordered countries have any further duty to compensate for economic inequalities on the basis of some ideal of global social justice. In his view, each people is responsible for its own prosperity, which is dependent on its work-ethic, political system, and birth policy. Since there is no world state to safeguard the conditions for fair global cooperation, all that liberal and decent peoples can do is to offer humanitarian assistance, promote fair trade, and protect basic human rights, in order to promote the autonomy of the least advantaged peoples. In short, in Rawls's view, there is an insufficient analogy between national and international legal orders to transpose full liberal justice to international relations.

10.7 Criticism of Political Liberalism

Viewed from the perspective of legal philosophy (something which Rawls does not do), Rawls's theory of justice exemplifies the thesis with which we earlier summarised political-liberal morality: in a world of conflicting and mutually incompatible ideals, the law is an indispensable instrument of public morality to regulate the free development of everyone's personal ideals – at least in modern Western societies. Liberal morality consequently presents a perspective on the right relation between law, order and freedom. Although political liberalism claims to rest on an overlapping consensus in the Western world, it has been met with fundamental criticism.

Within liberalism, it is contested how far the state may interfere with economic life in the name of distributive justice. Libertarians like Robert Nozick criticise Rawls's egalitarianism because it would unjustly impede market freedom. Instead, the state should confine itself to protecting the properties that citizens have acquired in a legitimate way.[6] (Obviously, the minimal liberal state should also protect their life and physical integrity.) On the other hand, socially minded liberals like Dworkin advocate more extensive social rights than Rawls's second principle allows for.[7]

Political liberalism is nowadays often subjected to criticism that shows perfectionist tendencies. Communitarians, such as Alisdair MacIntyre and Michael Sandel, caution that indispensable traditional communal values are threatened by the modern emphasis on individual autonomy (Section 9.1.2). In the communitarian view, human beings derive their identity from the communal traditions in which they are brought up. Autonomy, then, leads to anomy. Universal human rights are, according to MacIntyre, abstract arbitrary fabrications that belong to the rhetoric of liberal ideology. In fact, rights differ per cultural community, and cannot possibly belong to man as such. Liberalism, moreover, would encourage a one-dimensional consumerism, which has little to do with autonomy and self-development. Its stress on individual autonomy furthermore undermines the sense of social responsibility. This criticism of political liberalism harks back to thinkers such as Aristotle, Thomas Aquinas and Rousseau.

Neo-Marxists and socialists object that civil society and the bourgeois state (with its emphasis on 'human rights') are merely instruments of power of an elite of owners of private property (Section 9.3.1). As a consequence both the true interests of the exploited and of the exploiters are curtailed. Only in a communist society can the ideal of self-determination take shape: here people will spontaneously develop their potential, and nourish their social relations, without fear of being oppressed by others. The liberal praise of individual freedom is not compatible with altruistic cooperation, at most with cooperation on the basis of rational self-interest;

---

[6]According to Nozick's *entitlement theory* property is justly distributed if it results from initial acquisition of a *res nullius* (a good that belongs to no one), provided that one leaves enough to others (Locke' *proviso*, see Section 4.2.2); or from a legitimate transfer (sale, inheritance, exchange, etc.). The *proviso* may serve as a reason for even libertarians like Nozick to concede that the state should provide some minimal social security.

[7]We can reformulate all of this with the assistance of the terms negative freedom, positive freedom and essential freedom which were introduced earlier (Section 1.4). 'Positive freedom' is equivalent to an 'absence of negative impediments'. Gradually the insight has grown that people are limited in their freedom not only by 'positive impediments', such as external coercion, but also by 'negative impediments', such as lack of money, lack of knowledge and unemployment. A government which realises this cannot satisfy itself with the imposition of 'negative duties', duties of abstinence (primarily by the state), but must equally recognise the existence of 'positive duties', duties to do something, namely seeing that money, knowledge or employment is available to all citizens. Still, a state that grants social rights is not perfectionist, because it does not promote any essential concept of freedom. Negative and positive liberties are simply necessary means to the autonomous choices of individual citizens.

competitive individualism continues the civil war by other means. These critics seek affiliation with Marx, but can likewise be inspired by Hegel, and, via Hegel, by Rousseau and Aristotle.

Martha Nussbaum develops a non-metaphysical version of Aristotle's normative conception of man, which she calls *internal* essentialism (Section 9.1.6). People can thrive only when the political and legal system recognises ten essential human needs and capacities. A good human life entails at least that everyone can build up relations with others, develop his intellectual abilities and fantasies, can relax, etc. The state should promote this. Unlike Aristotle, Nussbaum maintains that individuals do not coincide with their social environment, but have a life of their own. More particularly, they have the capacity to design their own ideals and live accordingly. Therefore she stipulates that the state should guarantee the individual freedom rights of Rawls's first principle of justice. But Nussbaum rejects the egalitarian distribution of socio-economic goods of Rawls's second principle. According to Rawls, each individual may use his income in his own way; Nussbaum, on the contrary, argues that the state must use financial redistribution to promote the development of the essential human capacities, even against the preferences of individuals. Thus, the state may subsidise forms of high culture that are despised by the majority. This is a perfectionist element in Nussbaum's theory. Still, she subscribes to the liberal view that individuals may not be forced to participate in such cultural activities. The state should only create the possibility of enjoying them.

Liberal morality is criticised from a feminist perspective as well: Rawls wrongly confines his theory of justice to the participants in official labour relations, neglecting the informal labour within the family. This is to the disadvantage of women, who traditionally take care of the household. To be sure, Rawlsian justice gives women equal chances to attain positions in the formal sector, but it denies the division of labour between husband and wife. It leaves those out in the cold who are stuck in their traditional housewife roles; liberals thus allow women, in the name of freedom, to remain without freedom. Liberal feminists propose to amend Rawls by extending his principles of fair distribution to family life. In reaction, other feminists advocate an *ethics of care* that aims at restoring traditional feminine values. This critique does not want to include the family within liberalism, but, like communitarians and communists, rejects liberalism as such, as an expression of competitive individualism.

Rawls's law of peoples is criticised as being insufficiently cosmopolitan, as well as insufficiently egalitarian. Why not extend the liberal principles of justice to all human beings, irrespective of which society they live in? Why should liberals tolerate 'decent' peoples that do not recognise full religious freedom, exclude minorities from public functions, and deny their citizens democratic rights? Why not global social justice, implying a worldwide duty of economic redistribution between rich and poor peoples? As to the latter, can one not question Rawls's thesis that the poor economic condition of a people is exclusively determined by internal causes? Is it not just as well the outcome of asymmetrical international relations, such as a history of colonisation and slavery, economic barriers to imports from poor countries, and unfair trade conditions?

When one reflects on all these objections, it is noteworthy that, despite their rhetorical presentation (notably by MacIntyre), frequently no radical break with political liberalism is argued for. Some critics only want to extend liberal justice to wider domains (family life, international relations). Even those who are more critical still accept democracy and the rule of law, focusing their objections on the alleged individualistic atomism of liberal justice. Moreover, this latter critique turns Rawls into a straw man. First, the individual autonomy of metaphysical liberalism does not coincide with egoism, since individuals may just as well choose to embrace altruistic ideals. Secondly, unlike its metaphysical brother, *political* liberalism does not claim that autonomy is the true essence of man. It only assumes autonomy in the political domain as a fiction meant to guarantee peaceful cooperation on the basis of reciprocity.

Other critics completely reject political liberalism. Can liberalism, against these radical opponents, defend its original claim to universal validity? Or should liberals like Rawls withdraw to a more modest position in international relations? Or are the radical cultural relativists right in denying the universality of the liberal model? More about this in the next section.

10.8 Liberalism: A Universal Morality?

The principles of the liberal Enlightenment are embraced in ever more parts of the world, even though many feel somewhat uncomfortable about this (as we saw, communitarians, Neo-Marxists, internal-essentialists, and feminists, often do not support a radically divergent politics, but want to bring about corrections to liberalism). Admittedly, after the fall of the Berlin Wall in some regions nationalistic outpourings occur, and forms of fundamentalism gain in influence, but this is lamented in many parts of the rest of the world. To be sure, the fact that the Enlightenment ideals have the wind behind them only proves that many find them attractive, not that they are true. Critics of liberal morality may maintain that this process merely makes the human condition direr: human life becomes increasingly impoverished as idolatry, consumerism and conceit affect communal values. That many endorse liberal values does not show that they are right. Perhaps they are just an accidental and transient product of Western culture.

This is denied by the advocates of the classical Enlightenment, who claim that liberalism reflects a universal ethics. Their claim is supported by a doctrine of cultural evolution of mankind: human civilization demonstrates a tendency towards progress in knowledge and moral emancipation. In this view, cultures that are organised on the basis of objective scientific knowledge signify progress in comparison with 'primitive' cultures that are based upon superstition. This would also imply moral progress: science-based cultures would encourage an autonomous, assertive, individual way of life, guaranteed by a democratic constitution. In this the 'primitive', morally inferior cultures lag behind, ignorant of the Enlightenment ideals. These underdeveloped societies should be 'modernised', under the guidance of the enlightened ones.

However, this claim has been criticised by cultural relativism, which we encountered in its ultimate consequences with Winch (Section 9.2). Following the philosophy of language of the later Wittgenstein, Winch maintains that human knowledge depends on interpretation that is determined by the conceptual order of one's culture. Transcultural standards of truth and rationality are absent. Therefore, scientific knowledge has no privileged claim to objectivity. With regard to ethics, then, a culture that recognises freedom, equality and democracy is as good as a culture with the opposite values. In the Athens of Plato and Aristotle slavery was considered right, in contemporary Western society it is viewed as utterly unjust. To cultural relativists the claim of the Enlightenment that history shows moral progress is simply one more expression of Western ethnocentrism.

Philosophers like Habermas and Apel (Section 9.3) agree with Winch's emphasis on linguistic interpretation, but counter his relativism with the objection that one can go beyond the factual consensus that prevails in a cultural community. It is possible to reach a *rational* consensus on the basis of exchange of information and open discussion on an equal footing. In their view, this is even a universal duty, because man is essentially a communicative being, whereas the essence of communication consists in unimpeded argumentation, unfettered by asymmetrical power relations. This requires a narrow liberal ethics: man can only fully thrive in a democratic society that allows all its members to participate equally and freely. Therefore, the liberal values can serve as a universal standard for moral progress.

The difficulty is, however, that they derive this essentialist conception of human language from a one-sided selection of cultural reality. To be sure, language can be used for a free exchange of information, but equally well as an instrument of power and manipulation. Its critical function in open and sincere communication may even be typical of Western science, which brings us back to cultural relativism. As long as cultures are isolated from each other, this may not have insidious consequences. But as soon as they clash, their ideological controversies could easily end in war, without any universal moral standard to decide the conflict.

Is this indeed the final word? Recall at this point what was said in the first section of this chapter: narrow morality is not primarily a theoretical system that can be true or untrue, but a practical political morality that aims at fulfilling its pacifying function (and would be falsified by its failure to do so). The philosophical war between liberals and perfectionists can continue in the theoretical field, as long as in the political domain the conflicting parties respect the limits of public reason, which, for example, prohibits particularist arguments to underpin the use of state force, and, a fortiori, the enforcement of particularist ideals. By their agreement to disagree, political adversaries observe the very directives of liberal morality. To be sure, this does not prove the theoretical truth of liberalism, but all the more its practical value in politics.

This practical solution primarily applies to ideological conflicts within a modern national state. As Rawls recognises, for the time being in international relations the conditions for cooperation on liberal terms are lacking. All one can hope for is that liberal values may gain gravitational force in a future where global economic interdependencies increasingly discourage war. It may be argued that here we can learn from history by analogy with the learning process that Europe has experienced since its religious wars. As a result of this common experience, Western people now generally accept liberal democracy as the best regime. A similar process might be on its way on the world stage. In this vein Francis Fukuyama has even proclaimed *the end of history* in his 1992 book of the same name. At the end of the 20th century, Fukuyama argues, history has shown that liberalism is the only serious political theory that can be reasonably advocated. Its totalitarian rivals have proved to be unfit. Fascism surrendered as soon as 1945 (after all, the Arian race, represented by the Germans, turned out not to be the fittest in its struggle for survival). The Cold War between liberal and communist countries found a peaceful end with the implosion of Communism in the 1980s. Thus, the cultural evolution of mankind has reached its peak in liberal democracy, Fukuyama concludes. This does not imply that all wars and ideological strife are over, but only that alternative ideologies and forms of government are inadequate to cope with the requirements of modernity. The Shiite theocracy of Iran had its equivalents in the European Middle Ages; Saddam Hussein ruled Iraq like a Renaissance prince. That liberal democracy is the future is shown by the worldwide increase in democracies. This tendency to democratisation will further ensure that wars are replaced by free trade.

Such views are representative of the optimism that liberals expressed during the last decade of the 20th century – although they were also criticised as gross overstatements (pointing to the large-scale violence, famines and oppression that infest the world, in his 1993 *Specters of Marx* Derrida equated Fukuyama's 'end of history' with Christian eschatology). However, historical developments since the turn of the millennium have brought about a setback for liberal optimism. Muslim fundamentalists inside and outside Western countries have violently opposed Western supremacy by means of 'terrorism', with the attack on New York's World Trade Centre in 2001 as its major success. The successive invasions in the Muslim countries Iraq and Afghanistan under the leadership of the United States did not result in the exportation of democratic ideals that the conservative American Bush government had hoped for (while that government undermined its credibility as a liberal regime by its inhumane treatment of captured terrorists). The supremacy of Western democracies has also been challenged by the economic success of the former communist countries Russia and, particularly, China that combined capitalism with an authoritarian regime. As a new economic super-power, China was even able to support the American and European economies during a grave economic crisis in 2009.

The confrontation between Western and Muslim cultures was predicted by Samuel Huntington in *The Clash of Civilisations* (1997). In a critique of Fukuyama's *End of History* Huntington argues that after the fall of communism in 1989 the world will stage new conflicts around cultural identities, rather than around political ideologies. As main cultures or civilisations, each characterised by its particular religion and way of life, Huntington discerns the Confucian-Chinese, Japanese, Hindu, Islamic, Latin American, and Western cultures (and possibly an orthodox Russian, and an African culture). The major clashes, Huntington expects, will occur between Western and Islamic civilisations. Critics, however, have objected that Huntington too strongly identifies culture with religion. In reality the diverse Islamic peoples are divided by large ethnic gaps. Moreover, the Islamists advocating a Caliphate or Islamic state only represent radical minorities that mainly fight their own authoritarian governments. According to Fukuyama, the fundamentalists' 'terrorism' is just a pre-modern rearguard action against the worldwide modernisation process.

China's combination of capitalism and a one-party government, the latter justified with an appeal to Confucianism (Section 9.1.1), may present a more serious challenge to liberal democracies. However, it has to be seen whether in the longer run authoritarian regimes can adequately confront internal and external problems, such as bridging the huge gap between the richer, modernised parts of China and the poor, underdeveloped countryside. The lack of freedom of information and open critique may prove counter-productive. Moreover, the burgeoning well-to-do middle class may want to combine economic freedom with political and spiritual liberties. Political liberals, then, may still stick to moderate optimism about the course of history.

However, this is not all there is to be said about liberalism on the national and international level. Whatever the practical success of political liberalism may be, principled adversaries may still stand firm in their opposition. So far, political liberalism can only claim the status of what Kant calls a 'hypothetical imperative': *if* you want peaceful cooperation on the basis of reciprocity, *then* you should accept a liberal constitution. Rawls may consider liberalism as the superior political philosophy in a more unconditional way, but he presents no arguments to support this claim. Non-liberals will not be impressed. Someone who takes metaphysical values so seriously that he is willing to sacrifice his own life in their name, will not accept liberal tolerance. A fundamentalist will not, simply for the sake of peace, suspend his deepest convictions about the right way of life. Likewise, liberal morality is no remedy for adherents of a heroic ethics who are convinced that people should wage a life or death battle to establish who may impose his values on society.

Yet, political liberals need not worry too much about this, at least not at a theoretical level. Even if they cannot convince fundamentalist perfectionists of the desirability of liberal restraint in politics, for their part liberals have no reason to tolerate intolerance. After all, the fundamentalists do not present any *public* reasons why others should obey their rule. The ultimate liberal way out, then, is a just war out of self-defence.

10.9 Answers to the Questions of Section 1.1

Of the main philosophical problems that were summarised in Chapter 1, a number have now been answered. These questions are: To what extent does law relate to morals, specifically to justice? To what extent is law simply an instrument of power? How can legal coercion be justified? When must one obey law? Up to which point may the state interfere with the private lives of its citizens? After a journey through the history of Western political and legal philosophy, in the first section of this chapter these questions were systematically split up into three related themes that emanated from the diverse philosophical theories: (1) the *epistemological* theme of whether rational justification is possible in matters of practical and legal philosophy; (2) the theme of the relation between law and morals, that is, is it possible to formulate a specific *legal morality*?; (3) the theme of the character of legal morality, or, should the legal order be governed by a *broad perfectionist* ethics or a *narrow liberal* one?

In so far as the first two questions are concerned: in the modern worldview it is difficult to maintain that law has a necessary relation with any essentialist morality. Traditional natural-law doctrine presupposes a metaphysical view of nature, which is nowadays no longer regarded as acceptable. Yet it still appears possible to arrive at a 'narrow' concept of justice when one starts with the procedural criterion of acceptability for all. In epistemological terms (theme 1): although it is not possible to establish the truth of ethical theories on the basis of their correspondence with any metaphysical (including empirical) reality, justification may still be found in rational consensus. In Rawls's theory of justice, this takes the form of a hypothetical social contract. This procedure results in principles of justice that pertain to the constitution of the national state (theme 2), and represent a narrow liberal public morality, honouring the values of freedom, equality and democracy (theme 3). These principles of justice can subsequently serve as an independent critical moral test for positive law. This way of grounding law in a public morality can be seen as a form of natural law, when one does not interpret the latter term as an essentialist definition of the true nature of law, but as a search for a justificatory ground, and as a critical norm for the positive legal order.

These considerations concerning the relation between law and morality may also provide an answer to those other central questions of legal philosophy: when should one *obey* positive law, and when is *state coercion* justified?

In the view of Hobbes and the normative legal positivists (and, in his way, Kant) that the main function of law is to establish social order, disobedience to positive law is (almost) never justified. Indeed, they prefer a bad social order to disorder. Individuals should not have the opportunity to take the law into their own hands with an appeal to their particular sense of justice, for this would amount to collective disorder.

The narrow ethics of Rawls, on the other hand, imposes (in conformity with Locke) more far-reaching, moral demands on a legal order that claims obedience. In the first place, it requires that the state adopt a democratic form. Without a democratic say citizens have no duty to obey. Furthermore, one does not have to obey democratic laws that seriously violate the principles of justice. Yet the order-argument also plays a role in Rawls's theory of justice. Democracy is such an important achievement that one should to a certain extent accept unjust laws which came about democratically. Only in the case of very unjust law is civil disobedience allowed, but this requires a great degree of self-control from disobedient citizens. The illegal acts should be aimed only against the unjust part of the law, while showing loyalty to the legal order as a whole. Because of the indeterminacy of the idea of justice, Rawls moreover requires a very careful attitude: disobedience is permissible only when it is unambiguously clear that a principle of justice has been breached. This can clearly be established in the case of the violation of the classical fundamental rights that are guaranteed in the first principle. However, concerning the interpretation of the second principle, that is, the distribution of socio-economic goods, much room for debate is reasonably possible. Therefore, one must in this domain leave the decision to the majority, so that the democratic order can be safeguarded.

The notion of a narrow ethics, moreover, gives a decisive answer to the question concerning the *limits* up to which the state may interfere with the private lives of its citizens. Most versions of a narrow ethics have a liberal import. Whether they take the value of individual autonomy or ethical non-cognitivism as their point of departure, the conclusion is that the individual must establish by himself how to arrange his life. In contrast with a broad, perfectionist ethics, a liberal state may, therefore, not impose a specific mode of life on its citizens simply because it regards it as morally correct. Moral decisions belong to everyone's autonomous sphere of freedom, guaranteed by the classical fundamental rights.

On the basis of such considerations the 19th-century liberal John Stuart Mill proposed the *harm principle* to determine the limits of the use of state force: individuals should be free to act and think as they like, unless they threaten to cause one another harm. State coercion is permissible only to prevent this. On this basis Mill assigns a very minimal task to state and law, and maximum individual freedom to individual citizens, in accordance with the 19th-century ideal of the minimal state: only where one individual violates the freedom and property rights of another individual, should the state interfere. Mill's conception is thus akin to Kant's thesis that the central task of law is to protect the freedom of each citizen in so far as it is compatible with the equal freedom of all others.

Hobbes, on the other hand, starting from the very same harm principle, does not recognise any principled individual liberties, because he fears mutual harm from everywhere. In his sombre version of the state of nature even peace-loving people do not escape from acting selfishly and aggressively, so that freedom may easily turn into war. Only by way of absolute power can the government properly fulfil its task – the maintenance of social order. In spite of his state absolutism, Hobbes confines his political philosophy to a 'narrow morality': there is no all-encompassing norm for *the* good life; all norms have the exclusive function of making peaceful cohabitation possible.

In the present view of narrow ethics the state is accorded a task which is more extensive than the minimal state of Mill, but more restricted than the absolutist state of Hobbes. In the current view, the state must interfere actively in the socio-economic domain (in contrast with the free market economy of classical liberalism). This intervention in economic freedom is required by liberal freedom itself: redistribution should guarantee that all citizens have equal opportunities to make use of their negative liberties. The current welfare state is based on this idea. Furthermore, the state should provide 'public goods' from which everyone may profit. This broader view of the state nevertheless falls within the notion of a 'narrow morality' because it stresses the priority of the classical freedom rights that allow individual citizens to give shape to their own lives.

10.10 Conclusion

In the preceding section the central questions of legal philosophy that were raised in the first chapter have been answered from the perspective of political liberalism. At the end of Section 10.8, however, we came to the conclusion that we cannot theoretically settle the epistemological dispute between political liberalism and its opponents. Rawls claims to do no more than rationally reconstruct the prevailing overlapping consensus in Western culture. It thus remains a fundamental subject for debate whether human rights and the democratic constitution represent universal values, or whether they are simply a product of Western culture. In brief: What is the value of the project of the Enlightenment? Do the Enlightenment values really provide a standard for moral progress?

In post-metaphysical times the most important argument against a universal ethics states that the contemporary world is so radically fragmented that only a relative, very temporary, place- and culture-bound agreement can be reached. Different cultures, subcultures and individuals would adhere to such widely divergent worldviews or interpretive paradigms that mutual disputes concerning facts and norms cannot be settled in a rational way. This conclusion would lead to serious political problems, because in the Modern Age worldwide communication has increased to such an extent that conflicts between cultures with opposing worldviews cannot be avoided, both on the national and the international level.

Here the political variant of a modern, narrow ethics may still provide the solution, which is based on the insight that people, despite their deep ideological disagreements, nevertheless have to live together and cooperate with each other. The notion of a narrow morality is a morality of the second order that is reconcilable with the verifiability *and* unverifiability of moralities of the first order. Everyone who wants to avoid war and suppression has to agree to a compromise, based on the liberal tolerance of a narrow meta-ethics. This particularly applies to modern Western societies that already share a tradition of tolerance. Here political liberalism has outgrown the status of an unstable compromise, being generally accepted as a *fair* arrangement. The hope is that this model may gradually be extended on a global scale as a consequence of increasing worldwide interdependence.

However, the political choice in favour of such a narrow ethics cannot be grounded in a compelling way. In the first place, it is possible that someone prefers war to orderly freedom, even if that choice could be deadly. The motto 'peace and order forever' will seem quite boring to belligerent types who, like Nietzsche, favour a heroic type of ethics. In the second place: someone who, following Hobbes, indeed prefers order, does not therefore have to prefer a *just* order as well (thus a narrow ethics in the Rawlsian sense). If a universal, objective ethics is absent, one can, moreover, consistently choose in favour of one's unadulterated self-interest and become a free rider (as long as all other citizens do not turn into free riders as well). Thirdly: it is possible that one can indeed choose in favour of a just order, but still reject Rawls's narrow theory of justice. This especially applies to non-Western societies. According to cultural relativism, every culture establishes what is right in its own way. One cannot, therefore, criticise a culture where a broad ethics is generally accepted, and where the state indeed imposes a perfectionist mode of life. This conclusion is strengthened by the frequently repeated criticism of Rawls's theory of justice, that it reflects Western bourgeois society of the 20th century, and thus itself only has local validity. Similarly, within Western culture, communitarians may reject the model of political liberalism as too narrow, so that it should be completed with some traditional elements. In this, however, they will be confronted with the lack of generally shared traditions in the West. More threatening to political liberalism are Western fundamentalists of various creeds who are not willing to compromise in the name of social peace. With them, liberals are in a potential state of war.

On the other hand, cultural relativism may be invoked in support of Rawls's narrow political and legal ethics, because within Western culture the liberal constitution is accepted by an overwhelming majority. Political liberalism, then, can serve as shared moral point of departure for the design of Western societies, and as moral criterion for positive law. The further moral discussion within Western culture would then focus on the refinement of these ideals: What precisely does equality entail? When are inequalities justified? How must the different Enlightenment ideals be balanced in the case of conflict, as when freedom and equality collide, or when democratic majority decisions turn out to be unjust?

Viewed internationally, however, cultures with a liberal, narrow morality have not won the argument. On the one hand, the Enlightenment ideals of freedom, equality, fraternity, and the democratic constitutional state, are increasingly accepted all over the world. Most countries at least pay lip service to the values of the Universal Declaration of Human Rights. On the other hand, however, powerful non-Western countries, like China and Russia, do this in a rather cynical way. International relations are at least partly ruled by realistic power politics, also from the Western side. Here the practical solutions of a narrow political morality do not seem to work. In the case of an international conflict between a culture with a narrow ethics and a culture with a broad ethics, even Hobbes's order-argument does not provide a solution. Unlike in relations between individuals, between states enormous inequalities in power exist, so that stronger countries can without danger to themselves enforce their will on the weaker ones.

The consensus within Western societies is furthermore breached by cultural minorities with a more authoritarian perfectionist view of ethics, often imported from their non-Western regions of origin. Its members have, at best, an opportunistic reason to accept the liberal narrow ethics for the time being, as long as it safeguards their freedom to follow their own way of life (provided they do not bother others with it).

In brief: for someone who is prepared to compromise on reasonable grounds, the modern narrow political and legal ethics may be the right solution. However, no compelling arguments exist against persons and groups who regard their own perfectionist convictions as absolutely true, and therefore reject tolerance. Liberals may find some solace in the insight that their adversaries have no compelling arguments either.

Bibliography

Alexy, Robert. 2002. *Theory of constitutional rights*, 2nd ed., transl. Julian Rivers. Oxford: Oxford University Press.

American Anthropological Association, Executive Board. 1947. Statement on human rights of the American Anthropological Association. *American Anthropologist* 49: 539–543.

Apel, Karl-Otto. 1980. *Towards a transformation of philosophy*, transl. Glyn Adey and David Frisby. London: Routledge and Kegan Paul.

Aquinas, Thomas. 2002. *Political writings*, transl. R.W. Dyson. Cambridge: Cambridge University Press.

Aquinas, Thomas. 2008. *Summa theologica*. http://www.newadvent.org/summa/. Accessed 28 May 2010.

Aristotle. 1984. *The complete works of Aristotle: The revised Oxford translation*, ed. Jonathan Barnes. Princeton, NJ: Princeton University Press.

Aristotle. 2004. *The Nicomachean ethics*, transl. J.A.K Thomson. London: Penguin.

Aurelius, Marcus. 2006. *Meditations*, transl. Martin Hammond. London: Penguin.

Austin, John. 1954. *The province of jurisprudence determined*. London: Weidenfeld and Nicolson.

Barry, Brian. 1973. *The liberal theory of justice: A critical examination of the principal doctrines in A Theory of Justice by John Rawls*. Oxford: Oxford University Press.

Beccaria, Cesare. 2004. *Of crimes and punishments*. Whitefish, MT: Kessinger Publishing.

Benedict, Ruth. 1971. *Patterns of culture*. London: Routledge and Kegan Paul.

Bentham, Jeremy. 2005. *An introduction to the principles of morals and legislation*. Whitefish, MT: Kessinger Publishing.

Berlin, Isaiah. 1958. *Two concepts of liberty*. Oxford: Clarendon Press.

Berlin, Isaiah. 1969. *Four essays on liberty*. Oxford: Oxford University Press.

Berlin, Isaiah. 2000. *Three critics of the enlightenment: Vico, Hamann, Herder*. Princeton, NJ: Princeton University Press.

Burke, Edmund. 1982. *Reflections on the revolution in France*. London: Penguin.

Camus, Albert. 1991. *The myth of Sisyphus, and other essays*, transl. Justin O'Brien. New York, NY: Vintage.

Cicero. 2008. *On obligations*, transl. P.G. Walsh. Oxford: Oxford University Press.

Comte, Auguste. 1997. *Auguste Comte and positivism: The essential writings*, ed. Getrud Lenzer. Piscataway, NJ: Transaction Publishers.

Comte, Auguste. 2009. *A general view of positivism*, transl. J.H. Bridges. Cambridge: Cambridge University Press.

Cornell, Drucilla. 1992. *The philosophy of the limit*. London: Routledge.

Critchley, Simon, Jacques Derrida, Ernesto Laclau, and Richard Rorty. 1996. *Deconstruction and pragmatism*, ed. Chantal Mouffe. London: Routledge.

Dempf, Alois. 1971. *Ethik des Mittelalters*. Darmstadt: Wissenschaftliche Buchgesellschaft.

Derrida, Jacques. 1973. *Speech and phenomena and other essays on Husserl's theory of signs*, transl. David B. Allison. Evanston, IL: Northwestern University Press.

C.W. Maris, F.C.L.M. Jacobs (eds.), *Law, Order and Freedom*, Law and Philosophy Library 94, DOI 10.1007/978-94-007-1457-1,

Derrida, Jacques. 1976. *Of grammatology*, transl. Gayatri Chakravorty Spivak. Baltimore, MD: The John Hopkins University Press.

Derrida, Jacques. 1987. *The post card: From Socrates to Freud and beyond*, transl. Alan Bass. Chicago: The University of Chicago Press.

Derrida, Jacques. 1994. *Specters of Marx: The state of debt, the work of mourning, and the New International*, transl. Peggy Kamuf. London: Routledge.

Derrida, Jacques. 2002. *Acts of religion*, ed. Gil Anidjar. London: Routledge.

Derrida, Jacques. 2005. *Rogues: Two essays on reason*, transl. Pascale-Anne Brault and Michael Naas. Stanford: Stanford University Press.

Descartes, René. 1968. *Discourse on method and the meditations*, transl. F.E. Sutcliffe. London: Penguin books.

De Ville, Jacques. 2011. *Jacques Derrida: Law as absolute hospitality*. London: Routledge.

Diderot, Dennis. 1750. "Prospectus" d'octobre 1750, rédigé par Diderot. http://classes.bnf.fr/dossitsm/aprospec.htm. Accessed 28 May 2010.

Diderot, Denis, and Jean le Rond d'Alembert. 1751–1777. *The Encyclopedia of Diderot and d'Alembert*. http://quod.lib.umich.edu/d/did/. Accessed 17 June 2010.

Diels, Hermann. 1909. *Fragmente der Vorsokratiker*. Berlin: Weidmannsche Buchhandlung.

Dodds, Eric Robertson. 1959. *The Greeks and the irrational*. Berkeley, CA: University of California Press.

Dworkin, Ronald. 1978. *Taking rights seriously*. Cambridge, MA: Harvard University Press.

Dworkin, Ronald. 1986. *Law's empire*. Cambridge, MA: Harvard University Press.

Elster, Jon. 1985. *Making sense of Marx*. New York, NY: Cambridge University Press.

Epictetus. 1955. *Enchiridion*, transl. George Long. New York, NY: Prometheus Books.

Epicurus. 1994–2009. *The internet classics archive. Letter to Menoeceus*, transl. Robert Drew Hicks. http://classics.mit.edu/Epicurus/menoec.html. Accessed 27 Feb 2010.

Esser, Josef. 1972. *Vorverständnis und Methodenwahl in der Rechtsfindung*. Frankfurt am Main: Athenäum.

Finkielkraut, Alain. 1995. *The defeat of the mind*, transl. Judith Friedlander. New York, NY: *Columbia University Press*.

Finnis, John. 1980. *Natural law and natural rights*. Oxford: Clarendon Press.

Foucault, Michel. 1991. *Discipline and punish: The birth of the prison*, transl. Alan Sheridan. London: Penguin.

Franklin, Julian, H. 1973. *Jean Bodin and the rise of absolutist theory*. Cambridge: Cambridge University Press.

Freud, Sigmund. 2001. *The standard edition of the complete psychological works of Sigmund Freud*, ed. James Strachey. London: Vintage.

Fukuyama, Francis. 1989. The end of history. *The National Interest* 16: 3–19.

Fukuyama, Francis. 1993. *The end of history and the last man*. New York, NY: Harper Perennial.

Fuller, Lon. 1964, 1969. *The morality of law* (Storrs Lectures), Revised ed. New Haven, CT: Yale University Press.

Gadamer, Hans-Georg. 1997. *Truth and method*, 2nd Revised ed., transl. Joel Weinsheimer and Donald G. Marshall. New York, NY: Continuum.

Gaius. ca. 170 AD. The Institutes of Gaius. http://www.thelatinlibrary.com/law/. Accessed 27 Feb 2010.

Galenkamp, Marlies. 1991. Collectieve rechten: een review essay. *Nederlands Tijdschrift voor Rechtsfilosofie en Rechtstheorie* 20: 60–72.

Gay, Peter. 1966. *The Enlightenment: An interpretation – The rise of modern paganism*. New York, NY: WW Norton and Co.

Gay, Peter. 1969. *The Enlightenment: An interpretation – The science of freedom*. New York, NY: WW Norton and Co.

Goodrich, Peter, Florian Hoffmann, Michel Rosenfeld and Cornelia Vismann, eds. 2008. *Derrida and legal philosophy*. Basingstoke, Hampshire: Palgrave Macmillan.

Grotius, Hugo. 2004. *The rights of war and peace, in three books*, transl. Jean Barbeyrac. Clark, NJ: Lawbook Exchange.

Habermas, Jürgen. 1972. *Knowledge and human interests*, transl. Jeremy J. Shapiro. Boston, MA: Beacon Press.

Habermas, Jürgen. 1985. *The theory of communicative action*, volumes I and II, transl. Thomas McCarthy. Boston, MA: Beacon Press.

Habermas, Jürgen. 1990. *The philosophical discourse of modernity: twelve lectures*, transl. Frederick G. Lawrence. Cambridge, MA: MIT Press.

Habermas, Jürgen. 1996. *Between facts and norms: Contributions to a discourse theory of law and democracy*, transl. William Rehg. Cambridge: Polity Press.

Hare Richard Mervyn. 1963. *The language of morals*. Oxford: Clarendon Press.

Hare, Richard Mervyn. 1965. *Freedom and reason*. Oxford: Clarendon Press.

Harris, John. 1980. *Violence and responsibility*. London: Routledge and Kegan Paul.

Hart, H.L.A. 1958. Positivism and the separation of law en morals. *Harvard Law Review* 71: 593–629 (also published in Hart, H.L.A. 1983. *Essays in jurisprudence and philosophy*, 48–87. Oxford: Oxford University Press).

Hart, H.L.A. 1961. *The concept of law*. Oxford: Oxford University Press.

Hartogh, Govert A. den. 1992. Waarheid en consensus in de politieke filosofie van John Rawls. *Algemeen Nederlands Tijdschrift voor Wijsbegeerte* 84: 93–120.

Hegel, G.W.F. 1977. *Phenomenology of spirit*, transl. A.V. Miller. Oxford: Oxford University Press.

Hegel, G.W.F. 2002. *The philosophy of right*, transl. Alan White. Newburyport, MA: Focus Publishing.

Hobbes, Thomas. 1988. *Leviathan*. New York, NY: Prometheus Books.

Hobbes, Thomas. 1998. *On the citizen*. Cambridge: Cambridge University Press.

Hoerster, Norbert. 1974. Kants kategorischer Imperativ als Test unserer sittlichen Pflichten. In *Rehabilitierung der Praktischen Philosophie II*, ed. M. Riedel, 455–475. Freiburg: Rombach.

Hudson, William Donald, ed. 1969. *The is/ought question*. London: MacMillan.

Hume, David. 1969. *A treatise of human nature*. Harmondsworth: Penguin.

Hume, David. 2007. *An enquiry concerning human understanding and other writings*. Cambridge: Cambridge University Press.

Huntington, Samuel P. 1996. *The clash of civilizations and the remaking of world order*. New York, NY: Simon & Schuster.

Israel, Jonathan. 2001. *Radical enlightenment philosophy and the making of modernity* 1650–1750. Oxford: Oxford University Press.

Jacobs, Frans. 2008. *Een filosofie van emoties en verlangens*. Amsterdam: Nieuwezijds.

Kant, Immanuel. 1977. *Critique of practical reason*, transl. Mary Gregor. Cambridge: Cambridge University Press.

Kant, Immanuel. 1991. *Political writings*, ed. H.S. Reiss, transl. H.B. Nisbet. Cambridge: Cambridge University Press.

Kant, Immanuel. 1998. *Critique of pure reason*, transl. Paul Guyer and Allen W. Wood. Cambridge: Cambridge University Press.

Kant, Immanuel. 2002. *Groundwork for the metaphysics of morals*, transl. Arnulf Zweig. Oxford: Oxford University Press.

Kennedy, Duncan. 1976. Form and substance in private-law adjudication. *Harvard Law Review* 89: 1685–1778.

Kennedy, Duncan. 1997. *A critique of adjudication*. Cambridge, MA: Harvard University Press.

La Mettrie, Julien Jean Offray de. 1996. *Machine man and other writings*, ed. Ann Thomson. Cambridge: Cambridge University Press.

Legrand, Pierre, ed. 2009. *Derrida and law*. Surrey: Ashgate.

Lemaire, Ton. 1980. *Het vertoog over de ongelijkheid van Jean-Jacques Rousseau, of de ambivalentie van de vooruitgang*. Baarn: Ambo.

Litowitz, Douglas E. 1997. *Postmodern philosophy and law*. Lawrence, KS: Kansas University Press.

Locke, John. 1961. *An essay concerning human understanding*, ed. J.W. Yolton. New York: Dutton.

Locke, John. 2003. *Two treatises of government and a letter concerning toleration*. New Haven, CT: Yale University Press.

Lyotard, Jean-François. 1984. *The postmodern condition: A report on knowledge*, transl. Geoff Bennington and Brian Massumi. Minneapolis, MN: University of Minesota Press.

Lyotard, Jean-François. 1989. *The differend: Phrases in dispute*, transl. Georges van den Abbeele. Minneapolis, MN: Universty of Minesota Press.

Machiavelli, Niccolò. 1975. *The discourses*, transl. L.J. Walker. London: Penguin Classics.

Machiavelli, Niccolò. 2003. *The prince*, transl. George Bull. London: Penguin.

MacIntyre, Alasdair. 2007. *After virtue*, 3d ed. Notre Dame, IN: University of Notre Dame Press.

Magee, Brian, ed. 1978. *Men of ideas: Some creators of contemporary philosophy*. London: BBC Books.

Maihofer, Werner, ed. 1972. *Naturrecht oder Rechtspositivismus?* Darmstadt: Wissenschaftliche Buchgesellschaft.

Maris, C.W., and F.C.L.M. Jacobs, eds. 1996. *Rechtsvinding en de grondslagen van het recht*. Assen: Van Gorcum.

Maris, C.W. 2002. Legal positivism and the end of European private law. Duncan Kennedy's Critique of adjudication. *European Review of Private Law* 10: 111–132.

Marsilius of Padua. 2005. *The defender of peace*, ed. and transl. Annabel Brett. Cambridge: Cambridge University Press.

Marx, Karl. 1992. *Capital: A critique of political economy*, transl. Ben Fowkes, Volume 1. London: Penguin.

Marx, Karl. 1993. *Grundrisse: Foundations of the critique of political economy*, transl. Martin Nicolaus. London: Penguin.

Marx, Karl, and Friedrich Engels. 1848. *Manifesto of the communist party*. http://www.marxists.org/archive/marx/works/download/pdf/Manifesto.pdf. Accessed 16 June 2010.

Marx, Karl, and Friedrich Engels. 1975–2005. *Marx/Engels collected works*. New York, NY: International Publishers.

Marx, Karl, and Friedrich Engels. 1998. *The German ideology*. New York, NY: Prometheus Books.

McKirahan, Richard D. 1994. *Philosophy before Socrates: an introduction with texts and commentary*. Indianapolis, IN: Hackett Publishing Co.

Mill, John Stuart. 1963. *Collected works*, ed. John M. Robson. Toronto, ON: University of Toronto Press.

Mill, John, Stuart. 1982. *On liberty*. London: Penguin.

Mill, John Stuart. 2002. *Utilitarianism*, 2d ed. Indianapolis, IN: Hackett Publishing Co.

Montesquieu, Charles de Secondat. 2005. *The spirit of laws*. Clark, NJ: The Lawbook Exchange Ltd.

Moore, Barrington Jr. 1993. *Social origins of dictatorship and democracy: Lord and peasant in the making of the modern world*. Boston, MA: Beacon Press.

Multatuli. 1987. *Max Havelaar: Or the coffee auctions of the Dutch trading company*, transl. Roy Edwards. London: Penguin.

Nieuwenhuys, Robert. 1987. *De mythe van Lebak*. Amsterdam: G.A. van Oorschot.

Neurath, Otto. 1979. *Wissenschaftliche Weltauffassung, Sozialismus und logischer Empirismus*. Frankfurt am Main: Suhrkamp.

Nietzsche, Friedrich. 1980. *Sämtliche Werke, kritische Studienausgabe in 15 Bänden*. München, Berlin: de Gruyter.

Nietzsche, Friedrich. 1989. *Beyond good and evil: Prelude to a philosophy of the future*, transl. Walter Kaufmann. New York, NY: Vintage Books.

Nietzsche, Friedrich. 2003a. *Thus spoke Zarathustra*, transl. R.J. Hollingdale. London: Penguin.

Nietzsche, Friedrich. 2003b. *The genealogy of morals*, transl. Horace B. Samuel. Mineola, NY: Dover Publications.

Nietzsche, Friedrich. 2004. *Twilight of the idols; and the antichrist*, transl. Thomas Common. Mineola, NY: Dover.

Nozick, Robert. 1974. *Anarchy, state, and utopia*. New York, NY: Basic Books.

Nussbaum, Martha. 1992. Human functioning and social justice. *Political Theory* 20: 206–246.

Nussbaum, Martha. 1994. *The therapy of desire: Theory and practice in Hellenistic ethics*. Princeton, NJ: Princeton University Press.

Olivecrona, Karl. 1971. *Law as fact*, 2nd ed. London: Steen & Sons.

Paine, Thomas. 1961. *The rights of man*. New York, NY: Heritage Press.

Plato. 1997. *Complete works*, ed. John M. Cooper. Indianapolis, IN: Hackett Publishing Co.

Pope, John Paul II. 1993. *The Splendor of Truth*. http://www.ewtn.com/library/ENCYC/JP2VER.HTM. Accessed 27 Feb 2010.

Popper, Karl R. 1969. *The open society and its enemies*. London: Routledge and Kegal Paul.

Popper, Karl R. 2002. *The logic of scientific discovery*. London: Routledge.

Portalis. 2004. *Preliminary address on the first draft of the Civil Code*. http://www.justice.gc.ca/eng/pi/icg-gci/code/index.html. Accessed 29 May 2010.

Radbruch, Gustav. 1950. *Rechtsphilosophie*. Stuttgart: KF Koehler.

Raddatz, Fritz J. 1975. *Karl Marx – eine politische Biographie*. Hamburg: Hofmann und Campe Verlag.

Rawls, John. 1971. *A theory of justice*. Cambridge, MA: Belknap Press of Harvard University Press.

Rawls, John. 1985. Justice as fairness: political not metaphysical. *Philosophy & Public Affairs* 14: 223–251.

Rawls, John. 1993. *Political liberalism*. New York, NY: Columbia University Press.

Rawls, John. 1999. *The law of peoples*. Cambridge, MA: Harvard University Press.

Raz, Joseph. 1988. *The morality of freedom*. Oxford: Oxford University Press.

Rorty, Richard. 1978. Philosophy as a kind of writing: An essay on Derrida. *New Literary History* 10: 141–160.

Rorty, Richard. 1989. *Contingency, irony, and solidarity*. Cambridge: Cambridge University Press.

Rorty, Richard. 1998. *Truth and progress: Philosophical papers*, volume 3. Cambridge: Cambridge University Press.

Ross, Alf. 1956. *Towards a realistic jurisprudence*, transl. Annie I. Fausbøll. Copenhagen: E Munksgaard.

Ross, Alf. 1959. *On law and justice*. Berkeley: University of California Press.

Rousseau, Jean-Jacques. 1986. *Political writings*, transl. and ed. Frederick Watkins. Madison, WI: University of Wisconsin Press.

Russell, Bertrand. 1997. *Religion and science*. Oxford: Oxford University Press.

Sabine, George Holland, and Thomas Landon Thorson. 1973. *A history of political theory*. Hinsdale, IL: Dryden Press.

Sade, Marquis de. 1965. *Justine, philosophy in the bedroom, and other writings*, transl. Richard Seaver and Austryn Wainhouse. New York, NY: Grove Press.

Sandel, Michael J. 1982. *Liberalism and the limits of justice*. Cambridge: Cambridge University Press.

Sandel, Michael J. 1984. *Liberalism and its critics*. Oxford: WileyBlackwell.

Schlick, Moritz. 1974. *General theory of knowledge*, transl. Albert E. Blumberg. New York, NY: Springer.

Scholten, Paul. 1949. *Verzamelde geschriften*. Zwolle: W.E.J. Tjeenk Willink.

Seneca. 1917–1925. *Epistles*, transl. Richard M. Gummere. Loeb Classical Library. Cambridge, MA: Harvard University Press. http://www.stoics.com/seneca_epistles_book_1.html. Accessed 27 Feb 2010.

Spinoza, Benedict de. 1997–1999. Great Books Index. http://books.mirror.org/gb.spinoza.html. Accessed 27 Feb 2010.

Stevenson, Charles L. 1944. *Ethics and language*. London: Sage.

Sullivan, Roger J. 1980. *Morality and the good life: A commentary on Aristotle's Nicomachean Ethics*. Memphis: Memphis State University Press.

Swaan, Abram de. 1988. *In care of the state; state formation and collectivization of health care, education and welfare in Europe and America in the modern era*. Oxford: Oxford University Press.

Unger, Roberto Mangabeira. 1986. *The critical legal studies movement*. Cambridge, MA: Harvard University Press.

Voltaire. 2007. *Philosophical letters, or letters regarding the English nation*, transl. Prudence L. Steiner. Indianapolis, IN: Hackett Publishing Co.

Voltaire. 2006. *Candide and other stories*, transl. by Roger Pearson. Oxford: Oxford University Press.

Waldron, Jeremy, ed. 1987. *Nonsense upon stilts: Bentham Burke and Marx on the rights of man*. London: Methuen and Co.

Williams, Bernard. 1973. A critique of utilitarianism. In *Utilitarianism for & against*, eds. J.J.C. Smart and Bernard Williams, 77–150. Cambridge: Cambridge University Press.

Winch, Peter. 1958. *The idea of social science and its relation to philosophy*. London: Routledge and Kegan Paul.

Winch, Peter. 1972. Understanding a primitive society. In *Ethics and action*, ed. Peter Winch, 8–49. London: Routledge and Kegan Paul.

Wittgenstein. Ludwig. 2003. *On certainty*, transl. Denis Paul and G.E.M. Anscombe. Oxford: Blackwell Publishing.

Wittgenstein, Ludwig. 2007. *Tractatus logico-philosophicus*, transl. D.F. Pears and B.F. McGuinness. London: Routledge.

Wittgenstein, Ludwig. 2009. *Philosophical investigations*, transl. G.E.M. Anscombe et al. Oxford: Blackwell Publishing.

Name Index

GPSR Compliance
The European Union's (EU) General Product Safety Regulation (GPSR) is a set of rules that requires consumer products to be safe and our obligations to ensure this.

If you have any concerns about our products, you can contact us on

ProductSafety@springernature.com

In case Publisher is established outside the EU, the EU authorized representative is:

Springer Nature Customer Service Center GmbH
Europaplatz 3
69115 Heidelberg, Germany

www.ingramcontent.com/pod-product-compliance
Lightning Source LLC
Chambersburg PA
CBHW072040200825
31303CB00003BA/14
* 9 7 8 9 4 0 0 7 1 4 5 6 4 *